MORGAN TSVANGIRAI

AT THE DEEP END

WITH T WILLIAM BANGO

eye books

Challenging
the way
we see things

Morgan Tsvangirai: At the Deep End published in Great Britain in
2011, by:
Eye Books
7 Peacock Yard
Iliffe Street
London
SE17 3LH
www.eye-books.com

Cover design by Flame Design, Cape Town
Front cover image by Tsvangirayi Mukwazhi

Edited by Graeme Addison

British Library Cataloguing in Publication Data
A catalogue record for this book is available from the British Library

ISBN: 978-1-908646-00-2

CONTENTS

Map of Zimbabwe

LIST OF ACRONYMS

ADB	African Development Bank
AFC	Agriculture Finance Corporation
AIPPA	Access to Information and Protection of Privacy Act
AMWUZ	Associated Mineworkers' Union of Zimbabwe
ANC	African National Council (founded by Abel Muzorewa)
ANZ	Associated Newspapers of Zimbabwe
AU	African Union
BSAC	British South Africa Company
CAF	Central African Federation
CAZ	Conservative Alliance of Zimbabwe
CCJP	Catholic Commission for Justice and Peace
CFU	Commercial Farmers' Union
CHOGM	Commonwealth Heads of Government Meeting
CIA	Central Intelligence Agency (United States)
CIO	Central Intelligence Organisation (Zimbabwe)
COG	Commonwealth Observer Group
Cosatu	Congress of South African Trade Unions
DP	Democratic Party
DRC	Democratic Republic of Congo
EPZ	Export Processing Zone
ESAP	Economic Structural Adjustment Programme
ESC	Electoral Supervisory Commission
EU	European Union
Frelimo	Front for the Liberation of Mocambique
GALZ	Gay and Lesbian Association of Zimbabwe

GAPWUZ	General Agriculture and Plantation Workers' Union of Zimbabwe
GNU	Government of National Unity
GPA	Global Political Agreement
ICFTU	International Confederation of Free Trade Unions
ILO	International Labour Organisation
IMF	International Monetary Fund
ITAZ	Informal Traders' Association of Zimbabwe
IZG	Independent Zimbabwe Group
JOC	Joint Operations Command
LRF	Legal Resources Foundation
MDC	Movement for Democratic Change (first leader, Morgan Tsvangirai)
MK	Umkhonto we Sizwe (armed wing of African National Congress)
MKD	Mavambo/Kusile/Dawn (founded by Simba Makoni)
MLC	Movement for the Liberation of Congo
MMD	Movement for Multiparty Democracy (Zambia, Frederick Chiluba)
MNR/Renamo	Mozambique National Resistance
MPLA	Popular Movement for the Liberation of Angola
NAM	Non-aligned Movement
NCA	National Constitutional Assembly
NDP	National Democratic Party (headed by Michael Mawema, banned 1961)
NDU	National Democratic Union
NECF	National Economic Consultative Forum
NFAZ	National Farmers' Association of Zimbabwe
NSC	National Security Council
NWPC	National Working People's Convention
OATUU	Organisation of African Trade Union Unity
ORAP	Organisation of Rural Associations for Progress

PF	Patriotic Front
PF Zapu	Patriotic Front Zapu (breakaway party of Joshua Nkomo)
POSA	Public Order and Security Act
Renamo/MNR	Mozambique National Resistance
RF	Rhodesian Front (founded by Winston Field, Ian Smith)
RICU	Reformed Industrial and Commercial Workers' Union (formed 1946)
SADC	Southern African Development Community
SATUCC	Southern African Trade Union Coordination Council
SRANC	Southern Rhodesian African National Congress (banned 1959)
SWA	South West Africa (now Namibia)
SWAPO	South West African People's Organisation
TNF	Tripartite Negotiation Forum
UANC	United African National Council (founded by Abel Muzorewa)
UDI	Unilateral Declaration of Independence (November 1965)
UNDP	United Nations Development Programme
UNIP	United National Independence Party (Zambia, Kenneth Kaunda)
Unita	National Union for the Total Independence of Angola (leader, Jonas Savimbi)
UP	United Party (formed by Abel Muzorewa)
UPM	United People's Movement (formed by Jonathan Moyo)
UPP	United People's Party (formed by Daniel Shumba)
WAG	Women's Action Group
Zanla	Zimbabwe African National Liberation Army (armed wing of Zanu)
Zanu	Zimbabwe African National Union (founded by Ndabaningi Sithole, Leopold Takawira, Herbert Chitepo, Robert Mugabe, Enos Nkala, Edgar Tekere & others, 1963)
Zanu PF	Zanu Patriotic Front (Zanu renamed at insistence of N Sithole)

Zapu	Zimbabwe African People's Union (founded by Joshua Nkomo & others, 1961)
ZBC	Zimbabwe Broadcasting Corporation
ZCBC	Zimbabwe Catholic Bishops Conference
ZCTU	Zimbabwe Congress of Trade Unions
ZDERA	Zimbabwe Democracy and Economy Recovery Act (2001)
ZEC	Zimbabwe Electoral Commission
ZESA	Zimbabwe Electricity Supply Authority
ZESN	Zimbabwe Elections Support Network
ZFU	Zimbabwe Farmers' Union
Zimcode	Zimbabwe Conference on Reconstruction and Development
Zipra	Zimbabwe People's Revolutionary Army (armed wing of Zapu)
ZNA	Zimbabwean National Army
ZNWVA	Zimbabwe National War Veterans' Association
ZUD	Zimbabwe Union of Democrats
ZUJ	Zimbabwe Union of Journalists
ZUM	Zimbabwe Unity Movement (formed by Edgar Tekere)
ZURO	Zimbabwe Unemployed and Retrenchees Organisation

CHAPTER ONE

VILLAGE BOY

There is something unique about being the first child of a young Zimbabwean couple, especially a boy, largely because Zimbabwe is a patriarchal society. There is excitement in the home, within the community and beyond, as the first-born heralds a new era in the life of a black African family.

My father Dzingirai-Chibwe was ecstatic when he heard the news of my birth on 10 March 1952. A father naturally sees beyond the face of a baby boy; a son spins around a male African's mind and seeds wild dreams. A son stands for the perpetuity of the family line. A girl descendant will, one day, disappear to a different family and assume a new name. While this may sound like an unfair perception, to my young parents and to the entire Tsvangirai family, the arrival of a boy was a milestone marking a moment of unfettered celebration and joy.

My mother Lydia gave birth to me in the family's sooty, pole-and-mud kitchen, with the aid of traditional midwife. Mama had juggled her pregnancy with attending to the normal domestic chores associated with a young bride in a 'foreign' home. The home was not that foreign anyway: our culture dictated that unions be encouraged only among families that were familiar with one another within our communities. My father had followed the spirit of that cultural demand, stubbornly paying little amorous attention to the beauties he met travelling to and working in Johannesburg, 1 200 kilometres from our village of Buhera. He left his job in the South African mines for a courtship within the neighbourhood. Dzingirai-Chibwe Tsvangirai and Lydia Zvaipa had grown up together, knowing each other into their teens before settling down as husband and wife. That gave their respective families a chance to test their individual characters for suitability – an important factor that eventually nudged them into marriage.

Buhera in far western Manicaland, one of the ten administrative provinces of Zimbabwe, lies amid boulder-strewn hills and savannah thornbush. Its rural shops and government administrative centres and its remote hamlets are connected by narrow dusty roads. The wide open skies capture thunderheads billowing in from the Indian Ocean, but all too often the area is plagued by devastating drought and much of the surrounding area is low-lying and malarial. Although Buhera district is one of the poorest in the country it is still a wonderful place in which to grow up surrounded by the natural beauty of the African countryside. The nearby Nyazvidzi River cuts a rocky channel through terrain that is overlooked by rugged heights such as the Bedza and Dzapasi mountains.

The scattered villages maintain a strong sense of community and close family ties. At the time of my birth nearly all the land was communally owned and administered by chiefs and their headmen. Women still do much of the tilling and harvesting on subsistence plots, cultivating maize and the large-grained millet called sorghum, a staple food in dry areas of Africa – they have to, because many of the men are away working in urban -areas.

As is always the case with the first boy child, there seemed to be a silent but taut competition within the couple's home to raise a clone, a mirror-image of either parent. Sometimes my parents' expectations and demands came into conflict. Like all Zimbabwean rural fathers, Dzingirai-Chibwe sought to imbue manly responsibility, fearlessness and moral worthiness so that I would be ready to claim space and show leadership and resilience. My mother centred her early advice on survival skills, independence, empathy, passion, kindness and communal solidarity. I felt it all, as I grew up; I can feel it even to this day.

I was born a few months before the white settler administration formed the Federation of Rhodesia and Nyasaland comprising the self-governing territory of Southern Rhodesia (now Zimbabwe) and the British protectorates of Northern Rhodesia (Zambia) and Nyasaland (Malawi). Within the federation, Southern Rhodesia's white tribe dominated political activity and decision making. The period coincided with the rise of African nationalism across the continent and decolonisation which led to independence for many new African states, beginning with Ghana in 1957.

My life was destined to be closely interwoven with political, economic and social changes in Zimbabwe. As a youngster, of course, I was at first barely conscious of the realities of white supremacy and the unfolding drama of our liberation as a people. In my formative years, though, I suffered experiences that would leave a deep and lasting impression throughout my subsequent private and public life. Indeed, millions of Zimbabweans were subjected to similar experiences, so I can claim no distinction for myself.

At the raw end of injustices, we learnt that our humanity counted for very little in the eyes of those who had seized the country, exploited us, held power over us and exercised it in their own narrow interests. Our craving for human dignity, fairness, equity and the freedom to be ourselves was not something that arose out of the liberation struggle: it was the underlying force that drove people to demand what was rightfully theirs. So in telling my personal story I track the historical background at the same time. Zimbabwe's story is that background: it ultimately became, for me, the foreground of my life. Trade unionism and then national politics thrust me to prominence, with all the responsibilities and risks that come with leadership.

In our village there was both hope and anxiety: people sensed that freedom and independence, however desirable, might not be all that easy to attain. Dreams of liberation were especially strong among community leaders and a few literate officials, including teachers and low-level state bureaucrats who had experienced inequality and racial discrimination. They had access to information on global political trends through newspapers and local and external radio broadcasts and could foresee the struggle ahead. Migrant workers returning from South Africa told of the world of forced labour and poorly paid work, and brought news of the rise of African nationalism across the continent.

The political climate that shaped my young mind was a melting pot of sorts, where values and world views came into conflict. Resident, largely rural black African laypeople were confronted by a relatively advanced and sophisticated white immigrant group looking for space and opportunities away from a crowded, volatile Europe. Here were two sets of human beings brought up under vastly different conditions, living in different areas with different religious creeds. Their behaviour and mannerisms set them apart, let alone their skin colour, hairstyles, languages and even diets. A clash of cultures was inevitable.

It has taken me decades to fathom and follow the complex interplay of events, personalities and parties that delivered Zimbabwe as an independent state. It is important to sketch this background even though at the time I was only a child and understood nothing of any of it and could not have foreseen where it would lead me.

The capital city of the federation was Salisbury (now Harare) in Southern Rhodesia. The federation, also called the Central African Federation (CAF), was Britain's imperial exercise in state-building which turned out to be a serious mistake.[1] Under an appointed governor general, the federal government handled external affairs, defence, currency, intercolonial relations, and federal taxes. The larger vision was to create a decolonised, semi-independent state in the British Commonwealth by handing over power to white settlers, allowing for the gradual inclusion of blacks into the political system. The grand plan collapsed after a mere decade as

African nationalists challenged the vision, demanding that the majority, not the minority, gain power.

Although blacks in Southern Rhodesia were by 1940 loosely organised in various protest, interest and trade union groups, it was not until 1957 that they formally created a purely political organisation, the Southern Rhodesia African National Congress (SRANC). SRANC followed a moderate line calling for fairness, an end to racial discrimination, and economic opportunities for blacks. The federal government banned SRANC in 1959 and briefly detained many of its leaders in a forlorn bid to contain dissent. Arising from the calls for decolonisation and independence, Africans resisted the federation, leading to demonstrations in 1960 and 1961. Several nationalists from Zambia and Malawi were arrested and detained in Southern Rhodesia for organising the mass protests. Upon their release, the nationalists continued their pursuit of a strong reformist agenda and seem to have expected Britain to hand over Zimbabwe to black majority rule through a constitutional conference.

But immediate majority rule for Southern Rhodesia was not to be. In 1961, Britain convened a conference in Salisbury to which Joshua Nkomo, Ndabaningi Sithole and other nationalists were invited. A new constitution was agreed to but it allowed for a complicated, racially discriminatory voting system in which two separate voters' rolls were introduced: an 'A' roll for the whites and a 'B' roll for blacks. The 1961 constitution meant different things to whites and blacks: whites understood it as a way to pave the road for their independence from Britain while the black nationalists saw hardly any sign of progress towards their goal of majority rule. Britain retained its authority over the country. Although Nkomo signed the agreement on 7 February 1961, he changed his mind soon afterwards and instructed his supporters to boycott a referendum on the new constitution.

Under a new party hastily formed after the SRANC was banned, the National Democratic Party (NDP), headed by Michael Mawema, the nationalists tried to disrupt the referendum. Three days before the referendum, blacks mounted widespread protests and police shot two people dead in Salisbury's African townships, heightening the tension further. The vote was taken on 26 July 1961, opposed by a strange mixture of bedfellows: prominent white liberals led by former prime minister Garfield Todd and ex-chief justice Robert Tredgold; conservatives Winston Field of the Dominion Party and Selukwe farmer Ian Smith; and nationalists Joshua Nkomo and Ndabaningi Sithole. Despite – or because of – this combination of opponents, the government won approval for the proposed constitution. The premier of Southern Rhodesia, Edgar Whitehead, relied on the support of Roy Welensky, prime minister of the federation, and Humphrey Gibbs, the British governor of Southern Rhodesia, to gain the backing of the white majority. After the referendum, Whitehead banned the NDP.

White politicians who had rejected the constitution, including Field, the leader of the federal opposition Dominion Party, and farmer and MP Ian Smith, immediately began to campaign against the Whitehead government in preparation for the Southern Rhodesian elections in 1962.

When Sir Roy Welensky dissolved the federal parliament to make way for the elections, the situation in Northern Rhodesia and Nyasaland had taken a different turn. Britain seemed ready to allow for majority rule in the two countries, paving the way for the birth of Zambia and Malawi which became fully independent in 1964. But the picture in Southern Rhodesia was different. The British were unclear about the future, apart from the fierce resistance they faced from the settler administration. In the circumstances it seemed the best they could do was as little as possible.

In December 1961, Joshua Nkomo and the former NDP nationalists formed the Zimbabwe African People's Union (Zapu) and maintained a similar political line to that of the banned NDP, continuing to press Britain for democratic reforms. When it became clear to Nkomo and his leadership that they were making no progress, Zapu changed its tone and began to focus on the regime in Salisbury. This led to a rise in black militancy which attracted a hard-line response from the white settler population.

The deteriorating situation in the Congo added to the anxieties of the white community. In 1960 Belgium had suddenly abandoned the enormous Belgian Congo (which became the Republic of Congo, later Zaire, and is now the Democratic Republic of Congo).[2] In the ensuing chaos, Congo's colonial settlers stampeded for refuge and almost all trekked to the two Rhodesias where emergency committees received them with food packs, temporary shelters and medicines.[3] Instability in the Congo persisted for decades with civil war, rebellions, massive corruption and the brutal tyranny of Mobutu Sese Seko[4] who came to power in 1965. To white Rhodesians the Congo illustrated what Ian Smith later described as the danger of capitulating to metropolitan powers that seemed ready 'to cut and run at the drop of a hat'.[5]

Whitehead banned Zapu, reacting to the growing anti-black sentiment in his constituency and to shore up his fortunes. But his power base was crumbling. Field and Smith, backed by wealthy white businessmen, industrialists, miners and commercial farmers, formed a new party, the Rhodesian Front (RF). Whitehead narrowly scraped through the election in April 1962 but his administration remained strongly challenged by both the black nationalists, who boycotted the polls, and the RF. He was forced to call an early all-white election in December 1962. In that poll, the RF won 35 of the 50 'A' roll seats; another went to Dr Ahrn Palley, a white independent, leaving the hardliners, Field and Smith, with a working majority of five parliamentary seats. Field took over as the new prime minister and appointed Smith as his deputy and minister of finance.

Britain had granted Nyasaland independence as Malawi three months earlier, further hardening the position of Southern Rhodesian whites who dreaded the wave of liberation heading southwards. Zambia was next. In March 1963, Britain gave in to pressure from Lusaka, sounding a clear death-knell to the federation. The RF wanted a different type of independence under white control; they aimed to thwart moves towards majority rule, arguing that the history and situation in Southern Rhodesia was different from that of its erstwhile federal neighbours. Unlike Zambia and Malawi, Southern Rhodesia was not a protectorate under direct control from London but was self-governing.

The RF maintained that from as far back as 1890, Southern Rhodesia was the property of a private company until well into the twentieth century. This meant that settlers had always enjoyed some form of freedom to run their own affairs without undue interference from a faraway colonial capital. In 1889 British businessman, mining magnate and empire builder Cecil John Rhodes had received a Royal Charter from Queen Victoria to form the British South Africa Company (BSAC) to move into modern-day Zimbabwe and exploit minerals. The following year, he put together a team of 500 men to invade the territory north of the Limpopo River where, after a few skirmishes with the local population, the company conquered the country and set up a base and a settler administration outpost. No official British colonial administrators moved in to qualify Zimbabwe as an official colony, until it acquired quasi dominion status in 1923 somewhat resembling that of Australia and New Zealand.

Subsequent generations of Rhodesians saw themselves as no less African than the black majority. They were outnumbered 20 to 1 by the people they found already resident there but felt they had as legitimate a claim to the territory as the indigenous people. As early as 1931, for example, the Southern Rhodesia government allowed for the seizure of 48 million acres of prime land which was allocated to a few whites. The black majority were left to share a mere 28 million acres in low rainfall and arid areas. Not surprisingly, the settlers felt relatively free to treat black Africans as second or third class citizens without any external sanction. While they remained loyal to Britain and to the Queen, they were determined to frustrate plans for the same decolonisation pattern as in other parts of sub-Saharan Africa. With the federation now terminally in the intensive care unit, the RF felt it was time to make a move towards their definition of independence.

In March 1963, the federation collapsed. I was just 11 years old but my life had stretched over the entire short history of the federation which had come and gone. Now the government of Field and Smith seized the initiative. To assert control and authority, the RF moved swiftly to crush nationalist activism and set up much harsher forms of public control, throwing Zimbabwe's nationalist leaders into a crisis over policy cohesion. As a result, the nationalist movements began to fragment, with consequences that would stretch far into the future. Facing a combination of state-sponsored brutality, enemy infiltration and political conflicts over strategy, ideology and tactics, Zapu inevitably split. In August 1963,

Sithole, Leopold Takawira, Herbert Chitepo, Robert Mugabe, Enos Nkala, Edgar Tekere and others formed the Zimbabwe African National Union (Zanu). The divisions between Zapu and Zanu became so sharp that their supporters attacked one another, vying for political supremacy. The settler administration initially fanned black-on-black violence but later banned the two parties and threw their leadership into detention centres and jails without trial.

When Britain refused to grant the administration its wish for pre-emptive 'independence', the RF turned against Field who they felt was failing to push the British hard enough to achieve their goal. In their view, he failed to read the settler mood correctly; he had performed dismally in his dealings with the indecisive British who never seemed to see the urgency of the matter. In April 1964, the RF parliamentary caucus passed a vote of no confidence in Field and replaced him with the hardliner Smith. So deep was the mood of anger against Britain that those considered to be moderates or even mildly sympathetic to black majority rule were soon sidelined from politics. Opposition figures Welensky and Sidney Sawyer lost heavily to RF candidates in two Salisbury by-elections in October 1964.

Smith – the first Rhodesian-born white leader of the settler community – was seriously underrated in terms of his depth of sentiment and resentment of black African aspirations. He described himself as a white African with no other home, family or emotional attachment to Britain, unlike his predecessors.[6] He claimed to know the feelings and minds of people on the ground; he also claimed to understand the black African mentality, culture and lifestyle better than any former white leader.

In the initial search for a political solution, Smith avoided the nationalist leaders and their political parties. According to government estimates at the time, there were about 800 political activists loyal to both Zapu and Zanu who had managed to evade arrest and detention, and were leading the resistance. Smith began to court the favours of African chiefs. He planned a survey of the opinions of about 30 000 community leaders he believed to be the legitimate voice of the African people. One of his first moves was to meet with their representatives. As early as June 1964 his administration organised a trip for 29 chiefs to India, Pakistan, and to

Italy – where they met the Pope in the Vatican – and then on to London. British Prime Minister Alec Douglas Home refused to meet them, much to the disappointment of the chiefs and Smith himself.

Britain was in the middle of a campaign for a general election set for 15 October 1964. Smith, keen to have the incoming government send observers to evaluate his survey of African opinion, cabled an invitation to Prime Minister Home who quickly dismissed it. Smith went ahead anyway, meeting the chiefs and their headmen and later reporting that he had managed to secure their support for 'independence' in terms of the controversial 1961 constitution. On 5 November 1964, he took the question of independence to the settler community in another referendum. Again, he told the world that 89 per cent of the people backed him.

After a year of further attempts at prodding Britain to grant the settlers' wish, Smith could wait no longer. He announced the Unilateral Declaration of Independence (UDI) on 11 November 1965. The previously serene countryside awoke to the news, with many – especially African workers, teachers, agriculture extension officers and students – openly expressing revulsion.

To a 13-year-old, what was happening around me appeared so complicated as to make no immediate sense. All I heard at home and at school were constant discussions about the changing world, but not in any coherent way. Remarks were passed about changes in health care, education, politics, governance, beliefs and the church. Almost everything seemed set for disruption. Only slightly later in my teens did things begin to fit together. Or rather, only then did I begin to perceive that things did not fit together smoothly; politics, culture, religion and social lifestyles really were located at stress points between two worlds – between settler standards and African customs.

As with other African communities confronting change, there were fears and anxieties about a white-imposed lifestyle. We worried about the effect it would have on the people's values and the dangers it posed for age-old principles and codes of behaviour. Everything seemed so foreign, including voting, capitalism, national registration and religion. Our society was stressed by the imposition of settler Christian norms and the money economy which drove young men away from their rural homes in search of work in busy centres.

Debate in the rural areas seldom focused on the key issues. It was uninformed by national trends, muffled and confined to an attentive few. Repression, both subtle and open, was a fact of life everywhere, aggravated by official segregation. There was little reliable mass communication. Access to newspapers was a rare privilege while radio came loaded with alien ideas, music, fast talk and fashionable modern trends. There was as yet no television in rural areas, though when it was introduced in 1960 it carried heavy government propaganda. It was difficult for rural people – mainly illiterate women and the elderly – to follow national events in a systematic way.

Unlike the natural evolutionary processes that we had grown used to within our communities, colonialism overturned all that we knew and trusted. It came at us with a cross-cutting, often violent urgency which outpaced a black person's normal tempo of gradual assimilation and adaptation. It demanded serious adjustments in one's approach to daily life, contradicted established practices, upset patterns of thought, interfered in personal matters like courtship, love-making, marriage and sexual mores. Schools brought literacy, a written language and dress codes; health centres prescribed laboratory medicines to replace our herbal remedies; churches targeted our shrines, rituals and matrimonial practices; automobiles roared down newly paved roads all across the country, replacing the plodding donkeys and quiet footpaths that had carried us in the past. Our laid-back demeanour and unconsciousness of time management came under heavy attack.

The white person's lack of appreciation of, and total refusal even to understand who we were and what we stood for, confused us as a people. With our diversity ignored, our tranquil environment tampered with, and our traditions viewed with contempt, we were never allowed to embrace the new way of life voluntarily and in peace.

Young as I was, I eavesdropped on my parents and other villagers as they murmured their dismay and anger at the negative influence of whites.

Almost daily, the main discussion point appeared to be centred on the government's push against African traditional lifestyles. This was not just directed at symbols and belief systems: people were truly being pushed off their land, displaced from ancestral territory and sent into dry and rocky regions. They were forced to reduce their cattle herds, and at the same time those who hoped to travel to urban centres for better opportunities found that their movements were restricted.

Land and cattle occupied a special place in rural Zimbabwe. They were symbols of wealth, a form of family savings, and a black African's lifetime pension scheme. Cattle have many uses in an African family: some are for sacrificial rituals, others are reserved for marriage feasts or funerals. Many cattle remain on loan having been acquired from family opponents as compensation for offences. Chiefly rulings may have imposed cattle fines three or four generations before for transgressions or abuses committed within the clan. Without state-sponsored social security networks and income safety nets, cattle function as a form of savings and investment that can make an invaluable contribution to family welfare during hard times.

When the whites launched an assault on these resources, they touched a raw nerve. Whatever the intention in stripping people of their land, cattle wealth and traditional livelihoods – whether it was to lay hold of more commercial farmland for whites, remove competition by blacks, turn subsistence peasants into a labour reserve, humiliate us, or all of these – the effect was to breed anger and cause deep disillusionment with the government and its policies. Land, cattle and, later on, jobs became politically sensitive issues.

I witnessed how the government cut up our farmlands into units where we were forced to put up contour ridges; I saw our pastures being reduced drastically to limit livestock levels; and 'pass' laws were introduced to discourage and to monitor movement into urban areas. I heard how chiefs and their subjects were ordered off parts of Gutu, Bikita, Chirumanzu, Mvuma and Chivhu as large chunks of these districts were turned into white commercial farms. I recall when new terminology was introduced to define our home areas: they became known as the labour reserves, African reserves and tribal trust lands (TTLs), terms which those slightly older than me found derisive, offensive and insensitive.

The state uprooted thousands of villagers and forcibly resettled them in the 'reserves' – usually places where the soil was poor and rainfall unreliable – to make way for cattle ranches and commercial cropping. In no time, the 'native reserves' became so crowded that the administration opened up new areas in Gokwe and Silobela in the Midlands, areas which were previously classified as uninhabitable because of the presence of the tsetse fly. The mass displacements increased during the UDI years. The state forced blacks to sell their livestock to the new white owners at prices set by the administration.

To those who remained in their homelands eking out an existence as subsistence farmers, the colonial authorities inflicted further pain through taxation. Failure to meet a tax obligation attracted a harsh penalty, including being thrown into a forced labour camp. Through family networks, news quickly reached us in Buhera of how some chiefs, including Jojo Huchu of Chirumanzu, with the support of his people, put up a strong resistance. Taxation, an alien concept, drove many young men to escape from rural hopelessness. They fled to the cities or left the country for South Africa or newly independent Zambia and Malawi. Finding paid work elsewhere was a form of sanctuary as successive settler administrations kept on tightening controls on the basic freedoms of the general populace.

We lived under the watchful eye of the Native Affairs commissioner who commanded the police, agricultural extension workers (then known as land development officers and agricultural demonstrators) and nests of spies and informers on the state payroll. Initially peasant farmers had to work for the new white farmers to enable them to pay their taxes. But as tensions continued to rise, they were pushed off to Gokwe. By the time I was at high school, I realised through discussions with classmates that the pattern of mass displacements affected nearly all African people. Race relations were increasingly strained while nationalist calls for majority rule grew more strident.

At a spiritual level, I could feel that religion was an area of confusion within our culture. In my early life Christianity reached every hearth and was at the centre of the battle for the African heart and mind. White colonialists used the church extensively to attack our way of life, discouraging – and sometimes punishing – those who dared to express dissent. African reinterpretation of Christianity was regarded as a form of heresy against West European Christian doctrines.

Religion was not the only source of bewilderment in our lives. In a way, the spiritual conflict paralleled the political one, and not just between white and black but between black nationalist movements themselves. As the campaign for liberation and independence accelerated during my teenage years, so a proliferation of parties and leadership personalities sought the backing of the mass of black Zimbabweans. Confused spiritually, we were also pulled several ways politically. In the final years of white rule, widespread social upheavals, forced removals and the general turmoil resulting from the liberation war added to our perplexities, as my unfolding story will show.

That the poor shall have direct access to heaven and inherit all their earthly aspirations as soon as they embraced Christianity was the rallying call. This became a doctrine that found some easy takers among a people who, on a material level, had so very little and were often intimidated by the ceaseless propaganda about Western civilisation and the efficacy of religious conversion. To reach out to thousands of potential converts, white church ministers and their impressionable black assistants – frequently with the connivance and encouragement of colonial administrators – sought to turn an African villager's mind to accept poverty as a natural phenomenon, nothing to be ashamed of; poverty was God-given; and while on earth, poverty was a temporary reality that could translate into a faith-based blessing in eternity.

My mother was among the early converts and regularly attended the Methodist congregational services at a centre near the Buhera colonial administrative office. Dzingirai-Chibwe hardly took Christianity seriously, although he occasionally accompanied my mother to a Sunday service.

The main denomination throughout Buhera was the Dutch Reformed Church, an Afrikaner Protestant group rooted in South Africa, then on a determined evangelical drive throughout the south of Rhodesia. The church, in addition to religious services, conducted catechism seminars for potential converts, performed baptisms and ran schools.

Like many African women of the time, my mother struggled with the pressures of poverty. Having limited formal education and even less exposure to the ways of the modern world, women battled to feed, clothe and succour their children. It was a high achievement to put together the building blocks of a relatively stable family when spouses were away for long periods trying to scrape together enough to sustain themselves and send back remittances to their rural kin. I sensed the desperation, even in those early stages of my life. Child mortality was abnormally high. It took impeccable care and hygiene to look after an infant under the age of five. The commitment and care my parents showed towards the health and well-being of our family was so strong that none of the nine children succumbed to an early death. We all survived into the current century.

My mother told me how she used to secure me on her back when I was down with an ailment – measles, a cold or a bilharzia infection – and ride my father's rusty bicycle through untamed forests along the footpath to Gutu Mission Hospital, the only place with a relatively well-equipped church health centre. As I grew up, I saw a repeat of the same pattern: occasionally I would be left in the care of neighbours as my mother ferried my younger brothers to the same hospital for primary health care. A courageous woman, she braved wild animals on remote paths, sometimes for days on end, to safeguard our health.

It may seem from all this that we were helpless victims of change and oppression. That was not the case at all: beneath the surface our culture was robust and continued to thrive and survive, along with a strong feeling that an unfolding destiny awaited us. We took part spiritedly in occasional gatherings to support nationalistic calls for independence and the restoration of the dignity of black people. Meanwhile, the main activities in our village centred on peasant agriculture, African dances and rituals, and Christian church services. Peasants hardly missed a Sunday service and followed the rites with the zeal of young military recruits. As Bibles were expensive, those fortunate enough to possess such a prized item were held in high esteem.

Marriage rites and ceremonies never changed; offerings to our dead ancestors in the form of traditional beer, the blood of sacrificed animals and remembrance rituals continued unabated; our dances, cuisine, practices, clans and fellowships remained intact. Also unchanged were the roles, responsibility and place of African traditional doctors and practitioners, spirit mediums and herbalists – all seen by the church as primitive affronts to the new Christian canons.

Among most Africans there was certainly a widespread desire to overcome old habits and embrace change for the better, but the fast pace at which Christianity sought to transform our culture seemed improper. Many found it difficult to cast away everything that defined them as a people and as a community. As Africans practising various religions we had always recognised the existence of God. We differed with whites on how to view Jesus Christ in a general cosmology that remained African. How should we pray? How to make offerings and conduct rituals for spiritual healing? As individuals and families, Africans tender their service to God through the dead, which is not what has been called 'ancestor worship' but rather seeking intercession with the Almighty through deceased and highly respected family elders as well as clan leaders. At a communal level, we communicate with the holy world through our chiefs and 'spirit' mediums.

There was open resentment, especially among the elderly, of the way white missionaries looked down on our practices. They introduced a 'white' Jesus Christ and advised all, including young children, to talk directly to God – often in a way African traditionalists felt was disrespectful and reflected a deadly assault on our society and beliefs. The new way of religion had a strong impact on many among the poor and it divided the people, separating some from their culture and causing a gulf in relationships between generations. Some girls opted to train as nuns and to give their lives to God at a time when their families expected them to get married and raise families. The trend led to family rifts as the girls deserted their homes for missionary and pastoral work.

The majority made serious efforts to retain an African cultural identity. But to cope with a changing world a dual system emerged, albeit quietly, in which Christian principles were observed side by side with a time-honoured ancestral system. The practice remains common in our rural areas as black Zimbabweans simultaneously accept, observe and honour both the Christian doctrine and their hallowed customs. Those with a strong rural background enjoy the comfort of modern churches during the day. At night they take out their rawhide drums and dance easily to their rhythms as they 'talk to and consult with' the departed ones deep inside their homes. One can pray in church for a good growing season, with abundant rains and flourishing crops, then proceed to take part in a rain-making ceremony where a similar appeal is lodged with the ancestors.

Migrant mine and hotel workers drew from their exposure to South Africa's spiritual pluralism to produce hybrid systems of faith. In a bid to lessen the impact of conflict on our values, new church leaders emerged to set up separate religious sects. After they 'ordained' each other as apostles, prophets, bishops or church elders, the new sects devised flexible, alternative canons to make it possible for them to take some African practices into Christianity. In their skewed and elastic analysis of the Bible, based on specially selected sections of the Old Testament, the new churches embraced polygamy and faith healing. They shunned all types of modern medicines and herbs and came out against vaccination and immunisation. They followed a strict but simple dress and deportment code. They donned snow-white robes and kept their heads clean-shaven. The men maintained a neatly stretched, long beard and always carried long and well-polished walking sticks as their church symbols.

These churches composed their own hymns and designed their own sacred programmes and prayer codes. Some muttered words of Godly praise in unfamiliar tones – 'speaking in tongues' – claiming to have direct access to God who, according to their teachings, communicated through them in their sleep, while in a trance, or during their open-air sermons. The churches adopted names like Bethesda, Jericho Holy Spirits, Sacred Apostolic Church, *Mugodhi's Vapostori*, and Church of Africans; or they simply took on the names of their founders. Constant leadership squabbles and other internal disputes often caused the new churches to splinter into an assortment of sub-sects.

To me as a child all of this was fascinating, picturesque, and sometimes alarming. One could not fail to be intrigued by the strangely attired prophets and their followers who moved through the milieu of daily life in the village. At the same time, they brought bitter but subtle discord with seemingly unending, vicious contests to stake out their claims to the contested terrain where African culture and Christianity met and mixed.

Like all rural boys, my life consisted of herding cattle and other livestock, wearing a coarse jute sack as a raincoat and always going barefoot. I helped out in the fields at planting and harvest times, and at home tried to keep the free-range chickens in check while guarding their nests and chicks. When my mother was away I babysat my siblings. The bane of my life were the restless goats which, as if to punish me for all my boyish sins, deliberately sprinted into neighbours' millet fields and nibbled their highly prized crop. The goats infuriated them and got me into trouble.

We lived the way Africans had always cherished, with sheer simplicity and devoid of any Western trappings and competitive influences. Yet on Sundays entire villages donned a completely different mask. Clad in our best – though rudimentary – outfits we huddled our bodily frames inside makeshift, grass-thatched Christian church 'halls'. Closing our eyes devoutly we recited our biblical prayers, confessing what we thought were our sins and transgressions during the week. Our voices rose in carefully rehearsed Christian hymns that nevertheless bore the sonorous and unmistakable signature of African choral singing. We chanted for salvation and unconditional forgiveness, praising Jesus Christ and God, the Almighty. Africans love to sing and I loved the singing and the songs. The regular church choir competitions, with their compelling rhythms and rich harmonies, induced a sense that the community was at one with itself. It seemed as if heaven must open up to our appeals. We had sincere expectations of a better life after death beyond our earthly miseries when all spiritual promises would be fulfilled up there in heaven or beyond in some glowing infinity.

That was Sunday. On our return home, life reverted to the gruelling, poverty-stricken realities of our corner of Africa. In retrospect, the world we inhabited was richly varied and complete; though poor, we did not feel destitute and abandoned by God or the spiritual universe. We had our routine rituals and cultural expectations, reinforced by a strict observance of communal norms and standards. Politics, money and sectarianism may have disturbed us but they could never destroy us.

The crunch came when I was ready for school. Both parents valued education immensely but schools were few and far between, and cripplingly expensive if you had a large family to equip with books, uniforms and shoes. The missionaries never made choices easy for people: non-converts of a particular church found it difficult to enter into particular schools.

In 1959 I started off at Munyira Primary School, eight kilometres away, together with my childhood mates Enias Ndarambwa, Taruvinga Rwizi and Jephta Mapiye. My first teacher, Nhekanori Matimba, was a stern disciplinarian who insisted that we cram into our heads everything that he taught us, especially certain Bible verses. Teacher Matimba, or Mr Matimba as he resolutely insisted we should refer to him, left such an indelible impression in my mind that to this day I can recite Psalm 23 with ease.

By then I had a younger brother, Collins, who was born four years before I went to school, quietly snatching away from me the monopoly I had enjoyed as the sole focus and linchpin in my parents' home. At first, I was a little jealous of Collins but as we grew up he became a wonderful playmate and companion.

When out of school, I was Collins's babysitter while my mother continued with her seemingly unending domestic chores. I could see that an African woman's work was never done: watering the family vegetable garden, washing dishes, bathing us, making the fires for our warmth, lighting and cooking, weeding the crop fields, checking on the welfare of our livestock, pounding and grinding the millet flour for our meals – it went on and on as a carefully programmed, routine assignment every day.

One day, our cheeky cow Katsime (which means a tiny fresh water spring) gave birth. Katsime never liked young children around her, especially when lactating. When we tried to kidnap her calf and lock it away in a warm goat pen, she rushed at me and knocked me down, mooing loudly and trampling on my torso. The attack sent Collins scurrying into the homestead for cover, alerting my mother to my predicament. I still bear the mark of the injury.

Munyira had double classes for its first five grades, from sub-A (equivalent to a first grade) to Standard 3. But for the last three grades, Standards 4 to 6, there were only single classes. This meant that if one failed to make the grade at Standard 3, you either dropped out of school completely or had to look for a place elsewhere. As I was no better than average, I was squeezed out of Munyira after failing to make the grade for Standard 4 in 1964. The headmaster, Amon Gwata, could have used his discretion to let me in had it not been for an unpleasant clash with my father. Dzingirai-Chibwe alleged there was too much bias towards religious education at Munyira. Gwata would have none of it; he told my father off – and me, too!

A stubborn Dzingirai-Chibwe was wholly dedicated to seeing me through school, especially as I was the first-born. He studied our options and found an alternative. My mother's half-brother, Tafirei Murira, was already attending school in the neighbouring district of Hwedza. So in January 1964 I was sent off to St Marks Primary School, Goneso, run by the Anglican Church. Tafirei's school was nearby in Zviyambe village. My father arranged to transfer Tafirei to St Marks for his final year in primary school, Standard 6, so that he could be close to me. Meanwhile Dzingirai-Chibwe had found a place for Tafirei and me to stay in the homestead of a Mr Ndekwere.

I never found out Mr Ndekwere's first name, and the reason for that is quite significant. In a traditional African setting young children were rarely permitted to ask the first name of any adult and they were forbidden to refer to adults by their first names, either in private or in public. A number of the elders I met in my early life shall consistently be referred to by the family surname, for I honestly never knew their first names or initials.

Being away from home was unsettling. It was the first time I had travelled on a bus and I was exposed to what I thought was a weird family environment. Mr Ndekwere, though a hard-working peasant farmer, lived with his two children as a single parent since his former wife had moved to the town of Rusape and rarely visited the family. I had never lived in a home without a mother and wondered how life could be possible under such circumstances. The only consolation I had was the company of Tafirei. Mr Ndekwere had a teenage daughter and a son who was slightly younger than me. We prepared our meals and cleaned the homestead as a family. After a mere three months something disturbed Mr Ndekwere and he evicted us. I guessed he feared for his daughter after noticing what he thought were teenage sexual advances from Tafirei.

Undaunted, Dzingirai-Chibwe looked for another place. In my second school term, we moved in with the Shana family where we had our own room but shared meals with the rest of the family. This was a stable family unit with a father, a mother and two children. Conditions were much better – something closer to what I was used to – and I immediately struck up a friendship with the son Peter, who was my age.

Then something occurred at school that brought the outside world and its sinister features directly into our innocent young lives. One of our teachers, a Mr Chipunza – a young political activist – teamed up with some villagers in the dead of night and destroyed a cattle dip as part of a nationalist resistance campaign and protest against land policies. Following a tip-off, police swooped on St Marks, dragged Chipunza out of class, handcuffed him and shoved him in a police vehicle which roared away with bleeping sirens. This happened in July 1964, little over a year before UDI, and was a clear indication that the political temperature was hotting up as the government moved to suppress opposition – which would however not be suppressed.

It was the first occasion on which I witnessed an arrest under the command of a white police officer, and it was scary for all of us. We huddled in a classroom corner, darting quick glances at the beleaguered political campaigner whom we instinctively understood had done something courageous on behalf of all of us. Perhaps at that stage we could not consciously rationalise that he sought our freedom as an oppressed people, but in due course the lesson sank in. As pupils, we heard that police set about rounding up the nearby villagers to interrogate them and arrest their suspected leaders.

Chipunza was never seen at the school again.

Life went on. During the school holidays, Dzingirai-Chibwe urged me to persevere, telling me that a better education would surely set me free from poverty. He loved to tell stories about his experiences in Johannesburg where educated blacks drove their own cars and led a lifestyle he envied. He described how their superior education and knowledge gave them the courage to stand up for themselves and dare to challenge white managers. This was in apartheid South Africa which at that time was witnessing the trial and conviction of Nelson Mandela and others for plotting the armed overthrow of the white state. Despite these developments, Dzingirai-Chibwe regarded South Africa as a superb example of how a black person could move away from subsistence to a place of honour through a good education. He loathed his own social status, having attended school for only three years. For his children to be upwardly mobile and to adapt to competitive life in Southern Rhodesia, he needed to mould us and convince us of the benefits of Western education.

Dzingirai-Chibwe admired the few well-heeled clerks, teachers and other educated blacks in leadership positions. Himself a builder, carpenter, community organiser and a competitive communal farmer, he often told me that he detested the life he led and would not want his children to face similar limitations. He took a tough line; he was an ambitious parent, hyperactive and hard-working, resolute and unwavering in discipline, and he would always have the last word. He insisted on what he considered to be the best and he maintained a firm grip on family values.

At a very young age I realised that Dzingirai-Chibwe favoured a straight and narrow path for me. To have a more direct influence on my life and to lessen the burden of paying for my staying away from home, he decided that I should move from St Marks and live at home. At the end of 1964 I was on the move again, this time joining Chikara Primary School which was run by the Catholics. It was only three kilometres away from our village but situated in Gutu, a neighbouring district separated from us by the Nyazvidzi River. The river unfortunately presented a natural barrier.

As I started school in the middle of the rainy season, the Nyazvidzi was often flooded and too dangerous to cross on some mornings. There was no bridge. Dzingirai-Chibwe accepted the new challenge and negotiated lodgings for me with the Chidanguro family in Gutu – at least until the floods subsided. In the end this meant only a month or so away from home but it did demonstrate that if you lived in an underdeveloped rural area you had to be adaptable. Simply giving up was never on my father's agenda.

While nature put up natural barriers, politics invaded our lives and threw up obstacles to progress. My Standard 5 teacher at Chikara was John Makumbe, another young political activist fresh from a teacher-training school at Bondolfi Mission in Masvingo (at that time called Fort Victoria). Apart from his usual political statements on the disadvantages of colonialism for any black person, Makumbe could hardly contain his anger when Smith declared UDI in November 1965. He burst into the classroom after lunch expressing his revulsion and shouting that as black people our struggle for freedom was going to be a difficult and complicated process. Makumbe had picked up the story on the main afternoon news bulletin. He spent the whole afternoon explaining what Smith's move meant for our country and that we, as black people, must resist the move.

My own growing awareness was strongly reinforced by an encounter in a post office. In order to apply for places in various high schools I was buying postage stamps when a white official scoffed at my ambitions, saying he did not see any reason why I should worry as Africans were dull and unimaginative by nature. I concluded my purchase and limped out, my ego thoroughly bruised and anger seething through my nostrils.

Although our home was a mere seven kilometres from the government's administrative offices, I rarely came into contact with the officials and their families who lived there. We used to watch them shopping at the local shops, but hardly spoke to them. Generally, the presence of whites evoked mixed feelings of resentment and fear. I saw them as different and cruel, especially after what I saw happen to Teacher Chipunza in 1964. Villagers tended to minimise contact with the whites, going to the administrative offices only when it was absolutely necessary, like having to visit the 'pass' office for national registration papers.

My temporary displacement from home in 1964 and 1965 which required me to move between families, schools, religious settings and districts affected my academic performance. Although I was extremely competent with figures, arithmetic and mathematics, I had difficulties with both spoken and written English. There were insufficient English books around; no libraries; and the language was never widely spoken, either as a medium of instruction or by the pupils outside of basic grammar lessons. The closest I came to anything written in English was a government propaganda newspaper, *The African Times*. There was some copy in English, though the rest was in ChiShona and SiNdebele.

The African Times was published monthly by the Rhodesian Ministry of Information and Tourism. Distributed free to African residential areas, schools and townships it claimed to have over a million readers. The newspaper portrayed Rhodesian Africans as the happiest people on earth under white rule. African nationalist movements were denigrated and, naturally, black majority rule was depicted as quite unsuitable for Rhodesia. The lies were blatant and anyone on the ground could see they contradicted our day-to-day experiences. My English would improve as I learnt to decode these messages but, most of all, going to secondary school would get me talking and thinking about the harsh realities of white overlordship.

ENDNOTES

1   Hyam, Ronald (1987). 'The Geopolitical Origins of the Central African Federation: Britain, Rhodesia and South Africa, 1948-1953.' *Historical Journal* 30(1): 145

2   Gondola, Didier (2002). *The History of Congo*. Westport, Connecticut: Greenwood

3   Smith, Ian (1997). *The Great Betrayal: The Memoirs of Ian Douglas Smith*. Brisbane: Blake Publishing, p41

4   Gondola, op cit

5   Smith, op cit, p44

6   Smith, op cit, p67

CHAPTER TWO

WORKING LIFE

As a young adult I had an experience that underlined for me, as never before, the profound suspicion and persecution that surrounded us under white rule. The level of paranoia was astonishing: in every corner, it seemed, the intelligence services espied another communist-led black nationalist fomenting revolution.

During my high school years I grew increasingly alert to warning signs that indicated white disapproval of independent African thinking. Perhaps I would have become a political activist but my parents needed financial help to support the other children through school. My father, as always, pressed me to finish my studies and enter working life. After leaving school I landed a job in the town of Umtali (renamed Mutare in 1982) making elastic trimming for curtains and underwear bands. Known as Elastics & Tapes, the company gave me two weeks' basic training and set me to work among the wooden looms.

I had barely started to adjust to my new surroundings when a contingent of police turned up at the company for a word with my supervisor. The presence of police was always disturbing but I tried to pay no attention. Suddenly they dashed at me and placed me under arrest. Like Teacher Chipunza at St Marks primary school years before, I was handcuffed and manhandled off the premises. They took me to Umtali Police Station where the charge was that I was using a pseudonym. I was suspected of being a trained 'terrorist'.

I pleaded my innocence for I was not a member of any trade union or political structure. But they hammered away, asking me why I used the name Morgan when my 'real' name was Richard. The fact was that my mother had named me Morgan but the church had renamed me Richard after baptism as a Catholic. I rarely used the name Richard, not because I did not like it but it simply failed to appeal to my friends, my community and my parents.

Explanations did not help. I was detained for a night in a tiny cell full of criminal suspects. No doubt the police pursued their enquiries through the night. By the following morning they seemed satisfied and I was released. I went straight to my bosses who quickly understood the source of the misunderstanding.

I was totally bemused and a number of thoughts raced through my mind. Was there someone somewhere who was disturbed that I had found employment so quickly after leaving school? I had been attending some meetings and protest marches: could I have been spotted and reported to the authorities? Or was there an informer on the prowl in the hostel where I stayed with my father? He was deeply worried by this development, as was everyone at Elastics & Tapes. It was a warning to stay out of politics. This was in 1972.

I continued to attend meetings after my arrest, regardless of official intimidation and fears of being spied upon. The only difference was that I was now slightly more careful with my tongue.

However, all of this lay in the future as I prepared for my first year in high school. I had sat for final Standard 6 examinations in 1966 and did extremely well in all subjects except English which, predictably, I failed, having had so little exposure to the language. This was very demoralising but my parents won me another chance and I succeeded with the English paper in 1967. My natural high school should have been Makumbe Mission near Buhera. But this was an elite institution which favoured students from the Dutch Reformed Church schools in Buhera, Charter (now Chikomba), Hwedza, parts of Manicaland and Masvingo.

Even the placement of pupils at Chikara and other Catholic schools was competitive and before my admission I had faced a stiff pre-entrance series of workshops, prayer sessions and catechism seminars. The aim was to prepare us for conversion and baptism into Catholicism, a requirement for attending the school. Baptism came with a name change, implying a spiritually cleansed identity. Churches required baptised Africans to renounce traditional beliefs and customs, which we pretended to do. We were expected to cast off our animist modes of worship, shun our respect for the ancestors, and abandon our inherited rituals.

'Now you can go to a Catholic high school without any problems,' said my mother, apparently unconcerned by my name change, or my born-again status. My mother loved the name Morgan – I can't remember why – but at any rate having a dual name was not a bad price to pay for access to secondary school. Little did we know how this would get me into trouble one day.

It was the norm at Chikara for the Catholic Church to prepare their primary school graduates for high schools in Masvingo, in particular for Mutero Mission. I was initially destined for Mutero but new places became available when Silveira Mission, a single-sex boarding school in Bikita, Masvingo, was opened in 1967, and I found a place there. Silveira had two classes each for Forms 1 and 2, and acted as junior high school to prepare pupils for Gokomere High in Zimuto, also in Masvingo.

Life at the boarding school was a mixture of fun and, occasionally, homesickness. There were only two of us from Buhera at the school, Noah Makaza and I. All our schoolmates were from surrounding rural areas, which meant that we were exposed to new faces and ideas but also that we had little contact with others from Buhera district and Manicaland. As a new school, Silveira was adequately staffed and still smelt of fresh paint. The laboratories were well equipped, the dining rooms were neat, we had relatively new beds, and the library was well stocked.

Catholic schools in Masvingo fell under the Diocese of the Midlands and were run primarily by the Bethlehem Order. I got through my two years at Silveira fairly easily, taking an active part in the debating society, in science experiments and in various school competitions. The only unsettling element was the presence of a certain Father Fray, a German Swiss, whom we saw as openly racist and a supporter of the Rhodesian Front. So insensitive was he that when the Rhodesian government conducted its referendum on a new constitution to turn Zimbabwe into a white-run republic with a state president, he spent the day wearing a military uniform. This made us wonder whether he was indeed a priest. I have not been able to keep track of Father Fray's further involvement in the ministry, nor could I establish his first name, but immediately after leaving Silveira I put all thoughts of his attitude and behaviour out of my mind.

Abruptly, my formal schooling almost came to an end. Although I was keen to continue I could see that my father was now feeling the strain of putting his growing family through relatively expensive boarding schools. My young brothers, Collins, Samuel and Casper, were already at various stages at Chikara, preparing their way for high school education. They needed the family's attention at a time when my father earned very little as a semi-skilled artisan dependent on odd jobs, casual carpentry and occasional building contracts in the village. I knew I would not achieve much with only two years of high school, so in early 1970 I appealed to my father to be allowed to slog it out for another two years to enable me to complete my Ordinary Levels.

If it were not for my family's poor bank balance and weak asset base, I knew that Dzingirai-Chibwe would need no persuasion at all. It was agonising to see my parents selling off a few goats, a cow and tons of maize and groundnuts to raise my school fees and money for school uniforms.

When the schools reopened in January, I felt lucky to be part of the student community at Gokomere High School. Ten of us from Silveira, mainly those who came out at the top of the class, made it to Gokomere.

Both Silveira and Gokomere gave me tremendous insights into the world. Apart from making new friends from Catholic schools all over Zimbabwe, I was exposed to a variety of sources of history, politics, and information and current affairs. The libraries were relatively well equipped with an array of magazines, newspapers, books and periodicals on topical political issues. Missionaries, in particular the Catholics, tried to offer a holistic education, emphasising discipline and moral uprightness; encouraging debate, tolerance and compassion; and engaging us in sport. I was an avid soccer player, at one stage making it into the school's first team as a striker and mid-fielder. As pupils we had space to live, breathe and think.

During my time at Silveira I began to fill in many gaps in my understanding of current political issues. I began to put in context the source of attacks on black nationalists; the meaning of the emergence of independent, black-ruled African states, and the intricacies of racial discrimination against black advancement. Through reading and from discussions with other students whose political experiences were richer than mine, I was able to see the plight of Africans from a new perspective. The challenge to understand was also a stimulus to articulate ideas and explain the issues to myself and others. I remember telling a classmate how disturbed I had been on the day in 1965 when Ian Smith rebelled against Britain and declared UDI: thoughts that echoed the angry tirade of our teacher John Makumbe at Chikara.

At Silveira, schoolmates spoke of the difficulties of living in a racially discriminatory white world. It was especially hard for those whose homes bordered on white commercial farms – a world that I from the village could only imagine. I listened to their stories with deep interest, trying to comprehend features of the wider Rhodesian setting.

Gokomere was a well-established institution, with worldwide links and strong contacts throughout the Catholic community countrywide. The school's philosophy was to provide an unfettered climate for free expression. The mission influenced us to embrace solidarity and always preached fair play and the congenial atmosphere helped to boost my self-confidence. As my school performance improved, so did my appreciation of and interest in politics and society. I felt recognised as a key player and organiser of social events. In no time I became the overall leader of our sports teams, helping the sports master to organise and manage our swimmers, tennis players and the soccer team.

We followed and analysed the factional fighting between various nationalist groups, then confined to urban townships. Due to enemy infiltration and ideological conflicts, the nationalists often differed over strategy, which led to physical fights between youths aligned to different factions. Conflict intensified after nationalists led by the Reverend Ndabaningi Sithole pulled out of the dominant Zimbabwe African People's Union and formed the Zimbabwe African National Union in 1963. There were pitched battles in Salisbury's townships as the two groups sought to control their turf.[1]

We kept ourselves abreast of news about young activists across the borders in Botswana, Zambia and Malawi where blacks had recently gained independence. State radio broadcasts, though largely used as a white propaganda tool, were a source of vital information on the struggle against colonialism. At least we could tell through the biased news that the black people were resisting white domination. Though it was risky and could bring the police down on us, we sporadically checked the information by tuning in to external radio broadcasts from Zambia, Tanzania, South Africa and the United Kingdom.

Nearly all my dormitory mates, especially at Gokomere where several were from urban areas, told stories of strikes and small-scale acts of sabotage as blacks pressed for a fair deal. We shared small bits of information about how irate villagers torched and vandalised white tobacco farms and destroyed cattle dips. There was, of course, some youthful exaggeration – creating the impression that an immediate victory over colonialism was at hand and we could look forward to the imminent transfer of power. On the negative side, we were all conscious that forced removals were going on, ripping blacks from their ancestral lands.

While many students at the rural mission schools had never met any of the leading political activists, the exploits of their organisations were widely discussed at both Silveira and Gokomere. Early movements had included the British African National Voice Association, founded in the 1940s; the Reformed Industrial and Commercial Workers' Union (RICU), formed in 1946; and the Southern Rhodesia African National Congress (SRANC), most active between 1957 to 1959. These groupings, among others, were opposed to racial discrimination and campaigned, without success, for comprehensive reforms. Later, they transformed themselves into nationalist movements with an improved political approach.[2] Their main thrust was to put pressure on Britain to grant Zimbabwe political independence in line with a constitutional principle Whitehall was following throughout its colonies. At the time, the rallying cry was the need for a 'one person, one vote' franchise as an agenda for regime change.[3]

To teenagers like ourselves the tableau of revolutionary news was at once exciting, far-reaching, and incredibly promising as regards our own personal futures. We could hardly contain ourselves. At the same time the information reaching us, which we moulded with the imagination of youth, opened the way for a variety of interpretations and explanations from the African grapevine and rumour mill. We were sailing in deep waters and the issues would turn out to be more complex than they at first appeared.

Politics aside, I was increasingly concerned about the future of our own family and my role in pulling them out of poverty. How could I do that, given the inequality and lack of opportunity that faced black Zimbabweans and rural youth in particular? Despite the difference in their ages, my brother Casper caught up with Collins and they entered high school at Silveira in the same year. Between them they possessed one blanket and one spare pair of shorts which they swapped on laundry day.

After completing school, where, I wondered, would I get a job to help my parents end the family's humiliation and suffering – and what kind of job would it be? The only assured openings were in the teaching and nursing professions, areas I thought I could hardly master. Decent work and political rights preoccupied other senior students too. We stared, discouraged and enraged, at a world where the potential of a black person was unrecognised beyond that of a provider of raw labour. I seldom discussed politics with my father, not going beyond issues around racial discrimination and white domination. His issues were far more immediate. Finally, I decided that I would have to settle for any job I could find.

By the time I left school with eight O-Level subject passes in 1971, most of Zimbabwe's nationalist leaders were in detention. But the struggle, after initial hiccups in the mid-1960s, had resumed, this time in the form of a low-level guerrilla war against Rhodesia. Both Zapu and Zanu carried out raids through their armed wings, the Zimbabwe People's Revolutionary Army (Zipra) and the Zimbabwe African National Liberation Army (Zanla), attacking from the neighbouring territories of Zambia and Mozambique.

Limited success had attended the skirmishes mounted by Zanla guerrillas in the mid-1960s.[4] At the same time, Zipra, in concert with Umkhonto we Sizwe (MK), the armed wing of the African National Congress of South Africa, launched a joint offensive in the Wankie area near Victoria Falls in 1967. Zipra's links with MK paved the way for the direct intervention of South African security forces. Pretoria openly supported Rhodesia in the war – at least to start with; relations later soured. Similarly, Zanla later forged a new alliance with the Front for the Liberation of Mozambique (Frelimo) at the end of the decade. The alliance prompted Zanla to shift its tactical approach and launch attacks on north-eastern Rhodesia through the Mozambican province of Tete.

Details of the opening skirmishes of the so-called Bush War were sketchy at the time so it is worth recounting them for what they disclose about how the guerrillas operated at first, and how the regime responded. The first group of trained Zanla guerrillas, in particular the Crocodile Gang led by William Ndangana, ambushed and killed a white farmer, Petros Oberholtzer, in the Chimanimani area of Manicaland on 4 July 1964. According to Edgar Tekere, Oberholtzer died after being attacked by Ndangana, Victor Mlambo, James Dhlamini and Master Tresha. After this act, Mlambo and Dhlamini crossed the border into Mozambique, but the police there captured them and deported them to Southern Rhodesia. They were later convicted and hanged in Salisbury. Master Tresha, also captured, was sentenced to life imprisonment, escaping capital punishment because of his youth. Ndangana escaped into Malawi. Their effort was further complemented by an assault on Rhodesian forces by a group that crossed into Rhodesia in April 1966 and engaged in combat near the town of Chinhoyi. While the group is said to have perished, it signalled a definite shift towards direct confrontation with the security forces in the struggle for Zimbabwe's independence.

The change of tack in the struggle gave the two guerrilla armies invaluable experience, leading to a more radical approach, a fresh military strategy and linkages to other parties and organisations fighting for freedom in Angola, Mozambique, Namibia and South Africa.

In 1969, my father moved from our village to take up a job with the Umtali municipality as a builder/carpenter. He lived in the Matida Hostel in Sakubva, sharing a room with four other municipal workers. The hostel accommodation was utterly basic: rooms were subdivided into four compartments with cloth curtains strung on loose pieces of wire with sisal cords. Since my father was there, Umtali appealed to me as a natural destination for my first job search, especially as I had no close friends or family in the bigger cities of Salisbury and Bulawayo. Before setting out, my mother borrowed my grandmother's old jacket for me, saying it was important to look presentable to impress prospective employers.

I arrived in Umtali in February 1972 at a time when the story of the eviction of Tangwena people from their Nyanga ancestral homelands dominated political discussion in the township of Sakubva, then the main residential area for blacks. Chief Rekayi Tangwena had put up an excellent argument against displacement from his ancestral home and had resisted efforts to deport his people to Mozambique or to relocate them to Gokwe in order to make way for a white commercial farm, Gaeresi Ranch, in the Eastern Highlands area of Nyanga. The dispute began soon after Rekayi became chief around 1965 and the ensuing saga had extended over a decade or more.

In 1966 Chief Tangwena's community were ordered to leave their homes. The Tangwena people – members of the Manyika, one of the Shona-speaking peoples inhabiting an area in eastern Zimbabwe adjacent to Mozambique – had occupied their land before the first white settlers arrived. They refused to leave and for several years resisted the government's attempts to evict them. Then their huts and property were burned down and their cattle seized. Tangwena fled into the Inyanga Mountains and continued to press for justice, attracting a major national and international outcry over the obvious injustice of the forced removal.

Despite his lack of exposure to the media, Chief Tangwena made so much noise that the story became national headlines, particularly in Salisbury and Britain. The chief, now classified as a squatter, had on several occasions been prosecuted and fined for his refusal to move out of his Inyanga redoubt. Because of the proximity of the mountains to Umtali, the townspeople followed the Tangwena story with keen interest. I later gathered that the Manyika were among the first in Zimbabwe to hear the news that the British government had intervened and agreed with Ian Smith to settle the Tangwena land dispute.

I made sure I never missed a copy of the local newspaper, the *Umtali Post* for an update. Chief Tangwena finally left his hideout to put his case to Sir Alec Douglas Home and to Sir Peter Rawlinson, the British Attorney General, who were visiting Salisbury at the time. One had to admire the Chief's bravery,[5] in particular his reported comments to Rawlinson whom he boldly asked if a British Queen would agree to be moved by her government to Italy!

A White Paper from the British government had set out a proposal for a Rhodesian settlement. A copy of the White Paper was clandestinely circulating in Sakubva and I soon picked it up. Among other issues, it suggested a three-man commission to stop evictions from 'European areas' and the setting up of an independent Land Board to hear land ownership disputes. It also suggested a search for ways to end racial discrimination. This was encouraging but hardly definitive and we waited for more, in vain.

Prime Minister Ian Smith and the British Foreign Secretary, Sir Alec

Douglas Home had struck a deal for continued white control of the country – provided it could be shown that the majority supported it. A 20-member commission chaired by Lord Pearce, a retired English judge, was set to assess public opinion in Rhodesia. Naturally this provoked anti-Pearce Commission demonstrations and denunciations, with protests being held all over the country.

The bad news for the Rhodesian government was that a new political group, the African National Council (ANC), formed in 1971 and led by a then little-known Methodist bishop, Abel Muzorewa, also of Umtali, and a colleague, the Reverend Canaan Banana, immediately launched a national campaign to reject the plan. Muzorewa, Zimbabwe's first black man to be ordained a Christian bishop was well known and hugely popular in Umtali. He had once served as a resident bishop at Old Umtali Mission. When he formed the ANC, people understood him to be standing in for the nationalist leadership that had been detained in the 1960s. He occupied a leadership vacuum and for a while had a credible national profile.

Muzorewa would ultimately become prime minister of Zimbabwe/Rhodesia for a few short months before falling into political obscurity. Banana would later rise to become the titular president of an independent Zimbabwe in 1980, but was forced to retire when Mugabe abolished the position and introduced an executive presidency instead. Whatever their mistakes and failings, these two leaders managed to overturn the Smith-Home plan for white hegemony well into the future.

Early in 1972 the Pearce Commission conducted hearings to find out whether black and white Rhodesians would accept the independence deal. Laughably, the agreement would have recognised the white minority government and given short shrift to African hopes for immediate one man, one vote democracy. Although Smith initially supported the Pearce Commission, his government set about obstructing the investigation by refusing access to rural areas and disallowing an opinion poll. For its part, the ANC did much to persuade the Pearce Commission to report adversely by holding protests across the country. As far as the majority of blacks were concerned the proposed settlement was a non-starter. Meanwhile protests on the streets and in rural areas antagonised the regime which cracked down with police shootings and numerous arrests.

In the end, Pearce reported that blacks rejected the settlement on a massive scale. The British government accepted the findings, saying that sanctions imposed after UDI would stay in place, while Smith called the whole exercise a farce. Smith, who had served in the Royal Air Force during World War II, regarded Britain's approach to the crisis as a 'great betrayal' of its kith and kin in Rhodesia.[6]

I attended several secret meetings in Sakubva, most of which were held in the males-only hostels, at which the people debated the proposals, planned their campaigns and raised objections to the Smith-Home project. I was disturbed by the reaction of the colonial authorities to the people's views. Soon after my arrival in Umtali, two people were shot and killed as the police tried to suppress a demonstration against the Pearce Commission in Sakubva.

The atmosphere was tense as the people demanded total independence from Britain, not what we saw as the kind of cosmetic political reform and compromise solution Whitehall had put on the table. I remember being part of a group that attended a fiery and emotion-charged meeting at the Beit Hall in Umtali which was addressed by Canaan Banana. People were extremely angry with Britain for trying to appease Smith and his settler administration with a patched-up version of white supremacy that might never lead to an effective transfer of power – at least not in the foreseeable future. Not surprisingly, the plan collapsed. Britain quickly pulled out and Smith came out with guns blazing. He denounced the Pearce Commission and vowed to fight the national insurgency, now still confined to north-eastern Zimbabwe but spreading.

In my nascent reading of the political situation, the collapse of the Pearce Commission strengthened the view of black Zimbabweans that an armed revolution was inevitable. By 1973, Smith had begun to feel the pinch of the war and faced a mounting crisis of legitimacy. He tried closing the border with Zambia, but this seemed to have little impact and was too late anyway.

To me, coming from a village deep inside Zimbabwe, the Manyika seemed like a sophisticated people who understood the white man's thinking better than the rest of us. This was not surprising: the first mission schools, churches, trading missions and foreign manufactured trinkets had been introduced to the region by the Portuguese in neighbouring Mozambique hundreds of years before permeating into the hinterland.

The Manyika around Umtali looked more suave and elegant than any other African tribe I had seen before. For the first time, I saw a people who respected good food, knew restaurant 'etiquette' and table manners; they always used forks and knives when eating, even in their own homes, and exuded confidence, always smiling, spoke the distinct but soothing Shona dialect, and scarcely ever displayed their anger in public.

Unlike other Zimbabwean patriarchs, they were excellent cooks and knew the European cuisine well, together with its restaurant menu jargon. While we tended to cup our craggy hands around water taps to drink water, the Manyika were masters at hygiene: they used water glasses and tiny tumblers or cups. The men wore well-pressed clothes and well-polished leather shoes or bright white canvas sneakers, and had neatly cropped hairstyles.

Almost every Manyika household had a wireless set or radio receiver for current affairs and entertainment. The marginally well-to-do people had small jalopies or old luxury cars, some imported from as far afield as Johannesburg, Durban and Cape Town.

Sakubva was a peculiar place in a number of ways. It was built in a marshy area full of mosquitoes. Its residents – mainly workers in the municipality, timber sawmills, grading yards and cosy inns and hotels – shared tiny spaces in substandard houses, mostly with communal toilets and distant washrooms. Many lived in single-sex hostels where they shared kitchens and ablutions. One characteristic stood out sharply: the men, especially hotel waiters and cooks, were impeccably smart and always spoke in English.

For three months after my arrival in Umtali, I hit the streets on a daily basis, checking at factory fronts for work, visiting a government employment agency and looking out for newspaper advertisements for openings.

Umtali was hardly a promising choice for a young school-leaver with eight Ordinary level passes. It was quite a small town and apart from the timber processing yards, the hotels, a few shops and a car assembly plant there were few opportunities.

Most employers preferred casual and seasonal workers for short stints, depending on the demand for them. Anyone with a high school certificate was considered overqualified for their needs. Finally, my search paid off. In April 1972, I landed my first job as a trainee weaver in a textile factory, Elastics & Tapes. I hoped to use this as a starting point and to gain some experience in commerce and industry. The company was a small family business running on the basis of shifts with fewer than 15 workers in the factory at any one time.

In early 1973, my father was allocated a new municipal room at Chisamba Singles section in Sakubva. These were small, four-roomed, stand-alone units, each with a separate entrance and, as the name implies, meant for single male municipal workers. This was a slight improvement on the hostel complex where four strangers shared a single room, though we still had a communal bathroom and kitchen area.

By then Umtali and its surroundings was fast becoming one of the most highly politicised places in Zimbabwe. Something else was under way too that was destined to change my life fundamentally: labour activism was on the rise, especially in the textile industry. Phineas Sithole, a veteran unionist representing textile workers and based in Bulawayo, visited Umtali in March 1973 and addressed a union meeting at Moffat Hall. After listening to Sithole, I approached a workmate who was the leader of the local branch of the Textile Workers' Union and indicated my desire to join them.

Sithole's address inspired us. In the textile industry we worked long hours, were seriously underpaid and never enjoyed our rights as workers. I started off on a wage of Z$5 for a 40-hour week (around US$8 at the time). With that money, a single person could hardly afford the bare necessities of life, let alone maintain a large family, especially in an urban area, or send money to half-starved relatives in the rural hinterland. I never so much as dreamt of comforts like a vacation or decent household assets like furniture or a used car.

When I discussed Sithole's meeting with David Mapingire, a driver and neighbour at Chisamba Singles, I realised that there was a pattern of low wages in many sectors of the economy. Black workers in the transport industry earned roughly the same as we did.

The pace at my workplace was slow and frustrating. My family's poverty was keeping me in this type of job, so I put in a lot of effort to make it work, but it was deeply frustrating. Because my weekly wage was so low I decided to enrol for an accounting and cost management course at a local private college to improve my qualifications, but I was forced to abandon the class after a few lectures because of my changing shift-work. It was tough to be a first child and a man in a black African family. Our fathers eagerly bequeathed responsibility for our siblings to us. Many took early retirement, leaving the eldest son with the care of the entire family at an early age.

As a budding trade unionist, I quickly learnt to assess my white employers, who were openly racist in character and behaviour. Dealing with them took all my diplomacy and required some shrewd thinking. One had to persevere and be tolerant in the face of provocation, all the while remaining conscious of the pressing demands of workers and the needs of one's own family. People from diverse backgrounds depended on the trade unions to help them meet their needs, so I had to get to know them and respect differences of opinion. I was at school again, in a new and unexpected way, paying my dues and learning my lessons.

One misty morning at the end of 1973, my father woke up early and told me that his ancestors in Buhera had recalled him to the village. I knew exactly what he meant. He had decided to retire and return to his roots. He told me that he was the natural heir to the Nerutanga chieftainship and wanted to go back to prepare for that eventuality. I never doubted his strong belief in African customs and traditions, royalty and religion, but for him to wean me off so early and to turn me into the main source of support for the entire family was alarming. The family was large and very poor. None of my young brothers could fend for themselves, let alone support my parents. But that was it; it was the last time my father held a formal job in an urban area.

While this was a tough family assignment, ironically and for the first time, I felt a whiff of independence. I was now alone in the little municipal room, which gave me an opportunity to start building a lifestyle of my own. I could flirt with the local girls and go out drinking with friends and colleagues away from the shadow of a domineering parent. Throughout my stay with Dzingirai-Chibwe in the city, I could see that he cut a lone figure, having few friends and always worrying about his children's welfare and future. He kept himself very close to me.

I continued to search for new opportunities, checking out newspaper advertisements for training facilities and openings. In my free moments, I enjoyed taking a stroll to the market, talking to vendors, workers and rural farmers. I felt strongly connected to their stories and they kept me briefed on the way ordinary people were managing under the circumstances – circumstances which I fully understood having been brought up in the village.

Once in a while I might bump into someone from Buhera. We nostalgically shared stories about familiar people and places, comparing notes on the whereabouts of my peers. Much had changed since I left home, although much remained the same. Occasionally I was able to pay my mother a visit. It took a long time to save for such breaks, which I took during the Christmas holidays. Each time I went home to Buhera I noticed the changes. An increasing number of children were going to school; returning migrant workers had opened up small shops; more families had access to radio sets and were listening to recorded music. I bought my own small radio which I carried home to brighten our Christmas reunion. Most of the girls who had been in my primary school classes were now mothers, either married or out of wedlock. The world around me was changing fast. And I was too.

ENDNOTES

1   Flower, Ken (1987). *Serving Secretly: An Intelligence Chief on Record: Rhodesia into Zimbabwe, 1964-81.* London: John Murray Publishers

2   Sibanda, Eliakim M (2005). *The Zimbabwe African People's Union 1961-87: A Political History of Insurgency in Southern Rhodesia.* Trenton, NJ: Africa World Press

3   'Zimbabwe African National Union Central Committee Report', presented by R G Mugabe, at the second congress of the party, Harare, August 1984.

4   Tekere, Edgar Zivanai (2007). *A Lifetime of Struggle.* Harare: Sapes Books

5   *Rhodesia: The Ousting of the Tangwena.* London: Christian Action Publications for the Defence and Aid Fund, 1972

6   Smith, Ian Douglas (1997). *The Great Betrayal: The Memoirs of Ian Douglas Smith.* Brisbane: Blake Publications

CHAPTER THREE

WAR ZONE

While I was living and working in the textile industry in Umtali on the Mozambican border, the town was abuzz with the news of the rapidly changing scene in our neighbouring state, then a colony of Portugal. In Portugal itself, discontent with nearly 50 years of dictatorship had spilled into the open with army captains demanding an end to conscription. The country was waging wars on three fronts – Mozambique, Angola and Portuguese Guinea; its youth was dying on the battlefields and the economy was bleeding heavily from the expense. Finally, on 25 April 1974 a leftist military coup took place in Lisbon, ushering in peace overtures in Africa. Some 500 years of African colonisation was about to end. Mozambique was placed under a transitional government, leading to full independence in July the following year. A similar fast-track arrangement was under way in Portugal's other southern African colony, Angola.

The Portuguese revolution brought about a seismic shift in the politics of southern Africa as white regimes beheld the collapse of the colonial power that had bolstered their borders for so long. The support from Frelimo gave Zanla tremendous confidence and the guerrilla force gained credibility among the people. The changed political scene in Portugal was an added bonus as it pointed to an inevitable Frelimo victory, and by extension, raised hopes at home.

Another factor was that South Africa's Prime Minister John Vorster was applying unrelenting pressure on Ian Smith to find a political solution (partly because South African police were helping the security forces in Rhodesia and partly because chaos and collapse in Rhodesia would not help the cause of apartheid). Pressure of a different kind came from Presidents Kenneth Kaunda of Zambia and Julius Nyerere of Tanzania who provided moral and material support for the guerrillas.

Now that a Frelimo victory was a fait accompli, Smith and his regime started to feel the strain of a possible wholesale isolation of Rhodesia. Smith agreed to release the detained nationalists and to commence yet another round of talks which included Muzorewa and those he had recently released under the watchful eye of Vorster and Kaunda. Vorster had spent almost two years in 1974-75 promoting a process he called 'détente' in a bid to persuade Smith to talk peace with Zimbabwean nationalists and to smooth Rhodesia's relations with independent African states.

In August 1974, I met Richard Matekenya, a former Silveira schoolmate searching for work in Umtali. Richard had not achieved his goal of going to Gokomere High School and had joined the world of work, hopping from one odd placement to another as a general labourer. He had kept his head high, continuously looking for something better. On one of his visits to Chisamba Singles, he drew my attention to an advertisement in the *Rhodesia Herald*. Anglo American's Bindura Nickel Mine was looking for a variety of trainees for its operations. Initially, I was not much interested but Richard insisted that we try our luck and submit our applications.

Three months later the company invited me for an interview at Ranche House College in Salisbury. I boarded an overnight train in Umtali for a city I hardly knew – save for a very brief visit in 1968 when I went to collect money from my father who was then working for a construction company building houses in the high-density township of Glen Norah. It puzzled me that Bindura Nickel Mine, owned by the giant multinational Anglo American with plush offices in Salisbury, chose to conduct the interviews at that private college. It turned out that Anglo American had donated funding to the college; but in any case it was a prestige venue that the Pearce Commission had used too. Perhaps this all made a statement about the glowing prospects for new recruits.

The interview in Salisbury marked a turning point in my life. Youth always has high hopes for the future, but little did I realise as I boarded the train that I would be taking my first steps on a path towards national union leadership and, ultimately, a political career opposing the government of Robert Mugabe. As an exploited young worker in the textile industry I had become unionised but still had only vague ideas about the role that unions could play in the transformation of society. This would all change when – to my surprise and gratification – I was recruited to the mining industry and left Umtali to take up a job in Bindura.

Strongly motivated to do my best, I succeeded in the interview, being among 700 of the 2 000 applicants who managed to make it on to a shortlist. My friend Richard was not so lucky. The selection process continued, and eventually the company took only 14 of us to train for a six-month period in various mining operations. As I began my in-house apprenticeship in early 1975 I was conscious that another of my brothers, Samuel, was only starting his high school education and that family responsibilities lay upon me.

Before my interview in Salisbury in November 1974 I saw a newspaper report announcing the impending release from detention of liberation leaders Joshua Nkomo, founder of the Zimbabwe African People's Union (Zapu), and the Reverend Ndabaningi Sithole, founder of the Zimbabwe African National Union (Zanu), and their comrades. Among those also released were Robert Mugabe, secretary-general of Zanu, and Edgar Tekere, also of Zanu. Their organisations were due to take part in a conference with the government to be held in a railway coach on the

Victoria Falls bridge, high over the Zambezi River and linking Zambia with Rhodesia.

The famous, and abortive, August 1975 talks were held under the auspices of Vorster and Kaunda with Smith and Muzorewa in attendance. The peculiar choice of the bridge on the border allowed the Rhodesian delegation to sit in home territory while the black nationalist representatives sat on the Zambian side. The general strategy of the liberationists was to negotiate but keep their options open for armed struggle. The talks failed and the war continued for three more years. Smith was lukewarm about treating with the enemy, and his principal opponents in the Zimbabwean movements, who were not united, went their own ways to fight for liberation as they saw fit.[1]

I was back in Umtali in early December when the nationalist leaders were freed after periods of detention that varied from three to 12 years, sending wild cheers of excitement and hope through the ranks of political activists and sympathisers in the town. By then, I was preparing for my journey up north. In January 1975, clutching my meagre possessions and looking like a lost wanderer, I arrived in Bindura – far from tiny Buhera village where my umbilical cord lay buried.

Though much smaller than Umtali, Bindura had a character of its own. Situated in a rich agricultural zone, with moderate, energising temperatures and an inviting climate for livestock and cropping, Bindura provided Zimbabwe with the much-needed base of its agro-economy and an abundant labour force. The heavy presence of white farmers in khaki shorts, tractors and sophisticated farming machinery grinding away in the midst of lush, flat rows of crops and irrigation fields, lent the place an aggressively businesslike atmosphere. I was nonplussed, feeling the impact of my limited national exposure – let alone any knowledge or experience in mining. I threw my bag on to my head, asked around for directions and hit the road for Trojan Nickel Mine.

Other lucky recruits – Levi Mangadze, Sunny Chipungu, Ben Maidza and two others – were already there, sharing, I supposed, my nervous excitement. We were directed to our quarters where a waiting clerk cheerfully handed us keys to a separate section of the mine compound.

In Rhodesia, low income mine and farm housing areas were known as 'compounds' while those in towns and cities were classified either as hostels or townships – to separate them from whites-only residential suburbs. One's neighbourhood determined one's class in a racially segregated society. But we mine recruits were a slight cut above mere labourers. My new abode – a three-bedroomed, asbestos roofed house, was in an area reserved for the semi-skilled, lowest-ranked middle class mine staff. As we were young adults without families, we were allocated a single house.

After an intensive training programme as a plant operator in the mine smelter, I acquired the necessary skills to be part of this completely new environment. Everything was different: the people, the culture and above all the much better lifestyle. Even the climate seemed propitious with clear blue skies and regular rainfall, compared with the Eastern Highlands city of Umtali with its mists and unpredictable weather patterns.

The Korekore-Shona dialect of Bindura differed from the laid-back, soothing Manyika-Shona lingo of Umtali, presenting challenging idioms. My new situation was made all the more complex by witnessing the spillover of the liberation war from the north-east into the hinterland. Within two years, guns were crackling down in my home village of Buhera, some 250 kilometres away as the crow flies, and spreading further afield. Unlike Umtali, where the action was still mainly on the other side of the Mozambique border, in Bindura one felt very close to the war front.

The town was at the epicentre of government military operations. White administrators and residents initially tried to mask this by encouraging their community to engage in non-military activities. Racially segregated country clubs teemed with revellers and sports fanatics as if everything were normal; gardens and swimming pools in the whites-only areas radiated a sense of normal life in an unruffled society. The annual Mazoe Agricultural Show, a ritual to showcase the area's superior commercial farming produce, continued without interruption despite the war.

Trouble had started in the area shortly before Christmas in 1972, when the tranquillity of Bindura was shattered by rocket, grenade and rifle fire. Guerrillas attacked two farmhouses on successive nights, bringing a new intensity to the war that had already rumbled on for half a decade. Prominent local farmer Marc de Borchgrave scrambled miles through the bush to summon the help of security forces while his injured daughter Anne sobbed with fear in the farmhouse. When soldiers came to the rescue one of them was killed by a landmine planted in the road leading to the farm.

Darkness favours the guerrilla fighter. So it was that isolated white farmers and those living on the fringes of towns learnt to fear night attacks by the forces of liberation. They longed for the security of daylight when the Rhodesian army and air force could mount search and destroy operations against 'terrorist' bands. The events were widely publicised both at home and abroad, opening a new phase of the war. The Bush War, as it was dubbed by the white community, had started in April 1966 when more than 40 Zanla fighters crossed from Zambia into the northern part of Rhodesia. From then on throughout the 1960s sporadic incursions and engagements occurred along the northern and eastern borders. As the fighting escalated and more civilians were hurt or killed, white Rhodesians realised that their lives of plenty and privilege were beginning to cost them dearly.

African insurrectionists called the Bush War the 'Second Chimurenga' (a Shona word meaning revolutionary struggle for human rights). The First Chimurenga marked the fight against British colonisation in the 1890s. According to one account, the attacks on the Bindura farms were at first selective. The guerrillas identified farmers who were unpopular with their labourers and left the more popular farmers alone.[2] This was all to change as time went on, and eventually during the so-called Third Chimurenga – launched by President Robert Mugabe in 2000 to seize land owned by whites and turn it over to blacks – there was little to discriminate between farmers. But that's a later part of the story.

The 1965 Unilateral Declaration of Independence (UDI) was never going to be a success story. Resistance had started almost immediately. While Smith tried to reach a settlement with successive British governments over Rhodesia's legitimacy, armed resistance was gaining ground. Zanu lent its support to Frelimo and working together they gained a strong foothold in Mozambique's Tete province. By late 1972, Zanu, through its military wing Zanla, had established a rear base in the Tete province as a safe haven close to north-eastern Zimbabwe.

Bindura, the provincial capital on the north-eastern frontier, was always in the news. The farming and administrative areas and towns of Centenary and Mount Darwin – all serviced by Bindura – were subjected to many attacks. Buoyed by the success of the Christmas 1972 operation, Zanla embarked on a determined pattern to entice security forces into skirmishes in far-flung areas where ambushes and landmines could exact a price in life and limb. High school students and school-leavers were abducted from the area for military training. In 1973 the kidnapping of hundreds of students from St Albert's Mission and their subsequent enlistment into Zanla ranks dominated news media coverage for many months.

Although I was far away from the armed action in the north-east, I was a close follower of politics and the war, an avid newspaper reader and current affairs fanatic. The intense Rhodesian information and propaganda campaign projected Bindura on to the national map as being at the epicentre of the war.

I was also aware, through newspaper reports, that a dialogue was going on for the greater part of 1973 aimed at a separate political settlement between Bishop Abel Muzorewa, founder of the African National Council (ANC), and Prime Minister Smith. But the process was difficult to follow; details about these engagements were sketchy, and the information flow was extremely slow. All the newspapers carried were vague comments about how 'fruitful' the talks were proving to be.

Negotiations were taking place in the wake of the regime's strong disappointment with the outcome of the Pearce Commission in 1972 which reported that blacks rejected a settlement that would have left power in white hands.

Although Bindura looked undisturbed on the surface during my first year at the mine, there were clear signs of stress among both blacks and whites. Government troops from the operational areas took occasional rests at the town's whites-only Kimberley Reef Hotel for beer-drinking binges while their commanders relaxed at country clubs at the mine and in farming districts. Traumatised managers sometimes picked on innocent black workers, abusing them without provocation.

I could feel the tension; it was a kind of psychological echo from the nearby battlefields. The tenacity of the Korekore people in supplying guerrilla forces with food and intelligence charged the air with a sense of conspiracy. It was impossible to cover up, distort or influence the story despite the regime's well-oiled information machinery. Zanla had been in the area for nearly five years, and even boasted of 'liberated zones' along the border. Given the high illiteracy rate and grinding poverty among the blacks around Bindura, the guerrillas managed to appeal to traditionalists; they discouraged Christianity and Christian churches, invoked spirit mediums, and encouraged ancestor worship in a campaign they regarded as essential in asserting the original identity of the black African.

The guerrillas played up historical events in which African heroes and heroines had been humiliated by colonialists. The names and exploits of the 1890s African heroes who had resisted colonialism became potent propaganda tools to win the hearts and minds of the villagers. It was a historical mythology that the Smith regime found difficult to counter. In the 1896-97 war of resistance, African traditional leaders, led by Mbuya Nehanda and Sekuru Kaguvi of Mazowe near Bindura, mobilised the people for a spirited fight against foreign domination. The uprising was however crushed and Nehanda and Kaguvi were later tried and hanged by the colonial authorities. These stories were passed among generations in rural Zimbabwe mainly by word of mouth.

To contain the insurgency, Smith panicked and uprooted villagers from their homes, pushing them into fenced-off areas, colloquially called 'keeps'. The keeps, or protected villages as they were officially known, were meant to deny the guerrillas access to the local population, starving them of intelligence, materials, food and logistical support. Keeps were littered around the rural areas near Bindura. The plan was borrowed from British counter-insurgency tactics in Malaya in the 1950s. Its perceived success there at the time influenced the Rhodesians who had served in the colonial army. It was also tried in Vietnam, Algeria, Angola and Mozambique with varying but limited and usually counterproductive results.

The victory of Frelimo in Mozambique had shown that the liberators could win. Now home-grown guerrillas could move freely along the Mozambican border and gain support from rural people in the area. The Zambezi River was no longer a barrier preventing their incursion into Rhodesia from Zambia and Mozambique.

I was hardly three months into the new job when I heard of Herbert Chitepo's assassination by means of a car bomb in March 1975 in the Zambian capital, Lusaka. South African-trained Chitepo, a Manyika from the Umtali area and the first black Zimbabwean barrister, was a highly respected nationalist throughout southern Africa. When he left Zimbabwe, he initially took up a post as the director of public prosecutions in Tanzania before moving to Zambia to lead the Zimbabwean struggle on a full-time basis as Zanu's national chairman. He directed the struggle from both Tanzania and Zambia while all the other leading nationalists were in detention in Rhodesia.

His assassination received world attention, forcing Kaunda to institute an official international inquiry. Since then, much has been written about Chitepo's death, together with the controversies it generated within Zanu, Zanla and in Rhodesia itself. Although his murder has never been solved it has been variously attributed to agents on both sides. The controversy continues to unsettle Zimbabwe even today.[3] Smith claimed to have benefited from Chitepo's death as it divided the guerrilla forces, led to the arrest of their commanders, Josiah Tongogara, Josiah Tungamirai and others, and temporarily affected the pace of the war. After Chitepo's death, I began to hear more about Robert Mugabe.

Little was known about Mugabe, especially in Umtali and Bindura, until news began to filter through that he had left for Mozambique with the help of Chief Rekayi Tangwena, a traditional leader who had thrown in his lot with the liberationists. Mugabe had taken over the leadership of Zanu and its Zanla guerrillas and was reportedly based in the city of Maputo. The move did not affect Muzorewa's popularity, at least not immediately, as his senior officials kept on enlisting recruits to cross the border into Mozambique and to join Zanla in the war effort. To ordinary people, the distinction between Muzorewa's ANC, Zanu and Zanla was thin and negligible.

With hindsight, I think Muzorewa deliberately sought to mislead the nation about his control of Zanla guerrillas. He must have known that Nkomo, Sithole and Mugabe individually claimed to be in charge of the war effort, so he quickly changed the name of his party – after claiming to be an umbrella body representing all the liberation movements – to the United African National Council (UANC) and for a while people thought the party was a broad alliance of all nationalist movements. For a while Muzorewa managed to fill a political vacuum inside Zimbabwe.

With the release of Nkomo and Sithole after a period that lasted for close to a generation, there seemed to be a battle for the leadership of the African people. Muzorewa, Nkomo and Sithole finally split openly and claimed different identities for their political formations. As if to manage the disruption they all claimed the use of the name ANC. So we suddenly had activists referring to themselves as members of ANC (Nkomo), ANC (Sithole), and (United) ANC.

Muzorewa faced another problem. Banana and others had broken away from the ANC to form the People's Movement, a party they said was the internal wing of Zanu. Sithole seemed to be having further problems for he wanted to retain the leadership of both Zanu and the ANC (Sithole). The story went that Sithole lost his Zanu leadership position to Robert Mugabe, his secretary general, through a palace coup while the Zanu nationalists were in custody. This added to the confusion, but the impact was invisible to illiterate villagers, urban workers and ordinary guerrilla supporters on the ground.

There were other unexplained developments. Edison Sithole, Muzorewa's chief adviser and a prominent lawyer, was abducted outside a Salisbury hotel by suspected secret service agents and was never seen again. The fate of Edison Sithole has never been officially and publicly determined. There were stories that Rhodesian forces dumped him in an abandoned mine shaft; others said he was thrown into a crocodile-infested river. Curiously, neither Muzorewa nor the new Mugabe administration ever enquired into what happened to him.[4]

Zimbabwe remained on the international radar as the political situation became increasingly chaotic. It attracted the attention of the United States administration primarily because the entire region was becoming destabilised. South African forces invaded Angola to fight the revolutionary Popular Movement for the Liberation of Angola (MPLA), which had seized power in Luanda and was heavily supported by Cuba and the former Soviet Union.

Powers on both sides of the Cold War saw South Africa, Zambia, Mozambique and Tanzania as countries on the front line of the Rhodesian dispute and continued to pile pressure on Smith. The US dispatched Foreign Secretary Henry Kissinger to meet with Smith and Vorster in Pretoria, hoping to end the Rhodesian stand-off and reach a settlement strong enough to withstand a communist takeover. Kissinger, working with the British government, shuttled back and forth between African capitals. He told Tanzania's President Nyerere and other leaders that Smith had agreed to a transfer of power to the black majority within 18 months, but the reality was that Kissinger and Vorster had reached an understanding to abandon Smith and call for majority rule with protection of minority rights.[5]

Sithole, Muzorewa and Mugabe had left Zimbabwe, leaving Nkomo to try his luck with Smith. Again, for several months Nkomo and Smith were widely quoted in newspapers describing their talks as 'fruitful'. But nothing substantial was to come of it. By mid-1976, the war was being waged across almost half the country, much of it originating at the bases in Mozambique where newly installed President Samora Machel of Frelimo allowed Zanla to operate along the entire eastern border. Under siege, Smith hardened his position and launched cross-border attacks into Mozambique, culminating in a major raid on 9 August at Nyadzonya, 80 kilometres east of Umtali. In a radio broadcast, Smith claimed to have completely destroyed the guerrilla base, killing 500. In a separate broadcast through Radio Mozambique, Zanla put the figure at unspecified thousands of refugees, including women and children. Vorster, according to Smith, was against the raid and withdrew South Africa's helicopter crews then on a mission of solidarity to support the Rhodesians.

The escalating war saw Kissinger once again in southern Africa. After months of shuttling between capitals, another agreement was struck with the blessing of both the Americans and the British. But without the participation of guerrilla leaders, such pacts meant very little. By October 1976, I had heard of plans for another all-party conference in Geneva. Mugabe and Nkomo agreed to join forces under the name Patriotic Front and attended the conference, chaired by Britain, as a united group. However, disagreements persisted after nearly six weeks of talks and the war dragged on.

My friends and former workmates informed me that Umtali's Grand Reef military airstrip had become the centre of operations against Zanla. The atmosphere in the town was that of a war zone and there was pandemonium among the city's white residents as large groups of Portuguese nationals fled westwards into Rhodesia apparently fearing black rule in Mozambique. This did not surprise me as I had witnessed the initial trek into Umtali when I was preparing to leave for Bindura. Jittery and unsure about the meaning of freedom in Mozambique, the government closed the border in 1976 and Smith adopted an openly hostile attitude towards Maputo.

Watching these developments, I became confident that victory in the liberation struggle was within reach. In both Umtali and Bindura, I attended several secret political meetings at which black people sought to assure themselves that Zimbabwe was destined for freedom. The war was now everywhere. Zanla's operations had spread across three quarters of the country while Zipra (Zimbabwe People's Revolutionary Army, the armed wing of the Nkomo's Zapu) was most active in the northern and western parts of Zimbabwe.

With the constant conscription of white managers into the police and the army, I soon found myself with additional responsibilities at work which set the stage for professional growth. Mining is a serious business. One of the key lessons I drew from that environment was the importance of time management and the maintenance of sound labour relations. Smelting requires a strict, no-nonsense adherence to specific timelines and an alert workforce.

Bindura changed my life significantly, and fairly quickly. I was happy to help my young brothers out with their education: one was preparing to go to the University of Rhodesia. Because of my increased work responsibilities, Bindura Nickel soon recognised my potential. I was promoted to the post of general foreman. I was now able to concentrate on my personal and professional growth, and become actively involved in the Associated Mine Workers' Union of Zimbabwe (AMWUZ). While I never held office in the nationalist movements, by following politics closely and engaging in trade union activities my grasp of current affairs and the underlying issues improved enormously, as did my self-confidence.

With a steady source of income, I realised that it was time to settle down and raise a family. In late 1977, my colleague Levi Mangadze told me of the impending visit of his girlfriend, then due to be introduced to his family in Zvimba, north-west of Bindura. The girlfriend, who later became Mrs Mangadze, arrived in the company of Susan Nyaradzo Mhundwa. After a few probing questions, I realised Susan was from my home area. This couldn't have been more ideal: our tradition and culture in Buhera emphasised that we marry those from our close environs.

After a careful comparison of shared interests, we realised that we were deeply in love and had much in common. Susan had a mission to perform: the future Mrs Mangadze was related to her (as her aunt), and African custom demanded that Susan be a family witness at the 'inspection' of the Mangadze homestead by the prospective bride. So Susan left on her mission and then went home. But as was usual in those days, relationships were kept alive through the post. A year later, during the annual Rhodes and Founders holiday, I drove my first car to Buhera, picked up my father and proceeded to the Mhundwa family homestead in the Gunde Hills area near Dorowa Mine. Rhodesia always set aside two days in July to commemorate the life of Cecil John Rhodes. It was an annual holiday which black people hardly recognised though we enjoyed it for what was worth. It gave us an opportunity to visit our rural homes for wedding ceremonies and other traditional rituals.

Our marriage was the start of a 31-year partnership. We were destined to have six children and share a deep commitment to social and political goals. The name by which I was to refer to my beloved wife was 'Amai Edwin', although many continued to know her as Susan Tsvangirai. In Zimbabwe's traditional society, rarely is a married man or woman with children referred to on a first name basis. The custom is to use the terms 'father of' or 'mother of' their first child. Edwin was our first child, so Susan became 'Mother of Edwin' or Amai Edwin.

There would be times in the future when she literally restored me to life and health after vicious assaults and supported me and many others through thick and thin while we faced trials, persecution and false accusations. Truly, a man was never so blessed in a life partner.

After the marriage formalities, we drove back to Buhera, about 40 kilometres away. We had to leave before dusk as there was now a curfew and the village was in the middle of the war. In fact, the guerrillas had a base in the Gunde Hills, near my in-laws' home. I returned to Bindura and Amai Edwin soon followed to set up home as a mine foreman's wife in surroundings that were completely new to her.

At Trojan, we could all feel the heat of the war. In 1978 the tower on top of the main smelter where I worked was hit twice in the space of three weeks by guerrilla rockets. A heavy military presence restricted and monitored workers' movements. The experience was a particularly menacing one. I recall one day when I was drinking with friends in one of the mine's African beer halls and a white manager, dressed in military fatigues and fully armed, burst in and ordered us to lie on the cement floor. Then one by one we were screened, verbally abused, and told to run for dear life to our different compounds. After that experience I was terrified about the risks we all faced and became very concerned about what the country's future held – especially as Susan was now pregnant.

The Zimbabwean political dilemma refused to go away. As if unfazed by the collapse of the 1976 Geneva Conference on the transfer of power, Smith and our nationalists faced each other off, each maintaining a hard line. Rhodesia's political oscillations never ceased to swell the general debate at home and abroad, while wartime conflict increased tensions across the colour line. In late 1977, Smith changed tack and began to search for local partners whom he considered reasonable and conservative.

He courted Muzorewa, Sithole and Chief Jeremiah Chirau – the new leader of the Council of Chiefs, a body Smith had treated as the legitimate representatives of the black African people since his assumption of office in 1964.

Kissinger was no longer an active player, having been replaced by US Ambassador Andrew Young – again working with a Briton, UK Foreign Secretary David Owen, following changes in their governments. According to Smith,[6] the two acted in concert with Kaunda, Nkomo and British businessman Tiny Rowland, in an attempt to resuscitate the talks. Rowland owned the London and Rhodesian Mining and Land Company (Lonrho), a mining giant with interests in agriculture, textiles and other business, and he enjoyed cordial relations with several African politicians and nationalists in Rhodesia, Zambia and beyond.

Smith told Kaunda at a secret meeting arranged by Rowland that Muzorewa had the support of 60 per cent of the black people while Nkomo had 15 per cent, and Sithole and Chief Chirau shared 25 per cent. The plan was to bring Mugabe on board at the insistence of Nyerere, as Nkomo's deputy, but in the end, the talks excluded Nkomo and Mugabe.

There wasn't much optimism about any of these talks among the workers and ordinary people in Bindura and the surrounding areas. The war was taking its toll: levels of abuse at the workplace were increasing; simmering tensions were everywhere.

The pace of the initial internal discussions in 1977 was slow. In mid-January 1978, Britain convened a separate meeting with Nkomo and Mugabe in Malta, a move Smith thought was meant to divert attention from his dialogue with Muzorewa, Sithole and Chief Chirau. Smith claimed that when the British made no progress at the Malta engagement they encouraged the internal leaders to pursue their dialogue with him. After another two months of haggling, a deal that came to be known as the Internal Settlement was struck on 3 March 1978.

The agreement in essence changed nothing, nor did it generate any celebrations or widespread acknowledgement. Under the terms of the deal, an election would be held in a year's time and the country was to be renamed Zimbabwe-Rhodesia. I wondered how this could be possible before a comprehensive ceasefire was agreed with the external parties to bring about a return to normalcy.

By the time Zimbabwe-Rhodesia held its exclusive general election the following year, Muzorewa had been so discredited as a politician that the majority had lost faith in both him and his black colleagues. The election was exclusive in that it was contested only by the parties to the 1978 Internal Settlement. Muzorewa emerged from the election as the new prime minister of Zimbabwe-Rhodesia with former headmaster and Presbyterian minister Josiah Gumede as the titular first president. Neither the combined Patriotic Front nor Zapu and Zanu, led respectively by Nkomo and Mugabe, took part in the polls. The election failed to put a stop to the war, nor did it result in a legitimate government. At the United Nations, Council Resolution 423 declared the Internal Settlement illegal.

One of the biggest early blows to the Internal Settlement came with the appointment of British-trained barrister Byron Hove as co-minister of internal affairs, with responsibility for the police. Hove flew into the country and within a matter of days he sneaked out, fearing for his life and telling the world that Rhodesia was still intact and nothing had changed. Muzorewa was powerless to act, although he was the one who had invited Hove into the interim cabinet.

In a bid to assert his authority, Muzorewa committed serious blunders, allowing the security forces to continue their raids into guerrilla camps in Zambia and Mozambique, possibly killing thousands. His public utterances after these unfortunate forays did not help the situation either. His administration never managed to make far-reaching changes to the people's way of life; the regime remained firmly under the control of white Rhodesia.

To compound an already complicated situation, both Muzorewa and Sithole introduced their own militia with the express aim of enforcing compliance among the people. The militia, which was called *Pfumo reVanhu* (Spear of the People), inflicted much pain and suffering as it was under the direction of Rhodesian military officers. So serious were the brutal exploits of the militia that when a true election was held in 1980, with the participation of nationalist movements, Muzorewa only managed to claim three parliamentary seats in the 72-seat House of Assembly while Sithole won nothing. Ultimately, with Mugabe's 1980 victory, the militia, also known as the auxiliary forces, escaped to South Africa for their own protection.

Meanwhile, my life was taking its course. In August 1979, I drove Susan to Bindura General Hospital when she indicated that she was in labour. I went on to work as I was on the morning shift. Before my shift was over, I received a call from Dr Richard Laing with the good news that we now had a baby boy. It was a normal delivery, but of course Edwin had entered a troubled land. But the thought of having my own child dispelled my political worries for a moment, as I jumped up and down with joy, telling anybody who cared to listen that I was now a father!

Laing, a child specialist with a warm and open heart, clear political views and immense respect for humanity, was highly thought of in Bindura. He was a cut above the rest, showing respect to all and devoid of any hint of racism in a society where racial segregation was government policy.

I had read about the Commonwealth conference held in Lusaka in August 1979 at which Zimbabwe-Rhodesia was one the hottest items on the agenda. There had been a change of government in London. Prime Minister Margaret Thatcher succumbed to pressure and decided to bring together the warring Zimbabwean parties, including the illegitimate Zimbabwe-Rhodesia government, at Lancaster House in London. After months of tough negotiations, an agreement was hammered out providing for a ceasefire and a new constitution, and making it possible for Zimbabwe to achieve independence and freedom from colonialism and to conduct its first democratic elections – albeit with 20 seats reserved for white representatives. Although not a fully satisfactory deal, for the first time we could see real change on the ground: international peace-keepers arrived, the war wound down, political prisoners and detainees were released, and foreign guarantors of the agreement became directly involved. We eagerly awaited the return of our gallant fighters, the forthcoming elections and a genuine people's government.

We celebrated our first Christmas holiday as a family with feelings of hope. Combatants from either side had begun to move to assembly points and back to the military barracks. There was a lot of excitement in the air, save for a few incidents in some parts of the country where pockets of fighting were still being reported. Most rural roads were still impassable after years of neglect, so we spent the holiday in Bindura.

Edwin was born on the eve of this new era, a period of uncertainty but one which spurred hope for a lasting restoration of our self-esteem and dignity. I knew Edwin was destined for far greater heights than the rest of us in Tsvangirai family. He came into the world just as the past was sliding into oblivion and when change was simply inevitable.

ENDNOTES

1   Sellström, Tor (2002). *Sweden and National Liberation in Southern Africa (A Concerned Partnership (1970-1994))*. Stockholm: Nordiska Afrikainstitutet, p180

2   Petter-Bowyer, P J H (2006). *Winds of Destruction*. Bloomington, Indiana: Trafford Publishing, p256

3   White, Luise (2003). *The Assassination of Herbert Chitepo: Texts and Politics in Zimbabwe*. Bloomington: Indiana University Press

4   Only recently has there been a muffled explanation from Zanu PF that Sithole was, indeed, murdered by the Smith regime. Neither murder scene nor burial location has been identified, nor was there an official inquiry into his death.

5   South African Democracy Education Trust (2006). *The Road to Democracy in South Africa: 1970-1980. Vol 2*. Pretoria: Unisa Press

6   Smith, Ian Douglas (1997). *The Great Betrayal: The Memoirs of Ian Douglas Smith*. Brisbane: Blake Publications, p237

CHAPTER FOUR

MINE UNIONIST

For two years, Zimbabwe was a jungle. Armed forces could do as they pleased – extort, plunder, rape and murder – and it seemed that those responsible included bands of guerrillas, the militias of Muzorewa and Sithole, and the Rhodesian forces. Almost the entire country was under curfew, but this proved to be more of a cover for gross violations than a form of protection for the populace. We were still under a state of emergency, in force since 1964. This effectively gave the police and the security forces a free hand under the guise of maintaining law and order.

After the Internal Settlement the Rhodesian Front government had extended its draconian powers by proclaiming martial law in several areas where military operations were under way. Eventually much of the country was under martial law and Muzorewa's administration used the opportunity to place thousands under military guard in 'protected villages'.

Close to a million peasants who had been displaced now flocked to urban areas as squatters. The prison population was bursting at the seams with political prisoners, detainees and curfew breakers. To those still in their village homes, lawlessness was the order of the day.

All this was due to change following the Lancaster House Agreement of December 1979. The London conference agreed on the terms of an independent constitution and was signed by the British government, the Patriotic Front led by Robert Mugabe and Joshua Nkomo and the Zimbabwe-Rhodesia government represented by Bishop Abel Muzorewa. The staccato of guns that had begun in the mid-1960s fell silent and the nation emerged deeply shaken but hopeful that true national elections would now bring peace.

I was only 12 years old when the Second Chimurenga – the modern war of liberation – began, and thus grew up under wartime conditions. As an adult I was familiar with the factors that had contributed to the birth of the new Zimbabwe: the anguish of people without equal rights, the injustices of racism and repression, the fervour of black nationalists who saw the triumph of other African independence movements as a sign of things to come, the miseries of rural poverty affecting millions, the exploitation of farm and factory labour, and much more to make one angry, bitter – and yet hopeful at the same time. At last we were turning a corner.

We would be free! The mood of the nation could be likened to the first steps of an infant on a difficult and fraught life journey after surviving a traumatic birth. There was an air of expectation and promise all around us: the skies smiled widely, the rains were good and the season looked bountiful. The country was green with budding life; our being, our dignity and sense of existence were ticking back into shape. Peace was in the air and travel to the countryside was slowly increasing.

The period of transition from the Internal Settlement of 1978 to the Lancaster House Agreement in 1979 was harsh and confused. I have compared it to a jungle but perhaps it was more like warlord-ism gone wild with armed factions each controlling their share of the country's turf. Far from settling anything, the internal deal that led to the election of Muzorewa as prime minister of Zimbabwe-Rhodesia merely accentuated the levels of conflict throughout Zimbabwe. It quickly resulted in Muzorewa's plunge from the premiership to political oblivion.

In my opinion, Muzorewa's fall from grace was so shattering because he committed gross errors of judgement. This God-fearing cleric had tried his best; probably only he knew what turned good intentions into disaster at a time when Zimbabweans looked to him for their freedom. For the loyal supporters of Muzorewa's UANC, his demise was nothing short of traumatic. I was in Umtali back in 1971 when the Bishop thrust his tiny frame out of the crowd and took a clear lead in the political marathon (in what appeared to be a sincere hope) to reach a credible settlement. With the Internal Settlement seven years later, Muzorewa had clearly developed a political wobble and would soon be discredited as a stooge of the government.

He had won the Pearce Commission battle, but lost the war of hearts and minds. The real shooting war raged on. In the elections held in April 1979 under the Internal Settlement, there was still a possibility of change through people-power but this was a mere semblance of the real thing. The Rhodesian state machinery, the guerrillas, our neighbours – including South Africa – and black Africa remained in charge of the political process while Muzorewa had little effective control. Thus Zimbabweans faced their toughest transition challenge at a time when Muzorewa was at his weakest. His supporters fled from his side, embarrassed and dismayed, opting for more determined contenders.

With hindsight, I can see now that people-power alone can be an insufficient instrument for an effective power transfer. As long as a possibility exists for deep political subversion, both the people and the process must be right in order to achieve a desired goal. Change must be visible; change requires national ownership; change must have a meaning.

During Muzorewa's era none of that change could be seen or felt, apart from his physical move from a township home into State House as prime minister. He was a paper PM. He lost the plot and was finally forced to negotiate himself out of office, barely three months after assuming the appearance of power. And that was it!

As we sat with friends during the 1979 Christmas break, heavily engaged in small talk about what lay ahead, there were a number of issues on the table. I gathered later that the same concerns dominated the nation's mind at the time. These included the efficacy of the Lancaster House Agreement and the implementation of the ceasefire. Were we likely to have another Muzorewa? What went wrong? Why? Was real peace and independence possible? Could we now travel back to the village and rebuild our lives?

Families like ours asked these questions with an urgency born of fear and trepidation. I wondered what lay ahead for my baby son Edwin. No ready answers availed themselves; the course we were travelling remained blurred and rough. Under the circumstances, it seemed to me that the political party with the ability to stop the war had the best chance of making it to the finishing line.

As the Christmas holiday came to an end, the nation received another major shock: Zanla's supreme commander Josiah Tongogara, who was also Zanu's secretary for defence, died in a car accident in Mozambique. We could hardly believe the news. His death came just a few days after the signing at Lancaster House. A highly respected guerrilla chief, Tongogara is credited with building Zanla into a formidable force and directing the war effort from both Zambia and Mozambique. The news was a huge blow for an already anxious nation at a time when we all thought Tongogara was finally about to come back home to receive fitting honours and recognition.

In the absence of a steady and dependable flow of information, wild speculation filled the vacuum with many concluding that Tongogara was the latest victim of the furious Rhodesian resistance to real change. If that was true, I asked myself, what kind of transition lay ahead? We huddled around our radio sets, listening for bits of news from Radio Mozambique where Zanu ran a small but effective propaganda service. We also checked newspaper reports from Salisbury and listened for clues on the bulletins of the Zimbabwe-Rhodesia Broadcasting Service. Still, no clear-cut or convincing picture emerged. There were a lot of half-truths, misinformation and biased reporting on both sides.

Also disconcerting was the news that Zanla guerrillas were proving reluctant to leave their village bases and mountain hideouts to move to assembly points. Under the terms of the ceasefire agreement, guerrillas were supposed to assemble under the care and supervision of a Commonwealth monitoring force. Zanu largely ignored the demand, fearing that the Rhodesians might take advantage and wipe them all out at the assembly points. Zanu also wanted its guerrillas to act as the party's election campaign staff since it did not have a party structure countrywide.

Numerous stories reached us from Buhera about the continued presence of armed guerrillas among the hapless peasants. We heard about Zanu's compulsory all-night 'mobilisation' meetings. Regular skirmishes between guerrillas and the militia or the security forces seemed to be continuing, along with new arrests and shootings of curfew breakers. Travel restrictions remained, even between villages.

A desperate Muzorewa was now fully engrossed in the national campaign. He was a midget of a man, dwarfed in official photographs by white cabinet colleagues, but it was hard to miss his 'towering' presence in our lives. His party was well resourced and he received a huge amount of airtime on radio and television while splashing out with sizeable advertisements in newspapers. His campaign methods were sophisticated. Big noisy rallies attracted large crowds, drawn by plenty of food and drink. Helicopters and small planes air-dropped pamphlets and flyers. With a network of highly paid and agile canvassers driving new cars and mounted on shiny, well-polished bicycles, Muzorewa ensured that his name and image were literally everywhere.

Apart from his direct access to state resources and support, he had the open backing of South Africa. Even before the Lancaster House Agreement was officially ratified, three Puma helicopters, a DC3 transport aircraft and in excess of a thousand South African troops, advisers and election managers moved in.[1] Sadly for Muzorewa, his links with the white Rhodesian establishment and South Africa worked terribly against his campaign. The nationalist parties portrayed Muzorewa as an extension of black Zimbabwe's natural enemy, trashing his political brand and ultimately nullifying his legacy.

In contrast, Zanu relied on its guerrillas, now apparently in control of the rural population. Their campaign used rudimentary and crude tools: violence, anything anti-white, intimidation and coercion. Zanu was very clear: its Zanla soldiers expected the rural population either to toe the line through a no-questions-asked approach or face gruesome consequences which could include a mutilated ear, nose and mouth or, at worst, death. They made no secret of it. Their slogans were explicit: *Down with sell-outs! Down with whites!* 'Down' meant six feet under the ground. To the simple villagers this kind of political slogan carried a morbid and chilling message. It meant one thing: either Zanu won the election or the war would continue! The threats were expressed with force interspersed with war songs.[2]

War-weary villagers had to 'choose' between these two options. Little came their way about Zanu's policy positions, a plan for transformation or the meaning of independence. It was not even clear whether the ordinary guerrilla on the ground knew or understood any of the policy issues to enable them to put up a persuasive argument. Not surprisingly, debate was discouraged on what the future held, nor was there any information about the planned new face of Zimbabwe under a Zanu administration. Further, no other parties or candidates were allowed to set foot or to campaign in the areas Zanla now controlled. To ensure that nothing was left to chance, Zanla released a few of its fighters and thousands of untrained war collaborators to occupy the assembly points, leaving their experienced fighters firmly in a position to influence the voting.

As agriculture, the peasant's mainstay, had all but collapsed the guerrillas encouraged the villagers to scour the remaining few commercial cattle ranches and drive out the beef herds for instant slaughter and consumption. The practice was commonplace in the dying days of the war and went on right into independence. For much of the war, and especially towards the end of its final year, villagers consumed abundant quantities of quality beef from stolen livestock. Worried about the losses, the government passed a stock theft law with a mandatory nine-year jail term. This was imposed only if either the farmers or their guards failed to shoot the suspected thieves dead on sight.

As we inched slowly towards the election date, rifts began to emerge within the Patriotic Front (PF). Mugabe had decided that Zanu would break with the alliance and go it alone in the election, a move which incensed Nkomo who then announced that he would go to the polls under the name PF (formerly PF-Zapu but now with the Zapu temporarily dropped). We in the urban areas saw this as a plan to confuse voters who, during the period of the Lancaster House negotiations and their aftermath, had seen Nkomo and Mugabe as close comrades with a combined ability to stop the war.

In most rural villages, especially in Manicaland, Mashonaland and parts of the Midlands where Zanla had a foothold, the issue had always been clear. They had never heeded the alliance. They were repeatedly told of only one party, Zanu, as the main player in the struggle for independence. Nkomo's announcement, therefore, meant very little to them.

As political events rolled forward another surprise popped up. Sithole, the founding president of Zanu, claiming that he was the party's legitimate leader, filed a complaint with the High Court and forced Mugabe to change his party's name to Zanu-Patriotic Front or simply Zanu PF. With the guerrillas still on the ground, the name and the message were quickly absorbed together with that of the new party symbol – a cockerel. The cockerel, over the years, had assumed its own figurative meaning. During the war the guerrillas frequently demanded that villagers slaughter their chickens to provide food for the fighters. Those who failed to follow the order for 'chicken menu' paid dearly, mainly through beatings; so the cockerel – for a different, but brutal reason – was a war emblem with a meaning of its own.

Under one of the Lancaster House Agreement's compromise provisions, Rhodesian whites were to be on a separate voters' roll. This provision – part of what were termed 'entrenched clauses' – was to remain in force for seven years after independence and meant that whites were guaranteed 20 separate elective seats in the House of Assembly, with an option for a proportional number of appointees to the Senate. The common or black voters' roll allowed for 72 elective seats in the House of Assembly, and a sizeable proportion of appointees in the Senate. Chiefs were represented in the Senate only, after an exclusive election in their own chiefs' council.

Whites accordingly cast their vote ahead of the much more complicated national election and on 14 February 1980 the Rhodesian Front won all 20 of the reserved seats. The result did not elicit much excitement among us: we knew the white Rhodesians well and their tendency was to close ranks as a single united group each time they felt challenged.

The wider nation, however, waited for main game then scheduled for 27 February. The roll included incoming black voters who were destined to make their crosses for the first time. Most black Zimbabweans had never voted, save for the exclusive 1979 Internal Settlement election which brought in Muzorewa as prime minister. Even that election was largely confined to urban areas. Most rural voters had never had a chance to cast a ballot for political representatives.

I did not take an active part in the 1980 campaign, save for attending a few public meetings. From the reports I was receiving from all over the country, it was clear that Mugabe was destined for a massive victory. His main contestant, Muzorewa, had damaged his reputation irreparably; Nkomo still had a slight chance, but only among his traditional supporters and in rural Matabeleland. I never thought much about Sithole, Chikerema and about a dozen other smaller political parties which had surfaced on the eve of the election.

Far from being peaceful, the general atmosphere was still tense. It was risky to travel outside the cities and from all parts of the country there were reports of random bomb blasts, accidental and deliberate detonations of anti-personnel mines, and landmine explosions. Because Zanu PF held the ascendancy I was particularly concerned by attacks on their leaders which could once again destabilise Zimbabwe. One such attack was directed at Mugabe while he was on the campaign trail in Victoria and another targeted the home of Kumbirai Kangai, a veteran nationalist from a well-known family in Buhera. But, by and large, the violence did not interfere with the elections and a lasting solution looked possible.

On 27 February, the three-day general election commenced. I had remained in Bindura and, with Edwin neatly strapped on her back, my wife Amai Edwin joined me to vote early. This was new political territory for us but we were shaping our destiny and knew it. Like the majority, choosing between either Zanu PF or an unending war, in good faith we gave Mugabe a chance to test out his vision. As results began to come in on 3 March, Mugabe's victory margin did not surprise us. We knew it was going that way, for on our way to the polling station the people we met were using their hands to imitate a crowing cockerel. Mugabe's party garnered 57 of the 80 common roll seats; Nkomo took 20, mainly in Matabeleland; Muzorewa received three, while Sithole and Chikerema – despite their lifelong service in the nationalist struggle – failed to secure even one single seat.

The most gratifying part of Mugabe's victory came from his 4 March 1980 acceptance speech to the nation. The man came across well, delivering a mature, sobering address that helped to douse the simmering tensions which were still alive in the country. No attempt would be made to dislodge any officer from the public service, the judiciary, the police or the army, including those known to have been key elements of the state apparatus. The speech was well received; it was full of hope and encouragement, surprising many of my white colleagues in Bindura.

Zimbabwe was now clearly visible on the world's skyline as an unparalleled success story. Our leader appeared focused, was legitimately in charge and preaching unfettered racial tolerance and a home for all. He vowed to end the war instantly, much to our relief, and gave us a rare sneak preview of what the future held. I looked at Edwin who was sleeping on my lap, and muttered to myself: 'Lucky chap. The world is now all yours.'

More surprises and good news followed Mugabe's gesture. Nkomo was to come in as minister of home affairs, and some of his colleagues were up for cabinet posts. David Smith from the RF and Dennis Norman, a white commercial farmers' leader, were in the line-up for a government of national unity. The transition was billed to go smoothly and countries throughout the world, including the great powers, instantly recognised the new government. To cap it all, the Reverend Canaan Banana, an Ndebele, was appointed the new state president.

The jubilation and celebration went on for days in the streets, mines and factories, in the villages, and even beyond our borders. On the night of 17 April, the entire country hardly slept. The morrow was Independence Day. What a day! We had made it to our biblical Promised Land.

Suddenly I felt a surge of renewed interest to participate in politics.

A few weeks later, together with Amai Edwin, we made enquiries about joining Zanu PF, submitted our applications, and became part of the club of champions.

On the employment front things were going well for me. Since I was now a foreman, we moved from the mine compound into a home befitting my new status as a junior manager in Bindura's low density suburbs. Together with Norman Nyawo, a political activist, we began to build Zanu PF in the town. Nyawo was elected branch chairman and I became his secretary.

With Mugabe and Zanu PF now in charge, a serene mood started to envelop Zimbabwe. The smell of gunpowder, the roar of helicopter gunships and mortar fire were almost a thing of the past and in many areas had completely disappeared. People bustled from place to place picking up the pieces, restarting their lives. Nearly everyone I knew seemed to be in a hurry to prove themselves after generations of colonial bondage. Blacks were set to settle down, or so they thought, full of self-belief and with chirping confidence in the comforting knowledge that for the first time they were now in truly in charge.

The mood was different in the white community. They darted from here to there, uncertain about their future. To most of us at work and in the village, the whites' newfound insecurity was somehow tragicomic. During the Rhodesian era whites had been privileged from birth and they enjoyed the biggest slice of the national cake. Robert Mugabe's victory completely threw them off balance because they had come to believe their own propaganda. To stay or to go – that became a dominant question, while their nostalgia for the past and constant reminiscing over old times earned them the nickname of 'when wes'.

It was not funny for them, of course. In small towns like Bindura emotions among the whites ran extremely high and many could not stomach the transition from Rhodesia to Zimbabwe. Property prices in the former whites-only residential areas dropped drastically. Many empty houses were left in the care of friends, domestic workers or estate agents. The only other country on earth with a similar official discriminatory policy was apartheid South Africa – so it wasn't really a surprise when whites began to trek there en masse. Among those who grudgingly remained, to judge by their bursts of angry expletives against blacks, one could detect shocked denial that change had really come. There were some who remained because they felt they belonged and were committed to the new dispensation. Whether gravely nuanced, pessimistic, optimistic or even oddly boisterous, their language said a lot about their anxieties, fears and veiled intentions.

There were those who were open and friendly. At a social level, Dr Laing and others often stopped their cars by the roadside for chats with rural black strangers, enquiring after their health and wishing them well in a new Zimbabwe. But extreme elements shouted abuse, created unnecessarily ugly scenes in pubs and on the street, hurling profanities at blacks, crassly wishing them ill and denigrating the new Zanu PF administration. These 'Rhodies' would be a thorn in our side for years to come.

Depressed market prices forced white families to part with their assets at ridiculous prices. Elderly whites who were understandably reluctant to leave simply decided to sit it out. Younger families began to offer their homes for much less than their real value and in some cases sellers added a few carrots to their unwanted properties: the family's second car; all household furniture – fridges, sofas, workshop tools, a boat, a barbecue stand. Blacks were their target market, and they were willing to take advantage of once-in-a-lifetime bargains if the money could be found. Unfortunately the banks and building societies were yet to open up credit and still had to learn to trust ordinary 'men and women of colour' with loans. Only those with company guarantees or in the civil service could qualify for 25-year mortgage finance.

An acquaintance who managed to buy a property along Shamva Road told of a widow who prayed and pleaded with him to look after the property. He should never cut down any tree and must maintain the exotic grasses and daffodils she had imported from Europe. He even had to swear to replace broken window panes.

'I know you people,' she moaned, tears dripping down her cheeks. 'Very soon you will bring goats into this beautiful garden. The walls will soon turn black from burning firewood. Please, please, do not let me down …'

My friend, being black, said he did not know how to react to such entreaties with their racial overtones.

The once blue swimming pools, blooming flowers and manicured lawns in the white neighbourhoods started to look abandoned, the paint flaking off walls and the colours wilting. Their owners took sanctuary in Salisbury as a first step out of Zimbabwe on the way to South Africa, to Australia, to New Zealand, to Canada – anywhere for a fresh start. For a brief spell, all roads led to Salisbury. They no longer wanted to stay in the place they had called home and had fought to hold: Rhodesia was no more. The 'terrs' (short for terrorists) that they had dreaded, led by a sworn communist called Robert Mugabe, were now in charge. Radio and television, once their source of conceit, snobbery and a mirror of white culture, were now beaming cacophonies of inaudible sounds littered with war limericks and speeches of triumph.

Haulage and removal companies reported roaring business: mementos, family photos and everything that represented Rhodesia were thrown in. The rich moved to their apartments in Salisbury – complete with granny's ashes in the urn, the odd potted plant, a baptism certificate, a trophy from a shooting competition, all the junk that normally clutters any middle-class home. Poor whites – yes, there were poor whites – sold off their meagre possessions, mainly to their domestic workers, and flocked to the safety of the big cities. Professionals flew out to South Africa; so did former policemen and army officers who apparently feared a backlash. Long convoys snaked down the highways, pulling overloaded carts and caravans.

The children asked uncomfortable questions: 'Why are we leaving Loveness (the housemaid) behind? Will she survive the terrs?'; 'Are there no terrs where we are going, Mummy?'; 'Is our swimming teacher coming with us as well?'; 'Will the terrs allow us to come back to Sunday School next week, Daddy?'

For those of us who witnessed this exodus it was saddening, maddening, grim, amusing, and ultimately – we had to admit – a loss from which the country could not quickly recover. By the end of 1980 about 20 000 white Zimbabweans had left. That was about 10 per cent of their total number in the country. The figure may sound insignificant, but given that most of them were highly experienced public sector administrators and skilled artisans it meant a lot to a nation in the making. Almost none ventured to settle down in independent, black-ruled Africa as white Africans.

Emigration dominated dinner table discussions. Those who could not afford to emigrate no longer had their privileges to fall back upon and started to join the majority poor. Meanwhile the rich saw the black elite punching holes in the glass ceiling which had kept them down. Blacks entered through the same ceiling holes that some whites had fallen through into poverty. Now there were black residents in formerly white neighbourhoods; blacks in their exclusive clubs and on company boards. All previous symbols of racial and class supremacy were falling to the influx of the newly liberated.

White miners at Bindura Nickel Corporation retreated into themselves, showing visible signs of stress. 'Rhodesians will never die ...' one would blurt out, with a stiff upper lip. 'The fuck'n thickheads can never make it alone. They need us. Britain has let us down. Shit ...' Loss of racial superiority raised questions about the relationships they would now have to nurture with their black workers. And how were they supposed to handle integrated schools, hotels, sports facilities, cinemas and toilets – that had for so long been separated between black and white?

We could not hazard any answers. For their part, white politicians appeared politically moribund and never tried to explain the new Zimbabwe to their supporters. There was nothing to say. They, too, had their own questions – without answers – and were equally confused. All energies had been concentrated on winning an unwinnable war, or finding a solution that still left whites on top. They were ill prepared for the eventuality of black majority rule. It came as a shock and many fell back on fear and prejudice rather than looking forward to reconciliation and reconstruction. White Zimbabweans desperately tried to hold on to the past, but the pace of change made this impossible.

Bindura's few dozen mixed-race residents – 'coloureds', as they were known – seemed equally overwhelmed by the changed situation. Torn between two cultures because they were neither black nor white, many of them had allied themselves with whites but now searched for a sense of identity in the new black-run state. Most of them were third or fourth generation coloureds, thus they had built their own separate communities and did not have direct ties with their black or white ancestry. Through no fault of their own, such rootlessness often led to extremes of antisocial behaviour in the form of irresponsible drunkenness and licentiousness. Under the colonial system, they had enjoyed a semi-sheltered status, being below whites but above blacks. They had to decide quickly whether they were white or black – and usually chose to align with blacks after realising that they were also victims, though to a lesser extent, of a racist system.

Together with those of Asian ancestry (Indians and a few Chinese), coloureds had enjoyed a slightly higher level of privilege in a country of white racial supremacy, and rarely spoke indigenous languages. A significant number of coloured Zimbabweans established themselves as academics, poets, writers, pro-democracy activists and revolutionaries; others were managers, musicians and entertainers. There were also a handful of excellent soccer players, mainly with Arcadia United, a top Harare team which was their community club.

During the war, coloured men were conscripted into the Rhodesian military where they served for long periods. After independence, unlike whites who could easily emigrate, coloureds did not seem to have another place they could claim to be home. Zimbabwe was their only home; and in a short time many started to find the going tough. The sight of numerous poor coloureds on the streets and at shopping centres reflected the changed and changing times. The majority of coloureds had limited social options, so they learnt to speak the lingos of the Shona and Ndebele, tried out *sadza* (the maize staple), and frequented our beer halls to drink traditional sorghum beer – a thick, grain-soaked brew that was shunned when the whites were in charge.

One could easily revel in the discomfiture of our erstwhile masters and their juniors but a moment's thought brought less satisfying perceptions. If whites had not thought about their futures beyond the collapse of Rhodesia, nor, apparently, had we. We basked in the glow of freedom but perhaps this was all just a temporary respite from grinding realities. Returning fighters were traumatised; many were missing, whereabouts unknown; families had lost their breadwinners. In the rural areas, the war had left widespread devastation while whole villages were deserted due to the relocation of people into 'keeps'. These people had lost their homes and were penniless. Squatters crowded around the cities while unemployment gained ground. The mood of political euphoria could not conceal dark intimations that the ruling party would ignore constructive suggestions and be intolerant of dissent.

At first none of this disturbed us. Scenes of change flickered by as if in a fast-moving thriller, foreshadowing the changing political climate. We were entering into a new phase as a people with equal rights and privileges. Jobs, civil liberties and constitutional rights previously reserved for whites were now open to all. Years of colonial humiliation were melting away like a dispersing black cloud giving in to the power of a bright sun. Unbelievable! It was all over at the stroke of a black vote – the first ballot through which we were allowed to speak out; a ballot which we all fought hard for; a ballot which changed our lives and our personal and collective esteem. It was impossible to escape the feeling of national expectation and bliss.

Salisbury (soon renamed Harare) was the seat of government and possessed the keys to our political direction. The government – now controlled by a fearless but magnanimous guerrilla leader, the urbane and well-read Robert Mugabe, and his triumphant freedom fighters with their unquestionable legitimacy – was to guide us into a new epoch. For the first time, we looked forward to our national news bulletins for direction and vital information. The Voice of Zimbabwe was that of the people talking to themselves. Our hopes were rekindled. Principled bravery had paid off.

Visits to rural villages peaked after years of separation between town and country. The excitement brought by peace gripped the country as families sought for news about a long-lost brother, sister, child or any close relative. Elderly parents, brothers and sisters, nephews and cousins, children and grandparents all searched far and wide for clues to the fate of their loved ones. 'Did he or she survive the war?' This was an all too familiar question. 'Are they coming back as our own local heroes?' Enquiries were pasted up everywhere, with Zanu PF offices overwhelmed by similar queries.

The rumour mill was equally alive. 'He was last seen in Mutoko and Inyanga. He must be coming back home at any time.' Or: 'She is at the guerrilla assembly point at Foxtrot. I saw her there, with my own eyes.' 'Sure? What does she look like now?' I often heard such reassuring messages, triggering happy conjecture at street corners, at bus stations, or after a church service, as people comforted each other and shored up their mutual hope that loved ones would return.

Anxiety gripped many a Zimbabwean household at the time. Families just had to cope with the stresses, be they psychological or financial, in a situation of poor record keeping. Given the nature of guerrilla warfare and its lack of recorded detail, there was a serious information vacuum. Perhaps with better management of lists of recruits and fighters the PF could have assembled a register but the secretive nature of insurgency campaigns made this dangerous and difficult. After the war the PF's armed wings, Zanla and Zipra, were very slow with any details: they too seemed overwhelmed and out of the information loop.

Soon after the election in 1980, family reunions took place far and wide. Girls who had joined the struggle from school now nursed young babies; adult males, with young families in tow, were returning to their roots; our boys, our brothers or *vana mukoma*, as the ex-combatants were affectionately called, were now back home, many sprouting beards, maybe a moustache, greeting their relatives with deep voices. They came from neighbouring countries and from all over the world: from Eastern Europe (Romania, Bulgaria and Poland, among others), from Russia and China, from America, Britain, France and Germany, and from Cuba. They had mixed with freedom fighters from South Africa and Namibia and were worldly-wise about the Cold War and its impact on newly independent countries that strove to be non-aligned. Many were radicalised and spouted the language of Marxist-Leninism.

Those fortunate to be back carried a mixed and often depressing baggage of psychological and physical scars. Some were maimed, others were emotionally corroded, still others struggled to shrug off a bush psychosis, imagining themselves still out there under the stars ready to ambush the enemy. If they struggled to readjust, such were the scars of war.

War is never kind either to soldiers or civilians.

It was disconcerting for our young heroes to return from the war front without any psycho-social support in place. The paltry amounts of money that were supposed to get them started were looted by some of their commanders. There was no accountability and tin trunks full of cash are known to have disappeared without trace. It was a lawless game; there was nobody to complain to.

In Bindura and its environs – the zone which had borne the brunt of the war for the longest period – most of the war veterans were instantly demobilised. They were deemed unsuitable for retraining into the new national army because they did not have an adequate educational background. The war had not only deprived them of their schooling but now they were being punished for their bravery. Whole villages, especially in the north-east where I lived and worked, no longer existed and the veterans had no place to go.

A significant number of those who received start-up cash squandered it recklessly. I saw some hobble back to their villages without any means of support. Many were forced to start afresh entirely on their own, back on the tiny, sandy patch they had abandoned almost a decade before. Some now had families, but without assets, without food, a home or skills, they seemed desolate and doomed. In no time at all, they became destitute – abandoned by their own party, by the new government and by their communities.

The esteem and national recognition that should have been extended to our war veterans quickly fizzled out. Key military and government posts were snapped up by nimble-footed and educated former refugees and relatives of senior politicians and commanders who had spent the war years comfortably under cover at universities and colleges in Europe and the United States, picking up various professional and technical skills.

But to most of the survivors I met, one conviction thundered out and knitted them and the rest of us together: they were grateful to be home alive, with Zimbabwe as their prized reward. A national objective had been fulfilled and the nation was indeed proud of them. Peace had been made possible and freedom could be taken for granted.

I watched my own youngblood, Edwin, open his tiny mouth, displaying his first four budding front teeth and learning to recognise the family. He related happily to his mother, to me and a few friends. *'Ta-ta-aa, M-m-m-ama ... Mama ... Heeh-hehh.'* I loved to watch him while sipping a glass of beer after work. There he was: lift a foot here, fall over there, and try again and again, as he primed his first steps. Edwin's facial expressions and moods were vivid and bold, with a wide, still-forming, craggy laugh.

Here I was with my own first-born son, in circumstances very different from those of my birth but still with the expectations and dreams of the typical African father. With a young family, and my extended family responsibilities slowly diminishing as my brothers and sisters became self-sufficient, I looked forward to an unimpeded and leisurely emergence of my personal fortunes. It was somehow surreal and unbelievable after our family's difficult quest for education and my own desperate search for work. For once in my life an assured future in the new Zimbabwe beckoned. My position as a foreman came with a range of perks, a better salary, spacious accommodation, access to the mine's sports facilities previously reserved for my white colleagues, membership of the elite country club, access to company loans and general acknowledgement of my professional and personal status.

My circle of associates was growing; in addition to my position as secretary of the local structure of Zanu PF, I was elected to lead the local branch of the Mineworkers' Union. These two positions exposed me to a rich world of human relationships that enhanced my understanding of basic social and political dynamics and brought me closer to the people. Although I used to socialise often, take an after-work drink and a cigarette at times, as a respected family man I was moderate in my habits.

I started to sharpen my tools for effective communication and diplomacy, looking closely beneath the surface for complex meanings. Issues of management interested me very much, while I set about garnering more knowledge of the history and workings of trade unions and political structures. These turned out to be closely interrelated. At independence, Zimbabwe's labour movement was divided into six federations. Those representing black workers were often small, fragmented and underfunded, while white workers' unions were well resourced and better organised. Black workers occupied mainly the unskilled and semi-skilled category and earned so little that their unions could hardly manage to raise capital from tiny membership dues.

Although companies trained their own artisans through a national scheme, rarely did they enrol black students. I was lucky to be one of a mere thousand technical graduates to have been trained in 46 years – an indictment of commerce and industry if ever there was one. Apart from the state's open policy of racial discrimination, the powerful white unions blocked the enrolment and training of black apprentices, keen to maintain a supreme position for their ilk and fearing competition at the workplace. The white unions excluded the sizeable black, lower middle-class ranks of bookkeepers, senior clerks, artisans and the semi-skilled.

While discriminatory practices were widespread in business and manufacturing, the picture in the mining industry was slightly different. The Associated Mineworkers' Union (AMWUZ) had three categories of union membership: one for whites; another for semi-skilled and clerical staff, or A-group; and lastly the B-group which accommodated the unskilled. The A and B groups often had a single leadership which represented them in times of collective bargaining with the employers' Chamber of Mines. These groups were led at Trojan by Jeffrey Mutandare, then a senior clerk at the mine.

With the advent of the new Zimbabwe, the fragmentation of unions no longer made any sense. First came the departure of many white unionists out of trade union affairs. In our case, AMWUZ's white leaders withdrew all the money from the union's bank accounts, claiming it as their pensions, and blithely handed over the keys to Mutandare's office.

Kumbirai Kangai, the new minister of labour, found a heavily fractured labour movement which could neither speak with a single voice nor represent the workers effectively. The new government intervened to help workers across the board to establish a single labour federation. Kangai's plan was to have a single union for each industry affiliated to one umbrella body. He opened up 88 Manica Road, the tiny two-storey building in central Harare which housed the Zanu PF headquarters, to aspiring trade unions to set up shop.

Zanu PF became heavily involved in the formation of new unions. A number of party activists were selected and assigned to the hastily formed trade unions. In no time, 88 Manica Road resembled a huge assembly point – a political and social meeting place and grievance centre for war veterans, refugees, disgruntled workers, political activists, political opportunists, and even con artists and thieves.

Several other functions were also taken over by Zanu PF, including that of hearing family and domestic disputes. Overnight, 88 Manica Road assumed a supreme status: passing binding verdicts – which few dared to challenge – on labour issues, harassing errant spouses, punishing white business people, and extorting money from intimidated individuals. Thieves also took advantage of 88 Manica Road, waylaying their victims at, or near, or actually in the building before disappearing with their loot.

The place became notorious for cases of physical assault and harassment of spouses, businessmen and unsuspecting Zimbabweans. Soon the pattern replicated itself countrywide: every Zanu PF office turned itself into a little kangaroo court. Coming out of a brutal war, ordinary people seemed to excuse these actions. Workers, bruised and battered for a long time by inequality and seemingly baying for some form of revenge, put their faith in their former liberators and hardly raised their eyebrows. To the aggrieved, 88 Manica Road provided answers to nagging issues; it became the centre for instant justice and a symbol of conquest and victory. Any attempts to question or enter into a discussion over the party's behaviour or motives could land one at a Zanu PF kangaroo court – with dire consequences.

As the exiting unions had been largely ineffective, the government felt duty-bound to play a greater role in the labour market. Zanu PF justified its swift intervention in the labour market as a means of ensuring security of work. Party officials explained that they aimed to raise the standard of living for ordinary workers by narrowing inherited income gaps and managing inflation. As trade unionists we expected such a move because industrial unrest reigned countrywide for 18 months after independence. Kangai was in a helicopter nearly every day, from Hwange to Chiredzi, Kariba to Plumtree, Nyanga to Masvingo and back to Harare and

Bulawayo, trying to calm thousands of restless workers.

At Trojan we had our own strike which lasted ten days. In the end, the workers just returned to work when nothing could be done to attend to their grievances, which looked poorly thought-out and unclear. I found myself advising patience and endurance, arguing convincingly for both sides. My unique position in junior management and in the trade union movement was my point of reference. The arguments, concerns and frustrations of both workers and employers made sense to me and I sought a reasonable common ground. My motivation was to avoid unnecessary disruptions arising from difficult positions, racism or other external factors.

Although figures varied, the Zimbabwe Congress of Trade Unions (ZCTU) later established that there were at least 300 organised or spontaneous strikes at this time. Workers were on edge, complaining about what they thought was a slow pace of change. Some white business people, out of stubbornness or for the fun of it, provoked nasty scenes in commerce and industry, at farms and plantations, and in mines and hotels, referring to the new government with an array of derogatory terms. This led to strained workplace relations and invited the ire of edgy and expectant workers.

A commission of inquiry into incomes, prices and conditions of service was set up in September 1980 to, among other issues, provide baseline data and enable the state to attend to past imbalances. Earlier, parliament had enacted the Minimum Wages Act of 1980, primarily to bar employers (and even employers of domestic workers in private homes) from dismissing their staff without prior government permission. Under the Act, the state set annual minimum wages – an action that in effect undermined any attempts by unions to embark on a collective bargaining process with the employer bodies. It was clear that Zanu PF wanted to use the minimum wage as a populist move, in order to endear itself to the workers. Employers tended to follow government directives and ignored trade unions.

Our work in the unions suffered further after the state decreed that workers could now form shop floor workers' committees and works councils, operating independently of the unions. These structures were legally mandated to liaise directly with a local labour office in times of industrial disputes or tension. For a short period, the structures seemed to work well – but lack of training in the art of negotiation, collective bargaining, workers' rights and workplace democracy affected the work of committees and began to undermine their effectiveness.

After a 20 per cent devaluation of the Zimbabwe dollar in 1982, workers' basic earnings lost value significantly. The small gains we had accrued in the previous two years began to erode. To make matters worse, the state introduced a wage restraint policy in a bid to contain inflation which mainly affected the public sector and state-assisted companies. Salaries in the private sector became more attractive, causing a brain drain from the public service. One worrying outcome was that low incomes in government work tempted officials to engage in corruption, bribery and extensive moonlighting.

Given the tiny size of the private sector inherited from Rhodesia, the policy of minimum wages and other measures worsened the prospects for job creation. Companies were now barred from freely dismissing their workers without state approval, even in cases where business was down. Employers then became reluctant to engage new staff, fearing bureaucratic interference each time they tried to downsize operations for economic or operational reasons. It became increasingly difficult for them to deal with cases of open misconduct at the workplace. The government seemed to appreciate the role of trade unions, but preferred an organised workforce led by a generally supportive and pliant labour movement.

Kangai kept the pressure up, calling for the formation of a single body for each industry. His actions saw the registration of 52 trade unions by 1981, followed by the formation of the ZCTU soon afterwards.

The inaugural congress of the ZCTU in 1981 elected Robert Mugabe's brother Albert to the influential position of secretary general, along with a number of middle-ranking Zanu PF party officials or sympathisers into the executive. I did not know much about Albert Mugabe, nor did he stay long in the job: he was found floating dead in the swimming pool at his home in Ashdown Park, Harare, a year later. No one was prosecuted, nor was the nation informed whether or not foul play was suspected. Speaking in hushed tones, some who claimed to have been close to Albert later said he had committed suicide; others thought he died in a freak accident; other indications were that he was murdered by a close relative in a family feud. Beyond that, Albert Mugabe's death remains a public mystery. Emmanuel Chimwanda, then a senior police officer, later told me that the police were instructed by their seniors to stop the enquiry into Albert's death. No reason was given.

Albert Mugabe's death temporarily destabilised the ZCTU. However, with an acting secretary general, it plodded along, still under the heavy shadow of Zanu PF and the government. But our Bulawayo-based unions refused to toe the Zanu PF line. They aligned themselves to PF-Zapu, Nkomo's party, and remained that way – with Kangai making no secret of his disdain for such behaviour. Unions were unhappy with the leading role of the state as it made their offices moribund and irrelevant. Moreover, workers found no joy in associating with trade unions as they saw no immediate benefits from such an arrangement.

With Mutandare now at the helm of the Associated Mineworkers' Union, I found a colleague and experienced unionist to work with at close quarters. We knew each other's families well and often took time off together to share ideas and strategies. In 1983, I was unanimously elected second vice-president of the AMWUZ. By then I had helped Mutandare to train as a smelter and he was working in my plant. With his new full-time post of AMWUZ president, he left Bindura for the national office in Harare.

As second vice-president, I remained in my job but travelled extensively to build and strengthen the union and to attend to workers' grievances at various mines. This was my first direct contact with national affairs. Immediately I saw a clear disconnect between the Zimbabwe we had expected and the unchanging, grim reality of Zimbabwe as it really was, with its paucity of personal and collective growth prospects for workers. Our much sought-after independence as a country had yielded little, if anything, to show for the ordinary worker.

I wondered why this could be at a time when we as workers thought, together with the peasants, that the white oppression and colonialism that had held us down was now lifted. Each time I raised the subject of workers' welfare with colleagues in Zanu PF, in particular with our cabinet ministers, I was surprised at how quickly they dismissed my concerns as both uninformed and worthless. Their argument was that the plight of workers constituted the least of the government's worries and priorities.

Meanwhile I started to notice signs of resignation and desperation among mine workers: a loss of hope and inspiration. Whenever I spoke to senior unionists from other sectors on the few occasions I represented Mutandare at ZCTU meetings, I sensed an abundance of available, alternative options facing Zimbabwe, ready for effortless picking. But the absence of political will to attend to the pressing items on our national wish list seemed to be the main obstacle. There was no debate on job creation, nor were alternative sources of work explored.

The entire nation's mind remained fixed on a tiny and apparently overwhelmed formal business sector. In Smith's Rhodesia, the formal, private and public sectors had provided a small white population with almost all its basic needs. But after 1980, the formal business sector was expected to offer an instant cafeteria environment for all Zimbabweans. For this to happen, the state needed to create space for private initiative and to marshal fresh resources and incentives so that the business community could engage in accelerated growth. It also needed to encourage new black enterprises. Mugabe, our 'socialist' leader, discouraged small to medium-size enterprises, especially those owned by black Zimbabweans. The only avenue for job creation, we were told, was through cooperatives, set up in line with self-professed Marxist-Leninist philosophy.

Sadly, relations between business and the government were frosty at best. The private sector was viewed in Zanu PF circles as being dominated by unrepentant Rhodesian capitalists, bloodsuckers and profiteers. The same productive sector faced an additional pressure from a rise in demand for goods and services. This was the upshot of the state's minimum wage policy and a growth in public sector incomes for the new black civil servants. But the state, while raising wages by decree, put a cap on prices of basic commodities through price controls. There were signs of impending shortages as businesses cut their output on unprofitable production lines and switched to the manufacture of goods outside the state's zones of control.

There were lots of questions as to the effect of these policies on the quality of life. The reality was unpleasant. Zanu PF's public persona was that of a caring parent, yet it openly displayed intolerance towards dissent. I found the behaviour confusing: they preached socialism which in theory emphasises empathy, equality and respect across class and social station. But evidence of greed and ideological confusion was visible far and wide. High-level corruption involving ministers and senior officials was entirely evident – but was kept out of national debate. In Bindura, for example, army commander General Solomon Mujuru was known to be acquiring vast tracts of property and commercial farms. People spoke about these issues under the cover of darkness; none would dare raise such questions openly.

As a person, Mugabe radiated a reserved, deeply conservative personality. He ran the government and Zanu PF in a strictly hierarchical fashion, military style. While his public face was that of both an admirer of socialism and a practising socialist, his other side conveyed the picture of a devout Catholic and Zimbabwean traditionalist, a no-nonsense, decisive and domineering father figure bent on individual and group discipline; and a strong male role model everybody was supposed to look up to for order and guidance.

I listened carefully to the men and women I met at union meetings. Well-meaning and concerned workers' leaders described how our independence had brought temporary, psychological relief to most workers and their families, but nothing could be regarded as sustainable in the long term. While I agreed with them, I was unsure how best the people could reclaim their power and push Mugabe to listen, or at least notice these early alarm signals.

This worsening situation left me and fellow members of the union movement feeling distraught and powerless. We started to worry about cracks emerging in what was originally thought to be a perfect new Zimbabwe. The toddler on whom we had projected our hopes for a much better future was stumbling and we began to fear that something was seriously wrong.

ENDNOTES

1   Smith, Ian Douglas (1997). *The Great Betrayal: The Memoirs of Ian Douglas Smith.* Brisbane: Blake Publications, p322
2   Pongweni, Alec J C (1983). *Songs that Won the Liberation War.* Harare: College Press

CHAPTER FIVE

MUGABE RULES

In November 1980 outbursts of gunfire shattered the fragile peace that had descended on the city of Bulawayo in the wake of independence. Violence had erupted between former guerrillas loyal to rival political movements. The war we thought had gone away now returned in a new guise. The so-called Entumbane Uprising – named after the suburb where former guerrillas were housed – was to claim hundreds of lives in the next few months and leave Bulawayo reeling as homes were destroyed and people took cover from the fighting. The day before the outbreak, Enos Nkala, one of the founders of Zanu, had warned in a fiery speech that Joshua Nkomo's Zapu would be eclipsed in a bid to bring about their political destruction.[1] Although Nkala has claimed that he did not incite violence, members of the armed wings of the two political parties started shooting in the opening rounds of what was to become a civil war.

The elation of independence had not worn off when these events took centre stage. During the next few years my personal life would follow a trajectory from hope to disillusionment – and finally disaffection with the ruling Zanu PF. Full of enthusiasm, and regarding Robert Mugabe as a champion of freedom, I had joined the ruling party after the elections of 1980. I would leave it in 1984, after losing faith in both the party and its autocratic leader, giving myself over to national trade union activities. Many disappointments along the way fuelled my doubts and led to a process of questioning that would finally take me into outright opposition to the government – though that still lay more than a decade and a half in the future.

In the early 1980s it was scarcely possible to imagine the dark future that lay ahead. As I was now a national trade unionist and a Zanu PF activist, I felt that my biggest challenge was to understand the connection between Zimbabwe's political leadership and the impact of its public behaviour on people's lives. This entailed a grasp of our new government's policies along with the links between governance and economic growth. Politics carried weight in all facets of life so it was important take hold of the issues and explore them.

I took time to reflect and tried to follow Mugabe's actions much more closely than before. This was not an accidental or a casual need; it was essential, for in many instances I found myself in an embarrassing position when I failed to analyse situations and respond convincingly to the fears and anxieties of workers on the shop floor and employers in boardrooms. I talked to many people: trade unionists, politicians, church leaders, journalists and ordinary workers, trying to discern the national mood. What were the people up against? What did they expect from their government? From these private consultations, a complex image of what lay ahead started to emerge in my mind.

I worried about the suitability of Mugabe as the best man for our time. He came across as a two-faced personality, seldom predictable and difficult to assess. The massive investment set aside for the social, education and health sector reflected – on the face it – a legitimate leader and caring nationalist devoted to uplifting the disadvantaged. But on the flip side of the coin was a conservative introvert prone to dishing out orders and non-debatable directives. Here was a demagogue with an immense capacity to cause serious national fractures that could be difficult to repair.

From the day Mugabe made the famous reconciliation speech, the nation and the world felt assured of good things to come. As we set out to rebuild ourselves and the country, there was tremendous goodwill in most quarters. Mugabe ministered to us while we repaired war-damaged rural schools, churches and health centres or built new ones and opened up roads. Former combatants had surrendered their arms. We were open to interaction with our former enemies across race and tribe and we respected our government for the first time after 90 years of mistrust. There were impressive inflows of foreign funding, culminating in the Zimbabwe Conference on Reconstruction and Development (Zimcode) which took place in Harare in March 1981. This donors' conference pledged massive support, especially for the rural sector.

But the rifts inside our own national family were quick to rise to the surface. Towards the end of 1980 and contrary to public professions of the need for national reconciliation, Mugabe's ministers spent much of their time denigrating Nkomo, his PF party and white Zimbabweans. Pliant official media tended to amplify and stress past differences, stoking hostility rather than calming it.

Friction led to the fierce fighting between Zanla and Zipra guerrillas at Entumbane. Zipra combatants were crushed and many took to the bush for their safety. The story was that this group was largely responsible for a fresh wave of sporadic disturbances, mainly acts of banditry and murder, that swept across parts of the country.

There were signs of simmering tension from Matabeleland, with small pockets of insurgents beginning to cause trouble. Mugabe's response was swift and brutal, targeting Nkomo and PF officials whom he accused of fanning the then nascent acts of lawlessness. In his first cabinet reshuffle, Nkomo was the main casualty – demoted from the ministry of home affairs to the far less powerful post of minister of public service – a humiliation that stripped Nkomo of his control over the national police. Yet it was the same Nkomo who barely four months earlier had moved for an extension of the state of emergency that had been in place under Smith since 1965. As minister of home affairs he had clearly aimed to curb random unrest and political crimes. I found no quick explanation for the contradiction. (The Emergency was to remain in force with further renewals every six months until July 1990.)

Speaking at rallies, if Mugabe spared his attacks on Nkomo he vented his anger instead on the 'unrepentant' whites. As a unionist and employee in the mining sector, which was previously dominated by strong racial attitudes, I disagreed with Mugabe. Those whites who had remained were accommodating themselves to the realities of the day. I wondered about the credibility of Mugabe's sources of information as what he often loved to talk about smacked more of history than current attitudes. It was clear from the outbursts of Zanu PF officials, cabinet ministers and from Mugabe's own rhetoric that the government of national unity was unlikely to survive its planned five-year term.

Casting my mind further back, it was plain to me that while the combined PF of Zanu and Zapu had given an external impression of fighting against colonialism as a united front, that marriage of convenience really fell apart just before the February 1980 election. It flickered back to life in a weak form after Mugabe became prime minister.

Reading my Sunday newspapers in my Bindura garden, I could reflect at leisure on where we had come from and where we were going. But an uncomfortable thought struck me. I remembered the concern of a senior PF official who had confided in me during a beer drink while I was visiting workers at How Mine in Matabeleland North. He said that Mugabe was now comfortable with an inherited highly repressive state which possessed sophisticated machinery for brutality. The entire system abhorred black political opposition and was antagonistic to any form of dissent. At the time I could not believe that could be a correct assessment of Mugabe's character. But when I saw the way he began to treat his PF comrades, I understood it better. As head of government, Mugabe could use the state apparatus of senior civil servants and security officers as unquestioning enforcers of his rule.

Those who had previously caused untold suffering to millions of innocent civilians while trying to save Rhodesia from collapse were now unsure of their fate. They were naturally keen to prove their loyalty to Zanu PF and to the new regime by exploiting the rift between Nkomo and Mugabe. The situation was so fluid that it needed careful political leadership. Where would the worker fit into this complex contest for power supremacy, with Mugabe seeking to assert total control while harassing Nkomo, Smith and the former Rhodesians? Again, no answer seemed to present itself.

The government gave the British military a transitional mandate to integrate the three previous warring armies into a single force at independence. However, six months after the British started their work, a newspaper story said the government had entered into a separate agreement with North Korea to train and arm an additional brigade. How could we have an army trained by different countries with different philosophies? When I raised the issue with a Zanu PF colleague, he explained that this was important because the British were biased against Zanla. I meekly asked him why the matter could not be raised for debate in parliament. When he stumbled over his reply, I let the matter rest.

In February 1981, two months after Nkomo lost his interior ministry, there was another major outbreak of violence, again at Entumbane. It spread to the nearby areas of Ntabazinduna and further east to Connemara near Gweru. An estimated 300 combatants are said to have died in the disturbances. Mugabe showed some concern – remorse, perhaps – by setting up a judicial inquiry under a respected judge, Enock Dumbutshena, to examine the causes of the uprising and report on the fatal differences between Zanla and Zipra. The report was never made public, giving rise to a perception that Mugabe's men had been responsible for the flare-up. He continued with the anti-Nkomo crusade and never publicly indicated a desire to negotiate an amicable solution to save such an important coalition.

I scanned through the list of those countries that the government considered to be Zimbabwe's best friends. Mugabe was leaning to the East, constantly intimating that the region was a traditional ally. Naturally, I thought, he wanted to acknowledge the support Zimbabwe had received from the communist bloc during the armed struggle. But as far as business was concerned I could see no advantage in this at a time when we desperately needed Western donors and investors to help us rebuild the country.

Because United Nations sanctions had been in place against Rhodesia, most companies still depended on South Africa for essential spares, markets for finished goods (especially textiles) and a variety of services. Despite Pretoria's policy of apartheid, deeply resented by the majority of Zimbabweans, South Africa remained our biggest trading partner and a major source of tourism receipts. At the South African trade mission offices in what is now Nelson Mandela Avenue in Harare, there were always long queues of desperate women applying for visas to visit South Africa. They went there to buy essential consumables and trinkets and returned home with bags and baskets bulging with goods. As our small formal sector was already feeling the pressure from increased demand for basic items and spares, these women played a critical role in filling the gap.

Mugabe's general attitude did not help us, especially in that formative period of our transition. He played into Pretoria's hands by adopting an aggressive stance and the entire nation paid dearly as a result.

To punish us, Pretoria counter-attacked under the pretext of supporting Nkomo and a few ex-Zipra dissidents. Initial evidence of Pretoria's direct military involvement, in collusion with remnants of the old Rhodesian order, came to light in August 1981 when three white members of the South African Defence Force, two of them Rhodesians, were killed in a surprise attack at a remote corner along the eastern border. According to an official report in *The Herald*, the dead were part of a group of 17. It was suspected that they were on their way to blow up a railway line from Zimbabwe to Mozambique when they were ambushed. The effect of white South Africa's involvement was severe on our race relations. Zimbabwean whites became instant suspects or collaborators of subversion. Together with the assault on Nkomo, a new campaign directed at whites did not augur well for national reconciliation. The net effect of all this on national healing, economic cohesion and the moral authority of our leadership was negative. In the end, ordinary people suffered as violence and disorder once again began to erode their lives.

Further reports indicated the existence of a plan, dubbed Operation Drama, to support Mugabe's opponents. Directed by Colonel Jan Breytenbach – commander of South Africa's feared counter-insurgency units in northern Namibia and Angola – an organisation called 'Super ZAPU' was formed to undertake the task. The band was said to have been trained at four camps in the then Transvaal region of South Africa. The operation was minor compared with similar South African activities in Angola and Mozambique, but beyond the sketchy details very little information is available on the size of Super ZAPU or its military prowess, its leadership, links with Zapu – if any – and the degree of material support offered by South Africa.

To add to the confusion, suspected foreign saboteurs blew up a munitions store and armoury at Inkomo Army Barracks near Harare in August 1981. Another deadly attack followed on 88 Manica Road, the head office of Zanu PF. These events further raised Mugabe's suspicions about the loyalty of Zimbabwean whites to their own country. Relations between blacks and whites became highly polarised while the relationship between Mugabe and Nkomo hung on a thread. The risk of the entire constitutional agreement falling apart rose to a dangerous level.

In the circumstances, the workers and their welfare became secondary issues. All was not lost as the ZCTU was formed to represent workers, as described in the previous chapter. A now seemingly insecure Zanu PF made sure that it directed matters by installing Mugabe's brother Albert as congress leader and checking out the credentials of all senior executive post holders. The ruling party maintained its dominion over the ZCTU for some years to come but it was not destined to last forever, as the story of the 1990s will show. For the present, however, the development of an autonomous labour federation was to be hindered by government authoritarianism.[2] This did not augur well for Bulawayo-based unionists who remained loyal to Nkomo and PF. Most of Zimbabwe's nationalists and immediate post-independence trade unionists were aligned to political parties. Those from the southern region tended to maintain their loyalties to Nkomo while others belonged to various political parties and formations. It was for that reason that the unions formed at 88 Manica

Road were all loyal to Zanu PF, as if to balance the political representation between the main parties.

Given the non-partisan work of trade unions, their political allegiances never affected the common interests of the ZCTU and its constituency, as far as I could see. There was a common thread linking all trade unionists to what they sought from the government in terms of the recognition of the basic rights of the workers. To a government now facing what looked like a more serious security threat to its existence, the case for enhanced worker welfare was relegated to the bottom of the pile of national priorities.

Albert Mugabe's death nearly paralysed the ZCTU. He died at a time when the labour centre was barely on its feet and without a functional secretariat. Its affiliates were weak, disorganised and less respected by workers who looked to the government for annual announcements of statutory wage increases. The position of the ZCTU deteriorated progressively because of lack of capacity, state interference and a poor revenue base.

The rift between Mugabe and Nkomo reached a climax in February 1982 with what Mugabe said was the discovery of arms caches, all attributed to Zipra combatants and Nkomo's PF. These arms were said to have been found on properties owned by the PF which had bought commercial farms and hotels to accommodate its demobilised ex-combatants. The aim was to generate income for those who had failed to make it into the new national army. Matt Calloway – head of a branch of the Central Intelligence Organisation (CIO) – was credited with making the discovery. Calloway fled from Zimbabwe soon afterwards. When a newspaper reported that he had been exposed as a South African agent, I was forced to wonder what really lay behind the story of the arms caches.

By then, though, things were falling apart. The shaky coalition collapsed. Mugabe sacked Nkomo, his party's deputy president Josiah Chinamano, PF secretary general Joseph Msika, and senior party official Njini Ntuta from the government. Zipra commanders Dumiso Dabengwa, Lookout Masuku and four other senior former Zipra officials were arrested and charged with treason. Other senior political and military leaders fled

Zimbabwe in fear.

After a lengthy trial, the High Court acquitted Dabengwa, Masuku and their comrades. They were redetained soon afterwards under the State of Emergency and languished in jails for years. Masuku's health deteriorated rapidly while in detention, resulting in his death in April 1986, a month after his release. Dabengwa remained in prison until December 1986.

The case of the four Zipra commanders sent shock waves through the ranks of former guerrillas who saw no future for themselves either in the army or in an independent Zimbabwe. Desperation drove many – the exact figure may never be known – into exile or into the bush. The Zimbabwe they had fought so hard to achieve turned its back on them and closed off their prospects as veterans of the anti-colonial struggle. Unsurprisingly, they perceived Mugabe as totally anti-Zipra and were convinced that he hated Nkomo intensely. Mugabe's feelings were echoed by his entire government, with ministers and officials linking all acts of lawlessness and armed robberies to the work of Nkomo's 'dissidents' – charges Nkomo was always quick to dismiss.

When it was claimed that Mugabe's official residence had come under attack in June 1982, Zimbabwe slid into full-scale civil war. A curfew was imposed in large parts of Matabeleland, several PF politicians were detained and troops were deployed in the area. There are several mines in the area and I found my job as vice-president of AMWUZ hampered by the imposition of curfews and restrictions on travel to and from the area.

By July Zimbabwe resembled a nation at war. Six foreign tourists were kidnapped and killed on their way to Victoria Falls. Two were Britons, two Americans and two Australians. Random house searches for suspected PF supporters were commonplace in all urban areas. Thornhill Airbase near Gweru was attacked by saboteurs with explosives and 13 planes destroyed. The military went into action in Matabeleland and the Midlands. So serious was the war psychosis that Mugabe found it necessary to rush through parliament the reinstatement of the Indemnity and Compensation Act of 1975, granting immunity from prosecution to all government functionaries and agencies who took up arms to defend the state. In addition to a regular force, Zanu PF trained and deployed a party militia to help out in military operations. The Act allowed state officials and security forces to do anything in their power to contain what they considered to be acts of terrorism without any fear of prosecution for their decisions and actions. It was widely used during the final days of the liberation war. After dissidents murdered at least 33 white commercial farmers or members of their families the government also allowed farmers to rearm to protect themselves.[3]

The civil war and the deaths of the six foreign tourists hit Zimbabwe hard, especially the tourism industry. While the government tried to suppress the impact, Mugabe told a press conference three years later that the six tourists were part of a group of nine – six men and three women – who were force-marched to a village in Lupane where their bones were later exhumed. He said the three women were released unharmed and allowed to leave the country. The group's leader whom Mugabe did not name was also released and given a ransom note signed 'Zipra Forces'. The note demanded the release of Zipra leaders Dumiso Dabengwa and Lookout Masuku. It also demanded the return of the PF properties seized by the government after the alleged arms cache discoveries. It was unclear whether Mugabe had known these details at the time or learnt them later. The abductions were said to have been carried out by a group of 22 dissidents led by one Gilbert Ngwenya. Ngwenya was arrested, convicted of murder in the High Court in November 1985 and hanged in April 1986.

While dealing with the civil war, Mugabe decided to send troops into Mozambique to help the Frelimo government, then under siege from the Mozambique National Resistance (MNR, later Renamo) – again supported by South Africa. The matter never came up for debate in parliament, nor were the costs or the wisdom of the action explained to the people.

The media, under state control and operating in a State of Emergency, failed to fulfil its public duty and mandate. Under such conditions, also inherited from our past, there was a huge arsenal of laws governing the conduct of journalists and the media. Mugabe used these laws to maximum effect, deporting foreign journalists and imposing restrictions on the reporting of events in war zones. Those of us who lived outside

Matabeleland, the Midlands and even Mozambique, heard very little about what was going on there. The little information that filtered through merely centred on positive government successes and activities among the people, ministerial speeches and the so-called defections of PF supporters to Zanu PF.

Almost every weekend, cabinet ministers and veteran Zanu PF nationalists Enos Nkala and the late Maurice Nyagumbo visited Matabeleland to spread vitriolic propaganda against Nkomo and his supporters. The lack of open information had a negative impact on the entire society. It constrained us from debating the issues coherently.

By the time the North Korean-trained 5th Brigade moved into Matabeleland in January 1983, the situation was extremely confused. White commercial farmers had rearmed and there were daily reports of atrocities – all blamed on Nkomo's dissidents.

When the Catholic Church called for restraint, Mugabe emerged with guns blazing, accusing the clergy of siding with lawlessness. I learnt later that the instability in Matabeleland led to the neglect of nearly 200 000 hectares of commercial farmland, wholesale destruction of villages, schools, health centres and the collapse of government public services. Security agents fanned out to capture and kill dissidents. This prompted the Catholic Church once again to sound an early warning about the excesses of security agencies and their impact on the peasantry, a message Mugabe ignored. Mission hospitals bore the brunt of the instability, having to attend to thousands of brutalised villagers who flocked to their doors – sometimes creeping into their premises in the dead of night for fear of further victimisation.

By March 1983 Mugabe had placed Nkomo under house arrest. Accused of plotting a coup, his passport was seized and he was restricted to his Bulawayo home. Nkomo managed to sneak out of Zimbabwe, fleeing to Britain via Botswana, saying he feared for his safety. Thus did one of the fathers of national liberation remove himself from contention. In his autobiography, Nkomo documented his personal account of the difficulties he had had with Mugabe immediately after Independence.[4]

A month after Nkomo's departure, the Zimbabwe Catholic Bishops

Conference (ZCBC) and the Catholic Commission for Justice and Peace (CCJP) sought and were granted an audience with Mugabe. Nothing substantial emerged from this meeting, save for a brief withdrawal of the 5th Brigade, ostensibly for retraining, and a temporary lifting of the restrictive curfew in Matabeleland North. But within a month the brigade was back in the area.

International media reports began to trickle out of Matabeleland. As if to save face, Mugabe appointed another commission of inquiry, this time led by Harare lawyer Simplicius Chihambakwe, to have a fresh look into the disturbances. Just as in the case of the Entumbane inquiry led by Justice Dumbutshena, Mugabe once again suppressed the findings. The recommendations of the Chihambakwe Commission have never been made public.

I realised that while Mugabe could tolerate some criticism of his government from a few influential white business executives – those in commerce and industry raised problems during their annual conventions – he was particularly ruthless with his black opponents, especially Nkomo, Bishop Muzorewa and the Reverend Ndabaningi Sithole. Nkomo in particular, in Mugabe's view, asked too many questions. He was ambitious as well, with the potential to challenge Mugabe's credentials as a national leader. Nkomo was generally referred to as Father Zimbabwe, in recognition of his early role in the struggle – something Mugabe seemed to find profoundly irritating.

Mugabe and Zanu PF had no interest in participatory governance. The entire nation was excluded from their decision-making processes. At our party branch in Bindura, I tried to raise issues for debate and was advised that in Zanu PF decisions were made at the top for implementation at lower levels. This differed significantly from the way we worked in the trade union movement and as time passed I found it increasingly difficult to defend Zanu PF and its methods or policies. Both Zanu PF and the state reacted to calls for remedies in times of crisis in a dictatorial manner. Almost daily, I was disappointed by the way government treated workers and blocked unions from campaigning and functioning independently as autonomous, civil society institutions.

I was equally unhappy with the snail's pace of the resettlement of the landless, which began in 1980. I could easily relate to the rural poor, having come from that background myself. They were unable to secure employment in urban areas and continued to eke out a living in the communal lands. Each time I drove to my home village, my heart sank when I saw former friends and school-mates looking older than their years, with either emaciated or bloated bodies drained by poor nutrition and excessive beer drinking. They had no hope. For them, independence was yet to translate into a meaningful reality. Their lives and standard of living seemed to be deteriorating even further as the government concentrated on its own survival through the civil war in western Zimbabwe and its military support for Frelimo.

When would all this come to an end? Mugabe was a ruthless leader and I could see no signs of any soft spot. Deciphering his character became something of a fixation for many of us who were puzzled by the direction the country was taking under his leadership. How did he compare with the leaders of national liberation movements who had subsequently become presidents of other African nations? It became important for me to make some comparisons to see if there was any difference between our prime minister and other African heads of state in matters of governance, public policy and democracy. The enquiry gave me a rather mixed picture. On the one hand, once in government several nationalist leaders had adopted dictatorial ways; on the other, some were facing challenges from political opponents, including those with trade union backing, and might well be unseated in elections. Time would tell.

Was Mugabe a black racist? The question was certainly not an open one at the time, given that Britain had decorated him with a knighthood and countless Western universities conferred doctoral honours upon him with flowery citations each time he visited their countries.

Could he be a tribalist? It was difficult to say, given that he worked well with nationalists from other ethnic groups, including the Ndebele. If he was a tribalist, how could he settle for a Ghanaian wife; he could easily have married locally. I did not see the ethnic factor in his baseline or decision making.

Was he really a socialist? Of course not! I remembered a colleague in the General Agriculture and Plantation Workers' Union of Zimbabwe (GAPWUZ) whispering into my ear in 1982 at a collective bargaining training workshop that Mugabe had just acquired a huge commercial farm in Norton, 40 kilometres west of Harare. I laughed in utter surprise when he said that, as an employer, Mugabe, was underpaying his workers and often flouted his own government's labour laws. When I challenged the young unionist further he was quick to provide more evidence, but warned me against discussing the issue publicly. I kept my word, as he had spoken in confidence.

If one thought these were mere rumours, time would prove them not only correct but part of a pattern that has continued ever since. Mugabe purchased the 1 100-acre Highfield Farm soon after independence. At the height of his land-grab programme 20 years later, he proceeded to acquire additional commercial farms, estimated at a dozen, for his family. These include Gushungo Dairy near Bindura, refurbished with state-of-the-art equipment by South African experts, which sparked an international outcry when milk processor Nestlé refused to buy milk from the farm.

Was Mugabe put in power as the West's best hope of suppressing the working class and the peasantry? A story put about by Mugabe's nationalist rivals – which I had often dismissed as inconceivable – was that the United States had worked clandestinely to press Britain and South Africa to allow Zanu PF to take over Zimbabwe in 1980 in a bid to stop a possible Soviet dominance in southern Africa.

Zimbabwe had flatly refused to become an instant Soviet client at independence. It took Moscow three years to set up an embassy in Harare. At the time, we thought the Soviets were hated because they had backed Zipra in the struggle while Zanla benefited from China's support. Despite his open admiration for socialism, Mugabe preserved capitalism and safeguarded all major foreign investments, including South Africa's giant Anglo American Corporation and all its business assets. Nothing was nationalised, unlike neighbouring Mozambique and Zambia. Most Rhodesian capitalists remained secure and led a privileged lifestyle, apart from the occasional pot-shots Mugabe directed at them from time to time. It was business as usual for the mining companies whose workers I represented in their union.

With Zanu PF's regular disdain for the workers and its negative attitude towards trade unions, I was now beginning to believe the stories of American manipulation behind the scenes. As I was now flirting with socialism from a trade union perspective, I toyed with the question of Mugabe's real allegiances for some time, not quite sure whether I was right or wrong. It bothered me because it was all too apparent that none of Mugabe's cabinet colleagues seemed to have a clue what socialism was.

Having been to three Catholic schools, I was suspicious of Mugabe's claim to be a deeply religious person, a devout Catholic. The Catholic Church preached fairness, sympathy and solidarity – especially with the poor – I recalled that the motto of my high school, Gokomere, was *Vincere Caritate* – 'Conquer with Love'.

The hardest question for me was whether he was a corrupt political impostor. How could this be, given his impressive academic background and urbane poise? I remembered my parents' insistence on quality education and how it could transform a black person. One had to admire those lucky and determined enough to have bettered themselves through adequate schooling. Mugabe was certainly one of those – in fact, I had regarded him as my idol – but as time went on the contradictions made it increasingly difficult for me to defend Mugabe, his actions and his decisions.

At the centre of it all, I saw something that I thought revealed a key characteristic of Mugabe as a social being. Soccer, arguably the most popular sport in the world, was similarly a favourite pastime for Zimbabweans, either as supporters or players, followed by boxing and wrestling. While there were a number of white Rhodesian soccer clubs and star players, many changed their sporting preferences during that time. Mugabe quickly joined them and opted for cricket at a time when there was no black cricketer in sight.

The prime minister's public demeanour, deportment and body language classed him alongside business executives. He wore formal dress and carried himself with the air of a lord. At his party meetings, he donned his Cuban-style olive green suits, but rarely left out a necktie. All civil servants quickly followed that line, for Mugabe abhorred long hair and casual clothing. I knew from my Zanu PF and trade union colleagues that Mugabe was perceived as a person who loved to be feared; a consummate disciplinarian, a hater of alcohol and a non-smoker; a man who saw himself as a national beacon worthy of perpetual deification and adulation.

Was Mugabe under some deep psychological pressure to turn away from the real issues affecting Zimbabwe? It appeared his responses to questions about his style of governance were poorly thought out. At no time was there a concerted effort to identify, define, refine and address the root causes of our string of crises. We had plunged willy-nilly into a civil war and now, to the surprise and dismay of those who believed that liberation was for all, Zanu PF turned on Zimbabwe's women.

In patriarchal fashion, Mugabe appeared to have different sets of expectations for Zimbabwean men and Zimbabwean women. Women in particular risked his displeasure if they showed any sign of deviance or wayward behaviour. He seemed to expect Zimbabwean women to live under the permanent eye of a strict moral authority, the male master within the home. The cabinet pulled Zimbabwe out of women's beauty and modelling contests in 1981, arguing that catwalks and feminine parades were against Zanu PF's socialist philosophy.

Gender issues in Africa are always sensitive but women are standing up for themselves and have formed associations to advance their rights and get them into business and politics on an equal footing with men. Zimbabwe would have been no different except that the attitudes of Mugabe and Zanu PF fomented more women's activism.

Zanu PF believed in what it termed a process of re-education for those women whose behaviour it disagreed with. Using strong-arm tactics the party punished thousands of women, targeting them in all walks of life. There were only muffled protests. Two years later, for three nights in a row from 28 October 1983, the police and the army rounded up close to 6 000 urban women in a swoop code-named *Operation Chinyavada* (Operation Scorpion). The women's crime was said to be moving around the cities after sunset unaccompanied by men. Accused of prostitution, the women were dumped in Chikurubi and other prisons before being transferred to a makeshift camp in the Zambezi Valley for Zanu PF's so-called re-education retreat.

The personal liberty Zimbabwean women had dreamt of vanished. Colonial authorities had routinely raided urban townships and workers' hostels to flush out suspected prostitutes; now our own government was doing it. Operation Chinyavada caused outrage and confusion in trade union ranks because it seriously affected the livelihoods and family security of some of our members, especially nurses and factory workers on night shift.

Serious questions were asked about the government's commitment to the advancement of women. Not only did the operation subject Zimbabwean women to ridicule, but those found to be unemployed were ordered to leave cities for the rural areas. Absurdly, it seemed that the campaign led by state security minister Emmerson Mnangagwa regarded the presence of women on the streets at night as a national security risk. Meanwhile the new ministry responsible for women's advancement and welfare, headed by Teurai Ropa Nhongo, a former Zanla woman combatant, just looked on and did nothing to help the victims, among whom were officials from the ministry itself and scores of civil servants.

Instead of forcing women to comply with Zanu PF's desires, Operation Chinyavada spawned a backlash against the government. It exposed the ministry of women's affairs as a facade, an immobilisation tool and an appeasement tactic to muzzle debate on equality. Women came together, and after a series of informal meetings in their homes and offices, the Women's Action Group (WAG) was formed in 1983 to focus on women's freedoms. This was a significant event which would later have a profound impact on opposition politics.

Initially, the state dismissed WAG's activities as inconsequential, deriding its members as loose single mothers and failed housewives. Encouraged by this show of independence, a number of social movements sprang up. In came Musasa Project (for abused women and cases of domestic violence); the Zimbabwe Women's Lawyers Association (legal matters); the Zimbabwe Women's Resource Centre and Network (gender and development); Women Writers Association (authors, dramatists and poets); Women in Politics Support Unit (democracy); and the Women Support Network (information).

Our tiny civil society welcomed these newcomers and took heart from their example. Civil society had previously comprised farmers' organisations, the church and trade unions. Church bodies had already distanced themselves from party politics and now many unionists were becoming uncomfortable with their subordinate status under Zanu PF. The growth of the third sector after political parties and business was under way.

War veterans were another thorny issue. Not all the liberation fighters could be absorbed into the national army. Thousands were demobilised and paid off with an initial resettlement allowance. A few went back to school, but the majority – especially in the north-east where I worked – returned to the village and by 1983 their tiny payouts had dried up. In Bindura a former priest and returning war veteran, George Rutanhire, planned to hold a gathering to discuss the plight of those who felt they deserved better treatment after seven years of war. When Mugabe heard about the gathering, they were ordered to abandon it. I saw some who had sought to meet in Bindura and thought they looked traumatised.

Demobilised ex-Zipra combatants from Matabeleland had a particularly tough time. With their former commanders facing charges of attempting to topple the government, Mugabe's security forces saw them as the first suspects each time there was a murder or robbery. Those already in the army found the work difficult, because their comrades and ex-Zanla commanders distrusted them. Tensions were always high and when ex-Zipra fighters disappeared they left a cloud of suspicion behind. Where had they gone? Into exile? Into the bush? Had they been abducted?

One such case involved a certain Captain Edwin Bhundani Nleya, a 35-year-old officer in the Zimbabwean National Army (ZNA). His body was found on a hillside in Hwange in the western province of Matabeleland North two months after his apparent abduction in January 1989 from the camp of the 1:2 Infantry Battalion.[5] Protesting the lack of a proper inquiry by the Zimbabwean authorities, Amnesty International said it was widely alleged that Captain Nleya was killed because of what he knew about the ZNA's involvement in poaching and smuggling activities in Mozambique. Other cases of disappearances are well documented in the *Breaking the Silence* report of 1997. In interviews for that report, none of the respondents explicitly stated that they ever sought to further the aims and objectives of either Zipra or the PF. They saw themselves as a desperate group being hounded out of the country on allegations of anti-government activities. 'No one was recruited; we were forced by the situation, all of us just met in the bush. Each person was now on his own, running from death,' said one.[6]

Meanwhile key economic indicators declined while the demands for state support were on the rise. The economy was overheating with shortages of essential commodities starting to be felt. The general scarcity of vital tools and resources for increased production invited a plethora of state controls. The controls bred more corruption, and corruption began to fertilise the black market in the informal trading sector, creating avenues for enrichment outside of state control. It was a vicious and self-reinforcing circle.

The business community seemed hardest hit by a crippling shortage of foreign exchange which the government controlled strictly, together with import licences for essential spares. A thriving black market in import licences had taken root, involving top Zanu PF officials who were now in a race to amass wealth. The new trend widened the gap between the poor and an emerging class that was well connected to big business and to top Zanu PF officials.

The most visible case arose after the 1982/83 drought which led to reduced harvests in the communal areas. As donors moved in to help, the government contracted the new black business people to cart grains and cereals for distribution across the country. In concert with senior Zanu PF officials, Zimbabwe lost millions of dollars to one Sam Mwashata Paweni and several others in shady deals. While Paweni ended up in jail, the suspected Zanu PF officials were untouched as allegations against them never made it to a court of law.

Further reports of graft, abuse of office and costly maladministration came to light, in particular investigations into the manner in which business was conducted in government ministries. I followed the work of the parliamentary public accounts committee with particular interest, for it routinely exposed the decay in almost all government ministries. These issues made a mockery of Mugabe's dream of a socialist paradise. All indications showed a distinct move towards a full-blown capitalist society underpinned with corruption.

As we entered 1984 we began to see – for the first time since independence – visible signs of abject poverty in urban areas. Our streets became home to large numbers of forlorn toddlers, some as young as two. Our traditional coping mechanisms were collapsing: the extended family networks were getting weaker and the state's social welfare system was unprepared and inexperienced. Urban blight, squalor and squatters – issues long associated with the war – suddenly re-emerged. The picture was worse in Matabeleland and parts of the Midlands because of the civil war. Young people left in their thousands for Botswana and South Africa. The economy was performing far below par and Mugabe was at pains to contain public displeasure about avarice and greed within Zanu PF's top ranks.

A number of cabinet ministers and officials, who a mere four years before could hardly boast a decent wardrobe, were now owners of fleets of cars, large tracts of commercial farmland and well-established businesses. Some senior trade unionists in the ZCTU fell into the greedy trap, causing disaffection among the various unions. Numerous accusations involving misuse of donor funds and union subscriptions came to light. The ZCTU became mired in confusion as party loyalty and ideology conflicted with the need for good governance. Some called for increased government intervention while others sought autonomy for the union. Those on the left clashed openly with their conservative and liberal colleagues, causing the ZCTU to send confusing messages to its affiliates. In the end, the government placed the ZCTU under a caretaker administration.

It seemed to worry Mugabe that corruption in his party and in government were on the rise but his forlorn attempts to put an end to it failed to silence the growing disquiet among workers and peasants. At the first post-independence Zanu PF congress in August 1984, Mugabe imposed what he called a leadership code. The code limited newly acquired farm size to a mere 50 acres. In addition, all party leaders – at every level – were barred from owning assets with a value beyond a certain amount. As a branch secretary of Zanu PF I could not make sense of these regulations; they went to such extremes that they were rendered unenforceable.

I raised my doubts with the late Eddison Zvobgo, then a senior minister, about how the code was to be implemented. Sipping a glass of whisky at a private club, he mockingly stated that one could amass enormous wealth through non-party members and friends. He said he was about to acquire two multi-floor hotels in Masvingo, each barely occupying the ground-space of an acre.

Our national budget deficit was rising at an alarming rate. The state was so weak that it could scarcely find the money to service the civil war at home as well as military action in Mozambique. It could not inject any new capital into the economy by way of development projects, nor could it cushion the vulnerable from deepening poverty. Subsidies on bread and maize meal for the urban poor failed to stem a sharp rise in the prices of other basic essentials and unemployment was on the rise. The trend worsened with an increase in school-leavers now seeking work in an economy whose prospects for growth were dwindling because the government budget deficit was left unattended to.

The government was failing to meet targets it had originally set for itself in the transitional national development plan. The plan derived from a 1981 economic policy framework, Growth with Equity, which sought to transform Zimbabwe's economy from its sharp duality. A relatively sophisticated modern sector reliant on cheap labour and serving a tiny minority existed side by side with a subsistence economy dominated by a majority black peasantry. While there was an overall gross domestic product growth rate of about 12 per cent for the first two years of independence, our fortunes started to decline rapidly. Mugabe attributed this to drought and a global recession. This was partly true, but the government refused to acknowledge how it had accelerated that decline through reckless expenditure, corruption, an avoidable civil war and support for the Mozambican government. The operation in Mozambique cost Zimbabwe an average Z$2 million a day at a time when the economy could hardly sustain it; nor were there any benefits from such extravagance, apart from giving Mugabe the political mileage he needed as a donor and powerful regional leader.

All sectors were affected by the changing times, including the labour movement. Anxieties mounted, and answers there were none.

Zimbabwe held its first post-independence election in June 1985. By then there were emerging divisions in the white community whose majority party, the Rhodesian Front, had changed its name to the Republican Front. At the time of the name change in 1982, RF legislators split and half of them became independent MPs. Zanu PF threw its weight behind the RF rebels. As required by the Lancaster House Constitution, whites voted separately for their 20 legislators. The white 'independents' called themselves the Independent Zimbabwe Group (IZG) and ran against the Republican Front, itself renamed the Conservative Alliance of Zimbabwe (CAZ) but still led by Ian Smith.

Having seen little or no change in their lifestyles, most white Zimbabweans never had a serious problem with Mugabe. They were keen to retain their identity and stay that way: aloof and far from the madding crowd. The white electoral contest was, to me, merely an academic exercise although the IZG wanted closer ties with Zanu PF while CAZ said it stood specifically for the preservation of white interests. As it turned out, the election was quite revealing. With only 33 734 white voters, CAZ clinched 15 seats, the IZG only four, and a candidate called Chris Andersen who opted to stand as what he called an 'independent-independent' snatched the last seat from both CAZ and the IZG.

Mugabe was livid, accusing whites of clinging to their racist past while spurning his hand of reconciliation. He attacked them as misguided, nostalgic geriatrics lacking a common national vision with the rest of Zimbabwe.

On the campaign for the common electoral roll, Zanu PF deployed its militia, the state machinery, war veterans and the military in the four mainly Shona-dominated provinces to intimidate and coerce villagers to its side. In the volatile Matabeleland region that job was assigned to the partisan North Korean-trained 5th Brigade. The result was that Nkomo's PF, now contesting as Zapu, lost five seats to Mugabe's Zanu PF. Significantly, and despite intense brutality and intimidation against the villagers in Matabeleland, Nkomo's party maintained its hold in the area.

The five seats Zapu lost were mainly in the Midlands. Also surprising was Muzorewa's total loss while Goodson Sithole, formerly Ndabaningi Sithole's driver, campaigning under the banner of Zanu (Ndonga), secured a seat in his home area of Chipinge in the south-east. This seat had previously been held by Zanu PF. Muzorewa threw in the towel, retired from politics and returned to the pulpit.

Soon after the election, Zanu PF embarked on orgy of violence and retribution against Zapu supporters in urban areas, injuring several and destroying property worth thousands of dollars. They accused these residents of being Zapu dissidents and Nkomo sympathisers. The violence was particularly bad in Chitungwiza, outside Harare, and police took their time to quell the chaos. I was at a loss for words as to the rationale of this needless assault on people, many of whom were workers and trade unionists. After that incident, I simply stopped attending Zanu PF meetings and quit the party.

Meanwhile the union movement was becoming more assertive. Stronger unions, including AMWUZ and the Commercial Workers' Union, made a fresh push for the revival of the ZCTU. Mineworkers lobbied other unions and at a congress in Harare, Jeffrey Mutandare – our president – took over the ZCTU as the new leader in late July 1985, beating Alfred Makwarimba whose founding executive committee was accused of ineffectiveness and corruption. Lovemore Matombo (of the Postal and Telecommunications Union), Jerry Jaricha (Zimbabwe Motor Industry Workers' Union) and Edward Njekesa (Zimbabwe Building Workers' Union) became Mutandare's three deputies. Anselm Chitehwe became the new secretary general.

The change in the ZCTU took place before our own AMWUZ

congress. At that meeting I assumed the post of first vice-president, a full-time position. It was a tense meeting, with politics taking centre stage. Complaints from our regions and our branches about the deteriorating conditions of mineworkers had us on the ropes. Workers felt their salaries and wages were now worth much less than before due to a decline in the Zimbabwe dollar and the withdrawal of state subsidies on basic commodities.

My new role required that I move to Harare. I was granted leave of absence from Bindura Nickel and moved to the capital in early 1986. Susan was anxious about our move to Harare. The personal cost was high. My monthly allowances were low, and we lost the cushy perks then attached to my job in Bindura. Edwin had started school and we had been blessed with another boy, Garikai. Yet my election to the top post in AMWUZ was a turning point in my life. Personally, I enjoyed the new national responsibility. After settling down in a new home in the medium-density suburb of Ashdown Park, which we bought with the help of a building society mortgage of $30 000, I immediately set out to do my work.

Harare is one of those African capitals that has both profited by – and bears the scars of – colonialism. A compact city centre with high-rise buildings is partly ringed by plush suburbs lined with trees and tropical flowering shrubs; but then in the midst of plenty there is dire poverty. Townships built in the pre-independence period to house the black population are crowded with rural migrants. Many depend on extended family networks and the African spirit of sharing, or *ubuntu*, to provide for them when they are starving. Lying just south of the commercial heart of the city is the densely packed township of Mbare, where rough shacks, flaking churches and neatly maintained matchbox houses sit cheek-by jowl, sharing a dilapidated infrastructure of potholed roads and uncertain electricity and water supplies. Colourful vegetable markets and the unwavering cheerfulness of the people hide the realities of street crime, high child mortality, Aids orphans, and bleak job prospects. Although sometimes called the 'sunshine city' in tourist brochures, Harare can be cold and wet because it sits on the central high elevation ridge of the country. Since the 1990s the city has borne the brunt of the economic collapse brought on by government's failed economic policies and conditions for the poor are tough indeed.

But Harare was now my home. Urban conditions were destined to deteriorate a lot further in coming decades as Mugabe actively persecuted the urban poor for their growing support for the political opposition. For the present, my attention was directed to union matters. Upon arrival in Harare, I realised that the tensions between the labour movement and the government had risen considerably since the ZCTU July 1985 congress. As a former mineworker, I was acutely conscious that my colleagues throughout Zimbabwe had vested their fate in both our new executive and that of the ZCTU. Now I found the same mood among other unionists.

Calls for disengagement from Zanu PF were getting louder. But each time the matter was put to debate at the ZCTU general council meetings the unions failed to agree on the nature, scope and scale of the divorce. Some union leaders believed dialogue with Zanu PF was a better weapon; others saw no progress via that route. Zanu PF and the government did not tolerate disagreement or attempts at autonomy. I sensed that a combination of political allegiances and fear interfered with the debate. Whenever the unions were unsure of the consequences, the tendency was simply to do nothing.

Unlike other economic sectors, by 1986 the mining industry was doing well. Frederick Shava, the new labour minister, was talking of worker participation in industry, pushing – at least publicly – for worker representation on boards and calling for a share ownership scheme. But that was only a political and publicity stunt. It was never taken seriously by the government. Mining alone could not change Zimbabwe's fortunes overnight.

In our dire economic circumstances, I was surprised to hear Mugabe announce that Zimbabwe was to host the eighth summit of the Non-Aligned Movement (NAM) in August 1986. He planned to build a prestigious five-star hotel and dozens of presidential villas for heads of state and governments from 101 nations. The extravagance shocked us in the trade union movement, but we could do nothing to stop it. And so Harare played host to kings, emperors, life presidents, elected and appointed prime ministers, military leaders – including Muammar Gaddafi of Libya and Thomas Sankara of Burkina Faso, along with heads of liberation movements from Africa, the Middle East and even East Timor in the Far East.

Despite promises of increased tourism receipts after the NAM conference, our trade union colleagues in the hospitality sector recorded no significant changes. Mugabe was selected to chair this loose grouping of Third World countries for a three-year period. The nation was never informed of the cost of the mammoth convention.

After the summit, pressure continued to mount on the economy, forcing Mugabe to search for a way to end the civil war in Matabeleland. Talks between Zanu PF and Nkomo began in earnest, with State President Banana mediating. The dialogue, held secretly and while the civil war was still raging, ended on 22 December 1987 with an agreement which saw Nkomo disband Zapu. He took his entire party into Zanu PF and was immediately appointed a senior minister of government. No formal ceasefire was attached to the pact, which Nkomo and Mugabe called the Unity Accord. But in early 1988, a general amnesty was declared and a mere 113 former rebels formally surrendered to the authorities.

With Mutandare, a former close colleague and family friend, at the helm of the ZCTU and with peace having been achieved in Matabeleland, I thought we could work out a plan to influence the government to change its policies in favour of the workers in a measurable way. I expected Mutandare to have a deep understanding of the plight of workers and to direct the ZCTU along a productive path. But for some reason, he never quite succeeded. He tried and tried, but failed; and eventually succumbed to temptation, dipping his fingers into the ZCTU's cash box.

Mutandare was booted out at the 1988 congress; he was charged with corruption soon afterwards, convicted and jailed for an effective six months. The story was that he had fiddled with donor funds from an American labour organisation. By then, my relations with Mutandare had deteriorated to a very low level.

Mutandare lost the vote to Gibson Sibanda, a veteran railwayman and unionist from Bulawayo whose late wife, Zodwa, was actively involved in nationalist politics before independence. I found Sibanda to be a firm but easy-going, honest and reliable colleague, enabling the two of us to form a powerful alliance and to generate a productive work plan that eventually saw us together for nearly 20 years.

It was exciting to find myself at the centre of things, but depressing too. Listening to the stories from workers countrywide and the manner in which they felt let down by their government, I felt strongly that Zimbabwe was pursuing the wrong political options while not putting into effect sensible economic measures.

ENDNOTES

1   'Nkala wants Mugabe prosecuted for Gukurahundi'. The Zim Diaspora, 21 December 2009. http://www.zimdiaspora.com/

2   Raftopoulos, Brian & Sachikonye, Lloyd (2001). *Striking Back: The labour movement and the post-colonial state in Zimbabwe 1980-2000.* Harare: Weaver Press (distributed by the African Books Collective, Oxford). See also Book Review by Norma Kriger in *African Affairs*, April 2002, pp 260-261

3   *Breaking the Silence, Building True Peace. A report on the disturbances in Matabeleland and the Midlands, 1980-1989. Summary Report.* Catholic Commission for Justice and Peace & Legal Resources Foundation, 1999, Harare http://www.hrforumzim.com/members_reports/matrep/matreppart1c3.htm

4   Nkomo, Joshua (1984). *The Story of My Life.* London: Methuen

5   'Poaching and Unexplained Deaths: The Case of Captain Nleya'. Amnesty International July 1992 AI Index: AFR 46/02/92

6   *Breaking the Silence,* op cit, p38

CHAPTER SIX

DICTATORSHIP

The Unity Accord that marked Joshua Nkomo's capitulation to Robert Mugabe set Zimbabwe firmly on the road to authoritarian rule by a supreme leader who brooked no opposition. Throughout the 1980s and into the 1990s Mugabe had things all his own way. This does not mean that opposition disappeared, just that it was suppressed on every occasion that it raised its head – until, that is, our Movement for Democratic Change appeared at the end of the 1990s to mount a real challenge against the dictator.

Zimbabwe had the appearance of a multiparty system but in reality all power was consolidated in the hands of Mugabe and Zanu PF. Until Nkomo's surrender in 1987, the existence of Zapu as a strong regional party with its roots in Matabeleland kept the ruling party in check to some extent. After the Unity Accord any new populist parties stood little chance of success in a de facto one-party state. General elections demonstrated that dissent continued to exist as there was always some support for minor opposition parties.[1] But, having taken full control of the state machinery, Zanu PF proceeded to abuse power, ignoring constitutional protections in the 1979 Lancaster House Agreement. In its Declaration of Rights the Constitution had recognised a wide range of civil and political rights, including the right to life and personal liberty.[2]

Even Zanu PF's own Leadership Code, adopted at its Second People's Congress in 1984, declared that its leaders should respect the constitution and not 'deal arbitrarily and arrogantly with members of the public or indulge in any conduct which brings the Party into disrepute or ridicule'.[3] Later developments were to prove that neither Mugabe nor the party had any fundamental commitment to these principles. The torture of opponents became routine while large-scale brutality would be perpetrated especially against rural people. The party would be feared and abhorred. The Code said Zanu PF was a socialist party and it described corruption as an 'evil disease destructive of society'. It banned bribery and the receiving of favours while disallowing leaders from serving as directors of private firms or drawing more than one salary. All these rules were ignored once Zanu PF was firmly in the saddle and, indeed, turned capitalist.

Nkomo's capitulation gave Mugabe the relief he had always wished for. Former prime minister Abel Muzorewa was already out of the way, in forced retirement. Although Zanu's original founder, Ndabaningi Sithole, narrowly snatched a seat in his Chipinge stronghold from Zanu PF in 1985, he posed no serious threat. Nkomo conceded to the prime minister's long-term ambition of unbridled supremacy over all he surveyed; he had to dump Zapu or perish together with his supporters. With 11 short clauses, the Unity Accord unambiguously stated that its purpose was to subdue Nkomo and to get rid of Zapu, its name and symbols, its structures and ideology, and its political brand.

The terms were clear: 'That Comrade Robert Gabriel Mugabe shall be the First Secretary and President of Zanu PF; That Zanu PF shall have two Second Secretaries and Vice Presidents who shall be appointed by the First Secretary and President of the Party'. Nowhere in the agreement does

Nkomo's name appear, but Mugabe's is in on three occasions. Nkomo's signature stands visibly at the end.

There was a specific clause stating that both parties would take immediate vigorous steps to eliminate and end the insecurity and violence prevalent in Matabeleland. In effect, the only thing of which Mugabe assured Nkomo was an end to the killings and the release of Zapu officials from jails. There was to be no compensation for a whole decade of vanished opportunities; for loss of lives and property; no healing tools or platform for reflection; and no preferential support for regional development.

Now holding all the cards, Mugabe introduced a constitutional amendment elevating himself to Executive President. This removed the position of prime minister and forced the titular president, Canaan Banana, to accept a hefty exit package as he would not see through his five-year term. To minimise possible inconveniences to his rule through an oversight, Mugabe abolished the Senate. This upper house of parliament, argued Mugabe, was an unnecessary, costly and ineffective layer of bureaucracy that merely duplicated the main business in the lower, elected chamber. Years later he would forget these arguments and reintroduce the Senate in order to counter the opposition's challenge at the polls.

The entrenched clauses in the Lancaster House Constitution which required the abolition of special parliamentary seats for whites expired in 1987. Zimbabwean whites, as a bloc, became effectively immobilised. Smith had earlier been suspended from parliament and subsequently retired from politics following the allegation that he was using his position to denigrate Zimbabwe away from home. This followed a series of interviews he had granted to the media and his addresses to outside audiences while on foreign trips.

As the decade of the 1980s wore out, it looked as if Mugabe had achieved a personal best. The people seemed to go along with his complete control of the state.

I was stunned to note that the May 1988 amnesty brought only 113 rebels out of the bush. I wondered how so few dissenters had caused Matabeleland so much pain, suffering and misery. Never in the history of Zimbabwe had so few caused such grief to so many – if the Zanu PF version of events was to be believed. These few rebels had drained our national coffers to a dangerous level and attracted Mugabe's fury to a point where he sacrificed the national interest to his ambition to destroy Nkomo's political dreams.

It is true the Unity Accord ended the war on the ordinary people in western Zimbabwe, at least on the surface. Yet the whole thing turned out to be worse than a nasty joke, as later revelations of genocide were to show. The casualty figures from the five-year onslaught in Matabeleland have never been precise. Nkomo estimated the carnage at 20 000. Others believed the figure was much lower, with some even alleging a total toll as low as 700. Because of the veil of state secrecy, our nation was unable to reconcile these claims with the reality, whatever it was, or even handle the perceptions of a large-scale genocide.

The nation had weathered the *Gukurahundi*, hardly knowing what it entailed. The term 'Gukurahundi' was coined by Mugabe at the time he deployed the North Korean-trained 5th Brigade. Literally, in the Shona language, 'Gukurahundi' means the first rain that ends the winter, rain which usually brings joy as it bursts out of the skies for a short period between August and early September to settle the winter dust. The dry ground was watered for a new spring season – but in this case it was blood that flowed.

As I consulted with the trade unionists from Matabeleland, I could see that reconciliation and peace were still far off. Nothing was done to reintegrate millions of affected villagers and survivors into mainstream society. There was no visible effort to heal the wounds; to tell the nation the truth; or to compensate the aggrieved communities, either individually or collectively. The Accord, however, seemed to have immobilised the people in the entire region, turning them into passive political fodder. They had to be content with individual efforts to pick up the pieces and to mind their own business (or scrape whatever living they could from the soil) for years to come.

Many Matabeleland families have never been able to recover fully, having lost their loved ones and breadwinners. Neither psychological support nor any physical restoration of assets was ever made officially available to the victims. Fear and mistrust of the government was passed on from the survivors of the civil war.

As we entered 1988, the time was up for another ZCTU congress. Jeffrey Mutandare had led the organisation as its president at a time when most unions were weak and structurally dysfunctional because of the government's meddling in the activities of the labour movement. The government still barred us from collective bargaining, preferring to stick to its system of statutory minimum wage regulations. After successfully destroying Zapu, Zanu PF saw itself as a renewed, radical national liberation movement.

Unionists from well-established unions like AMWUZ had a strong asset base. They could afford to host regular workshops on trade unionism for shop stewards under the guidance of experts and consultants. For many years mineworkers were trained, advised and guided by Jim Roberts, a veteran trade unionist who was associated with the union before and after independence. Smaller unions lacked that kind of exposure. The only avenue open was for their leaders who, sporadically, were invited to Eastern European countries for seminars, study tours and workshops.

I went to Gweru for the 1988 ZCTU congress as a delegate of AMWUZ. It was clear that Mutandare was struggling to save his post, as many unionists blamed him for poor delivery. Various candidates jostled for power and busied themselves with their campaigns for various posts then up for grabs. I never thought much about positions; I just wanted the ZCTU to consider what I thought was a major issue: autonomy from Zanu PF. Eventually Mutandare lost to Gibson Sibanda.

The popular candidate for the post of ZCTU secretary general was Charles Chikerema, the president of the Zimbabwe Union of Journalists (ZUJ) – a successor to the Rhodesia Guild of Journalists. The ZUJ had been rekindled by Nathan Shamuyarira, then minister of information and tourism, in 1981. Initially led by *Herald* labour reporter Elton Mutasa, the ZUJ was heavily embedded in Zanu PF. It was a dud, ineffective union. It did not even have an office. Chikerema, an avowed communist, took over the ZUJ in 1985. An inflammatory Marxist-Leninist ideologue, nationalist and war veteran, he was fluent in Spanish and French after his military training in Cuba and Algeria in the early 1960s.

Because of his working class leanings I began to work closely with Chikerema. Without an office, staff or vibrant shop floor structures, he ran ZUJ from his desk at *The Herald* where he was a reporter. Occasionally he would issue a press statement, but generally avoided controversy. In his campaign to win leadership of the ZCTU, Chikerema convinced most delegates of his ability to assume the post of secretary general but carefully avoided saying anything critical of Mugabe and Zanu PF. In 1985, when Willie Musarurwa, the editor of *The Sunday Mail*, was unceremoniously dismissed by information minister Nathan Shamuyarira on allegations of failure to toe the Zanu PF line, the ZUJ remained mum. When Mugabe dismissed Henry Muradzikwa, Musarurwa's government-appointed successor, over a story alleging that Cuba was deporting HIV-positive Zimbabwean students in 1986, Chikerema let the matter pass without his union's attention. Geoffrey Nyarota lost a similar post at the Bulawayo *Chronicle* for a series of articles exposing corruption in government. Again, Chikerema failed to lift a finger in protest. Instead, Chikerema was promoted soon afterwards to the post of editor of *The Sunday Mail* before moving to *The Herald* in the same capacity.

Chikerema was a close relative and ardent supporter of Robert Mugabe so he was most unlikely to take a stand against media-bashing. By contrast, Chikerema's brother James was a former Zapu vice-president and a fearless nationalist who broke away from Nkomo, briefly joined Muzorewa in 1978, and later parted ways with the Bishop to form his own Zimbabwe Democratic Party which contested and lost in the 1980 election. *Murehwa*, as old James was affectionately known, was slightly older than Mugabe; they grew up together in the same rural neighbourhood of Zvimba – but never saw eye to eye. James had been the co-editor of a weekly liberation newspaper called *The Rise of Zimbabwe* but his non-conformist views caused him to be sidelined from the revolutionary movement and from government. In the year 2000, Mugabe listed James Chikerema's farm for seizure – as a punishment, James Chikerema said, 'because I stood against him'.[4] He died in America in 2006.

None of this tainted Charles Chikerema. The prevailing assumption was that as he had the ear of the president, he would convey ZCTU messages about the plight of the working class in an effective and forceful manner. On the eve of the election, Chikerema backed out. Late that night delegates from various unions came knocking on my hotel room door, in separate groups, sounding desperate and heavily let down by Chikerema.

Chikerema openly told his campaign team that he was scared of a potential collision with Mugabe. Attempts to persuade Chikerema to reconsider his decision failed. The field was now open and all kinds of vultures were on the horizon. 'There is an emerging consensus that only Tsvangirai can calm down the situation,' a delegate whispered to me at around midnight in my hotel room.

I politely asked for time to think about it. Reflecting on the offer took my mind back to April 1986 when I had spent six weeks on a study tour in Moscow with 38 other union leaders. I worked closely with them during that time and got to know them well. When we compiled a report for our government, I realised that most of my colleagues lacked the necessary depth to understand complex governance issues. I ended up doing the draft alone, which they gladly endorsed without any amendments.

The trip to Moscow was an eye-opener. The relatively young and urbane Soviet leader, Mikhail Gorbachev, had just assumed power at a time when that massive country was almost on its knees. Socialism was under serious pressure from within and without. On the one hand, a unique combination of Western conservatives, Ronald Reagan and Margaret Thatcher, did not conceal their hostility to the 'evil empire' (as Reagan put it). On the other, the USSR was fast becoming a Third World country due to its own inefficiencies.

I was in Moscow at the time of the Chernobyl disaster, the nuclear accident on 26 April 1986 when the lid blew off Reactor No. 4 and polluted vast areas with radiation. This was considered the worst accident in nuclear history and ranked at level 7 on the world nuclear events scale. Reports slowly filtered out from the official media but it was only in the outside world that much of the story was assembled from diverse sources. A huge fire raged for days, causing a major radioactive fallout and the evacuation of thousands of people from Ukraine, Belarus and western Russia. Of the 134 initially exposed workers, 28 died in 1986 due to acute radiation syndrome. The accident was blamed on old machinery and equipment.

The USSR now relied on archaic plant and machinery which, together with poor market coordination, had produced a depressed economy. The people were weary of their seemingly unending military engagement in Afghanistan, while demobilised troops spread the message that the war was unwinnable. Young Soviets were heavily hooked on vodka, the traditional favourite that is now the opiate of the working class. Gorbachev was busy dismantling centuries-old vodka distilling companies and turning them into soft drink manufacturing units, and pubs were being converted into crèches and children's foster homes. All this added to the demoralisation of the Russians.

There were serious shortages of basic commodities, although our hosts tried hard to hide this negative side from us. We travelled throughout the vast country, sampling vodka and *piva* (beer) and chatting to workers, intellectuals, politicians and unionists who seemed confused by Gorbachev's *glasnost* and *perestroika* (openness and transformation) policies. It was interesting and exciting, though all in all there were not many positives after seven decades of communist dictatorship.

I discussed these issues at length with my colleagues and we agreed that it looked as if this was the direction Zimbabwe was headed too. We made that observation in our report, which the government duly ignored. The positive aspect of our trip was that we developed strong, personal relations among ourselves as Zimbabwean trade unionists.

As I reflected on this trip in my hotel room I fell asleep – only to rise early to meet an emissary from the unions seeking my response on the ZCTU position that was being offered to me. I brushed him aside, saying I had no problem with any congressional wish. At the breakfast table, the pressure became more intense with some congratulating me on the election victory even before the ballots were cast. Before I could consult my family and close non-union friends, I found myself the new secretary general of the ZCTU. This immersed me in a deep reflective mood. What lay ahead was simply too much to contemplate. But I put on a brave face, showing little emotion.

Nonetheless, I accepted my new role, making a terse statement and thanking the congress for the confidence placed in me. There was jubilation, foot-stomping and wild, discordant singing as the congress hailed all the new appointments.

Back in Harare, I found a labour centre that existed in name only. At a small office in Jason Moyo Avenue, the ZCTU had operated largely as an appendage of Zanu PF. The tiny secretariat looked stressed out, trying to provide essential services to the centre and its 38 affiliated unions. On paper we had 38 affiliates, but many were very weak. The Commercial Workers' Union, led by the late Shangwa Chifamba, was the strongest, followed by the Engineering Workers' Union and that for the hospitality industry. Fragmented legislation prevented civil servants and other state employees from affiliation to the ZCTU.

The collection of membership dues was erratic, records were in shambles and no training programmes were in place. The ZCTU desperately needed a viable start-up programme in order to remain relevant. The centre itself badly needed institutional renewal. I was told that in 1981 Yugoslav unions had donated some prefabricated materials for the ZCTU to build a national labour college. Nothing was done and the materials were left to rot in an open space in Chitungwiza outside Harare. It was too late to revive the plan so I stuck it out in the old, dimly lit building where the lift had stopped working due to lack of maintenance. This was in downtown Harare – extraordinary!

Within days of my election, I sensed that I was being followed. I had attracted the attention of the government's secret service spooks, keen to know everything about my background, my thoughts and the direction in which I was likely to take the ZCTU. I paid little attention to their sneaking into my life and work, for I was convinced – naively so – that I meant no harm.

Behind an unpolished brown desk, surrounded by a few files, half-empty filing cabinets and empty shelves, I looked back on my uneven journey through life thus far. What a meandering and narrow path I had taken to get to where I now was! My education had always been uncertain and I was lucky to have reached O levels. The early years of my working life had been extremely tough as I scrimped to help feed and educate the rest of our family. My parents had done everything they could for me and I had tried to repay them with support for my siblings. I had managed to rise from fairly menial work to the position of mine foreman, then trade union organiser, and now I was national secretary general of the ZCTU. True, it was mostly just a shell, but something could be made of it.

One thing that was clear to me was that anything I had achieved in public service so far was entirely at the pleasure of the people that I served. I examined my weaknesses and my strengths, my interest in public affairs, my passion for workers' rights, a penchant for politics I could hardly explain, and my sociable approach to life as something shaped by my upbringing and experience of working with people.

It helped me to engage in personal reflection of the travails I was exposed to in my early life. The challenges of supporting my large extended family had made me dutiful and firm of will. Zimbabwe's independence was inspiring, but the dubious outlook for the country's future filled me with a mixture of determination and dread. I needed a lot of help from other people; I needed everybody to succeed. Clearly, I would accomplish nothing if I adopted a selfish, self-centred approach to my new executive function. Conscious of my obvious weaknesses – academic, professional, executive, lack of international exposure and general directorial inexperience – I resolved to learn fast and to consult as widely as possible in order to have a national impact through my new job.

The deep conversation I had with myself unearthed numerous possibilities. There was much to be done and with the right approach we could do it.

We had to get organised, apply ethical standards, and be visible. At my first meeting with Gibson Sibanda, we decided to professionalise the ZCTU, draft a five-year development plan, deal decisively with corruption, spur the confidence of ZCTU affiliates, increase our membership, strive for fairness, and help redirect Zimbabwe – through worker power – to reclaim its long-lost social and political conscience. Among our key priorities was the need to set up a professional secretariat with departments dealing with health and safety, training, legal matters, gender in the workplace, advocacy and international relations.

We discussed the manner in which the ideals of the liberation struggle had been hijacked by a tiny elite and the state's constant attacks on our basic freedoms. To free the workers and, by extension, our peasants, I suggested that the ZCTU needed total autonomy from the government and financial viability. Sibanda agreed. But we were by no means sure how we were supposed to see through the implementation of our ideas. We vaguely comforted ourselves by noting that in concert with others, nothing was impossible.

After that meeting I consulted all union leaders and officials. I felt humbled by the unending catalogue of nostalgic expectations spawned by our freedom from colonialism, back in 1980.

There were strong similarities between the situation now and my initial assessment of Zimbabwe's options when I first rose to national office in AMWUZ. An abundance of available alternatives for Zimbabwe's advancement was ready for easy picking. The absence of political will to attend to the pressing items on our national wish list was the main stumbling block. The government showed haphazard commitment – if any at all – to uplifting ordinary people. Socialist policies and plans that had been tabled in the early years after independence were being succeeded by the Economic Structural Adjustment Programme (ESAP) for Zimbabwe which was capitalist in spirit. Both approaches were in effect destructive. What today we would call sustainable development remained elusive, as did a political culture of tolerance to encourage enterprise and innovation.

We had to feel worried about rising unemployment, officially estimated at 26 per cent, up from 15 per cent at independence. Zimbabweans needed to make comprehensive changes to our way of life to meet the needs of the growing population. We had to put development on a firm footing. There was a national subsistence system of production and consumption which was evidently failing to cope with increased demand. The economy was too urban biased and, to a large degree, negligent of the broader needs of the mass of the population.

Meanwhile the government had embarked on a land reform programme, offering four types of resettlement options to the peasants. The state slowly acquired prime land for peasant resettlement, in terms of the Lancaster House Constitution, on a willing seller, willing buyer basis. But the process was slow. By applying the peasants' habitual methods of subsistence production, these new settlers could hardly make a go of things and they continued to depend on external support and remittances from urban workers. It was clear that since 1980 most rural farmers had been, and continued to be, excluded from the mainstream economy.

Output from each commercially exploited hectare on large farms was four times higher than on a similar-sized plot in the communal lands. The government was failing to find a practical and lasting solution to such a clear economic imbalance. The problem was recognised but the answer was not in the making. Robinson Gapare, the president of the National Farmers' Association of Zimbabwe (NFAZ), told a seminar I attended in my new role at the ZCTU that our national economic base was so weak that there was an urgent need to address the nation's two-tier agriculture system: communal and commercial. It was a good thing that, with the civil war behind us, it was now possible for people to speak out relatively freely. At least it seemed so. The prevailing fear of being labelled saboteurs or Nkomo supporters must give way to constructive debate.

Just how unlikely this was soon became evident. Gapare was a peasant leader. He posed a critical question on whether the state's proposal to redistribute land was the best way of answering the skewed historical equity imbalances within our society. Was land redistribution the best method of wealth creation, given the diverse socio-economic and political dynamics among Zimbabwe's village communities? None of the participants, including senior government officials, attempted to answer Gapare's question. Gapare was apparently exasperated; after a moment he shook his head, picked up his papers and left the room – never to return.

Gapare's association was one of the three representing various grades of Zimbabwean farmers. Lower middle class black farmers had a separate grouping, the Zimbabwe Farmers' Union (ZFU) which drew its support from small-scale commercial farmers in what Rhodesia had called the African purchase areas. In a clearly separatist format, white farmers belonged to the Commercial Farmers' Union (CFU), an all-white lobby.

The question Gapare had posed was vitally important in several respects. The government's intentions were unclear and confusing; indeed government was cautious and extremely conservative when it came to the land question. While there was much talk of assisting the landless and poor, there was too little action and the euphoria about land was evaporating.

By then, the state had acquired three million hectares for distribution, half of which were in arid zones, meaning that a large chunk of the land was totally unsuitable for serious crop farming. Despite a growing demand for land, 250 000 hectares – though acquired for resettlement – lay unused. No serious distribution of land was taking place at a time when the rural population was rising.

The rural areas were becoming overpopulated, overcropped and overgrazed, while the formal sector of the economy was failing to cope with an increased market demand for jobs, for basic services and for a fresh capital injection. The private sector desperately needed new plant, machinery and tools. In the years of Rhodesian UDI, international trading sanctions had forced businesses to develop import substitution industries. In some ways this had been a good thing because manufacturers became more self-reliant, but the reverse was also true: production was substandard and they could not compete on world markets. The Zimbabwe government needed to build on the sounder aspects of the industrial and trade policies by being entrepreneur-friendly and encouraging business to operate without fear or threat from state. Incentives to domestic producers would develop the capacity to produce certain needs from within.[5]

To survive, more people found themselves in the informal sector as vendors and small traders of smuggled and imported trinkets. With a rise in the rural drift to towns and cities, the informal sector was fast becoming a waiting room for job-seekers. The only source of relief was that the Unity Accord meant that expenditure on security and defence, which had gobbled up our national savings since independence, was likely to decline. Soon, however, we would enter a war in the Congo with all the heavy military costs that would entail.

I feared the presence of an idle and underemployed pool of young people, for this could be highly explosive and could lead to yet another bout of national instability. Almost the entire communal sector is situated in unattractive, arid, low rainfall areas – historically set aside as part of a racial segregation policy. According to Gapare, the 800 000 farmers who lived there received an average per capita income of Z$600 – an amount too low to stimulate either jobs or generate new capital for expansion.

I listened with keen interest to other presentations at the seminar. I felt that I needed background information to understand where Zimbabwe stood at the time. Between 1980 and 1987, the communal farmers harvested about half a tonne each. Considering that maize is the national staple, much of that was consumed in the village. The remainder, though sold, fetched so little that it was insufficient to meet the costs of inputs for the next farming season, deepening the peasant's dependence on credit and external handouts. Such a situation was unsustainable and dangerous.

With Zimbabwe now firmly a de facto one-party state, opposition began to emerge from within. Edgar Tekere, the man who had crossed the border into Mozambique with Mugabe way back in 1975 and rose during the war to become Zanu PF secretary general until the post was abolished at the party's 1984 congress, began to condemn the government publicly for lack of political direction. Tekere was strongly against the one-party-state system Mugabe and Nkomo had just endorsed, saying that it was never part of the founding principles of Zanu PF.

Mugabe's reaction was swift and unconcealed. Tekere had to go. Tekere upped the tempo with his outbursts, challenging Mugabe to take a stand against rising corruption which, he charged, was now rampant within his cabinet and among top officials.

Tekere's fall from grace and expulsion from the cabinet was predictable. He had embarrassed Mugabe when he shot and killed a white farm manager, Gerald Adams, on a farm near Harare in August 1980. The High Court freed him after the presiding judge was overruled by his assessors at the conclusion of the trial. The assessors believed Tekere and his bodyguards, who initially claimed to have been on a mission to hunt down supporters of Joshua Nkomo, strayed after failing to find any and had gone to a nearby farm where they found Adams. Mugabe dismissed Tekere from his cabinet on 11 January 1981. At the 1984 Zanu PF congress Mugabe abolished the post of secretary general from the party's structures and created a new order under which, as party president, he was now the first secretary of Zanu PF.

Tekere was not wrong about corruption in high places. In 1988, *The Chronicle* in Bulawayo published a series of stories involving a car purchasing scheme at a state-assisted motor assembly plant in Willowvale, Harare. 'Willowgate', as it came to be known, embarrassed senior officials who were exposed as being heavily involved. In any normal society, innocent car purchases would have gone unnoticed. But because of the shortage of new cars on the market, the government hatched a scheme under which ministers and top officials would get preferential treatment whenever a new vehicle was available. They acquired the vehicle at a controlled price and resold it immediately at an unbelievably inflated price.

Compared with Harare, Bulawayo may strike one as a sleepy provincial backwater, but this is far from true. Its wide streets, with few skyscrapers and homes decked with brilliant scarlet bougainvillea in a region of wooded bushland, lend it the impression of tranquillity. Zimbabwe's second largest city is located in the southwest of the country in the heart of Matabeleland, and its history has made it a multicultural city with, at times, a politically electric atmosphere. Bulawayo was founded in 1840 by the warrior king Mzilikazi whose Ndebele nation was an offshoot of the militant Zulu state far to the south. It was later annexed by white pioneers, who drove Mzilikazi's son, King Lobengula, into exile and established what was to become Rhodesia. Today, the languages of English, Ndebele, Shona and other tongues are spoken in this 'City of Kings'. Like all other Zimbabwean centres, Bulawayo had experienced a sharp decline in the standard of living – made worse by the terrors of the Gukurahundi campaign directed against opposition to Zanu PF in Matabeleland.

It was not surprising that a state-owned newspaper, *The Chronicle*, then edited by Geoff Nyarota, a fiercely independent journalist, uncovered the

Willowgate scandal. Political feelings ran high; and the fact that Mugabe's men were benefiting from illicit car deals rubbed salt into the wounds of the opposition. To placate matters, Mugabe commissioned a judicial inquiry into the scam. Among the casualties of the inquiry were Maurice Nyagumbo, Enos Nkala, Dzingai Mutumbuka, Frederick Shava and many others – all staunch Mugabe allies and close cabinet colleagues.

Nyagumbo committed suicide soon afterwards, but despite those circumstances of infamy, Mugabe declared him a national hero. Shava was convicted of perjury during the hearings and sentenced to jail. Mugabe quickly pardoned him before he had spent even one night in a prison cell. The whole thing was ludicrous but unsettling. In the end, no one was prosecuted although some of the ministers later resigned.

As for Nyarota, he paid dearly for the disclosure. The company claimed to have 'promoted' him to a public relations post. He was given a huge office with several telephone lines but no editorial responsibility. Bored and frustrated, he later resigned. In 1998 he and Wilf Mbanga would start the *Daily News*, a private venture, in Harare.

When university students took to the streets protesting the rise in government corruption, Mugabe raised the stick again. In 1989 he closed the University of Zimbabwe and detained the student leaders, led by Arthur Mutambara. Seeking to stem a further rise in student activism, the government amended the University of Zimbabwe Act to limit academic freedom. The move sparked a fresh wave of student demonstrations, leading to further arrests. I issued a public statement on behalf of the ZCTU condemning Mugabe. He quickly struck out, accusing me of being a South African spy who deserved to be charged with treason.

My short protest note to the media highlighted the students' right to speak out on corruption and against the state's plan to curtail their basic freedoms. I thought I had a simple right, also, to air my organisation's view. Taking advantage of the State of Emergency, Mugabe could lock me up for a long time, without trial. It had never occurred to me that I could land in trouble by merely issuing a press statement but it dawned on me that Mugabe was angry with me, as the new secretary general of the ZCTU, for leading the labour movement away from Zanu PF.

To my amazement I was arrested and held without trial.[6] Being confined in a police cell in an independent Zimbabwe was both a frustrating and terrifying experience. The police appeared confused by the order to arrest and detain me but suspects detained under the emergency law could be kept in 90-day detention without explanation.

I was held incommunicado without access to my family or a lawyer. My arrest caused a lot of anxiety for Susan, my friends, my brothers and sisters and my parents who did not understand why I had been arrested. The police questioned me about my work at the ZCTU and why I had supported the protesting students. Susan was eventually allowed to visit me and she came with Ben Hlatshwayo, then a junior law lecturer at the University of Zimbabwe, a family friend and a civil society activist. After six weeks in police cells, I was released without being charged.

As I walked out of the police station, I was quickly ordered back and informed that the state was now charging me with treason. I was immediately sent back to the cells, but later released as the charge had been dropped. Visiting the ZCTU office on the way home, I heard that my arrest had led to an international outcry. It was heartening to learn that the International Confederation of Free Trade Unions (ICFTU) had dispatched a special envoy to Harare to plead for my release. His treatment on arrival added to the publicity surrounding my case. The ICFTU emissary was Frederick Chiluba, secretary general of the Zambia Congress of Trade Unions, who was arrested and deported before he could meet with officials from the ministry of labour.

Although I was now free, I could feel Mugabe's shadow looming over me. Now it was apparent that when state security agents monitored my movements and closely followed my work they had every intention of acting against me. But I refused to be intimidated.

On a private family visit to Buhera after my release from police custody, I was disturbed to learn that my parents' marriage was on the rocks. Dzingirai-Chibwe, in his quest for the Nerutanga chieftainship, had argued with my mother and moved out of the matrimonial home. After the death of Chief Nerutanga, my father was supposed to be the natural heir to the throne. But a dispute occurred in our royal family and

Dzingirai-Chibwe started his own struggle to reclaim what was rightfully his position. It was hard to imagine that my parents would separate, yet my father remarried and raised another family much later in his life. The couple had two children, Chibwe and Manotsi. Our attempts to mediate failed, but my mother remained at home. We all felt very bad about what happened. By the time Dzingirai-Chibwe died in 2007, I was already in national politics and I knew that the government would never have allowed him to assume a powerful position while I was opposing Mugabe and his government. We buried him at the family cemetery at his original homestead, the place where we all grew up – and the place we still regard as home, where my mother lives to this day.

For the next two years, Mugabe's interest in the ZCTU's activities declined. He knew that we possessed neither the capacity nor the organisational cohesion to pose a sustained threat to his rule. While he maintained a dislike of some of my colleagues and me, he seemed to regard us as infrequent irritants. He had his hands full dealing with events within Zanu PF where a wave of discontent was beginning to emerge. Fanned by Tekere's unrelenting attacks on corruption, Zanu PF's one-party-state plan and general greed in the top echelons of the government, the comrades were getting restless. Mugabe took a major political risk by dismissing Tekere from Zanu PF. He was one of the old fighters, after all, and a most senior one at that. In the history of Zanu PF, especially under Mugabe's leadership, disagreements were often contained with extreme care to avoid rubbing the ex-fighters on their raw side.

The origins of this party sensitivity went back to 1974 when Raphael Chinyanganya (aka Thomas Nhari), a field commander in north eastern Zimbabwe, and Zanla colleague Dakari Badza led a rebellion sparked by differences over strategy and tactics. The Badza/Nhari rebellion, as it is known, was ruthlessly crushed and Nhari and Badza were later executed. In 1977, military commanders – led by Wilfred Mhanda (aka Dzinashe Machingura) – tried to wrest control of the party once more, for similar reasons. The two incidents led Mugabe to include the military in the civilian political structures of Zanu PF.[7] Tekere's dismissal had to be carefully weighed as it had the potential to lead to fresh conflicts between the mainstream Zanu PF and the war veterans, many of whom appeared to side with Tekere on his anti-corruption crusade.

To contain the restive war veteran community, in April 1989 Mugabe allowed the ex-guerrillas to form a representative association, the Zimbabwe National War Veterans' Association (ZNWVA), to keep them close to Zanu PF. He even promised them parliamentary representation in the pending general election in 1990.

Tekere moved quickly and formed the Zimbabwe Unity Movement (ZUM), openly stating a resolve to take on Mugabe in the 1990 election. Tekere's action coincided with the global revolution inadvertently started by President Gorbachev through his far-reaching reforms in the Soviet Union. To most of us in the ZCTU, evidence of a turning point in regional and international politics and a new world order came with the collapse of the Berlin Wall in late 1989. At the same time, we witnessed the decline of one-party-state systems in Africa.

The impending transition of the territory called South West Africa (SWA) into the independent state of Namibia – no longer under South African rule – came about as the Cold War ended. The USSR and Cuba had backed the SWA People's Organisation (SWAPO) in a long war against Pretoria which had reached a stalemate at the battle of at Cuito Cuanavale in southern Angola.

My understanding of this battle from media reports in 1988 was that it was an important turning point in the Angolan civil war – a war which began immediately after independence from Portugal in 1975. In that battle Angola, with the support of Cuba, launched a major offensive on Jonas Savimbi's National Union for the Total Independence of Angola (Unita) rebels in south-eastern Angola forcing Pretoria to intervene on the Unita side. With Cuban reinforcements, Angola held on to the town of Cuito. South Africa retreated while the Cubans used their superior air power to continue pounding Pretoria's forces. After failing to push back the Angolans, the South African Defence Force left Angola. SWAPO took advantage of the changed military power balance and intensified the war inside northern Namibia, forcing South Africa to resume peace talks in

Windhoek. A ceasefire was ultimately brokered on 27 June 1988, leading to an agreement for Pretoria's total retreat from Angola in September of that year. Namibia thus became assured of its independence through a peace accord, mediated by the United States, signed on 22 December 1988 in New York.

We were all inspired by developments in South Africa where the release of Nelson Mandela after decades of imprisonment seemed ever more likely. In February 1989, President P W Botha, who had suffered a stroke, was unable to continue as head of the National Party and was replaced by a reformer, Frederik Willem de Klerk. De Klerk immediately began to institute essential political reforms leading to the final demise of apartheid. His most notable achievement was the freeing of Mandela and the unbanning of the African National Congress and other political organisations, paving the way for negotiations for a democratic South African constitution.

Indications were that southern Africa as a whole was poised for peace.

All of this was cause for jubilation. Political change was sweeping through Africa and the world, giving hope to Zimbabweans. The one-party-state system was collapsing all around us, giving rise to calls for political pluralism and spurring the rise of civil society organisations.

Demands for change grew louder, especially in Zambia where Frederick Chiluba was leading a crusade against corruption and food prices and shortages. President Kenneth Kaunda's popularity declined, forcing him to introduce various structural adjustment prescriptions from the International Monetary Fund (IMF) and the World Bank. As popular discontent with Kaunda's slow reforms increased, food riots erupted in Lusaka which led to Kaunda's abandoning structural adjustment. The riots left 15 people dead, mostly urban workers, when police tried to intervene to stop widespread looting and attacks on supermarkets and shops by angry, hungry mobs.

Freedom had its costs, and we saw things in that light. Despite rising unemployment and a decline in the value of the Zimbabwe dollar in the second half of our first decade of independence, there existed bright prospects for economic recovery and peace in the region.

An election was due in Zimbabwe in early 1990. For the first time Mugabe faced a challenge from a serious opponent, Tekere, who could conceivably command substantial support. The ZCTU refused to back Mugabe in the 1990 election, claiming autonomy from Zanu PF. There was considerable excitement because voters felt Tekere represented a sizeable group of potential Zanu PF reformers with the capacity to turn the country in a more promising direction.

Regional stability was essential for Zimbabwe's economic prospects because of the direct and indirect costs of the various wars to our economy. In the eight years during which we had helped the Frelimo government in Mozambique against Renamo rebels, both our military operations and the presence of thousands of Mozambican refugees strained our national coffers. The refugee caseload rose threefold from 1987 to nearly 100 000 in December 1989, with similar numbers of stranded Mozambicans living quietly among Zimbabweans as a source of cheap labour. The government set up five camps for the Mozambicans along the eastern border at Nyamatikiti, Mazowe River Bridge, Nyangombe, Tongogara and Chambuta. There were hundreds of other refugees of various nationalities – Malawians, Ugandans, Ghanaians, South Africans and Namibians – living mainly in urban areas.

By June 1990, Maputo and the right-wing Renamo rebels began to talk peace. Their war had taken 100 000 lives and created 800 000 refugees, littered all over southern Africa.

The 1990 election campaign kicked off with much fanfare as the region prepared to enter a climate of peace and security. Mugabe looked fairly comfortable with Nkomo now on his side; at least the Unity Accord assured him of Zanu PF's acceptance in Matabeleland. In other parts of the country, Mugabe showed some jitters about Tekere's chances.

Tekere put up a brave fight, managing to field candidates in all 120 parliamentary constituencies. Mugabe upped the tempo, using state intelligence operatives to infiltrate the nascent party and resorting to open police and militia intimidation of ZUM candidates. In the final stages of the campaign Elias Kanengoni, a serving secret service officer, and Kisito

Chivamba, a Zanu PF youth leader, shot and wounded Patrick Kombayi, a Gweru businessmen and a senior ZUM official, then challenging vice-president Simon Muzenda for a parliamentary seat in the city. Kombayi was lucky to survive after he was airlifted to the United Kingdom for treatment. Kanengoni and Chivamba were arrested, tried and convicted of attempted murder. Although they were sentenced to a lengthy prison term, Mugabe pardoned them immediately.

The attack on Kombayi left ZUM candidates badly shaken. Almost two dozen pulled out at the last minute. The shooting had a serious psychological impact on voters, who ultimately gave Zanu PF and Mugabe another mandate. But Tekere refused to accept the result, citing numerous electoral irregularities, intimidation and vote rigging – although he did not mount a legal challenge in the courts. The manner in which Mugabe manipulated the 1990 election was exposed in a study entitled *Voting for Democracy*[8] by Professor Jonathan Moyo. Tekere's ZUM collapsed soon after the election when his deputy, Bindura doctor Emmanuel Magoche, and senior officials Wurayayi Zembe, Alois Masepe and others broke away from the party citing what they called Tekere's lack of vision and dictatorial tendencies. Magoche and Zembe formed a new outfit, the Democratic Party (DP). Initially Magoche claimed that the ZUM national executive had fired Tekere from the party for misconduct, only to invite a salty reaction from Tekere in which he told them that it was, in fact, he who had fired his entire national executive.

The DP eventually trickled away into nothing; when I occasionally bumped into Magoche and Zembe, they claimed the DP was still alive, although there was no evidence of it on the ground.

Mugabe's 1990 victory gave him a six-year term in office. The Tekere challenge had prompted Zimbabweans to look critically at his leadership style, especially his tolerance of corruption and his failure to deal with the rapid deterioration of the economy. As a people battered by both national and regional insecurity, we expected to earn a major peace dividend that would rekindle our economic fortunes and raise the overall quality of life. In the trade unions, our attention remained firmly fixed on our relations with the government. The decade was opening on a hopeful note and offered Mugabe a chance to prove his leadership qualities.

ENDNOTES

1   Laakso, Liisa (undated). 'Opposition Politics in Independent Zimbabwe'. *African Studies Quarterly* (online), 7(2&3) http://web.africa.ufl.edu/asq/v7/v7i2a6.htm

2   The Constitution of Zimbabwe: Schedule to the Zimbabwe Constitution Order 1979 (SI 1979/1600) of the United Kingdom

3   Zanu PF Leadership Code, 1984. http://www.zimbabwemetro.com/resources/downloads/zanu-pf-leadership-code/

4   'James Chikerema, firebrand revolutionary who was a catalyst in the transformation of Rhodesia into Zimbabwe'. *The Sunday Times of London*, 4 April 2006 http://www.timesonline.co.uk/tol/comment/obituaries/article701623.ece

5   Hurungo, James (2010). 'An inquiry into how Rhodesia managed to survive under economic sanctions: lessons for the Zimbabwe government'. Paper prepared for the Trade and Development Studies Centre, Harare

6   'Zimbabwe: Reconciliation, unity and conflict (1980-1989)'. Electoral Institute for the Sustainability of Democracy in Africa. Undated. http://www.eisa.or.za/WEP/zimoverview4.htm

7   As a senior Zanla commander, Mhanda helped Robert Mugabe come to power, a move he soon regretted. In an interview with the Helen Suzman Foundation soon after the formation of the MDC, he said that senior commanders, including himself, realised they had made a mistake in electing Mugabe as the new leader of Zanu. Mugabe, he said, didn't want to unite with Joshua Nkomo as he was scared of him. After his election Mugabe dissolved Zipa (the Zimbabwe People's Army) and 'abolished all the joint organisations between the liberation movements'. The commanders were upset by this, especially those who had worked hard for a united front. Mugabe asked Samora Machel to arrest the commanders to avoid a military rebellion. 'I was arrested along with some 600 fighters and the 50 top commanders,' said Mhanda. 'Some fighters were released, but the commanders stayed in jail for three years.' http://www.hsf.org.za/resource-centre

8   Moyo, Jonathan (1992). *Voting for Democracy: A study of electoral politics in Zimbabwe*. Harare: University of Zimbabwe

CHAPTER SEVEN

ECONOMIC MELTDOWN

The impending collapse of the Soviet Union in 1989 had come as an unwelcome surprise to many advocates and disciples of socialism in Zimbabwe, both in academia and in the trade union movement. I myself had visited the USSR on a trade union mission half a decade earlier and had seen the signs of industrial decay and human demoralisation. There was not much to inspire belief in central planning or the ideology of Marxist-Leninism. As Russians wondered what was becoming of their once all-powerful, all-seeing government, dramatic events unfolded in the USSR's Eastern European satellites.

I followed with interest the events in Poland where Solidarity, the trade union and social movement, won power in a semi-free election and eventually swept the communists out, setting off a domino effect. Equally dramatic was a bloody uprising in Romania that led to the execution of the dictator Nicolae Ceauşescu and his wife on Christmas Day 1989. Pictures of their corpses were splashed across the world media.

In my report after the mission to Moscow I had sounded a warning that the Zimbabwean economy could crumble in the same way as the USSR's through inefficiencies and a dispirited labour force. If Mugabe and Zanu PF ever read that report at the time they were not inclined to listen; but as the USSR collapsed progressively and finally disappeared in 1991, new thinking was forced on our government. The changing world created a major headache. For the first ten years of his rule, Mugabe had been an active Cold War player – a Marxist ideologue, a fiery demagogue and a master of political rhetoric against colonialism and capitalism.

There was no doubt that European colonialism was on its way out; at the same time capitalism seemed to have triumphed worldwide. Like others of his African nationalist generation with a socialist agenda, Mugabe seemed to be outpaced by the rapid international changes. One of the world's superpowers had fallen in a puff of popular sovereignty. To any close political watcher, it was impossible not to see that the other, the United States, was in a triumphalist mood, crowing about American democracy, the market-driven economy, privatisation, free trade, globalisation, and export-led growth for developing countries.

As a trade unionist, I could hardly escape the dominant presence of the IMF and the World Bank who implored and nudged Zimbabwe to forsake the centrist experiments of socialism for a more open, market-orientated economy. With a squeeze on the nation's balance of payments, in 1991 Mugabe buckled and blindly swallowed the IMF prescription, dubbed the Economic Structural Adjustment Programme (ESAP). He jumped out of the frying pan of socialism into the fire of neo-liberalism, choosing one evil over the other. The choice was to prove disastrous.

With that, all pretensions about socialism vanished from Mugabe's vocabulary and his way of life, leaving Zanu PF ideologically bankrupt and utterly confused. We cautioned Mugabe about the danger of taking the IMF medicine without consultation with trade unions, other stakeholders like the church, the student movement and the economically vulnerable.

Adopting ESAP was a radical policy shift; out went the centralised,

Soviet-style planning programmes and in came a totally different economic model geared to the efficacy of market forces, a free enterprise system and less state direction and intervention in the economy. State subsidies, fixed minimum wages and protective labour laws were out. We disagreed with the government; we thought that together we could craft a more sensible and humane alternative. But there was to be no argument.

Our fears were to prove justified both at home and abroad. By the end of the 1990s the world at large was learning that limitless capital flows could bring the economies of developing countries crashing down. It would emerge that ESAP exposed Zimbabwe to merciless globalisation in which we could not compete, and hence placed us in a position of dependency. For us, as for many in the developing world, the 1990s would turn out to be a lost decade for development. Financial crises hit Mexico, Thailand, Malaysia, South Korea, Indonesia, Russia, Turkey and Argentina. When the world turned the corner into the new millennium, further shocks were in store – this time not for the developing world but for the big capitalist economies themselves. By the end of the first decade of the new century a crisis of global proportions sent markets into a spin and major capitalist economies into recession. Billions of people across the planet suffered the consequences of unbridled free marketeering. In this fast-changing world, workers and their trade unions became the first casualties. There had to be a better way.

As the 1990s opened, it was back to business for Mugabe – the business of consolidating his power under the guise of a tightly controlled democracy. After securing the national vote that he needed as leader of a 'united' Zanu PF party, and with Joshua Nkomo now safely tucked under his arm and Edgar Tekere licking his wounds after a supposed electoral defeat, there seemed to be no need for a further extension of the State of Emergency. The law had been in place since Rhodesian times. It was repealed by parliament in July 1990.

With that colonial relic out of the way, I thought it was now time for the ZCTU to organise without fear of indefinite detentions and police harassment. We set out to grow the organisation, paying particular attention to workers' rights and economic management. We now boasted a vibrant secretariat with labour economists, lawyers, medical doctors, advocacy and gender experts, and a series of training programmes for our unionists. We streamlined our administrative systems, improved our capacity for collective bargaining and raised the ZCTU's profile to a level that put the labour confederation on the national and international map.

I was keen to see a strong labour movement, totally apolitical and fighting for the social rights and freedoms of ordinary workers. ESAP lacked a human resource development strategy; its thrust was mainly on cost-cutting measures. This became evident in our various analyses as trade unions; in our workshops and seminars with civil society; and in our daily observations on the route Zimbabwe was now being forced to take by the emerging global economic environment.

I regarded ESAP as a blunt instrument directed against the workers and I warned against its implementation in the form that was put to us. The programme discouraged self-reliance, especially when the government tried to justify it by saying that it was export-orientated. With our structural weaknesses, I knew that we would import more than we exported; I knew we would produce less because of our foreign exchange constraints. Our production base was tiny, relying on scientifically inferior and backward tools. We were not yet ready, technologically, to compete on a global scale.

In the ZCTU, we tried hard to make Mugabe see the pitfalls that lay ahead under the new economic thrust, only to be shoved aside. Instead, he turned on us calling the ZCTU leadership a coterie of excited amateurs who should not concern themselves with matters of statecraft and governance.

As if to reinforce the global changes and to reflect the new thinking, heads of state and governments of all the Commonwealth nations met for their biannual meeting in Harare in 1991 at which a critical document on governance was adopted, the Harare Declaration.[1] The declaration was a landmark document in that, among other issues, it emphasised the belief in 'the liberty of the individual under the law, in equal rights for all citizens regardless of gender, race, colour, creed or political belief, and in the individual's inalienable right to participate by means of free and democratic political processes in framing the society in which he or she lives ...' It also noted the end of the Cold War and totalitarianism.

Post-colonial Africa faced a new phase in governance. The Harare Declaration had little real effect at the time. African nations threw up populist post-colonial leaders who held out high hopes of change but instead delivered instability and disintegration. Presidents Kenneth Kaunda in Zambia, Hastings Kamuzu Banda in Malawi, Samuel Doe in Liberia and several others were voted out when their people demanded more open societies and greater respect for fundamental rights.

It was easy to promise change but far harder to bring it about. At least Zambia and Malawi had relatively peaceful elections, but in the Horn of Africa and Ethiopia the worst was to happen. In Somalia, warlords toppled the dictator Mohamed Siad Barre after 18 years of dictatorship, leaving Mogadishu without a functional administration; ongoing chaos led to the break-up of the country. In Ethiopia, the dictator Mengistu Haile Mariam murdered thousands of his opponents in the 'Red Terror', but was finally forced to flee the country in May 1991. He found refuge with a good friend, Robert Mugabe. Mengistu settled down as a respected guest in a Harare mansion and was granted permanent residence in 2001.[2]

Throughout the 1990s Mugabe charted his new course, regardless. From my observations, he appeared ill at ease with the ending of the Cold War but accepted, and indeed enthusiastically implemented, ESAP as the ideal prescription for growth. Although in public he seemed unconcerned, he was under increasing pressure to introduce major social and economic reforms. His bewildered party saw him cast away the socialist mask he had worn since 1980.

Throughout his rule so far, Mugabe had remained the darling of the Commonwealth and the United Nations, despite his repressive actions in the Gukurahundi era, and despite his socialist pronouncements and strange bedfellows. When he embraced ESAP he added leading financiers and corporate investors to his circle of world admirers.

Foreign governments were nervous about the rise of trade unionism, which they feared could propel 'Labour' into power in Africa and bring about a return to the failed policies of socialism. This was far off the mark. We wanted jobs, development and progress, not ideological formulae. In

Africa too, the black nationalist establishment began to suspect that trade unions could become a new challenge to their hold on power.

When trade unionist Frederick Chiluba won the presidency in Zambia after a campaign strongly supported by the unions and civil society, Mugabe's establishment was shaken to the core. Chiluba's victory sent out ripples of wild expectation in southern Africa's trade union movement.

For the first time, wherever I went on ZCTU business I fielded questions regarding my political ambitions, something that had never crossed my mind. I developed a standard response, persuasively telling anybody who enquired that our political situation was vastly different from that of Zambia. The Chiluba template was not appropriate for Zimbabwe, I opined.

Nevertheless, I developed a keen interest in economic affairs, and especially how the ESAP programme was set to affect the workers. The state was dismissing surplus workers; companies laid off those they saw as non-essential staff; the government created a 'social dimensions fund' with a view to cushioning the retrenched workers; but all indications pointed towards a negative position for the growing numbers of poor people and the traditionally vulnerable peasants.

In the ZCTU we began to ask questions after noting that the volumes and quality of goods and services produced in Zimbabwe was shrinking at an alarming pace. The small amount of foreign currency from limited exports was lost to high-level corruption and poverty levels were rising. Mugabe was quick to evade debate. He began to distance himself from our activities, and to avoid possible embarrassment from confronting a restless workforce he routinely turned down our invitations to address workers' meetings.

In the end, we became so desolate that we did not know where to turn. Mugabe's previous 'socialist' government was now much closer to the business community. Workers could be dismissed without following laid-down procedures. The ZCTU was inundated with calls for help from all over the country. What was to be done?

I took a closer look at the communal sector, thinking perhaps that was where the answers lay, but there was no comfort to be had. Subsistence agriculture was based on primitive technology and methods, virtually dependent on rainfall that came once a year, if it came at all in some areas. When the rains failed, as happened in the 1991/92 season, famine was sure to follow in a nation with a weak industrial and commercial base and without any form of social security. Throughout the 1980s, meaningful land redistribution had been endlessly deferred despite Zanu PF's claims that it was a priority. The promise to resettle huge numbers of households on millions of hectares was simply not realised, and by the mid-1990s most of the settlement areas were quickly reverting to communal subsistence.[3]

To compound an already deteriorating situation, Mugabe had, by then, abandoned the resettlement programme and was now working closely with white commercial farmers. Organisations like the Horticultural Promotion Council entered the scene and commercial farmers started to move away from food crops, especially maize, shifting to more lucrative export crops because of a deliberate policy thrust that suppressed producer prices. ESAP discouraged subsidies and other forms of state support to the small farmers. At the time, few qualified for assistance from the state company, the Agriculture Finance Corporation (AFC) and those who failed to repay their loans, for whatever reason, were struck off the registers and excluded from further borrowing. Combined with variations in rainfall, crop yields, especially of the staple maize, dropped significantly. Large-scale production of maize decreased from 1.7 million tonnes in 1981 to 0.7 million tonnes in 1991.

To make matters worse, Mugabe took advantage of the expiry of government farm leases of hundreds of white farmers in 1992 and began to dish out farms to his government ministers and top Zanu PF officials, leaving the peasant staggering for breath and sustenance. The new class of landowners, who were political beneficiaries, saw their acquisitions largely as status symbols; they were neither farmers nor business people. They began to retrench their workers in large numbers.

Our records at the ZCTU showed that a poor balance of crops and an overall reduction in the proportion of exports led to a decline in formal employment in agriculture, including forestry and fisheries. Research conducted by the ZCTU economics department, led by Dr Godfrey

Kanyenze, established that shortly after the war ended in 1980, agriculture had employed 327 000 people. By 1991, the figure had dropped to 150 000. Those out of the system retreated to the communal lands, joining the pool of the unemployed. Such developments dominated our work in the ZCTU, considering that fewer people were being resettled and no efforts were being made to seek alternatives. Unemployment and hopelessness were on the rise.

I watched Mugabe slowly develop into a full-blown capitalist, allowing his ministers and top military officials to pursue aristocratic modes of wealth accumulation. As capitalism officially became acceptable inside Zanu PF, a race for the 'good life' burst forth, with clear signs of a new class of the politically well-connected leading the scramble. This class included cabinet ministers, senior military officials, legislators, black business people aligned to Zanu PF and bankers. Many never created new enterprises; they simply acquired existing companies, ran them down and used their offices as avenues for fleecing the state through a corrupt tender system. Capitalism rendered Mugabe's 1984 leadership code completely moribund.

As the cake shrank, Zanu PF created new means of public asset-stripping and looting. With hindsight, I think South African businessman Moeletsi Mbeki put it most succinctly when he wrote that there is something inherently wrong with African nationalism; there is a major contradiction at its centre. Mbeki's observation was quoted by *The Mail & Guardian* when he launched his book, *Architects of Poverty* (Picador) at the Cape Town Book Fair in July 2009. 'Nationalism sets out to defeat its perceived enemy,' says Mbeki. 'But it sees the enemy's way of life as its model. This is the contradiction of nationalism ... It set out to emulate, through black economic empowerment, white capital.'

Given what we inherited as an economy, the trend was unfortunate. We came into a free Zimbabwe with three economies operating side by side: subsistence, informal and a tiny white-owned enclave of business activity. We needed to integrate the three into a single national economy; to look beyond subsistence agriculture as an economic model. With five natural regions, the first being rated the best for cropping and the last totally unsuitable, my view was that a separate business model was needed for the transformation of our communal lands.

Commercial agriculture thrived on state and private sector encouragement, intervention and direct support, while the peasantry and the informal sector were left to fend for themselves. ESAP worsened the gulf between the two, emphasising the supremacy of the market as a determinant for growth and survival. Naturally, the peasant was caught unaware and unprepared for this sophisticated economic challenge.

The absence of a deliberate, national policy to integrate the separate economies destroyed our once vibrant traditional communal farming system and transformed the peasant sector into a docile labour reserve. Staff cutbacks in government departments under ESAP resulted in fewer and poorly equipped extension workers to spearhead rural development.

In our view as trade unions, when ESAP started to cause economic confusion, we could see that we had inherited nothing positive from Mugabe's socialist experiment. The social agenda that Mugabe had pursued from independence faltered under ESAP, with devastating results. No meaningful development of any kind – socialist or market-driven – was visible in the communal lands.

The government's interventions in the economy were counterfeit and populist, intended to gain cheap political mileage. It failed to change the fundamental Rhodesian structures, their inequities and their inefficiencies, as a viable economic model. The reason was simple: there was never a development strategy to clear inherited economic rigidities. Focus seemed to be on ad hoc, short-term stabilisation programmes. Levels of investment – both local and foreign – had always been low.

Generally, in the period of Mugabe's socialist rhetoric the state discouraged black Zimbabweans from undertaking business ventures. Foreign investors, if not put off entirely, were uncertain about the economic direction Zimbabwe wanted to take. Disincentives were compounded by the introduction of a battery of centrally generated regulations and excessive state controls on the economy. Despite its heavy-handedness, or because of it, the state failed to guide the economy and to harness the dormant potential of the informal sector.

It is true that the state pumped massive resources into education and health. Yet little was done to prepare for tomorrow by expanding our industrial base to absorb the intended beneficiaries of the Zanu PF social agenda. In any case, the schools built for the new Zimbabwe started to collapse as the economy declined under ESAP. A rise in pupil and student enrolments up to university level produced mounting frustration for those who had nowhere to go after they finished school or graduated with degrees.

Our small finance sector, though fairly stable, serviced an equally small white population and soon became overwhelmed as new demands were made on it. Markets need credit, and credit needs banks. Zimbabwe's finance sector was heavily protected by the state and only separated according to function. Building societies specialised in mortgages, while commercial banks dealt with short-term finance. The state decreed a minimum lending rate while interest rates were left open to individual banks and institutions with minimum central bank supervision. This resulted in monopolies. Varied interests across other economic sectors used their financial muscle to strengthen themselves.

Up until the advent of ESAP, the Zanu PF government saw no immediate reason to open up the financial sector making entry into this area difficult for indigenous players and, by extension, it limited the availability of support for newcomers hoping to obtain short-term loans for their businesses. I knew that under the changed economic policy framework there was no way the formal sector, given its size and its traditional market, could suddenly rise to punch above its weight, so to speak.

In concert with ZCTU officials and economists, and with the aid of external experts from the University of Zimbabwe and the private sector, we debated ESAP in detail. We sought a deeper understanding of what the policy shift meant to the workers and agreed that as long as the structural rigidities inherited from Rhodesia remained intact, Zimbabwe was set to achieve little or very low economic growth under the programme. After a decade of rising budget deficits, ESAP's impact on rising unemployment and poverty was therefore negligible.

Mugabe's administration pushed itself progressively into a situation where it became impossible for it to service the national debt. About 25.5 per cent of the government's budget deficit went towards paying for operations of perennially failing state companies which were kept afloat as avenues through which political cronies could be accommodated and as vehicles for corruption.

We ran a series of workshops and seminars at which ESAP was on the agenda, alerting our affiliate unions to the dangers that lay ahead for their members. We told them that without an integrated economic model that took all Zimbabweans on board, a social crisis was threatening the national collapse of all our systems: health, education, employment, social services and the public sector. I insisted that by opening up an already distorted economy, Mugabe was laying a base for a crisis of governance that would eventually turn Zimbabwe into a disorderly, failed state.

Some of my colleagues felt that agriculture, as a labour-intensive industry, could provide answers. I disagreed. I told them that although the state had, by 1990, acquired 3.5 million hectares of land it had only managed to resettle 52 000 of a planned 162 000 families.[4] Out of these figures, a mere 19 per cent of the acquired land could reasonably be classified as prime land; the rest was in poor, sandy areas with erratic rainfall patterns. The new lands were unsuitable for crop farming or agriculture by normal methods. Figures showed that a mere 5 500 hectares – out of 16 million in the communal lands – was under irrigation in 1992. This was a drop in the ocean considering Zimbabwe's rapid population growth. Although we had a state irrigation fund, peasant farmers were uncomfortable with borrowing money because of tight lending conditions. I argued that the government only supported the production and marketing of exports, marginalising the poor from the economy.

Mugabe gave commercial farmers incentives for their crop exports, allowing them to keep a percentage of their foreign exchange earnings. These farmers were free to import inputs and lived in relative comfort. In the ZCTU we could see that the exports, originally meant to spur economic development, were unbalanced and foreign exchange earnings were unpredictable.

The little that trickled in was quickly absorbed by commercial farmers who, by then, had abandoned food crops, opting for wildlife management, tobacco, cotton, flowers and oil seeds. None of the peasants had the wherewithal to try out any of these exports. The share of marketed maize dropped from 70 per cent to 30 per cent. We began to experience food shortages. A rise in inflation became noticeable. By 1993, the value of wages was down to 15 per cent of their 1983 level.

ESAP demanded that the government devalue the Zimbabwe dollar, and when Mugabe complied with this requirement there was chaos across the country: prices of basic commodities shot up and the cost of living rose wildly.

I found myself in a particular dilemma. Seeing thousands of workers, ZCTU members, lose their jobs under ESAP I felt that Zimbabwe needed a national bias towards industrialisation to rectify the historical imbalances and to attend to the negative influences of our colonial inheritance of inequality. With ESAP, Mugabe found an excuse merely to replace the colonial and settler administrators with black faces; he rarely consulted the people and was intolerant of opposing views. Not surprisingly, then, our participation in all sectors of the economy as black Zimbabweans was still at two per cent. You could find this funny, or tragic, but the fact is that it was the outcome of many years of colonial discrimination and the later Zanu PF official discouragement of black business through socialist rhetoric.

In the ZCTU we were increasingly agitated by the callous decision to drive the entire country into wholesale capitalism. The state was now reduced to the status of passive observer, while we believed it had a role and a responsibility to put together an enabling environment for greater national participation in the economy.

On a national scale, cutbacks in the state funding of national institutions weakened them. Corruption, a brain-drain into neighbouring countries, and lack of accountability eroded confidence among professionals in the public sector.

A spirit of both survival and self-enrichment was taking root in our newly opened up capitalist society. What made our lives even more difficult as workers was that Mugabe outlawed workers' strikes and often ordered the army and the police to apply brute force if we tried to defy the ban.

We faced a particularly difficult time as trade unionists; workers demanded answers which we failed to provide. Even war veterans, now resident in remote communal villages, occasionally came to our offices showing signs of discomfort with the way Zimbabwe was turning out. They were concerned with Mugabe's apparent abandonment of land reforms to help the poor. Senior ministers and officials had embarked on systematic material deprivation of the pool. Almost all of them owned large tracts of land – which they hardly used.

As we struggled through this difficult period, a further development in the region led many people to turn to me for possible solutions. In 1991, I resisted suggestions from within our trade union ranks and among our admirers and supporters, to follow Chiluba's footsteps into national politics. Barely a year later another colleague, Chakufwa Chihana – a veteran Malawian trade unionist – entered the fray and dared to take on Life President Banda in an election. Chihana left a Southern African Trade Union Coordination Council (SATUCC) meeting in Zambia, publicly challenged Banda, and flew to Malawi in a bid to start a campaign against his ageing nationalist leader.

As was to be expected from Banda's ruthless regime, Chihana found the Malawi police waiting for him at the airport. From the glare of television cameras in Lusaka and Johannesburg, Chihana found himself in jail just minutes after his plane touched down in his native land.

For some time after Chihana's daredevil adventure, I received numerous calls and exhortations to emulate such bravery and start preparing to take on Mugabe politically. Again, I politely cautioned that our situations were different and required a different approach. My subsequent reflections on the lessons of trade unionists entering politics are covered in the next chapter. It was pointless to rush into politics without broad-based alliances, and even more foolhardy to do so without intensive brainstorming and policy formulation to bring about social transformation with justice.

When Chihana was released from jail in 1993, he resigned from SATUCC and opted for full-time politics. SATUCC immediately appointed me to take over his post as secretary general. I found the work cumbersome and difficult. The SATUCC head office was in Kitwe and I was in Harare so I temporarily moved the head office to Harare for better coordination and management. While I tried hard to execute my mandate at SATUCC, the situation at home was getting worse; our unions were becoming weaker, with steadily shrinking membership and leaders struggling to cope with job losses under ESAP. The situation threatened to make the trade unions irrelevant.

The government allocated only a small budget to land reform, further heightening the anxieties of retrenched workers who saw a piece of land as a form of security, in the absence of any formal work. They were simply looking for space to subsist. They knew that those resettled in the early 1980s were no different, in status and farming methods, to those they left behind in the communal lands. The economic decline was forcing workers back to an already disempowered peasantry. The folly of ESAP was that it alienated millions of potentially productive citizens from the development cycle. The entire state plan was shoddy, dealing mainly with symptoms, avoiding the structural inequities in the economy. There was growing disillusionment, lethargy and hopelessness.

In 1992, the government passed the Land Acquisition Act replacing the willing buyer, willing seller principle agreed to in the Lancaster House Constitution. Under the new law, the state had a right to seize any piece of land anywhere and to compensate the owner for improvements. Beyond the change to the law, nothing much happened to help out the landless. Whenever a new farm became available, state officials resorted to nepotism, bribery and directives from Zanu PF on the allocation of choice plots.

Looking back, I recalled that the plan to hand over prime land to the elite started long before ESAP. In 1985, the state tried to sideline peasants, sending them to the periphery, by identifying isolated projects along the Zambezi River, south-east of Lake Kariba, for the poor. One, named the Mid-Zambezi Valley Project, benefited from a US$25 million grant from the African Development Bank (ADB). The area is infested with the tsetse fly and is in a poor rainfall zone. The project targeted close to 7 600 families for placement on 12-acre rocky plots covering 2 600 hectares of desiccated, virgin land north of Guruve.

The plan was abandoned and only resumed during the ESAP era. And, in what was becoming typical Zanu PF fashion, the state engaged consultants from the Food and Agriculture Organisation to undertake a two-year feasibility study of the area without any input from the peasants, local government officials or even their district councils. I was still in Bindura at the time and officials at the provincial office told me that it was kept in the dark about the goings-on in the Zambezi Valley up until the time Harare was about to sign a loan agreement with the ADB in Abidjan, Ivory Coast, in 1985. When the news filtered through to the targeted villagers, they turned down the offer of land, arguing that they had not been consulted. Peasant resistance gathered momentum to a point where they armed themselves with spears, axes and other traditional weapons in a show of defiance.

The land reform policy failed the peasantry; it never considered their competences and limitations, their knowledge systems, or even their concerns as a distinct community. Even the church became worried as they began to process increasing requests for help from people. Thus the churches too became critical of the government's ESAP programme.[5] In 1994, a group of church-based charities launched discussion forums to review the impact of ESAP on their members. Together with the CCJP and the Methodist Synod, the churches entered the anti-ESAP crusade, taking up roles in policy advocacy, civic education, voter education and election monitoring.

By 1994, Mugabe seemed to recognise these failures and commissioned a group of experts and stakeholders, led by a University of Zimbabwe academic, Professor Mandivamba Rukuni, to study the imbalances in land ownership and usage and to chart a way forward. I made a written submission to the commission on behalf of the ZCTU calling for a radical structural shift of the entire economy to accommodate the communal and informal sectors in the mainstream financial system. Mugabe ignored the commission's report and recommendations, casting further doubt on his sincerity and desire for a lasting solution. We immediately convened a ZCTU meeting and decided on a comprehensive economic study in the forlorn hope of persuading Mugabe to change the direction Zimbabwe was headed. We knew that ESAP, as a programme, would ultimately come to an end.

We were worried about life beyond ESAP, so our study focused on the period afterwards. In our report, entitled *Beyond ESAP*,[6] we identified the distortions in the economy as the main impediment to national advancement. Naturally biased towards job creation and social security, *Beyond ESAP* argued against Mugabe's policy shift which promoted a passive labour market in a highly flexible and volatile environment. We suggested the adoption of a two-pronged approach to accommodate our existing realities and to integrate the non-formal sector into the mainstream economy. In the process, we felt, a vibrant, transparent and well-planned land reform programme was an invaluable part of the solution. Our proposal sought to discourage exclusive concentration on the formal sector as this tended to further entrench the enclave and dual structure of the economy.

Once again, Mugabe ignored our suggestions. I was surprised to see the government introduce new legislation offering communal farmers a paltry 10 per cent of Zimbabwe's water for irrigation. The Water Act was rushed through Parliament in 1995, setting aside a minimal amount for the historically dry communal sector. With that allocation, I became convinced that Mugabe was no longer interested in structural change or in redressing the imbalances in the economy, at least not through agricultural reform.

My concerns and fears were confirmed when the government in its 1995 national budget set aside next to nothing – by way of cash – for land reform, resettlement or water development. We debated the issue in various ZCTU meetings and concluded that Zimbabwe was slowly, but surely, destined for a failed state status. The communal sector now found itself completely under siege. The state reduced the number of commercial grain collection depots and did not involve small grain traders, transporters and food processors in the commercial supply chain. State support to the communal lands was cut. The cutbacks included research and extension services, further reducing direct government contact with communal farmers. State crop marketing boards were privatised, leading to massive staff retrenchments.

The informal economy played a vital role in economic activity, both in the urban and rural areas. As trade unionists, we could discern no dynamic linkages between land, labour and capital. In an informal or false economy the structure of wages and incomes is generally distorted. Cost margins and returns are never matched, leading to heavy losses. The state and the shrinking formal sector were always bound in a foreign currency and debt trap, partly because of their poor links to the rest of the country. By making the majority poor, the levels of savings collapsed. This happened at a time when local interest rates were rising, thus discouraging investment. Local companies began to look elsewhere for external sources of finance.

Our secondary schools were offloading 300 000 graduates on to the labour market every year at a time when the private sector was shedding jobs to cut costs. The clothing and textiles industry was hardest hit, registering a 21 per cent decline. The informal sector flooded the market with cheap 'used' clothes, leading to the deindustrialisation of the textile industry and clothing sector. Godfrey Kanyenze's 1996 study showed that some 72 companies closed down between 1993 and 1995, costing 4 000 jobs. ESAP forced the government to cut its staff by 25 per cent. To those still at work, real wages had dropped to about 60 per cent of their 1980 level.

By 1995 about 9 000 retrenched workers had attended five-day courses meant to turn them into small business operators. This measure failed to cushion the vulnerable groups. Although Z$89 million was set aside for this purpose, the numbers of beneficiaries were never officially made public – suggesting that corruption could have crept into that exercise in the end. The support was supposed to cover basic expenses like food, school fees and health care.

Mugabe and Zanu PF exposed their incompetence and wasteful behaviour in the ESAP era. They perpetuated underdevelopment and allowed entrenched systems and structural flaws to persist. This would later accelerate Zimbabwe's economic meltdown and deepen the crisis of governance. Mugabe was now in a trap. The political unpopularity of

ESAP could not be minimised, nor could he turn back to his discredited brand of socialism. Zimbabwe seemed to be flying without a pilot. ESAP bore no fruits as Mugabe and Zanu PF faced yet another election in 1995 with nothing to show.

As I travelled in the countries of the Southern African Development Community (SADC) on SATUCC business, I heard similar concerns about ESAP and its effect on the future of trade unions and workers. I was particularly worried by the decision to set up export processing zones (EPZs). The government felt that EPZs would help bring the economy in line with global trends, but my worry was about the welfare of the workers. I found a different response in the SADC region, especially at government level. In SATUCC, we were against these different approaches and wanted a common position on ESAP and EPZs.

SADC, despite a common public pronouncement for regional unity, still pursued a parochial and nationalistic line. Competition for investment and markets was high, creating tensions between member states. SATUCC convened a regional meeting and agreed that EPZs constituted a weak and inefficient way of achieving economic investment and growth. The cost to national economies, to the ordinary people and to the region far outweighed the benefits. Such a strategy was divisive and an attack on regional integration.

The strategy undermined the gains we had made through negotiated programmes and struck at the heart of our trade union work. We believed that prospects for job creation were dwindling. These zones had failed elsewhere because of minimal earnings and a high repatriation of profits. Moreover, workers employed in these zones were not covered by any labour laws. The zones never stimulated domestic growth; failed to develop skills; and never facilitated any meaningful technology transfers. Their greatest threat was local industry – which they sabotaged through substandard and cheap alternatives.

In my view, EPZs were a cost to the national purse, distorted our tax base and were unfair competitors to domestic industry. As trade unions, we were highly distressed by a deliberate government plan to make concessions on labour, the environment and health standards in the name of investment.

Job security was at stake, health and safety heavily compromised and workers felt exposed to unending poverty through the EPZ scheme. We feared that international criminals could use the zones to exploit workers during the life of a zone's concessionary period; and we feared that imports of hazardous raw materials could find their way into the country through these unregulated practices.

SADC appeared to contradict itself over this issue. While the grouping understood the benefit of working together to attract regional investment, the issue of EPZs meant a clear departure from that position. The region now competed for players and investors in these zones, promoting an extreme form of single-handed liberalisation, totally against group cooperation. When newly democratic South Africa became part of SADC in 1994, workers believed that prospects for a strong regional approach could now be realised. But these hopes were dashed as it became apparent that the political will remained subdued and lukewarm.

As the prospects for peace in Mozambique and Angola improved and open conflict appeared to be dissipating, we thought stability would bring development to the region. But for two years, SATUCC watched in dismay as no significant agreements were sealed on labour, trade, investment and other key areas.

The civil war in Mozambique had ended with the country's first multiparty election in 1994. Although Frelimo retained the national mandate, the former Renamo rebels made significant inroads into parliament, thus turning Mozambique into the only country in Africa with a strong opposition. With that election, Zimbabwe no longer had a military involvement in Maputo's affairs. In Angola the Unita rebels of Jonas Savimbi had signed a peace agreement in May 1991, paving the way for a 1992 election. But Savimbi refused to accept the election result. The agreement, known as the Bicesse Accords, was reaffirmed in 1994 by regional leaders in Lusaka as the search for regional peace intensified.

Instead, fresh conflicts began to emerge because of an inexplicable desire to harp on selfishness and counterfeit nationalism. As the SATUCC secretary general I could see that the urge to defend sovereignty and national interest is generally attractive to nations but easy to abuse. Those who define these terms on behalf of the people normally fail to reflect the national sentiment in its totality and use their theories for personal gain and aggrandisement. I discussed these issues at length with my colleagues at home and in the region. My conclusion was that a limited regional vision denies a nation a much-needed long-term dividend and is a recipe for future instability.

As we approached the 1995 general election, ESAP presented huge challenges to Zanu PF politicians inside Zimbabwe's de facto one-party state. The opposition came now from within Zanu PF and politicians started to jostle for power inside the party.

Margaret Dongo, former PF politician Sidney Malunga, together with Zanu PF's legislators Lazarus Nyarayebani, Mike Mataure, Gibson Munyoro and even Edgar Tekere tried to fight from within Mugabe's party for reform, often raising critical questions about the impending crisis of governance. But the opposition was largely symbolic and inconsequential, featuring loudmouths with little real influence. Those brave enough to stand up to Mugabe, like Edgar Tekere and Margaret Dongo, were soon expelled from Zanu PF.

The internal climax of the power struggles saw vice-president Simon Muzenda challenged by a retired military officer, Josiah Tungamirai, in Gutu North constituency. Muzenda, still under an embarrassing political shadow arising from the attack and near murder of Gweru businessman Patrick Kombayi by state agents at the time of the 1990 election, had decided to shift constituencies to his traditional home area of Gutu. He found former air force commander Tungamirai waiting and a new fight for political turf inside Zanu PF erupted. Other than that, the election should have passed as a non-event as there were no strong parties to fight Mugabe.

The only potential external challenger was the Forum Party, a loosely formed political grouping headed by two former Supreme Court judges – the first black Zimbabwean Chief Justice Enock Dumbutshena and his deputy, another senior retired jurist, Washington Sansole. In our view, the Forum Party was an upper middle class outfit with leaders whose political message meant very little to our impoverished population. The Forum Party, like ZUM, collapsed and disappeared soon after the low profile election in which 55 Zanu PF seats were uncontested.

Veteran nationalist Ndabaningi Sithole returned to the scene. With a comrade, Fred Sithole, from his Zanu (Ndonga) party, they defeated Zanu PF in the Sitholes' Ndau/Shangaan ethnic stronghold of Chipinge in south-east Zimbabwe. The reason was simple. The Ndau ethnic group, to which the two Sitholes belonged, appeared never to have forgiven Mugabe for taking over the leadership of Zanu from Sithole, its founding president, in what they saw as a 'coup d'état'. Ndabaningi Sithole was among the nationalists detained by Ian Smith in the mid-1970s and Mugabe made his move during this period. The Ndau group vowed to remain loyal to Sithole, affectionately known as *Musharukwa* (the old man), regardless of the difficult electoral conditions, community harassment and various, open and subtle forms of punishment and marginalisation applied by Mugabe's government.

At the conclusion of the polls, Zanu PF scooped 118 seats in the 120-member parliament. The significance of the 1995 election only emerged later. War veterans, seeing the economic chaos unfold and a rise in the gap between the rich and poor had earlier kept the pressure on the government through their organisation, the ZNWVA. A fight erupted between two young ex-combatants, Margaret Dongo and Vivian Mwashita, over a parliamentary seat in the Sunningdale township of Harare. Zanu PF endorsed Mwashita as the official candidate. Dongo refused to step down and contested as an independent. When the official results were announced Dongo was deemed to have lost. She took the matter to court. The court ordered a rerun after it unearthed massive vote rigging in the poll and exposed the manner in which Zanu PF always tampered with the vote. Dongo then emerged as the winner. She was immediately expelled from Zanu PF, making her a lone opposition voice in parliament. Details of how Mugabe and Zanu PF handled that low-key election are contained in a study by two eminent scholars who showed just how extensive electoral distortions had become.[7]

As the ZCTU, it was impossible for us to openly align the workers with a particular political party, or to endorse any of the contesting players and their organisations. The top leadership of various unions had divided personal and political loyalties. I was not surprised, therefore, to see Florence Chitauro, a ZCTU vice-president, and Edward Njekesa, another senior unionist, contesting the election on a Zanu PF ticket. They won, and joined the gravy train!

Mugabe immediately appointed Chitauro the new minister of labour – a move which I thought was meant to send a message to the unions that it paid off to play the game according to his rules. Chitauro subsequently earned herself a senior diplomatic post representing Zimbabwe in Australia, while Njekesa met a cruel death in a Chitungwiza hotel in unclear circumstances.

On the ground, voter apathy and despondency affected political participation, especially among the workers. The trend continued into 1996 when Zimbabwe was set for a presidential election. Under the constitutional amendment that created the executive presidency there were separate terms of office for parliament and for president. Parliament maintained its traditional five-year term while that of the president was raised to six years. The 1995 election was for parliamentary representatives and 1996 for the presidency.

As for others who used parliament as a platform to criticise government policy, Mugabe hardly responded, even when these wayward utterances found their way into the public media. He knew how to manage them, either through threats or by whipping them into line.

As for the military, their commanders were an important part of Zanu PF's Soviet-style politburo. Mugabe chaired the politburo, a body more powerful than cabinet or parliament as it was the highest decision-making body and all critical issues came before it. Mugabe clung to power against all odds and against any significant armed challenge or military takeover.

Bishop Abel Muzorewa tried a comeback in the presidential elections, saying he had managed to bring together all the small opposition parties under a new formation, the United Party (UP). Sithole refused to join him and decided to go it alone. But when the High Court ruled in favour of Dongo in her Sunningdale electoral challenge and published details of how Zanu PF had rigged the lacklustre 1995 parliamentary election, both Muzorewa and Sithole changed their minds. They pulled out of the race a few days before polling day. Mugabe refused to accept their withdrawal and insisted on an election, but Muzorewa and Sithole told their supporters to ignore the poll.

The 1996 presidential election was nothing less than a farce. Fewer than 30 per cent of the voters – so we were told, officially – bothered to come out and endorse Mugabe for a six-year term of office. Despite this, SADC leaders congratulated Mugabe for his lone-race, electoral 'victory'; so did Africa. The world simply watched from a distance and no one seemed to care.

Our concern in the ZCTU remained the need for relief from the economic squeeze. Yet each time I tried to raise issues about Zimbabwe's poor leadership style and crisis of governance, I encountered vastly divergent views among my trade union colleagues. Without consensus it was difficult to lobby the government and parliament in a robust manner. Nevertheless there was forward movement. After Chitauro and Njekesa left the ZCTU for parliament, the congress met in May 1996 and decided, as a matter of policy, to encourage workers to take part in national politics, in particular in economic affairs and governance. Our needs were so basic that we felt that any attempt to separate them from social concerns was misplaced.

Trade unions, as part of their natural rights, generally engage governments and business in employment creation and working conditions. The social sphere forms the bedrock of employee sustenance, which can only be supported by a political climate with guarantees for good governance. Our decision to encourage political engagement rested on the understanding that good governance implied legislative openness and accountability; a clear and transparent national direction; an inclusive national political value system; and a solid and consolidated political culture.

In terms of its mandate and general policy thrust, the ZCTU felt that Zimbabwe could make significant gains through a partnership between the state and the workers. We strongly believed that workers could benefit through social contracts, conflict management and a coherent national vision. ESAP had shattered worker confidence and undermined worker unity. The ZCTU resolved to keep on trying to develop a climate for serious and continuous dialogue with the government. But Mugabe seemed determined to alienate the workers and to keep the ZCTU out of the picture.

This was clearly demonstrated at the National Economic Consultative Forum (NECF) where we intermittently engaged various ministries and raised our concerns at national level on a range of issues. But one day in 1996, we were surprised to learn that Mugabe had unilaterally changed the terms of reference of the NECF. We were told by an official in the ministry of labour that the government was getting uncomfortable with the matters we were bringing to the table. The ZCTU had no option but to pull out of the NECF. That decision left the Tripartite Negotiation Forum (TNF) – a set-up between the government, the ZCTU and private sector employers – as the only avenue for dialogue. By the time we launched our 'mass action' events in 1998 the TNF had collapsed.

Mugabe claimed to have abandoned ESAP in early 1996 and replaced it with another economic policy but the workers saw no fundamental differences between the two. To us, it was business as usual: rising poverty and more job losses. Given the large number of company closures, relocations and disinvestment taking place, workers felt short-changed by the continued life of the Insolvency Act. Job losses through retrenchments were commonplace. Our struggle for meaningful amendments to the Insolvency Act to enable the plight of workers to take centre stage in case of company liquidations had led us nowhere. Nobody was listening to us.

To maintain our contact with the laid-off workers, the ZCTU formed a loose social network called the Zimbabwe Unemployed and Retrenchees Organisation (ZURO). Led by Dennis Murira, a young activist who had never been able to secure permanent work despite his academic qualifications, ZURO grew fast, its membership and structures spreading to most towns and cities.

We organised a series of workshops for informal traders in six provinces.

The traders, all retrenched workers, were united in a network they named the Informal Traders' Association of Zimbabwe (ITAZ). The two bodies, ZURO and ITAZ, showed a keen interest in national policy formulation and, like the ZCTU, called for transparency and political reform. They also put pressure on the ZCTU for additional support.

Whenever I raised these issues with cabinet ministers and Zanu PF politicians, both informally and formally, the oft-stated response was raspy and gruff. I was reminded time and again that Zimbabwe was far better off than 'African countries to the north of us'. What this meant was that as Zimbabweans we should be grateful for the little that was available, for the situation could be far worse. As if to hasten an already serious economic meltdown, Mugabe boasted at a meeting with traditional chiefs in Gweru that his critics lacked appreciation for the fact that no Zimbabwean could have run the economy better than him. In his view, a severely weakened Zimbabwe was still a strong nation – if only compared with the parlous state of those lying to the north of us!

The political environment required a visionary leadership to carry the entire population to a new mindset. Mugabe and the Zanu PF nationalists needed to move beyond what they knew; to get out of their 'war management' psyche; to listen; and to take cognisance of what others proposed to make the country successful. But our rulers clung to narrow, insular formulae. Their group egos and limited world view caused them to lose sight of Zimbabwean reality.

ENDNOTES

1   Harare Commonwealth Declaration, Harare, Zimbabwe, 20 October 1991, Commonwealth Secretariat http://www.thecommonwealth.org/

2   'Mengistu to stay in Zimbabwe', 22 March 2001, BBC News http://news.bbc.co.uk/2/hu/africa/1235828.stm

3   Moyo, S (1994). *Economic Nationalism and Land Reform in Zimbabwe*. Harare: Sapes Trust

4   Moyo, S (1995). *Land Question in Zimbabwe (Southern African Political Economy)*. Harare: Sapes Trust

5   For details, see Muzondidya, J (2009). 'From Buoyancy to Crisis, 1980-1997', in Raftopoulos, B and Mlambo, A (eds), *Becoming Zimbabwe*. Harare: Weaver Press, pp167-200

6   *Beyond ESAP: Beyond the Economic Structural Adjustment Programme (ESAP): Framework for a Long-Term Development Strategy*. Harare: ZCTU, 1995

7   Makumbe, J & Compagnon, D (2000). *Behind the Smokescreen: The Politics of Zimbabwe's 1995 General Election*. Harare: University of Zimbabwe

CHAPTER EIGHT

FALSE STARTS

In Malawi's 1994 general election – the first in 31 years – Life President Hastings Kamuzu Banda and his Malawi Congress Party lost, making way for Bakili Muluzi and the United Democratic Front. Chakufwa Chihana, who emerged a distant third, went into a coalition government with Muluzi, serving as his vice-president. In Zambia, Frederick Chiluba was set for second term as president. First elected in 1991, Chiluba was called a 'political dwarf' by President Kenneth Kaunda – referring to his diminutive stature – but his Movement for Multiparty Democracy (MMD) succeeded in wresting power from Kaunda, one of Africa's senior nationalist statesmen.

In Zimbabwe there was renewed pressure on the ZCTU and on me to consider going into politics. The calls increased after the 1995 parliamentary and 1996 presidential elections. I resisted the calls; I knew that the ZCTU was far from being ready for such a prime national service. There were diverse party affiliations inside the ZCTU, especially after our colleagues Florence Chitauro and Edward Njekesa openly joined Zanu PF and became legislators.

Despite my hesitation, I knew that calls to follow the example of labour leaders in neighbouring states did make a lot of sense. Zimbabwe was arguably in a worse condition than Zambia had been when food riots erupted in that country and President Kaunda was forced to terminate the structural adjustment programme. Our state too was in crisis. The proverbial law of the jungle in which only the fittest survive and thrive was now the order of the day. As a trade union umbrella body, we found ourselves stuck between a rock and a hard place; we lacked both the institutional means and a uniform political understanding to take on Mugabe and Zanu PF.

In my opinion, Zimbabwe's political problems stemmed from a weak national constitution. I began to agitate for both constitutional and economic reforms, while simultaneously pursuing my core functions as a labour leader at home and in the Southern Africa Trade Union Coordination Council (SATUCC).

I knew both Chiluba and Chihana as serious trade unionists. Now as senior leaders in government, I became confused as to the line each was taking. It seemed as if they were being compromised by more experienced old-style nationalist leaders in the southern African region and had forgotten about the workers' rights we all fought for in SATUCC.

Progressively, I began to lose confidence in both Chihana and Chiluba as former trade union allies with the capacity to spur our political leadership in the region to rally around the cause of the workers. I could no longer defend their legacy as ace trade unionists capable of bringing about change.

Our predicament in Zimbabwe would not be resolved if I or anyone else made a sudden leap for political power without a proper programme for national integration and reconstruction. Yes, the pressure was on to find an alternative to the failed policies and gross mismanagement of the Zanu PF regime. But, no, the time was not ripe for a political challenge – not until we had deeply considered the ZCTU's role in change and set out the principles upon which workers could unite with civil society to bring about real and meaningful change.

By 1996, Chiluba's political credentials as a democrat and a visionary were already in trouble. He had risen to political power from a trade union shop floor and then national office in the Zambia Congress of Trade Unions. Once in government, Chiluba appeared to be struggling to manage a fragile, broad-based and politically weak MMD. I had the feeling that he never had his hands firmly on the pulse of the state. He relied too much on disgruntled, old-time nationalists, many with a shady past, who were known to be politically mean and corrupt and were considered to have assisted in bankrupting Zambia for almost three decades.

Chiluba's loosely rooted MMD party's style of democracy and approach to politics mimicked that of Kaunda and his United National Independence Party (UNIP). As direct beneficiaries of the 'winds of change' that swept through post-colonial Africa after the Cold War ended, it appeared as if the MMD had never thought through their mission or really expected political responsibilities.

From our vantage point in nearby Zimbabwe, turning around Zambia's fortunes seemed a daunting task for President Chiluba. We watched carefully and picked up valuable pointers.

The MMD failed to realise that merely calling for change for change's sake was an insufficient formula. To unwind decades of misrule, bad governance and lost opportunities one needed more than empty political slogans. What people demand after years of living under a rigid centralised power is much more than promises of better times ahead. There is a need for consultation and participation leading to total transformation. Ordinary people have to be empowered in a meaningful way so as to be able to embrace new value systems and work ethics. An enabling environment is needed, rather like a cafeteria of choices – a kind of democratic menu – from which they select options for change and development.

All indications were that Chiluba was never ready to involve the entire Zambian nation in the redefinition of their political culture or to set up the requisite institutions to protect their newly found gains. To turn Zambia on to a new course and essentially create a new nation there should have been a broad-based process of participation, data collection, analysis, debate and scenario building. It didn't happen.

I discussed Chiluba's challenges in SATUCC and they agreed with me that the MMD's 'revolution' seemed to have lost direction. However, I feel compelled to note and to accept, as a matter of undisputed history, that Zambia under Kenneth Kaunda had never enjoyed peace and prosperity since gaining independence from Britain in 1964. Lusaka bore the brunt of supporting struggles against colonialism in Zimbabwe, Mozambique, Angola, Namibia and South Africa. Chiluba thus inherited a nation already on its knees.

Zambians were on the front line and arguably suffered more than any other southern Africans for the total liberation of the subcontinent. Colonial and settler regimes in Angola, Mozambique, Rhodesia and South West Africa – with blanket support from South Africa and some of its Western allies – were at war with their subjects. Kaunda's determination, and Zambia's geographical position of sharing its borders with the colonised neighbours, helped all of us. For that, we must recognise the role Kaunda played – notwithstanding his serious errors of judgement and leadership mistakes.

The West, together with Pretoria, was keen to block liberation movements from using Zambia as a safe haven for refugees and guerrillas. To complicate matters, Zambia's eastern neighbour, Malawi, was a strong South African ally, forcing Kaunda to look to Tanzania as a safety valve and dependable gateway to the world. Close to three decades of wars and instability wore down ordinary Zambians. Thousands of refugees and constant political headaches arising from regional evils took their toll on the country's citizens, their economy and their government.

With the end of colonialism in central Africa, Kaunda had every reason to hope for a peace dividend. He was seen as the fearless chairman of the Frontline States, a grouping of southern African countries fighting against colonialism and apartheid. That position automatically earned him a coveted and respected statesman status in Africa, and even beyond.

Southern Africa let Kaunda down, seemingly abandoning him when he needed them most. The region neither helped him to soothe tempers at home nor assisted in winning him any understanding abroad when he got into difficulties. They simply watched him tumble with his misfortunes. Some political leaders, especially in Zanu PF, seemed to enjoy Kaunda's predicament and regarded his regime as a victim in a fast-moving, globalising world.

The serious domestic instability that struck Zambia in the final stages of Kaunda's presidency resulted from a complex of factors, many of which he could not control. The rest of Africa was undergoing its own political evolution, the Cold War was over, and Namibia and South Africa were on the verge of independence. The turn of events simply proved too much for the veteran nationalist and Chiluba became the man of the moment.

Unlike his close comrade, Tanzania's founding president Julius Nyerere, Kaunda and UNIP, to add to their final bungling act, never had a clear leadership succession plan. The party collapsed like a deck of cards when faced with its first real challenge. Two post-colonial generations of Zambians had grown up under Kaunda and they were tired of shortages, excuses and poverty.

Chiluba's record as Zambia's post-colonial leader born out of the trade union movement and fed by social unrest is in the public domain. It has been documented, described and debated at several forums and I do not wish to repeat the same here. One ugly error, however, rises to the surface. Chiluba turned viciously against Kaunda, labelling him a foreigner of Malawian ancestry. He harassed him and barred him from challenging him politically.

Chiluba's weak and vindictive attempt at retribution was laughable, if not outright stupid. It was a pathetic and poorly thought out case of primitive xenophobia: after 27 years in power, surely a man of Kaunda's stature could not suddenly be treated as an unwanted alien in his own country! Chiluba's behaviour lacked respect not just for Kaunda but for the diverse Zambian nation which includes many of foreign descent and foreign ancestry.

By the time he was forced into retirement (or rather, chased away) by irate Zambians, Chiluba carried the baggage of many mistakes and false starts – a mixed bag of political misfortunes, untested theories and wayward experiments. He made enemies when he dismissed close colleagues from government for unclear reasons. Like Kaunda, who many believed had a raw deal after leaving State House, Chiluba fared no better. Chiluba appointed Levy Mwanawasa as his successor, in the belief that Mwanawasa was weak and pliable and would protect him in retirement. Mwanawasa had been his first vice-president but resigned in 1994 in protest against corruption. After Mwanawasa won the 2000 presidential election he immediately declared war on economic plunder, setting up a commission to investigate his predecessor's government. Chiluba was charged with stealing funds but was acquitted after a six-year trial.[1]

Chiluba displayed personal shifts of character, unchecked avarice and greed. He had an inexplicable religious appetite for imaginary, spiritual purity. There were stories that Chiluba abandoned his wife for a domestic worker. He tried to steer the constitution and the people of Zambia into a born-again Christian nation.

Whatever Chiluba's mistakes and faults as an individual trade unionist turned politician, he led the people of Zambia, through the MMD, to upset a former liberation movement and unseat it from government. This unsettled Kaunda's nationalist colleagues in the region and caused them to clench their fists to defend their power base.

Africa's liberation parties and icons enjoyed unquestioned legitimacy at home and beyond. The world tended to ignore the excesses of liberation parties and when they erred, gave them the benefit of the doubt. Dictatorships in Zaire, Malawi, Uganda and elsewhere attracted feeble criticism. These regimes were never officially condemned or discouraged. For that reason, Mobutu Sese Seko of Zaire and Idi Amin of Uganda rose to prominence during their reigns, and even chaired the Organisation of African Unity for 12 months each.

It was unthinkable for post-liberation players to confront the icons of national liberation – let alone in an election. Black-on-black oppression was not spoken about. The clenched fist in response to Chiluba's unwelcome rise to power in Zambia kept some nations in line – but not Malawi. Chiluba's success gave hope to the people of Malawi, who for many years suffered under political conditions seemingly far worse than those in Zambia.

This small, impoverished, landlocked country flanking a great lake had been dominated since 1966 by its liberator, Dr Hastings Banda. Once a medical doctor in Scotland, he had returned to take Malawi out of the Federation of the Rhodesias and Nyasaland (now Malawi). The eccentric and dictatorial Banda was born to a peasant family in Kaesong, Malawi in 1898, became a medical practitioner, and finally assumed a sort of kingship over his native country as President for Life. By the time he was replaced in 1994 he was nearly 100 years old.[2]

Chakufwa Chihana was a Malawian trade unionist who gained fame as a leading pro-democracy campaigner. Detained for six years without trial in the 1970s, he went into exile until the end of the 1980s. Chihana became SATUCC executive secretary at its August 1984 congress in Maseru, Lesotho, which I did not know at the time as I was not then involved in regional trade union politics. Ironically, his candidature was recommended by Chiluba because of Chihana's vast international experience and his deep interest in southern African affairs. Chihana made SATUCC a politically visible organisation and tried hard to influence SADC's policies and development programmes. He was credited with crafting numerous policy papers on regional issues, introducing a newsletter on trade union issues and suggesting various policy realignment positions – sterling work that earned him a high regional profile.

As the politics of the region began to change rapidly at the end of 1989, Chihana and SATUCC suddenly found themselves in difficulties. The dynamics were shifting and Chihana recommended that governments should begin to refocus their work ethic and engage civil society in a cooperative manner for both national and regional programmes. The nature of the engagement in a changing region, according to Chihana, would spin off positive economic effects on transport, customs, trade, and the movement of people.

SADC governments turned down SATUCC's numerous proposals for reform, accusing Chihana and the trade union organisation of being puppets of imperialism. This only revealed a serious lack of drive and political will among governments to extend freedom to ordinary people and bring about change. SADC, according to Chihana, enjoyed tremendous international goodwill and had the potential to obtain healthy donations – resources which could facilitate change in all aspects of people's lives. In his view, he told me in 1991, SADC was overly political and fared badly in the economic field.

In 1985, after a year in office as executive secretary of SATUCC, Chihana was inexplicably deported from Botswana. Some left-wing unionists thought his differences with James Dennis Akumu, then secretary general of the Organisation of African Trade Union Unity (OATUU), might have contributed to a negative attitude from the Botswana government. Akumu was highly respected in official African government circles as the voice of the African worker. I never got close to him, but I often wondered why he enjoyed so much fame. Later I was informed that he was a firebrand nationalist and shared the same philosophy and ideology of Africa's traditional nationalists.

Chihana's high-profile status may have been the cause of his deportation from Botswana. Or perhaps Banda's Malawi government had encouraged Botswana to adopt a hostile attitude towards free trade unions; the matter remained unclear to us in the ZCTU. Chihana relocated SATUCC to Maseru in Lesotho where he operated from a hotel room for four years. After Chihana had met and pleaded with a senior Malawian government minister for SATUCC to be accommodated in Malawi, he returned home to Lilongwe in 1989 and set up the SATUCC office there.

But the situation changed three years later, after a meeting in Lusaka of Malawian exiles opposed to Banda. Chihana attended this meeting and on his return home was jailed for two years for sedition. The SATUCC workers were arrested, together with a visiting US trade unionist, Tom Medley, who was briefly detained and then summarily deported. SATUCC was forced to move again, this time to Kitwe in Zambia. It was at that time that I took over the post from Chihana.

As it turned out, Chihana served only nine months of his sedition sentence. He was released in 1993 and immediately resigned from SATUCC. His release coincided with a referendum in which Malawians voted overwhelmingly for multiparty democracy. In 1994, as leader of the Alliance for Democracy, he came third in the race for president of Malawi and was appointed as second vice-president under Banda's successor, Bakili Muluzi.

Political liberation dominated Chihana's work, with campaigns for freedom in South Africa and Namibia featuring high on the agenda. But his bookkeeping skills were often cited as being fairly weak. While he used his high profile to SATUCC's best advantage, introduced gender programmes as a SATUCC priority and had a fantastic talent for raising funds, his record as an administrator was poor.

Chihana's political foray put pressure on us in the ZCTU as workers saw him as a hero, despite his electoral loss to Muluzi. The new Malawian president, Muluzi, represented a change from one nationalist to another. A former cabinet minister in Banda's government and a businessman, Muluzi went along with pro-democracy sentiments after assuming power. He initially agreed with the proposal for presidential term limits. But, like Chiluba, he sought to extend his term in office in a third election. Malawians, like Zambians, would have none of it. They kicked them all out of office.

Unfortunately Chihana was caught up in this undignified charade. After initially resigning from Muluzi's cabinet he agreed to return – apparently strengthening Muluzi's bid for a third term. He died in Johannesburg in 2006.

I feel I must place on record that one of Chihana's achievements while in SATUCC was the creation, in 1985, of a women's wing in the regional body, led by Alice Gondwe Siame. Siame was a senior unionist from the Zambia Congress of Trade Unions. In that position, the fiery lady successfully pushed for a constitutional amendment seeking the recognition of women on the SATUCC executive board. And for many years Siame sat on that board, along with Miriro Pswarai from the ZCTU, Maudline Castico from Tanzania and Onalenna Letamo from Botswana.

Apart from generic trade union work targeting female workers, the women's committee worked hard to raise awareness of equality in the workplace and encouraged female unionists to venture into politics. An early beneficiary was one of our vice-presidents, Florence Chitauro.

Women unionists kept pressing for better deals and forced SATUCC to convene a special conference on the empowerment of women and gender integration in the SADC region. As the SATUCC executive, we examined regional labour laws that affected women and general labour laws and their specific impact on female workers and suggested remedies and strategies for reform.

My disappointments with fellow African trade unionists made me think carefully about my own position in a political challenge to Mugabe. Many were urging me to follow the lead of Chiluba and Chihana, but how could I? After the way they had performed, and with my perception that a flash-in-the-pan style of leadership for 'change' – as a mere slogan – would get us nowhere, it was evident that a very different strategy was required. Any political opposition with a serious chance of winning power must have a real plan for transformation, and this could come only from the people themselves.

While these thoughts went round and round in my mind, more immediate concerns claimed my attention.

Macroeconomic policies of structural adjustment had done serious damage to the economies of both Zambia and Zimbabwe. I often raised the issue of the social impact and economic devastation of the ESAP programme on the welfare of the workers. But I received a lukewarm response from both my SATUCC colleagues and from SADC government officials.

I tried to raise alarm, voiced my worries and suggested a variety of alternatives – but none seemed ready to debate the subject. Each time I tried to reason with SADC labour ministers at regional meetings at which I represented SATUCC, I could sense a strong whiff of mistrust. I spent a lot of time trying to defuse tensions and to reassure government officials that our main concern was worker welfare and advancement.

At a policy and planning workshop in July 1995, I saw growing polarisation and inequality between the countries in the SADC region. I suggested that attention be paid to the primary causes of the shift. My plea had no takers as governments pursued a selfish line.

During the struggle against colonialism and apartheid in southern Africa, unity was taken for granted. There was an obvious bad boy, a bully, in the neighbourhood. But after South Africa's historic election, there were signs of retreat; of attempts to show off, to peddle political seniority and to claim political leadership over the region.

Nelson Mandela's stature overshadowed that of all the nationalist leaders, a scenario that made them uncomfortable and, in some cases, openly hostile towards Pretoria.

Our colleagues from the Congress of South African Trade Unions (Cosatu) argued that their country was being flooded with unskilled labour from neighbouring states. South African employers exploited and abused these migrants because they were desperate and remained out of local trade union structures. Cosatu called for a regional commission on labour migration.

Other suggestions included the need for a single regional investment centre to minimise competition among states. Our ideas were clearly spelt out in SATUCC's social charter, where we expressed a desire for a basic regional standard of living for all workers. Governments were uneasy with the charter and deliberately delayed its implementation.

In essence, the charter emphasised broad principles underlying the basic tenets of labour legislation in the region. In it, we spelt out our trade union rights and reflected our social, economic and cultural roots. What seemed to irk governments was our insistence that basic rights for workers should add force to any future regional development strategy.

As far as ESAP was concerned, the charter called for tripartite economic forums to decide on investment and to be part of any national and regional economic transformation policies. It placed a responsibility on governments, employers and trade unions to work towards worker education and training.

Governments, through the SADC employment and labour sector, discussed the charter at length. But each time there were differences over its adoption and disagreements about our desire for the free movement of workers throughout southern Africa. Employers were also against the charter, emphasising a right to lock-outs.

We tried hard to be flexible, making several changes to the charter. But its adoption remained a major problem, particularly among South African employers. Pretoria's commerce, mining and industry sectors demanded that if a right to strike was considered fundamental, they should also be allowed to lock workers out of the workplace – a demand even the ILO considered abhorrent and unacceptable. The charter was finally adopted at a SADC employment and labour sector meeting in Windhoek, Namibia, in 2001. By then I had left both the union movements.

Meanwhile, inside Zimbabwe, Zanu PF came under extreme pressure to meet the nation's baseline demands for survival. Ex-fighters wanted land, compensation and war-time pensions; civil servants called for a living wage. War veterans and government workers started to share the views of the ZCTU that government should be made to respond. The war veterans based their claims on the desperation of their comrades who had been disabled by the war; civil servants threatened strikes in order to be heard.

Mugabe responded positively, first to the war veterans' claim and put in place a War Victims Compensation Act under which a state medical officer was to recommend each ex-combatant's degree of disability to help the government work out a suitable form of compensation. Initially he ignored the issue of a lifetime pension.

When the civil servants saw the ex-fighters' partial victory, they hauled out their own weapon; Zimbabwe was plunged into a nationwide work stoppage. That was in 1996.

The ZCTU mediated in that strike, although under our labour laws civil service unions were barred from ZCTU membership. Again, the issue was partially resolved and the state conceded to a modest wage increase. The civil servants then came back with new demands, forcing Mugabe to make further concessions: his government helped them start a housing scheme to cope with homelessness. The scheme meant that the government was to collect a monthly subscription from each state worker for a revolving housing fund.

Seeing these developments, the Zanu PF capitalist vultures raised their appetite for easy pickings. In Zimbabwe, almost every senior public official could claim to have suffered during the war and to qualify for compensation. The same public officials also claimed to be homeless, needing help from the new housing scheme. Under the plan, each qualifying civil servant was entitled to a Z$200 000 loan facility which would be sufficient to cover the cost of a standard, three-bedroom house.

To our surprise in the ZCTU, among the first beneficiaries were our young First Lady, Grace Mugabe, and police commissioner Augustine Chihuri. Grace Mugabe scooped close to Z$6 million, while Chihuri took slightly more than Z$1 million. In the end, a total of Z$200 million ended up in the pockets of top government officials, leaving the poor civil servants still homeless. The scandal spilled into the courts, but although High Court Judge George Smith called for an official investigation the matter soon died down.

New cases of corruption emerged. Disabled war veterans, languishing in poverty in the rural areas, woke up to the news that Z$450 million from the War Victims Compensation Fund had been cleared by cabinet ministers and senior officials. Again, Commissioner Chihuri was among the main beneficiaries, claiming 95 per cent disability, although he remained Zimbabwe's top police officer.

A seemingly confused Mugabe set up a judicial commission of inquiry, led by Judge President Godfrey Chidyausiku, to investigate the matter. The commission unearthed more embarrassing information, but the issues were never followed up.

Take, for example, the case of one Alveria Kufeneta, a nurse at a government hospital who claimed more than Z$500 000 using different aliases. Her combined level of disability was estimated at 146 per cent! Or that of Colonel Lazarus Gutu, the commander of the Presidential Guard, who helped himself to Z$515 000 in three separate tranches. A separate claim, this time with a 20 per cent disability tag, was pending when the Chidyausiku inquiry was in session. The claim could have put Gutu's total disability rating at 103 per cent – at a time when he was in charge of Mugabe's personal, elite military unit.

A significant cog in the war veterans fund scam was Chenjerai Hunzvi, a former Zipra combatant who claimed to have been trained as a medical officer in Poland. Hunzvi, then attached to Harare Central Hospital as a junior medical officer, determined the levels of disability of the ex-fighters. He used the opportunity to campaign for the leadership of the war veterans' association.

Thanks to his role as disability assessor, he made sure that the needs of senior Zanu PF officials and those in government were satisfied through the War Veterans Compensation Fund. Ordinary war veterans in remote communal villages were not amused. Senior ministers and officials, almost all of whom owned large tracts of land which they hardly used, had embarked on a systematic material deprivation of the poor. Some 17 years after independence, a mere 50 000 families were said to have been resettled although the number of those demanding land was estimated at about half a million.

Mugabe sought to pacify the restless war veterans by promising them land among the nearly 2 000 farms the state had identified and designated for forced seizure. Not trusting the promise, the veterans continued to press for action, this time under Hunzvi. They held a series of rowdy demonstrations and threatened to march to State House to have their case heard.

Zimbabwe's small privately owned media exposed more cases of Zanu PF's baseness and greed. The District Development Fund (DDF), then tasked with the building of infrastructure for water reticulation and sanitation in the rural areas, spent close to Z$5 million drilling water wells at homes of senior Zanu PF officials, mainly in urban areas. This looting deprived close to 60 000 villagers of access to clean water. In that free-for-all environment, senior DDF officials helped themselves to a whopping Z$12 million's worth of plant and machinery. Herbert Murerwa, then finance minister, pleaded for reimbursement of the misused funds. Nothing happened.

By then war veterans were solidly under the leadership of Hunzvi. After a series of demonstrations for lifetime pensions, Mugabe started to feel the heat and finally gave in. The day came when war veterans besieged Mugabe and his leadership in his office and Mugabe ordered Zimbabwe's central bank to print Z$3 million for the veterans' gratuities and pensions. This move, in November 1997, collapsed the Zimbabwean dollar overnight from an average US$1 to Z$10 to US$1 to Z$25. It slid further to US$1 to Z$39 in matter of days. The nation was horrified; the value of our money simply evaporated. Obviously, government did not have the funds to buy off the war veterans and had taken a huge inflationary risk.

For war veterans – many of whom had not handled a single coin in many moons – the payout was a marvellous windfall. An individual sum of Z$50 000 (about US$4 500) sent them into a spin. Many hired buses and trucks, immersed their heads in alcohol and ordered confused drivers to take them to their rural homes to celebrate their newfound booty. Some married second wives; others bought maize hammer mills, wheelbarrows and bicycles. In no time, the money was gone – and the veterans were back on the street, making new demands, asking for a share of their promised land.

To Mugabe, war veterans were a potent force and had to be handled with care. He feared what he perceived to be their grassroots organisational skills and must have wondered how he would survive if they teamed up with civil society to work against his regime. Hunzvi sometimes called for leadership renewal in Zanu PF and, like those of us in the ZCTU, he also thought the Lancaster House Constitution was the source of our national problems. The key question then was who was best suited to contain the emerging black capitalists, who neither contributed meaningfully to economic advancement nor created new job opportunities through their speculative behaviour. There was agony everywhere as the economy shrank. Mugabe told the nation that the money for the war veterans would be raised through an additional tax on workers' wages and salaries.

Publicly, I raised the concern of the workers over Mugabe's directive to print money and to introduce a new tax. For this audacity, I almost paid dearly.

One morning, a group of war veterans pitched up at the ZCTU office and asked my secretary Edith Munyaka if they could see me. When permission was granted, they shoved their way in and attempted to throw me out of a tenth floor window of Chester House in central Harare. I was dumbfounded but I managed to hold them off. Edith, suddenly summoning her motherly instincts, screamed hard for help, alerting our colleagues in the building. The assailants immediately fled, leaving me in a state of shock with minor bruises and head injuries. I ended up in hospital, regardless.

After my assailants' arrest and prosecution, they were acquitted. This assured them and other thugs of a measure of invincibility and, I think, turned a rogue section in Zimbabwe's war veterans community into a largely lawless and arrogant gang devoid of sensitivity or reason.

Thus we ended 1997 on a pretty sour political note. I had almost been assassinated. Those who hated my role as a catalyst for change would stop at nothing to get rid of me. Change must come – but how? There had been false starts among trade unionists turned politicians in our neighbouring countries. It would not be a good idea to emulate them. The situation in Zimbabwe demanded action, but our unions could not embark on change without alliances and without a ground plan.

While Mugabe always tried to thwart the unions, the way he gave in to the war veterans' demands proved to me that he was unable assert total supremacy over an entire nation. I started to look around for fresh options to maintain the heat, and to question his glaringly lopsided public policy and leadership style.

ENDNOTES

1 'Ex-president Frederick Chiluba walks free after Zambian corruption trial', *The Sunday Times of London*, 18 August 2009 http://www.timesonline.co.uk/tol/news/world/africa/article6799424.ece

2 'Obituary: Dr Hastings Banda', *The Independent*, 27 November 1997 http://www.independent.co.uk/news/obituaries/obituary-dr-hastings-banda-1296534.html

CHAPTER NINE

A COUNTRY ADRIFT

In a large room at State House, Mugabe appeared totally absent-minded. The leadership of the Zimbabwe Congress of Trade Unions – I among them, as secretary general – was giving a presentation on what we saw as worrying signs of dangers facing the nation.

The meeting came about because the ZCTU had called for a week-long stayaway from work in March 1998, a move that prompted the government to invite us for talks. Among our publicly expressed demands was the need for price control on basic commodities and the scrapping of a range of new taxes.[1] Life was getting much harder for everyone. The fact that Zimbabwe had entered a war in the Congo had placed a huge burden on state finances while our soldiers seemed to be dying in numbers. In January, food riots had erupted over price hikes. The economy was in steep decline while corruption and officially sanctioned brutality were spreading.

Mugabe was supposed to be chairing the discussion. He suddenly stood up and dismissed us, charging that we were trying to hide our clearly visible frames behind what he called a single finger: the plight of the workers. Our real intention was political, he charged, with furrows of anger bulging on a sweaty forehead. He dared us to go ahead, convinced that we were political lightweights without any liberation war credentials, legitimacy or national standing to take him on. We left his office feeling humiliated, heartbroken, thoroughly shamed, and confused.

In retrospect, this was a make-or-break moment both for the government and for the unions. It would lead to the launch of an opposition party – the very thing Mugabe had challenged us to do. We came into the room to discuss grievances and concerns; we left it with no option but to take up the political struggle.

The country seemed adrift in a sea of problems. Our president decided to send troops to the Congo to rescue President Laurent Kabila from a rebel uprising. We had watched the situation in the Congo as former Zairean President Mobutu Sese Seko suffered a humiliating defeat at the hands of Laurent Kabila and a small force that gained control of the capital Kinshasa. Mobutu was a kleptomaniac in government: he had reportedly stashed multi-billions in banks abroad. His legitimacy reached zero as he ruled through a combination of brutality and bribery.

Now his successor was in trouble.

Apart from the war in the Congo, a rushed decision by Mugabe to silence war veterans with a massive, unbudgeted payout led to the collapse of the Zimbabwe dollar. The payout forced the government to impose new taxes which struck at the heart of a broad stratum of society, pushing up the cost of living and provoking food riots. The Zimbabwe economy was imploding from a cumulative assault on the Treasury and escalating corruption in government.

Meanwhile, the Catholic Commission for Justice and Peace (CCJP) and the Legal Resources Foundation (LRF) had revisited the horrors of the 1980s civil war in Matabeleland and the Midlands. After a decade of research, in 1999 they published a record of interviews and an analysis of what took place in the two areas.

Mugabe swiftly expressed his displeasure at the move, arguing for what he called sensitivity and national unity. It appeared his main fear was what impact the report would have on the people after more than a decade of suppressing the information. But before the state could intervene, the report was already on the Internet. Entitled *Breaking the Silence: Building Peace – A report on the Disturbances in Matabeleland and the Midlands 1980 to 1988*, the CCJP/LRF report provided ordinary Zimbabweans with a penetrating insight into Zimbabwe's immediate, post-independence era.

I read it again and again. It was a painful indictment of Mugabe's excesses; it shamed his administration and his colleagues for their failure to respond to the needs of the people for communal therapy and healing. The government still refused to accept any responsibility for what had happened, nor was there open debate or discussion.

Former PF-Zapu politicians and officials have always been reluctant to discuss the past. None went out of their way to help survivors to cope with their losses and the attendant disadvantages arising from nearly a decade of conflict. A generation was denied official information on the fate of their loved ones: many children in the area grew up as orphans. In the ZCTU, we were shocked by the stories of unchecked brutality against innocent civilians and an apparent refusal to put in motion a set of mitigating programmes to alleviate the burden on the people. What unsettled us further was the attempt to keep the entire nation ignorant of a matter that was so important for national integration.

The wounds remained fresh and painful, no matter that Mugabe tried to avoid the subject. No individual or community compensation was ever paid or even contemplated. The report led me to understand the Ndebele people's perception that the region was deliberately marginalised; development initiatives meant for the area were diverted elsewhere, and the entire ethnic group was subjected to an official hate campaign.

I was appalled by the regularity with which whole villages had been rounded up, made to dig their own graves and shot dead – for no apparent reason other than their ethnicity – by military units acting beyond their supposed constitutional mandate.

According to the report, the casualty figures had never been precise. Nkomo estimated the figure at 20 000 dead. Others believe they were much lower, with some even alleging a total as low as 700. Because of the veil of state secrecy, our nation was unable to reconcile these claims and disparities with the reality or even to handle the perceptions of a large-scale genocide.

As a result, there was fear and mistrust of senior government officials in western Zimbabwe. Mugabe's actions and omissions during and after the civil war had contributed to a culture of dread and silence.

I met with Mike Auret, a former director of the CCJP. We discussed the report and the manner in which Mugabe was handling the subject. He believed part of our problem lay in a flawed national constitution – a supreme law without sufficient guarantees for individual freedoms. I agreed with him and explained the need for civil society to support an initiative from the Zimbabwe Council of Churches for the formation of an advocacy group, the National Constitutional Assembly (NCA). The ZCTU was part of the founding NCA task force which began consulting civil society in August 1997. We believed, right from the start, in political pluralism and wanted a broad-based mass organisation that could take in members from Zimbabwe's diverse communities.

The NCA had a specific plan to develop public interest in the Lancaster House Constitution, identify its shortcomings and start serious work on proposals for constitutional reform. The debates and discussion were supposed to act as a precursor for fresh inputs into a new constitution. The idea was to extend the people's freedoms through popular participation in national affairs. In our preparatory meetings, we emphasised the need for an inclusive leadership of the NCA, straddling all ideological persuasions and groupings. I specifically remember Auret arguing strongly for all shades of opinion to be accommodated. He even suggested that the organisation be called the Movement for a Democratic Constitution!

I continued to consult with Auret and other civil society leaders and formed an interim organising committee to prepare for the official launch of the NCA. I was uncertain how the new organisation would work, given that it was such a loose coalition, a mixture of activists from trade unions, political parties, academic institutions, business and student bodies and human rights organisations, professional associations, media advocacy groups.

How would the group function with its varied ideological complexion? Were we mismatched? Our initial work was particularly difficult, seeking to popularise a seemingly academic and legal issue like the need for a new constitution – which often requires that one has to unpack a number of contentious issues in order to be understood. In small, isolated meetings, workshops and seminars we tried to sensitise our various constituencies to constitutional matters. It was difficult to get the people to own the process and to drive the campaign.

At the centre of our quest were governance, citizenship and a desire for political space. We believed that the constitution-making process in itself was as significant as the result that it might produce. There was a negative perception that the main proponents for constitutional reform were members of the middle class, urban-based elite – a development which initially made me uncomfortable. Although we tried to simplify the subject as much as we could, we seemed to fail to register success or to generate sufficient interest at an impressive pace. We failed to follow up the discussions with much vigour.

Food riots had broken out in January 1998 as people responded to state-sanctioned increases in the prices of staples. Mugabe ordered the army to restore order, leaving ten people dead, hundreds arrested and scores injured. For the first time, I saw an alliance of workers, students, intellectuals, women's groups and human rights organisations speak with a single voice about the emerging national crisis. With a rising budget deficit as a stimulus, the ZCTU started to engage our budding civil society to rally the nation for constitutional reform as a precursor to a holistic solution to the economic crisis.

I felt strongly that it was time to move beyond the shop floor and to spill the issues on to the nation. The demand on the ZCTU was beyond the labour centre's ability to handle on its own. Soon after the food riots, we officially launched the NCA at the University of Zimbabwe on 31

January 1998.

Mugabe laughed us off and ignored our calls for reforms, with Eddison Zvobgo, the Zanu PF secretary for legal affairs, deriding us as a misguided bunch of dreamers. In an interview with a local newspaper, Zvobgo asked how a few people could sit under a tree and claim to be a National Constitutional Assembly. 'They are neither constitutional nor an assembly,' I remember him saying.

The state dismissed us, I think, partly because of our omnibus structure; Mugabe saw us as a rag-tag assembly of disgruntled social opportunists, too weak to mount a serious political challenge.

Constitutional discussions may have seemed academic and pointless, but one could not laugh off what was happening in the country. Now, to add to the already parlous economic situation, the government wanted money to pay a bonus to war veterans. In the ZCTU, we continued to press for the scrapping of a battery of taxes imposed on the workers to raise money to pacify the restive war veterans. We advocated consultations on economic policy in line with our recommendations in *Beyond ESAP*. In April 1998, I told a ZCTU general council meeting to start thinking beyond issues around collective bargaining and to shift the debate to the national crisis. With civil society on board, we believed that workers' issues had become a national concern and, by extension, a cause for serious anxiety. The meeting decided to press for mass action to push Mugabe to listen to our grievances. We set out to organise another round of protests. At every stage, I could see that the workers' calls for a better deal were turning political. As the workers hardened their attitudes against Mugabe, his public response remained cold and indifferent.

The crisis of the state reached a climax in August 1998 when Mugabe ordered Zimbabwean troops into the Democratic Republic of Congo (DRC) – as an international donor – to help the beleaguered government of President Laurent Kabila. Kabila's regime was under pressure from rebels, then supported by Rwanda and Uganda. When Kabila asked SADC for help, only Namibia and Angola joined Zimbabwe. I could understand why Angola was interested in the Congo: the Luanda government had fought against Mobutu Sese Seko because of his support for Unita, and it still wanted to subdue Unita which had remained active. But, like Zimbabwe, Namibia did not seem to have an immediate interest there and its intervention was unpopular at home.

The ZCTU's assessment of the situation in the Congo indicated a simple bilateral disagreement between Kinshasa and its immediate neighbours, Uganda and Rwanda, who had backed Kabila in ousting Mobutu. We saw no reason for Zimbabwe's involvement, given the distance between Kinshasa and Harare. In July, when Kabila fired his Rwandan chief of staff, James Kabarebe, and replaced him with Celestin Kifwa, a Congolese, Kigali appeared to be disturbed. The matter reached boiling point when Kabila deported all his Ugandan and Rwandan military advisers. I learnt this from the ZCTU international relations officers after the war began.

When Zimbabwe marched in, tensions rose and the Rally for Congolese Democracy (RCD) established its rebel headquarters in Goma. The fighting became messier, with Uganda helping a supplementary rebel group, the Movement for the Liberation of Congo (MLC) to take on the Zimbabweans.

A desperate Kabila also enlisted the help of Chad, Libya and Sudan, which led to even more confusion in the fighting. With troops from so many nations involved, widespread fighting, and casualties escalating into the millions, the wars in Central Africa and Congo have appropriately been termed 'Africa's World War'.[2] We were on the fringes, but that was bad enough. Kabila's government almost collapsed in September when the rebels moved closer to Kinshasa. Mugabe flew in specialised military units with sophisticated and expensive equipment, and saved Kabila.

Early reports from the war were shrouded in secrecy until it became clear that we were suffering heavy military losses and Mugabe was under severe strain. Our ZCTU members reported the arrival of lots of body bags and funerals in their families. Newspaper publisher Ibbo Mandaza and his reporter Grace Kwinjeh were arrested over a story about one such secret burial although they were later released without charge.

Mugabe told the nation that the country stood to benefit from the vast and untapped economic potential of the Congo. To most people, the Congo was simply too far away from home to invoke emotions of immediate solidarity. Ill-feeling remained etched in people's minds especially considering that Zimbabwe's intervention in Mozambique had put us under serious economic pressure. Zimbabweans generally expected to reap a post-apartheid dividend, especially in Mozambique. Our proximity to and cultural links with Mozambique, plus the traditional relationship between the ruling parties and their combined exploits during the liberation struggle, made Zimbabwe a top favourite and natural beneficiary of peace in that country. Yet, surprisingly, Maputo invited South African white business people and farmers – who, we were told, previously sustained the opposition Renamo rebels – to exploit the new opportunities in a peaceful Mozambique. For that reason, we did not trust Mugabe's push into another foreign territory, saying Zimbabwe stood to get something out of it.

On the few occasions when Mugabe publicly responded to doubters, he lamented our loss of opportunities in Mozambique and exhorted Zimbabwean business people to follow the military excursion into the Congo. Yet those who ventured to set up shop there faced serious risks, with lots of sad tales to tell: lawlessness, chaos, no formal banking systems, and no business culture. Most gave up in the end.

As the gory details of the war began to trickle in, it became clear that Zanu PF and top military officers were involved in questionable activities in the Congo which earned the attention of the United Nations. Highly secretive military-run companies and corporations were set up, gobbling millions of taxpayer dollars and contributing significantly to the historic economic meltdown which later paralysed the Zimbabwean economy.

According to a UN investigation, a company called COSLEG was hastily set up numbering among its key players Laurent Kabila's son, Joseph; the Speaker of the Zimbabwe Parliament, Emmerson Mnangagwa; and the commander of the Zimbabwe Defence Force, General Vitalis Zvinavashe. It had interests in diamonds and other precious minerals, timber and general supply contracts to the military.

An inner circle of army diamond traders instantly turned Harare into a significant illicit diamond trading centre. This circle included Brigadier

General Sibusiso Moyo, Air Commodore Mike Karakadzai, and Colonel Simpson Nyathi. Defence Minister Sidney Sekeramayi was cited in the UN report as a political coordinator and a shareholder. None of these findings were publicly refuted by Mugabe, by the government or by the persons named in the United Nations report; nor was there an alternative explanation.

At a governance level, the military assignment in the Congo started to weaken civilian systems of accountability and parliamentary checks and balances. I began to notice a rise in the personal enrichment of military leaders, an increase in their visibility as an upper class – especially members of the Joint Operations Command (JOC), a body including all the Zimbabwean military and paramilitary leaders.

None of the proceeds from the military-run businesses found their way into the public purse at home. A real vacuum cleaner mentality had taken root and was mutating fast, benefiting a tiny elite. The benefits of the Congo war to Zimbabwe were never quantified or explained, nor were any details of the precise events disclosed. Acting on a directive from the ZCTU affiliates, I wrote to Mugabe's office seeking a meeting to discuss what the unions saw as worrying signs.

The unions insisted on a change of course. Many felt the nation was too frail to undertake giant projects like our intervention in the Congo; to pay lip-service to rising corruption; and to sustain a bloated state bureaucracy.

Against this background, Mugabe agreed to meet the ZCTU leadership. At State House he was brusque and offensive, and his attitude towards the ZCTU was negative and, indeed, devastating. He treated us with disdain, like imbeciles and delinquents. He was not prepared to do business with us so long as we kept on raising issues related to matters of general governance and welfare. He was so rough that he left us wondering why he had agreed to meet with us in the first place. Some of my colleagues saw no hope in further dialogue with him while others suggested that we widen the engagement to include parliament and other arms of the state.

I realised that without essential information on the mindset of Zimbabwe – information that could only be obtained through a comprehensive survey – it would be difficult for me as the secretary general to provide professional advice to the ZCTU on our next course of action. In terms of our mandate and general policy thrust, we felt slighted as we believed in a strong partnership and dialogue between the government and civil society to deal with misunderstandings.

But at this meeting, Mugabe demonstrated unrestrained mistrust and widened the gaps in policy. As labour leaders, we committed ourselves to campaign, demand and struggle for labour justice. We wanted equitable and reasonable labour laws and the observance of our democratic rights. We knew that part of our national problem stemmed from political corruption.

While the delegation felt a deep sense of rejection, I was able to review my turbulent relationship with Mugabe, dating back to 1989. The ZCTU's interaction with Mugabe had been frosty and suspicious for almost a decade following our decision to declare our autonomy from Zanu PF. Our efforts to develop a climate for serious and continuous dialogue had generated, at best, a lukewarm response and, at worst, open hostility. Our supporters were convinced that we had reached a dead end in our efforts to strive for harmony between Mugabe and the workers.

In the meantime, peasants in the Svosve area, 70 kilometres east of Harare, invaded an abandoned farm after accusing Mugabe of a slow resettlement programme. Although the police moved in and evicted the 'squatters', the event triggered a series of activities which ultimately involved the government, major international donors and the United Nations.

With the support of the United Nations Development Programme (UNDP), Mugabe convened an international donors' conference in September 1998 on the historical issue of land, as it had taken on both a local and an international dimension. This was an odd move, considering Mugabe's inconsistent handling of Britain's donations for land.

Between 1980 and 1985, Britain gave Harare £47 million for land reform: £20 million as a specific land resettlement grant and £27 million in the form of budgetary support. But by 1988, the grant was already used up. When the British government indicated further interest in the programme, Mugabe began to dilly-dally. And, up to 1996, the government never bothered to respond to the proposal – according to British public records which were never officially refuted. The grant was subsequently closed, with £3 million still unspent.

The conference was obviously an important occasion and we were keen to take part as the ZCTU, even if only as observers. The CFU, seen as an important player through its international connections, attended the conference while the rest of civil society, the churches and trade unions and the generality of ordinary Zimbabweans were left out. In our discussions, we expressed concern about the exclusion of civil society from the donors' conference and our displeasure at the new attitude of both Mugabe and Britain over the resolution of the land issue.

On 5 November 1997, Clare Short, the British Secretary of State for International Development in the newly elected Labour government, had refused to commit the Blair government to any future land dealings with Harare. In her much-quoted letter to Kumbirai Kangai, the Agriculture Minister, Short said:

> I should make it clear that we do not accept that Britain has a special responsibility to meet the costs of land purchase in Zimbabwe. We are a new government from diverse backgrounds without links to former colonial interests.
>
> My own origins are Irish and, as you know, we were colonised, not colonisers. We do, however, recognise the very real issues you face over land reform. We believe that land reform could be an important component of a Zimbabwean programme designed to eliminate poverty. We would be prepared to support a programme of land reform that was part of a poverty eradication strategy but not on any other basis.

We believed from our informal interactions with diplomats that the conference would seek to tackle land reform in phases, as part of a holistic economic recovery plan. But a sly Mugabe tried to mislead the conference with a pledge to resettle 150 000 families for which, to start, Harare needed an upfront handout of Z$40 billion. The visitors turned down his request, insisting on a carefully worked out, phased plan with transparent benchmarks.

Mugabe revised his targets downwards. He assured the meeting that he wanted only 700 000 acres of white commercial farmland just before the general election in 2000. The UNDP agreed to coordinate the project. The conference agreed to establish a task force constituted of government and donors willing to substantially contribute to the programme.[3] Britain, as a former colonial power, was relieved of sole responsibility for the resolution of the matter. An international committee, excluding Britain, met in October 1998 to follow up the resolutions and decided to set up a technical support unit in Harare.

Mugabe turned his back on the proposed committee and showed no interest in the UNDP initiative, so the unit was never set up. Then he changed his tone and message, heaping all the blame on Tony Blair and he no longer referred to the donors' conference. It was all very puzzling: why run a conference and then forget about the support that was offered?

To the outside world, Zimbabweans entered the penultimate stages of a second decade as a relatively free people, but those of us at home found ourselves in a bewildering climate with the horizons seeming to darken. Hardly a day passed without a previously unthinkable event taking place. Our misfortunes and national crisis became a hard-to-believe but daily fare. What incensed us most in the ZCTU was that the symptoms of decay arising from Mugabe's poor leadership style seemed to escape the notice of his admirers in SADC and in Africa.

After two decades of watching Mugabe and Zanu PF closely I needed to do something meaningful to help Zimbabwe escape the consequences of what I considered unacceptable government behaviour. An interesting case in this regard was that of Phillip Chiyangwa, a close relative of Mugabe who had started off as a vegetable vendor in the farming hamlet of Chegutu, 100 kilometres west of Harare. In less than a decade, Chiyangwa was a flashy business tycoon with nauseating audacity and a habit of blowing his own trumpet, often publicly, citing his association with Zanu PF as a source of his wealth. Beneath the loud swank lay the real message of a blighted Zanu PF, rotten to the core. The majority rural poor were, indeed, still in Zanu PF. But they were nowhere near gaining preferment to enjoy Chiyangwa's level of open opulence.

Another example was that of Roger Boka, who claimed to be an ardent advocate of black advancement and an admirer of Mugabe and Zanu PF. At the end of 1998, Boka saw his empire collapse like a proverbial deck of cards.

Like Chiyangwa, Boka started off from humble beginnings. But he was quick to use corrupt Zanu PF channels to access monopoly contracts, supplying books to newly opened schools soon after the war. That opportunity thrust him into gold mining, cosmetics, tobacco and commercial photography. During the ESAP era, Mugabe personally supported and defended Boka as a revolutionary businessman and a super patriot. From that connection, Boka was the only black man to have a tobacco merchant's licence.

With varied interests in publishing, retail, banking, mining and tobacco, Boka regarded himself as a symbol of the much yearned for success of black Zimbabweans. He claimed to own the world's largest tobacco auction floor in Harare. He spoke of the need to break the white man's business spine, and often commissioned full-page advertisements in the official *Herald* newspaper full self-congratulation and self-praise. The advertisements, usually covering a number of choice broadsheet pages, were openly racist and denigrated white Zimbabweans and foreign capital.

But soon Zimbabwe's rising economic and political viral load caught up with the flamboyant Roger Basil Nyikadzino Marume Boka – and led to his irreversible downfall.

Boka used his political connections to get a banking licence, and in 1995 the United Merchant Bank of Zimbabwe opened its doors. He traded in bills running into multi-millions of dollars but since he had a government guarantee he was not concerned with profitability but rather with ensuring that he would get liquidity to launder funds internationally. He deposited money in Botswana, South Africa and the United Kingdom. Depositors' funds were mingled with personal funds and used to acquire properties.[4] The bank finally succumbed to mismanagement and was declared insolvent and deeply in debt – heavily borrowed from by senior cabinet ministers and Zanu PF officials.

In the ZCTU, we knew the collapse would lead to serious job losses and that it could trigger a national debt crisis especially when we learnt that Boka had issued a large number of fake bank cheques and about Z$52 million of state-hedged promissory notes. Economists in the ZCTU's secretariat estimated the damage to the nation's wealth at between two and five per cent.

In his heyday, Boka offered cash, plane tickets and free holiday packages to Zanu PF officials and cabinet ministers, even though some never asked for such favours. Now, clearly humiliated, Zanu PF and the government ditched Boka and launched an immediate probe into his activities – too late. Boka escaped Zimbabwe, leaving behind a messy political crisis, a vulnerable tobacco market and many a company and several banks in the intensive care unit. He was destined to die soon after his rapid departure.

As a parting shot he blamed his sorry state on Mugabe's government departments and was quick to accuse Zanu PF politicians of over-borrowing from his bank, often for personal gain. Before his final demise, Boka reminded Mugabe that his government owed him Z$26 million and that he wanted it all back. He even threw in a veiled threat – what he called 'serious consequences' if the state ignored his claims.

But it was water off a duck's back. Mugabe – under pressure from the war in the Congo, with his Treasury hopelessly broke and under the watchful eye of the IMF and other multilateral institutions – simply kept quiet. Boka's case was among numerous stories to dominate the newspaper columns of our normally pliant, laid-back and lily-livered media.

An unpleasant national scandal hit the headlines in late 1998. It revealed that people in the highest office could have feet of clay. A young former police officer, Jefta Dube, told a High Court hearing that he murdered a colleague after suffering from years of psychological trauma arising from being regularly raped and sexually abused by former State President Canaan Banana, now an academic and a Methodist Church minister.

As happens with high-profile court cases, there were some embarrassing and worrying details, including indications that Mugabe knew about and suppressed information about Banana's activities soon after independence. The abuse ran for seven years while Banana was Zimbabwe's ceremonial president and continued into his retirement.

Several witnesses – mainly former bodyguards, security staff, assistants and those close to his office – testified that for a long time they were either victims of or knew about Banana's 'weak waist and ever-sharp loins', as Zimbabweans say.

The patriarchal society and a widespread practice of polygamy meant Zimbabweans generally turned a blind eye to private sexual matters, even promiscuity. But if senior public figures ravage their own staff, such behaviour is frowned upon. What the public found unacceptable in Banana's case was that he turned on innocent members of staff within his official home and abused them. When he was exposed, many people recalled Banana's ventures, which included a soccer team, State House Tornadoes, which he set up in the early 1980s. Young teens flocked to the team seeking proximity to the state president, only to tell hair-raising tales after a training encounter or two. Banana is said to have loved those fitness exercises. When the team was finally disbanded, Banana frequented the University of Zimbabwe sports pavilions for routine exercises with students.

The general discussion among Zimbabweans, though initially about Banana's escapades, quickly switched to Mugabe, whose public views against gays and lesbians were openly antagonistic. In 1995, Mugabe had banned Zimbabwe's Gays and Lesbian Association (GALZ) and directed the police and organisers to close down their literature stand at an international book exhibition in Harare. He went on to describe gays and lesbians as worse than 'dogs and pigs'. Now here was one of his respected former colleagues embroiled in this scandal. The people accused Mugabe of covering up for Banana.

Banana, then 62, initially escaped to South Africa. When he returned home after a flurry of diplomatic activity, he was charged and convicted and spent a year at an open prison near Gweru. He died a few years later.

One of Banana's wayward sons was sentenced to 18 years in jail for an armed robbery on a jewellery shop in Harare, using an AK-47 rifle he stole from the family cabinet for the purpose. Another son, an airman, was also prosecuted, but acquitted of a murder charge involving a love triangle. His mother Janet and other siblings left Zimbabwe soon afterwards. By the time he died Banana's family was in disarray. His wife Janet had gained asylum in the UK and could not be with him in the final moments of his life. Mugabe later described Banana as a 'rare gift to the nation'. As custom demands, Mugabe followed a reflexive and cultural requirement which demands that the dead be showered with positive accolades immediately after their demise. But he stayed away from the funeral.

I felt sorry that Zimbabwe's founding president had died in such disgrace. Zanu PF did not offer Banana a place in the National Heroes Acre, where Zanu PF luminaries are laid to rest with military gun salutes, flowery speeches and the usual pomp and pageantry. Buried at his rural village, deep in Matabeleland, Banana had fallen from grace in bizarre circumstances.

I met Banana on a few occasions while trying to broaden my understanding of Zanu PF's inner workings. I found him to be an experienced politician with interesting views, apart from his sexual preferences, which never bothered me. I also had several private meetings with Eddison Zvobgo, right up to his death. Zvobgo, Edgar Tekere and many other not-so-lucky Zanu PF nationalists used to give me useful insights into Zanu PF thinking and leadership style. The stories I have cited as examples were mere tips of the iceberg. The rot was literally everywhere. In the ZCTU we recorded a minimum of 19 major official corruption scandals that rocked Zimbabwe in 18 years. Corruption was now endemic and institutionalised.

For two years, I witnessed the spectacular collapse of our systems of governance, hastened by corruption, policy flip-flops and deepening mistrust of the government. I decided to do something about it – a year before we entered the new millennium. But I was unclear what it was that could ultimately help the nation out.

I put together a ZCTU team to assess the national mood, led by Timothy Kondo, our senior advocacy officer. Kondo was a former Zanu

PF political commissar and an ex-combatant. From July 1996, he had pursued a vigorous advocacy programme in line with the provisions of the *Beyond ESAP* document. He specifically tackled issues related to the ZCTU policy development, undertook numerous lobbying missions with the government and parliament and was heavily involved in our capacity-building activities.

Kondo and the team travelled around Zimbabwe interviewing community leaders as well as ordinary people. They consulted with many groups and notable opinion formers, communal farmers, retrenched workers, rural-based social networks, women's organisations and clubs.

I wanted the ZCTU to have a detailed report and analysis of the dominant social, economic and political issues countrywide. For three months at the end of 1998, Kondo – in concert with officials and staff in our regional offices in Mutare, Masvingo, Bulawayo, Gweru, Chinhoyi and Harare – was away from home, listening, engaging and recording a variety of views. From Beitbridge to Nyanga, from Plumtree to Hwange to Kariba, Kondo was able to discern a pattern from which the ZCTU and I managed to look into Zimbabwe's mindset as a nation.

ENDNOTES

1   'Government seeks dialogue with ZCTU'. Zimbabwe News Online, 1 June 1998 http://www.africa.upenn.edu/Newsletters/zmno21.html

2   Prunier, Gerard (2008). *Africa's World War: Congo, the Rwandan Genocide, and the Making of a Continental Catastrophe.* Oxford University Press

3   Communique Issued at the End of the International Donors' Conference on Land Reform and Resettlement, Harare, September 1998 http://www.raceandhistory.com/Zimbabwe/1998conference.html

4   Fundira, Bothwell. 'Profiling Money Laundering in Eastern and Southern Africa.' Institute of Security Studies (ISS), Pretoria, Monograph No 90 http://www.iss.co.za/pubs/Monographs/No90/Chap6.html

CHAPTER TEN

BATTLE LINES

We Zimbabweans are fantastic critics: what I loved to call 'desktop revolutionaries' when I was at the ZCTU. As a people, we are generally slow political strategists, hesitant to come up with alternatives to the existing state of affairs. Formulating new content to replace what has failed is not, in my view, our strong suit. By 1999, Zimbabwe boasted the largest number of university graduates per family in sub-Saharan Africa. The same intellectuals could easily shrug their shoulders in despair, ready to quit a simple political discussion – let alone join a call to action.

If the political party project was to succeed, I told myself, it had to be led by ordinary workers, peasants, ordinary women and men, with the help of truck and train drivers – practical organisers like shop-floor stewards – not theorists, but doers. Sure, we would depend on the support of a varied collection of followers riding on the train – a cultural potpourri, an assortment of true believers with different beliefs; a chequered movement indeed, but united in spirit. Those at the front line would need a no-nonsense mindset to focus the energies of the assembly.

A nation of relatively well-read theorists, we were victims of our educational success. Our appetite for theories and theoretical debates, for religion, for relaxation and a good personal life, plus an unexplained habit of boasting in public about modest individual exploits, turned our people into their own unconscious enemies.

As a people, we are quick to appropriate and lay claim to successes that are hardly the result of our own efforts, preferring to urge on a brave few with exhortations like: 'We are behind you! Go on ... We are fully behind you!' – only to retire to our backyards and watch the drama unfold. More importantly, we fear anybody and anything with a semblance of authority – real or perceived.

We needed change-makers, not dreamers. We needed the whole nation on our side. Courage, commitment and consistency would be our watchwords. Our modus operandi should be to work consultatively, in the open, with no hidden agendas and a large welcome sign above our heads. Over the years, many a champion of change had spouted forth promises and programmes that came to nothing: it all dissolved into hot air in those backyards and homes where ideas came cheap and the living was safe and easy. But now the country was not safe and the living was certainly not easy. There were good reasons for masses of people to join the cause.

We trade unionists had become the movers and shakers of political transition more by default than design. We found ourselves in a gap that no one else seemed prepared to occupy – or at least no one seemed willing or able to take the first steps to organise a countrywide opposition. Trade unionism conferred certain advantages in that we already had nationwide links, nodes and networks with members agitating for change. Our work had equipped us with a range of organisational and communications skills that would prove vital in the struggle ahead.

Only the labour movement and its civil society allies had the capacity to come together to form a political opposition. Business would lend moral and financial support but would not take the initiative itself. Academia could be called upon to do research and add intellectual weight to our policies and programmes, although some professors would rather stay off the streets. The country had lacked a political alternative ever since the 1987 Unity Accord subjugated Joshua Nkomo's Zapu to Mugabe's Zanu PF, handing total control to the dictator. Any further political opposition – such as Edgar Tekere's Zimbabwe Unity Movement – was sporadic and unsuccessful.

By the late 1990s the labour movement was already viewed as a political threat to the ruling party. We could see, however, that the issues went far beyond our mandate as the labour movement. We decided to convene an all stakeholders meeting, including our partners in civil society to chart a path out of Timothy Kondo's study. We did not take that decision lightly. We knew that Mugabe wanted confrontation, and believed in intimidation and the use of force to cow and silence the ZCTU and the workers. We understood our weakness as trade unions, and could not risk taking on Mugabe alone.

Timothy Kondo, in the capacity of ZCTU research coordinator had, as mentioned earlier, led a team around Zimbabwe to collect people's views on the economic situation and listen to suggestions for social and political change.

To guide the project, the ZCTU secretariat and I suggested that Kondo and his team confine their work to issues related to the quality and delivery of health and education services, the standard of living, the fate of vulnerable groups, employment opportunities and incomes, business and investment avenues, the economy, and the availability or scarcity of basic commodities.

At the same time, I was receiving reports from the women's advisory council officials – Miriro Pswarai, Thokozani Khupe, Kumbirai Makore and Paurina Mpariwa – that, based on the surveys conducted by the education department during the course of its programmes, the country was ripe for another political party. I took these reports seriously, but decided to wait for Kondo's final report for additional information.

On politics, I stressed that special attention needed to be paid to voter behaviour and the causes of voter apathy. Kondo was expected to record specific national views on the question of land reform, the conduct and efficacy of parliament, the limitations of the Lancaster House Constitution, party politics, and general governance matters.

In a combination of live interviews, questionnaires and formal meetings, Kondo and his team posed questions, listened, engaged and recorded Zimbabwe's story. In one of his regular briefs to the ZCTU in November 1998, I advised him to go deeper into the rural areas to avoid what was clearly emerging as an urban bias in his preliminary findings.

I insisted on an inclusive study after realising that Zimbabweans in the communal lands tended to be a conservative lot, with a collective mindset that requires considerable effort to shift. The catalyst for change, as with most recent developments, still rested with the urban population, partly because of easy availability of communication channels and a high population density. To address the weakness, in particular the absence of the rural voice, Kondo spent another month with villagers in Esigodini, Umzingwane, Chidobe, Tsholotsho, Binga, Hwange and Filabusi in Matabeleland and Vusisizwe, Vukani, Silobela, Makobozhori, Zhombe, Cicelalisaci, Siyazipiliza and Lower Gweru in the Midlands.

The work in these rural areas was made possible by the cooperation of the Organisation of Rural Associations for Progress (ORAP). Kondo approached ORAP because of the organisation's strong grassroots structures in Matabeleland and parts of the Midlands where it had worked for more than a decade since the end of the post-independence civil war. (Ironically, a Zanu PF stalwart, Stembiso Nyoni, ran ORAP for a considerable period of time.)

In ORAP, Kondo received immense support from the organisation's field and programme officers, Nomalanga Zulu and Grace Moyo. The two facilitated meetings, interviews and discussion forums. In addition, Kondo and his team interviewed Dumiso Dabengwa, then minister of home affairs; Welshman Mabhena, the former governor of Matabeleland North; Zenzo Nsimbi, the deputy minister of transport and energy; parliamentarians Sikwili Moyo, Lazarus Nzarayebani and Mike Mataure; and Lovemore Moyo, then associated with Imbovane YaMahlabezulu – a

Bulawayo cultural pressure group. (Lovemore Moyo entered parliament as an MP for Matobo in 2000 and would rise through the party ranks to become the national chairman of the MDC and Speaker of the House of Assembly during the Government of National Unity.)

All in all, consultations were held in 26 towns, cities and districts around Zimbabwe in which nearly a thousand people took part. Those sampled included unionists, teachers, civil servants, human rights activists, members of the secret service, the police, business people, informal traders, legislators, villagers and staff from non-governmental organisations.

In January 1999, Kondo compiled two detailed reports, *The Raw Data*, which covered mainly the views and suggestions of people in urban areas; and the *ZCTU/ORAP Consultative Report*, with a strong rural bias. From the two reports, it was clear that all indicators for recovery and progress pointed downwards. I wondered how we could proceed with this information, or simply to what use I was supposed to put it. I circulated the reports within the ZCTU and later convened a meeting in a bid to get guidance from the leadership.

It remained my conviction that a truly national political solution could be found only when all interest groups and stakeholders participated in policy formulation, decision making and implementation. Broad consultation based on a decentralised approach was the only guarantee that the process would yield results acceptable to the people in democratic elections. Hence our decision to convene an all-stakeholders meeting to consider Kondo's reports.

The country had a frail institutional base for the protection of democracy and a loosely rooted political culture. To correct this we needed to create or rebuild strong, independent institutions and instil the idea that government was accountable to the people and not the other way around.

I felt relieved that Kondo and his team, together with Khupe, Mpariwa, Pswarai, Makore and all the ZCTU women in the education department, had managed to read the mind of Zimbabwe correctly. According to the findings, the situation was far worse than we originally thought. Every town, city, village and growth point showed signs of rapid decline, and the conditions of ordinary people were deteriorating almost daily. The most affected sectors were national delivery in health and education services, an economy in a rapid decline, poor and no investment, and, plainly, bad politics.

Questions surrounding our politics and Zimbabwe's political culture generated the deepest emotions. While there were similar experiences, concerns and suggestions for solutions across the board on social and economic issues, there were vast differences on political issues. However, while opinions differed radically, depending on people's cultural and traditional practices, preferences and political affiliation, it was possible to discern a common national pattern that later proved invaluable in our planning sessions. But a broad thread was clearly visible in these separate findings: Zimbabwe had a fragile and easily corruptible system of governance.

Mugabe's government lacked political will for orderly land reform; there were deep concerns about tampering with our voting rights and a perception that Zimbabwe needed multiparty politics; opposition to a de facto one-party state was widespread; people wanted national guidelines on candidate selection for public office and they were well aware of electoral rigging and voter intimidation; state-sponsored violence was a burning issue; and to top it all there was criticism of our weak parliamentary system and unsatisfactory and flawed national constitution, both of which allowed for lack of transparency and public accountability.

The reports made it clear that the ZCTU was expected to fill the political vacuum arising from an unresponsive political system.

Concerns from the rural areas were simple and plainly stated: better health care and education services, unemployment, and lack of investment. In much of rural Zimbabwe – particularly Matabeleland and the Midlands and in Chipinge, Chiredzi, Mwenezi and Beitbridge – our young people saw no future prospects for themselves at home. They were being driven out to Botswana and South Africa, often without formal travel and immigration papers. Desperate for opportunities, they took all sorts of chances. Some would succeed in finding jobs and creating a better life for themselves but many were to be haunted by refugee status, living impermanently in neighbouring states that barely tolerated them.

With close to half a million school-leavers every year, it was disturbing that less than 30 000 managed to secure jobs in the formal market. Evidence of the youth's disillusionment with their own country was everywhere. So much talent was going to waste and the costs to Zimbabwe were substantial because as soon as a youngster had an Ordinary or Advanced Level matric or a university certificate he or she would leave the country.

A significant part of these reports dealt with what people had said when asked to suggest alternatives. The dominant view was swift, unambiguous and unconcealed: they wanted a broad-based attack on Mugabe to change course. At first, I had mixed feelings about this position. It was difficult to build such a movement in Zimbabwe, given our distorted inheritance along ethnic, historical, racial, religious, urban and rural and class lines.

Though the suggestion made sense, the task appeared too daunting and fraught with serious dangers. It was a bit late to start now, I thought. We should have built such a movement based on the positive groundswell of opinion against one-party systems in the early 1990s. At that time there was euphoria around democracy following the collapse of the Soviet Union.

The 1989-1991 period marked a turning point for Zimbabwe, as it did for Cuba, Eastern Europe and even China. A universal demand for systemic changes to bring about free and fair elections spread across the world from Moscow to Tiananmen Square. In Africa the popular surge was felt much more strongly in the early 1990s than in 1999; in other words, the era of the Chilubas, Chihanas and other post-colonial reformers was now history. Nowadays allies for the people's cause would be hard to find – at least in Africa which had become disillusioned by the failures of popular democracy led by labourites. We were in an unfortunate position. I thought any vision for democracy in Zimbabwe would fail to resonate with the views of African leaders or even common public opinion.

With that in mind, I reasoned that a serious political party, strong enough to take on Mugabe and Zanu PF, required extensive popular mobilisation and meticulous planning. I quickly discarded the temptation to follow in Chiluba's footsteps.

Kondo's report and the supporting documentation from the women's education department saw me reading, again and again, as I pondered where to go from here. At meetings, some in the ZCTU appeared to backtrack; others pressed on for a new political party. Some even suggested that we do nothing, arguing fearfully that Mugabe was too powerful and brutal.

After arguing for hours with my colleagues in the ZCTU, without success, against political recklessness and for a comprehensive situational analysis, I found myself confronted with a serious dilemma. We needed a solution which only an inclusive convention could craft out of our findings. Now that we had all the data, how did it translate into action?

Zanu PF and Mugabe were shrewd masters at the game of divide and rule. There was a broad understanding that any isolated skirmishes with this government could easily lead to one group being played against the other. The result would be massive losses mainly on our fragile side – as several people had warned us through their inputs to the report.

A number of examples of previous projects with mixed outcomes came to mind. I recalled our failure in November 1996 to press the government to resolve a crippling doctors' and nurses' strike which had paralysed the health delivery system. We could have done better, but the state emerged victorious in the end. I could also vividly recall the highly successful national shutdowns of 1997 and early 1998. But in the end, we were infiltrated and divided – with the result that the actions progressively began to lose steam.

What was not in dispute was that as leaders we were under intense pressure to help from our members, from civil society and other advocacy groups and from ordinary people.

Life in Zimbabwe was increasingly difficult. The 1980s had been a well-watered paradise compared with the drought-ridden, economically catastrophic 1990s. Mugabe's embrace of the Economic Structural Adjustment Programme (ESAP) had taken us into a dead end. Manufacturing output had fallen by 40 per cent from 1991 to 1995, with a similar decline in workers' real standard of living. Terrible inflation had sucked the value out of savings and devastated the informal economy in particular. The national crisis was becoming more pronounced as each day passed. We had failed to convince the government to talk to us. We were rebuked and derided for lack of patriotism each time we raised the alarm.

Mugabe was no longer in the mood to entertain our concerns: he saw us as irritants and spoilers. He turned down invitations to officiate at ZCTU meetings; to attend our public functions; and even to see us as labour leaders. Mugabe, in typical macho and bully-boy fashion, appeared always ready to sharpen his sword for combat. That has always been his style: to shoot first before asking questions. He took wild swipes at Sibanda, the ZCTU president, describing him in contemptuous terms.

'A mere train driver wants to take over this country,' I heard him one evening on national television telling a jubilant Zanu PF rally. He was referring to Sibanda's previous employment at the National Railways of Zimbabwe. 'Never, never, ever …' he vowed, his face angry and furrowed.

Taking advantage of a nation in fear and confusion, Mugabe's pillars of support – mainly the military, security and senior party officials – had requisitioned the national cake for themselves. They were not going to slice it up further just because a 'train driver' and his friends said it was unfair.

I recall telling my family in 1999 that, from my experience of dealing with Mugabe while I was the ZCTU secretary general, the man detested difficult conversations. One of his strengths was his technique of calculated procrastination; he could delay the discussion until it began to flow his way. Perhaps there was something to be learnt from this but at the same time it meant he approached any dialogue in bad faith. With hindsight I could see that what Mugabe did when challenged and cornered was to drag things out to wear down an opponent before making insincere concessions.

Mugabe always saw disagreement, no matter how minuscule, as conflict. He would never accede to a generally preferred position in our meetings with him. Any outcome had to satisfy his desired outcome first, before he could make slight shifts – but then, only slight – to portray him as a generous giver. To me, Mugabe was a leader who would readily burn down a house rather than live in it with a colleague or compatriot who had differences with him.

In our dispute with the government during the 1990s each side understood the cause of the national impasse differently. We never agreed on what had gone wrong, how to rectify anomalies, possible solutions – let alone who was to blame. To us in the ZCTU, the whole issue was simple, but it was deliberately made to appear complicated. All we desired was a better deal for the workers, a rise in the standard of living and an extension of our freedom. Dialogue was therefore essential for both sides to move away from the blame frame, but that was proving to be extremely elusive. Mugabe was in a permanent state of aggression and denial, we thought, and this made him outrightly stubborn.

Things were looking especially bleak for us in the labour movement. The ZCTU could no longer respond to the needs of a dwindling and largely threatened workforce. Many retrenched workers took refuge in the rural areas, although starvation there was a real possibility as even basic sustenance was at a premium. There were no new jobs anywhere – except those handed out to Zanu PF partisans – while those who did have work lived in fear of retrenchment.

For the first time, we started to experience serious fuel shortages as the country could not afford to import enough oil and preference was given to the elite.

Zimbabwean troops were still in the Congo with government expenditure spiralling. The budget deficit had ballooned to a dangerous level at 4.6 per cent of the gross domestic product, according to a brief I received from Dr Godfrey Kanyenze, our chief economist. Inflation stood at 32 per cent in January 1999 – much higher then than that of Burma and Somalia. Lack of fiscal controls led to a rapid rise in poverty and food shortages were forcing people to tighten their belts, literally.

Many believed that the time was ripe for the ZCTU and the workers to pull the country out of serious trouble by ousting Mugabe and his corrupt minions. Mugabe refused to budge. He would neither entertain the thought of a new constitution nor a cut in government expenditure. Our calls for the withdrawal of troops from the Congo attracted harsh official rebukes.

I often took a walk from my ZCTU office to the mall in central Harare at lunchtime, observing and talking to ordinary people. I was almost always accosted by desperate youths, asking me what they could do to make a difference. I reiterated that the nature of the crisis was beyond the ability of a trade union movement to handle alone. An experienced Mugabe had for nearly two decades managed to cling on to power without any significant civilian or armed challenge. We required a comprehensive national approach. To those at the end of their tether, such a response sounded too late, lame and weak. They wanted action. Some even suggested taking up arms, which I deemed insincere and adventurist.

During quiet moments at home, I took time to study what had happened in Zambia when Chiluba swept to power. In particular, I looked carefully at Chiluba's successes and mistakes and realised that our situations were worlds apart. It was impossible to apply the Zambian template to a democratic struggle in Zimbabwe.

Zambia, with an urban population close to 70 per cent at the time of Chiluba's rise to power, could mount a formidable opposition from the cities. From information I gleaned from discussions with colleagues, newspapers, magazines and anything I could lay my hands on, I realised that much less than 40 per cent of the people in Zimbabwe lived in urban areas; the majority were in the rural areas. Nothing could move without input and support from the rural areas where villagers placed exaggerated faith in Zanu PF because of their exposure to the movement during the liberation war.

Mugabe's mentality and political strategy had never moved out of the ideological shell with which he had surrounded himself during those years. His ideas on governance were permanently rooted in the defeat of white Rhodesia and colonialism. To him, defeat of those twin evils was both symbolic and terminal; it was in a sense the end of his story, an achievement in its own right. Those who sought to move on in a post-colonial framework were treated with the utmost suspicion. To Mugabe, an anti-colonial ideology was sufficient to rally the people: it was the ultimate answer and sole point around which a system of governance should be built. Imperialism and white people were the enemy and any black person who questioned Mugabe's world view in that regard was the enemy too.

The reality was otherwise. We now had an entire generation of 'born-free' Zimbabweans, an educated corps without any emotional attachment to the liberation struggle. The new generation came of age at a time when things were falling apart. Independent Zimbabwe had made the most of the infrastructure inherited from the prior Rhodesian settler regime and had made health and education the foundation for future progress. Thousands of new clinics and schools were built with extensive state support and external aid. By the late 1990s the infrastructure was falling apart and both aid and investment were drying up due to economic mismanagement and corruption. We were going backwards.

Zanu PF refused to see this, insisting on a sense of entitlement to the ownership of Zimbabwe. The feeling of supremacy deluded the ruling party into thinking that it could hold the torch and direct the national compass forever. In such circumstances, any political challenge merely represented counter-revolution. Those who led the challenge were puppets of imperialism. They were vassals of the hated and defeated white man, in particular the racist Rhodesian who had refused to accept the new dispensation but continued to live off the spoils of the past. Political opposition was perceived as a serious threat to a supreme ideal.

Indeed, any challenge amounted to an invasion of Zanu PF privacy. They were masters of all and accountable to none. A pastiche of individuals seeing themselves as a political opposition was construed as breaking and entering a serene home like robbers. This provided sufficient justification for a violent rebuttal in order to protect a glorious God-given cynosure; a hard-won revolution destined for eternal recognition. Violence and a desire to protect this make-believe political edifice thus became the only means through which to repulse and humiliate rivals, often publicly.

It became more and more apparent to me that to debase opponents formed part of the so-called revolutionary cult of violence, in order to cultivate public fear and ensure national conformity. The danger of communal fear is that it drives everybody into the undergrowth; it immobilises a nation and spawns apathy. Fear has always been the number one enemy of most Zimbabweans. Fear always extinguished our hopes, dreams and aspirations in spite of a deep sense of betrayal by those we had trusted to lead us into a better future.

Dictatorships loathe public participation in national affairs; they thrive on close, pliant networks; they do well in a climate of exclusion. Our demand for inclusion in policy formulation was not simply an annoyance to Zanu PF – it was an insult, an act of disrespect and obduracy. Who were we to claim a place in the councils and anointed inner circles of heroes, heroines and the liberationists? We were the governed, expected to live and work as directed by a superior wisdom, that of Mugabe, the supreme leader.

The local diplomatic community had never paid much attention to the ZCTU, to the National Constitutional Assembly (NCA) or to the varied agenda of our tiny and fragmented civil society and interest groups. Many saw the ZCTU as containing remnants of the Soviet communist era, still clinging to a dying leftist ideology. There was an unquestioned understanding that Mugabe was too strong for any feeble political contests or acts of defiance from loose organisations that Harare-based foreign envoys thought were led by sporadic hecklers and political novices.

The ZCTU, it is true, was too weak to make a difference on its own. The logical conclusion was that unless we were very careful we would soon be crushed by Mugabe's well-oiled state machinery of repression. A rising but uncoordinated and disorganised tide of emotion and spontaneous outbursts of political rhetoric gave hotheads in the opposition movement the idea that a political party to take on Zanu PF would just spring into being. The notion that the ZCTU would miraculously transform itself into a Labour Party, as some colleagues romantically thought of it, was not tenable. Exasperated, I took a deep breath but stood my ground: we needed firm foundations.

Even Zanu PF wanted to see the ZCTU form a political party. I could imagine Mugabe staying put, unfazed, like an old crocodile feigning death – open-mouthed and basking in the sun – hoping to deceive and to draw a curious young duiker to a vantage point within striking distance.

As I examined a variety of options and perspectives, a dark and dangerous tunnel seemed to gape ahead of us. My fear was that a rushed launch could lead to quick defeat and this would feed into the traditional analysis of an indomitable Mugabe, nourishing and extending the culture of fear.

Work stayaways were no longer the answer. I saw diminishing returns from more national business shutdowns when it was clear that we had no plan for a change of identity; for a change of strategy. Many in the ZCTU still favoured that option, even when the people's demands were in reality turning political. Our challenges to Mugabe through the national shutdowns were becoming meaningless. This was partly because Zimbabwe made allowances for a nominal democracy; and partly because we were part of a metaphorical, but largely ornamental, multiparty state system with symbolic, periodic elections through which Mugabe laughed all the way to State House – picking up international accolades as a suave, caring and reasonable statesman.

In the absence of further industrial pressure on the government, what options lay on the table? We could not just sit on our haunches. Our ZCTU members also posed these questions, getting only a mealy-mouthed response from a hesitant and terrified trade union leadership. A number of mid-level professionals and academics regularly came up with incisive, well thought out criticism of Zanu PF and government structures. When this happened, Mugabe either co-opted the intellectuals into his party's ranks or bullied them into silence. Academics were appreciably in awe of Mugabe, who was at that time ranked among the best educated leaders the world. Few in university positions had the necessary backbone to stand up for themselves and others.

But a few started to come out openly. Professor Masipula Sithole, though clear and resolute, was somewhat tainted by his association with his blood brother Ndabaningi, a founding president of Zanu who lost his post to Mugabe in a vicious power struggle while the nationalists were in detention. Masipula Sithole and some of his peers at the University of Zimbabwe seemed comfortable working with the budding civil society groups under the cover of academic freedom and also to supplement their meagre incomes through seminar and workshop presentation fees.

Since independence, I had observed a number of opposition parties take off in a hurry, only to crash on their own or to be pushed off the political cliff by Zanu PF. These parties had one thing in common: they emerged from hotel rooms and private homes. Aspiring politicians raised their heads and shoulders only in times of elections. Their flimsy organisations – often with high-sounding names, symbols and impressive manifestos – had little foundation in the people and were crafted mainly by professional consultants. They fizzled out soon after the polls.

With years of experience in handling the opposition, especially in its infant stages, Mugabe was by now an accomplished but rough player. He managed to wipe out PF-Zapu, the United African National Council (UANC), Zanu (Ndonga), the Zimbabwe Unionist Movement (ZUM), the Democratic Party (DP), the National Democratic Union (NDU), the Forum Party, Zimbabwe Union of Democrats (ZUD), and many others had come and gone.

While Mugabe handled these challenges with passion and unbridled ruthlessness, I think the threat these little parties posed to Mugabe was always overplayed. Many small parties existed as decorative artefacts, built around a perceived, charismatic leader – a nationalist or an old-timer, a priest, an intellectual, a jurist, or an ex-combatant – but without a national following. They posed no real danger to Mugabe's legitimacy or to his national and international stature. Their following was too fragmented, often ethnic-based and without a holistic vision for the country. But Mugabe took no chances, descending hard on them with a ton of anger.

There had been spirited attempts by individuals to challenge the liberation movement. Their motives may have been honourable but their strategies were misguided. They would suddenly jump on to a political podium and claim to represent our battle-hardened Zimbabweans, one and all. Voters checked them out and ignored their political promises with smiles denoting Zimbabwean politeness.

In general, these parties or messianic campaigns never moved away from the narrow circles of their originators. At best, they were short-lived challenges to the regime which at least alerted people to the possibility of opposition. At worst, they were nothing but paper proposals carried about in hand luggage. My experience had taught me that a party formed without a viable base involving key sectors of Zimbabwean society and embracing a strong grassroots feeling, was doomed. We in the ZCTU were not ready, or so I thought. But the dilemma remained: the pressure was on us to do something – soon.

On Mugabe's side too pressure was building for a 'Third Chimurenga' – a continuation of the guerrilla war, this time directed at repossessing land occupied by whites when they colonised the country. A nervous Mugabe looked over his shoulder at the increasingly militant war veterans who felt they were not receiving what they expected at the end of the liberation struggle. Many former guerrillas had ended up back on their subsistence plots in rural areas feeling abandoned by the state.

In 1997 Mugabe had imposed levies and taxes to fund compensation for war veterans. Revelations that the fund had been bled dry by high level corruption spurred public anger, leading to street demonstrations and work stayaways. The state suppressed the public flare-up but the problem of the veterans had not gone away. Now, using the tremendous power at his disposal, Mugabe sought to kill two birds with one stone: on the one hand, inflict severe damage on the ZCTU, and on the other mount a hasty land repossession campaign to give the war veterans what they wanted. The Third Chimurenga would unfold on a horrifying scale from the year 2000 onwards as Mugabe faced his first serious electoral challenge since taking power, but already we could see the momentum building for a dramatic state-driven land grab.

The battle lines were being drawn between a virtual one-party state and mounting opposition. Mugabe and Zanu PF were an immovable object about to be confronted by an irresistible force – a people demanding their rights and freedoms.

The entry of a new opposition party into the fray for the first time might have gone largely unnoticed both at home and abroad had we not taken pains to consult widely. The work of the ZCTU's education department and Timothy Kondo's valiant research effort yielded more than raw data: it lent credibility to the grassroots strategy we were determined to pursue.

Although we had decided on a broad convention to consider the Kondo study, some senior unionists, including my deputy Isidore Manhando Zindoga and the late Shangwa Chifamba of the powerful Commercial

Workers' Union, were against trade union conflict and confrontation with government. That worried me greatly for I was not sure that many in the ZCTU understood where the process would eventually take us.

Labour unions the world over might get drawn into politics but it is not their primary role. The ZCTU had never regarded itself as a spearhead for a new political movement. Lack of political cohesion gave the ZCTU a very fragile base for a measurable attack on Mugabe, Zanu PF and a ruling party-controlled state. Even close colleagues claiming to have deciphered the growing national consensus for a new political thrust had hazy ideas about what forming a political party would actually mean for all of us. If I insisted on forming a political party, I could be taking the ZCTU into a dangerous trap. To some, persuasion was a better option. I kept on pushing for a convention to formulate a correct approach, and at last my persistence paid off: the ZCTU embraced the idea.

The tragedy of being associated with civil society for too long was that we depended too much on government and its leader to come to our rescue. The temptation was always to cry out to Mugabe for reforms and for space, not to mount a direct political challenge to the status quo. For close to 20 years Zanu PF had dominated the political scene; Zimbabweans knew only one national leader, Mugabe – and he had a vile disposition towards dissent or even discussion. Why bite off more than we could chew?

While there appeared to be a national concurrence that Zimbabwe was yearning for change, I was not sure if it was wise to take a wild plunge and put together a direct political challenge at the time. There were strong signs of uncertainty. The majority could not picture a lucid outcome from confrontation with Mugabe and Zanu PF. Could anyone forecast the outcomes, matching our intentions to what was likely to happen when we took on the entrenched powers that be?

As a leader, I often searched deeper for the subtext in conversations – the meaning of the lyrics in the song, the mood and sense of it – to get a real grasp of what Zimbabweans said in their veiled way. I was now a middle-aged African male and I knew our communication and cultural systems well. I had never left the country for long periods, nor had I joined the liberation war as a front line fighter. I harboured no external influences;

I had never been 'contaminated' by influences from other distant cultures and unknown lands.

I knew that in our African society decision making is always a group effort, with heavy influences from kinships, families, clans, tribes, social circles and interest-based groups. Behaviour was conditioned by communities. The strength of African culture was that it lent the advice and guidance of others to the individual, limiting the scope for impulsive and selfish behaviour. The weakness was that it could enforce conformity at the expense of the individual conscience and good sense. There were advantages and disadvantages to these systems of influence: they could strengthen common sense or lead one down a garden path to a proverbial slaughter house.

But it was not all doom and gloom: each time the ZCTU leaders and I addressed both public and private meetings, I detected a strengthening of minds and a rising groundswell among various sectors for a coming-together that would initiate real action for change. While Margaret Dongo, a Zanu PF dissident and now independent legislator, and a few others made noises which excited many from time to time, the lack of a robust challenge confined these anti-establishment sentiments to public bars and to one-on-one discussions behind closed doors. Dongo, Sidney Malunga, Lazarus Nzarayebani, Gibson Munyoro and even Edgar Tekere were essentially internal reformers seeking some form of influence in Zanu PF.

Given that the opposition in parliament was titular and largely inconsequential, some allowance was given for their loud mouths. Zanu PF hardly responded, even when these wayward utterances were sneaked into the public domain and the state-controlled media. Zanu PF knew how to manage them, either through direct expulsion or threats, whipping them into line through salty reminders or tough talk.

In the eyes of the world and many at home – despite a rapid fall in the standard of living and our declining political fortunes – Zimbabwe presented a visible cut above many African countries. It appeared very little of our predicament was obvious to Africa and beyond. Mugabe's skilful use of a mixture of coercion, political patronage, diplomacy and low-level brutality to keep a firm and secure lid on Zimbabwean society had pulled the wool over outsiders' eyes.

Whenever I travelled outside the country, I was astonished to hear remarks in praise of solid political leadership in Zimbabwe. People eulogised the country as one with an assured, fairly predictable future, a safe destination for business and all forms of external capital. Imagine – an African country with a negligible crime rate, plus a highly educated and disciplined workforce. To them it seemed admirable.

At international conferences, seminars and workshops, then a regular feature in Harare, guests seemed to marvel at the friendliness of Zimbabweans and our excellent race relations. We had a varied and abundant nightlife, with the dark corners of our towns and cities remaining relatively safe. General urban blight was absent and we had a clean and well-managed environment. Even poor backpackers on holiday from faraway lands noted how they enjoyed camping without any fear of highway thieves or felons. There seemed to be no danger for travellers anywhere in Zimbabwe at any time. Our people smiled and were always willing to help, while our fluency in regional and other foreign languages made communication easier and added to the respect we showed visitors. Lastly, our fear of authority kept Zimbabweans in line which seemed like a seventh heaven to those who expected Africa to be chaotic.

I usually failed to respond to this kind of flattery, for I thought I knew better. I simply blushed and retreated but, as custom demands, I smiled nevertheless. The surface impressions were all true – Zimbabweans were a friendly, orderly people and proud of their hospitality – but beneath the surface we all knew things were bad and getting worse.

These accolades and the general respect Mugabe enjoyed as well-read scholar, gentleman and no-nonsense pan-Africanist, ready to commit troops and give external aid to poor neighbours to help them achieve order and stability – even without parliamentary approval – insulated him whenever he used a blunt instrument to contain scattered pockets of dissent and muffled voices at home.

Those at home were not fooled. To most workers, Mugabe had long assumed a feared national position through a tapestry of measures, a complex system of political nimble-footedness and a sophisticated dictatorship. I convinced myself that as long as I was alive, I was going to persist in my objective of founding a comprehensive opposition movement. I shared this thought with Amai Edwin one Sunday afternoon and she laughed her heart out. It sounded like a foolish, careless joke – unimaginable!

The personal risks of opposition leadership would be immense. Stories and evidence abounded in 1999 of the endemic terror of the secret service, the CIO; numerous allegations were thrown around of unexplained abductions of dissenters and reckless loudmouths. Mugabe had driven Zimbabwe into a state of political evil supervised by his flamboyant tyranny.

Given the general melancholy in our midst, the lost opportunities, and the constant cries of emaciated babies and hopeless workers who were being retrenched almost daily, the ignorance and short-sightedness of outside observers and visitors was deplorable. My colleagues and I felt bitter that a clearly bungling leadership style and record of human rights abuses could be so easily camouflaged. As visitors enjoyed our hospitality, dishevelled workers scrounged for scraps in dump sites along the Mukuvisi River on the periphery of Harare's spotless city centre. Many battled to eke out decent lives in the communal lands. Other centres contained similar scenes of grime and grit, so near but seemingly so far away from a foreign eye.

Our professionals had begun the great trek to previously unimaginable places searching for work, food and economic security. Clear signs of family failure were becoming evident. Aids and HIV infection rates were rising as a result of diminishing state support.

For many years, every day, we in the ZCTU discussed the matters linked to our deteriorating economy and the growing plight of workers. It became clear at every stage that the crisis stretched far beyond the confines of labour disputes. We found no solace in the state's reaction to a plainly collapsing society. What irked us most was the absence of political will, not only in the government's failure to listen to any voice of reason, but among those who had it in their power to nip in the bud an impending catastrophe.

Mugabe's intolerant leadership – previously understood to be hostile mainly towards the Ndebele minority in western Zimbabwe – was covered up in public media until much later. Now his shadow fell across the entire territory: workers and peasants had begun to ask each other what had befallen the nation.

Little did they know then that the worst was yet to come.

Before the stakeholders' convention I wrote to Mugabe, once again seeking a meeting to discuss what the ZCTU saw as the major signs of danger to Zimbabwe. The request was turned down.

In terms of our mandate and general policy thrust, as labour leaders we had felt slighted at our last meeting with Mugabe and by his subsequent refusal to meet us again. We strongly believed that workers and the nation could benefit immensely through partnerships with government, civil society and business through social contracts and a patriotic approach to resolving misunderstandings and crafting strategies for a national vision. I yearned for the day when workers would take part in the establishment of a national patent: a guiding philosophy on advancement and a safe leadership succession arrangement.

What Timothy Kondo termed 'a worker-driven and people-centred development process'[1] in his reports to the ZCTU was now an imperative. I felt strongly that politics must seek to enhance the welfare of society through good governance. And with good governance come questions of legislative openness and accountability; a clear and transparent national direction; an inclusive national political value system; and a solid and consolidated political culture and frame.

We had always thought it was clear that we were desperate for relief – or at the very least a hearing from our government or head of state. That was not to be. I recalled our seemingly unending quest for a fair deal with regard to unfair labour laws since 1980. While we made some headway with the enactment of the Labour Relations Act in 1985, we lost a sizeable chunk of our legal benefits in 1992 when the Act was amended to accommodate ESAP. One of these was the right to strike, and in some cases – particularly in the public sector – workers were even denied the right to collective bargaining.

As we entered 1999, the ZCTU knew that part of our national problem stemmed from political corruption and political partisanship. Our efforts to develop a climate for serious and continuous dialogue had generated, at best, a lukewarm response and, at worst, open hostility. Our supporters were convinced that we had reached a dead end in our efforts to strive for harmony between the government and the labour movement. We felt that we were being pushed to the wall.

Through my contacts with state officials with whom I often interacted in the Ministry of Labour, I began to hear that the government wished to start a process of drafting a new constitution. This was a direct reaction to our campaign for a new constitution which was by then gaining momentum. Other officials, mainly from the secret service, told NCA officials that civil society would not be part of this process because of the government's belief that it was contaminated by the ZCTU.

While I was happy that the ZCTU agreed to organise the National Working People's Convention (NWPC), I knew that without a credible outlet for public information, our views were likely to be distorted in the government-owned media. Help was at hand. At the end of 1998, Harare was awash with news of a coming daily newspaper – a project initiated by veteran journalists Geoff Nyarota, who had earned his credentials as editor of the *Chronicle* in Bulawayo, and Wilf Mbanga, who was running about half a dozen tiny, state-owned rural newspapers whose coverage of news and current affairs had very little impact on the nation at large. By then, the state had imposed a total blackout on its military activities in the Congo war. Local journalists courted trouble by publishing casualty figures or any stories about the looting that involved senior army and Zanu PF politicians during that war.

For a long time, Zimbabweans had relied on limited daily news coverage from a single company, Zimbabwe Newspapers. Nyarota and Mbanga now proceeded to set up three small weeklies: *The Express* in Chitungwiza, the *Eastern Star* in Mutare and the *Dispatch* in Bulawayo. I believed that if transformation was to be possible, the people needed a diversity of news outlets through which they could share ideas. Access to information is vital to the formulation of informed choices.

After 11 years at the helm of the ZCTU I had never felt the strain as much as I did in early 1999. We were about to enter completely new terrain, totally different from the day-to-day routines of the labour movement. Here stood a people, across the board, on edge and impatient with their black, post-colonial government. They looked superbly steeled for the pain – many awaited only a clear goal. A peasant had told Kondo bluntly: 'Come hell; come storm; come rains; come fire: please just go ahead and do things as we resolved here. Do not look back. And, be always aware that the road is rough and dangerous. But do we have any other choice?'[2]

Our nationwide study of the mindset of Zimbabwe had raised the hopes of those who took part. They sincerely believed that the ZCTU possessed the capacity to help and placed their entire faith in the labour movement to drive the process of change. I understood them. Never mind that the government had succeeded in marginalising the population and stood ready to swipe at any attempts to undermine the state. People felt their former liberators were now preying on them, riding roughshod over basic graciousness after having fallen hard into the trappings of power, ambition and avarice.

Come hell, come storm, the opportunity for us to oppose the government's constitution-making and propose a broad-based alternative was what we had been seeking. The ZCTU and civil society were well placed to organise such a national project at a time when private newspapers had broken the monopoly of the state media on the publication and broadcasting of alternative viewpoints and public information.

ENDNOTES

1   Kondo, T F (2000). 'The worker-driven and people-centred Development Process for Zimbabwe'. ZCTU publication (internal document)
2   ZCTU/ORAP Consultative Report, Harare, 1999, p56

CHAPTER ELEVEN

CHINJA!

Naming a political party can be a tricky business. The name asserts the brand, and a brand is an intangible but powerful element of success. What should we call ourselves?

The name of our proposed political party was decided on 7 May 1999, some months after the convention, when the senior leadership met the technical team to consider the matter. A number of suggestions were thrown around, including *The New Alliance*. The idea failed to resonate as it hardly captured the spirit of the convention, nor did it fit our mixed identity or carry an emotive message that would also position us as a democratic party. We threw in other words and phrases such as the *New Alliance for Civic Organisations* – but how would such a name be received by the unemployed and those in the rural areas? Could it be called *The Labour Party*? That would alienate other civic organisations. What about *The New*

Party? No. All suggestions that included the word 'party' were deemed unsuitable. Although the ZCTU was facilitating the process, we wanted an all-embracing, inclusive movement as dictated by the convention. After hours of debate we narrowed the exercise to specific words that conveyed the intentions of the alliance. Eventually we arrived at the *Movement for Democratic Change* – the MDC. We looked at it deeply and agreed that it summed up what the people wished to see. That was it. The MDC.

With a name in place, we needed a slogan. Ernest Mudavanhu, a young activist from Zaka who worked in neighbouring Bikita, had come across a striking phrase used by organisers in the community. In its original form the slogan exhorted villagers to change their hygiene habits for a safer and cleaner lifestyle: 'Change your ways, change your hygiene habits'. To this, the Bikita community simply roared: 'Change!'

Our team worked on it and settled for: '*Chinja Maitiro, Maitiro Chinja*' in ChiShona and '*Guqula Izenzo, Izenzo Guqula*' in SiNdebele. Literally translated into English, this means 'Change your behaviour'. But the dynamic political meaning is rich. The slogan appealed to Zimbabweans to change their political behaviour.

We had to pitch the message that the whole system needed transformation and this could only happen if people moved away from passive acceptance of the Zanu PF style of top-down leadership. Top-down meant bottomless suffering for many. Violence was endemic and, to a large extent, part of our inheritance. We lived in a violent society, initially perpetuated by colonialism and later by Mugabe for many generations.

To show our abhorrence of violence, retired Colonel Tichaona Mudzingwa, a veteran of the Zimbabwean struggle and a military doctor, insisted that the MDC use an open hand as a party symbol. We agreed. An open hand in Zimbabwe's culture is a symbol of peace; it assures friend and foe alike of the absence of malice or a hidden agenda. Zimbabweans live in a world dominated by symbols. In fact, symbolism is so deeply embedded in our culture that it can be seen as second nature.

We wanted to reverse the symbolism of the clenched fist. Our symbol signified a new way of life. Colonel Mudzingwa said that an open hand would represent the MDC as an alternative with nothing to hide –

compared with Zanu PF's clenched fist which represented threat and intolerance. Normally, we open our hands, especially the right hand (even if one is left-handed), to welcome and to greet each other. It denotes the pleasure of being together; it is reassuring in that one can see the full hand, outstretched. Slow and carefully measured claps after a handshake and a greeting are an expected custom, especially among the Shona tribes, to demonstrate unconditional respect for age and social standing, to honour a stranger, or convey a greeting after long family breaks.

With a name, symbol, slogan, draft policy documents and interim structures now ready, the interim committee looked set to launch a public campaign. We drew up an election manifesto, and tied up a number of loose ends: posters, ceremonial objects, a logo, badges, pamphlets and membership cards.

All of this took a lot of planning and none of it had come about haphazardly. After dwelling on all the issues of representivity, participation, long-term strategy and political mission that had troubled us for so long, I put together a technical team to organise a three-day meeting called the National Working People's Convention (NWPC).

At the same time, Gibson Sibanda, our ZCTU president, launched a private, parallel mission to consult veteran politicians that he knew from the liberation struggle. He travelled extensively, especially in Matabeleland and the Midlands, conferring with peers on the role the ZCTU should play. The outcome was that the ZCTU should continue to guide the process.

Sibanda told me that he benefited immensely from the wise counsel of his wife Zodwa and other former PF-Zapu stalwarts in Bulawayo. Zodwa was a veteran human rights activist. She appeared to be more politically astute than Sibanda and was his close adviser and mentor.

The technical team drew up an agenda and a programme for the convention, based on *The Raw Data* and the *ZCTU/ORAP Consultative Report*. A venue was secured at the Zimbabwe Women's Bureau in Harare. Some 700 civil society delegates from all over Zimbabwe took part. Three hundred were women drawn from social clubs, church groups, human rights organisations, student associations, the unemployed and communal farmers.

The conference began on 26 February 1999 with a hectic morning of sharing information and clarifying issues and objectives. The gathering then broke into eight committees to work on specific themes.

Leading civil society activists and academics Godfrey Kanyenze, Phineas Kadenge, Blessing Chiripanhura, Charles Halimana and Brian Raftopoulous worked in the economic and labour market group. They identified economic marginalisation, poverty and the lack of a political platform as the main factors affecting the majority. Capital constraints, entrepreneurial inabilities and landlessness featured in their findings. A non-integrated economy leading to an uneven, separate development model hindered growth and the state had done nothing to address the inherited dichotomy. Zimbabwe had a semblance of a modern economy but the communal and informal sectors were totally left out. Sharply critical of the Mugabe administration, the committee found that the state seemed to promote inequality and poverty through public policy confusion.

Zimbabweans were 'voiceless, root-less and future-less' – a view the team said it adapted from the 1996 UNDP Human Development Report. Sustainable growth right across the economy required a democratic culture and a cogent plan for mass empowerment, along with the promotion of a distinct cultural identity.

Hindrances included lack of transparency in the labour market; general backwardness in formulating economic strategies; uncertainty about the state's role in business; poor product competitiveness; the absence of a social contract; and poor planning generally.

Imports far outstripped exports and this was extremely dangerous. Our national debt was 158 per cent of the country's 1997 gross domestic product. This meant that 37 Zimbabwean cents were needed out of every dollar raised in revenue to service the interest on debt.

Women's activists Rudo Kwaramba and Ona Jirira, along with unionists Gertrude Mtombeni, Miriro Pswarai and Enna Chitsa, headed the gender relations committee. They examined the impact of cultural values, customary law, access to resources, the feminisation of poverty, violence, working conditions for female workers and child labour practices.

Zimbabwean women were under pressure from a runaway HIV/Aids pandemic and had been forced to assume increased family and social responsibilities.

Jose Martins, Regis Mushininga and Paul Themba Nyathi led the session on land reform and recommended the adoption of a combined policy of agricultural development and industrialisation. The team felt that Zanu PF politicians should stay away from the land reform programme because of their history of interference and bungling.

Other committees included one on governance led by Isaac Matongo, Gandi Mudzingwa, Dennis Murira, and lawyers Welshman Ncube, Lovemore Madhuku, Ben Hlathwayo and Tendai Biti. They looked at broad issues related to governance, the restoration of basic habits of citizenship, local government, and the roles of the government secret service, the Lancaster House Constitution, election management and administration, and the public media.

After three days of hard work, we ended the convention with a plenary session at which we concluded that Zimbabwe had a negative scorecard on most primary indicators for a free society. There was state-sponsored violence, a democracy deficit, a lack of a human rights culture, a high unemployment rate, and a spectacular collapse of the public sector. To cap it all, we identified the absence of a viable, national constitution to protect democracy as a major obstacle to national development. The immediate impact of a weak constitution was evident: poorly rooted national institutions and a deficient political culture. Further, the state and Zanu PF worked as a single unit, threatening democracy and diversity.

The convention resolved to reverse Zimbabwe's potential slide into anarchy. It called for a new constitution along with a comprehensive review of our electoral system. To promote national integration we called for a Truth and Reconciliation Commission similar to the South African model, to probe past injustices.

After considering all the recommendations for change, we decided to form a political movement to challenge Mugabe and Zanu PF in the 2000 general election. We recognised that everything had to rest on a strong, democratic, popularly driven movement of the people. Such a movement should protect the discrete and independent role of its constituent bodies including the labour movement, informal traders, women's groups and others such as peasant farmer associations.

The convention left open the question about which organisations would coordinate the formation of the political movement. It seemed there was a tacit understanding that the ZCTU would undertake the assignment. It was also felt that our resolutions should be endorsed by the ordinary people. Amidst the wild singing and celebrations marking the end of the proceedings, the delegates swore to report back and to start mobilising their members and supporters to take on Mugabe and Zanu PF.

The public media downplayed the story. There was a tiny reference in the inside pages of the state newspaper, *The Herald*, to the effect that the ZCTU was now a political party. So small was the story that I presumed it escaped the notice of the newspaper's ordinary readers. The omission highlighted a major failure of the media in Zimbabwe as a supposed early warning system on matters of public interest. The public media had been so abused that facts were deliberately misrepresented to please the ruling elite.

Nevertheless, we attracted the attention of the state. Although it was only one among many founding organisations, Mugabe announced that the government was considering banning the ZCTU. There was no legal basis for such a move. We had a constitutional right to safeguard our interests as trade unionists and to associate with any group, even if it meant taking part in an openly political forum. The ZCTU was free to facilitate the formation of a workers' party, just as similar parties existed all over the world. The Labour Party in the United Kingdom, for example, owes a great deal of its continued existence to the support of British workers; and closer to home, the link between the African National Congress (ANC) and its alliance partners, the Congress of South African Trade Unions (Cosatu) and the South African Communist Party is a matter of common knowledge.

We made no secret of the ZCTU's involvement, or that we wished to maintain the labour movement's autonomy from the proposed political alliance of civic groups. The ZCTU would play a role in the political movement as this would benefit the workers and other marginalised Zimbabweans. A political movement with our input would be better positioned to deal with the wider agenda of good governance, freedom, macroeconomic matters, public safety and national security. In terms of tackling community-based development the ZCTU was too small to make an impact. Our main role so far had been to identify, define and refine pressing national needs and to provide the technical organisation for the national convention.

Indeed, all the groups at the convention aimed to retain their independence, serving their memberships in the normal way while participating in the new movement. The churches, human rights groups, farmers, teachers and others shared a direct interest in a corrective action for change. Workers and others had suffered and had to be unified on an agenda for action, just as they had once participated in the liberation struggle.

As I left the convention I witnessed a surge of excitement and optimism among delegates filled with confidence and hope. Their zeal and patriotic fervour were humbling. The thematic teams had worked long hours and would have put a hive of worker-bees to shame! Naturally, the state's secret service moles and their informers had carefully planted themselves in the meeting, taking copious notes and reporting back to their handlers. None of the delegates appeared worried: we knew we were being spied on but carried on, convinced of the rightness of our cause.

Back at the ZCTU office, I was unsure how the process was going to proceed. Many in the ZCTU did not expect to assume a pivotal role. We embarked on a series of post-convention consultations, inviting new players to our meetings and setting up interim structures. I believed as long as we kept an open door policy, remained considerate and compassionate and worked hard for inclusion, the proposed political movement would one day become a formidable force.

Realising that we were political novices, we co-opted retired Colonel Tichaona Mudzingwa into the main organising structure. Others who contributed their organisational expertise included Sekai Holland, another veteran nationalist then working with the Association of Women's Clubs, and Dr Reginald Matchaba-Hove, a medical practitioner who had acquitted himself superbly as the leader of ZimRights – the first post-independence human rights advocacy group. Those invited on to the national steering committee were drawn from the student movement, women's groups, informal traders, the unemployed and other groupings.

Our planning sessions were chaired by the ZCTU president Gibson Sibanda, assisted by his deputies Isaac Matongo and Enna Chitsa. Assisting me as secretary general of the ZCTU were Nicholas Mudzengerere, one of my deputies, and Remus Makuwaza, the general secretary of the Chemical Workers' Union.

The initial process was not without its setbacks. Some civil society organisations failed to put in the expected effort, to consult further and reach out to their membership. Others quietly disagreed with the approach and did nothing other than follow their daily routines; or they feared the consequences of what we intended to do – and went back to Zanu PF.

In April 1999, Nyarota and Mbanga launched *The Daily News* – much to my relief. It joined other privately owned weekly and monthly publications – *The Zimbabwe Independent* and *The Standard*, the *Financial Gazette*, and *Horizon* and *Parade* magazines. The difference was that this was now a daily newspaper, set to take on *The Herald*. The newspaper's entry on to the market created a public sensation as it countered the state-owned media through its diverse coverage of views and events.

As we were not yet a political organisation, at the beginning we tried to steer away from premature publicity and did not use *The Daily News* very much. We did not address any public meetings, nor did we issue any press releases. Neither *The Daily News* nor the public media followed any of our early, preparatory work or reported on it. To the general public, Zanu PF still appeared to be firmly in charge and Mugabe invincible.

Events in the country took their course and as each day drew to a close so the MDC's relevance increased.

Police arrested journalists Mark Chavunduka and Ray Choto and handed them over to the military for interrogation over a story published by *The Standard* newspaper alleging a looming coup plot against Mugabe. Chavunduka was the newspaper's editor and Choto was his chief reporter. The army assaulted them both severely before they were proved innocent. Amnesty International was forced to intervene and to airlift the newsmen to London for treatment.

Within the state sector, there were cases of unrest over pay disputes. Public servants wanted a pay rise the state could hardly afford because of its commitments in the Congo. University and college students were involved in running battles with the police after the students took to the streets in protest at Mugabe's intention to privatise accommodation and catering services at tertiary institutions.

Another political player emerged in the name of Zapu 2000 in early 1999. Though initially vocal in Bulawayo, and with prominent playwright Cont Mhlanga as one of the leaders, the party appeared to be targeting only the Ndebele vote. Prominent Zanu PF provincial officials in Matabeleland led by Reuben Donga and a former mayor of Bulawayo, Elliot Dube, quickly joined the new party. I discussed the issue with Sibanda and he quickly dismissed Zapu 2000 as a tribal outfit unlikely to affect our plan for a mass movement. Mhlanga claimed to be reviving the old PF, but none of the old Zapu guard tilted in his direction.

Margaret Dongo, the only independent in parliament following the controversial 1995 election, had formed the Zimbabwe Union of Democrats (ZUD). But her party was too small to make a difference. She seemed to face a tough time as a loner. In one of the parliamentary debates, Dongo accused fellow male MPs of being Mugabe's wives. The statement incensed former army commander Solomon Mujuru who had to be restrained from physically assaulting Dongo. She was fined for the 'unparliamentary' remark.

With our ZCTU interim committees, we continued with our plan for the launch of the new movement. In the National Constitutional Assembly (NCA), a key ally of the ZCTU, I was already working with Michael Auret, national director of the CCJP. His work in the rights movement spanned many decades – he had helped dozens of detained nationalists in

Smith's Rhodesia. Auret never relented in his work challenging Mugabe's human rights record.

David Coltart and Eddie Cross, both from Bulawayo, joined us. Coltart, a human rights lawyer, was known for his sterling contribution to the CCJP/LRF report. Cross, an industrialist, knew Zanu PF well after years of consulting for several government ministries. A former general manager of the state-assisted Cold Storage Company and the Beira Corridor Group (BCG), Cross was highly respected in Zanu PF. The BCG was set up in the 1980s to keep Zimbabwe's access to the Indian Ocean open after several attacks on the rail and pipeline by Renamo rebels. The idea was to minimise costs of imports and exports, and reduce reliance on South African ports as part of a broad fight against apartheid. Landlocked Zimbabwe also needed shorter alternative routes to seaports.

At our first meeting I sensed that Coltart's political inclination was liberal, while Cross stood a few paces from the centre, towards the right. In my view, the two – like most Zimbabwean whites and coloureds in Bulawayo and Matabeleland – see themselves as white Ndebele. In our meetings, both argued for the case of minorities in western Zimbabwe in much stronger terms than most ethnic Ndebele traditionalists. Notwithstanding their clear biases and blind spots, the two were seriously committed to national integration and democracy.

Coltart and Cross helped us to understand the feelings of the white population which, after the defeat and departure from politics of Rhodesian leader Ian Smith, seemed holed up in a political closet. The whites tended to retreat into a laager; they wanted a relatively quiet and safe lifestyle on their farms and in their businesses.

Apart from a small number of individuals, other white Zimbabweans seemed hesitant to join us. They saw the ZCTU as a leftist organisation that was anti-business. That perception arose when communists like Enoch Chikweche aka Munyaradzi Gwisai, a law lecturer, openly aligned himself with the ZCTU. But this never bothered Gertrude Stevenson, an activist with the Harare Ratepayers' Association; Roy Bennett, a former Zanu PF activist, Chimanimani farmer and businessman; Alan McCormick, a Mashonaland Central farmer; and filmmakers Edwina and Newton Spicer and their teenage son Tawanda.

As we were behind time for the 2000 election, we made allowances for four separate groups to speed up the organisational development process. We set up a steering committee with the responsibility for policy formulation; a working group, whose role was to oversee the routine administration of the project; and a technical committee to craft founding documents and position papers, and also to recommend a mobilisation and campaign strategy.

The technical teams were led by the ZCTU secretariat, with the help of volunteers Gandi Mudzingwa, Deprose Muchena, Dennis Murira and Dr Rene Loewenson, a public health specialist, organisational development expert and trade unionist.

For the Matabeleland and the Midlands regions, we requested ORAP to go into overdrive, holding post-convention report-back meetings. The ORAP meetings resolved to start mobilising ordinary peasants to register as voters, to muster courage and to overcome fear. From Gwatemba and Nkakezi in Filabusi to Pashu, Mulindi and Nakapande in Binga, ORAP helped our teams set up committees to spearhead the formation of the new political movement.

In the meantime, through Auret and others in the NCA, we continued to pile on pressure for a new constitution. We knew it would be difficult for Mugabe to justify the continued use of the Lancaster House Constitution nearly 20 years after independence. Zimbabweans saw the Lancaster House Constitution as a ceasefire document crafted by the British for a transitional period. Mugabe amended it 18 times to try to align it to his own political needs but such moves never gained popular acceptance. He was therefore embarrassed about continuing to defend it as a supreme law of the land.

As if to undercut us and to pre-empt the plans, in April 1999 Mugabe appointed a constitutional commission led by Judge President Godfrey Chidyausiku. We immediately convened a meeting of the NCA and resolved to oppose the work of the government-appointed commission. The government should not be taking charge of the constitution-making process as the task belonged to the citizenry. Zanu PF, of course, reacted by dismissing the concept of a people-driven constitution. Mugabe invited neither the ZCTU nor the NCA to join the commission. Although Eddison Zvobgo, a cabinet minister then managing the process, understood our position, he wanted it to be directed by Zanu PF.

Zvobgo was a maverick ensnared in the trappings of the nationalist politics of his generation. He was easy to engage, but had an inexplicable habit of attacking us viciously whenever he deemed it necessary to ingratiate himself with his colleagues. At the same time, Zvobgo's political reading of the situation was correct and it unsettled Zanu PF. He warned his party that it risked losing the election if it did not attend to the demands for a new constitution as a matter of urgency.

As the NCA, we argued for a commission defined by and accountable to representatives of civil society as the legitimate voice of ordinary Zimbabweans. Those appointed by Mugabe had a common agenda and would find it difficult to disagree with his personal political wishes. I noticed, with some amusement, that a few of our colleagues decided to join the government-appointed commission despite having been party to the resolutions of the convention.

Among them was my family friend, University of Zimbabwe law lecturer Ben Hlatshwayo. Hlatshwayo's decision surprised me, considering the work he had done as a civil society activist and sympathiser of the ZCTU since the late 1980s. Hlatshwayo, with Jonathan Moyo and newspaper publisher Ibbo Mandaza, led the information and public relations unit of the commission, now termed the Chidyausiku Commission.

While Mandaza had always been aligned to Zanu PF, Moyo was well known as an acerbic critic of Mugabe. His sudden change of heart, like that of Hlatshwayo, was equally shocking. Moyo began to shift his position radically, turning himself into one of Mugabe's most vocal, militant and uncompromising supporters. He had made a sterling contribution to the Zimbabwe democracy debate; he even produced a damning report on the 1990 elections, conveying the image of a promising activist and progressive comrade. At the time he was a lecturer at the University of Zimbabwe. He left Harare after a messy domestic dispute in the early 1990s and spent some time in Kenya before moving to South Africa. Stories about the circumstances of his return vary, but given his known anti-Mugabe stance, he is understood to have negotiated a job with Zanu PF, many believe, for personal protection after a murky lifestyle while in exile.

With Hlatshwayo and Mandaza, Moyo mounted a serious propaganda drive for Zanu PF, using the Chidyausiku Commission as a platform. Under the direction of Zanu PF, Moyo left a trail of cruelty and insensitivity that polarised the nation and visibly delayed the resolution of the national crisis.

I felt both Moyo and Hlatshwayo were acting in bad faith. Hlatshwayo and I had been very close. When I was arrested in 1989, he had helped my family immensely, providing support and legal advice freely. He accompanied my wife to the police station and facilitated my family's access to me. He contributed to the debates and to the formulation of our resolutions at the NWPC. I had also worked with Moyo in 1990s when he predicted the collapse of Zanu PF and the rise of the ZCTU to fill an impending political vacuum. Their history seemed to have been forgotten by both academics in early 1999.

As we argued with the government over the efficacy of the constitution-making process, I was further surprised by the behaviour of some senior officials in the NCA. I was advised that Welshman Ncube, another University of Zimbabwe law lecturer and civil society activist, was also working quietly with officials in the Chidyausiku Commission. When I confronted him, he admitted it but argued that he only advised the commission in his personal capacity, not as a representative of the NCA.

In the ZCTU, we intensified our work on the formation of the party. We set up interim structures with our trade unionists acting as the leaders. The changed agenda from trade unionism to politics created a national sensation and a countrywide hype about the prospects of a national political party. I then realised that it was important for the ZCTU to officially announce its position on the new developments as they seemed to be causing anxiety among some in the leadership.

Much of our work needed an explicit endorsement by the broader ZCTU leadership. The general council felt that it was not sufficiently mandated by the ZCTU statutes to take a position on the matter. Basically, what was being sought was a caretaker responsibility for coordinating the formation of the movement on behalf of civil society organisations. Zimbabwe was due for an election in a year's time. If we were to challenge Zanu PF, we had to move fast.

I was keen to see the launch of the movement by the end of August 1999, but a lot still had to be done. We set up a national steering committee and started a massive membership drive. The committee agreed to call an extraordinary congress of the ZCTU on 7 August 1999. After failing to secure a venue for the congress – frightened private hotels seemed unwilling to associate with the ZCTU – we quietly booked a conference room at a government training centre owned by the Zimbabwe Electricity Supply Authority (ZESA), in Belvedere, Harare. We had used the centre before for our workshops and the management saw nothing wrong with our work this time around.

The congress specifically considered the declaration of the NWPC and its implications for the labour movement and the entire country. At the time, the ZCTU had 24 affiliate unions, which were represented by 149 delegates. Four other unions, though members but not fully subscribed and paid up, were allowed into the congress as observers. Nine others were not in good standing and were excluded from the proceedings.

At the beginning, we observed a minute's silence in honour of Joshua Nkomo, veteran nationalist and vice-president, who had died in July. After receiving a report from Sibanda, I took the floor and presented a NWPC resolution calling for the formation of a mass-based political party.

I read through the resolution very slowly, to make sure everybody understood my position clearly. I explained the gravity of our national crisis, emphasising that as trade unions we were unable to handle the situation alone. We needed a political party or movement to take on Mugabe and Zanu PF. After scanning my audience's body language, I could gauge a sense of excitement, hesitancy, doubt and even fear. I suspected that a large part of the audience may not have fully understood the implications of what I was saying.

From my experience working with them for more than a decade, I knew many preferred painless remedies; they were comfortable with following easy routes and often avoided difficult situations. I recalled a number of cases involving some senior unionists who headed back to their villages, away from any confrontation in the city, whenever we called for mass action. They bounced back quickly and claimed credit in times of success but criticised us strongly when things went wrong. So I coloured my presentation with constant references to our core business: trade unionism, worker advancement and worker welfare. I explained that we were in a very difficult position; there seemed to be no safe path open to us: to avoid action or to confront the situation – that was the question.

Repeatedly, I insisted that our support for the political alliance should be conditional on the proposed political movement's desire to uphold and advance the interests of workers, failing which the ZCTU would walk away. The political movement was not a workers' party, but an alliance of interest groups and classes keen to shape public policy in Zimbabwe. I assured the congress that the ZCTU should guard its basic freedom of association principle jealously, allowing its members and unions to carry their political differences and support political parties of their choice. I concluded with a plea for reason, saying that the whole country looked to us for guidance and salvation.

As I finished my address, I felt like a man holding a hand grenade with its safety pin already removed. I could either direct it at a target or let it blow up in my hand. After all, I was not sure of the position the congress would ultimately take on the issue. Personally, I had taken a huge risk and put in a great deal of work. I had kept Sibanda and others in the leadership fully briefed on the work that I had already started on the ground, using ZCTU resources and staff. I had committed the ZCTU name and brand to the formative stages of the political movement, without congressional approval.

The first words of support came from a representative of the Energy and Electricity Workers' Union. After a lengthy attack on the government, he endorsed my proposal. Then came a bolt from the blue: Lyson Mlambo of the Urban Councils Workers' Union said his union was concerned about a growing perception that the ZCTU belonged to either Sibanda or Tsvangirai as individuals. The ZCTU would outlive the tenure of individual leaders and the two of us were free to go if we so wished. He wanted to use the extraordinary congress to get us out of the ZCTU. He added that the ZCTU should stay out of the proposed movement, and was quickly supported by other delegates. Others differed, dismissing Mlambo's idea and saying the forum was an inappropriate one for a leadership change.

After that the debate swung in different directions. At the centre was the issue of funding for the political movement. Delegates felt the ZCTU neither possessed the wherewithal nor capacity to be part of the project, let alone to lead it. I knew that after the extraordinary congress, it would be impossible to use the ZCTU facilities, vehicles, offices and money for the political project. The question of lack of resources sounded too threatening.

To break the impasse, Zvavamwe Shambare of the National Union of Railwaymen asked if the proposal could be put to a congressional vote. Amid murmurs of disapproval, many delegates shouted him down, saying that it was unnecessary. After persuasive contributions in favour of the project from Remus Makuwaza of the Chemical Workers' Union and Isaac Matongo of the National Engineering Workers' Union, the congress unanimously passed the resolution.

It was gratifying. In fact, the congress went even further in allowing the ZCTU free rein on the project. It granted the entire leadership permission to hold on to their union offices until the general election, then scheduled for April 2000, even if they opted for political positions in the new movement.

I checked my wristwatch. We had started at 8.30am and the time was now fifteen minutes after midday. It had seemed like an interminable morning. Sibanda sent the delegates off with a simple, positive message: 'Although our child is still to be born, that baby is expected to learn to crawl, to stand, to walk and to run. Change is coming to Zimbabwe.' I noted his words down immediately.

After a closing prayer, the high-ceilinged hall echoed with unrehearsed song and foot-stomp dances of unrestrained joy – the kind of wild ecstasy I had last seen in a township beer hall in Bindura on Zimbabwe's Independence Day in 1980.

As I drove home from the ZESA training centre, I wondered what tactics were needed to unseat Zanu PF, a party under the firm grip of a nationalist strongman and in power for two decades. How were the voters going to receive us? What was going to happen to the ZCTU?

I never thought about the part I would play or the position I would hold, either in a new movement or in a renewed ZCTU after the normal August 2000 congress. With this mandate, the question was how we would manage to conduct a launch at the month end and move on from there. Building a national party from a loose movement to contest the April 2000 election was what they called in politics a Big Ask. When I arrived home I phoned Sibanda at his hotel to share my anxieties with him but was told he had already checked out, heading for Bulawayo.

In the end I consoled myself by pushing the thoughts aside. Mugabe was in a worse crisis than any of us. Could he see his political future, which would be determined in the next few months? We had the initiative now and saw things positively. Mugabe was gleefully waiting for us to enter the ring and might resort to violence, but he did not necessarily control the future.

What was certain was that we needed the people's backing in overwhelming numbers, or we would be attacking a hungry lion with our bare hands and in an open space.

Back in the ZCTU office, it was business as usual. Buoyed by the latest developments, our teams were in high spirits, putting together the final touches for the launch ceremony.

A few days later news broke that there were moves in the IMF to suspend financial support to Mugabe's government because of shoddy bookkeeping. The IMF's proposal triggered a string of reactions from other multilateral quarters. The International Development Association suspended all structural adjustment loans, credits, and guarantees to Harare, citing an unbecoming economic management style. And, like a spreading virus, these moves marked the beginning of a line of negative international decisions on the Mugabe regime.

Slowly, loans and cash advances from international organisations, even for existing projects, started to dry up. The signs were clear. Zimbabwe was sliding into the status of an untrustworthy, international pariah state. Coupled with the general agitation for political change on the ground, it was difficult to see where Zimbabwe was set to land.

As non-state actors, there was nothing we could do at the time. We were excited about our plans to launch an alternative movement, organising ZCTU structures to play their part in the MDC. Although we had an impressive reservoir of organisational skills and experience in the trade union movement, we lacked a political brand and our fangs as a potential political force were still immature and weak. Further, whether or not we posed a threat depended on the goodwill of a loose coalition – without a unifying ideology – which must have appeared totally vulnerable to Mugabe.

For our part, it remained unclear as to who among our senior ZCTU leaders were ready for a dramatic career move from the comfort of their unions into the political arena. It was never going to be easy. Zimbabwean politics was murky, the ground underfoot uncertain, and the zone of public visibility highly dangerous. Who was likely to support us? Where would we get the money and other resources?

The ZCTU general council met to establish the officials for secondment to the MDC. Several senior officials volunteered, among them myself, Sibanda, Matongo, Mudzengerere, Makuwaza, Esaph Mdlongwa, Mpariwa and Khupe. Mpariwa was chosen to lead the interim Women's Assembly, with Khupe as the secretary and Kumbirai Makore as the organising secretary. Makore later dropped out. Mpariwa and Khupe then co-opted Sekai Holland, Grace Kwinjeh, Emilia Chamunogwa and Yvonne Mahlunge to their interim executive committee.

The issue of resources nagged at me. Zanu PF allocated itself a generally non-debatable allowance from the national budget through parliament. For close to 20 years, a tradition set in allowing for a vague line between Zanu PF as a party and the government. Mugabe could use state resources with gay abandon to support the party through what he called the Ministry of State for Political Affairs.

The term 'political affairs' referred to ministries and departments, specifically created to service the Zanu PF youth and women's leagues, and the party's general administration. This was in addition to the unquestioned support from the police, the secret service, the army and other state departments. In the more extreme cases of public fiscal abuse, quasi-state companies provided vital logistics and staff to Zanu PF at the taxpayer's expense.

My enthusiastic colleagues looked totally unconcerned about the potential landmines that lay ahead. Instead they focused on the end of August, the date set aside for the official launch of the MDC. I knew then that the success of the project lay squarely on the preliminary work of the ZCTU secretariat. We were lucky still to be covered by the ZCTU for our basic operational needs: salaries, allowances, the use of our facilities and offices and the services of our structures.

Together with the NCA and some volunteers carefully selected from the original convention, we put together a party launch coordinating committee. Wobbly interim provincial and district structures emerged everywhere, initially led by activists from the ZCTU, ZimRights or NCA local organs. In Harare, Bulawayo, other towns and cities and in parts of the Midlands and Matabeleland, these temporary structures became contact and political liaison points.

Our affiliate unions played a significant role in mobilising their memberships to advance the new movement. Among the leading lights were the Agriculture and Plantation Workers' Union, which rallied the majority of farm and agro-industrial workers, and the Domestic and Allied Workers' Union which worked throughout the low density, conservative and middle-class areas.

I held numerous meetings with politicians who had previously attempted to form and organise political parties. I wanted to learn from their experiences and impress upon them the need for a united front.

Patrick Kombayi, ZUM and DP official, needed no persuasion. He quickly offered us one of his suburban properties in central Gweru for use as a provincial office. At the time of his death in 2009, Kombayi was a Senator after being elected on an MDC ticket. A nationalist fighter, he had impeccable liberation war credentials. Zanu PF refused to honour him, despite his impressive record.

I met with Margaret Dongo but she was reluctant to work with us. Dongo's ZUD was nothing more than a loose coalition of activists; people who believed they could mount a challenge against a ruling party as independent candidates. When ZUD tried to set up proper structures and turn itself into a real political force, it split into even smaller units.

I continued with my consultations, meeting with retired politicians and Zanu (Ndonga) officials. Among those who joined up was college lecturer Fidelis Mhashu who threw himself tirelessly into our formative committees. A number of low-level officials defected from Zanu PF to render their help. Given the structure, attitude and values of the new party, there was now a possibility that down the line – who knows? – a person from a minority group could actually be president of Zimbabwe.

For me, it was a good and a natural progression to mobilise people across race, across tribe and across any other form of culturally constructed separation. The ZCTU had taught us that one worked with anyone who shared common values and concerns. Trade unions, like churches, are open organisations, admitting members at face value without any ideological, ethnic, gender or other distinctions.

After the steering committee had appointed Sibanda as the interim party leader and completed all the preparations, we realised that it was impossible to have the launch at the end of the month. We settled instead for 11 September 1999 at Harare's Rufaro Stadium.

Close to 20 000 people attended the launch of the MDC. There was jubilation everywhere among workers and peasants from all over Zimbabwe. With much fanfare, the stadium roared into life as we formally presented our election manifesto, our founding documents, our flag, and our slogans. And, in no time, the crowd was abuzz with waving hands, chanting: *'Chinja, Chinja! Maitiro Ako Ayo; Hezvoko – Bwa-a!'* Used in conjunction with a raised and open palm, the slogan showed a major shift from the furious clenched fist of Zanu PF. Ours was a peace movement with a clear and open purpose. I knew the slogan and the gesture were set to change social interactions in Zimbabwe.

After 11 September we went straight into a rapid process of building the movement while campaigning against the draft constitution and the work of the government's Constitutional Commission. The support for the MDC countrywide grew phenomenally within a short period of time and there was a huge turnout – almost 30 000 people – at the first meeting I held in Bindura.

We were fortunate that *The Daily News* was now up and running. The newspaper gave positive coverage to the launch while the official media tried hard to play down the event. Contrary to the Zanu PF propaganda that the MDC was a cluster of disgruntled workers and the unemployed on the payroll of Britain, the European Union, the USA and white farmers, I had actually seen fewer than a dozen local whites in the crowd.

Further, the accusation that the MDC had been formed to stop the land reform programme was equally out of step with the prevailing mood. Mugabe never talked about land reform in the manner in which he finally implemented it. He had yet to commit himself to the pact he had sealed with the international community of donors at the 1998 conference.

Up until 1999, whites had faith in an orderly land reform programme following the resolutions of the 1998 donors' conference. They were not sure about the route the MDC would be taking. After the collapse of the Rhodesian Front and its successor, the Conservative Alliance of Zimbabwe, and following the demise of the breakaway Independent Zimbabwe Group of the 1980s, the Forum Party of the 1990s and other small opposition parties, most Zimbabwean whites retreated to their business associations to lobby for their separate political interests. In the interim committee of the MDC we decided that any white person who wanted to join the party was free to do so. We had a policy of inclusion, but we were not looking at special racial privileges for them.

There were still pockets of resistance or mistrust among whites. I set out to engage them in their own communities and I realised that we were seeing things differently. Many whites wanted a collective white role in the MDC as a bloc – not as individuals. It was important to put them right on this point because it would set a dangerous trend of in-group thinking and separate value systems. By pushing for a distinct political voice and shoring up the CFU they risked further isolation and attack. I insisted that they become part of the broader Zimbabwe instead of seeing themselves as an elite.

Having been born and raised in white-ruled Rhodesia where racism was official policy, I believed I knew white Zimbabweans well. As a shop-floor worker, a miner and trade unionist, I had endured a lot of white racism. I hated it. I fought against it. In my discussions with them while preparing to launch the MDC, I tried to make them see the folly of their separatist attitudes and their negative behaviour.

In the 1980s, most whites clearly spurned the policy of national reconciliation. They tried to perpetuate their advantages and racial superiority. Some even worked with Zanu PF politicians and benefited from the party system of patronage in their pursuit of their interests. With fresh memories of colonialism, black Zimbabweans saw whites as an offspring of that past who regarded themselves as a privileged group. Many whites reinforced this stereotype by clinging to racism and hunkering down in their exclusive social clubs. They displayed loathing for the poor; frowned at interracial relationships and marriages; and openly obstructed efforts at economic justice. Any fantasies about Zimbabwe's excellent race relations and racial stability aside, many local whites still saw blacks as filthy, primitive tribesmen and women – a whole 19 years after independence.

To the ordinary peasant and worker, the CFU was an added problem. As a bloc it fought hard to frustrate equity in land ownership when it knew that the majority remained on the periphery of the economy and lived in perpetual penury.

Mugabe's relations with wealthy white Zimbabweans appeared to complicate matters. The people looked to him for leadership, but over the years he seemed to be leaning closer to white capital, firstly through ESAP, then towards big business in general. Socially he became the patron of Zimbabwe's game of cricket, mainly a white sport. Mugabe, always a darling of the West, led the poor to think that he had abandoned them for a new life with the rich and famous – a view deeply held by the workers and peasants.

Against that background, I still believed it was important to include whites in the MDC. Whites must, of necessity, have a role to play in a racially integrated society in Africa if the continent is their natural home. Mugabe selectively used only prominent whites and marginalised the rest of the community. Similarly, he believed in black patronage and selectively used a few leading blacks, but isolated the majority – especially the rural poor. He treated the rural poor as permanent hostages, threatening them at will because of his liberation struggle credentials.

In due course, as the movement grew, especially among agricultural and agro-industrial workers, led by their union, more whites saw the MDC's potential. We included some of them in the interim leadership of the party as a demonstration of our policies and values. A few had worked hard for the party, including Coltart, Stevenson, Cross and others.

Zanu PF started to denounce white Zimbabweans, forcing them to turn to us for political help. Even some of the traditionally ardent Zanu PF supporters found comfort in the new movement, because in their view it was better than Zanu PF. They came in as individuals, partly because the business community as a whole did not quite trust me. I came from the labour movement, considered then the natural enemy of white capital. I knew they didn't like me and that they thought I was a radical leftist.

Whenever the opportunity arose, I explained to them that this new movement was committed to democracy, non-racialism and inclusion, emphasising that whites must work with others as a matter of survival. Towards the end of the year, many whites, especially in rural Mashonaland, began to enquire about the role they could play in the new movement. But they set up their own structures, in the form of support groups. These groups comprised both whites and influential blacks who were not keen to be seen at the forefront of political activism at the time. They were interested in working behind the scenes, supporting the movement's programmes and activities on the ground.

Growing white support for the MDC brought more condemnation from Zanu PF. This never bothered me. I thought it was not important – perhaps naively so. I asked myself: what can a small group of whites do by way of influence? They would neither manipulate the MDC, nor shape our policy significantly along the lines of their self-interest. To Zanu PF the few Zimbabwean whites were hardly a threat. In the 1985 election, there were about 30 000 registered white voters in Zimbabwe. By 1999, that number had dwindled.

Generally, I have had an interesting relationship with white Zimbabweans. At some point a number drifted away with my colleagues when the party split in 2005, only to return to the mainstream MDC after the breakaway faction made a poor start. At one time, even Western diplomats gave up on me and my prospects for success, using an un-African reading of African systems and African mindsets. I knew that one day I would prove them wrong; so did many black Zimbabweans. I strongly believe that, from the cradle to the grave, white Africans and other minorities always look out for a steady home. We need to find a way to deal with it.

The few whites in the MDC exhibited both their strengths and their own idiosyncrasies. Our cultures are different – and that resulted in friction over policies, organisational styles and mass mobilisation activities. Whenever we came out of our confidential and strategic meetings, white officials quickly dashed to their laptops and mobile phones to inform their families and friends of the decisions taken and the progress made. The information soon came into the public domain. So by rushing to show the world what we were doing, my white colleagues unsuspectingly and inadvertently briefed Zanu PF long before we executed our carefully worked out plans.

In their quest for what I thought was an act of exaggerated transparency, our secrets hardly survived. They were splashed everywhere: in the foreign media, at bowling clubs, around dinner tables, through internet blogs and in printed fliers. At the beginning I tried to caution them, only to abandon the effort upon realising that they would still go public – and broadcast even my whispered warnings!

When Mugabe and his vast state machinery saw these messages spreading, they were livid. He thought the whites were driving the agenda to unseat him; whites wanted Rhodesia back, he opined. Mugabe's comments appeared to be well received in traditional Zimbabwean circles and within his peer groups in Africa. That delayed the MDC's growth and when spiced with Zanu PF propaganda it distorted what the MDC stood for. Mugabe turned to war veterans as a careful ploy to handle the spirit of 1999 – a massive groundswell of black opposition – and to keep himself in office. But with the passage of time, Mugabe could fool only a few at home and abroad.

Top: Morgan Tsvangirai with trade union colleagues

Above: With his brother Collins, father Dingirai-Chibwe and brother Manase

With his wife Susan and his brother Samuel

Top left: The Tsvangirai family

Left: With the twins, Millicent and Vincent

Below: Susan with her sisters

With his mother-in-law on the left and his own mother on the right

At the ZCTU office in 1988

With Gibson Sibanda

Campaigning in the rural areas in 2000

With Robert Mugabe

CHAPTER TWELVE
NEW MILLENNIUM

As a budding politician, I found myself in an atmosphere that resembled an exciting, fictional thriller. The year 1999 was ending and the world was turning the corner into a new century. Hope was on the horizon.

Most people I met tended to take the proposed referendum on a new constitution seriously, seeing the plebiscite as a rare opportunity to be heard. We intensified our party-building effort while campaigning against the Chidyausiku Commission. People expressed measured optimism about the MDC. Misfortunes had become part of their daily fare but they calculatedly steeled their souls in the hope that the end could be aproaching.

In public discussions people said that they regarded the 1990s as a totally wasted decade. Our slide into chaos as a nation had its roots in the 1980s but had accelerated during the past decade. Either Zanu PF actively pushed us downhill or they could no longer cope with the crisis. The situation was aggravated by the government's supposedly charitable engagement in the Congo's complicated civil war. Such benevolence baffled many, given the realities on the ground in our own beleaguered society.

With the country on a knife-edge and muffled calls for Mugabe's departure, interspersed with the traditional factor of fear among Zimbabweans, I saw the work of the Chidyausiku Commission, and in particular the way it was constituted, as an insincere attempt to deal with fundamental issues. Mugabe maintained his obsession with power, so we never trusted him to direct the constitutional reform process through his appointment of Chidyausiku and yes-men and yes-women on the commission.

Some Zimbabwean whites saw the merits of our argument and came to our side, while others remained ambivalent and seemingly unconcerned. We began to engage with those who picked up our message, mainly from their highly unionised farm workers, on their farms and their nearby agro-industrial towns. Soon, our voice penetrated these constituencies through our members, our literature and our leaflets.

While the whites had their own biases because Zanu PF denounced them daily, we needed access to their workers whose views could have been different from those of their bosses. The state media preached racial hatred, thinking that was the best way to reach out to the black workers – a mistake since the workers had their political grievances against Mugabe and Zanu PF, apart from anything they may have thought about their employers. In panic, whites desperately sought pockets of safety. Some joined the NCA; a few braved it out and declared their allegiance to the MDC; others kept their heads low, working quietly in the MDC support groups.

January 2000 was a particularly busy month for me. I was doing my normal trade union work at the ZCTU while taking part in the National Constitutional Assembly (NCA) campaign against the government-appointed constitutional commission. There were thousands of MDC party-building chores to attend to, and we were simultaneously organising an inaugural party congress. Mugabe would have us believe that the election would be held in March – in fact it happened in June – so the pressure was on.

Our party did not yet have a properly elected leadership – that would be up to the congress – and I could not immediately tell where the referendum pendulum would swing given the people's excitement and attendance at the Chidyausiku Commission's hearings. Even if we were to go into an election, where would we find the required 120 candidates strong enough to take on Zanu PF?

Mugabe and Zanu PF dismissed the national mood as petty and inconsequential and this attitude gave us a lot of space as we were able to do our political and advocacy work without much interference from the state apparatus. Even diehard Zanu PF supporters had no problem with us as they did not suspect that anything could be amiss.

The open waving of hands was a customary way of expressing appreciation, a form of respect, a greeting and a farewell gesture. To our organisers, this was the measure of approval of the MDC. Only later did the party symbol give us a major problem. But by then, Zimbabwe was already another country.

Attempts to prevent people waving their open hands were farcical. In most rural homesteads, people normally warmed their hands by opening them to an open fire in a rural kitchen stove. To Zanu PF this simple human gesture was tantamount to supporting the MDC. Zealots banned the use of an open hand for greetings or a casual wave to acknowledge a passing friend or stranger. The situation became so ridiculous that education minister Aeneas Chigwedere asked parliament to ban the MDC's symbol. Chigwedere's argument was that a number of innocent villagers had become targets of public misunderstandings and violence after merely raising an open hand while greeting each other.

Not dissuaded, people resorted to touching each other with clenched fists as if they were rival boxers teasing each other out before a bout. Our rural folk would close all their fingers while sitting by the fireside at all-night funeral vigils or relaxing in their own homes, just in case they were misunderstood by a Zanu PF zealot.

Schoolchildren – who were always commandeered to line up and welcome the president while his unusually long motorcade wound along – were ordered never to wave an open hand. Headmasters were told to retrain the children to give victory salutes with clenched fists to acknowledge Mugabe's passage. Even newspapers found the situation amusing. When Mugabe arrived for a campaign rally in Gokwe, central Zimbabwe, in early 2000, he raised his characteristic clenched fist – but his wife Grace enthusiastically waved her hand in the air. The moment was caught in a *Daily News* photograph. It raised anger inside Zanu PF and a public chuckle in the MDC. Did Grace also desire change? That question dominated casual pub talk for a day or two.

Compared to the government's public media blitz, our countermeasures spread mainly through small gatherings and whispers. As our membership grew, the NCA became more experienced and focused. Some of my conservative colleagues in the ZCTU, uncomfortable with a direct challenge to the government, began to question our role and status as a labour movement in this increasingly 'militant' line-up. All I needed to say was that we were mandated by the NWPC and the ZCTU extraordinary congress to oppose the Chidyausiku Commission.

It was interesting to decipher the political trends. On the surface, our supporters appeared to be following the constitutional debate, but deep down they saw the exercise as an opportunity to kick Mugabe out of power completely. The matters they raised with the government-appointed commissioners were telling. Objections were levelled at the powers of the executive, bloated government and unbridled government waste and corruption.

The people called for term limits for presidents, leadership age limits, food and jobs, free and fair elections, the abolition of superfluous ministerial portfolios and provincial governorships – a gamut of issues. There were great similarities countrywide, whether the objectors were from rural areas, far-flung provinces, villages, towns or major cities. Even discussion in private homes echoed the concerns about our nation's future. Mugabe and Zanu PF were hugely unpopular, everywhere.

In retrospect, I have realised how unfortunate it was that the MDC's inexperience led us into a corner. The nation misunderstood our opposition to the draft constitution and we did not grasp this at the time. People thought a negative referendum result would be sufficient to spur an automatic ouster or the graceful resignation of Mugabe from office. The broader political danger in this approach did not strike me until a few weeks later, so I continued to urge our supporters to send a clear message of discontent to the government.

We agreed to hold our inaugural congress on 29 January 2000. As this was the first time I had been involved in a political congress, I had no knowledge of the unnatural world of politics and the associated complexities of power dynamics on such a national platform. In my contributions in meetings and through my work, I merely expressed myself honestly and fully out of a personal commitment to transparency and respect. A week before this historic occasion, I noticed a flurry of activity – both positive and negative – involving lobbying for senior party posts. Jostling for space in the leadership of the MDC brought with it the emergence of interest-based alliances and political camps. This was politics, after all, and the shape of things to come.

Neither Sibanda nor I were involved; we simply watched from a distance. For me, it did not matter what post I would finally hold, if any at all. I was still the secretary general of the ZCTU. My goal was to help in the formation of a legitimate political alternative to Zanu PF.

On the last Thursday of January, the interim leaders of the MDC met at Adelaide Acres, a private convention centre eight kilometres west of Harare, to put the last touches to our party's founding documents and the election manifesto. We had to find ways to accommodate and to feed the thousands of delegates we expected to grace the Chitungwiza Aquatic Centre to attend the inaugural congress in 48 hours' time.

During one of the tea breaks, as I engaged in idle talk with colleagues, Paul Themba Nyathi, a former combatant and activist who ran Adelaide Acres, came to me and whispered that he wished to pass on a private word. Nyathi had an inexhaustible supply of jokes and an amazing capacity to lighten tense moments and break communication ice blocks of any size with his funny stories. I hastily dismissed him, thinking he was pulling another one on me. When he persisted, I accompanied him to a place between two granite boulders under a leafy Msasa tree.

Suddenly his face turned serious – totally unusual for him – and he said: 'Look, we must talk.'

Had something gone wrong? I wondered, my thoughts racing through all the issues we had discussed that day. Maybe the venue for the congress had been cancelled, or Mugabe had banned us before we were even on our feet. 'What do you want to discuss, Paul?' I asked, guardedly.

Paul Themba Nyathi, a smart lobbyist and nimble-footed political player, took a deep breath. 'You know, we have talked a lot about this. We have been in consultation with our colleagues right across the spectrum in the MDC. The general feeling is that you are probably the one who has contributed more to this party than anybody else,' he paused, checking my expression and body language.

'You know, it is a tough call. But there is a general consensus that you must lead the MDC. Gibson (Sibanda) has done a lot as well. But it is important for you to realise that in this game there is more to leadership selection and choice than just hard work. Gibson is from Bulawayo – like, you know what I mean,' he said, indicating that as a person from a minority Ndebele tribe, perhaps the time was not yet ripe for Sibanda to run the MDC.

Leadership of the party had never crossed my mind. I had a fantastic working relationship with Gibson spanning a 12-year period. I tried to argue that as far as I could see, Gibson's being an Ndebele did not matter. Joshua Nkomo, an eminent nationalist leader, was well respected countrywide despite coming from a minority tribe, the Kalangas.

'A lot has changed since the Zapu and Nkomo days,' Paul Themba Nyathi, himself a former Zapu stalwart countered. 'And, mind you, we have had some problems in Matabeleland.' I assured him that I was following his argument and I knew that the area and its people had endured a lot in the years following our independence. Mugabe could easily isolate the Ndebele again and target them for reprisals. All of that I had considered

– but how was I supposed to work with Sibanda should I be elected as the party leader? I asked Paul Themba Nyathi, after a long pause.

'We have spoken to Gibson,' was his straightforward answer. 'There is no problem; you must go for it.'

For many years, I had been guided by Sibanda and the ZCTU general council in my work. Sibanda was a man I respected tremendously. How could he suddenly become my subordinate, in whatever capacity? Paul Themba Nyathi allayed my fears and anxieties. He said that Sibanda had agreed to step down as interim leader of the MDC and would be comfortable being my prime adviser and deputy. This sounded strange, so I asked Paul Themba Nyathi: 'Has Gibson explicitly cleared this position? We wish to see an inclusive political party emerging out of this, so the question of tribe or race is not an issue as far as I am concerned.'

Paul Themba Nyathi insisted. A decision had already been taken. Most trade unionists and founder members agreed that Sibanda should make way for me. Still unconvinced, I asked for time to think through this unexpected turn of events. I hardly had time to organise my thoughts before a number of senior colleagues buttonholed me and advised me that the decision for Sibanda to step aside had been unanimously taken by the majority in the interim committee. By then the sun was setting. My participation in the remaining conversations was now somewhat subdued.

Sibanda did not even talk to me about it. His behaviour left me wondering whether what was being said made sense to him. I decided not to ask him either. We exchanged a few glances in the final session of the preparatory meeting but I decided not to give any indication that I knew anything about the leadership issue.

Are these the kinds of intrigues normally associated with politics? I wondered. Why would a man with such impeccable credentials as a nationalist during and after the liberation struggle, a leading trade unionist and effective politician; a man who had worked so hard to see this project through to its penultimate stage, suddenly agree to assume a lower post? Was he that magnanimous? Was he afraid of something? Mugabe, perhaps? I could not find a ready justification for Sibanda's change of heart.

By the time I arrived at Chitungwiza for the congress, the place was buzzing with confidence. There was a lot of singing and dancing. Delegates had come from far and wide and the numbers kept on swelling: people were buoyed by our visibility in the referendum campaign. Students, unionists, business people, church leaders, grassroots advocates, politicians, women activists – all cheered as I drove into the seldom used Aquatic Centre, built five years before for the All Africa Games, and abandoned since then.

Our choice of venue was symbolic of where we stood in the country's politics at that time. We were newcomers and as long as we wanted a place to meet, the authorities were willing to oblige. The Aquatic Centre often stood empty. After the Games, the local council had tried to hire out the complex to anyone who could make use of it: churches, musicians, wedding ceremony organisers, burial societies, as a venue for private parties or to any large group in need of a convention centre.

The reason for the limited use of the Aquatic Centre was simple: swimming was a relatively new sport to black Zimbabweans. There were few local trainers, the kits were expensive and none of the schools in Chitungwiza had a swimming pool.

Meeting in the Chitungwiza residential area said something about our socio-economic profile as a new political party. Built in the late 1960s and 70s along the same lines as the vast township complex of Soweto in Johannesburg, Chitungwiza was meant to be a 'dormitory' for people working in the shops, offices and factories of Harare. It lacked a visible industrial base of its own. Workers living in tiny two-roomed, tin-and-asbestos-roofed, matchbox houses commuted to and from Harare to work from early morning until late at night. Nothing changed after independence in 1980.

By 1999, Chitungwiza was home to an estimated one million people, the majority of whom were either unemployed or very poor. It bordered on the Seke communal lands, a desolate rural area that had been heavily denuded by deforestation to feed the fuel demands of the city. Its sandy soils were depleted.

By lunchtime, there must have been more than 14 000 people milling around the centre, loitering and eavesdropping on discussions. There was near chaos when we ran out of food. An assistant, Dennis Murira, rushed up to alert me to the fact that we were short of food for the delegates and observers. The tiny Harare catering company, *Happy Eater*, was failing to fill the rising number of open mouths. *Happy Eater's* routine customers were the few company employees they served at workplaces at industrial sites. They had never had to deal with such a large crowd.

As Murira and I went aside quietly to address the seemingly overwhelming congress logistics, a thought raced through my mind: money and congress expenses. Our kitty was virtually empty – yet we had to pay *Happy Eater*, and the bus companies we had hired, and even for the chair I would be sitting on. The enthusiasm was electric, but how was I supposed to run a party without a steady source of income? I decided to shelve the thought, comforting myself with the huge turnout at the inaugural congress. No doubt the very fact that the congress had been so well attended would generate funding from well-wishers.

Looking closely at the audience, I recognised a number of familiar faces; unionists and civil society activists from as far afield as Hwange near Victoria Falls, Chipinge and Mutare in the east, Gweru in the Midlands, Masvingo and Beitbridge in the south, and Binga and Kariba in the north. Large numbers were from Harare and Bulawayo.

Sibanda, as the interim president, directed the proceedings in a calm and professional manner. The congress ran smoothly, and without any hiccups we adopted the MDC policy documents, a party constitution, logos, slogans and manifesto. Our technical committees were thoroughly prepared, organising delegates into various discussion groups and guiding the process at every stage.

After the brainstorming, congress wound up with the election of the MDC's substantive leadership. Dr Lovemore Madhuku of the NCA took over the proceedings and conducted the polls. Although I suspected that I was set for nomination, I was actually surprised to have a total endorsement from all the provinces without a challenge. The same happened to Sibanda for the post of deputy leader.

Isaac Matongo, a former ZCTU vice-president, became the founding national chairman, after a stiff challenge from Dr Tichaona Mudzingwa. When it came to the post of secretary general, there was a tie. Gift Chimanikire and Welshman Ncube received an equal number of provincial nominations. After intense lobbying by senior unionists from the western region, in particular by Gertrude Mtombeni, Milton Gweru, Esaph Mdlongwa and Sibanda, congress persuaded Chimanikire to give way. Ncube's backers included academics and student leaders, including Learnmore Jongwe. Coming from the trade union movement, I was more inclined to go along with my like-minded colleague, Chimanikire. He stepped down but the congress offered him the post of deputy secretary general, again without a challenge.

Sibanda then brought in Fletcher Dulini-Ncube, a veteran nationalist and former PF-Zapu official, as the new treasurer. There were hardly any objections, partly because of the people's respect for Sibanda and partly because of our desire to infuse diversity and experience into the top echelon of the MDC. Rusape businessman and farmer Valentine Ziswa had been treasurer of our interim executive. He later ran for parliament in Makoni against Didymus Mutasa of Zanu PF. For close to a year, he had a raw deal from Mutasa's thuggish supporters until he threw in the towel – and went back to Zanu PF.

Esaph Mdlongwa, a senior trade unionist from Bulawayo, scooped the position of national organising secretary, while Paul Themba Nyathi settled for the post of director of elections. Khupe, Kwinjeh and Sekai Holland were elected directly into the main wing, while Gertrude Mtombeni came in from the provinces. Other women in the national executive included Mpariwa, Mahlunge, Stevenson and Chamunogwa. Khupe became the secretary for transport, logistics and welfare. Mpariwa took up the labour portfolio after Remus Makuwaza was forced by a strong women's lobby to step down. Holland took the foreign affairs post, pushing out Learnmore Jongwe as the women mounted a spirited campaign for recognition in the new party's top decision-making structures.

Women and youth units – assemblies as we called them in the MDC – were elected after the main congress, separately, and in fierce contests. In the end, a fearless student leader, Nelson Chamisa, took charge of the youth, while blistering orator and trade unionist Lucia Matibenga became the founder-chairperson of the women's assembly.

The morning after our Chitungwiza congress, I awoke later than usual having spent the night starry-eyed, thinking about the road ahead. The referendum on the draft constitution, along with parliamentary elections, was a few weeks away. We did not even have candidates and nor had we thought through the selection process.

I dreaded the thought that Zanu PF had a perfect and experienced infiltration machine. Edgar Tekere's Zimbabwe Unity Movement (ZUM) had suffered heavily in the 1990 election when nearly 30 of his parliamentary candidates dropped out of the race a few days before polling under a heavy Zanu PF coercive influence. I saw these candidates blurt out their regrets on prime time television news. It was like a circus. Their public retractions destroyed the fighting spirit of ZUM supporters as Mugabe, assisted by a partisan and docile media, watched Tekere's candidates shout on national television: 'After serious thought, I have now seen the light! Zanu PF is my home. I have dropped ZUM. Please forgive me ...'

How would we fare against the ruling party's machine?

I began to think seriously about the calibre of men and women I could field as candidates, how we would select them and go through their political credentials.

When Justice Chidyausiku delivered the government commission's draft constitutional proposals to Mugabe at the end of November 1999, our head of state was unhappy with what he found there. He unilaterally amended the findings.

Despite being hand-picked to serve Mugabe's expectations, I later heard an unconfirmed report that the commission proposed that he should step down and become a 'ceremonial president', with power passing to an elected prime minister. The same report, from a fairly reliable source, indicated that at a secret meeting between the presiding judge and Zanu PF this upsetting clause was deleted. Mugabe also added a clause allowing the government to seize land held by white farmers, with the provision that the British government should pay compensation. He saw the nationalisation of land as a priority. He further ordered the deletion of, or wholesale amendment to, other clauses which struck at the heart of the people's aspirations. Mugabe accused Britain of hypocrisy for reneging on its Lancaster House commitment to pay for the land required for resettlement. While people had raised land reform as important, it ranked low in their hierarchy of urgent needs.

By tampering with the recorded views of the people in the original draft, Mugabe further alienated himself from the national feeling. People felt short-changed and decided to show him that this was unacceptable. In the new party and in the NCA, we shared this view and the information war intensified.

We waited anxiously for 12 February 2000, the referendum day. Many voters would choose not to go to the polls as a way of protest, so the turnout was low. Nevertheless the result was a rejection of the proposed constitution. There were wild scenes of jubilation as the results began to come in. Mugabe had lost. He had totally misread the mood of Zimbabweans, thinking that every person was crying out for a piece of land.

As the MDC, our interests were aligned with those of civil society around common national grievances – how the state was run outside the rule of law and the economy mismanaged. We claimed 54 per cent of the vote, forcing Mugabe to admit defeat for the first time in his political career. Given our inexperience in politics, we failed to see the impact of this rejection on a ruthless dictator – in power for two decades – whose reaction to the national verdict would be both callous and savage.

To Mugabe the loss was a loud wake-up call. Voters had seen the constitutional review process and its result as something akin to a verdict or referendum on Mugabe's rule. The debate around the constitutional proposals was for many a side issue. In the end, all the political excitement and the fuss about the hearings had not been about the technical process of redrawing the national constitution: it was whether or not the people supported the government. Realising this, Mugabe panicked. So did his party. They could not countenance that at the ripe and experienced age of 37 Zanu PF might be destined to go the same way as UNIP in Zambia and the MCP in Malawi. Surely impressive fighting spirit during the colonial era gave it the right to govern indefinitely?

To console himself for the defeat, Mugabe blamed white Zimbabweans and vowed to deal with them mercilessly. He refused to accept that his black kith and kin had turned their backs on him.

I was convinced that Mugabe's days were now numbered. Given Zanu PF's plunder of Zimbabwe's resources, the nepotism of its ruling elite, the fact that they had turned their backs on the poor, and the stifling of growth, Mugabe was surely on the way out. During two decades of independence we had witnessed only ornamental political challenges from a weak opposition. This, despite serious human rights abuses; genocide in Matabeleland and Midlands where the simmering conflict remained unresolved; the foolhardy and costly intervention in the Congo that led to the looting of that country; and many other political obscenities.

Mugabe and his associates quickly retreated, regrouped and charged furiously at the entire nation. Not unexpectedly, our victory celebrations were short-lived. By publicly humiliating Mugabe, we probably made a mistake. With the benefit of hindsight, we could have handled our opposition to constitutional reform and the referendum campaign with greater care and political sensitivity to avoid a result that spawned more of a curse than a blessing. We should have carefully examined the 'morning after', thought through the scenarios, and prepared fully for the consequences.

My analysis of this is that if we had accepted that draft constitution and kept cool heads, Mugabe would have been out of power within a much shorter time. I totally believe this. We could have saved ourselves ten years of political chaos, economic havoc and a hazardous struggle to achieve democracy. Within a short space of time, circumstances would have forced Mugabe to accept what SADC and Zimbabweans finally pushed him to do after losing the presidential election in March 2008. He would have worked out an exit strategy fairly early on.

All indications showed that he was already tired; he had lost control of Zanu PF and he had limited options. If we had accepted the draft, chances were that we could have had elections in March or April 2000 and would have avoided the violence and bloodletting with which we were doomed to live for a long time to come. The chaotic invasion of commercial farmlands might have been averted along with the disruption of commercial agriculture.

We could have achieved the transfer of power in a much more clear-cut and orderly fashion than what we eventually had to go through on the way to the compromises of the Government of National Unity. We could have lulled the old man until the parliamentary election – due then in a few weeks – had taken place. In that election a landslide victory for us was on the cards, with so much popular support that rigging would have been impossible.

We had muscled together a formidable alliance from all over Zimbabwe, across class, race, ancestry and social location. Even when Mugabe behaved like a rabid animal, taking a rough bite at anything that moved in the opposite direction, if we had given him an affirmative vote, he would not have decided to burn down Zimbabwe for his political survival.

We had failed to read the political temperature correctly.

The MDC became overexcited about the possible defeat of a once mighty monolith. We convinced ourselves that our slogan for change – Chinja! – would bring about the reality. The new generation had almost seized the deck of the ship of state and saw themselves on the captain's bridge manning the tiller. Instead of looking at our popular approval in strategic terms, we were consumed by the feeling that we could wipe out Mugabe and his party in the forthcoming parliamentary polls and in the 2002 presidential election. We were naive to assume the situation would remain normal and unchanged and that Mugabe would never sink the entire nation into a sewer for the sake of power.

With the illusion of a clear victory in the coming parliamentary election, again we failed to see a difference between winning an election in a dictator's territory and assuming political power. Were Mugabe and Zanu PF ready to give up power at that stage? No. Mugabe was not. Nor were his fanatical and corrupt supporters who ran the key institutions of state.

Mugabe was not prepared to negotiate. Refusal to talk to those he perceived as enemies was a widely recorded weakness of character ever since he had entered Zimbabwean politics. He never saw value in negotiations as a mechanism to end a disagreement. His peers and former African diplomats speak of hard times whenever they proposed talks to resolve the Rhodesian crisis in the 1970s. In almost all the recorded cases, Mugabe had to be threatened, blackmailed and eventually forced to accept dialogue of any kind. During his political career, he had developed a very thick skin that hardened him against humane, sensible and carefully managed conflict resolution.

Mugabe lost numerous opportunities to seek ways to talk to anyone he viewed as an opponent. He would quickly slide into a trance and veer off the topic, as I was to learn in my personal dealings with him. In the MDC's case, he rushed to pronounce the mantra that we were puppets of colonialism and sources of evil within the body politic, intending nothing other than the ruin of liberation's legacy and the destruction of Zimbabwe's sovereignty.

As if he held the monopoly on the concept of national interest and patriotism, Mugabe saw us as vassals trying to reverse the gains of the liberation struggle. It was nonsense. With this attitude, it was fairly easy for political criminals to manipulate him – which is exactly what happened after our referendum 2000 victory. Zanu PF was dead; it had created a vacuum. No wonder thugs, opportunists, rogue elements in the military and the security establishment, and murderers wormed their way into the political fray with ease.

CHAPTER THIRTEEN

LAND, VOTES, FOOD

The loss of the referendum was so shattering to Mugabe and Zanu PF that they marshalled all available resources to thwart a repeat of the same result. Using a lethal combination of war veterans, thieves, police, military, officials and greedy Zanu PF politicians, Mugabe went out of his way to reverse the people's gain. In March 2000 the military launched what it called *Operation Tsuro* (Operation Rabbit). Tellingly, he turned to the Joint Operations Command (JOC), a relic of the Rhodesian Security Forces but now under a new command, to coordinate Operation Tsuro. The JOC included the armed forces, police, intelligence services and even the war veterans, now suddenly elevated to conflate the councils of state.

The JOC assigned the forces at its disposal to various parts of the country to seek out and punish opposition communities and individuals.[1] I learnt later that the work involved about 2 000 war veterans, 1 000 soldiers of the highly partisan 5th Brigade, 300 CIO officers, an undisclosed number of civilian informers, 500 police officers and close to 7 000 Zanu PF volunteers, mainly from the party's militias – all with a single objective: to mete out violence on the opposition in order to bring about our annihilation.

Whites, especially commercial farmers, along with their farm workers, opposition party activists and civil servants in the rural areas, teachers and nurses, were targeted for attacks. Suddenly, the entire country was smoking with the fires of hell and became a war zone overnight.

Operation Tsuro sought to drive whites off their farms; to force the peasants to 'fall in love' with Zanu PF; and to assault, harass and even kill known and suspected MDC officials and supporters. Farm workers on commercial farms were specially targeted. The combined operation at first confused the police and some influential Zanu PF politicians. It took time to bend the security forces to Mugabe's will and to co-opt some senior officials, including vice-president Joseph Msika, into the cycle of violence. They tried to protect white farmers and called for alternatives to the violent land takeovers.

The international community needed to support land redistribution, but not Mugabe's version of it. His main motive was not black empowerment (except to feather the nests of the ruling elite). It was not even revenge against whites. One of the primary aims was to deal with the farm worker threat to Zanu PF in elections, as I shall explain. Land reform was used to justify a concerted campaign against political opponents and it involved murder, assault, torture and the destruction of property.[2] To give the whole exercise a gloss of legal authority, in May 2000 parliament passed the Rural Land Occupiers (Protection from Eviction) Act which blocked legal action to evict persons illegally occupying land in anticipation of being resettled by the land-acquiring authorities.

At the beginning, however, things did not always go smoothly for the invaders. There were reported skirmishes between certain police units and the land invaders. One such encounter took place in the farming district of Mvurwi at the end of May when police openly clashed with the invaders, leading to the death of a war veteran.

The trouble erupted after war veterans stormed the police station to force the release of 12 of their colleagues who had been arrested for violent behaviour. In the melee, 13 war veterans were injured. Both the reluctant politicians and the police officers later joined in the chaos after receiving official instructions from Mugabe to stay out of what he called the people's peaceful demonstrations for their ancestral land. He promised them their own pieces of land and looted equipment.

In Harare's central business district, war veterans and Zanu PF supporters moved around the streets with war drums, axes, spears, machetes and long, sharp hunting knives. They grouped at their offices and street corners in assorted party regalia, awaiting deployment into white-owned commercial farms.

Under the direction of armed military and secret service men, they were ferried in party and government vehicles to targeted areas in full sight of the police. As their convoys snaked out of the city every morning, the apprentice invaders bellowed war slogans and chants, bunching their tightly clenched fists in a frenzy that scared generally peace-loving and reserved Zimbabweans.

The pace at which Zimbabwe was thrown into confusion was rapid and the lawlessness so sweeping that it is difficult to describe the pandemonium to anyone who did not actually witness it. A cacophony of sounds blared in the previously tranquil commercial farmlands in scenes akin to medieval European battles – only this time there were no knights in armour, just ragged party men in colourful regalia. The pattern mutated, fast cascading into the communal lands. There, villagers were forcibly driven from their homes to nearby commercial farms to claim their plot of prime land before it was too late.

White farmers, besieged and terrorised, found no one to protect them. With their traditional two-way radios, mobile phones and cameras, white farmers were talking all the time: to themselves, to the CFU, to their families and friends, to the police, to us in the MDC. Nobody could help! Those with a history of bad labour relations on their farms suffered doubly: some of their workers instantly turned against them, siding with the invaders.

Political swindlers, extortionists and Zanu PF aligned criminals claimed their space on farm carts, promising trembling white farmers protection in exchange for hefty sums of money. I heard of shocking cases of blackmail almost daily throughout the year 2000. Many whites were lulled into a sense of false security in exchange for loyalty to Zanu PF. Not even our peri-urban farmers, the main horticultural supply line for our major cities, were spared. Zanu PF swung into action, with the military in tow, staking their claims on residential plots.

Behind the marauding bands of looters were food vendors, feeding urban residents who joined the queue for newly acquired vegetable gardens. Amateur signwriters cashed in too, charging a fee for putting up a scrap metal plate with a new stand owner's name and address.

Harare airport and the area around the runway was divided into claims and dished out to grateful desperadoes. Leading Zanu PF officials, seeing an opportunity for quick money, charged the homeless for their new finds. At day's end, sacks full of cash were seen around beer stores. War veterans and all sorts of crude crooks had a wonderful time. Normally reticent, conservative middle-class professionals were psychologically energised and swung into action.

The Ministry of Agriculture called for applications from aspiring black commercial farmers who were lured into believing that they would be treated specially, and with respect. One only needed to collect an application form, fill it out and attach a projected cash-flow statement. Boom! That was it. You qualified for a commercial farm. A Zanu PF membership card was an added advantage. Bookkeepers and typists recorded a roaring trade preparing dud and imaginary project proposals and cash-flow projections; so did photocopier owners and commissioners of oaths as they assisted with document certification and replicas.

For almost three weeks, I was surprised to see the names of supposed beneficiaries – including many luminaries I knew well – published in state newspapers. They drove their shiny vehicles into nowhere; some even began to fight over farm houses.

After the election, they were told to wait and they gave up when they saw that they had been duped into voting for Zanu PF through this vote-catching tactic.

All of these developments, supported by Mugabe's blazing and uncompromising speeches, disturbed me deeply. The looming dangers were obvious. The CFU, as the quasi-political voice of white farmers, reacted swiftly. It was clear through their frantic responses that the only recourse they had was the law – and they filed, and filed, and filed papers and complaints with the courts, winning at every turn – but still getting no respite. Mugabe refused to budge. His regime ignored the verdicts and court orders.

It was as if the head of the family had decided to sell the family silver and throw away the family savings. Three months into Operation Tsuro, Zimbabweans were feeling the heat. Close to a thousand white farmers were driven off their land; 135 opposition supporters – mainly from the MDC – had been killed and thousands of ordinary villagers were displaced from their rural homes. Looking back, there was probably no way what happened could have been avoided, given Zanu PF's desire to destroy the MDC at any cost.

Marondera farmer Iain Kay is lucky to be alive today. He was badly injured after long hours of beatings and only escaped by swimming – which none of his Zanu PF captors could do – across his farm dam to safety. Kay's neighbour, Macheke farmer David Stevens and his supervisor Julius Andoche were besieged, beaten and taken to Murehwa, where they were shot dead.[3]

Stevens's neighbours, who tried to rescue the pair, were overpowered and severely assaulted before being dumped in the bush. Surprisingly, before their ordeal they sought sanctuary at Murehwa police station. They were dragged out of the police station, in full view of senior police officers, and taken to a nearby thicket where they were beaten. Stevens's farm – the tobacco warehouses and barns, his home, and the workers' quarters – was set alight. His murder led to an exodus from the prime farming lands of Virginia, Macheke, Goromonzi, Murehwa, Hwedza, Imire, Igava and Marondera.

Across the country in Nyamandlovu near Bulawayo, state agents and war veterans placed rancher Martin Olds under siege for several hours on the morning of 18 April. Police ignored calls for help from Olds, a known MDC sympathiser. When his neighbours tried to rescue him, the police physically blocked their entry to the farm. Olds's assailants shot and killed him before burning down his homestead. The police had set up a traffic checkpoint near the farm and turned away traffic, including an ambulance that had responded to his call for help during his last moments.

What were we to make of this devil's carnival? A number of reasons – if you could call them that – presented themselves. They were not reasons so much as rationales to carry out plunder. Now that it was clear Mugabe could be defeated in a national election, within the non-nationalist generation there were fights for supremacy among academics, young student leaders, trade unionists, civil society activists and business people. Opportunists of every kind surged into the gaping holes in the economy. The MDC was left reeling in disbelief but we knew we had to come up with an oppositional strategy to offer voters a stable and meaningful future.

To Mugabe, the argument for a redress of historical grievances sounded like a noble idea at home and in Africa: it portrayed Mugabe as a victim of a vast Western conspiracy; it covered up the real story of retribution and racial hatred and a desire to punish the nation for rejecting the state's plan in the February 2000 referendum.

I knew from our previous interaction with government officials that Mugabe was no longer interested in the land question. He believed he had done his bit. I know this very well because, in *Beyond ESAP*, we had raised the issue of land reform with all government departments and got no response. We failed to convince anybody, including Mugabe, that our dual economy was likely to present serious problems in the future. During the first decade of independence, Mugabe did something about land. But in the 1990s, he forgot about the peasants, cutting out choice plots and farms for his top officials. Hardly a thousand families were allocated land in the ten years beginning 1990.

Mugabe, who considered himself a scholar and a gentleman with a British knighthood, never wanted to upset or to destabilise the white community. The referendum result irked him so deeply, however, that he adopted a surprisingly hostile attitude towards whites. The land question was a facade. I doubted his sincerity, for I knew that his main target was the farm workers' vote.

From the last week in February 2000, Zimbabwe's politics became a matter of global interest. Africans in other countries saw what was happening and watched from a secure distance. Often bullied by Mugabe politically, Africa sympathised with his exaggerated plight and thought that he was a victim of colonialism. The West appeared more appalled by Mugabe's anti-white crusade than the fact that democracy in Zimbabwe was in the intensive care unit. It took Western countries a long time to understand the MDC. They were interested in the fate of white farmers, not the people's democratic struggle. So we really had no support from anywhere.

Despite our victory in the referendum, our party was still scattered, weak and disorganised. We lacked permanent structures; we were still to consolidate our support base, elect substantive grassroots leadership structures and mount a cogent national campaign against an experienced ruling party. We were in a bind, but we had committed ourselves to playing a political game and built a team for the purpose: either we entered the race or we perished.

With Zanu PF's newly oiled, violent machinery and political experience, it was never going to be possible for us to challenge their power on a broad front unless we could be sure of making a difference in the parliamentary election.

For long hours my mind circled around a range of demanding scenarios, sometimes sparking doubts, uncertainty and gloom. My salvation, as always, rested with the people who kept on urging my colleagues and me never to give up. Their solidarity and goodwill gave us the necessary courage and tenacity to soldier on.

In a national crisis one looks to thought-leaders for sound opinions and strategic guidance. There were academics who advised us and helped us chart the way forward, but others shamed themselves by climbing on Mugabe's bandwagon. I could see that the sources of rivalry were rooted in their college days. Those who failed to get into senior positions in the

MDC sought to fill in what they thought to be a political vacuum in a dying Zanu PF; they saw Zanu PF as a party lying comatose by the roadside and thought the time was right for them to pick it up and to continue with their college feuds – but now on a different terrain.

Jonathan Moyo, Ben Hlatshwayo and many others with a long history of fighting for change with us at the ZCTU and in civil society, opted to wade into the ranks of Zanu PF. They took up the fight against the MDC as advisers and technocrats. There were those who cautioned against taking Mugabe on in the current gruesome circumstances. At first I was in a dilemma. Should we go into such an election or should we stay away from it? But people kept pressing for the MDC to finish Mugabe off.

Campaigning was becoming impossible, especially in the rural areas. The level of violence was rising every minute. Yet we had no choice as we had jumped into the pool at the deep end. An election was the only available instrument for change. Either we were in, or we risked death.

Mugabe himself hesitated about calling for an immediate election. He postponed the polls to June 2000 in order to buy time and reorganise his campaign. At the same time, he quickly positioned himself in Africa, clamouring for help and sympathy by sending out an early warning signal that Zimbabwe's liberation heroes were under threat from recolonisation.

To Africa, Mugabe branded the MDC as a front for the Western world, a front for white colonialists. He painted us as a misguided cabal trying to undo Zimbabwe's liberation gains and its legacy as a champion of the black person's struggle against racism. So in Africa's eyes, we became instant reactionaries. Britain's response to Mugabe's actions was regrettable and unfortunate – and did not help us in the least. While trying to rescue the white farmers, London created an impression that the MDC was its vehicle for regime change.

Reports from Harare created hysteria and sensation in London. They focused on white farmers, crying out against what they saw as reverse racism and discrimination but did not highlight the general political violence against the black population. An attack on a white farmer was instant news. The impression left was that Mugabe must go, for the sake of white interests. As could be expected, this only made him dig in his heels further, and he made the most of the fact that the MDC was little featured in world media. With observers looking the other way, he targeted us.

It was ironic that in the MDC we strongly believed in the land redistribution exercise. Our founding manifesto clearly stated that we needed at least seven million hectares of former white-owned commercial farmland for the poor. We wanted an orderly land reform programme, part of a broad poverty alleviation thrust and economic advancement. Our policy was more radical than that of Zanu PF which initially targeted only five million hectares for redistribution.

Mugabe quickly reversed the position, took over our agenda, and now swept the entire country in search of land to be grabbed, reducing much valuable land to dead capital overnight. It did not matter to him if he lost white votes: the white vote was relatively insignificant; it remains so today. But white farms possessed a critical mass ready to make a difference in Zimbabwe. Removing one white farmer from his or her piece of land and turning it into a communal settlement was never the intended goal. Rather, the reasoning was to stop the MDC's chances of defeating Zanu PF in an election.

Of importance was the threat posed by the groundswell of support among the farm workers, who by that time numbered about half a million. With their families, this translated to almost a million votes. Zanu PF saw that. The party had realised that grinding poverty and the neglect of the rural areas had weakened its hold on the poor. Farm workers, together with our urban base, would tip the scales in our favour in an election. It became important that the farm worker vote be destabilised. Zanu PF knew that it was impossible to win an election without that constituency.

Through a ruthless 'scatter and disenfranchise' strategy, nearly a million voters were eventually dispersed, denied a vote or forced to vote for Zanu PF in return either for their lives or for a place to stay. The invasion of commercial farmland was not specifically aimed at whites although many were to think so. Nor was it for black empowerment. It aimed to smash, scatter and scuttle a potential MDC captive vote.

The war veterans used by Mugabe and Zanu PF to undertake this mission would realise the truth soon after the presidential election in

2002. The majority were kicked out and retreated back to the communal lands; back into poverty. They were used as cannon fodder for a political objective, what Zanu PF dubbed the *Retain Power Project*. No one in Africa would argue against attacks on colonialism or resolving the land question, so Zanu PF used its liberation credentials as a perfect cover for black-on-black oppression.

Africa has vivid memories of racial oppression. Race and historical inequality are still a burning issue, particularly in southern Africa. The roles played by the British, the French, the Germans, the Portuguese and the Belgians in sub-Saharan Africa raise heated emotions. History – especially distorted, patriotic history – often provides a rationale for instability, corruption, abuse and dictatorship. So when Britain criticised Mugabe, Africa thought it was wise, natural and logical to be on Mugabe's side.

London became incredibly paranoid about Mugabe, particularly the British press. On a business trip there I was asked what I wanted Britain to do. I told them to stay out; I said Zimbabweans had a right to fight over their mother's breast milk without any external interference. The British ignored me and vied to assume a front line position, much to the MDC's political disadvantage. British colonialism can never be justified, least by any black African. I warned British diplomats in Harare that by falling into Zanu PF's propaganda trap they were complicating our case – but my pleas fell on deaf ears.

I raised the subject with my colleagues on a number of occasions. The British, I argued, were about to muddle our case. The utterances of politicians Peter Hain and Tony Blair confused our message and made it impossible for us to market our case in Africa. We were talking about democracy; Mugabe was talking about patriotic history. We were talking about the rule of law; Mugabe was talking about colonial subjugation and the need for restitution for past wrongs.

Mugabe may not have had a resounding message for Zimbabweans, but he possessed the right propaganda tools and he used them to maximum effect. What was happening from South Africa and SADC's side? There was Thabo Mbeki watching the drama unfolding. He bothered little about the contagion of the dictatorship in the region – he was only interested in expanding South Africa's influence beyond its borders. As long as Mugabe was in charge and Zimbabwe was stable, an opposition party in Zimbabwe was an irritant to Pretoria's plans to turn the entire continent into a giant retail outlet for South Africa's economy.

As was the case in South Africa, Mbeki was of the opinion that opposition parties must accept being junior partners in government. The feeling was the same in Angola, in Mozambique, in Namibia and in many other African countries. Those nations with a different view preferred to stay quiet. To them, Mugabe was the neighbourhood bully – belligerent and capable of humiliating weaklings. He could easy attack nations as far afield as Uganda and Rwanda with a superior fighting machine.

The colonial struggle in Africa had died after Nelson Mandela's victory in 1994. The post-colonial struggles for pluralism and democracy took time to emerge from the era of the Cold War. Early challenges to one-party rule – such as those mounted by Zambia's Chiluba, Malawi's Chihana, the armed struggles of Laurent Kabila in the former Zaire and Afonso Dhlakama in Mozambique – were already history. So, when we came on board and expressed our vision for a democracy in Zimbabwe, our message made no sense and our views failed to resonate in Africa. Yet we represented the cause of good governance and our strategy was to gain power peacefully through the ballot box. Could they not see that?

Political stability builds confidence; confidence is often the bedrock of national prosperity. There was no way Zimbabwe was ever going to recover from the political crisis without an election. There was a serious political dispute; it had to be resolved by all our people through a clean ballot. Despite the signs of an extremely dangerous storm ahead, I knew we had to plunge in and swim to the shore, to freedom.

Freedom on its own could not save the country from catastrophe. We needed a comprehensive redevelopment plan and a government with the political will to implement it.

Starvation now stalked the rural areas. What convinced me more than ever that Zimbabwe was crying out for relief were the pathetic scenes

I witnessed whenever I visited the villages and subsistence farms where the majority of Zimbabweans lived. There is nothing more heart-rending to a parent than seeing one's children crying with hunger when one is genuinely unable to help. Following his election setbacks, Mugabe ordered a food blockade on all opposition supporters in the rural areas at a time when food shortages were beginning to pinch hard. Food sanctions were meant to starve people into submission. State agencies told villagers to join Zanu PF or risk starvation.

Each time I visited a rural area I faced numerous distressing pleas for food. These encounters were both harrowing and infuriating. Seeing their suffering for myself was enough to spark angry thoughts, but to react recklessly would undermine the MDC's steadfast commitment to winning power peacefully at the ballot box.

The elections, however, were rigged, so we had to resort to the courts for justice. And there the problem was – as a study by the Solidarity Peace Trust in March 2005 found – that 'freedom of election has been consistently subverted in Zimbabwe with the complicity of the judiciary'.[4]

The use of food as a political tool was first tried and tested during the Gukurahundi era in the 1980s in Matabeleland South. Taking advantage of three consecutive years of drought, Mugabe inflicted punishment on the community by preventing all movement of food into and around the region. Drought relief was stopped and stores closed. Almost no one was allowed in or out of the region to buy food and private food supplies were destroyed. Partisan state officials, largely in the form of the 5th Brigade, actively punished those villagers who shared food with starving neighbours, according to several witness accounts captured and published in the CCJP/LRF report of 1997.[5]

The physical and psychological effects of the food embargo were profound and would not soon be forgotten. Now, heading towards the 2002 presidential elections, a new food embargo was imposed. The threat of famine was spreading throughout southern African due to several years of severe drought, but in Zimbabwe the situation was made far worse.

By 2002 the World Food Programme estimated that nearly half the country's 12.5 million people would need food assistance.[6] The violent land seizures carried out in Operation Tsuro resulted in an alarming fall in commercial food production. Food shortages were now accentuated by deliberate moves to direct food to Zanu PF supporters and away from potential opposition strongholds. While many agency staff detested the practice, they found little room to manoeuvre as they were constantly under surveillance from the CIO, Zanu PF and war veterans.

Sensing danger, the MDC sourced maize donations abroad but when the grain arrived at the Beitbridge border post from South Africa, Mugabe took the gift and gave it to his supporters. This time the strategy covered the whole country. Against this background, I visited the United States and Europe in July 2001 to promote the MDC and inform foreign leaders about our goals and strategies. I sought pledges to provide independent observers for the following year's elections.[7]

Once the people had tasted the MDC's first victories in the 2000 elections, we had momentum for further challenges. We set about selecting the right candidates. We were on course, whether Africa and the world understood us or not. We were determined to change Zimbabwe's face.

ENDNOTES

1   Chitiyo, Knox & Rupiya, Martin (2005). 'Tracking Zimbabwe's political history: The Zimbabwe Defence Force from 1980-2005.' In: Rupiya, Martin (ed.), *Evolutions and Revolutions: A Contemporary History of Militaries in Southern Africa.* Institute for Security Studies www.issafrica.org

2   'Politically motivated violence in Zimbabwe 2000-2001: A report on the campaign of political repression conducted by the Zimbabwean Government under the guise of carrying out land reform.' Human Rights Forum, Harare, August 2001 http://www.hrforumzim.com/evmp/evmpreports/polmotviol0108/polviol0108j.htm

3   Smith, Ian Douglas (2008). *Bitter Harvest: Zimbabwe and the Aftermath of its Independence.* London, John Blake Publishing, p430

4   Solidarity Peace Trust (March 2005). *The Role of the Judiciary in Denying the Will of the Zimbabwe Electorate since 2000,* p36 http://www.solidaritypeacetrust.org/download/report-files/subverting_justice.pdf

5   CCJP/LRF (2008). *Gukurahundi in Zimbabwe: A Report on the Disturbances in Matabeleland and the Midlands, 1980-1988*. Columbia University Press

6   'Mugabe tells farmers to down tools: Order given to abandon wheat crops in hungry Zimbabwe'. *The Guardian*, 25 June 2001 http://www.guardian.co.uk/world/2002/jun/25/zimbabwe.andrewmeldrum

7   'Zimbabwe: US, Europe Promise Election Monitors'. 6 July 2001 allafrica. com news http://allafrica.com/stories/20010706175.html

CHAPTER FOURTEEN

PRESIDENT TSVANGIRAI?

'"Tsvangison" will never rule this country,' Mugabe told radio listeners in April 2000 ahead of the June elections. Derisively, he nicknamed me 'Tsvangison' in a forlorn attempt to prove to the voters that I was a stooge of the whites. Suddenly Tsvangirai was no longer a minor irritant but the man that the nation had to fear. Mugabe assured the nation that I would never be allowed to take power:

> 'Tsvangison' will never rule this country. Not in my lifetime or even after I die. My ghost will certainly come after him and all of you if you allow that to happen. He is a dreamer, who after his wife sucks his ears while in his sleep, he thinks he can take over Zimbabwe as President. Never, ever ... The MDC is a Rhodesian puppet; a front for Britain. Zimbabwe will never be a colony again.[1]

From April, Mugabe raised the frequency, volume and rhythm of his threats, talking like his predecessor, Rhodesian leader Ian Smith, during the liberation war. Smith had vowed that there would never be majority rule in Rhodesia in a thousand years. Mugabe put it differently, but with the same meaning nevertheless.

Changing my name to sound non-Zimbabwean was a deliberate smear on my patriotism. Mugabe further referred to me as a white man's 'tea boy', an uneducated fool, a deserter from the liberation struggle, and anything else he thought might be useful in denigrating my person. If I had tried to do the same in reply, the police would immediately have pounced on me for lowering the public esteem of a sitting state president, an offence that could attract a jail term under Zimbabwean law.

Politically motivated violence was now the norm. From the time that Mugabe and Zanu PF commenced Operation Tsuro to seize white farmland, a brutal campaign unfolded in which violence was used extensively against defenceless opposition supporters.[2]

When the election campaign began, I had been president of the MDC for barely a month. For three months, and as the June election date drew closer, I could see my world closing in on me. I saw my prospects and misfortunes clashing like doves and hawks in the sky. I had taken on too much, I thought. I needed an urgent makeover: from an innocent, cushioned role as leader of the labour movement to that of a state actor in waiting and, perhaps, the future president of Zimbabwe.

Mugabe now knew he faced a personal challenge from me and he hit back in a frenzy. I began to think that I could easily have stayed on as leader of the ZCTU and avoided this situation for myself. My dramatic rise to political office brought with it a whole new set of demands – and dangers – about which I felt both excited and terrified.

In June 2000, the MDC would come close to winning a majority of the elected seats in parliament and may well have done so had the election been free and fair. The MDC took 57 of the 120 elected seats while Zanu PF took 63. In October 2000, Mugabe issued a decree granting a general amnesty for politically motivated crimes that occurred between 1 January and 31 July 2000. The pattern of threats, belittlement and brutality was now well established and would continue against the MDC and commercial farmers in the run-up to the presidential election in March 2002. At that point, Mugabe knew there was a real possibility that President Tsvangirai could unseat him.

I never thought Mugabe would go as far as to allow innocent peasants to be killed as part of an election campaign. I misled myself into believing that after 20 years in office, and with his advanced age and stature as a founding political figure of modern-day Zimbabwe, he would show restraint, decorum and respect for the people. But I had no experience of politics in a virtual war zone. I would have to learn – and fast.

I had long been a keen follower of politics. I knew about the fate of opposition politicians in Zimbabwe, including Kombayi's near-death encounter with the CIO in the 1990 election campaign – and after the MDC's good performance in the February 2000 referendum, I felt that in some ways the whole national burden was now on me – and this responsibility had a direct impact on me and my family.

Amai Ed and my young children had to adjust to the new reality. We had to be constantly on the alert. We had to accept that I could easily, very easily, lose my life in unexplained circumstances. The CIO was notorious for that. Even among the few in the MDC with a political background, none dared to counsel or make suggestions on how a potential first family should behave or protect itself. Nobody offered to train us, nor did we have the resources to seek professional advice. At a family level, we were completely vulnerable: everybody around me or linked to the Tsvangirai name was suddenly exposed. The young MDC simply stared at me; the people of Zimbabwe expected a solution from me; the world was sizing me up.

Shifting from the leadership of a tiny interest group to dealing with an entire nation is no mean task. One needs to take a huge leap in almost all spheres of one's life. Everywhere people would ask themselves: Can we invest in this person and in this party? I knew I had built a brand as a trade unionist, but that was wholly insufficient for the new office. The MDC had still to make its mark independent of the perception that the referendum result was a mere protest at Mugabe's overstaying his welcome as leader of the country.

My understanding of my surroundings, my personality and disposition, behaviour and attitude, public interaction and social outlook all needed a radical facelift. And time was never on my side. Mugabe is an extremely rough political player, a cunning pugilist, well trained for any bout with a newcomer to the ring. He invents his own rules and changes the pace of the game at will – to a point where he can even attack the referee and the spectators while fighting his enemy – totally without scruple or shame. All Mugabe wants is a self-fulfilling fallacy that he has won.

With my four months' experience as a politician, I was taking on a shrewd academic, a former guerrilla leader and sitting president with a 40-year political record behind him. Mugabe had been in the game since I was a seven-year-old rural kid. Experience may be the best teacher, but inexperience can be fatal.

Zanu PF and the state employed political scientists, psychologists, strategic planners, political schemers, sociologists, and military and security experts. I relied on a few, one could say, enthusiasts and optimists for advice and direction. Gandi Mudzingwa, my personal aide, was a labour economist who had studied in the Soviet Union. Although he came from an illustrious family with an impeccable history of colonial resistance, he had his own limitations and inexperience in politics.

Even at a very mundane, individual level I had to rethink and restructure my lifestyle. Although I was 47, I was never a consistent wearer of business suits. As a factory worker, a miner and a trade unionist, I probably had one business suit which I rarely wore. I remember the outfit as a cheap, formal suit which I turned to on those rare occasions when I attended the odd wedding or a memorial service at a church. The kind of work I was in and my circle of friends generally allowed for casual, informal clothing.

My favourite jacket I got by accident – it is a story that I like to tell. I was sipping a cold Castle lager with a friend at our local Feathers Hotel in Mabelreign, Harare, one Saturday afternoon when I told the friend, a fellow trade unionist, about a family ritual down in Buhera which would involve the slaughtering of an animal, traditional brews and a reunion. He suggested I bring back the hide of the old ox, from which he, a member of the Leather and Allied Workers' Union, would try to make a jacket for me. I took him up on his offer.

After Gatooma or Jamburutu – I think one of those was the name of the slaughtered old ox – was skinned I demanded the hide, much to the chagrin of an old village friend who earned a small income through the sale of hides and skins. I folded it neatly, shoved it in an old hessian bag and threw it in the back of my old Peugeot 504.

By the time I met my friend three days later, Gatooma's skin had begun to emit an unpleasant, pungent smell. He quickly took it and disappeared – and about two weeks later he brought me a shiny black leather jacket – from old ox Gatooma!

I was amazed! After thanking him and trying it on, I immediately fell in love with it. By the time we parted, I was in my neatly ironed jeans and a fresh leather skin. As I had worked underground at the Bindura mine, I found comfort in the steel-toed miners' work boot. My favourite colour was black. My leather jacket and work boots became my favourite attire – indeed, my signature garb which made me instantly recognisable – and as I wore them to important workers' meetings, during labour forums and open discussions they almost became part of me.

I liked to go out to meet and chat with friends and have a drink with them in public places. But now a casual drink at the local pub or a Sunday soccer match at the stadium required planning and security. It had been my style to show up unannounced at factories for casual chats with workers. It was the same with family, friends and colleagues: my surprise visits usually turned into social occasions. Now I needed a new form of personal time management and an appointments schedule.

I was left with very little time for genuine social interaction. I could hardly take a walk to the nearby shops, or stroll around a vegetable marketplace or go to a township auction floor looking for odds and ends as I used to do. I would be mobbed – welcomed or taunted. My presence could disrupt normal business. I retreated to my tiny home in the lower-middle class suburb of Ashdown Park, Harare.

I learnt that as a leader I had to be conscious of my entry point in any debate with friends and strangers alike; how serious I had to be or not; how to express my vision, privately and publicly; even when to smile. Leadership requires no flattery, no iron fist, no self-delusion; but plenty of respect for difference and careful weighing up of personalities. One has to accord people a hearing; adjust to their space. There were many times that I had to bite my tongue and suppress my anger. Leadership is a tough call. Be prepared for public humiliation, provocation and derision, even without having done anything to attract such behaviour!

One of my early mistakes was a public statement saying that Mugabe should go peacefully or risk facing a violent uprising. The message received a roaring response from a politically charged and enthusiastic audience. But it was a gaffe, the consequences of which hounded me for a long time. As I shall explain later, I was prosecuted for it, taking much of my time away from productive party work. The other glaring mistake I made led to another long, grinding treason trial. I was quoted in a recorded conversation saying some things casually, without the necessary careful political consideration.

I was naive enough to believe that we could change Zimbabwean politics simply through an election, but we should not have expected fairness. The Electoral Supervisory Commission (ESC) was staffed with retired and serving army officers, with Colonel Sobusa Gula-Ndebele appointed to ensure that Mugabe always had the upper hand.

Changing the power balance in Africa can never be a leisurely stroll in a tropical garden. African power transfers are complex processes because of history, corruption, dictatorships and outright national bungling. The generation of nationalists who fought for Africa's independence saw itself as ordained to remain in power till death and were unkind to any challenge, even from their own children.

Inside the family, Amai Edwin literally took over the dual role of father and mother. She, too, was thrown into a completely new world without any warning or training. She was an uncomplicated mother and an extremely honest spouse, a devout Christian, and a consummate listener and personal adviser. After my election, Amai Ed (as Susan was known in Zimbabwean public life) suddenly found herself hosting diplomats, senior politicians, business people, political activists and political crooks alike. I knew she needed training, but both the MDC and I failed her.

She too learnt the hard way, weaving her way through clothing colour combinations and making selections of appropriate attire for special occasions. There is a social discipline I call 'dining room dynamics' which goes together with diplomacy and the etiquette of wining and dining. It combines preparing after-dinner desserts with engaging in meaningful – as well as meaningless – conversation, as is expected from a high-class host. It was difficult, but there was only one way to go: learn on the job.

Our home was open to endless numbers of visitors. People thought they could just pass by to say hello, only to stay into the wee hours of the morning engaging in idle chat. Many meant well though a few became overbearing, offering all kinds of unworkable advice and ideas. Some thought we had lots of money and were quick to make this or that request for us to endorse their not-so-honest ventures, in writing, to potential donors. We saw through all of this fairly early and often referred them to the office where my colleagues had time to think through the issues before acting on them. Many were turned down.

When visitors pitched up unannounced, Amai Ed would lift her well-built, lanky frame and dash to the kitchen, initially to make a cup of tea, but often ending up preparing a full meal. Most times there was no money; no food, no drinks, no tea leaves, no sugar or salt. Amai Ed would whisper into my ear for some cash, and if I had nothing – as was usually the case – she would wander into the garden, pluck some vegetable leaves, and cook a large pot of *sadza*, a Zimbabwean staple, a thick maize porridge, normally taken with sour milk, meat or vegetable stew.

I said that the party and I failed Amai Ed. It is true. I knew the party well: we were cash strapped. I could not even press for a regular allowance or support for entertainment. We lived off my brothers, friends and well-wishers whose support was erratic and unpredictable. After I left the ZCTU, we never had money in the house. Our MDC financial management system was an extremely strict and complicated one. Only the national treasurer, the secretary and his deputy had access to our coffers and bank accounts. They only showed me the bank statements, usually after we had exhausted everything. I was nowhere near party funds or bank accounts – a situation some in the national executive committee felt was untenable. The reasoning, however, was that I should never allow myself to taint my reputation over money disputes, as had been the case with previous opposition parties whose leaders ended up suing each other in courts over resource distribution and money matters.

Amai Ed made numerous mistakes because of the absence of an assistant or other external support. At a very simple level, sometimes she failed to guess visitors' consumption patterns or hunger levels and ended up with excessive leftovers. She soon learnt how to turn left-over *sadza* into *mahewu*, a sweet traditional brew, with which she could fill the glasses of the next day's callers.

The visitors were of all kinds: traditional and faith healers, pastors, church members and their friends, family members and friends, party activists, avid political and ordinary gossips, general proximity seekers and political prostitutes, seasoned politicians, local and foreign journalists, business people, the poor and the vulnerable, the disabled, traditionalists, gays and lesbians, villagers, vendors, and the merely curious. In time, Amai Ed learnt to be careful what she said, when to say it and even why, because she could easily be misquoted by those seeking opportunistic mileage from their presence in our home.

Before her new role, Amai Ed worked hard to supplement the family income. Using two small sewing and knitting machines, she produced thousands of rural school and church uniforms and low-end of the market jerseys. When business picked up after a number of years, she dropped the school uniform side and concentrated on knitting jerseys, developing unique styles that found their way to the flea markets of Pretoria and Johannesburg. She travelled often to South Africa with cases full of jerseys for sale. As a family we found the extra income particularly welcome, for it contributed to the children's welfare and freed me to concentrate on my trade union work which, as always, paid miserably.

After my election as party leader, the increasing numbers of visitors interfered with the knitting business and she engaged a helper. But because she was now paying little attention to the business, the helper often dipped her fingers into the family cash box, licking out the little that was available. Even worse: she sometimes helped herself to either the yarn or the finished jerseys for side-marketing and sales.

Amai Ed's schedule now included preparing food for and visiting arrested activists at police stations, jails and remand prisons. She realised too late that her business was making serious losses. She then asked her sister Leah to supervise the operation, for the income was vital to our family's day-to-day survival. Continuing with the cross-border trips to South Africa, Leah broadened Amai Ed's market to cover our rural areas and farming communities. In no time, wherever I went, I saw our supporters clad in what became known as 'Amai Tsvangirai jerseys' – in a myriad of colours and zigzagging stripes, which became her distinctive label.

When the pressure on Amai Ed proved too much – and compounded by our customary lack of resources – I raised the issue with the MDC. With the little cash I received, I decided to buy a small, decades-old jalopy to help Amai Ed get around. Like all used cars in Zimbabwe, the vehicle was very old, rickety and unreliable. Before I could even get the car repaired, the news leaked to the state media that I had bought Amai Ed a vehicle as a birthday present using money from the British government through its funding to the MDC. The news caused the family and me extreme embarrassment.

The story was that I was getting millions of dollars from London as a British puppet. In any normal society, a party worker at the level of Amai Ed might have received a car and no one would make an issue of it. But in Zimbabwe, where the majority were extremely poor, a car as a birthday present is normally associated with the rich. I towed the battered vehicle away from our home and gave it to Edith Munyaka, my secretary.

The state-controlled media was particularly ruthless towards my family and me. It mounted a vicious disinformation war, using the same pattern the

Rhodesians applied against the nationalists during the liberation war. In Smith's Rhodesia, the state and the people were always at loggerheads on the availability of objective information. At the time, black Zimbabweans developed their own networks and succeeded as a nation in defeating Rhodesia's propaganda and a battery of legislative impediments designed to thwart the smooth flow of unbiased information.[3,4]

After their loss in the 2000 referendum, Zanu PF and Mugabe adopted the Rhodesian information management style against its critics, the MDC and me. For example, when a demonstration organised by a civil society was violently disrupted by the police and war veterans on 1 April 2000, cabinet ministers, diplomats, war veterans and Zanu PF officials blamed the protesters and tried to justify the attacks. They also blamed the MDC, accusing us of organising the protests.

The Herald and state radio and television never attempted to disguise their bias as they were now under much stricter and more direct control of the state. Chen Chimutengwende, the information minister, surprised us further with a wild allegation that commercial farmers had cached large quantities of munitions on their properties, supposedly under the guidance of the MDC and me for a violent takeover of the government. Stories like that damaged the credibility of the public media and propelled *The Daily News* into a market leader's position, almost overnight. Bornwell Chakaodza, *The Herald*'s editor, had totally lost control of the publication.

The competition between *The Herald* and *The Daily News* peaked and the state realised that official media were fast losing credibility as a source of public information. As *The Daily News* started to assume a reputation as the newspaper of record through its persistent and courageous reports, this seemed to push Jonathan Moyo and Zanu PF to the wall. They took a bizarre, barbaric step against *The Daily News*. On Saturday, 22 April 2000, a powerful bomb exploded at about 9.15pm in an art gallery on the ground floor of the newspaper's offices in the city centre.

The art gallery was situated directly below the office of the newspaper's editor, Geoffrey Nyarota. At first, it looked as though the move was designed to intimidate Nyarota and his staff. To save face, police arrested a foreign news photographer and accused him of planting the bomb. They released him soon afterwards when he had argued that he rushed to the scene after the blast to photograph the damage.

The state intensified its crusade against the MDC, any perceived supporters of our cause from civil society, my agents, staff and my family. At first I felt the pressure from the negative publicity, deliberate falsehoods and open defamation. But on realising that my character and the level of seriousness of the MDC were being put to the test, I devised various ways to cope with the vitriol. One of my first moves was to ignore the hatred expressed through the state media. I switched my mind off the local news bulletins and hardly bothered to read the state-controlled newspapers. Eventually, I stopped tuning in to our local radio station and I never watched the local television programmes.

Our children were not spared the strain of our new standing. They had to select friends carefully and without any advice or support from a trained governess or coach, as is normal in most political families. The children were exposed to a dangerous situation at a very young age. I had a problem with my eldest son Edwin, for instance. I didn't have time to pay attention to him when he was at his most vulnerable age. At one time he almost tried his hand at drugs, as any young man might do, and as a family we almost lost control of him. Eventually he overcame the problem. For a long time, though, I was totally in the dark about his problems – and only became aware of them when it was almost too late.

Our second son, Garikai, did not bother to complete his A-Levels. I had no time to concentrate on Gari and was unaware of this decision until I asked him for his academic results. He quickly shot back, saying that was water under the bridge. I realised then that I was not paying attention to my family at the most critical moments.

Occasionally, I played with my lovely twins, Millicent and Vincent. In my eyes they were still infants and too young understand what was going on – the large numbers of visitors, police raids and searches, and an absentee father. For the first time, it became difficult for me to attend their school activities, to cheer for them on sports days, to read them nursery rhymes like any other parent, or to be at school meetings. Nor could I be seen at their school's open days. The public attention I was getting was simply too much and it tended to interfere with the school's programmes for parents.

We decided that the twins be placed at a nearby boarding school so that they could concentrate on their studies during their formative school years. We settled for Bryden Primary School near Chegutu and Amai Ed had the responsibility of picking them up every weekend to be with us at home. But in terms of my role as a father, my performance was never impressive. I was building a party – and weekends were the best time for me to be doing this, away from home.

The girls, Vimbai and Rumbi, were in their teens. I hardly spent sufficient time with them. The burden fell squarely on their mother as they went through the normal changes of adolescence and metamorphosis into adulthood.

All my six children can, to some extent, narrate a story about how my role in politics affected them in a very negative way. Yes, I was in the house, but even my wife had to put up with loneliness and the pressure of my absence – even though I might be physically in the home. Despite all this, Amai Ed never expressed any doubts about what I was doing. She was very supportive. She knew the risks – and she knew me. She knew that when I did something, I did it wholeheartedly and with total commitment, and she supported my new political career without question. I am fortunate to be able to say that my wife and I had minimal conflict in our marriage despite the hardships we faced.

My brothers and sisters lamented the manner in which they, too, paid the price for my sudden fame. Some lost their jobs; others saw business opportunities disappear. Morgan Tsvangirai was being vilified on a daily basis and they paid the price of being associated with the family. Every time there was an attack, an arrest, a court case or whenever there was a trial involving me, they would rush to check for details. That meant abandoning their routine chores, work and families. These were very anxious times for them.

The first time I was arrested two weeks passed without anybody knowing where I was. My own family and my wife's family were concerned about my fate. They tried to follow state radio news bulletins for clues. They might hear a propaganda line saying this or that had happened and try to tease out its real meaning, causing more anxiety and fear. I am quite certain that both my wife's and my own families suffered terribly solely because of my entry into politics.

One of my wife's sisters was married to a soldier, an ex-combatant. She was shown the door, pushed out and forced to divorce him because of my involvement in politics. The story was that they disagreed all the time.

She supported what we were doing – but her husband would have none of it. Eventually, they parted ways and she came to stay with us. I felt very embarrassed, wondering whether to apologise or not. In the end, I was encouraged by her determination to help me to succeed in my new role.

My father, Dzingirai-Chibwe, was pursuing the Nerutanga chieftainship, stolen from him by a cousin, Kenneth Manyonda of Zanu PF, when he was the governor of Manicaland. My desire to lead an opposition party on a national scale affected my father's struggle to claim what was rightly his. Up until his death and to this day, the Nerutanga chieftainship of the Save clan remains unresolved. It is part of our family's long-cherished tradition and entitlement – and something we still hope to obtain.

My mother and my mother-in-law were very supportive, as was my late father-in-law. In fact, he died just two weeks before the June 2000 election, denied his wish to see the victory of his son-in-law.

What was the MDC bringing to the table and what was the essential difference between us and Zanu PF? These were fairly common questions raised with me in the early life of the party.

In short, Zanu PF is nationalist outfit with a liberation war legacy. It is structured like a pyramid and run directly from the top like a military unit with a commander whose orders are ignored at one's peril. It is administered like an army, understandably so, because it was a liberation movement.

The MDC allows for greater decision making at the bottom of its structures, at a local level. As a post-liberation party formed by social movements with a culture of debate and discussion before decisions are made, the MDC's main thrust is to extend the concept of freedom through popular participation, one of the ideals of the liberation struggle which the founders of the party felt Zanu PF had abandoned. We believed that the nationalists had betrayed the people, usurping their power and denying them their freedom after a national battle against colonialism.

The majority in the MDC were at one time in Zanu PF. When we structured the party, there appeared to be a tendency to mimic Zanu PF's structural models. Former unionists preferred to inherit ZCTU structural systems, coming up with executive and policy councils. Those who joined the party from civil society believed in the power of local structures as major determinants of policy and needs. The MDC structure therefore is a combination of influences from labour and from practices in civil society and other social movements.

Unlike Zanu PF, the MDC has no party cell. We felt that that was too militaristic and outright rebellious and terroristic. In the end, we devised one of the most democratic structures possible, both in terms of the participation of the people and in policy formulation, policy development and policy advocacy.

I have never found the structure of the MDC cumbersome. In fact, I feel comfortable with the robust debates in the MDC structures which culminate in resolutions and positions that make it easier for me to articulate as a leader. It is impossible for any leader in the MDC, including myself, to impose a personal preference or viewpoint as a party position. In Zanu PF, Mugabe could wake up one morning and declare a national holiday without consulting anyone. For example, he ordered the central bank to print money for ex-combatants' gratuities without reference to financial advisers; he deployed troops in the Congo without parliamentary approval. In short, what Mugabe said became policy.

The only thing I would say is a seeming structural deficiency relates to the position of our members of parliament. The MDC is an open party that allows any member to stand for office in the legislature or local council. They do not have to hold a position in the higher party structures in order to qualify for candidature. At the initial stage, our constitution was silent about the position of MPs within the party. This sometimes created conflict when legislators convened party meetings in their areas.

They lacked the necessary standing to call such meetings, unless they wanted to hold a general, non-partisan, report-back session.

I can understand how that came about. We were still out of parliament. The post of MP was a June 2000 phenomenon. We had to devise a mechanism to fit the MP into the structures so that there could be a link between the legislature and our district officials. Initially, we created an ex officio position for the MP in the district. Later, we realised that an MP must have a distinct political form of authority within a structure in his or her constituency. The relationship has to be carefully managed because, once elected, an MP becomes a servant of the entire constituency. Their constituents may include large numbers of non-party members, so it is important that their relations with their own party have some form of constitutional sanction.

The most important organ of the party is the ward structure. It selects and campaigns for a councillor and for an MP. Working with the councillors, the MP is a legislative representative of the collective voice of that constituency. An MP has to enjoy the blessing of the local political structure and must be answerable to it.

As I searched around for candidates for the 2000 parliamentary election, I discovered that most of the leading officials wanted to contest in urban areas. It was easy to assess the political trends and mood in towns and cities. Further, the violence Mugabe had unleashed in the rural areas made them unattractive and dangerous for MDC officials. I tried to convince them that the real election was due to take place in the rural areas. Zanu PF had totally abandoned the people there for 20 years. It was important for us to see how the poorest of the poor would respond to Mugabe's violent behaviour. Rural areas thus presented the plebiscite with a unique experience.

Take Mashonaland Central. Here was an area I knew well and the one that had suffered most in the liberation war. By 1998 Mugabe had completely abandoned the people. They had lost everything during the independence struggle. The villagers still relied on rudimentary hoes for tillage and barely made ends meet, despite a fantastic agricultural climate and superb soils. Skeletons of former fighters regularly got washed out of the ground from shallow graves, but Zanu PF failed even to give them decent burials, despite knowing their exact locations.

The June 2000 election was only for parliament. A direct challenge to Mugabe as president was only possible at the expiry of his term in 2002. I decided to lead the MDC in the parliamentary election as a candidate to enable me to gain experience before I challenged Mugabe for the presidential office in 2002. I convinced most senior founder members of the MDC to expand the party beyond its visible urban worker base into the rural areas. That was why I contested in Buhera North.

With the late Nicholas Mudzengerere, Remus Makuwaza, Sekai Holland, Gift Chimanikire, Lucia Matibenga and others, we opted to take on Zanu PF in the rural constituencies. There were 120 parliamentary seats up for grabs, although Mugabe had the constitutional power to appoint an additional 30 supposedly drawn from other interest groups, like traditional leaders. The 30 were always sympathetic to Mugabe and Zanu PF. To control parliament, the MDC needed to win at least 100 seats.

When Mugabe postponed the election to June to assert his hold on the ground through violence and intimidation, he inadvertently gave us the breathing space to organise our party primary elections and to strengthen our candidate selection processes.

We agreed that since the party comprised the majority poor, who had no money to back their campaigns, issues of merit must take precedence in candidate selection. There were some rural areas where it was a matter of identifying a suitable individual. I was concerned about sporadic reports that some aspiring MDC candidates were using tactics inherited from Zanu PF to secure nominations for parliament: violence, vote-buying, patronage, and the abuse of the youth. Some were set to brook no nonsense until they got what they wanted, even if it meant peddling influence by whatever means – including a combination of deceit and violence. It wasn't that widespread but I was nevertheless worried.

I was happy when I found that we were the only post-independence opposition party to field candidates in all 120 constituencies. For such a young party, I felt that by taking on Zanu PF in every constituency, we had got off to a great start, unprecedented in Zimbabwe's electoral history. Our calculation was that we were going to win in all the urban areas, but we were less certain about the level of support in the rural areas.

Many thought Mugabe would concede defeat if he lost the election by a wide margin, but he was battling to narrow the gap. The stakes were high. The MDC was building itself up and increasing its momentum. Our message differed from that of Zanu PF in substance and in style. We were charting a democratic culture whereas Zanu PF favoured the imposition of its candidates and its ideas with impunity and violence where necessary. We spoke loudly about the value of tolerance. By and large, that value and culture is still predominant within our ranks.

Our inclusive character had its own early setbacks. I had to manage the natural divisions, the ideological rifts, sometimes a clash of visions, different background dynamics and sharp personality traits carefully and with patience. There were some glaring ideological conflicts. Trade unionists and businessmen clashed often. When I appointed Eddie Cross secretary for economic affairs, for example, he came out with an economic blueprint with sections that were clearly in conflict with the social democracy ideology of the party. Cross would propound an unbridled free market philosophy and some of the new leaders from the labour movement felt social democracy as a guideline was preferable, with limited state participation in the economy. They were right. We had agreed that we were a social democratic party, following social democratic values. Cross and others progressively had to adjust their thinking to the party line.

There were moments when lack of policy clarity confused some. One of the ironies came to light when our internal foreign affairs officials applied for membership to various international political solidarity groups. Some of us wanted to affiliate with the socialist international grouping so as to become part of the social democratic family. But there were invitations extended to individuals like David Coltart and others to attend the Liberal International forums. Those fault lines were there.

Right-wing Afrikaner political parties in South Africa wanted to engage us, while Renamo, the opposition party in Mozambique, was keen to talk to us. Renamo's past as a rebel movement supported by the previous South African government was likely to create problems for the MDC.

Mugabe could have seized on that and used it to tarnish our image as a surrogate of the West. I cautioned the party against rushing into dialogue with Renamo, especially at a time when we were facing an election. It was a difficult time for me, and I had to wriggle out of uncomfortable situations with the agility of a cornered cheetah.

Although we were young in politics and inexperienced some of us had immense organisational experience from the trade union movement. I knew that it was going to be difficult for me initially, but not impossible. I believed our supporters wanted real change. They were not only anti-Mugabe: theirs was not just a protest vote against a leader who had gone too far, it was a vote for an alternative to Zanu PF. Our policies and ideals had been set out at the NWPC and the general policy thrust was for democratic change, in the real sense of the word. We had said that we were social democrats: we believed in a clearly defined but limited role of the state in governance and in the economy.

Compared to Zanu PF's stance, we were even more ideological. Zanu PF was just a nationalist movement whose agenda ended with independence in 1980. We had emerged as a political movement and moved towards consolidation as a political party and we positioned ourselves as a centre-left party. Because of the diverse nature of the party some would say that it was an omnibus taking on board everyone who was against Mugabe. To an extent, this could be true for our general membership as we never set out to screen anyone or to impose specific qualifications for membership.

We were a natural formation arising from the failure of a nationalist movement. The failure was evident, even among the same nationalists, which was why some of them joined us, why war veterans like retired Colonel Mudzingwa were, and still are, part of our leadership. What was clear was that Zanu PF had reduced itself to an elitist club at the expense of the general welfare of the people. We grew our national audience quickly because there was a national consensus that the way things were going were not in the best interests of Zimbabwe.

Considering our inexperience, I knew that we would have struggled to control the state, to have a meaningful impact. I didn't think that we were mature enough to take on the entire mantle of the state. But from the

Zambian example, I was determined that we would not rely on recruiting from the old establishment. We had our own people. I think Frederick Chiluba made a mistake in recycling the old politicians back into a new formation. We would have stumbled and struggled because of inexperience – the inexperience of a people with a new vision.

We had some of the youngest parliamentary candidates who had never worked in a formal setting in their lives – the likes of Job Sikhala, Learnmore Jongwe and Tafadzwa Musekiwa who were fresh graduates from the University of Zimbabwe who went straight into politics as a first call. They were very young – and vulnerable.

The negative factors on the ground, including the state's violence against the opposition in the rural areas where we were prevented from campaigning, made it difficult for me to prepare adequately for a complete overhaul of Zimbabwe's political system. We knew that we would win the election, but not by a sufficient margin to form a government on our own.

At best what we were hoping for was that the election would result in a hung parliament. We expected to form a coalition with Zanu PF, should such a development present itself. But the onslaught on commercial agriculture, violence, intimidation and the displacement of the farm workers' vote meant that Zanu PF was likely to emerge with a false victory.

In my dual role as party president and parliamentary candidate, I spent much of the first half of 2000 in both Harare and Buhera. I also travelled countrywide supporting the various party candidates. Occasionally, I flew overseas to garner international support and to explain the MDC to foreign governments and foreign audiences. Many wondered why I could not wait for the presidential election, which was two years away. But there was nothing to stop me from getting parliamentary experience before the 2002 election. The plan was that if I could get into parliament, I would get two years' legislative experience to then take on the bigger responsibility for the state.

I was particularly keen to observe the impact of the changing times in Bulawayo, rural Matabeleland and the Midlands. The MDC had the unique advantage of having worked with ORAP in its formative stages.

Zanu PF was hesitant to unleash violence on a full scale in Matabeleland, lest it reopen old Gukurahundi wounds. This time, they caused havoc in Mashonaland, Masvingo, Manicaland and parts of the Midlands.

In the MDC, we tried hard to downplay the ethnic factor. I was intent on finding a careful and sensitive ethnic balance within the party – especially within the top leadership. All ethnic minorities, from the Ndau-Shangaan in Chipinge, the Ndebele in the west, to the Tonga, Nambia and Shangwe in Victoria Falls, Hwange and Binga, had literally been abandoned by Zanu PF. In response, the minorities collectively abandoned Mugabe as well. The Ndebeles' action as a bloc was effected in spite of the 1987 Unity Accord between PF-Zapu and Zanu PF. They did not go along with that elite pact. Ndebeles and Kalangas respected Joshua Nkomo as a leader, but disagreed with him on the Accord. They had had a raw deal and they hated Zanu PF with a passion.

In structuring the MDC leadership, we signalled the emergence of a new kind of politics in Zimbabwe. Offering some of the key leadership positions to the minority Ndebele and a handful of white Zimbabweans, we managed to build a party that was national in character but portrayed a movement away from nationalistic politics. That won us the support of the Ndebele people.

And that was why, in terms of MPs, we almost wiped out all the Zanu PF candidates in Matabeleland. I was for broad participation in a new Zimbabwe and for this reason Steven Mudenda, a senior unionist and an ethnic Tonga based in Hwange, mobilised the people in the area. Zanu PF became history in an instant. In Chipinge and Chimanimani, Mathias Mlambo and Roy Bennett worked hard among the Ndaus and Shangani and we wrested the seat from Zanu (Ndonga). Paul Themba Nyathi and Moses Mzila-Ndlovu worked hard with the Kalangas and Xhosas in Bulilima, Mangwe and Gwanda, throwing these parliamentary seats into our bag with utmost ease. Renson Gasela, our agriculture spokesperson, easily claimed a seat in Lower Gweru, a rural area.

We cleared the entire Bulawayo metropolis. Harare and Chitungwiza had already turned their backs on Zanu PF. We became a respected movement overnight. Given the structure and the attitude and values of our party, opportunities for a non-ethnic based succession plan within the leadership were wide open. Perhaps that gave everyone much-needed hope.

I had come from labour where, if you are leader, you don't choose people for specific positions based on where they come from. You are either with them or not. Trade unions see issues as they are. I had the advantage of having worked in such a non-discriminatory environment; leading a political party was like a natural movement up the leadership ladder.

In an ideal situation, a parliamentary contest can be exciting game. But Mugabe was now totally paranoid about retaining power. While I received reports of beatings, harassment, farm invasions and deaths almost every hour from all over Zimbabwe, the state finally decided to come directly for me.

Soon after boarding a plane in Sweden on my way to London, an aide leaned towards me and informed me that two of my campaign staff in Buhera North – unionist Tichaona Richard Chiminya and a young activist, Talent Mabika – had been murdered by Zanu PF and state agents. I was told they were firebombed by armed state security agents and war veterans near Murambinda business centre, a mere 20 kilometres from my traditional family home. I was horrified by the news.

Chiminya was an experienced organiser and an activist close to me. With his favourite pinch of traditional snuff firmly cupped in one hand, sniffing and wiping off brown-black, dusty droppings from his well-cropped moustache, Chiminya was a convincing go-getter. In Buhera North, he had teamed up with Talent Mabika for my campaign. I knew Chiminya well, but I had no information about Mabika. The two were killed on 15 April 2000 by local war veterans, led by CIO operative Joseph Mwale – a notorious officer with a history of harassing us at ZCTU meetings and who I believe was specifically assigned to track me down when I entered politics.

On arrival back in Harare, I was informed that Chiminya and Mabika were first assaulted before their vehicle was set alight by Mwale and Zanu

PF Kenneth Manyonda's election agents. Chiminya died on the spot while Mabika died later in hospital.

As I mourned Chiminya and Mabika, reports of further deaths and chaos were streaming in. Patrick Nabanyama, David Coltart's election agent, was seized by state and Zanu PF agents in Bulawayo and disappeared, never to be seen again – presumed murdered.

Elliot Pfebve, our candidate for Bindura, was in trouble. The state was tracking him down. After failing to locate him, they abducted his father and brother and assaulted them severely. The brother, Matthew, died soon afterwards. Also in Bindura, Trymore Midzi – an MDC activist – was abducted and murdered by security agents.

In Kwekwe, our candidate Blessing Chebundo was forced to go into hiding. His opponent, Emmerson Mnangagwa, was known to have a particularly vicious and violent streak. Chebundo survived several assassination attempts and his home was razed in a bomb attack. So serious were his injuries that he was unable to present his own nomination papers confirming his candidature, sending an agent on his behalf.

As party leader, I felt overwhelmed by the scale of state-sponsored brutality and attacks on the MDC.

Inside Harare's Budiriro suburb, Chenjerai Hunzvi converted his private health centre into a Zanu PF torture camp. Several party activists were abducted and severely tortured at the clinic. The police hardly bothered to investigate these barefaced crimes and Mugabe blamed the violence on the MDC. The murders paved the way for uncontrolled looting and vandalism. Mugabe refused to acknowledge the lawlessness, still insisting that they were 'peaceful demonstrations'.

White commercial farmers suffered from abuse and torture as the war veterans turned the heat up. Some were murdered; many were forced to take refuge in nearby towns and cities. Clearly feeling vulnerable, white farmers abandoned their homes and pressed the CFU for dialogue. At the meetings, Mugabe was assisted by his deputy Joseph Msika, senior military commanders and Chenjerai Hunzvi and his war veterans. Nothing came of it, although the CFU offered Mugabe large tracts of land in exchange for peace.

But Mugabe was never interested in land. He wanted to break the backbone of the farm worker community – that captive constituency which he believed supported the MDC and me. He wanted the vast countryside as punishment reserves, away from public scrutiny, and to seal off a swathe of territory from the MDC campaign staff.

As the June election approached the climate of violence became unbearable. By May, most of the MDC's rural candidates had been driven out of their constituencies. By the time we went into the election a month later, the MDC could hardly campaign freely in 95 of the 120 constituencies because of violence and intimidation. We were, however, able to sneak in and out of 46 constituencies, mainly in the peri-urban districts.

An attempt by civil society in April to demonstrate against lawlessness in Harare was ruthlessly crushed and scores were injured in city-centre skirmishes involving war veterans, the police and ordinary people.

White farmers and MDC activists who braved intimidation in order to protect their property and crops paid dearly. They were publicly humiliated and some had to pay bribes or give away food and fuel for protection. Many lost vehicles and valuable assets.

The courts had been rendered totally impotent; often the state did not bother to oppose legal papers served by the CFU or the MDC and it treated High Court judges with derision, ignoring their orders with impunity.

I was seldom home during the first half of 2000. I was either helping out MDC candidates or attending the funerals of murdered activists. There certainly was no time to concentrate on my own constituency in Buhera North. Around mid-June, when I finally got to Buhera, I was appalled at the impact of the violence in my own area and its effect on the lives of the people I knew so well.

Kenneth Manyonda had set up Zanu PF's campaign based on violence and intimidation working with agents that included war veterans Bernard Makuwe, Tom Zimunya, another using the false name Kitsiyatota, and a certain *America Mudzvanyiriri* (a liberation war pseudonym, which literally means 'the US is an oppressor').

After the murder of Chiminya and Mabika, the intimidation of villagers intensified. MDC supporters were ordered away from my meetings and threatened with reprisals if they resisted. The inaction of the police induced fear among the people, so that many opted to stay out of 'trouble'.

Kitsiyatota owned a small grocery shop at Gaza in my constituency. When I arranged a meeting there, very few people turned up, repeating similar stories of intimidation. I was told of numerous cases of widespread arson in the constituency, in particular at Manjengwa and at Tafiramorera, deep inside the constituency. From Gwebo, Nerutanga, Gombe, Mombeyarara, Chitsunge to Garamwera, I began to experience very low attendances at my meetings. The story was the same: intimidation, violence, arson and beatings at night by Zanu PF gangs and army officers.

The war veterans revived the language of threats and intimidation they used during the war. The phrase 'sell-out' came back to life, sending shivers down the spines of villagers with war experience who knew the fatal consequences of being labelled as such. Zanla guerrillas had killed many an innocent villager merely on suspicion that he or she was a sell-out. Zanu PF knew that such labels would reach others: the message meant death, so the villagers took it seriously. Teachers, a respected core of professionals in poor, dusty communal lands, were particularly targeted. They were assumed to sympathise with fellow urban workers and, by extension, were perceived to be MDC supporters. True, many were on our side. They had watched their profession lose their previously coveted social status as community leaders because of a rapid decline in the quality of their earnings due to rising inflation.

In the middle of my campaign, I was invited to assist an MDC candidate in Mutare West. On arrival, I came face-to-face with Mwale. He burst into our meeting brandishing a loaded AK-47 assault rifle. People scurried for cover and in no time the whole gathering dispersed in panic. I did not talk to him; I just watched him before I ambled to my vehicle and drove off to a meeting at Mwenge in the same area. Here I found only 20 people who told me that Mwale had been there already and ordered them to abandon the meeting.

On 24 June, the first day of the election, I woke up early and voted at a station near my rural home. I then moved around the polling stations where I saw voters standing quietly in queues, waiting to cast their ballots. Many told me that they were happy that the campaign was over. They had had a hard time from Zanu PF, to put it mildly. I was concerned that only half of the registered voters turned up at the polling stations: the other half were too frightened or confused or could not be bothered.

Despite the total closure of campaign space and the ensuing apathy, I put up what I considered to be an impressive challenge as a first-timer. I was soon informed by the blatantly partisan electoral commission, the ESC, that I had lost by less than 2 000 votes. I refused to accept the result and immediately lodged a court challenge.

Countrywide, the picture was brighter. Many of our candidates had swept in. Though Zanu PF forcibly usurped 62 contested seats, we took 57. A small regional party, Zanu (Ndonga) squeezed out one seat in Chipinge in the east.

The Commonwealth had sent observers to monitor the election. In their report[5] the group said it 'commended' the people of Zimbabwe for their commitment to democracy, despite the violence and intimidation leading up to the poll. The report noted the bias of state media; the fact that large numbers were turned away from voting; lack of transparency in the counting process; and lack of neutrality in the ESC. Despite all this, said the report, the election marked a turning point in the country's history because for the first time the generation born after independence (1980) – the 'born frees' – were able to vote in a general election. Also for the first time there was a viable, nationwide political alternative based not on ethnic differences but on a different political platform.

From the MDC's perspective, we had firmly challenged Mugabe's control of parliament. I immediately returned to Harare. The place was jubilant. Despite the odds, we thought we had broken Mugabe's back. With the MDC's impressive showing, barely five months into our existence as a fully fledged party, I was happy that Zimbabwe was now another country where things really could change.

ENDNOTES

1   State radio broadcast, 18 April 2000.
2   'Human rights and Zimbabwe's June 2000 Election: A report by the Research Unit of the Zimbabwe Human Rights NGO Forum. Special Report 1.' Harare, January 2001 http://www.hrforumzim.com
3   Frederikse, Julie (1984). *None But Ourselves: Masses Versus the Media in the Making of Zimbabwe.* London: Penguin
4   LLC Books (creator) (2010). *Zimbabwean Media: Media of Zimbabwe, the Herald, Zimbabwe Broadcasting Corporation, Tsotso, Zimbabwe Daily News, Zim2day.com*
5   *Election Observer Group Report on the Zimbabwe Elections, July 2000* (2001). Commonwealth Secretariat

CHAPTER FIFTEEN

INTO PARLIAMENT

I had already announced that I would challenge my defeat in the Buhera North constituency when two boxes full of ballots were discovered floating in a nearby river. The CIO quickly snatched them and they disappeared in a ball of fire, according to villagers. The villagers told me they were threatened with death if ever the story was leaked. Well, despite the intimidation, the information could not be concealed forever.

The first hundred days of a new party in parliament would be seen, in most other countries, as a honeymoon period when MPs, fresh from poll victories, could find their feet, get to know the protocols, and rub shoulders with more experienced parliamentarians. But there was no honeymoon for the new opposition on the block, inside or outside parliament. The MDC had inflicted unprecedented losses on Zanu PF and there would be no truce during the battle that now loomed, leading up to the 2002 presidential elections. During our first hundred days the real power structures in Zimbabwe showed their hand, dampening our optimism for a peaceful and democratic takeover of power.

Elated and frustrated at the same time, I would let slip a remark that got me into trouble. In calling on the government to meet our democratic demands, I went a step too far, warning that the people's anger could turn to violence. Our opponents were to take the fullest advantage of this seeming threat, and it was a lesson to me to watch my words.

The ruling party was running scared and reacted with characteristic passion, malevolence, and force. Given the volumes of varied reports that I received from all over the country, it was clear that Zanu PF had actually lost the June 2000 parliamentary election. This was to be the first of several stolen elections. The ruling party took advantage of its control of the polls and the MDC's inexperience in poll monitoring – basically, our technical weaknesses at the ballot stations – to rig the final outcome.

Mugabe proceeded to form what he called a 'war cabinet' – confirming our suspicions as to the underlying reality of his administration which now ran along the lines of a civil-military junta with him in charge. As the first decade of the new century advanced, an ageing Mugabe would increasingly cede power to the security establishment. At last, after the 2008 elections, it would appear that the country had been taken over by the junta which simply kept Mugabe floating at the top of pseudo-civilian administration. In the meanwhile there was the depressing fact that military generals, senior police and intelligence officers now dominated in Zimbabwe. If not yet fully in the driving seat, the increasing role of the security forces in government served as a warning sign of worse things to come.[1]

While so-called 'land reform' extended its chaotic tentacles over the country, generating massive media coverage, the real crisis in governance went virtually unremarked among African leaders who feared to be the first to say the Emperor had no clothes. The true depth of the crisis was equally overlooked by Western leaders who focused on the losses and sufferings of white farmers. In spite of our poll victories, the MDC remained isolated and misunderstood abroad while being persecuted at home.

Mugabe routinely banned or caused the disruption of MDC meetings while large parts of Zimbabwe became no-go zones. Urban workers and visitors who attempted to enter the rural areas found themselves negotiating the risks of what had literally become war zones. The state was particularly ruthless with the peasant, the farm worker and the commercial farmer. Representatives of NGOs or members of civil society and even civil servants who attempted to intervene were given short shrift. Teachers and religious leaders who tried to awaken some moral consciousness, and nurses who treated the wounded and the dying, were singled out for cruel punishment.

Although the MDC had performed well in the parliamentary election, from the reports I received back in Harare I could see that we had faltered at the finishing line due to lack of experience. We did not put in place sufficient mechanisms to foil Zanu PF's rigging machine at the vote-counting stations. Our agents had never done the job before and none were properly trained. In many instances they were barred from polling stations in the rural areas. Voting took place over a two-day period which required that the ballot boxes be ferried from the polling station to a government office at the end of the first voting day. They would be returned the following morning for a continuation of the process.

Police and other security agents dismissed MDC officers at the end of voting after telling them to put their party seals on the boxes and return the next morning. I picked up from the polling officers, mostly teachers who supported the MDC, that Zanu PF replaced the seals with fake ones either during the night or while the boxes were in transit and tampered with the contents. The other weakness related to mobile voting stations. Our agents were not provided with transport to see what was happening either at the temporary stations or while the voting officials moved from one place to another.

Inside the counting stations, state security agents often brought in satchels full of papers, claiming that they were genuine ballot papers mainly from government employees on official duty elsewhere. These included the army and the police. These satchels surfaced only a few minutes before the end of the counting, making verification difficult, if not impossible.

Counting was done at a central place in the constituency at the end of the voting period. The use of dubious postal ballots helped Zanu PF to save the political careers of most of its senior officials. Among them was Sidney Sekeramayi, then minister of state security, who survived in Marondera West through a recount of the ballots during which 300 fake votes in his favour were added to the box as postal ballots. In the end, Sekeramayi claimed to have won by 65 votes against the MDC candidate, Didymus Munhenzva. In Makoni East Zanu PF diverted Nicholas Mudzengerere's votes to another party's candidate, leaving him 29 votes short of those of his main rival, a former CIO director, Shadreck Chipanga.

Zanu PF was keen to maintain a stronghold in the rural areas after realising that their loss margins in the urban areas were too high to play around with. They looked for constituencies where the MDC had narrowly scraped through to beef up their fortunes with postal votes.

In Mashonaland, Masvingo, Manicaland and the Midlands, fake postal ballots were actually transported in army helicopters to deal with this type of 'emergency', as one former security agent described it to me six months later. It was much easier to rig the election in areas where MDC candidates had been driven out by violence during the campaign. The polling stations literally had no MDC polling agents.

After carefully studying reports from the MDC candidates and thousands of election agents, I called a meeting of the national executive committee to review the results. The committee accepted the advice of our legal department to challenge the results in 39 constituencies. We expected the courts to grant us the legal space to be heard, as a matter of urgency. But this was not to be.

Before the election, Mugabe had amended the Lancaster House Constitution 17 times in 13 years, using the Zanu PF parliamentary majority to endorse the changes. To change the Lancaster House Constitution again, Mugabe needed a two-thirds endorsement from parliament. I knew after the June 2000 election that this would now be impossible, for he no longer enjoyed such parliamentary support.

Mugabe feared the worst. He knew our lawsuits had the potential to overturn the balance of power and gain us majority representation in parliament. The evidence we had against electoral malpractices was so overwhelming that in a normal democracy Mugabe's regime would not have survived for a single day after he proclaimed his false victory.

Yes, Mugabe would have remained as state president, but with a legislature whose majority was from the opposition. That would have forced Mugabe to negotiate with us for a power-sharing arrangement. That is why I believe that if we had given the draft constitution our blessing in February, it would have been impossible for him to be in power to this day. The draft, despite its clear flaws, sought to abolish the presidential authority to appoint 30 non-constituency legislators and eight provincial governors who are also automatic, but unelected, parliamentary representatives. Mugabe had retained this prerogative and now used it to pack parliament with his yes-men.

Vote-rigging and the packing of parliament was only part of Mugabe's plan to hold on to power. He had already announced that he had formed an administration led by what he called a 'war cabinet'.

As Zimbabwe was now out of the Congo following a regional peace deal in mid-1999 that required the withdrawal of all foreign forces, the 2000 election allowed Mugabe to redeploy the military in local politics, primarily to suppress the MDC. The Joint Operations Command (JOC) quickly became the actual political managers of Zimbabwe. Zimbabwe's military had vast experience in dealing with internal opposition forces after lengthy missions in Matabeleland and in Mozambique soon after independence. It was used effectively to destroy PF-Zapu, to strengthen Frelimo's hold on Maputo, and to thwart Kabila's ouster in the Congo.

A new armed elite – whose political culture thrived on an infusion of a war psychosis, customs, commands and blood – took control of almost all civilian public institutions, agriculture and land reform. These included fuel procurement and distribution, public transport, banking, national parks and wildlife management, commerce and industry, mining, and food security and delivery.

The JOC, chaired by Mugabe, co-opted the Zimbabwe National Liberation War Veterans Association, headed by Chenjerai Hunzvi. To the outside world, Mugabe was in charge. But at home, we saw that there was a strong, parallel administration working as an alternative to a civilian state. The parallel administration's mission was to keep the face of Zanu PF on the surface. This entailed the maintenance of a formal, but ineffective and politically decorative cabinet to handle external political critics of military regimes.

Meantime, war veterans, used to having their way with Mugabe, were demanding key ministerial posts and governorships to seal off rural Zimbabwe from opposition political influence ahead of the presidential election in 2002.[2]

Apart from Mugabe, the new public policy chiefs were General Vitalis Zvinavashe, Lieutenant General Constantine Chiwenga, Lieutenant General Philip Sibanda, Air Marshal Perence Shiri, CIO director general Brigadier Happyton Bonyongwe, Police Commissioner Augustine Chihuri, and retired Major General Paradzai Zimondi, the commissioner of prisons. They worked with a pool of advisers who included Air Vice-Marshal Henry Muchena, Brigadier Douglas Nyikayaramba, Hunzvi, and Zanu PF hardliners, Emmerson Mnangagwa, Patrick Chinamasa, Jonathan Moyo and Didymus Mutasa.

Senior military officers, out of the inner circle but privy to what was happening, informed me that the JOC was bound by a shared memory and fear of possible collective punishment should Zimbabwe's leadership change hands. The team remained intact due its collective and personal loyalty to each other after long service to Mugabe and Zanu PF.

I believe after spending their entire lives in politics – both before and after independence – and in the military, the officers sought to protect their JOC brand. This gave them unchallenged power, supremacy and influence; and, naturally, they feared change. In their view, change would never guarantee them the privileges and the security they enjoyed under Mugabe, especially after the violence in Matabeleland in the 1980s and before the June 2000 election. Genuine fears of national retribution seemed to dominate their decision-making processes.

Mugabe said his new 'war cabinet' was necessary to confront the West, led by Britain, and to protect Zimbabwe from regime change. It was his sincere belief, he constantly told the nation, that the West was using the MDC and me as its puppets to recolonise Zimbabwe and to expose him to danger. As he swore into office his civilian-military team in early July 2000, he even had the audacity to bring in Lieutenant General Mike Nyambuya as cabinet minister responsible for energy development.

Other state departments, though headed by civilians, were run by chief executives or senior officials drawn from the military's ranks: Colonel Christian Katsande (Industry and International Trade), Colonel Joseph Mhakayaora (Public Construction), ex-CIO officer Justin Mpamhanga (Energy), Air Commodore Mike Karakadzai (Transport), Major Anywhere Mutambudzi (Information), while Brigadier Elisha Muzonzini and Major Generals Edzai Chimonyo and Jevan Maseko were placed in the foreign service as ambassadors.

It was clear from these moves that Zimbabwe would never be the same again. The new civilian faces in the 'war cabinet' comprised some young, but hard-hearted technocrats and proven Mugabe loyalists. They included Joseph Made, an agriculturalist; Simba Makoni, a chemist and former executive secretary of SADC; Nkosana Moyo, physicist and businessman; Francis Nhema, a banker; Patrick Chinamasa, a lawyer; J B Matiza, an architect; Jonathan Moyo, a university lecturer; and Saviour Kasukuwere, a former ministerial chauffeur later recruited as a raw intelligence gatherer.

Although some members of this 'war cabinet' are unworthy of discussion, I would like to explain why they should be discussed, and how they failed at their tasks by choosing to abuse their positions for corrupt and selfish ends.

Nkosana Moyo was plucked out of nowhere. He was neither Zanu PF nor MDC in the June 2000 election. He contested the polls as an independent candidate in central Harare and lost, only to be co-opted into Zanu PF as the trade and industry minister. He stayed in the job for a few weeks and then left Zimbabwe in unexplained circumstances. He faxed a resignation letter to Mugabe's office from Johannesburg, saying he had given up on Zanu PF.

Mugabe gave Simba Makoni the national purse as the new finance minister. At the beginning, big business thought Makoni – an executive secretary of SADC for ten years – held a magic wand, only to see the photogenic technocrat and administrator stutter and stammer in despair after failing to knock sense into Mugabe's head over the need for a rational economic policy. Makoni stayed on for a while, trying to manage the dictator's finances. He, too, gave up and quit, but remained attached to the Zanu PF coat-tails, ensconced in the inner politburo circle until the heat became too much. He resigned as finance minister after disagreements with Mugabe on key issues including the currency devaluation and the printing of money. Mugabe accused Makoni of trying to follow universal economic management practices at a time when the government wanted to try a different route in order to survive.

Jonathan Moyo had failed to steer Zanu PF and Mugabe to victory during the constitutional referendum, but Zanu PF nevertheless rewarded him with one of the special 30 seats that the amended Lancaster House Constitution allowed the president to impose on an elected parliament. Moyo became minister of state for information and publicity.

As if to prove himself, Moyo immediately went ballistic, introducing radical media reforms which changed the face and operations of national media institutions. Radio, television and state newspapers switched their news agenda to a more aggressive, racial and anti-colonial line. Twenty years after independence, news and commentaries focused on Zanu PF's supposed victory in the Rhodesian war. Material previously stashed in media libraries was unearthed and rebroadcast and republished. Moyo reduced the number of foreign programmes and music to the bare minimum, forcing producers to air liberation war-time songs and old films.

Moyo's drastic restructuring of the official media staff was aimed at weeding out potential MDC sympathisers. Among the first senior scribes to go was Bornwell Chakaodza, editor of *The Herald*. The retired journalists were replaced with young reporters, so inexperienced that they would toe the government line without question.

He vented his anger on the private media, especially *The Daily News*, and pursued a harsh line against foreign journalists. Beyond the state media, Moyo landed his first punch on Capital Radio, a private station set up by a group of journalists. He directed the police to seize the station's equipment and to stop their limited broadcasts. Capital Radio immediately sought relief from the Supreme Court, but the hearing was delayed for two months.

Mugabe placed Joseph Made, his long-time private farm manager and conduit for state support at his personal farms, at the head of the ministry of agriculture. The CFU was initially optimistic about Made's appointment, thinking that as a professional he had the capacity to get Mugabe to spare the destruction of commercial agriculture, but the white farmers soon realised their mistake. Made smashed commercial agriculture. Incredibly, he asked Zimbabweans to change their national diet and forgo their staple, bread, for cassava and a local variety of sweet potato. He superintended the country's dramatic fall from being a net food exporter into a major importer, causing widespread famine and starvation in the process. At the time of writing, he remained Mugabe's chief farm manager and a cabinet minister.

Francis Nhema, son of a Midlands chief and former Mugabe aide, is married to one of Joshua Nkomo's daughters. Nhema almost ran a building society aground and narrowly avoided jail through a string of questionable financial deals before his new job as tourism minister.

Patrick Chinamasa became Mugabe's prime hatchet man against the judiciary. As the new justice minister, he relentlessly picked on individual judges and either forced them out of Zimbabwe or into retirement. One of his main targets was Chief Justice Anthony Gubbay, whom he described as a colonial relic and literally chased out of office, sparking a serious stand-off between the executive and the judiciary.

The 'war cabinet' immediately allocated Zanu PF the entire budgetary allocation set aside for political parties represented in parliament, forcing the MDC to – once again – object. Chinamasa argued that before the election the MDC had failed to lodge the necessary notifications to access the funds, which was untrue. We took him to court. Again, Zanu PF lost. With the state funding we received, the MDC was able to cover a huge outstanding election bill. After the election, the MDC's reserves were dangerously low. Zanu PF had infiltrated, intimidated and decimated our support groups, local donors and volunteers in the run-up to the polls.

At the same time, the state's national director of elections, Tobaiwa Mudede and Justice Minister Chinamasa started to change the voters' rolls, removing the names of voters with a known foreign ancestry. Because Zimbabwe is a small country with few tribes, the people tend to use their clan or tribal identity and totems as part of their full names. It is therefore fairly easy to place a Zimbabwean ancestral origin from the family name. For this reason, the government could easily pick out the names of whites and blacks whose parents or families had moved into Zimbabwe during the past hundred years and strike them off the roll at will.

But our single largest headache was the increasing number of displaced persons. Evictions, beatings, murders and arrests spread an all-pervading atmosphere of perpetual fear. Most of the victims who survived needed medical attention but state hospitals refused to admit them for treatment.

Those arrested on flimsy charges needed legal cover. Hardly a day passed without an incident – either on the farms or in some remote village, or in urban public bars and private homes – of soldiers harassing ordinary people. Our new legislators were not spared either. The police and war veterans, under the direction of the military, barred our MPs from addressing public meetings and often brutally assaulted them. Nearly all faced one charge or another. The legal costs were astronomical, and rising every day.

This was a war of attrition, intended to drain the MDC by bleeding all our resources dry. Although the presidential poll was still two years away, Zanu PF and Mugabe had evidently shifted into high gear to prepare for it, with intimidation as their main tool of public appeal.

Meanwhile it had dawned on me that politicians are an ambitious pack, something I now realised I had underestimated. Inside the MDC I saw amazing scenes as everyone's natural ambitions grew. Some among those who made it to parliament started to think of their success as an end in itself. Others assumed an air of superiority over their colleagues, both in and outside parliament. Our different backgrounds made these conflicts and tensions inevitable. As leader, I tried to play down the differences, advising that we remain focused on our political goals. I emphasised that as a political family we needed to keep our different styles as individuals in check to avoid unnecessary misunderstanding.

What upset me, though, were traces of division within the very top leadership, some based on minor, personal differences and others over interrelated character traits and impulses which, though repressed and difficult to define, influenced thoughts and behaviour. There were three members from Matabeleland, one from Mashonaland and another from Masvingo. I am from Manicaland. A tendency was creeping in to undermine the leadership, directed at me.

To do so, one of us had to be isolated and frustrated – and in this case, the dice fell on national chairman Isaac Matongo. The others knew about my confidence in Matongo, and so their plan was to pretend to attack him as a way of getting at me. If Matongo stood his ground, they would go for organising director, James Makore. Matongo and Makore, both former trade unionists, had worked closely with me right from the beginning to get the party up and running.

There were also some individuals, academics, who had difficulty fitting into our trade union culture of mass organisations. They were a minority so they failed to exert any influence. I worked hard to close these fissures and to manage delicate feelings and discouraged sidelining.

Personally, I abhor the use of too much executive authority. I believe in sharing. I believe that it is always better to start by random sharing, brainstorming as it were, whatever we have on our minds before we set out to gather and collect what is best for the party. Perhaps this is a weakness. I have always believed in reaching a consensus, in affording all a voice, so that as a party we can carry everyone along the same path to progress.

I sincerely believed in a collective position, although I later discovered that such an attitude sometimes leads to role conflicts in a political party. There were instances where, as the party leader, I felt I had to take a firm stance and drive the political agenda and process. Dictatorial as it may sound, the truth is that in the end the buck stops with the party leader – not a committee or the executive team. The people ultimately turn to the leader for an explanation; an effective leader cannot hide behind a committee resolution and get away with the consequences.

From an early stage – following our victories in February and in June 2000 – there was widespread confidence that an MDC government was a viable future possibility. Those victories were useful, much as they were instructive, in encouraging me to push on. I set out to grow the party in preparation for the 2002 presidential election. Leadership cohesion and a strategic approach were critical to the realisation of this goal and I started to search for constant avenues for strategic advice and to build a consistent and cogent political argument.

Local and international experts voluntarily helped the MDC leadership to develop the art of organisation and membership motivation. We had to stay on the party's message and engage in meaningful political communication through effective election campaign management. As leaders, we met regularly to assess the situation facing the party and craft responses to the increasing violence. It would have been hard enough to run a campaign against an entrenched government that put up obstacles everywhere, but the violence made it more difficult and harrowing still.

On the external front I saw the need to engage Africa and sent emissaries to various capitals to explain our position. I visited Botswana, Ghana and Nigeria where I was well received. At first their leaders looked hesitant to embrace the MDC cause; they listened but did not do anything to assist us. I called on a number of African embassies. Wherever I took my message, Zanu PF had been there already. Zanu PF had done its work – and efficiently too. They had an important tool and they used it to maximum effect: a liberation war legacy.

In the uncertain world of international diplomacy, other African countries simply told me that they were hearing me. Nothing else! I expected them to take on Mugabe, and try to convince him to respect the people.

South Africa was a bit tricky. Although low-level government and party officials talked to me, they politely explained that they had an official position that barred Pretoria from interfering in the affairs of its neighbours – essentially, that was the initial view of President Thabo Mbeki's administration.

I began to feel that Africa was shunning the MDC and that the continent saw us as an embarrassment to its liberation war legacy. When I tried to explain what was happening in Zimbabwe my story seemed to fall flat on the ground. Perceptions rested on misinterpretation: Mugabe's propaganda and diplomatic efforts were directed at a crisis over the land question which he had tackled in the most brutal manner; I was talking about a crisis of governance which had to be resolved in the interests of justice, peace and security for the people.

I tried to point out the most obvious issues: widespread violence, the complete subjugation of the people, and a flawed electoral system. Violence sounded so normal in Africa and meant very little to many a leader. The road was long, bumpy and winding: we carried our message far and wide, knocking on many doors and putting our case as persuasively as we could. Africa just watched from a distance. Out of politeness, African diplomats urged me to wait for the presidential election in 2002, seemingly content to believe that that election would ultimately clear any doubts about our transition.

Were it not for the simple fact that Zimbabweans in general knew the truth about their own situation, neither my MDC colleagues nor I could have survived a casual stroll in a Zimbabwean street. The propaganda and the vitriol were so intense and sustained that one could be forgiven for thinking Zimbabwe was at war. Indeed, it was experiencing a low-intensity civil war of a different kind. Almost daily, and on every public platform – even at funerals – Mugabe attacked the people for supporting us. He vowed that he was prepared to go all the way to survive.

Britain, through the Commonwealth, finally pushed South Africa to act. A troika of South Africa, Nigeria and Australia was formed to seek ways to help out but in my view their delegates never took the MDC seriously. Mugabe remained adamant, pursuing the same old theory that Rhodesians and colonialists were plotting a comeback through their puppets in the MDC.

While the Commonwealth diplomats tried their best to engage Mugabe, they paid little attention to us. No one really took up the issue of trying to get the two contesting parties together. I was concerned by such an attitude because I knew that the West had a strong influence on global affairs. And, in terms of what we were trying to achieve, we shared certain concerns with the West: democracy, transparency, observance of human rights, and free and fair elections. I was never a darling of the West. If anything, judging from my initial meetings with their diplomats and politicians, they did not seem to understand what I stood for.

But I knew that if I could convince the West about what we were trying to achieve in Zimbabwe, they would see value in my work. Africa claims to have its own value systems. Africa is mainly worried about stability, not about democracy in terms of principles and effective practice. For that reason, no African country would support a struggle for democracy in another African country without the risk of being accused of external interference. Africa looks to the sovereignty of African governments, not the sovereignty of African people. Britain, through Prime Minister Tony Blair, was the leading voice in the criticism of Mugabe, yet Britain was primarily concerned with the treatment of the few white farmers – in particular, the deaths of farmers David Stevens and Martin Olds – not the millions of black Zimbabweans under the heel of Mugabe.

As the former colonial power, which to an extent bungled the resolution of Zimbabwe's land question, Britain appeared eager to clear its name. Mugabe seized on the moment and followed Blair with the zeal of an attack dog. His main mistake, though, was to link Blair to the MDC.

For the record, and contrary to the Zanu PF perception and Mugabe's regular whimpers, Blair and Britain never sponsored the MDC with money or material support worthy of note. The only support we got – and which Zanu PF relied upon for propaganda – was £12 000 sterling from the Westminster Foundation for the training of our election agents. When our semi-literate activists failed to account for the money properly, the issue was raised in public and that gave Mugabe the proof he needed that we were a British lapdog. That marked the end of our relationship with the Westminster Foundation, fairly early in the process. Beyond that, we received nothing from London, either in the form of cash or ideas. To eliminate all doubt, as President of the MDC, I challenge any person in Harare, London or anywhere else to prove me wrong on this basic historical fact.

On 16 September 2004, I was flabbergasted to hear Blair claim in the British parliament that he was working closely with the MDC on a regime change agenda. That statement was false and severely damaged our cause. Blair played into Mugabe's hands, bolstering his position in our battle for African opinion; such utterances were totally unhelpful, for they buttressed Harare's view that we were a British creation. After Blair's statement, Mugabe jumped on to the podium, claiming finally to have obtained the proof he long craved of my collusion with Blair.

I immediately summoned the British ambassador to Harare to my residence and protested strongly. I was informed that the gaffe came in the heat of the moment during a parliamentary questioning session in the House of Commons. Blair, I was told apologetically, confessed that he hadn't applied his mind to the consequences of such a careless and wholly untrue utterance. British politicians never cease to amaze me.

A few years later, former foreign minister David Miliband told the British parliament that the MDC influenced Whitehall's foreign policy towards Zimbabwe. The gaffe, once again, came out during a debate on the question of sanctions. I called the British embassy and protested again. But Mugabe and Zanu PF had already taken note of this and used it to hit back at us.

For all the Zanu PF hype, neither Zimbabwean whites nor Britain influenced the MDC and me in any way. All London could do was to raise the Zimbabwean question at international meetings, which I believed was its sovereign right to do, not at our request as a party.

Zimbabweans, including Zanu PF-aligned businesses, contributed close to 90 per cent of the money, vehicles, fuel and other resources for our cause. Some made the most vociferous noises against us publicly to cover up for the substantial amounts of cash and support they disbursed to us secretly. They were not helping me personally. This was never a Tsvangirai struggle. They were contributing to a national project, their own struggle, and they believed in what they were fighting for even if some would not declare so openly.

With Jonathan Moyo now driving the Zanu PF propaganda machine,

Zimbabwe became a one-agenda country: the only issue was the cry for 'Land!' After an initial confrontation in which the CFU legally succeeded, Mugabe and Zanu PF dug in, ignoring court orders. White farmers realised they were going nowhere; the dispute was political and Mugabe, backed by his military and security forces, was set to take them on.

The CFU split into two organisations after disagreements about how to deal with Mugabe and Zanu PF. Those who left formed the Justice for Agriculture Trust and continued to lobby anyone who cared to listen for – as the name implies – justice, while the traditional CFU remained, though substantially weakened by the flight of its members to neighbouring countries or away from their farms. Neither faction was spared continuous, state-sponsored harassment.

Inside Zanu PF, and with the help of the public media, all previously reasonable men and women started to behave like real clowns, singing the land message at every turn, and I am sure even in their sleep. The way they articulated that message resembled a coordinated gold rush in some faraway, uninhabited territory. In political terms, they followed the party line but this meant preying on the powerless and exploiting a historical grievance for personal gain. Whenever they encountered questions, they resorted to violence and force: it was a case of obey or get beaten into submission.

Border Gezi, the new minister of youth, assumed immense powers, rounding up unemployed rural teenagers and driving them into militia camps for what he called a national service programme. In effect this was a conscription exercise to turn innocents into a giant killing machine. Gezi's plan was quickly approved by Zanu PF when Mugabe realised that the majority of young people were giving their support to the MDC. The intention was to counter the opposition's dominance of the youth political market.

With the majority of genuine war veterans approaching middle age, the training of a youth militia was meant to assure Zanu PF of a continuous source of partisan 'shock troops' to maintain a form of war psychosis in the rural areas as a principal campaign tool.

I know that a lot has been written about the subject so I shall avoid the temptation to delve in greater detail into what I believe is already in the public domain.

Zanu-PF had mobilised about 15 000 war veterans for emergency calls and to give direction to the agile and active youth militia which numbered slightly over 20 000. They were equipped with rudimentary tools and weapons for assault and intimidation such as axes, clubs, knives, knobkerries and spears. The people derisively called the youth 'Green Bombers', taking their cue from their olive-green uniforms. Deserters from the youth training camps have publicly stated that they were taught basic assassination skills, arson, rape and how to suffocate MDC activists and sympathisers.

The army commanded the militia's operations and provided them with food and transport. They patrolled the rural areas and camped at houses on commercial farms, beating drums to scare away the white owners, disrupting production, looting food and slaughtering livestock, and conducting all-night 're-education seminars' for farm workers.

The groups, led by Hunzvi and Joseph Chinotimba, a Harare municipal security guard who abandoned his job for the task, had a field day terrorising the nation at will. It was a tough time for the whites, their workers and all MDC supporters. As a party, we had our own information network and we tried to keep a record of the chaos. Farmers worked through a complex network, managed by the CFU. They recorded these activities daily and published a variety of bulletins highlighting their plight.

Their farm workers had a harrowing time. Many were displaced and dispersed, their houses and property seized by the marauding crowds as they were pushed into the bush. Some, following their ancestry, crossed our borders into neighbouring Mozambique, Zambia and Malawi in search of work and to obtain the assistance of kith and kin. A 2009 study of the catastrophic 'land reform' gave a detailed record of what happened to these poor trapped souls at the time. The study by GAPWUZ[3] found 'extremely high' figures of human rights violations with 1 in 10 respondents reporting at least one murder amongst fellow farm workers, while 38 per cent reported that children on the farms were forced to watch public beatings or torture.

The workers were subjected to even greater violence, torture and evictions than their white employers. A few who remained are now working for the new settlers. An estimated 40 per cent have since died. The decimation of GAPWUZ membership fell squarely into Zanu PF's original plan to destabilise the constituency as punishment for supporting the MDC during the referendum. With 150 000 members, GAPWUZ was one of our largest affiliates in the ZCTU. Today, that membership has been reduced to less than 10 000.

Traditional leaders joined the fray, claiming historical ownership of the commercial farmlands. Suffice to say, some traditional leaders took advantage. The attacks on commercial farmers and their workers exposed the purported land reform exercise as a systematic onslaught on nearly two million people to force them into the ranks of Zanu PF.

The aim was to deny me any support in the run-up to the 2002 presidential election. What I found distasteful was the use of a genuine historical grievance, land, as an excuse for the debilitating crisis of governance, the real issue which had led us to form the MDC. Mugabe used land as a ruse to blind Africa and the gullible in our own backyard and in the corridors of world power. Our economy, once the promise of Africa, was allowed to collapse, causing untold suffering to millions.

History will pronounce its verdict on the misguided who, even if they did not support Mugabe, more or less accepted his rationalisations. Future research will be necessary to assess the social costs of the chaos as lives were lost and Zimbabwe was reduced to dust during this period.

Mugabe had completely abandoned his constitutional responsibility and undertakings he had earlier committed himself to. In Zanu PF's 1980 manifesto promises were made to minorities that were later to suffer the lash:

> Zanu wishes to give the fullest assurance to the white community, the Asian and coloured communities that a Zanu government can never in principle or in social or government practice, discriminate against them. Racism, whether practised by whites or blacks, is anathema to the humanitarian philosophy of Zanu. It is as primitive a dogma as

tribalism or regionalism. Zimbabwe cannot just be a country for blacks. It is and should remain our country, all of us together.[4]

Twenty years later, Mugabe was now openly discriminatory. In one of his many racially divisive public speeches, he said:

> These whites do not deserve to be in Zimbabwe and we shall take steps to ensure that they are not entitled to our land in Zimbabwe. These, like Bennett and Coltart, are not part of our society. They belong to Britain and let them go there. If they want to stay here, we will say 'stay' but your place is in prison and nowhere else. Those who are compliant, let them come out and let them show they want to be part of us; otherwise time is not on their side.[5]

Such statements poisoned race relations and hardened individual and collective attitudes towards reconciliation; they were against our national interests as they tended to fuel greed among those with power. They also opened floodgates for corruption under the cover of nationalism. Mugabe openly encouraged the official discrimination against his political enemies and made allowances for anarchy.

As Zanu PF heightened its election campaign against the MDC, so did the vilification and violence increase. Although the presidential election was still 18 months away, any person listening to state radio and television broadcasts at the time would be forgiven for thinking the plebiscite was due in a matter of days.

Government ministries and departments started to announce phony 'development' projects for youths, women and rural communities to woo them away from other political parties. Nearly every cabinet minister, senior government official, traditional chief, some church leaders and Zanu PF executives at all levels were deployed in the campaign, with all sorts of election promises mixed with threatening war messages. As a political player, we could not simply watch from the sidelines. We responded, with our own messages, low-level and underground party activities and programmes.

I was encouraged by the manner in which our communities responded to the rising wave of brutality. They displayed a lot of resilience. Individuals, families, communities and our young party dealt with these pressures in an extremely mature manner.

By August, the levels of violence and intimidation had reached unprecedented heights. Hardly a day passed without a new case of assault, arson, a farm invasion, the death of an opposition activist or the displacement of a family in the rural areas. The police force publicly announced that it had asked army units to maintain order at what they called 'flashpoints' in Harare and other towns despite people's protests that they were being harassed. Armed soldiers were deployed in urban areas, rounding up late revellers at social meeting points and beer-drinking outlets in the townships and assaulting them. Both the army and the police argued that there was a potential for violence in the urban centres.

Human rights organisations and *The Daily News* documented hundreds of cases of abuse by the army, usually late at night and especially in Kwekwe, Chitungwiza and Harare. Among the people attacked was Edwin Mushoriwa, our new member of parliament for Dzivaresekwa in Harare.

In April 2000, South African President Thabo Mbeki had indicated his interest in brokering international funding for land reform, with the help of the UNDP, out of what he said was his concern for the breakdown in the rule of law.

As this was in the middle of an election campaign anchored on violence and intimidation, Mugabe ignored this, forcing the UN Secretary General, Kofi Annan, to appeal to him in writing to end the lawlessness.

In August 2000, Mbeki, with his ministers of finance, trade and industry, and agriculture, was in Harare for talks with Mugabe during which I understood he raised his concerns about the assault on commercial agriculture. After the meetings, Mugabe announced that he wished to end the lawlessness and promised to remove the war veterans from the farms by September. At the same time, he indicated an intention to seize 3 041 farms, a move the CFU immediately challenged in the High Court. Before

Mbeki left Harare, he promised Mugabe Pretoria's help to recover from the economic crisis. At a joint press conference with Mbeki at the end of their meeting, Mugabe vowed:

> We will be resettling those who are in need of the land both those on the farms, who have invaded the farms, and those who have not done so in the communal areas and elsewhere. We will, in the process, be removing all war veterans from the farms that are not earmarked for resettlement. The time frame I cannot really say, but certainly I want to say it will be within this month.[6]

For a moment, I thought the chaos was coming to an end, especially when Mbeki publicly stated that the United Nations had taken over the resolution of Zimbabwe's land ownership problem. He said more than US$6 billion was needed to pay compensation for the acquired farms and the issue was now on Annan's desk for immediate action. A week before Mbeki's visit, a UN team of experts was in Harare to underline the link between land reform, the rule of law and the availability of international financial support. Mugabe, however, did not seem to be convinced by their arguments.

The news appeared to irk the CFU which immediately sought the nullification of the process in the Supreme Court, arguing that it was illegal. The CFU offered 200 farms freely, a number Mugabe felt was inadequate for his needs. He now wanted about half the 12 million hectares then in the hands of whites. But his deputy, Joseph Msika, and the new agriculture minister, Joseph Made, appeared to differ, saying the land already seized by the state would be sufficient.

There seemed to be conflicting messages from the state on the way forward. Some officials appeared eager to halt the process while others, with a tight grip on Mugabe, advised him to act differently. A week later, Mugabe threw away his earlier assurance to Mbeki and told Hunzvi and the invaders to ignore Msika and Made. 'Whatever we do after the 3 041 farms will be purely complementary, but we are not stopping there,' he told a Zanu PF campaign meeting in Bindura. 'Our roots are in the soil and not in the factories. We can never allow a return to racial oppression.'[7]

At the same time, the military intensified its involvement in the farm takeovers, visiting commercial farmers and enquiring about the farm ownership structures and compiling annual production statistics. Farmers who visited our offices said armed military officers made them fill in a questionnaire, saying they needed the data for military use.

Rufaro Gwanzura, a Zanu PF MP for Marondera West – 60 kilometres south-west of Harare – died in a car crash in August 2000. In the MDC we saw an opportunity to test the party's strength following two months' intense post-election violence. But Zanu PF wanted the occasion for a different purpose: to prepare and test new rigging systems for the 2002 presidential election. The Marondera West poll was set down for 25 November 2000. This time the military made no secret of its direct interest to enter into politics and support their Zanu PF civilian administration.

Brigadier Ambrose Mutinhiri was the official Zanu PF candidate. We fielded Shadreck Chipangura, a simple activist from our party structures. When our campaign teams tried to move into the area, they found it sealed off from the opposition. For much of the final school term starting in September, most pupils never sat in classrooms and teachers, assumed to be sympathetic to the MDC, fled in fear as war veterans took over school premises for campaign meetings.

In the heat of politics and the excitement of the moment it is easy to make mistakes which are amplified by media coverage. In a dictatorship like Zimbabwe this can have serious personal consequences.

On 11 September 2000, we organised a public meeting in Harare to commemorate the MDC's first anniversary. The turnout was overwhelming: more than 40 000 people found their way to the soccer stadium for the celebrations. As party president, I was the last to rise and address the jubilant, high-spirited crowd. After thanking the people for receiving the party so well and mandating us to take on Mugabe and Zanu PF in the June election, and amid wild cheers, clapping and ululation, I veered off course. 'What I want to tell Mugabe today, is please go peacefully,' I said, in the full glare of state television cameras, and much to the delight and endorsement of the crowd. 'If you do not do so, the people of Zimbabwe will remove you violently ...' I continued with my speech, predicting the collapse of the Zanu PF government before the Christmas holidays.

A vote alone did not bring freedom: democracy was stillborn without economic liberation. I reminded the audience that in this stadium 20 years before, Robert Mugabe had announced the independence of Zimbabwe. But Zimbabwe had moved from the hands of one oppressor to another. There could be no freedom where there was no rule of law; where people were not safe; where there was hunger and no jobs.

One of our major concerns was the intrusion of the military into government and I urged that we needed to set up a National Defence Council which would be structured with input from all role players, to assess the threat to Zimbabwe and give recommendations to government on how to transform our defence forces into the protectors of the people, rather than their persecutors.[8]

Soon after I retired to my seat, I was amazed to see my colleagues, especially the lawyers in the MDC, rush towards me, whispering that I had made a serious mistake. Why? Mugabe could find no excuse to arrest me for any statement I had made. But my advisers pointed out that my remark about the people removing Mugabe violently would be seen as an open threat. Initially, I laughed it off. But after some thought I could see the sense of what they were saying.

I quickly advised the MDC information department to arrange a press conference after the rally. At the media briefing, I tried to explain that my statement was well meant as a piece of advice, a word of caution and an opinion in which I was counselling Mugabe to find a speedy resolution of the national crisis. I further stated that the MDC was a non-violent party, with no policy of unseating Zanu PF violently.

But it was too late. The regime would exploit my verbal slip to the hilt.

ENDNOTES

1   Scarnecchia, Timothy (2006). 'The "Fascist Cycle" In Zimbabwe, 2000-2005'. *Journal of Southern African Studies*, 32(2)

2   *The Daily News*, Harare 10 July 2000
3   *If something is wrong ... The invisible suffering of commercial farm workers and their families due to Land Reform.* Report produced for the General Agricultural & Plantation Workers Union of Zimbabwe [GAPWUZ] by the Research and Advocacy Unit [RAU] and the Justice For Agriculture [JAG] Trust, 2009 http://www.zimonline.co.za/Article.aspx?ArticleId=5381
4   Zanu PF 1980 Manifesto
5   *The Daily News*, Harare, 20 August 2002
6   Reuters, 3 August 2000
7   Mugabe misleads Mbeki www.zimbabwesituation.com/aug5.html
8   'Tsvangirai's speech at Rufaro Stadium'. 19 June 2000, MDC background papers http://www.afrol.com/Countries/Zimbabwe/backgr_tsvangirai_speech.htm

CHAPTER SIXTEEN

AGAINST ALL ODDS

During a trip abroad to try once more to impress upon the world what we were up against, I received an alarming message. My officials in Harare informed me that the police were looking for me in connection with my speech during the MDC's first anniversary celebrations at the Rufaro soccer stadium in September 2000. Unsettled, I cut short my trip and headed for Johannesburg, en route to Harare. As it turned out, the affair would blow over, but not before I had been taught a fundamental lesson in politics: don't hand your opponents a stick to beat you with.

Zimbabweans would be regularly misinformed through the state media that I wanted to see Mugabe assassinated so that I could assume power through violence. After the matter fizzled out because the police could not sustain a charge that would stand a judicial test, I could feel that state security agents had increased their surveillance on my home and members of my family. Mugabe continued to refer to my statement to justify an epidemic of violence against the MDC and for propaganda purposes to support his view that I had a dangerous disposition.

After the MDC's first anniversary celebrations, I had left for Europe, visiting a number of capitals and meeting with state officials to explain the MDC's position. The response was mixed: in some places I was well received; in others I could see that the governments were trying to size me up, to understand what I stood for, my motivations and my vision.

Two weeks later I returned home. The situation was worse than ever. Farm 'repossessions' continued to be highlighted while the terrorisation of the mass of rural people continued unchecked in the shadows.

There was some respite when the Supreme Court, sitting as a constitutional court to hear an appeal from Capital Radio, declared that the ZBC's monopoly, as the sole broadcaster, was illegal. The court further ordered that Capital Radio be permitted to start broadcasting once more. The police were supposed to return the station's broadcasting equipment, seized soon after Moyo's appointment as the new information minister. The relief was short-lived: Mugabe intervened and used his Presidential Powers (Temporary Measures) regulations to keep the ban in place. Unable to make headway using the legal route, Capital Radio relocated to London and set up a new station, SWRadio Africa, which broadcast specifically to Zimbabwe.

Moyo began work on a new law to protect the state broadcaster from local competition and to limit the private sector's access to the broadcasting industry. His concerns were not just political; he complained bitterly about the fact that I had been granted an interview on a private television station, Joy TV. The station, like Capital Radio, was also forced off air and closed down. Joy TV came into the market out of both necessity and economic accident. Established during the Non-Aligned Movement (NAM) summit in 1986, the station was then known as TV2. The intention, we were told, was to have an educational channel. But poor funding turned TV2 into a farce, forcing ZBC to lease it for five hours a day to Flame Lily Broadcasting Limited, owners of Joy TV, in July 1997. Flame Lily was owned by a consortium of elite Zanu PF officials, Leo Mugabe and James Makamba. Joy TV rarely produced its own news bulletins; it was merely a conduit for US and British fare. But, significantly, the station carried the BBC World's news bulletin in the evening. After the June election, Makamba tried to anchor a current affairs programme on Joy TV. He interviewed me on one of these programmes.

On 6 October 2000, Mugabe came up with another surprise. Using his constitutional powers as head of state, he issued a general amnesty for perpetrators of electoral violence and other politically motivated crimes in the run-up to the June parliamentary poll.[1] The amnesty excluded the 'specified offences' of 'murder, robbery, rape, indecent assault, theft, possession of arms and any offence involving fraud or dishonesty'. The pardon covered the six-month period between January and July. It meant that neither the murderers of white farmers and MDC activists nor the looters, robbers and farm invaders who caused chaos in Zimbabwe could be prosecuted for their dirty handiwork.

The decision shocked the MDC, leaving us with no option than to tender our verbal protests, which no one at home or beyond could even follow up with a recalcitrant Zanu PF.

Our neighbours in southern Africa pretended to have heard nothing from Harare and never raised the issue at their regular state summits. Mugabe's amnesty differed in a fundamental respect from an amnesty that I had promised in my Rufaro Stadium address if we came to power. I had said that truth must go hand in hand with forgiveness. We would give amnesty to those who told the truth to a national commission looking into the causes of the violence after the election. We did not seek revenge but honesty and healing for a nation that had been tortured for too long.[2] Mugabe's amnesty allowed his thugs to get away with murder and never be held accountable.

We thought about challenging the move in court, but soon realised that even if the amnesty was revoked, there was nothing we could do about the negative attitude of the police. They allowed perpetrators to walk scot-free, even in cases of overwhelming evidence against them.

After cushioning his constituency from possible danger, Mugabe maintained a firm grip on the MDC. On 17 October, police swooped on the home of Justin Mutendadzamera, the MP for Mabvuku in Harare, at dawn and assaulted him and his family for no apparent reason. Mugabe had upped his campaign significantly and Mutendadzamera was among the first victims of the renewed onslaught.

News of fresh cases of harassment and attacks on other MPs reached my office, with 40 of our 57 legislators being chased away from their homes. Their lives were disrupted as many advised their families to flee Zimbabwe. Those who decided to stay lived like nomads – constantly moving around for personal safety.

Before the end of the month, police informed me that they were interested in interviewing me in connection with my MDC first anniversary speech. As I was not required to do anything then, I simply had to wait for their date and time. And the police took their time.

Meanwhile, disaster struck in the MDC. Amos Munyaradzi Mutongi, our MP for Bikita West, a rural constituency east of Masvingo, died of liver cancer on 4 November – necessitating a by-election. Mugabe swiftly set 13 January 2001 as the date for the by-election. Again, the military fielded another soldier, Colonel Claudius Makova, as the Zanu PF candidate.

By the time we contested the other by-election in Marondera West on 25 November, I knew that we had a slim chance of making it. The MDC found campaigning impossible. It was an abnormal contest in that most of the commercial farms around the area had been invaded and new voters, not there in the June 2000 election, had been added to the roll. We were told they were new settlers who had recently moved into the area from surrounding communal lands which, before June, fell in different constituencies. We had never had access to these voters and the secret ballot was highly compromised.

The army was firmly in control and the area was awash with guns, often in the hands of people totally unwilling to subject themselves to any civilian election management authority. I was happy, at least, that despite our loss, Chipangura secured 4 366 votes against Mutinhiri's 7 376. The rest of the people, in an area with more than 30 000 registered voters decided to stay at home in protest.

While the MDC did all it could to defend Bikita West, one of its few rural seats, I could see a similar pattern to that used in Marondera West being played out. Zanu PF was determined to overturn the 2000 result and to reclaim the seat. In the fight, hell broke loose. Mugabe unleashed his entire arsenal of resources into the scattered villages in the middle of an agriculture season, disrupting normal life as voters were driven to meetings and subjected to nightly 're-education workshops'.

Unlike Marondera West, then surrounded by invaded commercial farms, Bikita West is in the middle of a vast communal land. The only way Zanu PF could coerce the people into joining them was by holding them as hapless hostages.

I took time to address a public meeting in Gwanda in the south west. The meeting, organised by Paul Themba Nyathi, our MP for the area, was a normal political rally and attended by local villagers and a few people from the small town. A few days after the meeting, as I was about to go into a planning session with my Bikita West campaign team, I was told the police wanted to arrest me for calling Mugabe a 'stinking skunk' at the Gwanda meeting. I could not recall making any such reference.

When our lawyers pressed the courts about the fate of our June electoral petitions, Mugabe pulled another surprise card. On 8 December 2000, he issued an executive order saying:

> Recognizing that the general elections held following the dissolution of Parliament on the 11 April 2000, were held under peaceful conditions and that the people who voted did so freely ... the election of a (Member of Parliament) shall not be rendered void ... and the doing of anything in connection with, arising out of, or resulting from the general election referred to in Section 2 which is or may be such a contravention (of the Electoral Act) is to that extent hereby validated and shall be deemed not to be such a contravention.[3]

Once again, the MDC saw the executive order as a violation of its members' rights and it clearly usurped the constitutional obligations of the judiciary. We requested an urgent hearing in the Supreme Court.

We persevered with our desperate attempts to enter Bikita West to campaign for the by-election. Our teams were mainly based in the town of Masvingo, 80 kilometres to the west, and in parts of Bikita East, occasionally making forays into the constituency to meet the people.

We tried the door-to-door method but encountered fresh problems as Zanu PF had set up a web of informers who caused further disruptions of the campaign. I realised in December that it was virtually impossible for the MDC to address open meetings in Bikita West because soldiers, war veterans and Zanu PF youths – drawn from the country's ten provinces – saturated every corner of the area armed with guns, axes, pick heads, knives and other weapons to force compliance from the voters and to block our defence of Bikita West.

On 21 December 2000, Chief Justice Anthony Gubbay took a swipe at the government's attitude towards the restoration of civil order and the rising levels of lawlessness. 'Wicked things have been done, and continue to be done,' he said. 'They must be stopped. Common law crimes have been, and are being, committed with impunity. Laws made by Parliament have been flouted by the Government.'[4] Gubbay was delivering a judgment on a separate challenge brought by the CFU against the continued farm seizures.

Judges and other judicial officers were routinely threatened and demeaned, as Mugabe fuelled a campaign of judicial subversion, initially directed at Gubbay and later spreading to prosecutors and magistrates. It became clear that the judiciary must play ball according to Zanu PF's agenda or be forced out.

In my view, by tampering with the rule of law, Mugabe made a serious political mistake. Modern society loathes and flees from anarchy. Business quickly shuts up shop and investors look elsewhere. The government's political legitimacy is eroded and if lawlessness continues the descent into a failed state can be fast and irreparable. Through its repressive and uncontrollable behaviour directed against anything moving in the opposite direction, Zanu PF cost Zimbabwe dearly. Mugabe inflicted deep wounds – wounds that will take generations to heal.

Concerned about the rapid deterioration of the rule of law, the International Bar Association (IBA) sent a fact-finding mission and tried, in vain, to get Mugabe to see reason. Mugabe nursed and nurtured a culture of impunity despite assuring the IBA delegation that he was ready to respect the rule of law and judicial freedom. He took no action to ensure police impartiality.

Particularly worrying were incessant attacks on the Law Society of Zimbabwe. Mugabe even suggested legislative amendments to curtail the ability of lawyers to speak out, especially on key issues which included a selective application of the law against the MDC and other opposition parties. The selective line of attack, through the abuse of the law, contravened Zimbabwe's international obligations which demanded equality through justice.

An example of the ruling party's blatant bias was the arrest and prosecution of war veteran Joseph Chinotimba for shooting and injuring an MDC supporter in the suburb of Glen Norah in Harare. Chinotimba was convicted of the crime but never spent a day inside a jail. By turning the government into the main law breaker, Mugabe turned the people away from the law, perpetrators and victims alike. Respect for the police vanished. While Mugabe and Zanu PF suffered immeasurably, the real damage was the loss of the people's trust in government.

Despite the selective application of the rule of law, Zimbabweans were lucky to have a vibrant judiciary that provided strong checks on Mugabe's behaviour. Judicial steadfastness, honesty and integrity posed a serious problem to Zanu PF's pursuit for political bias. Despite this strong stance against lawlessness, Mugabe persisted with his political programme.

So what Gubbay was saying in his December judgment reflected a common public policy pattern, though implemented with varying degrees of severity. In our case in Bikita, the situation was untenable. Each time teams from the MDC tried to enter the area, there were skirmishes and violent clashes. One person died in the melee. But the police arrested only MDC supporters and left those from Zanu PF alone.

The result of the by-election was fairly predictable. Claudius Makova forcibly scooped 12 993 votes, while Boniface Pakai of the MDC took

7001. After the polls, Pakai was hounded out of Bikita and went into exile.

Two weeks later, in a unanimous decision on 30 January 2001, after considering the MDC's challenge to Mugabe's December executive order barring us from being heard for the June electoral malpractices, the Supreme Court held that:

> ... the applicants had the civil right to partake in an election that was free and fair and devoid of corrupt or illegal practices, to challenge the result of an election which was claimed to have been tainted by corrupt and illegal practices, and to seek practical and meaningful redress in the form of a High Court order certifying that the results were tainted. The notice effectively deprived them of that right. The right of full and unimpeded access to courts is of cardinal importance for the adjudication of justiciable disputes.[5]

Three days after the ruling, Chinamasa visited Gubbay and tried to force him to take an early retirement package. He stood his ground and refused to go, sparking a serious constitutional crisis between the judiciary and the executive. Unconcerned, Chinamasa met with the other Supreme Court judges and 'advised' them to quit the bench, reportedly saying 'the President (Mugabe) does not want you to come to any harm'.[6]

After a positive Supreme Court ruling in our favour, the High Court started work with our lawyers on the electoral petitions. Out of the 39 original June 2000 election petitions, two were dismissed on procedural grounds; 16 of our candidates withdrew their cases; and five of the petitions were either never set down for hearing or were never completed by the High Court. The five involved challenges in Gokwe West, Marondera East, Mazowe East, Mazowe West, and Mberengwa East. The Chivi North and Murehwa South petitions were dismissed after our candidates failed to turn up on the first day of the hearings.

In another five areas, the petitions were abandoned after the deaths of Zanu PF candidates: Bindura, Chikomba, Hurungwe West, Makoni West and Marondera West.

Candidates withdrew their cases for various reasons. Many felt prejudiced by the continued delays. Some felt threatened about continuing to fight for justice; others simply fled into exile. For example, Philemon Matibe, a commercial farmer from Chegutu, lost his property to invading war veterans and Zanu PF militias after he filed his election petition. They demanded that he withdraw the petition. When he refused, they forcibly evicted him and he left Zimbabwe soon afterwards.

The Daily News tried hard to keep the nation informed about Zanu PF's excesses and its owners and reporters paid dearly for their stance. State agents and war veterans banned copies of the newspaper in areas outside the big cities in a forlorn bid to keep the nation in the dark. But, as happens in most repressive societies, newspapers were often smuggled to outlying areas by MDC activists and aid workers. Together with a small but vibrant foreign media corps, the story of what was happening in Zimbabwe spread far and wide.

There were instances when war veterans mounted random traffic checkpoints and searched for copies of *The Daily News* on unsuspecting bus travellers and private motorists. Those found with copies of the newspaper were assaulted. Copies were impounded and burned. I recall watching the news on the local state television, ZTV and, to my horror, saw a batch of privately owned newspapers, including *The Daily News*, going up in smoke – in full view of a police officer in Mutoko, 143 kilometres north-east of Harare.

On 23 January 2001, a horde of Zanu PF supporters and war veterans marched through Harare city centre shouting profanities and insults at *The Daily News*. Four days later, Jonathan Moyo declared that *The Daily News* was a security risk. The following day, Sunday, 28 January, the use of the law and intimidation seemed insufficient for Moyo, Hunzvi and other hardliners in Zanu PF in their quest to silence *The Daily News*. The newspaper was bombed.

I believe the state assigned its bomb experts to blow up the newspaper's printing factory. The powerful bombs reduced the printing machines to heaps of scrap metal. It was beyond doubt that *The Daily News* had been destroyed by military experts, who skilfully set up either a TM46 or a TM57 anti-tank mine, used on solid objects like bridges and buildings in times of war. No ordinary garden thieves would dare undertake such a delicate and complicated military mission. The newspaper made alternative printing arrangements and remained in business and on the streets, but with a much reduced print-run.

The bombing of *The Daily News* took place a few days after the MDC dismissed John Nkatazo, the director of security, and replaced him with Michael Hogan. The bombers sought to drive a wedge in the MDC by imputing that there was a rift between pro-white intellectuals and 'nationalistic' former trade union officials. The bombers tried to use their attack on the newspaper to get at the MDC, leaving crudely hand-written notes at the crime scene indicating that the work was done by a faction within the party.

The notes, purporting to be from an unknown group calling itself the 'Authentic MDC' read:

> This is the work of the Authentic Movement for Democratic Change (MDC Trade Unionist). This is a warning to the 'intellectuals' within the MDC who are flirting with the racist white minority. *The Daily News*, as the mouthpiece of our party, has done much damage our (sic) reputation by portraying us as puppets of the whites so causing us to lose the Marondera West and Bikita West by-elections. We are Zimbabweans and true patriots. To portray us as puppets of the white minority and the British imperialists is folly of the highest order. Remove Michael Hogan from our security department and reinstate John Nkatazo.

The aim was to keep Zimbabweans a captive people, to make politics and the practice of journalism extremely hazardous careers and to ensure that the MDC and I had no access to the public, or any media, at any time. Again, it did not surprise me when Mugabe and the state showed no interest in investigating this crime; Mugabe, through Moyo, believed the newspaper belonged to the MDC which was completely untrue.

War veterans and militias burned down the home of our candidate in Kariba, Luka Sigobole, whose loss in the June 2000 election we had challenged. He later disappeared. I persuaded the other 'losing' candidates to remain focused on their petitions and to persevere with the fight. I believed that after Mugabe granted amnesty to perpetrators of violence, the election petitions offered the people a platform that could alert the world to the scale of anarchy in Zimbabwe both before and after the June election. So, it was important that the challenges remained on the court roll.

That *The Daily News* maintained its strong editorial stance against Zanu PF excesses angered Moyo even further. He branded the publication an MDC mouthpiece and a creation of the enemies of Zimbabwe, controlled by Britain. Such comments incited Zanu PF supporters to shun the newspaper and the now lily-livered police ignored attacks on the newspaper's staff, both on and off duty. War veterans and security agents started to kidnap, abduct and assault staff of *The Daily News* while they were on assignments, especially at Zanu PF meetings and on the invaded farms.

When these measures failed to cow the newspaper into submission, Moyo tried another tactic. One morning, the state announced that the Zimbabwe Investment Centre (ZIC) had cancelled the investment licence of the Associated Newspapers of Zimbabwe (ANZ), the parent company of *The Daily News*. ZIC, the nation was told, had unearthed a crime committed by the ANZ at the time the company was registered. In short, the ANZ was accused of falsifying information to obtain a publishing licence and violating foreign exchange control regulations.

The newspaper argued that as a local venture, ANZ was exempt from conditions and operating rules meant for foreign companies wishing to invest in Zimbabwe. Mbanga and Nyarota were arrested, nevertheless. The company challenged Moyo's action in court. The matter was thrown out by a magistrate's court and *The Daily News* survived once more.

Moyo then made his first move on foreign journalists deemed to be sympathetic to the MDC. Mercedes Sayagues, the correspondent of the South African weekly *Mail & Guardian* was declared a prohibited immigrant and given 24 hours to leave Harare. Barely hours after Sayagues was deported, the BBC's Joseph Winter was sent packing under similar conditions. Winter had earlier had a tough experience while reporting for the BBC in Zimbabwe. He was once thrown out of a Zanu PF meeting on allegations of making up a story. David Blair of the British *Telegraph* suffered the same fate. All three journalists were officially barred from ever entering Zimbabwe again on any type of business. Their deportation set the tone for the subsequent harassment and forced departure of another foreign correspondent, Andrew Meldrum.

Virtually all major international media networks were banned. The state-sponsored squeeze on Zimbabwean journalism knew no legal bounds. Whenever the courts acquitted a journalist or media house of some trumped-up charge, war veterans and security agents were given tacit permission to mete out punishment – in a primitive and extra-judicial style.

From numerous conversations I had with media managers, journalists and my colleagues in the MDC, it was clear that Mugabe no longer cared about the need for a free press: he simply wanted to hold on to Zimbabwe regardless of local or international opinion. He did not care about the consequences. With a determined desire to smash the MDC against all odds, Mugabe and his new 'war cabinet' had sunk to a very deep level of depravity. They considered themselves to be super-patriots who believed in nothing but national indoctrination to ensure blind loyalty, the efficacy of lies, command and compliance. They were committed to the perpetuation of conflict and saw only themselves as right.

The assault on the private media and on the independence of the judiciary in early 2001 worried me a great deal. In particular, the attack on Gubbay, and the constitutional crisis it spawned, sent confusing signals to us in the party. Zimbabwe was now fragmented and polarised. Mugabe was not prepared to listen to anyone, harping on a nationalist mantra that considered any criticism as a negative development. There was no attempt at rapprochement, conflict analysis or resolution.

The spirit of 'us' and 'them' dominated the state media. Mugabe now controlled and distorted the 'truth' and freedom of expression. I, Morgan Tsvangirai, was made into an instant scapegoat for Zimbabwe's mounting troubles.

Countrywide, fear was now endemic: on farms, in villages, in factories, at mines and along roadsides. Mugabe became completely indifferent to the people's suffering and their quest for a better society and – with Moyo's rabid enthusiasm and foul language – distorted the Zimbabwean way of life to a level from which this nation may take many decades to recover.

Shunning any meaningful feedback from an impoverished populace and a mass of desperate young job-seekers, Mugabe used a vicious information and propaganda war to pursue a fear-based, deification style of leadership and to heighten the political temperature. He constantly blamed the MDC and me for his own lack of foresight and wasted opportunities.

In the meantime, the stand-off between the executive and the judiciary persisted after Gubbay vowed to stay. In the MDC, we were no longer sure what would become of our electoral challenges should the stand-off persist. The whole spectacle sounded surreal, but that was the shocking Zimbabwean reality. Mugabe took umbrage at both the MDC and the CFU for legal challenges and went all out for the judges, especially the whites.

Chinamasa and Moyo led the vitriolic campaign against Gubbay and his colleagues. 'It is like we have an English court on Zimbabwean soil,' said Chinamasa in a statement to the state media, referring to the composition of the Supreme Court. 'We must begin to exorcise from all our institutions the racist ghost of Ian Smith. We will do so by phasing out Smith's disciples and sympathisers …'

When Gubbay continued to turn up at his office to carry out his duties, Zanu PF deployed a large group of war veterans to storm the Supreme Court building. This happened a few minutes before the full bench was to hear yet another CFU challenge over its new losses of land. The rowdy, placard-waving crowd descended on the tiny building, shouting profanities, singing war songs and using threatening language. The police who escorted them simply watched from the sidelines. Gubbay protested; he appealed in vain for protection from Mugabe. Mugabe responded publicly by telling his party's convention that no judicial decision would stand in his way.

As the stand-off continued, Godfrey Chidyausiku, the head of the High Court and a former deputy minister in the Zanu PF government who had chaired the 1999 Constitutional Commission, entered the fray and publicly attacked Gubbay for his judgments, accusing him of siding with white Zimbabweans in the land dispute. Gubbay once again pleaded for protection, resulting in vice-president Simon Muzenda's summoning him to his office. Gubbay took colleague and respected jurist Wilson Sandura to the meeting – which turned out to be another farce. Tension between Mugabe and the judiciary had reached a point of no return, the two were told bluntly. In fact, Gubbay was so insulted that he threatened to resign.

The next day, Chinamasa called on Gubbay and informed him that Mugabe had accepted his resignation, which he had never tendered. When Gubbay, then 68, tried to clarify the position, he was threatened once more. Zimbabwean judges are compelled to retire at 70. Although this requirement can be waived, Gubbay still had the energy to pull through the remaining two years of active service on the bench. The government told Gubbay that it could no longer guarantee his safety if he refused to go.

When he finally threw in the towel, Chinamasa moved at lighting pace and tried to push him out of office immediately. He publicly announced that Gubbay was expected to vacate his office and official residence in a matter of hours. As that was clearly inhumane, Gubbay once again refused to budge.

The following morning, Mugabe mobilised a fresh set of vicious war veterans, led by Joseph Chinotimba who labelled himself the top commander of farm invasions, to invade Gubbay's office at the Supreme Court. Chinotimba was at the Supreme Court building twice during the day, each time howling abusive expletives in halting English. The police simply stood idly by, claiming they were under orders to do so.

Gubbay managed later to extract concessions from Chinamasa to stop the personal vilification, withdraw all malicious statements and allow him to remain chief justice for four more months while he prepared for a dignified exit. Clearly angered by Gubbay's momentary victory, Chinamasa discharged another set of arrows at Gubbay's colleagues, Nicholas McNally and Ahmed Ebrahim. The two were threatened and forced to agree to take early retirement.

Three new judges, who in Chinamasa's wisdom were supposedly sympathetic to Mugabe and Zanu PF, were quickly promoted to the Supreme Court as immediate replacements. From that time, the tone of the Supreme Court judgments changed. Among the first rulings of the newly constituted Court was a stunning decision to overturn an earlier judgment of the same Supreme Court in which the seizure of commercial farms was declared illegal.

Against this background I had every reason to worry about the fate of our June 2000 electoral challenges. We were feeling the effects of the presidential amnesty through witness intimidation. I received reports that in Chiredzi North, for example, Zanu PF had started to burn down the homes of potential witnesses to these challenges. During the hearings, many witnesses broke down and pleaded for protection after their testimonies. In Mount Darwin South, a witness was abducted three weeks before the date of the hearing, never to be seen again.

When the hearings started, my case against Kenneth Manyonda in Buhera North was the first to come under judicial scrutiny. I presented to High Court Judge James Devittie hard evidence of violence, electoral malpractices and the subversion of the entire process, which inevitably led to a flawed outcome.

Among the main points of my submission were the murders of my campaign manager, Tichaona Chiminya and his assistant Talent Mabika, burned to death at gunpoint by Joseph Mwale, a state intelligence operative, and Manyonda's Zanu PF agents. A number of witnesses supported my plea to nullify the result. Manyonda tried to escape culpability, protesting his innocence. But given the strength of the evidence, Justice Devittie concluded that, while Manyonda might not have been personally, willingly or knowingly involved, his agents – for whom the law made him answerable – were guilty of unduly influencing the result through their actions in his name.[7] He nullified Manyonda's election, thus necessitating a rerun.

Justice Devittie ordered the arrest and prosecution of Mwale and Manyonda's agents involved in the murder of Chiminya and Mabika. Specifically, he instructed the court to forward all the evidence to the Attorney General's office for immediate action. He stated in the judgment:

> … If I were to indulge my feelings on the matter, I would say that it is a conclusion I have arrived at with sadness; not because I have been

bound to follow the law as I have stated it; the law must be obeyed for the well-being of all of us, and in order that freedom of election may be bequeathed to future generations ... the killing of Chiminya and Mabika was a wicked act ... in terms of section 137 of the Act, the record of evidence must be transmitted by the Registrar to the Attorney General with a view to the institution of any prosecution proper to be instituted in the circumstances and the attention of the Attorney General is drawn to the evidence on the killing of Chiminya and Mabika.[8]

The order was ignored.

To remain in parliament, Manyonda quickly lodged an appeal to the Supreme Court. My victory showed that democracy had been short-changed in Buhera North. As I celebrated, just hours after Justice Devittie's ruling, police – in riot and crowd-control gear – raided my office and arrested my four security guards, Joel Mapaura, Ernest Chifomboti, Matthew Musokere and Nhamo Musekiwa as well as Freddy Kafantenganga, a worker from a nearby private shop. After detaining them for a night, the police came up with a trumped-up charge of their having undergone military training, for the purposes of banditry, in Uganda in 1999. The five were denied access to the lawyer who had immediately rushed to Harare Central Police Station to intervene. The charge was later dropped.

Manyonda's appeal was never heard. When Sheila Jarvis, my lawyer, followed up on this court officials told her that a substantial part of the record had mysteriously gone missing. Several tapes of the record were stolen from a locked office at the High Court. Some of the remaining tapes were said to have been damaged and were inaudible, while the Judge's notebooks were missing. Consequently, I was told, there was nothing that could be done about it. The matter died, and Manyonda served a full five-year term as a legislator.

After presiding over four other hearings, Justice Devittie noted that: '... at the heart of the spirit of the Electoral Act, lies the principle of freedom of election'.[9] He said that a people's freedom in an election vanishes when intimidation overwhelms a community, adding that he had heard incontrovertible evidence of torture, assault, and harassment of MDC supporters, enough to subdue voters of 'ordinary nerve and courage'.[10]

After nullifying another result in Hurungwe East against Zanu PF's Reuben Marumahoko, Justice Devittie said:

> I must uphold the oath of my office and therefore the idea of a nation governed by law; I must apply the law as it is, and not how I may wish it to be and that shall be my duty for so long as I shall sit as a Judge of this Court. In terms of section 136 (c) of the (Electoral) Act, it is my duty to pronounce that the respondent was not duly elected.[11]

Like Manyonda, Marumahoko appealed against the judgment. But again a whole section of the appeal record vanished from the High Court. However, when Justice Devittie summarised the evidence in his notes and the contesting parties agreed to proceed with the record as it was, nothing further happened.

Instead, Mugabe appointed Marumahoko to the post of deputy minister of home affairs. He remains a senior Zanu PF politician. He contested for a Senate seat in Hurungwe in 2008 and claimed to have won, again. Mugabe further appointed him as the new deputy minister of regional integration and international cooperation in the transitional government that was consummated in February 2009.

In the Mutoko South election petition, Justice Devittie nullified the election of Zanu PF's Olivia Muchena, now a cabinet minister, and stated, as a matter of record, that she was 'responsible in law' for the suffering, pain, misery, kidnapping and torture of MDC supporters.[12]

Similar to his verdict in the Buhera North petition, Justice Devittie again ordered that the evidence led on the murder of Mationa Mushaya, the MDC branch chairman, and his son Onias be submitted to the Attorney General's office for action. The order was ignored.

In other courts, Justice Devittie's colleagues, Justices Vernanda Ziyambi and Rita Makarau, nullified Zanu PF's victory in Chiredzi North and Gokwe North on the same grounds of violence and intimidation.[13]

Our candidate's case in Gokwe North was particularly interesting. The appeal by the Zanu PF candidate was thrown out by the Supreme Court. The court's registrar should have formally informed the Speaker of Parliament that the seat was now vacant, to pave the way for a by-election. Before that could be done, the Zanu PF candidate lodged a fresh set of papers to have the appeal reinstated and reviewed by the same court. No date was ever set for that fresh application, further stalling the need for a by-election until the life of the 2000 parliamentary session expired in 2005.

Justice Makarau held a similar view on the Gokwe South petition where the MDC candidate was attacked during the campaign period. He sustained serious injuries and a rumour was spread around the area that he was dead, fuelling further fear among the voters.

Terrible testimonies were heard from Makoni East where Nicholas Mudzengerere told Justice Paddington Garwe that his opponent, Shadreck Chipanga of Zanu PF and a former director of the dreaded CIO spy agency, through his election agent, one Chimombe, disembowelled Francis Chingonzo for reading an MDC campaign pamphlet. Chingonzo died as a result. Justice Garwe refused to condone such behaviour and ruled that Chipanga was not duly elected as a legislator.

I have deliberately picked on these random examples from Kariba, on the border with Zambia; Mutoko, near Mozambique; Chiredzi, in the far south and close to the Limpopo River; Gokwe, in central Zimbabwe; and Makoni in eastern Zimbabwe, to show that a systematic pattern of violence covered the entire country in the run-up to the June 2000 election.

I believe that if all our election challenges had made it for judicial scrutiny, the final result would show that the MDC had mounted a formidable challenge against Mugabe, just seven months after its formation, and had won the June 2000 parliamentary election. Had it not been for the intervention of the military, wearing a civilian mask, Mugabe could have long been gone from the Zimbabwean political scene.

I must accept, though, that the MDC lost some of the petitions. In all, these four High Court judges annulled the election results in seven areas and affirmed six in the initial batch of 13 petitions. The six, though they mattered, would not have affected the overall election result.

The nation followed the hearings with keen interest, as the MDC emerged victorious in eight petitions in succession. Similar to Justice Devittie's verdict, each of the other High Court judges appointed to hear the petitions – except for the newly appointed Judge Ben Hlatshwayo – nullified at least one of the election results.

Hlatshwayo summarily dismissed the election petition for Goromonzi and never bothered to give any reason or written explanation for his decision, making it impossible for the MDC to take any further legal steps because of the strict appeal procedures.

In all Zanu PF's losses their candidates lodged appeals with the Supreme Court. As in my case, that was the end of the story. Zanu PF candidates completed their terms of office while our petitions gathered dust on the shelves of the Supreme Court. High Court decisions were of little consequence in our search for relief and remedies. Out of the final 16 High Court judgments, there were 13 appeals. The MDC decided to ignore two others: Mwenezi and Shurugwi.

Zimbabwe's electoral law was clear. It mandated that election petitions be dealt with urgently, but the Supreme Court – now under Godfrey Chidyausiku – could not be bothered. Yet the world, let alone SADC and Africa, never raised a finger in protest or sought to exert pressure on Mugabe to recognise the impact of his actions on his legitimacy.

Not surprisingly, in a short space of time three of the remaining Supreme Court justices and nine of the 18 High Court judges, including James Devittie, apparently resigned in protest, were suspended and eventually pushed out; or otherwise retired early. Professional judges could not tolerate the manipulation of court rolls, cases of selective prosecutions, and other forms of executive interference which rendered their work untenable.

The damning evidence from the hearings and the subsequent international publicity around the challenges irked Mugabe and Zanu PF, while Jonathan Moyo once more set his sights on the media, both local and foreign.

I left Zimbabwe again on a foreign trip to try to impress upon the world what we were up against. I was shocked when my officials in Harare informed me that the police were looking for me in connection with my speech during the MDC's first anniversary celebrations in September

2000. The police had placed me on a wanted list for terrorism because of my remark about the people seeing violence as a last option.

Unsettled, I cut short my trip and headed for Johannesburg, en route to Harare. My officers at home, using information they had gleaned from their sources inside Zanu PF, said the police planned to arrest me soon after my arrival at Harare International Airport.

The party had begun to prepare for a showdown with Mugabe, as the dominant feeling was that we had had enough of the harassment. Through our Harare structures, the party organised the people, in large numbers, to meet me at the airport. As my anxious supporters and journalists milled around the route to Harare International Airport, police fired teargas and live ammunition to disperse them.

Some retaliated by throwing stones and logs at the police, resulting in skirmishes for much of the morning. I was scheduled to arrive in Harare around noon. Realising the danger of the volatile situation that was developing, our senior officials led by national chairman Isaac Matongo made alternative travel arrangements for me. For my safety, they decided that I should stay away from Harare International Airport. With the help of a well-wisher, I chartered a small aircraft in Johannesburg. Isaac Matongo, Timothy Mubhawu, Tapiwa Mashakada, Roy Bennett, Kisimusi Dhlamini, Gandi Mudzingwa and many others spent long hours working out a safe passage.

Eventually, the small plane was cleared and landed at a quiet Buffalo Range airstrip near Masvingo before taking off for an even smaller landing field on a private chicken farm, 8 kilometres west of Harare city centre. I then drove to my Ashdown Park home, north of the city. The place with its tiny garden was teeming with journalists and diplomats. I briefed the media about my trip and fielded questions about the police's intention to arrest me.

I could hardly settle down, so my lawyer and I drove to the police headquarters after contacting Augustine Chihuri, the police commissioner, through his spokesperson Wayne Bvudzijena. On arrival, I gave the police my side of the story.

I explained that Mugabe, as the leader of Zanu PF, was my political opponent. At his public political meetings, he took his gloves off and landed a barrage of bare knuckles on my character, my family and the MDC. Mugabe variously described me in extremely unpleasant terms, calling me a vassal of imperialism, a puppet of whites and the West and a 'tea-boy' – a demeaning term used in racist Rhodesia for black workers who prepared and served tea to the white rulers at home and at work. I challenged the police to accept that I had every right to hit back as a person and as a politician. Given the nature of the political contest in Zimbabwe, it would be fair game if I responded to Mugabe's insults in like manner. Why should I find myself in trouble with the law?

Bvudzijena and other senior officers simply looked at me and listened. As I drove home, I reflected that Mugabe was using arrests, harassment and court cases to wear me down. I decided to be extra careful about what I said. In public utterances from then on, I stuck to the core issues affecting Zimbabwe, concentrating on explaining my vision and on mobilising people for change.

Mugabe had beaten me remorselessly – if only figuratively at this stage – with the accusation that I had tried to foment violence against him. Spying on me intensified. Everywhere I went, I saw strangers in unfamiliar vehicles seemingly tracking my movements. Occasionally, I was attacked in my vehicle: at Patchway Mine near Kadoma, in Chivi South in Masvingo and in Mvurwi, either before or after addressing a meeting. Here and there a stone was thrown at me or I was verbally abused.

I withstood the behaviour of Zanu PF zealots as I drove into towns or rural areas, quickly dismissing the taunts which I believed were intended to frighten me out of politics. Mugabe had all the tools to take me out, if he seriously wished to do so. My personal security system was basic and rudimentary: nothing more than a few bodyguards who were not allowed to carry weapons. I did not even use a bullet-proof vehicle – just reinforced steel and glass to protect me from stones and iron bars in volatile and dangerous areas.

The country was awash with murderous gangs and Zanu PF fanatics who sincerely believed in Mugabe's cause. Nothing was stopping them from killing me – in fact, it could have been a fairly easy job. The capacity was there but I think Mugabe may have been afraid of the consequences. In the end, he just put me under tremendous pressure, hoping for co-option. If that failed, he believed he could crush the MDC.

But thousands of my agents, party candidates, MPs, activists and politicians were unlucky. They bore the brunt of Mugabe's intolerance. Hardly a day passed without a murder, destruction of property, a beating, a displacement or an arrest.

State-induced pressure, economic hardships and the seemingly slow pace of change disillusioned our urban base and displaced it, forcing young people into exile. Thanks to our large youth base, we quickly replaced the departing party organisers. Mugabe scattered the commercial farmers and their workers. Many relocated to the cities, others emigrated. But the MDC – against all odds – survived. That was the greatest source of my inspiration.

I felt I owed it to the people to be their symbol of resistance. I knew they believed in me. If I were to abandon this struggle, what would they say? They had suffered for so long. I knew that as long as the MDC remained close to the people, the nation would never abandon its spirit and the will to see change.

I decided to support the people in their resistance to Mugabe's offensive with what I thought I knew best: keeping hope alive through intensive grassroots organisation. So I went out often, meeting all kinds of people at all levels and engaging them in dialogue about the future. The plan worked. I found an unyielding spirit in the community – Zimbabweans who quickly saw through Mugabe's antics and were determined to persevere, willing to use their courage to overcome fear, violence and intimidation.

Much to Mugabe's displeasure, the crowds turning out at my meetings kept rising. The people valued the MDC message and made sense out of it. Slowly, Mugabe was unable to sustain his drive to recapture lost hearts and minds, despite sophisticated campaign jingles and highly imaginative messages crafted by Moyo. I began to think that Mugabe had never really understood what was going on, despite creating hard boundaries between Zanu PF and the MDC, and between himself and me. The so-called revolutionary party, the 'national liberator', Zanu PF, could no longer defend itself against what they saw as a puppet, the MDC. Zanu PF was now the oppressor; the MDC was with the people.

Even a spirited attempt to appeal to a historical grievance of race and racialism was failing to stick to the Zimbabwean mind. The battle for the soul of Zimbabwe was never going to be an easy one. To the outside world, which expected people-power demonstrations in urban streets, the people may have looked unassuming and meek. In Zimbabwe we regard silence as a form of self-expression which, depending on the circumstances, can be dangerously deceptive. On the surface, Zimbabweans can behave in an extremely polite and law-abiding manner – but they are a resilient lot. The minute they take a collective, moral position on a particular issue, especially on a national grievance, they stand by that decision. Our history is replete with numerous examples supporting this. In the election conducted by the 1979 transitional government that created Zimbabwe-Rhodesia, millions came out and voted for Bishop Abel Muzorewa and his UANC. Later they abandoned him to give solid electoral support to the incoming nationalist parties. The position of the masses was quite consistent: they wanted freedom and true independence.

On the numerous occasions Mugabe took to the podium – at home and abroad – he excelled as a demagogue and sent chills of fear down many an African leader's spine. He used a combination of political rhetoric and threats – delivered with an impressive turn of phrase. He abused historical facts and never hesitated to pull out a race-card. With abandon, he portrayed a personal victim image and rounded off his messages with the bravado of an unwavering revolutionary icon – always for martyrdom. At these meetings, Mugabe never missed an opportunity to strike, with utmost derision, at the MDC and at me.

I could sense that the old man had his moments of pleasure when dealing with the MDC – times when he really relished the use of dehumanising language to rubbish our cause. I deliberately developed a thick skin to ward off the pressure. This reflex worked, most of the time.

Still viewed by some as a father-figure, Mugabe's supporters at home sealed off their hearts and even attacked their own families in defence of his cause. Zanu PF could hardly permit any form of alternative reasoning. It was totally intolerant to differences even between husband and wife – as was the case with my sister-in-law – causing nasty family ruptures. This was very dangerous, as it left children stranded and confused. It smashed communal harmony, fragmented extended families and undermined Zimbabwean family values. With hindsight, I think it is fair to accept that, by 2001, Mugabe already excelled in his pursuit of tyranny. By then it was clear to most Zimbabweans that we had been too slow in intercepting Mugabe before he went too far.

With the MDC and me as a symbol of a struggle to remedy an intolerable situation, the people persevered and became a formidable groundswell of opposition to Mugabe. He knew it. For my part, I vowed to remain close to the people. I never dreamt of leaving Zimbabwe and flatly turned down suggestions to go into exile. There were some in and outside the MDC who suggested that I leave and direct the struggle from outside Zimbabwe. They said they feared for my life and for my family and that the party would collapse instantly should anything untoward happen to me. My argument was always that I had learnt a lesson from Joshua Nkomo's experience with Mugabe and Zanu PF, when he escaped at the height of the disturbances in Matabeleland in 1983. Thousands of his supporters felt that they were heavily exposed in Matabeleland, without a leader to guide them.

I decided to stay in the game.

ENDNOTES

1   General Notice 457A of 2000 – Clemency Order No. 1 of 2000
2   'Tsvangirai's speech at Rufaro Stadium'. 19 June 2000. MDC background papers http://www.afrol.com/Countries/Zimbabwe/backgr_tsvangiraispeech.htm
3   For full details, see Statutory Instrument 318 of 2000, Electoral Act (Modification) (No. 3) Notice, 2000
4   For further details, see Commercial Farmers Union v. Minister of Lands 2000 (2) ZLR 469 (S), at 486
5   See Movement for Democratic Change v. Chinamasa, 2001 (1) ZLR 69 (S),

at 70

6   Quoted in the International Council of Advocates and Barristers, the State of Justice in Zimbabwe, 49, 2004

7   For full details, see Tsvangirai v. Manyonda, HC 8139/2000, Buhera North Election Petition Judgment, 26 April 2001, pp62-64

8   Quoted in *The Role of the Judiciary in Denying the Will of the Zimbabwean Electorate since 2000*, a paper published by the Solidarity Peace Trust, Harare, March 2005, p23

9   Ibid. p23

10 Ibid. p23

11 Reported in 2001 (1) Zimbabwe Law Reports, 285

12 See, among other judgments: Muzira v. Muchena, HC 8231/2000, Mutoko South Election Petition Judgment, 27 April 2001, at 17; and Chadya v. Marumahoko, HC 8277/2000, Hurungwe East Election Petition Judgment, 21 April 2001, at 4, quoted in *The Role of the Judiciary in Denying the Will of the Zimbabwean Electorate since 2000*, a paper published by the Solidarity Peace Trust, Harare, March 2005

13 Mare v. Chauke, HC 8068/2000, Chiredzi North Election Petition Judgment, 20 June 2001, at 23.110 *Id.* p23; and Mlandu v. Mkandhla, HC 8228/2000, Gokwe North Election Petition Judgment, 15 January 2003, pp17-18

CHAPTER SEVENTEEN

THE TREASON TRAP

Our opponents were ceaselessly active devising new schemes to undermine the MDC, and me in particular. Slanders and smears were par for the course but more serious plots were being hatched that would eventually embroil me in a treason trial. Being charged with treason – knowing that capital punishment could follow a conviction – and having to face a gruelling trial was the worst personal experience I had ever faced. The whole nightmarish saga spanned several years, from 2002 to 2004 – years during which I carried on as MDC leader, campaigning in elections, reorganising the party, proselytising at home and abroad, fighting to overturn fraudulent election results, preparing major policy documents, and dealing with party spats that threatened our unity.

How does one carry on with a treason charge hanging over one's head? Well, one just does.

The trial was born of the ruling party's determination to destroy me. In August 2001, Mugabe seemed desperate. As often happens in such situations, international crooks wade in with suggestions on how a beleaguered political party can sneak out of danger. But in fact the crooks end up exploiting the situation for their own benefit. I think this is how Ari Ben-Menashe, a fraudster, insinuated himself into the scene, although it has never been clear what role the Mugabe government initially played in getting Ben-Menashe on board.

I understood much later that Ari Ben-Menashe had tried to enter Zimbabwe in the 1990s with a plan to sell military aircraft and spare parts, but he was rebuffed and went away. It is possible that he smelt an opportunity to get back after seeing that Zanu PF was in disarray. He came up with a plan to entice the party and its leader to hire him in its quest to crush the MDC.

When Ben-Menashe arrived in Harare in October 2001 with what he claimed was a taped recording of a discussion I had had with him, he met with Air Vice-Marshal Robert Mhlanga. The latter referred him to the CIO. This seems to indicate that there were no firm links with the government until then. Ben-Menashe might have known Mhlanga as a commander in the air force from his previous attempt to promote his 'military aircraft' business.

Ben-Menashe came in handy. The ultimate aim was to get me out of the 2002 presidential election race.

The ploy was to approach someone inside the MDC to propose a way to promote the party's image abroad. Using his shady international connections and after a careful study of our structures and leading personalities, Ben-Menashe settled for Renson Gasela, the MDC's parliamentary spokesman for agriculture. I am not sure that Gasela was aware of the game plan. A farmer from Gweru, Gasela was the general manager of the Grain Marketing Board in 1992 when Zimbabwe was hit by a serious drought. In organising grain imports from South Africa, he worked with one Rupert Johnson. The two later became so close that Johnson once organised a holiday for Gasela and his family in Cape Town.

One morning in 2001 while I was in the office, Gasela approached my personal assistant, Gandi Mudzingwa, asking to see me about a proposal he had worked out with Rupert Johnson involving a Canadian lobby, Dickens and Madson, which he, Johnson, was now working for. Gasela told Mudzingwa that Dickens and Madson could help to market the MDC in North America.

Unconvinced, Mudzingwa sent him away saying he needed more details before placing the plan on my desk. Gasela went away only to return a few days later with MDC secretary general Welshman Ncube. I had told Ncube that I was concerned about how best we could market the MDC in North America and mandated him to pursue the matter. I believed in Ncube, a law professor, and assumed he would do the background checks to verify the authenticity of Johnson's offer. Matters went no further until September 2001 when Ncube reported back, suggesting that we meet Johnson and his colleagues in London.

At our first meeting at Heathrow Airport's Terminal 4, Ben-Menashe boasted of an array of international connections, links with Zimbabwe's top military officers, and even direct contact with former US President Bill Clinton. He said he had worked extensively with Clinton, trying to persuade Mugabe to step down and retire gracefully. He claimed Clinton had been disappointed by Mugabe.

Ben-Menashe said he knew that I was set to win the presidential election, but was quick to play on my fears as to whether the military and state machinery would honour the result. He offered to use his close links with senior security officers and service chiefs to ensure a smooth transition. But for that to happen, he needed to sign a contract with the MDC, and required a $100 000 deposit.

In their earlier discussions, Ncube and Johnson had agreed on the content of the contract and appended their signatures to the document. Under the deal, Dickens and Madson were supposed to get the ball rolling with the job of raising our profile in North America where, according to Ben-Menashe, Zanu PF was making impressive political inroads through the lobbying firm Cohen & Woods.

At the end of October 2001, I was advised that Ben-Menashe had made some progress and that there were new developments he wanted to discuss with me. I was busy with the presidential campaign for the 2002 election but Ben-Menashe insisted that I see him personally, or he would not be able to move forward with the MDC project in terms of our London contract. I decided that I would make the visit a very quick one: fly into London, arriving in the morning for the meeting, and fly back to Harare on the same day so that I could catch up with my tight campaign schedule.

The London meeting turned out to be totally unnecessary and unhelpful. Ben-Menashe, accompanied by his assistant Tara Thomas, said he had nothing to report, save for the information that following the 11 September bombings at the World Trade Centre, he had been unable to get an appointment with General Collin Powell, the US Secretary of State. This message could easily have been relayed to me either by phone or letter.

I began to doubt Ben-Menashe's intentions. The $100 000 we had paid him bothered me a lot. Meantime, Ben-Menashe sneaked into Harare and met Air Vice-Marshal Mhlanga at his home. None of us in the MDC knew about this meeting, nor did he seek us out. On this trip, Ben-Menashe had brought what he claimed was a recorded transcript of my discussions with him in London. His intention, it later emerged, was to strike a separate deal with Mugabe and Zanu PF so that he could swindle them as well. At his meeting with Mhlanga he tried to convince him that he had evidence of my plot to kill Mugabe before the 2002 presidential election.

According to Mhlanga, what Ben-Menashe was saying could not be backed up by the largely inaudible recording. Tara Thomas had not done a professional job! Mhlanga was presented with an alleged transcript of the recording, of which he could make no sense. So he referred Ben Menashe to senior CIO officers who, I later understood, also failed to grasp what Ben-Menashe was trying to convey. However, they saw an opportunity and advised him to do another recording, not an audio one but on video tape.

At my last meeting with Ben-Menashe in October, he must have read my body language correctly as we parted and understood my strong desire for him to proceed. A major goal of the project was fund-raising from supporters abroad, as promised at the time we signed the contract in September.

Now working under the direct control of the CIO, Ben-Menashe moved swiftly. I am sure by then he had a contract with Zanu PF and the government. In December, he sent word that he had arranged a meeting for me in Washington, ostensibly to introduce me to senior state department officials to market the MDC. I was told I would transit in Montreal for a briefing at Dickens and Madson on my way to the United States.

From the moment Rupert Johnson and Ben-Menashe picked me up in Montreal I felt extremely uncomfortable. They seemed overexcited and their demeanour was suspicious. I was ushered into a boardroom at their offices where two other men and Tara Thomas were waiting. Ben-Menashe introduced one as Alexandre Legault, his business partner, and the other as Edward Simms. Simms, he said, was a senior director of the Central Intelligence Agency (CIA) with special responsibility for Africa.

The change in the arrangements came as a surprise to me. I had expected to travel to Washington, but was now told that everything was to be done at Dickens and Madson, with people I had never expected to meet. I had been looking forward to meeting US state department officials, congressmen and senators.

Unsettled, I asked Ben-Menashe what the latest developments were and he snapped at me: 'Have you seen the military yet?' I was slow to respond as I wondered why he would pose such a question. I told him I had no official contact with the Zimbabwean military.

I explained that I thought, in terms of the contract, that Ben-Menashe was supposed to do that on the MDC's behalf. Suddenly Ben-Menashe raised his voice angrily and confusingly. 'Look, sorry, we are not hired guns, nor are they,' he said, pointing at Johnson and Simms. 'Then assassinate or eliminate, or whatever, and then come back and say now there is a constitutional process. This isn't what we do for a living, to assassinate the head of state.'

I wondered what Ben-Menashe was talking about. It was a very strange meeting. The entire discussion was disjointed. I did not know what to expect from it and tried to steer our discussion back on track, reminding Ben-Menashe of the issues we had dealt with earlier. I kept reminding him that our expectations had nothing to do with Mugabe's assassination or physical elimination. He would not listen or even follow the thread of my conversation. In exasperation, I stormed out of the room. Johnson quickly followed me and pleaded for patience.

I told him that I was unhappy with the content and tone of the meeting. As he tried to respond, Ben-Menashe interrupted him: 'Look,' he said. 'Mr Simms wants to go now. If you still want the Americans to help the MDC, the meeting must resume now.' I reluctantly agreed.

Ben-Menashe continued, this time seeking my views on what was likely to happen if Mugabe was eliminated. I said his deputy would assume power immediately. He then raised a number of unconnected issues. I remained quiet, feeling very uneasy.

I was keen to hear from Simms. But he was silent for most of the time. Sensing my discomfort and perhaps expectation, Simms finally chipped in. He said the US government was ready to give the MDC $2.5 million immediately. He asked for our London bank details, which I gave him. He stood up and left.

At dinner with Legault that evening, Ben-Menashe joined us. He was not interested in eating but pressed for an earlier undertaking that an amount of US$400 000 be paid to him. I refused to commit myself, insisting that Dickens and Madson must first fulfil its part of the bargain. He took me to the airport the following morning – and that was that.

I left Canada a frustrated man. I found it difficult to believe Simms's promise. My distrust of Ben-Menashe was growing every minute and the whole exercise seemed an utter waste of time. Soon after my arrival in Harare, I briefed my colleagues and voiced my suspicions about the whole matter.

We decided to sever ties with Ben-Menashe and his gang. But, as things later turned out, the damage had already been done. The MDC had been swindled out of $100 000. It had never occurred to me that my two meetings with Ben-Menashe were being recorded. In the end, Ben-Menashe was in for a double kill: he took both the MDC and Zanu PF for a ride, and was rewarded handsomely. Zanu PF lost more than one million US dollars.

I never thought that the matter would go beyond a cash loss to international swindler.

As preparations got under way for a Commonwealth Heads of Government Meeting (CHOGM) at Coolum, Australia in March 2002, a heavily doctored video of my meetings with Ben-Menashe and his team was aired on Australian television. First broadcast on 13 February 2002 by Australia's Special Broadcasting Service (SBS) as an hour-long documentary on the programme *Dateline*, it was clear that its main intention was to influence discussion on Zimbabwe at the upcoming Commonwealth meeting where Zimbabwe topped the agenda. Clearly the conspirators hoped that the TV show would swing the balance in favour of Mugabe. Instead, the heads of government expressed their deep concern at the violence and intimidation in Zimbabwe and decided that appropriate action would be taken after a Commonwealth Observer Group (COG) had reported on the imminent presidential election of 9-10 March 2002.[1]

So far so good for me and the MDC. But the game was not over.

On Australian TV, some eight and a half minutes of footage had shown me supposedly discussing a murder plot against Mugabe. The original footage was so grainy that it was difficult to see what was going on. When the material was handed over to the Zimbabwe Broadcasting Corporation (ZBC), it was further distorted to suit Zanu PF election needs. The recordings were played almost daily on radio and television and published in state newspapers right up until Election Day. The documentary filmmaker, Mark Davis, stated that I had offered Ben-Menashe's Canadian firm of political consultants, Dickens and Madson, US$500 000 for the job.

Davis quoted Ben-Menashe saying, 'The MDC represented by the top man who's sitting here right now commits to, let's call it whatever you want to call it, the coup d'état or elimination of the president.' And later, 'OK, Mr Mugabe is eliminated. Now what?'

I addressed a press conference in Harare in which I admitted having met with Ben-Menashe but denied that the purpose of the meeting was to hire him to kill Mugabe. The ZBC ignored my protests and continued rebroadcasting an edited version of the Australian documentary. Presented as a journalistic scoop, the negative publicity I received as a result of this story almost threw me off balance. Many Commonwealth governments, especially in Africa, began to doubt my standing as a credible alternative to Mugabe. I could feel it each time I tried to engage African diplomats in Harare. They simply listened to me, as if they felt obliged to grant me an audience. Others avoided me, claiming to be busy with prior engagements.

I have kept three copies of the video recording. The original copy which Ben-Menashe and the state had to give to my lawyers, the one that was broadcast in Australia, and another reworked version that was aired by the ZBC are in my family archives.

On 25 February 2002, Mugabe landed what he thought was a killer punch: I was summoned to Harare Central Police Station and charged with treason on the strength of Ben-Menashe's recorded video tape.

As I was in the penultimate stage of my campaign, I steeled myself and pushed harder towards the finishing line. Seeing that I still had the energy to continue, Mugabe fired another shot on 1 March, adding a fresh set of election rules and regulations to the already restrictive system.

Predictably, the official election results awarded the lion's share of votes and seats to Zanu PF, while Mugabe was returned as president for another six-year term. But, despite all he had done to denigrate, obstruct, and demotivate me, the old man must have been shocked by my showing at the polls. According to the official election figures, the final count was 1,685,212 votes for Robert Mugabe and 1,258,401 for me, his main opponent. Mugabe was now facing a real crisis of relevance. His self-styled victory left his political future in doubt.

But he was still determined to crush the MDC and grind me to dust. Nine days after the election, I was formally indicted on the treason charge arising from the Ben-Menashe video recording along with Welshman Ncube and Renson Gasela. It would be an agonising 11 months before the three of us actually faced trial, beginning in February 2003. Because of the seriousness of the case and its potential effect on the MDC and on me, we had hired a highly experienced team of lawyers led by renowned South African anti-apartheid legal icon, Advocate George Bizos. Bizos was assisted by senior counsel Chris Andersen, Advocate Eric Matinenga and my family lawyer, Innocent Chagonda. I knew we had a solid defence team. My only fear was that the state had subverted the judiciary to such a degree that, despite our innocence, the verdict could go either way.

There was chaos on the opening day of the trial. The government tried to limit the number of people in the courtroom – against custom as this was supposed to be an open trial. Bizos had to protest to presiding judge, Justice Paddington Garwe, who ruled in favour of open proceedings.

We pleaded innocent and the trial commenced. Early on, I felt a measure of relief when the state case, led by Deputy Attorney General Barat Patel, suddenly began to show signs of floundering. The case was weakened by star witness Ben-Menashe's admission that, while purporting to work for us, he was on Mugabe's payroll as a public relations consultant and lobbyist.

Ben-Menashe made other startling revelations, one of which was that the British government planned to pay £6 million to air force commander Perence Shiri for a coup against Mugabe. Ben-Menashe accused the US government of supporting the plan, as evidenced by their alleged secondment of a Mr Edward Simms to the Montreal meeting which Ben-Menashe recorded on video. At the same time, Ben-Menashe conceded that he recorded the video with the intention of handing it over to Mugabe. I felt relieved again when, in cross-examination by Advocate Bizos, Ben-Menashe became incoherent and confused. In the end, he became extremely abusive and failed to answer questions, prompting Judge President Paddington Garwe to warn him against contempt of court.

At that point Bizos and his team applied for a discharge, arguing against presenting the defence case as this would be, in their view, a complete waste of time. Judge Garwe dropped the charges against Ncube and Gasela after Bizos successfully argued that for a treason charge to be validated, justified and substantiated there had to be at least two credible state witnesses to support the state's evidence. This was not the case for either Gasela or Ncube. Although I understood the legal argument, it still left me under pressure. It meant I had to face the gruelling procedure on my own.

Matters became simpler when Bizos called Ncube and Gasela as my first witnesses. Ncube stunned the court with the evidence that he had discovered, to his surprise, that Ben-Menashe's firm was fairly new, with no more than two employees and no contracts before or after it was engaged by the MDC.

Earlier, our lawyer filed papers in a Canadian court against Dickens and Madson seeking to reclaim our $100 000. In his defence against the claim, Ben-Menashe denied that he owed us the money, arguing that he had fulfilled his lobbying contract with the MDC. What Ben-Menashe said in his defence contradicted the evidence he had given earlier that he had done nothing to help the MDC, but simply listened to our views in order to inform the Zimbabwe government.

From then on, I knew it would be extremely hard for Garwe to pronounce a guilty verdict. The state case had collapsed. In addition, Bizos insisted that the state must bring Rupert Johnson, Alexandre Legault and Edward Simms to testify against me.

Neither Ben-Menashe nor the prosecution managed to track down the three men to compel them to appear in court as witnesses with supporting evidence.

The trial was adjourned for yet another long period as Garwe studied the evidence.

In mid-July 2004 the High Court informed my lawyers that Justice Garwe would deliver his judgment on the treason trial on 29 July 2004. The news left me with a mixture of nervousness and relief. I knew I was innocent. My conscience was clear. Should Garwe pronounce a verdict of guilty, with its possibly fatal consequences, my family would be devastated. A conviction would also impact seriously on the unity of the party.

I felt a rush of emotions about the possibility of a tragic end to my risky political career. When I decided to take on Mugabe and Zanu PF, I knew the pitfalls and all along I had in a way been preparing myself for the worst. A lengthy jail sentence? Or capital punishment? I was well aware of that possibility.

If capital punishment was to be the result, then so be it. I would go to my grave knowing that I had been unjustly persecuted for taking a stand for freedom against a dictatorship. This could be a major rallying point for the people, as I could easily become a symbol for political mobilisation. Not that I sought martyrdom! I felt strong, but was deeply uneasy at the same time. *What a strange contradiction!* I thought.

Perhaps I should have been more careful and avoided the likes of Ben-Menashe, I chided myself. And what about some of my utterances? Now, if I were convicted, Mugabe could use the case to destroy the MDC. Even if I was acquitted he could find an excuse to further humiliate me and so force the MDC to capitulate. An immediate consequence of my departure from the political scene would give Mugabe unlimited options to deal with the MDC.

A conviction would compel me to show remorse in mitigation of sentence; but what would I have to say? After all, I had committed no crime. I recalled that Ndabaningi Sithole, the founder of Zanu and Mugabe's predecessor, died with a prison sentence hanging over his head. Sithole was convicted in 1997 on a charge of treason for attempting to assassinate Mugabe with a claymore mine. Sithole died on 12 December 2000 and was buried at his farm in Chipinge. His supporters and fellow associates in the nationalist movement felt strongly that he should have been declared a national hero for his contribution to the liberation of Zimbabwe.

It was almost amusing to think how anyone could imagine such an assassination plan succeeding, given that Mugabe, as president of Zimbabwe, drove in arguably the longest motorcade in the world, with a personal security cordon of unimaginable size even in war zones – complete with gun snipers, a mobile, fully equipped and staffed hospital, plus doctors, nurses and military first-aid staff. Aside from the high-intensity human security surrounding him around the clock, Mugabe used a custom-built, bullet-proof car and travelled sandwiched between solid walls of vehicles directed by police outriders with sirens. The leading police bikers cleared the entire road before Mugabe zoomed past at maximum speed.

In such circumstances, how Sithole's claymore mine could have made an impact if he had wished to carry out the mission beggars belief. But he was convicted, nevertheless. A conviction of Morgan Tsvangirai was, indeed, a possibility regardless of the quality of evidence against me.

I set these thoughts aside as I shifted my mind to the state of the party and its chances should another election avail itself soon. The MDC had just published a fresh set of policy documents enunciating our political philosophy and vision for a new Zimbabwe.

In *Restart*, we used our policy proposal, *Restore*, as a basis for domestic education and diplomatic engagement. I approached Harare-based foreign envoys from SADC, using *Restore* as part of my search for a lasting solution to Zimbabwe's problems. I explained that we were keen to see an improvement in Zimbabwe's electoral machinery.

In the proposal, the MDC emphasised the importance of the rule of law, basic freedoms and rights, an independent electoral commission, public confidence in the electoral process and the need for ballot secrecy. We were heartened by the news that SADC, in preparation for an annual summit to be held in Mauritius in August 2004, was working on a similar set of election management guidelines for the entire region.

As I campaigned for SADC to hear us out, my lawyers told me that Garwe had postponed the judgment to 15 October. No reason was given.

The news did not reach my mother in Buhera. On 28 July she boarded a bus and arrived at my Harare home, hoping to be with me in court the next morning. I found her at home when I took a break from the office. She was obviously worried about me, but it was not apparent in her body language. She assured me that only God had the answer.

There was wild speculation in Harare over the reasons for the postponement. I heard various versions. One that seemed to gain currency was that assessors Misherk Nyandoro and Joseph Dangarembizi prevented Justice Garwe from passing judgment, demanding to see and to review the full transcripts of the trial. That they had objected, which I was unable to confirm independently, was the subject of a story in the local weekly newspaper, *The Zimbabwe Independent*, a day after the postponement.

Under Zimbabwe's judicial system assessors act as a kind of jury in the High Court. Procedurally, they are allowed access to recorded tapes and transcripts to enable them to make informed decisions and a fair and just contribution to a judge's verdict. A judge hearing such a serious case would not have made a ruling without the views of the assessors. Garwe needed the support of at least one assessor to either convict or acquit.

Police arrested two journalists and the general manager of the newspaper and detained them for six hours under the Access to Information and

Protection of Privacy Act (AIPPA) for publishing the story. Editor Vincent Kahiya, reporter Augustine Mukaro, and general manager Raphael Khumalo were charged under Section 80 of the Act with 'publication of a statement that is injurious to the reputation, rights and freedoms of the State, recklessly or maliciously or incorrectly representing the statement as a true statement'. Police said they arrested the journalists following a complaint from Justice Garwe. To my knowledge, their case never went beyond that stage.

The August 2004 SADC summit adopted a regional framework for elections with clear guidelines.[2] I saw this as a major breakthrough for the MDC in the region. Slowly, but surely – so I comforted myself – SADC knew that Zimbabwe was a problem: manipulating voters' rolls, manipulating votes, intimidating voters, and breeding conditions for electoral disputes.

At last SADC had realised that Mugabe had manipulated the 2002 election result. Would they declare him an illegitimate leader? They had to see that the real crisis in Zimbabwe was a crisis of confidence in Mugabe's leadership.

SADC was excellent cover for some southern African leaders who saw the guidelines as an effective, diplomatic avenue to deal with Mugabe. When Mugabe grudgingly accepted the protocol, we watched with interest how he would implement the guidelines. Mugabe's movement in a positive direction, no matter how slow, boosted our morale.

We had more pending by-elections arising from the deaths of Zanu PF's Eddison Zvobgo of Masvingo South and the MDC's Bennie Tumbare-Mutasa of Seke, but the national executive committee decided to stay out of the race until Mugabe and Zanu PF implemented the new SADC protocol in full. Zanu PF went ahead, nonetheless, and two of its candidates Walter Mzembi (Masvingo) and Phineas Chihota (Seke) walked into parliament without a challenge.

The day of reckoning dawned. On the morning of Friday, 15 October, a senior trade unionist and a close family friend from the ZCTU arrived at my home looking visibly shaken. I cannot disclose his identity as the information was given to me in strict confidence. He asked for a private conversation and we retreated to my small office at the back of the garden.

'One of your senior colleagues,' he said, mentioning his name, 'has just left the ZCTU office. He had asked for an audience with us in the executive and to brief us on what is happening inside the MDC.' I thrust my head forward to hear more. 'This former senior trade unionist says the top leadership of the MDC knows that you are going to be convicted, jailed, and maybe hanged afterwards. He says he was sent to the ZCTU by your top party colleagues to secure our support for Sibanda, your deputy, who would naturally take over until the next MDC congress.'

I felt torn to pieces.

In a bid to cross-check the information later I asked who else from the ZCTU had attended the meeting. 'Are you sure he said he was an emissary of all the top five leaders in the MDC?' I asked lamely, feeling confused. 'That is the position,' he said. 'Look, I have to go. I just felt that I had to share this with you in advance.'

Devastated and alone, I contemplated my bleak future. The party would move on without me. Perhaps I would never know the outcome of our long struggle.

In terms of the MDC constitution, Sibanda would automatically become the leader of the party. But why was there panic in the party? Could there be a conspiracy that involved Mugabe, Zanu PF and some of my colleagues in the MDC? I found no answers, and could not even hazard any guesses based on possible political scenarios. I kept my thoughts to myself.

I left home early with Amai Edwin to hear Justice Garwe's verdict on the lengthy treason trial which had hung over my head since February 2002. On arrival at the High Court, opposite Mugabe's official Munhumutapa office, there were scenes of chaos as diplomats, journalists, senior MDC party officials, armed soldiers, police and ordinary people jostled to enter the court building.

I was surprised to see a CNN news crew and wondered how they had been allowed into the country from Johannesburg when all other networks were now officially banned from Harare. As I observed this, another thought crossed my mind. Could it be that Mugabe wanted the whole world to watch my conviction live on their television screens? Was there any connection between what my ZCTU colleague had said and CNN's invitation to Harare? Was I being pushed out of the political scene in a conspiracy that involved my closest political comrades and Mugabe?

I steeled myself and strode inside.

My close relatives, my brothers, sisters and other family members, did not make it into the courtroom, let alone some of my key officials and staff. Inside, the room was already full of state security agents and plainclothes police officers, prison warders, lawyers and a few journalists from the state media. I entered the dock and waited patiently for the judge.

I watched Sibanda, Ncube, Mdlongwa and other senior MDC members come into court. I was keen to read their body language. They avoided direct eye contact and sat on the court benches, sharing small talk. Justice Garwe, sitting with his assessors, opened the judgment by narrating a year-long compilation of the proceedings leading to the day of reckoning. I was heartened when he began to cast doubts on Ben-Menashe's character and quality of evidence before declaring that the state had failed to prove its case in a manner sufficient to secure a conviction.

Not guilty! It was all over!

Relieved, stunned and smiling, I left the dock. But before I did so, I cast another glance at my colleagues. Sibanda was visibly surprised, so was the rest of the group. One by one, they stood up and shook my hand saying 'Congratulations' – and left.

Outside the court, Harare and the whole of Zimbabwe erupted in spontaneous elation and ecstasy. For once, police and soldiers withdrew quietly from the streets. It was a short-lived moment of triumph.

ENDNOTES

1   CHOGM Statement on Zimbabwe, 4 March 2002 http://www.chogm2002. org/pub/statements/zimbabwe.html
2   SADC – Principles and Guidelines Governing Democratic Elections http:// www.sadc.int/index/browse/page/117

CHAPTER EIGHTEEN

UNFREE AND UNFAIR

Mugabe never took me seriously – until he was forced to. In 2002, his eyes were on the presidential election, which he thought he would easily win by hobbling me with a treason charge and parcelling out pieces of seized land to his supporters. By destroying the MDC's rural base in villages and commercial farms, he would have nothing to fear from people who could be coerced into voting for him.

I was in the rural areas in November 2001 when I heard that Cain Nkala, a notoriously violent war veteran, had been murdered in Bulawayo by unknown assailants. Within a few days, police picked up our treasurer Fletcher Dulini-Ncube and a number of activists and charged them with the crime. Dulini-Ncube, a member of parliament and a diabetic, was lucky to survive; he was so badly treated that he lost an eye during the interrogation. He was kept in filthy police cells without food or medication. Nkala was declared a national hero and buried at Heroes Acre. In his customary address to mourners, Mugabe viciously attacked me and the West, and accused Dulini-Ncube of Nkala's murder. Moses Mzila-Ndlovu, our MP for Bulilima Mangwe on the Botswana border, was accused of kidnapping and assault in the same case. He, too, was detained and heavily interrogated by the police, the CIO and the army before being freed unconditionally.

After a string of court applications to secure his release on bail, Dulini-Ncube was temporarily released, pending trial, but the other activists remained in jail for nearly two years. In the end, they were all acquitted in May 2003 after a full trial. It is instructive to note that no MDC politician was convicted of any crime. But the toll of the state's action on our finances and our time was immeasurable. They cost my presidential campaign effort dearly.

Three other MDC legislators and scores of activists died as a result of internal injuries from violent attacks. Some 14 MPs had survived assassination attempts at various places since 2000 and another 20 lost property worth millions of dollars to Zanu PF gangs. None of the perpetrators were arrested and prosecuted. In addition, individual family members and friends of MDC activists and leaders became targets for state-sponsored harassment, with no recourse to the law.

Mugabe and Zanu PF particularly targeted 50 of our 57 MPs and 28 MDC election candidates for assault and harassment. At a Zanu PF convention in December 2001, Mugabe gave the MDC some telling hints about the forthcoming 2002 presidential election, in particular the way it was going to be conducted. Unfortunately, we did not pay much attention as we were too occupied with trying to cope with a deadly combination of violence, a vicious legal battle and a non-stop information and propaganda war.

Mugabe formally announced his intentions to erase the constitutional dividing line between Zanu PF as a party and the government; to openly restructure the relationship between Zanu PF and the military; and to make way for the further politicisation of the security sector where loyalty, and not professionalism, was to be the guiding philosophy. The military was to be ordered to take positions closer to the levers of state power.

'We shall run the election like a military machine,' said Mugabe, in a live broadcast from Victoria Falls. 'Zanu PF has assumed a commanding position and has a duty to drive the nation, military style, to comply in order to save Zimbabwe from recolonisation.'

When I heard this, I laughed and didn't take it seriously. It was the kind of rant we expected from a cornered, incumbent presidential candidate. Barely two weeks after the Zanu PF convention, Mugabe set up a national command centre, military style. Initially with headquarters at a local hotel, the centre later moved to Manyame Air Base, behind Harare International Airport, to coordinate the presidential election. The centre's brief was to ensure that Mugabe won the election at all costs. We were heading for an unfree and unfair election.

The military took over the functions of the Electoral Supervisory Commission (ESC), the Election Directorate and, more significantly, the administration of the voters' roll and other aspects of civilian electoral administration. The ESC was placed under retired Colonel Sobusa Gula-Ndebele, with staff drawn from the army under the leadership of Brigadier Douglas Nyikayaramba, a serving officer. In all, the management of the entire election was to be run like a military operation, with a reporting structure that led directly to the JOC and Mugabe.

The mass attendance at the few campaign rallies the police permitted the MDC to hold must have jolted the JOC and Mugabe. Our turnout was so high that the military operation faced the real prospect of failing to achieve the intended results. A decision was taken to tighten the screws further.

The regime declared total war on anyone who opposed it. Peasants, farmers, NGO workers, nurses, teachers and rural civil servants now found themselves on the front lines of this war – not waging it but under attack. Mugabe's efforts were futile as far as shifting hearts and minds was concerned. The nation became more agitated by his actions against the MDC, and when all indicators pointed towards my victory in the presidential race, the military and, in particular, the JOC panicked.

General Vitalis Zvinavashe, the commander of the armed forces, convened a hastily arranged news conference on 10 January 2002, flanked by other service chiefs, and announced that all the service chiefs fully supported Mugabe. In remarks aimed directly at me, he said the armed forces were not prepared to salute a president, or a Zimbabwean leader, who lacked liberation war credentials.

I knew that the top commanders had seen that the people were behind the MDC and ready to ditch Mugabe in the presidential election. They now sought to subvert the entire electoral process with an open declaration that they would refuse to serve a properly elected leader who did not meet their criteria. The service chiefs clearly went far beyond their constitutional mandate. Their statement alienated them from the nation, the collective sovereignty of the people they had sworn to protect. It was unfortunate.

From that day, I believed strongly that I would win the election, but that victory was unlikely to translate into an instant regime change. Mugabe – through the senior service chiefs – sent out a signal that he was preparing to defy a democratic power transfer, even if he lost the election. That complicated and confused the Zimbabwe situation both in the minds of the people and internationally.

While I pondered General Zvinavashe's statement, I received a call from Lupane in Matabeleland North. David Mpala, the MP for area, was on a life-support system at a local hospital after Mugabe's supporters had sliced open his abdomen. He had been abducted while on his way to the funeral of an MDC activist, murdered in a separate bout of politically motivated violence.

Mpala's attackers, local war veterans and Zanu PF supporters, dumped him – unconscious and bleeding profusely – about six kilometres from Lupane business centre. They drove his truck away and abandoned it in the neighbouring district of Tsholotsho. The caller, a relative, told me that Mpala could hardly speak. He was airlifted to Bulawayo for surgery.

As if that were not gruesome enough, Zanu PF used its parliamentary majority to fast-track the Public Order and Security Act (POSA) while Jonathan Moyo brought in the Access to Information and Protection of Privacy Act (AIPPA). POSA replaced the colonial Law and Order (Maintenance) Act of 1960, used extensively in Smith's Rhodesia to suppress dissent. The Rhodesian law was one of the most repressive and unjust measures used against political opponents. Mugabe inherited it and used it to silence the opposition for 22 years until the Constitutional Court declared the law unfit for a democracy as it infringed the basic rights of the people. Mugabe replaced it with POSA, which unfortunately was even tougher on the opposition.

POSA allowed the government to outlaw any group likely to cause or do anything the government thought might cause disaffection among the police and security forces, or be deemed prejudicial to the state, and prohibited anyone – peasant, worker, church person or politician – from doing anything the government considered to have the potential to undermine the authority of, or to insult, a sitting president.

How, in such an environment, does one build a political party or mount a political challenge without being deemed to be undermining or trying to insult an incumbent?

AIPPA was a Jonathan Moyo invention designed to silence *The Daily News* and other emerging voices. This law contained a raft of measures requiring newspaper licences, a complex accreditation system for both local and foreign journalists, codes of conduct and tight registration requirements. Both laws further restricted basic rights and freedoms of opinion, expression and information.

The United Nations Commission on Human Rights noted that 'the provisions [of AIPPA] infringe on the right to freedom of opinion and expression as guaranteed in Article 19 of the Universal Declaration of Human Rights and the International Covenant on Civil and Political Rights to which Zimbabwe is a Party'. In a letter to the Zimbabwe government a UN Special Rapporteur Abid Hussain argued that 'the provisions of this Bill will give rise to excessive government control over the media'.

An advocacy group in Harare, the Media Monitoring Project of Zimbabwe, pointed out that the public media was partisan and produced unbalanced news items that shamelessly favoured Mugabe and his regime during the election campaign.

Mugabe's measures provided clear testimony of his inability to contest a free and fair election. His legitimacy was on the line – and he has not recovered it to this day. Instead, he has done much to ruin his own personal legacy of liberation war icon, determined fighter for freedom, perceptive academic, and senior African statesman.

When the national sentiment remained unshaken, Mugabe went further. He flouted the constitution, ignored parliament and embarked on a series of illegal acts to change electoral rules, working with Justice Minister Chinamasa. After I submitted my papers and they were accepted as valid, I was in a do-or-die position. I was inside the field, waiting for the whistle to blow. But Mugabe was moving the goalposts.

Chinamasa had rushed the General Laws Amendment Bill through parliament, inserting allowances for changes to the Electoral Act late in the process. The bill sailed through parliament, improperly, and passed into law. I challenged it in court and won. The Supreme Court, by a majority of four to one, ruled in my favour and scrapped the new law from our statutes. The decision meant that the election was to proceed under the law as it was on 3 February 2002, before the latest act was gazetted into legislation. No new rules or goalpost shifts were to be permitted. It was as if Mugabe's proposed law never existed. Again, that was a blow to Mugabe but, undaunted, he persevered.

The regime ignored the Supreme Court ruling. And to clothe Mugabe's action with a veneer of legality, he turned to statutory decrees, using the existing electoral law. Chinamasa was even more brazen: he altered the election rules based on the new law the Supreme Court had just declared null and void. He claimed to be using the electoral law, but the changes now on the table were never covered by that law in the first place.

According to the Human Rights Forum of Zimbabwe,[1] Mugabe used his powers under section 158 of the Electoral Act to reinstate provisions nullified by the Supreme Court. The effect was to take the vote away from two categories of his perceived political opponents – some 5 000 non-citizen permanent residents with a constitutional right to vote, and an estimated million or more Zimbabweans living outside the country who had previously been entitled to postal ballots. Postal votes were to be restricted to members of the uniformed services and public service on polling duties.

The new rules denied any voter who happened to be outside his constituency or outside Zimbabwe on Election Day while on business, in hospital or for whatever reason, the opportunity to vote in the presidential election.

With a few days to go to the election, the world became increasingly curious about Mugabe's antics and pressure was mounting for international observers to validate election results. To make their entry into Zimbabwe difficult, if not impossible, Chinamasa and the state's director of elections, Tobaiwa Mudede introduced observation fees. The first time the regime had sought to bring in observation fees was when it introduced the General Laws Amendment Bill that was thrown out by the Supreme Court. The state proceeded anyway to charge both local and foreign observers a fee, illegally. Chinamasa was clearly acting outside his powers as minister of justice.

The fees for observers made it difficult for civil society groups to deploy the numbers they originally desired, and foreign observers had to be cleared by the government before they could start work. In addition, new observer rules came into force, tightening the registration requirements of election observers, monitors and even polling agents. The raft of measures caused anxiety and fear as the state's intentions were unclear. In many areas, our polling agents, now afraid of exposure, resigned saying the new rules compromised their safety and security.

All polling agents were required to provide the ESC with their physical addresses and contact numbers. This was impossible, given that in the rural areas, traditionally, a local post office box number, schools, villages and business centres were used as people's addresses and contact points.

The government ordered them to comply or risk arrest. On this basis alone, the legitimacy of the election was now already in doubt. Chinamasa's behaviour was both ridiculous and malicious. He wanted to subvert the Supreme Court ruling for the ultimate benefit of a cornered Mugabe. The manner in which Mugabe acted made the judgment of the Supreme Court[2] worthless, thus negating the concept of a fair hearing before an impartial tribunal in matters of dispute.

As if that were not enough, Mugabe introduced the Electoral Code of Conduct for Political Parties and Candidates just hours before voting began. Some of its provisions – outlawing threats of harm, provocative and intimidatory language, false or defamatory allegations against competitors, and racial and other discriminations – had repeatedly been abrogated by his own side. To allow a candidate at the centre of the contest to abuse his power of incumbency, and for to him get away with such behaviour, undermined the principle of legality as provided for in the national constitution.

A supplementary voters' register was reintroduced and any leftover voters who wished to place their names on the books were allowed to do so right up until the Election Day. This was a major departure from the norm. In any election, there must be a deadline for voters to register their intention to participate. But now they had the opportunity to come in at the last minute. I could see that the JOC and election director Mudede wanted to have a chance for a last sweep of the countryside, looking for new voters loyal to Mugabe even after the official cut-off date. Why else would Mugabe issue such a notice just hours before polling booths opened for the election?

For the first time in Zimbabwe's history, the responsibility for the management of the supplementary voters' roll was given to the army. Under the fresh regulations, uniformed military officers were allowed to enter polling stations to supervise the voting. In the past, while the law allowed for ordinary civil servants to assist the ESC in running an election, it specifically excluded the security and uniformed forces.

But Mugabe, through the new presidential decree, changed the law, allowing for any government minister to assign such persons in the employment of the state as may be necessary to perform secretarial or administrative functions for the ESC in an election. The arrangement opened the way for the army, the police and prison officers to occupy positions in election management and administration. Brigadier Nyikayaramba, war veteran and serving senior military officer, was now firmly in charge.

Not wanting to just give up, I filed more than eight court cases before the High Court and Supreme Court. In my protest, I stated that the ESC was set up in terms of the national constitution and it was supposed to function independently. If any government minister could assign staff from any government department to the commission at will, then the independence of the ESC was now in doubt. Further, and at the same time, the ESC was not properly constituted. While the constitution required that there be five commissioners, there were only four. I considered myself cheated by having to go into my first major election under such disgraceful arrangements.

My court submissions challenged, among other items, the illegal removal of names from the voters' roll; the continued, clandestine registration of voters after the close of voter registration; the restrictive residency and citizenship requirements for voter registration; the legality of the General Laws Amendment Act; the illegal use of military personnel as staff on the ESC; and the unconstitutionality of Section 158 of the Electoral Act which allowed Mugabe to abuse the law. The court found I lacked *locus standi* to bring the application due to the absence of any allegation establishing the infringement of a fundamental right.[3]

Among the government decrees published by Mugabe changing the electoral regulations was one that reduced the number of polling stations in urban areas, our strongest base, by 60 per cent. Mudede kept the information secret, making it impossible for us to plan the deployment of our election agents. Even observers and monitors were kept in the dark. Two days before polling, we learnt that Harare, with nearly a million voters, was only allocated 167 stations. More stations were relocated to the rural areas.

Mugabe's total disregard for integrity in the 2002 presidential campaign was roundly condemned by the European Union observer mission who felt Zanu PF's conduct was an affront to universal democratic principles, electoral norms and standards. In response, the government deported Pierre Schori, the head of the mission, accusing the EU of interference in Harare's internal affairs. Schori was fingered for being in the country illegally.

Although he had scored a major propaganda coup against me with the

Ben-Menashe story, Mugabe remained unsure about his fate. I attempted to wind up my campaign in the farming town of Marondera, 70 kilometres south of Harare, on Thursday 7 March. As I tried to enter Marondera, I saw that all roads leading to the place were burning and effectively blocked: used vehicle tyres doused in paraffin and petrol were in flames. Not a single side road or thoroughfare was spared.

Along the roadsides were hordes of Zanu PF militias with heaps of stones and logs, ready to attack any perceived MDC supporters destined for our public rally in the town's Rudhaka Stadium. As I tried to exit and negotiate a return to Harare, a hail of stones was directed at my car. The police, already spineless spectators, stood blank-eyed, watching the spectacle from a distance. I made it back home and waited for the final whistle.

The night before polling began, hundreds of my polling agents were attacked, especially in rural Mashonaland. Many abandoned their stations and sought refuge at our party headquarters, Harvest House in Harare. We called in international observers to witness and interview these unfortunate men and women, but it was too late for us to organise replacements. Nearly 95 per cent of the polling stations in rural Mashonaland ran their elections without MDC polling agents. The violence made it totally impossible to work there.

On Saturday, 9 March, Zimbabweans, especially in urban areas, came out of their homes in a manner that had never been seen before. Thousands of people turned up at their nearest polling station. They queued patiently as the voting officials took their time opening the stations, processing the papers and allowing people into the voting booths. Unfazed, people waited as the process proceeded at a snail's pace.

I was at my local station fairly early. Together with Amai Edwin and my two aides, the voters gave us the privilege of walking through, straight into Avondale Primary School, and within minutes we were out again.

The day before I had received numerous reports from all over Zimbabwe indicating that voting had already begun, especially in military, police and prison camps. Officers were casting ballots under the eagle eye of senior officers and war veterans. Secrecy was already compromised.

In Harare, despite the shortage of voting stations, people were supposed to vote for a president, a mayor and a local councillor. In nearby Chitungwiza, another MDC stronghold, the picture was even messier. Here, voters were expected to cast two votes: for a president and for a mayor. The decision to reduce the number of stations, particularly in these two cities, aimed at slowing down the voting process to deny as many people as possible the opportunity of voting, especially in areas known to have large numbers of MDC supporters. In the rest of the country, voters posted only one ballot: that for the president.

After Amai Ed and I had voted, I drove around Harare and was amazed by the large turnout, although disappointed by the painfully slow pace of the voting process. As a result, the voting went on into the night and spilled over to the following morning. I met with our senior officials and we decided to make an urgent court application for an extension of the voting period beyond the prescribed two days. Despite Zanu PF's spirited arguments, we won an extension. We wanted an additional two days for Zimbabwe to complete the election, particularly in urban areas where thousands of voters had been unable to cast their vote because of deliberate bureaucratic delays.

After the court had physically visited various polling stations, Justice Ben Hlatshwayo ordered all polling stations to be reopened for just one extra day. Mudede, however, failed to comply with the court order and instead reopened the polling stations late, and only in Harare and Chitungwiza.

He ordered all the stations to close at 7 pm, even in cases where as many as a thousand people were still queuing to vote. I brought another urgent application in the High Court for Mudede to be held in contempt of court for failing to comply with the court order, and insisting that polling should be extended to a fourth day. The High Court, however, dismissed the application.

Interestingly, it was Justice Hlatshwayo who initially indicated that he would be comfortable with limiting the extension to Harare and Chitungwiza only, but Zanu PF made a sudden U-turn and insisted that the order should cover the whole country. That was granted, and Mudede was authorised to extend the poll by another day. He never opened the stations outside Harare and Chitungwiza. In these two cities, apart from the delays, Mudede's officials seemed reluctant to work.

The public media gave the High Court's decision to extend the polling very little publicity, which meant that many voters only heard the news through the grapevine. Despite the setback, people turned up at the polling booths, only to be met by a hostile riot police force, which harassed them, accusing them of trying to vote twice. Hundreds of MDC supporters were arrested outside polling stations and only released the following day. None of them had had a chance to vote.

The Harare and Chitungwiza stations closed at 7 pm sharp, regardless of the electoral law that required a polling station to be open for at least eight hours continuously on each polling day. According to this same law, voting officers were compelled to permit every voter who happened to be inside the polling station, room, tent, vehicle or such other place where voting was taking place, at the time fixed for closure, to cast a ballot. These officers are even allowed to take in any voter who is unable to be inside the room because of congestion or other reasons when the time is up. But none of this was adhered to. Instead, those voters still in queues were violently dispersed by the riot police.

There were wild scenes outside stations as the police sprayed tear gas and tear smoke on eager but hapless voters, telling them to go straight home and remain indoors. In no time, the streets of Harare were deserted as terrified voters huddled in their homes for personal security. Their innocent attempt to exercise a universal right of citizenship had been criminalised at the stroke of 7pm. So much for democracy!

There were numerous cases of police trucks picking up large numbers of voters from their stations purporting to transport them to nearby stations after hoodwinking them into believing that there were shorter queues there – only to drive them straight into police holding cells, normally used for criminal suspects. Mothers who had left their infants at home only managed to return to their families after a night in crammed police stations, without food or water. Of the 878 715 registered voters in Harare, barely 50 per cent made it to the polls, whereas countrywide an average turnout of nearly 70 per cent was recorded.

In the rural areas where no monitors or international observers dared to check, and where our polling agents were denied entry and had been physically attacked the night before, the field was open for Mugabe to work out the voting patterns as he pleased. I was told there was a 100 per cent turnout in the rural areas, with numerous cases of multiple voting.

We were totally at the mercy of a frightening, state-manipulated system, led by a ruthless rival who regularly assumed the position of referee, match commissioner and player – all in the same contest. The ballot, in an entrenched African dictatorship, was insufficient on its own to bring about change.

We waited patiently for the official results. The system was so skewed against the opposition that to expect victory seemed far-fetched. The government refused to announce the results at the polling stations. They brought them to Harare, where they passed through the military-staffed and Zanu PF-controlled national command centre at Manyame Air Base, for what it called a verification exercise before being announced to the nation. None of our agents, or any from the other opposition parties or independent candidates, were allowed into the war-room type national command centre where a nation's destiny was being shaped.

Acknowledging that Zimbabwe was on a knife-edge at the time, I issued a public statement calling for calm and counselling patience, tolerance and political maturity. I thanked the people for their resilience in reclaiming their rights, as expressed by the massive turnout. I made it clear that I felt overwhelmed to see a people, in the face of such brutality, who had managed to retain such gracious exuberance and determination. I noted that the tide of change was irreversible and that people must be prepared to pay the price for freedom. I pledged to remain focused as their messenger and to remain strong against all odds.

Eventually, the military – using Tobaiwa Mudede, the civilian national director of elections – informed Zimbabwe and the world that Mugabe had won the presidential vote by 56 per cent; they gave me 42 per cent.

This translated to 1 685 212 votes for Mugabe and 1 258 401 for me – a difference of about 400 000. That difference equalled almost the same number of people in Harare alone who had deliberately been denied an opportunity to cast their ballots.

The other contestants, Shakespeare Maya of the National Alliance of Good Governance (NAGG) and Paul Siwela, an independent, were too far behind, with figures too inconsequential to make a difference.

I rejected the result immediately and called for its nullification.

Mugabe had claimed another six years in office! Harare, Bulawayo, Gweru, Mutare and other towns and cities retreated quietly after the election result was announced. There were no celebrations anywhere in the streets or in homes; no post-election partying. The country was uncomfortably quiet.

Two days later, Mugabe organised a victory celebration at his ancestral village of Zvimba, 60 kilometres from Harare. Even there, he sounded tormented and wounded, warning Zimbabweans against demonstrations and protests. I understood his anxiety.

As I coped with my personal heartbreak – exhausted but with the conviction that we should have won yet knowing the cards had been stacked against us – there were occasional but significant political successes which rekindled my spirits. The presidential election was conducted simultaneously with local council elections in Chitungwiza and in Harare. We won comfortably in both cities. Engineer Elias Mudzuri and 45 local councillors took over Harare, while Misheck Shoko became the new executive mayor of Chitungwiza. Mudzuri was the new executive mayor of the capital city in which Zanu PF was represented by a lone elected military officer, Colonel Hubert Nyanhongo.

Earlier, we had won the mayoral seat in urban Masvingo, Zimbabwe's oldest town. There another engineer, Alois Chaimiti, was now in charge. The same pattern had repeated itself in Bulawayo where economist Japhet Ndabeni-Ncube was the new mayor. That was a source of comfort. With all the parliamentary seats in Harare, Bulawayo, Mutare, Gweru, Kwekwe, Chitungwiza and urban Masvingo under the MDC, Zanu PF was now confined to the rural areas.

We had been denied outright victory but we were taking over the country bit by bit. By now Mugabe should have got the message and begun to prepare his own exit, but he did the opposite.

ENDNOTES

1 'Human Rights and Zimbabwe's Presidential Election: March 2002: Special Report 4.' May 2002. Report compiled by the Research Unit of the Zimbabwe Human Rights NGO Forum http://www.hrforumzim.com/special_hrru/Special_Report_4_2002%20Election/SR4_0.htm

2 The judgment nullified the General Laws Amendment Act under which Mugabe would have had a free hand in amending the electoral management regulations without having to go back to parliament for approval

3 For more details see, for example, Tsvangirai v. Registrar General, SC 76/2002, Judgment SC 20-02, 4 April 2002, at 7. For a critique of the Supreme Court's decision, see Geoff Feltoe, *Legal Standing in Public Law*, Zimbabwe Human Rights Bulletin (2002)

CHAPTER NINETEEN
SEEKING JUSTICE

International observers of the sham 2002 election, including the European Union, the Commonwealth, the United States, civil society and the generality of Zimbabweans, roundly condemned the conduct and outcome of the polls. A few African countries privately expressed concern, but the African Union as a whole backed Mugabe. Even South Africa, whose observer mission had a tough time with Zanu PF militants while on duty in rural areas during the campaign and polling period, issued a mealy-mouthed and contradictory statement which, in the final analysis, endorsed Mugabe. The Commonwealth said it was concerned about the slide into disorder and tasked three of its members, Nigeria, South Africa and Australia, to initiate dialogue with Mugabe and to plan a way forward. I agreed with this move, as I now believed that a much more holistic approach was needed to resolve the national crisis.

The international outcry against Mugabe's rule and the stolen election seemed to enrage him. Just three months after allegedly receiving a six-year mandate from the electorate, he listed another 3 000 commercial farms for an abrupt takeover – giving the farmers a mere 45 days to leave their properties. Surely, after a victory, if it was a genuine one, a political leader would sober up and get on with the business of the state, embrace opponents and govern the country?

South Africa favoured a negotiated settlement that could lead to the formation of a government of national unity, preferably with the MDC as a junior partner. Soon after the election, ANC secretary general Kgalema Motlanthe and Professor Adebayo Adedeji of Nigeria were tasked with bringing together the MDC and Zanu PF. Previously, Adedeji was a United Nations Under-Secretary General and Executive Secretary to the United Nations Economic Commission for Africa. In the early 1970s he had served for five years as Nigeria's federal commissioner (minister) for economic development and reconstruction. Motlanthe was then a senior ANC official with an impeccable liberation war legacy. He was destined to take over South Africa as caretaker president when Thabo Mbeki resigned and he later became deputy president.

The MDC's team for the talks included Professor Welshman Ncube, Professor Elphas Mukonoweshuro and businessman Ian Makone, while Zanu PF sent Patrick Chinamasa, Jonathan Moyo and other senior officials. At first, Mugabe appeared to be in favour of this approach and sought to take advantage of the eminent facilitators, Motlanthe and Adedeji, to get around the doubts about his disputed legitimacy.

When I queried the slow pace of the talks, I was informed that Mugabe was deliberately taking his time to stop me filing a challenge within the specified legal timeframe in cases of electoral disputes. As time was running out, and to back my negotiating position, I formally lodged papers with the High Court. Mugabe responded swiftly, condemning me for challenging his claim to victory, and promptly scuttled the talks. He argued that since I was keen to pursue the issue of the stolen presidency through the courts, Zanu PF was pulling out of the dialogue.

When Nigeria and South Africa tried to dissuade Mugabe from

withdrawing, he insisted that at all their meetings I should first recognise him as head of state and government, a position I refused to accept. The Commonwealth persisted in its effort to help resolve the crisis, but Mugabe remained stubborn. Nigerian President Olusegun Obasanjo and Thabo Mbeki made several visits to Harare, as did Malawi President Bakili Muluzi, then SADC chairman, in a bid to persuade Mugabe to soften his position. He refused to budge. We were back where we started.

Mugabe's refusal to talk peace, at least with the MDC and me, presented policy headaches on all sides and we heard that our situation dominated dinner table conversations right across the globe. Meanwhile SADC countries and the UK had begun to feel the weight of Zimbabwean immigrants and refugees. The UK imposed stringent entry visas on all classes of Zimbabweans and began to deport those who overstayed their brief welcome.

Inside the party, tragedy hit us. Our young, politically agile spokesperson, Learnmore Jongwe, killed his wife in a domestic dispute over allegations of infidelity. Jongwe, a member of parliament for Kuwadzana in Harare, briefly escaped from Harare to the Midlands before his arrest in July 2002. His actions affected me badly because I felt that as a young lawyer, a former student leader, and now a politician, he was full of promise.

After the state and the Supreme Court denied him bail, we all knew that he would either be hanged or given a lengthy sentence. The murder case generated a lot of negative publicity for the party.

After a few weeks awaiting trial in prison, Jongwe was found dead in his cell – indications were that he had committed suicide. Jongwe's sudden departure weakened our message delivery system for he was a key cog in the party leadership. It came at a time when the people felt let down by a flawed election and depressed by the thought of another six years of Mugabe's rule. We had to keep spirits up by communicating a positive message about our future. The national executive decided to fill Jongwe's position as information chief with Paul Themba Nyathi, an articulate former teacher. At the same time, I hired T William Bango, a senior journalist and a former trade unionist, to help me out as my personal assistant and presidential spokesperson.

In December 2002 I became aware of behind-the-scenes manoeuvres to edge me out of the political scene. The manoeuvres involved strange bedfellows, among them the military, some foreign governments and local business people. Leading the fishing expedition was one Colonel Lionel Dyke, a retired serviceman with close links to Vitalis Zvinavashe and Emmerson Mnangagwa.

Dyke put a strange proposal to me, indicating that the British government, working with South Africa and senior Zanu PF and MDC politicians and the military top brass, were keen to work out an exit strategy for Mugabe and save Zimbabwe from further decline. When I requested further details and asked what the team saw as my role in this arrangement, Dyke failed to provide a cogent explanation. I went public and denounced the plan, inviting the ire of Welshman Ncube, Paul Themba Nyathi and other senior MDC officials – although I had refrained from accusing or name-shaming anybody for their part in the plot. I gathered later that the secret team, working behind closed doors, wanted Mugabe and me off the political stage completely as it saw us as stumbling blocks to stability, progress and good business.

I had surrendered my passport to the Clerk of the Court as part of my bail conditions which meant that it was impossible for me to leave Zimbabwe until after the conclusion of the treason trial. Another condition required me to notify the police of my presence in Harare twice a week: on Mondays and Thursdays. This was a tough restriction. It meant that I could hardly get about and was denied the exposure I needed, at home and abroad. I had to rely on emissaries to articulate the MDC position, even in circumstances that required that I, as the party leader, should have been there to explain my vision for Zimbabwe.

The treason trial opened in February 2003, some 11 months after the three of us – Welshman Ncube, Renson Gasela and I – had been formally charged. In meetings between the long court sessions during the treason trial, I convinced the national executive of the need for a sustained, confrontational approach against Mugabe. I then planned a two-day national shutdown for March 2003. The people were simply urged to stay at home. Commerce, industry, mines and other economic activities were to be suspended for two days of protest over the national crisis. On weekends, I went around the country, mobilising our structures in preparation for the protests. My message was well received and the party structures devised a national, roll-out programme for a national shutdown.

On 18 March 2003, Zimbabwe came to a virtual standstill. Businesses and government offices closed shop, halting normal activity across the nation. Buoyed by the success of the mass action, I set out to organise another one which the media dubbed the 'Final Push'.

The MDC's mass action strategy coincided with two electoral campaigns. Earlier, our national council had dismissed Munyaradzi Gwisai, MP for Highfield in Harare, from the party over policy differences and indiscipline. The dismissal meant that Gwisai lost his parliamentary seat, resulting in a by-election. We also had another by-election in Kuwadzana, also in Harare, to replace the late Learnmore Jongwe.

The ruling party tried to use violence to re-enter the political field in Harare but failed. Nevertheless they still claimed a number of casualties. Zanu PF members imposed a curfew in Kuwadzana following a series of violent clashes with our party youths at one of the militia bases Mugabe had set up in the suburb. In nearby Chitungwiza, police arrested and severely tortured our MP, Job Sikhala, his lawyer Gabriel Shumba, and activists Taurai Magaya, Bishop Shumba and Charles Mutuma.

The police accused Sikhala of violating the Public Order and Security Act (POSA) but the matter was later thrown out of court. The generally intolerant attitude of the police towards the broader society had become so negative that 23 church pastors mounted a protest. When the pastors and other members of the clergy from Northside Community Church in Harare's northern suburbs attempted to deliver a petition to the Commissioner of Police they were intercepted, attacked and arrested before they reached the police headquarters.

Our continued participation in elections under such conditions was a matter of great concern to me. I put out word to our structures, hinting at the possibility of boycotting the Kuwadzana by-election but was overruled by the MDC. At every forum, the people argued that elections were our only weapon to achieve democracy. People assured me that they were determined to expose Mugabe through the ballot; any talk of alternatives to an election never found any takers. I was constantly reminded that there was no substitute for what lay inside the people's hearts and minds. Mugabe would one day find it difficult to rig an election and would have to go.

The party strongly believed that with carefully organised protests and constant participation in elections, Mugabe would finally give in. In the by-election on 30 March, we retained both the Kuwadzana and Highfield constituencies. Our candidates, Nelson Chamisa and Pearson Mungofa, sailed through despite the Zanu PF violence, torture and intimidation. Zanu PF responded to its loss with a random wave of post-election retributive attacks on the residents, led by military officers in uniform. The army kept up the pressure, patrolling the streets of Harare and Chitungwiza.

They worked with the CIO and Zanu PF militias who identified MDC targets for assault. The onslaught led to yet another death, that of Tonderayi Machiridza, an MDC organiser in Chitungwiza. When the community gathered for Machiridza's funeral, police in crowd-control gear arrested 70 MDC supporters. They seized the body and threw it into a grave at Chitungwiza cemetery while Machiridza's mother and family, his comrades and neighbours were barred from the proceedings.

While the MDC was making the final preparations for the national strike, I received an unexpected message from Father Fidelis Mukonori, a Jesuit who acted as chaplain to Mugabe, indicating that he wanted to see me. He drove to my home and tried to persuade me to abandon the mass action. I asked him for a trade-off, but he had none. I asked whether Mugabe had sent him or whether he was pursuing an individual initiative, but he was evasive. I took the opportunity to make a counter overture to Mugabe, asking him to consider a private meeting at his rural Zvimba home at which I could discuss my concerns with him. Mukonori, who I believe knew his man well, said Mugabe insisted that I abandon mass action before any meeting between us could take place. I could see through Mukonori's insincerity and refused. We parted without reaching any agreement.

The Ben-Menashe treason trial dragged on, wearing us down, but worse was to come. On Sunday, 1 June 2003, police commissioner Augustine Chihuri sought an urgent High Court order barring the MDC from engaging in the 'Final Push' protests. But it was already too late. The protest was highly successful, bringing Zimbabwe to a total standstill for a week. The state blamed me for the nationwide protests, saying I wished to remove Mugabe from office through the use of force.

I was arrested and detained on Friday, 6 June, the last day of the mass action. Sibanda called an emergency national executive meeting at the weekend but I received reports that he had failed to chair the meeting and it collapsed. No decisions were taken as the gathering disintegrated prematurely.

Despite the setback, it was clear that 'The Final Push' showed Zanu PF and Mugabe that they had underestimated our organisational capacity, while the enthusiastic response was a clear statement that popular support had swung in favour of the MDC.

I appeared before a magistrate after a weekend in police cells and was slapped with a fresh treason charge. The magistrate denied me bail, which meant that I had to go to jail while awaiting the outcome of an appeal for relief at the High Court. I spent two weeks in jail, now attending the Ben-Menashe treason trial from Harare's Remand Prison. As I languished in a filthy, flea-ridden prison cell, Ben-Menashe and his two Canadian workers, all witnesses, lived in luxury in a five-star hotel for several months at the taxpayer's expense.

I had not been held in custody since 1989 when I was arrested for supporting striking students at the University of Zimbabwe. This time the situation was worse. I was the oldest inmate; the majority were young adults aged between 18 and 25. Many had been inside for months after failing to raise even paltry amounts of surety, or were awaiting trials for petty crimes. Food was critically short and there was an outbreak of scabies, kwashiorkor and pellagra – all nutrition and hygiene-related diseases. I was lucky to receive food from home. Amai Edwin made sure she prepared a lot of it so that I could share it with my youthful, emaciated fellow inmates.

The MDC took advantage of the presence of Bizos and his legal team and instructed them to lodge a bail application in the High Court, causing a temporary suspension of the running treason trial. The appeal was heard by Justice Susan Mavhangira. She granted me temporary relief, with a fresh set of conditions and restrictions. It was difficult to raise the bail money, for the state insisted on a cash payment of Z$20 million – an amount that could not be raised easily because of cash shortages in Zimbabwe. With the help of well-wishers, we managed to raise the cash. It came in ten cardboard boxes and was in small denominations. It took the lawyers several hours to count it.

The treason trial before Justice Garwe then resumed. During a tea break, Ncube whispered to me that Chinamasa had approached him with a proposal that the MDC and Zanu PF should resume talks. I encouraged him to pursue the proposal. The two of them discussed positions of common constitutional principles for many weeks. Ncube later informed me that Thabo Mbeki was prepared to lend his support to the initiative. But the Chinamasa-Ncube secret talks were causing a lot of anxiety in the party. I recall one stormy national executive meeting at which Ncube was forced to accept that the MDC's representation be expanded.

Anticipating the reopening of the MDC-Zanu PF talks, the meeting appointed a negotiating team led by Matongo and including Ncube, Chimanikire and Lucia Matibenga. I understand that Ncube – as our contact person – communicated our position to Zanu PF through Chinamasa and a draft agenda was worked out. But Ncube remained secretive about his dealings with Chinamasa and continued to work on his own, leading to an agreement signed by the two of them, indicating their points of convergence.

When he gave me a copy of the signed document, I told him that there was nothing I could do with it unless the plan was passed by the national executive committee. I expressed my reservations over the manner in which he had conducted himself, going as far as appending his signature to an agreement without the party's endorsement. Ncube defended himself, saying he and Chinamasa decided to sign the agreement to avoid fresh differences emerging afterwards. He did not trust Chinamasa and feared that he was likely to change his mind from the agreed position.

I asked him if Zanu PF had agreed to talks on the basis of what Chinamasa had committed himself to. Ncube was not certain, indicating only that Chinamasa had promised to table the document at the earliest Zanu PF leadership meeting. Nothing happened. The whole plan collapsed as the document was never formally presented to either party.

Two other peace initiatives were under way during the treason trial. South African Anglican Archbishop Njongonkulu Ndungane flew to Harare and met Mugabe and me separately, but failed to make headway. Ndungane said he was on a peace mission, supported by various South African churches because of their concern about the worsening situation in Zimbabwe.

At the same time, three Manicaland bishops, Patrick Mutume (Catholic), Sebastian Bakare (Anglican) and Trevor Manhanga (Pentecostal) also tried to get involved on a separate mission. They said their effort was equally supported by their South African counterparts. Again, they met Mugabe and me on separate occasions, but they hardly moved beyond the preliminary talks.

Now facing two treason charges, I had to present myself at different courts depending on which case was up for a hearing. The new one was still at the initial judicial stages. This meant that I had to present myself before a magistrate from time to time for a further remand. The trial involving Ben-Menashe had already started and would continue until the state had exhausted its entire body of evidence.

As a free man, Ncube secured his passport, enabling him to travel outside Zimbabwe. For a while I relied on him to continue our international campaign and urged him to take the case of the MDC far and wide.

About this time I began to notice a disturbing pattern in the relationship between my deputy, Sibanda, Ncube, Dulini-Ncube and other top officials from the western region. They were spending almost all their political time in Bulawayo and the surrounding areas. I took Sibanda aside and tried to impress upon him the need for all of us to build national profiles and to refrain from regional biases. He seemed to understand my point, but nonetheless ignored my advice. There were unhealthy reports from

Matabeleland that our regional office was terrorising any officials deemed to support my leadership.

Suddenly, there were a lot of made-up disciplinary hearings and suspensions from the party structures. I tried to curb the practice, with limited success. I suppressed my frustrations and turned myself into a voracious reader of a myriad of books and texts on leadership, donated by well-wishers and friends. I devoured all that came my way, from medieval and biblical scrolls to contemporary academic surveys and memoirs of kings, queens, dictators, politicians and captains of commerce and industry. In the process, I built a comprehensive personal library with many works on leadership ideas, experiences and stories – from ancient Greek icons to Nelson Mandela.

Despite natural conflicts, inevitable in any organisation the size of the MDC, I managed to keep the MDC together at a time when it was most susceptible to splintering. The biggest threat to the MDC, so I thought, was the massive state arsenal for violence at Zanu PF's disposal, spearheaded by a youth militia that was now resident in every constituency. Intimidation through food aid was perhaps their most subtle technique; more straightforwardly, they just threatened people or used brute force without warning.

As I waited for the resumption of the main treason trial, the MDC scored another round of victories in local government elections in September 2003. I kept urging Sibanda and the MDC leadership to try to cover the whole country, to assure the people of our presence, and explain my absence on trumped-up charges. We now controlled all the major towns and cities. Again, that gave me hope and courage. If the ground had been level, I believed, we could emerge with far better results, even in the rural areas.

For example, because of violence and restrictions put in their way by the Registrar-General's office, MDC candidates failed to register in dozens of municipal wards. In Bindura, they were unable to gain access to all the ten town wards; in Chegutu, Zanu PF barred them in all eleven wards; in Karoi, the MDC was blocked in four out of nine wards; in Marondera, five out of eleven wards were sealed-off to the opposition; and in Rusape, the

MDC candidates dared not walk in any of the ten wards.

As a result, Zanu PF candidates were declared unopposed winners in Marondera, Chinhoyi and in seven rural district councils. Yes, the MDC was under siege. But Mugabe and Zanu PF did not rest either. The gruelling struggle required perseverance and determination.

Local Government Minister Ignatious Chombo's relationship with Mudzuri and the Harare City Council broke down irretrievably. In the end, Chombo sacked Mudzuri and appointed Sekesayi Makwavarara, the deputy mayor, to act as the new city chief. Makwavarara disappointed the MDC when she later crossed the floor and joined Zanu PF. After her defection, the city council collapsed and Chombo used the law to suspend the entire council. He appointed Zanu PF cronies to what he called a 'special commission' to run the capital for five years.

Chombo fired Blessing Dhlakama, the Chegutu mayor, for reasons similar to the instance of Mudzuri. The same happened to Misheck Shoko of Chitungwiza and Misheck Kagurabadza, the mayor of Mutare. The Urban Councils Act allows the minister of local government to dissolve a council and appoint a commission, as a transitional authority, to run a town or city's affairs for a maximum period of six months. This was to enable political parties to prepare and field new candidates for a democratic election. As Zimbabwe was now a place with no rule of law, Chombo's commissions stayed on forever, despite numerous successful legal challenges from residents and ratepayers.

The whole game became a mixture of victories and setbacks. It was disheartening to know that the people had made their choice only to have Mugabe ignore it.

I kept pressing the High Court to hear my legal challenge to Mugabe's March 2002 presidential election victory. I could see that by insisting on my right to be heard, I was being an irritant to Mugabe. I was pressured by many a Mugabe emissary to drop the case so as to pave the way for a negotiated settlement. Whenever I asked them what Mugabe was offering in return, I received no guarantees that he was prepared to make any political concessions, in any direction.

The end of 2003 was approaching without my challenge to the March

2002 election result being heard. This was yet another case of justice being denied through inordinate delays. Further, in the months following the filing of the election petition, Registrar-General Tobaiwa Mudede flouted several court orders in a bid to thwart the MDC's legal 'discovery' requests from my lawyers. In one particular case, Mudede flatly refused to allow my lawyers and officials to inspect the voters' roll and would not release the used ballot papers for inspection.

The ESC played its own part in subverting the petition. It ignored the court orders and failed to comply with my requests for public information from its records. To cap it all, the High Court Registrar could not be moved to set a date for the hearing, despite numerous requests from my lawyers.

I fought hard for 12 months just to get a date for a hearing, without success. Eventually, on 9 May 2003, circumstances forced me to file an urgent application in the High Court for what lawyers call a *mandamus* to compel the High Court Registrar to set the hearing down as a matter of urgency. It took a further two months for the High Court to grant the order. By then, I was in the middle of the two treason trials.

To avoid being drowned by despair during this legal war, I turned my attention to strengthening the party. I reshuffled the portfolio committees' policy secretaries; reshuffled the shadow cabinet; started to revise our party policies to reflect the changed political environment; and – in concert with Ncube and the national executive committee – mounted an aggressive international campaign for legitimate, free and fair elections in Zimbabwe.

Tendai Biti and Tapiwa Mashakada assembled a team of eminent economists and scholars and started to revise our economic policy. Gideon Gono, previously Mugabe's family banker, was now the governor of the Central Bank and had embarked on a series of dangerous experiments. He abolished money, replacing it with what he called local travellers cheques, subsequently renamed bearer cheques.

Real cash, legal tender as Zimbabweans knew it, was scarce and all our coins had become worthless due to a runaway inflationary spiral. Food, fuel and foreign currency were critically short. As a country, Zimbabwe was struggling to find trading partners or to buy supplies on the open market.

When a regime is under siege as a result of its own shortcomings, the tendency is to target the truth. Dictators despise the truth; they suppress the free flow of public information as a form of control. *The Daily News* became one of the first casualties of Mugabe's intolerance right from its inception. In his memoirs, Geoffrey Nyarota gives a personal account of his experiences as the founding editor of *The Daily News*.[1] The owners of *The Daily News* and its sister newspaper, *The Daily News on Sunday*, refused to obtain an official licence to publish. There were internal boardroom squabbles that eventually saw the departure of Nyarota. Apart from what was publicly known about the fate of the newspaper, I was unfamiliar with the finer details of how the newspaper was infiltrated and pushed to defy the law which required that all publications have operating licences or risk state-sanctioned closure.

Minister for information and publicity in the President's Office, Jonathan Moyo, then descended on the newspaper. In October 2003, after a string of unsuccessful court applications over its truckload of troubles, Moyo succeeded in silencing the newspaper. Although we had no stake in the newspaper, the ban was a big blow to the MDC and to Zimbabwe, leaving us totally at the mercy of a hostile state media.

Even minor media were not spared. In August 2002, a tiny Harare studio used by an externally based radio station, the Voice of the People, broadcasting into Zimbabwe, was firebombed. Police arrested the station's journalists on unspecified charges and the state did not bother to investigate the bombing.

The difference between our reasoned approach to national issues and a basically emotional, self-serving party line was to be clearly demonstrated in the court challenge to Mugabe's claimed election victory in the 2002 presidential election.

In the middle of working on *Restart* – one of our policy documents for the reconstruction of Zimbabwe – I was advised of a date for a pre-trial conference on my election petition. At the meeting under the direction of Justice Garwe, we agreed to split the election petition into two phases.

The first phase would comprise the legal and constitutional arguments. The court should establish whether there were, indeed, fundamental constitutional infringements in the conduct of the election that would be sufficient to nullify the outcome. The understanding was that should the High Court rule against Morgan Tsvangirai in the first phase, then a second phase would be scheduled to hear the evidence of violence, intimidation, corrupt and illegal practices, voter fraud, vote rigging, and polling irregularities.

After persistent efforts to get a date, the first stage of the hearing was set down for 5 November 2003. I hired another South African legal and constitutional expert, Advocate Jeremy Gauntlett SC, to lead my team which comprised Advocates Adrian De Bourbon SC, and Happius Zhou, assisted by Bryant Elliot. Lawyer Terence Hussein represented Mugabe.

On 5 November, after a long wait for the proceedings to begin, Justice Ben Hlatshwayo walked in and took the chair as the presiding judge. Of the High Court judges assigned to hear the 2000 parliamentary election petitions, Justice Hlatshwayo was the only one not to have ruled against Zanu PF in any of the cases he heard. Consequently, I was worried by Hlatshwayo's apparently casual approach towards the MDC's petitions. He seemed not to take them seriously – as evidenced by his reluctance to provide a written judgment or even give us the reasons for his dismissal of the MDC's election petition in the Goromonzi constituency.

Advocate Jeremy Gauntlett outlined the legal arguments for setting aside the election. In summary, we sought to emphasise that an election outcome deserved to be nullified if it failed to meet the expected standard of being free and fair. In particular, I had briefed the team to challenge Section 149 of the Electoral Act, which I felt had been published with errors by the Law Reviser causing a difference in meaning and a contradiction with the general spirit of the law. My understanding was that for an election to be set aside, the evidence need not demonstrate that the irregularities in the conduct of the election actually affected the outcome of the election. All that I was required to show was that the poll was not conducted in accordance with the basic, generic principles of a free and fair election.

I argued further that Mugabe enjoyed unlimited powers to

amend electoral laws when the responsibility for any such changes is constitutionally a task for parliament, not that of a single contestant in an election. Mugabe derived that power from the Electoral Act which allowed him to play around with the electoral law as he wished. By so doing he literally usurped the power of the legislature, thus interfering with the principle of autonomy and separation of public service duties. I challenged the regulations Mugabe introduced under a flawed law that had been overturned by the Supreme Court, a non-existent law, the General Laws (Amendment) Act.

The rules should have had no force of effect because constitutionally, the Electoral Act was a bad law. I cited, as an example, Mugabe's refusal to allow large numbers of citizens to exercise their right to vote after he declared that they were foreigners. I strongly objected to Mugabe's discriminatory practice over the use of postal ballots when he decreed that this opportunity was open only to the military and to Zimbabwean diplomats. I disagreed with his unilateral decision to reduce the number of polling stations in urban areas in an attempt to strike at the MDC support base, and further queried his intentions when he repeatedly and secretly extended the cut-off day for voter registration in order to accommodate his own supporters. These issues, in my view, posed a fundamental assault on the constitutional rights of Zimbabwean voters.

Through such devious means, I argued, Mugabe's behaviour had significantly affected the conduct of the election. For this reason, the outcome should be declared invalid.

I then took a swipe at the ESC which with only four members instead of five was improperly constituted in terms of the constitution. Because of that flaw, the ESC could not legally carry out its constitutional mandate of supervising a credible and legitimate election. The constitution provided for an independent ESC. But the 2002 election was conducted under the direction and control of the military.

I made sure the High Court placed on record that Mugabe – a mere four days before the election – issued an executive order directing government ministers to appoint staff to the ESC, thus compromising the independence of the commission. I raised the issue of other infringements which I had noted in the run-up to the voting day as irrefutable evidence of electoral malpractices which should never be allowed in a democracy. I believed we had a solid legal argument.[2]

After Gauntlett and his team concluded their submission, Terence Hussein, Mugabe's lawyer, totally ignored the legal arguments. He digressed, saying his client was a head of government, a president, who took a bold and brave step to embark on a land reform programme to redress the imbalance in land ownership and restore it to its rightful owners. He described Mugabe's move as 'brave' because it came at a price: the British government had vowed that one way or the other, Mugabe would be removed from office. In conclusion, he said it was inconceivable that the election of the president, the highest officer in the land, the Commander in Chief of the Armed Forces, and the signatory of all laws should be set aside because of 'the flowery language of three lawyers'.

Justice Hlatshwayo adjourned the proceedings, saying he was reserving judgment. Before the hearing ended Gauntlett pleaded with him to speed up the process so that the matter was concluded early. That was the beginning of yet another long wait.

While the High Court was considering my challenge to Mugabe's claimed electoral victory, Sibanda informed me that he had received a letter from Tafadzwa Basilo Musekiwa, one of our MPs, who was resigning his seat because he feared for his life. Barely three years into his five-year tenure as a legislator, he had fled Zimbabwe and entered the UK on a visitors' visa, before he applied for asylum and decided to settle in London. He was reluctant to return to Zimbabwe.

At 24, Tafadzwa Basilo Musekiwa was the MDC's youngest lawmaker – perhaps the youngest ever in the history of our parliament. Representing the Zengeza constituency in Harare was his first job. A former student leader but never a radical activist, Musekiwa came into politics, I think, circumstantially. Those who knew him well say Musekiwa, who had a quiet demeanour, was close to the main actors in the student movement in the late 1990s and happened to be in the right place at the right time when the MDC was formed.

In the 2000 election, Musekiwa pulled out a convincing 14 814 votes on an MDC ticket, defeating his more experienced political challenger, businessman Christopher Chikavanga Chigumba of Zanu PF, who only managed to get 5 330. Others in the same race were Evelyn Chimwaya of Zanu (Ndonga) who got 172 votes, and Gideon Chinoyerei, with a paltry 90 supporters.

Now he was jumping ship. True, young Tafadzwa, like most of the MDC legislators and candidates, had suffered at the hands of Zanu PF who heard the news of his departure with glee, seeing this as an opportunity to pick up a little of the propaganda mileage it had lost through Mugabe's feeble legal defence to my courtroom challenge, and to re-assert its political supremacy on the periphery of Harare.

A by-election would now have to be held in the Zengeza constituency. At the time this included the town of Chitungwiza, 27 kilometres from Harare, and given our strong support in Chitungwiza I was sure we would win, regardless of the stature of the candidate we fielded. After all, when Musekiwa waded his way to the legislature as a fresh school-leaver, he had hardly any political credentials. But I underestimated Zanu PF's desire to recover its lost political footprint in our towns and cities.

Our candidate selection procedures were unduly delayed, leaving the preliminary steps unattended to until it was too late. Choosing candidates for public office in political parties can be a highly divisive process. It needs to be done over time so that the various factions created by competitors can have time to close ranks, unite and mobilise the people for the election.

A week before the nomination court, I was informed that the selection process had not been done. Aspiring candidates – Charlton Hwende, Goodrich Chimbaira and James Makore – were busy fighting each other for political turf. Neither Isaac Matongo, the national chairman, nor Esaph Mdlongwa, the organising secretary, was in Harare to resolve the issue. Eventually, I found myself entangled in the dispute although under normal circumstances as party leader I am not involved in candidate selection for individual constituencies.

I invited the aspirants to my office. After intense discussions during which I implored them to settle on a single candidate, we all agreed that Makore would be the official party candidate. I then called the representatives of the party structures from the Zengeza district and announced that as the official position. Immediately after that there were lots of negative media leaks, accusing me of imposing Makore.

Unknown to me, there were some within the party who genuinely felt that I had imposed Makore as a candidate. I could understand why. Makore was close to Matongo; I had worked with the two of them for many years in the ZCTU and during the formative stages of the party. The smears were directed at me. While I tried to explain that I intervened only because senior officials with the task of selecting candidates were unavailable, it seemed to have no persuasive effect. Makore received lukewarm support in his campaign. It appeared as if most senior leaders became complacent and took a back seat on the assumption that Zengeza was a safe seat for the MDC. That attitude, together with Zanu PF's spirited onslaught to win Zengeza at any cost, eventually hit the MDC hard. Confidence in the MDC's chances in Harare's tiny foreign diplomatic community plummeted.

Doubts started to enter the minds of many, especially within the dwindling but still influential middle class, about our ability to withstand Mugabe's non-stop pressure on the people. Even newspapers began to raise questions over our ability to sustain the momentum.

As the campaign started in earnest in January 2004, Zanu PF turned Zengeza into yet another war zone. Militias and war veterans besieged the area, making a free campaign virtually impossible. Elliot Manyika, the new Zanu PF political commissar, and Information Minister Jonathan Moyo fought hard to break down the MDC, using all forms of propaganda, coercion and intimidation. I tried to help Makore on two occasions, but the police banned my meetings and allowed Zanu PF to set up militia bases in the town.

The MDC's campaign teams were overwhelmed by Zanu PF's massive presence, created by the regular bussing of the party's supporters from faraway rural areas to cow the urban residents. While we were in the middle of this election fracas, I was surprised to hear Thabo Mbeki announce on the South African broadcasting service, the SABC, that Zanu PF and the

MDC had agreed to a draft agenda for formal talks to end the national crisis.[3] Although Mbeki and Nigerian President Olusegun Obasanjo had spent a lot of time trying to persuade Mugabe to talk to us, I was not aware of any such breakthrough. When I asked Ncube about the statement, he denied any knowledge of what Mbeki was talking about.

As I was preoccupied with the final stages of my treason trial and the campaign in Zengeza, I did not find time to establish what had led to Mbeki's optimism. He had sounded categorical and clear, insisting that we had agreed to peace talks with Mugabe after many months of informal talks. He said that the draft agenda had been agreed to in December 2003 but talks had been delayed by the Christmas break. Beyond that statement, nothing further transpired for the time being.

The hearings in my Ben-Menashe treason trial ended in February 2004. Justice Garwe wanted time to study the voluminous amounts of evidence before reaching a verdict, so I was not totally off the hook yet. Another treason trial with separate bail conditions awaited me, following the 'Final Push' arrest.

On the ground in Zengeza, Zanu PF seemed unsure of the final outcome of the by-election as the people quietly returned to their homes. The uncertainty forced the military into the area, leading to a surfeit of guns in the usually quiet neighbourhood. As if to reinforce the Zanu PF message that the party meant business, on the last day of the voting, 28 March, a Zanu PF activist pulled out a gun and shot dead Francis Chinozvina, a young MDC activist. Chinozvina's death confined the majority of our supporters indoors, scared of venturing to the polling stations. It sent shivers down the spines of Makore's election agents, forcing many to abandon their work.

Independent observers noted an unusually large number of voters, mostly young people – claiming to be visually impaired, sick or unable to read or write – requesting to have their ballots cast on their behalf by polling officers drawn from the military and the secret service. Usually only illiterate elders required such help. To intimidate voters the polling officers at each polling station noted down the names and national identity numbers of all those who cast their ballots. This was abnormal and an obvious bullying tactic. Voting guidelines and instructions on wall posters outside the polling stations showed examples indicating that voters should mark their preferences on the blank space of the ballot paper officially reserved for a Zanu PF candidate.

Predictably, Zanu PF propelled itself to victory – not without a fight, even under those difficult circumstances – for Christopher Chigumba of Zanu PF managed to squeeze out 8 447 votes while the official result showed that electoral officials had decided to give Makore 6 706 votes.

A week later David Mpala, our MP for Lupane, died after failing to recover from internal injuries inflicted by Zanu PF thugs two years previously. Now, with the victory in Zengeza behind them, a triumphant Zanu PF immediately moved into Lupane for another round of elections. Lupane is a rural constituency in Matabeleland North, a safe MDC stronghold, and Zanu PF felt it imperative that it re-establish itself in the area which it had lost dismally in the 2000 election. A pattern similar to what had happened in Zengeza now repeated itself.

Lupane was facing serious food shortages and Zanu PF used traditional leaders and state institutions to apply both food and violence campaign tools.

I visited Lupane during the final stages of the campaign, to find only a handful of activists brave enough to await my presence at a local business centre. It took me an unusually long time to reach Lupane from Bulawayo as there were many police checkpoints along the way. At each of the points, police searched my vehicle and asked unnecessary questions about my itinerary. It hardly surprised me when we lost Lupane to Zanu PF.

To call both the Zengeza and Lupane circuses real elections is a mockery of what democratic voting is supposed to be all about. The MDC's loss of these two constituencies, however, seemed to point to a downward trend in the party's fortunes.

The incessant pressure raised the level of political polarisation to a point where nothing lay outside the political arena – all conversations turned to politics. One incident that comes to mind was the case of Roy Bennett. Bennett, the MDC legislator for Chimanimani, had been in trouble with Zanu PF since he defected from that party in 2000.[4] On 18 May 2004 during a parliamentary debate on a proposal to increase penalties for stock theft, Bennett found himself in trouble again. The debate became heated after several MDC legislators suggested that Zanu PF's interest in raising the penalty for stock theft was motivated by the fact many of its senior officials were now stock owners, courtesy of the land reform programme. In response, Chinamasa began a tirade, accusing Bennett's ancestors of murder, rape and looting of African resources. Bennett felt personally provoked and interjected. When Chinamasa persisted, Bennett stood up and charged at him. He and Chinamasa went tumbling to the floor. In the ensuing melee, which was broadcast on the state television's main news bulletin, Didymus Mutasa kicked Bennett in the back.

Bennett was charged with contempt of parliament. On 20 May, parliament set up a committee comprising three Zanu PF and two MDC legislators. When the matter was heard, Bennett said in his defence that he found the statement intolerable, coming as it did from the minister of justice whose department had a history of ignoring Bennett's successful court orders against Zanu PF and the police. He did apologise, however, for overreacting during the debate. I thought the matter would end there. But it did not. Zanu PF was determined to get at Bennett at all costs.

I kept on pushing for the two High Court judgments relating to my cases: one on the main treason trial and the other on my challenge to Mugabe's claims of electoral victory in 2002. Meanwhile I was still attending routine remand hearings on the 'Final Push' treason charge. It was an agonising grind, traipsing from court to court in a perpetual, frustrating attempt to get justice.

I was irked by the behaviour of Justice Hlatshwayo who, despite promising that he would make a quick ruling following Gauntlett's specifically recorded request, had not done so. To me this was morally unacceptable and I instructed my lawyers to approach the Supreme Court urgently to compel him to do so. The court complied and a day before the hearing Justice Hlatshwayo issued a terse, one-page ruling summarily dismissing my petition. Again, without giving any reasons! This was seven months after the hearing began.

In the Supreme Court, Gauntlett protested about what he said was a show of contempt for the rules of the court that specified that election petitions be dealt with as a matter of urgency. But the protest turned out to be academic as the court could not help. By handing down such an incomplete judgment, Justice Hlatshwayo made it impossible for me to appeal his ruling. I did not know why he had turned it down, so my lawyers found themselves unable to argue against his judgment. Much later – in November 2005 – Justice Hlatshwayo gave his reasons for dismissing our petition for an electoral review,[5] but by then the issue was merely academic and it was too late, anyway, to lodge a fresh appeal against his verdict.

ENDNOTES

1   Nyarota G (2006). *Against the Grain: Memoirs of a Zimbabwean Newsman.* Johannesburg: Struik Publishers (Zebra Press)
2   Tsvangirai v. Mugabe, HC 3616/2002 Petitioner's Heads of Argument, 13 October 2003
3   Reuters, Sunday, 8 February 2004 http://www.reuters.co.uk/
4   Matyszak, Derek (2005). *Roy Bennett: A Record of Political Persecution: 2000-2005.* The report is held at MDC's library, Harare
5   Hlatswayo, J. Morgan Tsvangirai Petitioner and Robert Gabriel Mugabe. High Court of Zimbabwe. Harare, 28 November 2005. HH 109-2005. HC 3616/2002 http://www.law.co.zw/downloads/judgements/

CHAPTER TWENTY

POSITIONING

The MDC was formed not just to counter Mugabe but to offer an alternative future to the citizens of Zimbabwe. The problem we faced was how to position ourselves, giving meaning to the brand so that our policies and programmes would gain assent at home and abroad. To do this we had to deal with a wide range of players in business, the churches, foreign governments and international associations.

It would take time, much trial and error, and careful analysis to pitch our message in the right way to the right people on the right occasions. We brainstormed the way ahead and developed a number of important policy documents. All the while, we had to watch our step. The MDC or individuals in it could easily be drawn into plots to catch us out or make us willing accomplices in the hidden agendas of others. It worried me that elements within the MDC could become distracted by this and lose sight of our overriding mission.

After several years of negative growth, business was becoming increasingly restless as it appeared that the election campaign, instead of ending with the June 2000 parliamentary election, was set to hot up as Zimbabwe geared itself for the 2002 presidential poll. An election campaign like the violent power struggle of 2000 had a serious effect on business confidence in Zimbabwe. Both local and international business people were unsure which way the country would drift, given the widespread violence and instability that punctuated the political campaign. They had good reason to be concerned about their future and to believe that it was time to do something to save the little that remained. Apart from commercial agriculture, commerce and industry dreaded the effect of the collapse of agriculture in an economy that is heavily agro-based. I became aware that some commercial farmers and industrialists had started to make concessions to Mugabe in the hope that he could stop the onslaught on the farms.

Even tourism, a major contributor to the economy, dried up. One industrialist, Clive Puzey, chairman of the Petrol Retailers' Association, claiming to have a mandate from big businesses, approached my office to establish whether I was amenable to dialogue with Mugabe. At a subsequent meeting with Puzey, I showed my interest in his initiative, especially as he claimed acquaintance with Zanu PF-linked businessmen, Nhlanhla Masuku, Goodson Nguni, Colonel Dyke, Saviour Kasukuwere, Ephraim Masawi and others.

Puzey further claimed to know senior US state department officials, among them Walter Karnsteiner and John Dunlop. I doubted him, but listened to his story. A few days later, Puzey advised me that he had approached Zanu PF with the same proposal and had received a positive response.

I interpreted Zanu PF and Mugabe's purported agreement to talks as a ploy to pulverise the MDC. They had seen the desperation of the white community and sought to use it as a weak entry point through which they could get at the MDC and force us to align ourselves with their agenda, particularly on the land issue. In that way, Mugabe could divert national attention from the MDC's core message of bad governance and the need for political change.

I assessed the Puzey initiative and the threats it posed to the MDC. I saw the ruse Zanu PF was keen to put on the table; I saw Zanu PF's insincerity, as in my view Mugabe was not then ready for constructive dialogue. I hesitantly allowed a low-level pathfinder mission to proceed. I assigned my assistant Gandi Mudzingwa to follow up Puzey's initiative.

Puzey, now with Goodson Nguni in tow, took Mudzingwa to a meeting with Mugabe's confidant and friend, the Catholic priest Father Fidelis Mukonori, at his base at Silveira House outside Harare. Their aim was to ask Mukonori, a Jesuit, to facilitate dialogue between Mugabe and me – a request he quickly embraced. I recalled that in late 2000, the CFU was particularly upbeat when Mukonori agreed to mediate in the talks between Chenjerai Hunzvi and CFU chairman Tim Henwood on ways to stop the farm invasions. But Mukonori did not help much and the impasse remained.

At their first meeting, Mudzingwa told me, it emerged that Nguni and Mukonori were childhood friends. It was interesting that Nguni also told Mudzingwa that he was related by marriage to Emmerson Mnangagwa, another Mugabe confidant. I wondered why Nguni would volunteer such information to Mudzingwa; it made me suspect that Mnangagwa could be the main driving force behind the scenes. In their discussion, Nguni used the Zanu PF language of land and revolution extensively. To Mudzingwa's surprise, Puzey was also speaking the same language, much to the glee of Mukonori who, it appears, sincerely believed that the MDC was a white man's puppet.

In several follow-up meetings, and at Mudzingwa's request, Puzey and Nguni dropped out, leaving Mudzingwa and Mukonori to search for a common position on which meaningful discussions could be anchored. As the preliminary talks did not appear to be getting anywhere, I advised Mudzingwa to ask Mukonori to bring in others from Zanu PF, preferably politicians.

In my view, Mukonori, Nguni and Puzey held no positions in Zanu PF and could not speak authoritatively on Zanu PF's concerns. Mukonori brought in Frederick Shava, then a director at Zanu PF headquarters, in the company of senior Zanu PF official Itai Marchi and a CIO operative I got to know only as Mugadza. At that point, I asked Gift Chimanikire, the MDC deputy secretary general, to step in. Chimanikire was close to me. He doubled up his role as my intelligence chief.

After a series of discussions, they finally agreed that Mugabe and I needed to meet. But for that to happen, Mukonori insisted that I write to Mugabe, in my own handwriting, expressing a desire to resolve our differences in the national interest.

I wrote the letter, acknowledging Mugabe's role as the founding father of modern-day Zimbabwe and the historical role he had played in the liberation struggle, and urging him to consider a negotiated solution to the rising political stalemate. Mukonori assured me that he would personally deliver the letter to Mugabe. That was in March 2001.

Mukonori reported that he had delivered the letter and I waited, and waited, and waited, for a response. Nothing came of it. Mugabe simply ignored the overture. Mukonori, however, remained in contact with me, through Chimanikire, for almost two years.

The church, like business, was equally concerned about the political stalemate. While a number of denominations – some in the leadership of the Anglican Church, a few Apostolic Church sects and Pentecostals – sided with Mugabe and Zanu PF, the majority voiced their disgust about the rising violence against innocent people. Others professed neutrality. Reverend Andrew Wutawunashe, with the backing of businessmen sympathetic to Zanu PF, Mutumwa Mawere and Philip Chiyangwa came up with his own peace initiative.

In my discussions with them, I maintained that unless Mugabe agreed to meet me so that we could share our different visions for Zimbabwe nothing substantial would come out of the whole exercise. The Wutawunashe idea failed to take root because Mugabe refused to a meeting.

While Mugabe continued to hammer the MDC, there remained on-and-off, low-level contacts with Zanu PF. Occasionally Ncube would report to me that he had met with Chinamasa to explore ways of breaking the political gridlock. I saw these forays merely as pathfinder efforts, and encouraged Ncube to pursue that route. My desire was for an agreement on the form of dialogue, followed by proper, interparty negotiations.

Mugabe now pursued a two-pronged approach against the MDC: hitting us hard at home while trying to talk the world into accepting Zimbabwe as it was, despite the confusion and repression. To reach out to the international public, Mugabe enlisted the services of a lobby then owned by a London-based Ugandan exile, David Nyekorach Matsanga, to spruce up Zimbabwe's image.

Matsanga claimed to have a research company called *Africa Strategy* with strong links in all the Commonwealth countries. What he achieved in Zimbabwe, if anything, was inconsequential as Mugabe increasingly found the Zimbabwe story a difficult one to sell. On one of his frequent visits to Harare, Matsanga claimed that he was Mugabe's public relations adviser.

Matsanga, who was from eastern Uganda, had a chequered and controversial political profile. He had escaped from Kampala, citing political persecution from President Yoweri Museveni's government, and was the chief negotiator for rebel leader Joseph Kony during the on-off peace talks to end the war in Northern Uganda.

Mugabe also turned to North America, hiring political consultants Cohen & Woods to help in telling his story and to lobby the Bush administration. Again, it does not appear as if Cohen & Woods made any breakthroughs that brought anything of value.

In the meantime, Mugabe assumed an even harder line against the MDC and white commercial farmers as he campaigned for the 2002 presidential election. Soldiers and war veterans drove thousands of Zimbabweans to his campaign meetings, crowds Mugabe mistook for a growing, voluntary support base for his cause.

The world, which originally thought Mugabe's behaviour was a temporary measure to stem a passing national revolt, started to shift its opinion. Zimbabwe was already an international flashpoint of conflict; inevitably, it invited more world media interest as it slowly descended into pariah status – especially over its casual attitude towards human rights and the rule of law. Whenever such a situation develops anywhere in today's world, the international community is likely to raise questions and investigate. In the West, in Britain and in Nordic countries, Zimbabwe and Mugabe were now frequent points of discussion.

Under the new world order in which decisions on governance, trade and other fundamentals have shifted from single nations to regional groups, Harare started to feel the signs of being part of a Western diplomatic agenda. While at home Mugabe gave the impression that he loathed the West and could bank on diplomatic support from Africa and other parts of the developing world, the reality was different. Zimbabwe's economy and culture are inextricably linked to the West more than anywhere else.

The flawed elections of March 2002 prompted the Commonwealth to suspend Zimbabwe's membership for a year. This decision was taken in April 2002 after leaders in Australia, Nigeria and South Africa agreed with Commonwealth observers that the election campaign had been marred by violence and intimidation. The Harare Commonwealth Declaration of 1991,[1] signed by member states including Zimbabwe, demanded a commitment to fundamental Commonwealth principles including freedom to participate in democratic processes, human dignity, and equal rights for all regardless of race or creed.

Now Zimbabwe was being held to account. Britain had felt obliged to take action because Mugabe constantly blamed Whitehall for Zimbabwe's predicament, owing to the unfinished colonial dispute over land reform. Unable to go it alone, Britain had turned to the 54-nation Commonwealth because of the club's obvious historical links. Working together with the so-called troika of Australia, Nigeria and South Africa, the Blair administration had sought a diplomatic outlet to resolve the crisis.

So it was that the Commonwealth became a leading crusader for peace in Zimbabwe, although in fact little would be achieved. On 7 September 2002, Commonwealth ministers met in Abuja, Nigeria, and debated the Zimbabwean situation. While acknowledging that land reform was at the core of the crisis, the manner in which it was handled should embrace the rule of law, respect for human rights, democracy and the economy. They insisted on fairness because the problem was equally a political one.

In a similar assurance to the one given to Mbeki in August 2000, Mugabe's government assured the Commonwealth that no further farm invasions would be permitted. In Abuja, Mugabe pledged to surrender some of the occupied farms and promised to follow the dictates of the law in future land allocations. Other promises included respect for the rule of law, freedom of expression, and an immediate end to violence and intimidation. The meeting, however, failed to craft a protective framework for farm workers – 70 000 were already destitute after being evicted from their homes. Angola, Botswana, Malawi, Mozambique, Namibia, South Africa and Tanzania immediately endorsed the decision taken in Abuja, but inside Zimbabwe nothing changed.

By late September 2002, Mugabe and Zanu PF were claiming that Abuja had endorsed their programme in its original form and that international donors must now start to move in to support it. No donor responded to the call. Commonwealth ministers had agreed that compliance with the Abuja resolution would be monitored for a full endorsement by heads of state and governments. Rather than endorsing Mugabe, the Commonwealth extended the suspension for a year. Mugabe stuck to his guns, claiming that he had done everything to meet the demands.

A Commonwealth delegation came to Harare to check progress on the ground. Mugabe conveniently announced that he had released 20 farms back to their owners since the Abuja meeting. The truth was that the ruckus was continuing unabated. Mugabe blamed the MDC and white commercial farmers for what he called misleading reports that invasions were still the order of the day. Farmers were said to be stage-managing new invasions to tarnish Zimbabwe's image. Britain was not spared either: Information Minister Moyo accused London of fanning instability on the farms.

Contrary to perceptions in some quarters, the MDC played very little part in Zimbabwe's suspension from the Commonwealth or in providing information. Mugabe and Zanu PF threatened to pull Zimbabwe out of the Commonwealth completely, and finally the decision to do so was announced in December 2003 – without any consultation with parliament.

As a party, I think we should have challenged the Commonwealth to act much earlier. The Commonwealth's 1991 Harare Declaration is very specific about the need for member states to be held accountable for human rights abuses. On the basis of the Harare Declaration, the Commonwealth was forthright in its dealings with Fiji, Pakistan and, to some extent, Nigeria, in a bid to restore civil order and democracy. But when it came to Harare and Mugabe, the Commonwealth had great difficulty enforcing its own declaration. We did our best to spread the word about Mugabe's excesses to the West and to countries in Africa, Asia and the Caribbean, but with limited success.

Across the Atlantic, the US – through Senator Bill Frist – had, by December 2001, started work on legislation called the Zimbabwe Democracy and Economic Recovery Act (ZDERA).

Basically, the proposed law sought to direct all US citizens on boards of multilateral lending institutions to oppose future lines of credit or support to Zimbabwe until Mugabe changed his style of governance, respected the rule of law and democratic elections, and introduced a legal and transparent land reform programme.

For the record, a lot has been said about this American initiative, with wild accusations that the bill was drafted at our party headquarters at Harvest House in Harare. Nothing of the sort happened. The MDC as a party was tiny and fragile at the time, and it lacked the necessary influence to craft and steer legislation through the giant US Congress.

Following the US proposal to exert pressure on Mugabe, in 2001 the European Union (EU) came up with a raft of travel restrictions aimed at 19 Zanu PF officials it deemed to be the masterminds of repression and tyranny. The list was later extended to 35 and then reviewed yearly so that by 2009 it included 160 Zanu PF officials. An arms embargo and asset freeze formed part of the sanctions package. The measures cited the ejection of the EU presidential election observer team from Zimbabwe in February 2002, the absence of the rule of law and the increasing political violence as the main reasons.

In the US, ZDERA became law. By the time President George W Bush signed an executive order barring Mugabe from Washington and freezing assets held in the US by 75 Zimbabwean officials, Zimbabwe was already in a parlous state and unable to access loans from the IMF and the World Bank's International Development Association for reasons which had nothing to do with ZDERA. Harare was facing serious arrears to those institutions for debt payments – a situation which landed Zimbabwe in a high risk position, ZDERA or no ZDERA.

It is worth noting, again, that despite the new US restrictive package of measures, normal trade between Washington and Harare remained unaffected. The British Parliament had already taken action and banned Mugabe's inner circle from setting foot in London, starting with a few individuals but later expanding the list to about a hundred. Australia and New Zealand soon followed what was becoming a trend in the West.

Notwithstanding these measures, these countries remain Zimbabwe's biggest donors of food and other forms of humanitarian aid to this day. The measures should not have affected their humanitarian efforts but Zanu PF made sure that much of the aid was routed towards its supporters.

As the economic situation worsened, with rampant shortages across the board, I engaged in a series of walkabouts and road shows to show my solidarity with suffering Zimbabweans and to enhance my visibility on the ground. I was well received as people came out of their homes and businesses to meet me, offering words of encouragement and urging me to remain resolute. I travelled throughout Zimbabwe on the few free days I had because of the travel restrictions imposed as part of my bail conditions during the long treason trials, consolidating the party and consulting people about the future. It emerged from these meetings that people were pressing for mass action.

Before we could complete our preparations for mass action, the National Constitutional Assembly, through its chairman Dr Lovemore Madhuku, informed me that it had organised some protests and wanted the MDC to back them. I responded positively but the proposed action, set for the first fortnight of January 2003, was a flop. The whole thing was poorly organised.

Clearly, we would have to do better. Organisational structures for mass action were needed but before we could get any sort of programme rolling a faction in Zanu PF – led by Emmerson Mnangagwa – set out on a fishing expedition to establish a way of getting the MDC, and me in particular, either into some kind of political accommodation or silenced completely. Through an emissary, retired Colonel Lionel Dyke asked to see me. Dyke, a former military officer, was a close business associate of Mnangagwa. His company, Mine-Tech, had received lucrative mine-clearing contracts from the Zimbabwe government, allegedly through Mnangagwa. We knew that Dyke had close links to senior military commanders and top Zanu PF officials.

As I listened to Dyke, I saw an intricate political web involving some local businessmen, top military officers, some leading MDC officials and a few Western embassies in Harare, particularly the British. I asked him about Mugabe's position, but he said everything depended on my response. Mugabe could easily be persuaded, he said, to take an early retirement package with sufficient security guarantees as Mnangagwa, General Vitalis Zvinavashe, South Africa, the United Kingdom and many senior officials in Zanu PF were fully behind the plan.

And me? What role were the MDC and I expected to play? On that, Dyke was unclear. He stammered and stumbled along. It did not take much to detect that this little scheme was designed to swallow and destroy the MDC. Given the involvement of some of my senior officials in the MDC, I was not sure how to handle this delicate issue.

After deep reflection, I came to the conclusion that the group was motivated by the need to preserve their business interests. As to Britain's concerns, it seemed that Mnangagwa had given them the assurance of a smooth transition that would enable London to maintain its long interest and influence in Harare. In my view, London had figured that Mnangagwa enjoyed the support of the military and was largely seen as Mugabe's heir apparent. In essence, their main fear, together with that of Thabo Mbeki and the local business community, centred on the question of national stability – and not democracy.

The group considered itself a well-positioned faction representing a reformed Zanu PF, said Dyke. The faction preferred to identify and work with what it saw as a like-minded 'committee of the reasonable' from inside the MDC. It emerged from what Dyke said that I was not to be part of the so-called committee, nor was Mugabe. Mugabe and Tsvangirai, in their view, were the main stumbling blocks to a smooth transition and the preservation of vested business and political interests among the politically ambitious in Zanu PF, along with some wily and power-hungry MDC politicians, Mbeki and certain Western embassies in Harare. What would Africa's position be in that plan? I asked. Well, Dyke told me, Mbeki could easily go along with it and promote it, given South Africa's economic influence on the continent.

On 18 December 2002, I called the MDC's parliamentary caucus to Harvest House and issued a statement denouncing the plan along with its alleged originators – Dyke, Mnangagwa, Mbeki and the British. To most of the legislators, the statement came as a surprise. But I sensed that a few had known in advance about the plan. I deliberately steered away from mentioning any involvement of MDC politicians, but chose my words carefully to indicate that I was aware of their connection to the group.

After my statement, Welshman Ncube, the secretary general, and Paul Themba Nyathi, the information secretary, stormed into my office in a fit of rage, demanding to know why I had gone public on the issue and insisting on more details from me. I stood my ground, maintaining that as party president, I had a mandate to issue any statement on any matter and at any time. I told them that I knew what I was talking about, as I had all the information about the plan.

Mnangagwa, Mbeki and the British embassy in Harare never responded to my statement, although it was widely published by the local media, including the state-controlled *Herald* newspaper. Dyke quickly vanished from the scene and made no fresh overtures. But the story did not end there. The saga was the beginning of a long drawn out process calculated to destabilise both the MDC and Zanu PF in order to make room for a new secret force.

I felt vindicated three years later when details of the plan resurfaced. To keep the party together at its nascent stage, I believed I had the right to fire early warning shots each time the MDC faced real danger.

In January 2004, the MDC published two documents, *Restart* – our economic policy which we tailored to suit our social democratic ideology and values; and *Restore* – a guide reflecting our views on the restoration of legitimacy and good governance through democratic elections.[2] When we tried to launch *Restart* officially at a public meeting in a local hotel, the police attempted to block us, forcing us to seek a High Court order. By the time the order was granted, it was late in the day but the news filtered into the Harare community and the occasion was a huge success.

In short, *Restart* captured the founding spirit of the MDC's original policies, developed from the National Working People's Convention in 1999 and the party's internal participatory and consultation processes. This five-year plan replaced an earlier one, *Bridge*, a key element of the 2002 presidential election campaign. *Restart* thus became a restatement and a recommitment to our ideals. The main objectives of *Restart* were to reconstruct Zimbabwe's social fabric and economic infrastructure; to stabilise the macroeconomy; to recover levels of savings, investment and growth and to transform the economy in a radical way.

One important feature that set the MDC apart from other political parties in Zimbabwe, past and present, was our engagement of our grass-roots structures on policy formulation and scenario planning. Nationalist parties that fought for liberation were so focused on the war that they came to power with socialist slogans to drive the process of national development forward. But these contained nothing by way of insights from the majority poor.

The nationalist parties vowed to meet the needs of the poor and ensure equity but the ruling elite soon turned to enriching itself instead.[3] Further back, the regime of Ian Smith had a kind of zero-sum approach to winning its war against the 'terrs': either the whites would retain power or ... there was no real plan for what might follow a settlement involving black majority rule.

We sought to overcome the hiatus of ideas, the negation and cruel abandonment of the views of the poor. The MDC had been founded in 1999 at a convention which weighed up the *Raw Data* and *ZCTU/ORAP Consultative Report* that came out of our survey of the national mood.

Listening to people's concerns had laid the groundwork for remedies and solutions to the country's problems and had formed a central part of our push for change. We came from a tradition of broad-based consultation and analysis.

By contrast, Mugabe had risen to power in the secretive, conspiratorial world of guerrilla insurgency, boardroom coups (although in his case, he unseated Ndabaningi Sithole in his prison cell) and Cold War politics where spying, murder and intimidation were often the norm. These habits remained.

The MDC's loss of the Lupane and Zengeza constituencies in by-elections seemed to point to a downward trend in the party's fortunes. The democratic struggle was taking longer and was more fatiguing than many an activist had originally anticipated.

Some among our allies in civil society were clearly exasperated by the slow pace of the struggle; others appeared paralysed by constant state harassment. They turned on the MDC and laid various shades of blame on me, variously accusing me of being weak on policy and strategy; of lacking what they called a 'killer-punch'; of being naive; and of surrounding my office with clueless advisers. I understood their collective fears and anxieties. Many had fallen into the trap of putting time frames to a non-violent democratic struggle. I knew that civil society, in its various components and shades, normally pursues single interest issues to create specific space for their narrow group mandates. That tends to limit their boundaries of analysis.

Some civil society groups felt the MDC was too diverse and fractured. That trait slowed down the party's response to their needs; others feared that the MDC might end up swallowing them if they tried to form a united front with us. They stayed at a safe distance, partly because of apprehension and a desire to be seen as autonomous and impartial. Still others were plainly selfish. Legally, Zimbabwe forbids external political party funding. They feared that their source of support could easily dry up if Zanu PF aligned them directly with the MDC as this could affect their purses, often fattened through external donors.

Zanu PF and Mugabe could see this and naturally they exploited it. They used the state media to heighten the perceptions of conflict and to raise tensions in the broader democratic movement. Insecurity, fear and uncertainty were rising in a manner that threatened to fragment our relations with these erstwhile traditional allies.

To worsen an already complicated situation for the MDC, a survey conducted by *Afrobarometer*,[4] an independent collaborative enterprise of the Institute for Democracy in South Africa (Idasa), the Centre for Democratic Development (CDD-Ghana) and Michigan State University, put a further damper on our effort to keep the flicker of hope burning. The survey established that Zimbabweans were losing faith in democracy and increasing numbers acquiesced to the idea of a single-party rule. At least 83 per cent felt uncomfortable discussing politics openly. Apathy was settling in and half the population preferred to stay out of active politics, saying that party competition led to social conflict. The results of the survey, published in August 2004, rated Mugabe's popularity as having risen from 20 per cent in 1999 to 52 per cent.

However, *Afrobarometer* noted that its researchers had been unable to assess public opinion in Zimbabwe fairly. Their findings showed a clear contradiction, an absurdity.

Poverty levels were much higher than in 1999; inflation was the highest on earth; there was no food, no fuel, no foreign currency, and no jobs; hunger was everywhere and the economy had collapsed – but support for Mugabe had actually increased? The report explained the paradox by attributing the shift to propaganda and fear.

I refused to accept *Afrobarometer's* general findings as a correct record of the feelings on the ground. The researchers' final observation was that Zimbabweans were tired of the seemingly unending stand-off between Zanu PF and the MDC.

The long and short of it was that respondents to the survey favoured dialogue between Zanu PF and the MDC. Mugabe himself arrogantly dismissed calls for dialogue in a Heroes' Day speech in 2003 when he said those who wanted unity must first repent, and act, walk and dream 'like us'.[5] For my part, I had said that the MDC wanted to raise the tempo on the government to come to the negotiating table.[6] The problem did not lie with us.

ENDNOTES

1   Harare Commonwealth Declaration. Harare, Zimbabwe, 20 October 1991. Commonwealth Secretariat http://www.thecommonwealth.org/

2   *Restart: Our path to social justice* – the MDC's economic programme for reconstruction, stabilisation, recovery and transformation, Harare, 2004; and *Restore! Minimum Standards for the Restoration of Genuine, Democratic Elections in Zimbabwe*, Harare, 2004

3   Dashwood, Hevina S (1996). 'The Relevance of Class to the Evolution of Zimbabwe's Development Strategy, 1980-1991'. *Journal of Southern African Studies*, 22(1), p27

4   Chikwanha, A, Sithole, T and Bratton, M (2004). *The Power of Propaganda: Public Opinion in Zimbabwe*. Afrobarometer, Working Paper No. 42

5   Quoted in 'An overview of youth militia training and activities in Zimbabwe, October 2000-August 2003'. Solidarity Peace Trust, 5 September 2003 http://www.swradioafrica.com/Documents/Youth_militia.doc

6   'MDC still willing to talk to Mugabe'. SABC Radio, 29 June 2003

CHAPTER TWENTY-ONE
TRICKY TACTICS

My acquittal on the main treason charge in October 2004 was a great relief to me and the MDC. For the first time since March 2002, I was entitled to my passport and could travel as a free person. But for Mugabe and Zanu PF, Justice Garwe's judgment caused anxiety, anguish and embarrassment. They had rested all their hopes on a conviction which would have silenced me and allowed free rein for calumny against the MDC at home and abroad. To save face, their initial reaction was that they wished to appeal against the judgment. The plan fell apart, for unexplained reasons.

In August 2005 the government finally dropped the 'Final Push' treason charge against me. They had never had a case and knew it, but had kept up the pretence to ensure that my time was wasted in court and my spirits taxed by anxiety and stress. I had endured two and a half years of daily vilification and state demonisation during the Ben-Menashe case, only to be freed on this and the other charge. The treason cases were a worthless attempt to divert attention from the issues confronting our nation. The ruling party had underestimated the resilience and resources of the MDC, and our commitment to due process in law. We remained firmly fixed on the principle and benefits of a multiparty political environment after 25 years of an unhealthy dictatorship that had presided over the collapse of our political, economic and social fabric.

The hype that had followed the Australian ABS television programme and the subsequent distortion of the Ben-Menashe video clip on local radio and television and in state newspapers had initially given Mugabe a huge propaganda advantage in the run-up to the 2002 presidential election and beyond. Now the tables were turned. When the treason charges failed to stick, alternatives were explored. At first, they tried to sell the idea that my trial had vindicated Zimbabwe's judiciary and reaffirmed its independence. But that failed to overturn the reality that the state was pursuing a scorched-earth policy against the opposition and Morgan Tsvangirai in particular.

A mood of euphoria surrounded me after my acquittal, but it did not take long for the ruling party to hit back. Two weeks later, to my surprise, Mugabe and Zanu PF demanded the conclusion of the work of a special parliamentary committee that had investigated the case of Roy Bennett during the previous session of the legislature. This was an abuse of parliament. Constitutionally, any outstanding business should have been expunged at the end of a parliamentary session.

Section 63 (8) of the constitution stated: 'On the dissolution of Parliament all proceedings pending at the time shall be terminated and accordingly every Bill, motion, petition, or other business will lapse.' The effect of this was that Bennett was in the clear – or so we thought.

Parliament had been prorogued on 19 July bringing the Fourth Session to an end. The Fifth Session started on 20 July, with a set agenda for business which did not include the resuscitation of unfinished motions and items from the Fourth Session.

Nevertheless, with Emmerson Mnangagwa in the chair as Speaker, on 27 October 2004 the parliamentary Privileges Committee proceeded to present its findings and recommendations. The committee refused to consider the years of harassment endured by Bennett as a factor in mitigation, saying what happened to him was not a justification for his action in parliament in May when he had tried unsuccessfully to punch anti-corruption minister Didymus Mutasa. The two MDC legislators on the committee disagreed and even suggested that a custodial sentence was unwarranted. To my horror, the majority from Zanu PF recommended that Bennett be sentenced to 15 months in jail, with hard labour. Three months of the sentence were to be suspended.

This sort of action was unheard of and unprecedented in Zimbabwe's history. Parliament sat as complainant, prosecutor and judge. This was a simple case of assault, which normally attracted a small fine – not imprisonment – and in any case Bennett was a first offender and had apologised, showing contrition for his actions. Now he was unable to appeal. There was nowhere to lodge the appeal, since parliament works independently of the judiciary and the executive.

When the matter came before a full parliamentary session, Zanu PF used its majority and Bennett was sent to jail. He was taken to Mutoko, a rural prison, 143 kilometres north east of Harare. I was devastated. The punishment was too harsh. I visited him while he was in prison. Here was a man who had lost nearly everything to Zanu PF: his thriving farm, Charleswood; large amounts of money through litigation; personal assets; and now his freedom. But I found him in high spirits. Bennett never wavered in his beliefs and commitment to our struggle.

The people of Chimanimani, Bennett's constituency, decided to honour him by asking his wife Heather to contest as a candidate in the 2005 elections while Roy was still in prison. The party respected that decision. Heather Bennett mounted a spirited campaign for parliament but as usual Zanu PF rigged the election and somehow contrived to hand over a huge chunk of her votes to its candidate, Samuel Undenge. Heather Bennett was officially credited with 11 031 votes and Undenge with 15 817 – a Zanu PF gain from a ruling in parliament that had unfairly locked up our MP.

Now that I was free, I scanned the broad political environment and found that a lot had happened without my knowledge, particularly after the High Court released Ncube from his treason charge a year before. My intuition told me that there was something unusual happening inside the politics of the MDC that I did not quite grasp. Across the political divide, in Zanu PF, there appeared to be a similar shift, hinting at a possibility of a split in both parties.

From what I had heard from my ZCTU friend on the day of the treason trial judgment, something was taking place behind the scenes – but what? Nothing was clear; it was difficult to discern a pattern. I kept my head down, observing and watching Zimbabwe's political dance floor from the proverbial balcony.

I received numerous reports from South Africa indicating that President Mbeki appeared comfortable working directly with Ncube on both MDC and Zimbabwean matters, instead of dealing directly with me as the party leader. And he made no secret of it. Mbeki had always wanted the MDC to assume the role of junior partner in a coalition with Zanu PF. That view set the pace for my numerous disagreements with him, as he exerted far more energy in pursuit of stability than he did for the cause of democracy.

To some extent there were senior politicians in the MDC who believed in that approach. It was something I refused to accept. For the sake of party unity, I avoided hasty decisions as I examined the impact of Mbeki's approach on my colleagues and on the broader MDC. We convened a national conference in December 2003 for a review of policies and an assessment of the strength of the party.

At the end of the review, we needed to fill posts in the national executive committee left vacant either by deaths or resignations of senior officials. In caucus as the top leadership, we decided to fill the late Learnmore Jongwe's position in the national executive with a senior woman politician. This was a deliberate decision, and veteran trade unionist Enna Chitsa, deputy chairperson of the Women's Assembly, was nominated for the position. The decision required that we should campaign to raise her profile in the party. Unfortunately, I soon realised that I was alone in the campaign as my five top colleagues on the executive had other ideas, despite having earlier agreed with the caucus suggestion.

To my amazement, Renson Gasela entered the race and easily clinched the post. He had spent several days working with the party's provincial chairpersons, and suddenly rose from a junior provincial party post to a powerful position in the national executive committee. Gasela had the support of my deputy, Sibanda, as well as Ncube and others at the top.

Here was the man who, through his links to Rupert Johnson, had plunged me into a serious trap and a gruelling treason trial. Instead of cautioning or sanctioning him for his political miscalculation, the party had, instead, awarded Gasela with a promotion to the national executive committee. It was now plain from the behaviour of my senior colleagues and some provincial chairpersons that something was definitely not right.

As we concluded the conference, Zanu PF was due to meet at its own annual convention. The meeting was to culminate in the election of one of Mugabe's deputies to replace Simon Muzenda who had died in September 2003. Naturally, the campaign for Muzenda's successor both excited and divided Zanu PF as hawks and doves vied for the position. I could see from the fights – which occasionally spattered into the columns of state newspapers – that Zanu PF faced an even deeper internal crisis than we did. There were two distinct camps in Zanu PF: one led by General Solomon Mujuru and the other by Emmerson Mnangagwa.

Remembering how I had been approached in December 2002 with a scheme that seemed both manipulative and underhand, I had a fairly good idea how the competing groups in Zanu PF were likely to be operating. No doubt these groups were secretly approaching senior leaders in the MDC to devise a political pact that would eventually edge Mugabe – and me – out of politics. As I did not know which of the two was ahead of the other, it was important to remain alert and pick up whatever signals came my way.

Dyke had intimated that the Mnangagwa group had the support of Mbeki and some Western embassies in Harare. All sorts of conniving was going on that could impinge on the MDC, particularly if our reputation in the eyes of voters or our international standing was damaged, so I had to observe events in Zanu PF very carefully.

After Muzenda's death, and in particular between October and November 2003, I heard a lot about the secret meetings of Zanu PF factions trying to find a suitable replacement. By December 2003, Mnangagwa emerged as favourite but at a conference in Masvingo, Mugabe delayed Muzenda's replacement by a year.

Solomon Mujuru's camp then regrouped on the understanding that whoever replaced Muzenda would ultimately lead Zanu PF. Mnangagwa, as the Zanu PF secretary for administration, had schemed his way towards the apex, getting the support of six out of ten provinces. With the backing of Jonathan Moyo and Chinamasa, Mnangagwa was sure to assume the post with ease.

Ironically, Mnangagwa's ambition claimed the scalps of six Zanu PF provincial chairpersons, along with Jonathan Moyo himself. The story was that Moyo organised the secret meeting which allegedly resulted in what Zanu PF called the Tsholotsho Declaration of 18 November 2004 when six provinces agreed to back Mnangagwa ahead of Joice Mujuru for the post of vice-president. Some of the Zanu PF political luminaries suspended from the party for attending the secret meeting were Midlands chairperson July Moyo, Daniel Shumba of Masvingo, as well as Jacob Mudenda of Matabeleland North, Lloyd Siyoka of Matabeleland South and Mike Madiro of Manicaland. These chairpersons led areas perceived to be Zanu PF strongholds.

Joice Mujuru took over as the new Zanu PF vice-president in a move that further ruptured the party. The real power behind Joice Mujuru was her husband Solomon, a retired general touted as a kingmaker in Zanu PF.

After he temporarily quashed the possible internal rebellion, Mugabe started to assemble a team to contest the parliamentary election set for March 2005. He dismissed Jonathan Moyo from his government in February 2005 after he defied a Zanu PF directive to stay out of Tsholotsho, a parliamentary seat he desired. Moyo would contest the seat as an independent candidate and he won narrowly.

A series of articles written by Jonathan Moyo for various publications after his fall-out with Mugabe and Zanu PF was fairly illuminating, although one had to take what he said with more than a pinch of salt.

He had already proved that he was an arch spin doctor and a specialist in negative campaigns. According to Jonathan Moyo, the Mujuru faction identified Simba Makoni as the preferred successor to Mugabe.[1]

One of the dismissed chairpersons, Daniel Shumba, formed his own party, the United People's Party (UPP), while Moyo tried, unsuccessfully, to set up another party, the United People's Movement (UPM). These developments gave the MDC an opportunity to exploit the fissures in Zanu PF. While we made some significant inroads, especially in Masvingo, our own internal weaknesses and a difficult political terrain prevented us from growing the party substantially ahead of Zanu PF before the 2005 election.

Mugabe adopted a few changes from the SADC protocol on the conduct and management of democratic elections, putting the MDC in an extremely difficult position on whether or not to take part in the polls. Although our candidates were ready, I was not convinced that Zimbabwe could come up with a credible election. The playing field was still bumpy and a number of flaws were glaringly obvious.

Parliament created a new institution, the Zimbabwe Electoral Commission (ZEC) which officially started work only two days before Mugabe announced a date for the election. The ZEC only became operational on 1 February 2005 and yet was expected to conduct a legitimate election a month later. It had no time to recruit staff and was simply given staff by the government.

To compound the situation, the ZEC found all its core functions – such as voter registration, the compilation of a voters' roll and other administrative duties – had already been performed by the state. The voter registration exercise was carried out from May to July 2004 by the same partisan institutions that had presided over the disputed 2000 and 2002 elections. Mugabe appointed a new ZEC chairman, George Chiweshe – from the military – without consultation.

The MDC was deeply concerned about Chiweshe's appointment. Although he was a High Court judge, his military background and association with Zanu PF appeared to compromise his integrity. For instance, he had passed questionable judgments denying Fletcher Dulini-

Ncube bail while on remand for the alleged murder of Cain Nkala.

Before assuming the new post, Chiweshe chaired the Delimitation Commission which drew up constituency boundaries in a manipulative way. Three additional constituencies were created in areas deemed to be in Zanu PF strongholds. Two constituencies in Harare and another two in Bulawayo, previously won by the MDC, were abolished. The reasons given for the changes did not make sense, especially after the 2002 national census confirmed that Harare's population had risen by 500 000 in ten years. Chiweshe's commission also took out Gwanda North and Mbare East and created new constituencies in perceived Zanu PF strongholds far out in the rural areas.

By the end of February 2005, only weeks before the election, the ZEC still had no phones, no permanent offices and only two members of staff. It operated from one of the visitors' lounges of the Sheraton Hotel in Harare and had no other structures countrywide. Its late start and lack of resources rendered the new body – purportedly set up to run the polls in line with SADC's guidelines – a peripheral player in the voting process. The whole pathetic performance was no more than a gesture, superficially adhering to the SADC guidelines. The reforms Mugabe introduced were woefully inadequate and failed to meet the basic framework set out by SADC in Mauritius in August 2004.

To cap it all, Chiweshe barred civil society organisations from helping out with voter education, further eroding public confidence in the integrity of the electoral process. Under the SADC protocol, Zimbabwe was supposed to use translucent ballot boxes for the first time in history. Because of civil society's inability to educate voters in an impartial manner, Zanu PF told voters that the boxes would enable the party's militia to see how individuals voted. Many, especially elderly voters, hesitated to cast their ballots for the MDC out of fear that Zanu PF would spot their crosses.

It was impossible for MDC candidates outside the capital city to liaise with the ZEC which had no visible presence elsewhere. We could not lodge complaints about malpractices or get guidance on election procedures. Without constitutional backing, the ZEC derived its powers from legislative support which made it subject to a government minister, compromising its status, authority, autonomy and legal weight.

After exhaustive debate inside the party at the end of 2004 and into early 2005, the MDC leadership succumbed to pressure from its members and supporters and decided to take part in the election, under protest. Personally, I was not in favour of getting into this election after my experiences in 2002. Yet the pressure from within the party, and in particular from the MDC parliamentary caucus, was intense. Our MPs, especially those from urban constituencies, knew that they were assured of clear wins and they argued for participation, partly out of selfishness. Control of the parliamentary caucus had begun to slip away from my grasp into the hands of Sibanda and Ncube. I chose to avoid the risk of taking a divided army into battle on the eve of a national election.

Compounding my dilemmas as leader was the fact that our traditional civil society partners were against our participation in the election, citing an uneven electoral playing field. I could take the MDC into the election and be damned, or boycott the election and be damned again. Personally, I decided not to fight for a parliamentary seat this time around.

Inside the MDC, the fissures started to widen. I was already seeing signs of unease over Ncube's activities. Our provincial executive committees and some MPs were heavily involved in attempts to wrest the party from my control, especially since the MDC congress was due in a few months' time.

Some of our parliamentarians began to see themselves as independent from the party. I was not to be a member of parliament so Sibanda, my deputy, became the official leader of the opposition. Under the direction of Sibanda and Ncube, our parliamentary caucus was slowly turning itself into a separate, autonomous power centre which sometimes sought to compete with the party's portfolio committees. Some MPs took instructions directly from Sibanda and Ncube and not from the party leadership in general, or me in particular.

It was my belief that we should launch the 2005 party's parliamentary election campaign in Masvingo. I argued, in vain, that I had managed to open up a new flank in Masvingo: our support there was rising daily. My colleagues in the top leadership disagreed. They said the MDC should launch the campaign in Bulawayo. I saw no reason for this, as Bulawayo and the entire western region were firmly behind the MDC. I maintained that it was important to exploit fresh Zanu PF wounds arising from the Tsholotsho fall-out in Masvingo and the opportunities that beckoned. Ncube stood his ground, insisting on Bulawayo as the venue for the launch. To strengthen his case, as the political head of the secretariat, he relocated the entire staff from our headquarters in Harare to the Bulawayo office – a move that was to have serious repercussions when the eventual split in the party came.

Even at the time, as party leader, I saw Ncube's move as an act of defiance and an attempt at a showdown with me. I knew that the bubble would one day have to burst, but for a while I did not know what to do.

With the help of the party's provincial leaders in Masvingo, I continued to insist on launching the campaign there, but Ncube would have none of it. Working with Dulini-Ncube, the treasurer, he refused to release money for the launch. I raised some cash from the Harare business community and kicked off the 2005 campaign in Masvingo anyway. Ncube and other top officials arrived late as if they were guests and left soon after my launch speech. This confirmed my suspicions that something was brewing.

Despite their own internal squabbles, Mugabe and Zanu PF maintained their pressure on the MDC. With the help of a pliant, state-dominated press and broadcasting and electronic media establishment, Mugabe and Zanu PF saturated the country with their campaign messages.

For instance, and in clear defiance of the newly pronounced SADC guidelines on the management of national elections, the launch of the MDC campaign received a mere two minutes and 35 seconds of airtime on television during the campaign. But when Mugabe launched the Zanu PF campaign on 11 February 2005, Zimbabwe television on that day alone allocated 18 minutes of airtime on the prime-time evening news bulletin. This was in addition to four hours of live coverage of the same event during the day, with television presenters clad in shirts and other regalia emblazoned with Zanu PF campaign messages.

State newspapers, with a total monopoly on the daily market, flatly refused to accept MDC advertisements and campaign messages, even though these newspapers were publicly owned. The refusals contradicted government gazetted regulations permitting opposition parties what was called reasonable access to the state-controlled media. This was another false nod to SADC's guidelines. Privately owned newspapers, which accepted our advertisements, were published once a week and had a very limited circulation, even in urban areas.

Mugabe made it clear throughout the campaign that he wanted Zanu PF to win by at least a two-thirds majority in parliament to enable him to make fundamental constitutional changes. Since June 2000 he had been unable to alter the Lancaster House Constitution because of a depleted majority in parliament. On the eve of the election, the MDC exposed the ZEC's bias towards Zanu PF, its structural weaknesses, and lack of capacity to supervise the election.

In terms of the law, election campaign managers were required to notify the constituency election officers of the names and addresses of election agents. Political parties were obliged to advertise these details in national newspapers at least three days before the polling day. The MDC complied with this requirement; Zanu PF deliberately did not do so. On 30 March 2005 our lawyers notified Chiweshe of this transgression but the ZEC ignored the protest.

As if in retaliation, the ZEC suddenly became openly hostile towards the MDC. I received reports that election officers, who were mainly members of the CIO and the military, refused to accredit MDC election agents on the grounds that they needed to show them original copies of the newspapers carrying the advertisements listing election agents.

Given the limited print-runs of Zimbabwe's newspapers, there was no way each one of our 24 000 election agents would have an original copy of a single publication. In a few areas where our agents had the newspaper copies, election officers insisted that they needed original letters from the MDC attesting that the agents officially represented the party.

I complained about the state of the voters' roll and demanded that we be given an electronic copy. Chiweshe refused, releasing only a hard copy which made it difficult for us to audit the roll on computers. The MDC carried out a limited audit of the roll and found, for instance, that in Bulawayo alone out of a sample of 500 voters, barely half were listed correctly – and about a fifth of those named were dead! In Harare North constituency, an MDC survey established that 64 per cent of the registered voters were not known at their given residential addresses.

The voters' roll was a major source of electoral doubt and fraud because it was a shambles, inflated and inaccurate, making it impossible for Zimbabwe to adhere to the principle of 'one person, one vote'.

In the final stages of the campaign, Mugabe and Zanu PF became even more brazen. Zimbabwe was facing serious food shortages. For many months leading up to March, the government had been importing the staple, maize, and stockpiling it at secret locations for use during the penultimate stages of the Zanu PF campaign. During the last week, Zanu PF openly sent out a ruthless message: *'Vote Zanu, or starve'*. Once again food was used as a political weapon. It was sheer blackmail, but the fact was that the message reached an estimated five million hungry people and must have affected their behaviour in a significant way.

The food was distributed by partisan traditional leaders in the rural areas who insisted that beneficiaries should identify themselves with a Zanu PF membership card. The leaders had received a hefty 150 per cent salary rise in January. Their seniors, traditional chiefs, were now proud owners of sleek SUV vehicles. In addition, Zanu PF directed the chiefs and their assistants to shepherd their subjects to the polling station on Election Day. In many areas, ZEC either employed or accredited local village heads, Zanu PF youths and chiefs' assistants as election officers, allowing them entry in and out of the polling stations during the voting.

In line with the piecemeal reforms Mugabe had made in terms of the SADC protocol, voting took place on a single day and ballots were counted at the polling stations.

Given the glaring evidence of the scale of the pre-election rigging and other malpractices, I tried to persuade Sibanda, Ncube, Dulini-Ncube and Paul Themba Nyathi to return the MDC secretariat to Harare for ease of communication. They argued that they were too busy with the campaign in Matabeleland. On Election Day, 31 March, I tasked Lucia Matibenga, the women's assembly chairperson, with running our information desk at Harvest House in Harare. Countrywide, I received reports that close to 150 000 people had been turned away from the polls for a variety of reasons. Either their names were not on the voters' roll or they were said to have incorrect identification papers.

After the voting, results began to trickle in. The ZEC adopted a two-tier announcement system, first reporting the total turnout at the close of the polls, and later giving a breakdown of the voting patterns. After telling the nation about the turnout in 72 constituencies, it abandoned the practice, saying it was now announcing only the actual results.

We were unable to analyse the accuracy of the number of votes cast in Mashonaland Central, Masvingo, Matabeleland North and in the Midlands as the ZEC flatly refused to release the figures. In the areas where figures had been announced earlier, we began to notice serious inconsistencies and unaccountable gaps between the actual vote tallies and the results. The figures did not add up. In at least 11 constituencies, the differences in the figures accounted for Zanu PF 'victories'.

Just a few examples reveal the extent of the massive fraud that took place in 2005. In Manyame, near Harare, ZEC said 14 812 people voted. The MDC candidate, Hilda Mafudze, received 8 312, which was a clear lead. But when ZEC finally announced what it said was the official result, the Zanu PF candidate was declared the winner with 15 448 votes. Beitbridge constituency was said to have recorded a total of 36 821 votes, but when the final results were given out, the combined total for the two competing candidates only added up to 20 602 voters. The pattern was the same in the 30 constituencies where ZEC officially broadcast the figures on radio and on television. The discrepancies varied between 2 000 and 12 000.

I met the South African observer mission and showed them these discrepancies. They just stared into space and promised to communicate the message to their government.

With a straight face, Chiweshe declared Zanu PF the winner, with 78 seats to the MDC's 41, and one independent. Predictably, Africa affirmed the election as having been free and fair. Mugabe now commanded the two-thirds parliamentary majority he desired in an election he boastfully declared to have been run according to the new SADC protocol on democratic elections.

Our estimates, however – based on the confusion at ZEC counting centres and the inconsistencies in the final figures – indicated that the MDC must have won the 2005 election with a much larger majority of parliamentary seats.

If Mugabe's attitude towards an election was so contemptuous, and he was ready to ignore the people's verdict, any plebiscite he conducted had nothing to do with Zimbabweans. He saw elections as a way of deceiving the world into thinking that he was a democrat and a statesman worthy of respect. Zimbabwean elections were, therefore, never meant for Zimbabweans.

The MDC was naturally apprehensive about the future. When some top officials suggested that we go to court, I laughed my heart out and wished them good luck! The aggrieved candidates tried to challenge the results, only to learn that the Electoral Court was improperly set up. That was the end of the story.

ENDNOTES

1   'Tsholotsho saga: the untold story (Tsholotsho Declaration)' http://www. prof-jonathan-moyo.com/

CHAPTER TWENTY-TWO
TERMITES

One would have thought that any political leader who claimed to enjoy such massive popularity as the election of 2005 had delivered to Mugabe could now take a rest and run the country smoothly. Not so. The so-called election victory was clearly a hoax, enough to deny Mugabe peace of mind. Although the country seemed calm and quiet, anger boiled beneath the surface. Through his CIO – what the *Los Angeles Times* called 'the Zimbabwe version of the KGB'[1] – Mugabe received regular reports on the mood of the populace collected by spies in beer halls, at gatherings, in shops and offices and villages throughout the country.

The economy remained in a state of collapse with shortages of food, fuel, electricity and even water. Life in the cities was bad enough, but in the rural areas the government had failed to distribute adequate food aid and people lived on the brink of survival. Once known as 'the breadbasket of southern Africa', Zimbabwe was now dependent on external food donors and chronic malnutrition stalked the land. With nothing to offer to pacify rising emotions, Mugabe became ever more desperate, casting around for scapegoats.

He found the ideal victims among the urban poor.

The MDC had won most of the urban constituencies in the 150-seat parliament, so Mugabe devised a response that would penalise urban residents and drive them out of the cities. Among the poor and the marginalised were those who had previously worked in the formal economy. The trade union movement which had been the basis of our political challenge to the regime in the first place, back in 1999, was rapidly eroding.

Membership of the national Zimbabwe Congress of Trade Unions (ZCTU) had dwindled substantially because of continuous company closures. Most workers were now on the streets, scraping a living from vending in the informal sector, doing private businesses in shacks littered around urban areas. The ZCTU had remained in touch with them and maintained some structures for retrenched workers but lines of communication and support were weak. In a bid to disperse them, Mugabe went for them.

In one of the most ghastly episodes in the country's history, the state launched *Operation Murambatsvina* ('Drive out the Trash', or 'Remove the Filth'). In May 2005, without warning, armed police and army units using bulldozers swooped into inner-city suburbs and shanty towns in Harare, razing homes, businesses and unauthorised extensions to buildings. The blitz spread to other towns and cities, targeting mainly the poor. Mugabe's aim was to scatter that constituency into the rural areas where he could control them through violence and partisan food handouts. The three-week 'clean-up', Mugabe said, was to reduce urban crime and vice, grime and money laundering, and to improve the people's general hygiene.

From Mutare in the east to Bulawayo in the west, from Mount Darwin in the north to Beitbridge in the south, the nation was swept by a tidal wave of vengeance against those who had already suffered the most and, in reaction, had dared to vote for the opposition.

Zimbabweans referred to the assault as a *tsunami,* a reference to the Indian Ocean disaster of 2004. In the language of international observers and local campaigners, Operation Murambatsvina amounted to 'urban cleansing' and was described as a 'humanitarian disaster'.[2] A disaster it was, but not the result of natural causes. Human rights campaigners and NGOs representing the informal sector were appalled by what was happening but could do nothing to stop it except report the excesses. This was the month of June and it was cold. Photographs showed toddlers clinging to each other in distress, traders moving office furniture into the streets as buildings were cleared out, a woman using a sledgehammer to knock down the walls of her own dwelling.

Once again Mugabe came under international spotlight. The United Nations secretary general despatched a special envoy, Anna Tibaijuka, to Harare to investigate. Tibaijuka's damning report, published in July 2005, saved the day. She forced Mugabe to stop this new war against the people. But by the time Tibaijuka arrived in Harare, the city had already been 'cleansed'.

According to the UN study, the disaster affected at least 700 000 people directly through loss of their homes or livelihoods and could have indirectly affected around 2.4 million people.[3] The whole episode seemed to be an act of madness. It made sense only to the perpetrators. The motive within the higher ranks of Zanu PF was both vindictive and self-enriching. The state ordered that those displaced should return to the rural areas or take up jobs on the new farms seized by Zanu PF officials.

In a country which already had a vast internal refugee population with little or no food security, the informal sector upon which so many depended to eke out an existence was devastated at one fell swoop. Did Zanu PF and its leader have no compassion whatever?

Interestingly, there were sporadic contradictions: some of the front line troops leading the attack were shocked to return home and find their families homeless after their colleagues had indiscriminately levelled their own residences and tuck shops. The operation was haphazardly carried out and it affected everyone, both MDC and Zanu PF.

I saw Operation Murambatsvina as part of Mugabe's relentless determination to destroy the MDC's urban base. The move was nothing but an act of retribution and an atrocious but ultimately fruitless attempt to weaken us. Through the evictions, the state violated international law and confirmed for all to see that Zimbabwe's rulers felt they could attack their own people mercilessly and get away with it – which they did. Police Commissioner Augustine Chihuri, in a public statement, callously claimed that Operation Murambatsvina was a way to clear the crawling mass of maggots bent on destroying the country.

To the MDC's shame, because of internal dissent and residual turf wars from the 2005 election, we failed respond to the operation in any meaningful way. We had just come out of a stolen election and our organisers and supporters were weak, tired and frustrated. It was difficult to know how to react at a time when both people and party were at their most vulnerable. Punch-drunk and slow to realise the widespread nature of the disaster, we had little energy to engage in a fresh confrontation with the state – especially a heavily armed regime that had shown again and again that it was ready to kill. People simply complied with Murambatsvina in agony, yearning for leadership. As a party, it must be said, we failed our supporters.

The 2005 election had clearly been rigged in favour of Mugabe. The SADC Principles and Guidelines Governing Democratic Elections, adopted in Mauritius in August 2004, had not been implemented in full. Certainly the spirit of those guidelines had been cynically disregarded.

The ruling party claimed to have won 78 of the 120 directly elected seats while the MDC had 41. Using his powers as president, Mugabe proceeded to pack the House with unelected non-constituency MPs (20 ordinary members along with 10 traditional leaders). This gave his party much more than the two-thirds majority that allowed for the constitution to be changed at will. In addition, Mugabe selected provincial governors loyal to the party. He could now run the country as he pleased.

Now that the will of the people had been denied once again, there was intense debate in the MDC about our continued presence in parliament. Party structures questioned the efficacy of attendance in a legislature in which we were unable to make a difference.

I put the matter before the national executive committee and we failed to reach a consensus on the way forward. There were strong feelings for a boycott of parliament, right from the first day, to protest Zanu PF rigging. Equally strong were views that we should stay there to keep an eye on Zanu PF at close range. Our people were agitated and at odds. In the end, MDC vice-president Gibson Sibanda and secretary general Welshman Ncube threw their weight around and ordered the MPs to attend parliament, regardless.

Behind the facade of implacable and unassailable power Mugabe was facing growing challenges, from inside as well as outside his party. There appeared to be no jubilation regarding the election outcome. Because of the massive scale of the rigging, which Zanu PF itself was aware of, Mugabe was unsure whether or not he remained invincible. He seemed firmly entrenched, capable of ruthlessly stifling all perceived rebellion in his own ranks, but he needed to prop up his administration to avert challenges from within.

He now talked of introducing several constitutional amendments, one of which was to push back the presidential election from 2008 to 2010. Justice Minister Patrick Chinamasa was instructed to draft the amendment which would effectively extend Mugabe's current term as president for two years. The pretext was that the presidential and parliamentary elections (due again in 2010) should be held simultaneously to save money. To our surprise and delight, Zanu PF's feuding factions temporarily united to oppose Mugabe's plan and his term was not extended. This meant the MDC could have a run at the presidency in 2008.

Inside the MDC, meanwhile, the rifts and fissures started to widen over strategy, means and goals. Termites had got into the foundations from our own ranks and from those who wished us ill. Frustration was creeping in and the first to feel it were our younger members who agitated for action, leading to internal skirmishes at Harvest House over minor differences. At first, I thought this was natural as the struggle was taking so long while the use of the ballot to effect change was letting the nation down.

The problems went deeper than mere youthful impatience. There was jockeying for position and influence among the more mature members. Most worryingly, the party was in danger of losing its integrated vision. Factions emerged that in some ways mirrored the national picture of social and political dislocation. Turf-hungry politicians ignored the effects of the broader, systemic disturbances in Zimbabwe to concentrate on exclusive and isolated issues which affected the cohesion of the MDC. I refused to be drawn into the melee, preferring to wait and study the situation. I was not interested in dealing with only parts of the problem but searched for opportunities for the entire party.

To me, the imperative was how to build bridges to link the diverse interest groups whose narrow focus had turned destructive because of external factors. Parliament was rigged, the country was a mess, and people saw no signs of change for the better. Grinding poverty forced many to go cap-in-hand to Zanu PF pleading for handouts and appointments.

As usual, Mugabe's secret service took advantage of our problems and infiltrated some of our party organs and activities, directing the more guileless members to stir trouble routinely. When we identified troublemakers we kicked them out of the party.

The CIO calculated that our provincial structures were weak and constituted an entry point for infiltration. Saboteurs wormed their way into the party as Zanu PF agents in order to defeat the MDC from within. We began to have serious problems with splinter groups in the provinces as structures were dissolved and new ones set up, led by individuals of questionable political standing and integrity. Some even supported Zanu PF.

Ncube and other senior leaders began to accuse me of relying too much on the advice of my staff to run the party, alleging that I had a 'kitchen cabinet' of loyalists who advised me behind closed doors and did my bidding.

As party secretary general Ncube dismissed two of my bodyguards, accusing them of fanning violence inside the MDC. I refused to accept this and from that time my relations with Ncube deteriorated progressively. A political party's administrative personnel are drawn from a pool of activists who share the same ideology as the full-time politicians. There was no time when my staff took a position outside the organs of the party – I would never have allowed that.

The members of my staff understood the political temperature. They saw and read into what was happening with regard to Ncube's behaviour and constantly advised me of the plots, dangers, fears and opportunities confronting the MDC.

To refocus the party and direct it to pay attention to our broad goals, I suggested at a national executive committee meeting that the MDC adopt a confrontational approach towards Mugabe and Zanu PF. The proposal was adopted. Mass action would unify the entire party through active pursuit of our goals. Politicians, by their very nature, love conflict – often unconsciously. They are fascinated by short-term gains and thrive on humiliating their opponents, both internally and outside their organisations. In our case, I believe, if left to his or her own world, a Zimbabwean politician's horizon stops after successful election to public office.

It was vital to engage civil society and to this end we sought to form an alliance with the National Constitutional Assembly, a coalition of pro-democracy civil society groups, including labour, founded in 1997. It was to be expected that it would take time to cement the relationship but because of internal differences, the alliance hardly took off. In the circumstances, no action was possible.

As a leader of a party as broad and as diverse as the MDC, I refrained from prematurely rushing into initiatives or intervening in some of the petty conflicts that had emerged. Any reckless act on my part would jeopardise the party's mission, opening further scope for political cannibalism. I took my time and waited, extending the foundations on which to anchor a firm leadership of the party. Working through the internal contradictions within the MDC was never easy because the movement remained fragile, with varied interests exerting pressure this way and that. All the diplomatic skills I had honed during my years in trade unionism had to be exercised, exhausted and new ones created to keep the sinking ship afloat.

The time was rapidly approaching when internal bickering needed to stop.

The next MDC congress was now due but we decided to postpone it to the end of the year. This was in order to renew and rebuild our disjointed grassroots structures, especially the provincial ones compromised by Zanu PF infiltration.

In June 2005, Ncube, in his capacity as secretary general, ordered the election of new leaders in the lower structures. The process was to lead to provincial congresses in October and as soon as new provincial bodies were in place the MDC would convene a national congress. All this was to be done before the end of 2005.

On the opposite side, as Zanu PF factions jostled for turf and supremacy, they kept reaching out to Ncube, our weak provinces and some of our members of parliament. Other events inside Zanu PF, emanating from parliament, concerned me. For instance, when Joice Mujuru became vice-president, the Women's University conferred a degree on her in some dubious discipline, claiming she had done a course on a part-time basis and qualified. There was a clear reason for this. Soon enough I was informed of attempts to push through a constitutional amendment requiring any future presidential aspirant to have *earned* an academic university degree, not merely to be in possession of an honorary one. At the time of Mujuru's controversial selection, Mugabe had hinted that for her political advancement the sky was now the limit. The proposed university degree requirement for future presidential candidates was clearly designed to disqualify me from standing in future elections. To my horror, I was told that the proposal originated from the MDC.

I called in Sibanda to enquire about the development and what it meant. He was non-committal, advising me to check with David Coltart, our secretary for legal affairs, but he too was evasive, telling me that details of the bill were on a compact disk somewhere. The matter of the MDC's complicity might have ended there, but soon afterwards I received telephone calls from concerned party officials worried about a photograph of Sibanda and Innocent Gonese, our parliamentary chief whip, on the front page of *The Herald*, both wearing smiles, and having tea with Mugabe at State House.

I spoke to Sibanda again. He told me that courtesy required that as leader of the opposition in parliament, he should have occasion to see Mugabe in his capacity as Head of State! When I asked him about the content of the discussions at the dictator's tea party, he stammered something that made no sense.

While enmeshed in these carefully devised propaganda ploys, Mugabe still faced serious problems within his party where dissatisfied elements were demanding their share of the political spoils following the elections. How was he to reward hard-line loyalists who, since 2000, had been losing elections to the MDC in the urban areas?

Through a rushed constitutional amendment, he re-established the Senate in order to hand out lucrative seats and so look after the interests of the Zanu PF old guard. Ironically, when the Senate was abolished in 1987, Mugabe argued that it merely rubber-stamped the work of the House of Assembly and was an unnecessary drain on national resources. Zimbabwe then was much richer than in 2005, but now the alarming expense did not worry our president who needed his rubber stamp for cronies.

I argued vehemently against this move, saying it was a waste of money in a nation that was as poor as it had been in 1970 under the white regime. Fewer were in formal sector jobs and life expectancy was far lower than in 1960. But MDC colleagues in parliament failed to see my point. Ncube campaigned in the provinces, persuading them to back the re-creation of the Senate. The carrot he offered, as I discovered from some of them, was a chance to contest in the proposed Senate polls.

Numerous reports reached me of secret meetings involving Ncube and a Zanu PF faction aligned to Emmerson Mnangagwa, a close Mugabe ally and Speaker of Parliament, and headed by Chinamasa. Ncube had the backing of Sibanda, Gasela, Priscilla Misihairabwi-Mushonga, Paul Themba Nyathi and others, mainly from the western region.

I understood that Ncube and Chinamasa were working with Pearson Mbalekwa, a relation of Mnangagwa from Zvishavane and with Chinamasa's good friend Jonathan Moyo. It appeared Zanu PF had managed to convince Ncube and some parliamentarians that to secure the interests of the Ndebele minority, it was important that they join hands with an influential section of Zanu PF. By 'influential', I mean a faction that enjoyed the backing of the military and South African President Thabo Mbeki.

The Mnangagwa group was weakened by Mujuru's rise in December 2005; it was natural that his faction sought out allies from the MDC to upstage their Zanu PF rivals. In fact, Mnangagwa had blamed his loss to an MDC candidate in the 2005 elections on the Mujuru faction, claiming they had manipulated the situation so that the MDC could win. The fact that he had previously been beaten by our candidate Blessing Chebundo in the 2000 elections did not seem to add up in his mind to an admission that the voters did not want him. He was now looking to rebuild his political fortunes.

As I maintained my strong opposition to the Senate proposal, the matter finally came up for discussion at the national executive committee meeting in July 2005. We agreed that because of differing positions, we needed to consult the people. We convened provincial council meetings at which the issue was put to debate. The same divisions that emerged in the national executive committee surfaced here too. I could see a clear division between our district executives and their provincial bosses, with the districts totally opposed to reinstating the Senate.

As much as I resented it, I could see a looming split in the MDC. After our consultations, Ncube and his group disagreed with my analysis of the feedback from the provinces. They insisted that we take the matter to the party's national council, knowing well that many councillors were either members of the provincial structures or had just lost their parliamentary seats in the stolen election in March. If the case was brought to the national council for discussion, councillors would certainly urge us to support the Senate proposal, purely out of self-interest. Many wanted to stand in the contest as senatorial candidates, especially in safe, urban constituencies.

On 12 October 2005, the national council finally met in a tense session chaired by Isaac Matongo, who – unknown to me – was in favour of the Senate. For hours, councillors argued the issue, but as I listened to the disputes, I could see a carefully planned strategy unfolding.

My main fear was that the party was likely to split into two equal groups – right down the middle. There was reason for hope in the fact that the powerful youth and women's assemblies, headed by Nelson Chamisa and Lucia Matibenga respectively, were totally opposed to the Senate. I stood my ground. I knew that Mbeki was in favour of a party split. He wanted the splinter group to join a Zanu PF faction in the hope that their combined force would weaken and eventually destroy the remaining MDC. Mbeki would then pronounce to the world that he had resolved the Zimbabwean crisis.

For his part, Ncube saw an opportunity to undermine me by advancing his own and Mbeki's strategy. I had suppressed the split for the sake of the party and the country. They thought I would do anything to prevent a split. I hung on to my thoughts until the situation became so serious that a split had to be faced.

As things were to turn out, both the breakaway group and Mbeki miscalculated the outcome of the whole game – but not before a few setbacks to my cause. My political reading was that the mass of MDC supporters were fully behind me, so I decided to let Ncube go. This decision was fraught with uncertainty, although my instinct warned me not to take a divided army into a battle with the ruling party. Doing so would definitely have led to self-destruction.

Ncube won the first round. His hand had been clear from the beginning. He had started preparing the ballot papers before the meeting. Anna Chimanikire, a Chitungwiza councillor, told me later that she received a substantial amount of money for casting a vote in favour of the Senate proposal. With the five senior leaders in the management committee and a number of provincial executives, Ncube succeeded in getting the national council to vote 33-31 in favour of participating in Senate elections. Our parliamentary caucus followed a similar pattern. Out of the 40, 21 supported my position.

To allow for a vote on a major policy issue in the MDC was out of line, unconventional and never part of our custom and practice. Isaac Matongo, chairing the session, nevertheless allowed the process to go ahead. As I have said, he was in favour of the Senate, although in the end he told me that he voted against it.

Sekai Holland, Grace Kwinjeh and Yvonne Mahlunge, three other councillors against the Senate proposal, were abroad. They could have tilted the vote in my favour, I thought. With the buy-in of provincial leaders, Ncube thought he could control the provinces. Little did he appreciate that the MDC, as a party, is firmly grassroots-based and that consequently the districts would disown their provincial executives and maintain their grip on the ward and branch structures.

After the divisive vote, I picked up my papers and announced that I was against the move. I was unwilling to take the MDC into the Senate election. I left and drove home. With dozens of journalists in hot pursuit, I informed the world that the MDC was out of the contest for the Senate. I went into my home, chatted briefly to Amai Edwin, and decided to leave Harare for a break.

I desperately needed time to myself. I wanted to reflect on the day's events and simply needed to rest – though not in Harare but at my birthplace in Buhera. As we got into the car, Matongo and Chimanikire arrived. I did not even bother to talk to them. I was very angry. I had realised that I was on my own at the meeting where my most senior and trusted colleagues had let me down, and I felt betrayed. To make matters worse, while I was literarally unreachable by telephone in rural Buhera, MDC spokesperson Paul Themba Nyathi issued a counter statement to mine, saying the MDC was going into the Senate election. Thus, for 72 hours, without my knowledge, the story of the confusion in the MDC dominated the news.

In politics, apparent victories may be illusions and seeming defeats turn out to be successes in disguise. Soon after my arrival at my Buhera home and after a brief chat with my mother, I retired to bed. I spent the weekend with close family relations, my neighbours and friends while reflecting on the way forward.

I was lucky to have built up a loyal staff component in my office in Harare where Makone, Gandi Mudzingwa, Professor Elphas Mukonoweshuro and Dennis Murira handled the political and diplomatic questions in my absence. My spokesman, veteran journalist T William Bango, dealt with the clamorous media, managing to argue my case with ease. I was grateful to my staff for defending my decision and advising the world that the MDC would emerge stronger after a temporary political hiatus.

Ncube meanwhile set up shop in our Bulawayo office, taking our secretariat with him as well as all the party records and computers. Apart from my office staff, only Brighton Matimba, our social welfare officer, remained at Harvest House.

Ncube and the others failed to read my mind correctly. They thought I was still the same trade unionist they had persuaded to take over the leadership of the MDC, a position I reluctantly accepted in January 2000. Little did they know that over the years experience had transformed me, teaching me to live with diversity and to manage adversity. In public office, if you are to be responsive to the demands put upon you it behoves you to explore your inner self and make discoveries there that strengthen you. I had come to understand my inner voice; if others thought I was making a mistake, so be it; I could live with that if I was convinced I was doing the right thing.

What I know is that I never set out to make mistakes for the wrong reasons, deliberately putting myself at odds with subordinates and followers. When I was wrong, I was the first to admit it – and to apologise.

In a struggle of our nature, a political party cannot function effectively when it is run by a committee. I had spent the better part of my tenure babysitting some of my highly unpopular colleagues, including Ncube. I fought hard for collective responsibility, only to take the flak each time things went awry, often without the collective defence and support of those I had shielded. For a long time, these senior politicians insisted that I should never address a meeting alone. They all wanted to be where I was, especially at mass rallies, in order to benefit from my personal political brand.

My colleagues were simply riding on my popularity, in the forlorn hope that part of it would rub off on to them. They were uncomfortable with me as a person and a leader and I sensed that they wanted to build their political careers using Tsvangirai as a seat warmer who could ultimately be dislodged as soon as the right opportunity presented itself. Little did they know how easily I saw through that.

My personal style involved consulting widely. At the end of the day, though, I was expected to carry the burden of whatever decision the party made and people looked to me for an explanation. In order to defend decisions with conviction I needed to be convinced first about the good sense and strategic value of what we were doing. From mistakes and failures I learnt that unless I took a step back and listened to that inner voice – intuition, and perhaps some wisdom of the ages – I could never make a cogent decision or sort out priorities among a myriad of immediate chores.

My staff were among the mirrors now at my disposal that enabled me to see what lay behind appearances and I drew encouragement and stimulus from people who expressed genuinely supportive sentiments and ideas.

In the streets, in corporate boardrooms, within civil society and even among my colleagues and friends, I shouldered the blame for not doing enough to unseat Mugabe. The country was weary beyond words. I was variously described in newspapers and on internet discussion forums within tired social networks as shallow-minded, weak in policy formulation, lacking a decisive killer-punch, a pathetic leader and a poor strategist. I absorbed everything like a sponge and turned it all over in my mind. Taking these punches was never the high point of my day but I had no choice and if I kept my wits about me I could learn valuable lessons. No quitter, it never occurred to me that I should throw in the towel or escape to some foreign capital, even when the political furnace became unbearably hot.

Yes, Mugabe had persevered and won a major battle to split the MDC. My top generals abandoned the troops just when the movement needed to get its ranks in order. But the war was still far from over. Our struggle would remain non-violent even if we opted for a more confrontational approach. The people, especially the majority poor, knew their destination, and that became my main source of inspiration. It was impossible to put a timeline to a non-violent struggle, especially with an opponent like Mugabe who often boasted that he had 'several degrees in violence'.

I readied myself to be bullied and damned whatever I did, but through deep inner reflection I tried to maintain the direction that the ethos of service to people demanded of me. It was an extremely difficult and trying time.

To a leader, clarity of thought is essential in today's confused world. Awash with consultants, nimble-tongued motivational speakers, experts and specialists in almost every sphere of life, one is surrounded by self-anointed advisers, con-artists, social and political prostitutes and smooth-talking crooks. You have to resist their blandishments. At the same time, the propaganda and spin put out by the other side has to be countered with effective arguments and valid information.

State media and Zanu PF crowed about how I had caused the MDC split. Recent events were perceived and written about as a major test to see who would ultimately carry the day between those who wished to continue with our opposition struggle and those keen on a compromise solution with Zanu PF.

Admittedly, the MDC split was a big blow to me personally – far bigger than Mugabe's relentless persecution – and my standing as a political leader was severely dented. But what was the issue? Mugabe had failed to justify the efficacy of the Senate. There was no need for it and our economy could hardly support another legislative chamber.

At the beginning, I was unsure about Tendai Biti's position. Later it emerged that Ncube had tried to recruit him to lead the splinter group but he refused and joined me in the anti-Senate campaign. So did Zimbabwe's vibrant civil society.

There was a strong perception that the Ncube group was nothing but a tiny, power-hungry and sectional outfit. Nevertheless, it inflicted much damage on the MDC's cause. The group was working against me, even planning my final ousting as party leader.

The splinter group now invoked their man in Pretoria to put me at a disadvantage. President Thabo Mbeki had shown antipathy towards me and the cause I represented on several occasions but he was now pulled directly into the MDC's domestic dispute.

On my return to Harare on Monday morning, 15 October 2005, Sibanda telephoned me suggesting that we meet. He came to my home and I told him that for our discussion to make sense, we needed the other four senior members of the management committee. Sibanda pretended to hear me out and left, promising to bring them along. But he never returned. Instead, and without my knowledge, Ncube had already booked flights for the five top leaders to see Mbeki that afternoon. As I waited at home, they were already in the air on the way to Pretoria.

Matongo, now unsure about his political future, had refused to accompany them, but he made some serious allegations about my leadership qualities in a discussion he had with Ian Makone. According to Makone, Matongo was very emotional. He suggested that I had failed and must hand over the leadership to a more capable replacement, but did not name possible alternative candidates.

Mbeki immediately granted the four an audience. He phoned me during their meeting – the first I knew that they were in South Africa. 'Well, I have got some of your leadership here ...' Mbeki began. 'I understand there is a problem ... Can you come here and we talk? I think we need to talk over the fall-out in your party.'

I was stunned. After greeting him politely, I asked bluntly: 'What has the politics of the MDC got to do with you? This is an internal matter which should not bother you as I understand you have much more serious matters of state to attend to.' After a long pause, I continued, 'I am not coming to South Africa. Tell them that I said they must come back and we will discuss the issues here.'

To that, Mbeki replied: 'I thought it may help if you come and we thrash out the issues.' I felt Mbeki had gone too far, and I snapped, 'Mr President, with all due respect, those people have no right to be there. They have to come here so that we can discuss and sort out the matter. I am open to discuss matters. As I speak to you, Your Excellency, I am waiting for Gibson [Sibanda] to bring the others here for a meeting at which I hope we can thrash out our problems.'

'Well, let me talk to them ... they are here with me,' he replied.

Sibanda and his group were listening in as Mbeki had switched the conversation on to a speaker-phone. I asked Mbeki to let me talk to Sibanda, but Mbeki refused, saying, 'No. No. No. Let me talk to him first. I will call you later.'

As I clutched my mobile handset, anxiously waiting for Mbeki to call back, an array of scenarios raced through my mind. What was going on? Why Mbeki? What role had he played in the MDC split? Where was Mugabe in all this? What were the implications for democracy?

When an acquaintance innocently called for a chat, I said, 'I am busy; I am in a meeting. Call me later!' I had not eaten anything for the whole day. A worried Amai Edwin asked me to take a break and have something to eat. I looked at her, then got up and paced around the garden, my mobile phone squeezed in my sweaty palm.

Finally, Mbeki was back on the line. 'Mr President,' I said, in a stern and exasperated voice, 'this is a party issue. It has nothing to do with anybody but ourselves. There is no reason why a head of state and government of another country, a foreign country, can come and involve himself in the opposition party politics of a neighbouring country.' No response. 'Hello. Hello. Mr President ...? Your Excellency ...?' Mbeki was gone – never to return.

But if I thought that Mbeki had backed off I was wrong. After that incident, his involvement in the MDC's affairs became even more obtrusive. It was clear to me now that the entire MDC split was externally influenced. It had nothing to do with our internal fights; and Mugabe and Zanu PF were involved in the matter.

I believe Ncube was externally supported by none other than Mbeki, and encouraged by many senior Zanu PF officials to have a go at me. I heard later that Mbeki was even financing the Ncube group to destabilise the MDC; among other things, he covered their travel expenses. In discussions with diplomats, journalists and his colleagues, Mbeki went out of his way to pursue an international crusade against the MDC and me. Every effort was being made to isolate me.

The attack on my authority had everything to do with manipulation by Zanu PF in connivance with Mbeki and Welshman Ncube. It was extraordinary – a conspiracy in all but name, stretching across the border.

On reflection, I found myself arguing with my inner voice. Never before in my political career had my leadership been tested at this level. If I pulled through this conflict – this split which was the result of pure mischief – then I would survive to fight another day and possibly win the struggle for democracy in the national interest.

Led by Ncube and now with the support of David Coltart, the group went around the world saying I was a dictator; that I had violated the party constitution; that I was a violent person; that I was unfit for leadership. Coltart has a personal website which I believe he used extensively to publish disparaging remarks about me and my leadership style.

When they returned home, Sibanda – then acting as their leader but firmly on Ncube's leash – tried to oust me from the party. I asked him what gave him the authority to do so. I had been elected at congress and only congress had the power to dispense with me if it saw fit to do so. Our congress was just weeks away. Not satisfied, the Ncube group went to the High Court seeking an order for me to step down. This course of action was perplexing and unfounded. Justice Yunus Omerjee ruled in my favour, emphasising that I was the legitimate leader of the MDC – a judgment which left the group with egg on its face.

I had known Sibanda for close to 20 years; Ncube for almost a decade. Ncube is a superb boardroom idealist but lacks a popular or grassroots insight. He never tries to get to the level of the people on the ground. I often saved him from angry activists who seemed unhappy with his leadership style. His manner enmeshed him in technical niceties in situations where they were totally unnecessary. An avid debater, Ncube is at his best in a meeting with executives. I realised for the first time, after many years of working with him, that Sibanda is neither an organiser nor politically smart as a player. I failed to understand his reasoning when he allowed himself to be fooled into trying to destroy all that we had achieved in making the MDC a household name.

Matongo returned to the party; so did Blessing Chebundo and many other senior executives. The provincial leadership in Manicaland, which initially looked hesitant and unsure, succumbed to the pressure from our grassroots structures and fell into line. Ncube meanwhile controlled the top structures in Matabeleland and continued to run his affairs from our office in Bulawayo using the party's vehicles, resources and secretariat.

Mugabe proceeded with the Senate elections in November 2005. Ncube and his group struggled to explain their actions as they faced a strong grassroots anti-Senate election feeling. They fielded candidates under the MDC banner but did not have sufficient candidates or resources to cover the whole country. To most Zimbabweans the election was a joke. It was marred by widespread apathy and recorded the lowest turnout since 2000.[4] Except for Bulawayo and a few rural Matabeleland constituencies, the Ncube splinter group was heavily trounced by Zanu PF in the Senate election. They only managed to get seven seats out of the 50 that were contested. I felt vindicated.

The offensive on the MDC was regionally motivated, I told myself, and the fact that it was ethnically driven would eventually help to defeat its whole purpose. It was simply a case of five senior leaders, three of them from one region with an ethnic motivation, who tried to highjack a national project away from the broader mass of people.

As for Gift Chimanikire – he sided with the splinter group, thinking his time had come. His view was that the Ndebele leaders would naturally resort to an ethnic Shona politician to help them to build a national following. He knew them well; he knew their limitations as leaders, so he simply hid behind them, waiting for an opportunity to strike and take over the leadership of the splinter group.

Chimanikire took a pronounced stance against me in this clear demonstration of his desire to bide his time and eventually take over. Ncube and others – unsuspecting perhaps – urged him on. But when the group finally approached Arthur Mutambara in Johannesburg – again, I understand with the help of Mbeki and others keen to see the splinter's continued survival – Chimanikire could not take it. He approached me through an emissary and asked for forgiveness.

The reason for my decision to stay on as president of the MDC was very clear, even when I was under tremendous emotional pressure.

When the split occurred, preparations for the second national MDC congress were already well under way. In terms of the MDC's constitution, we were bound to start at our grassroots structures in a bottom-up approach, leading finally to the national congress at which top leaders were elected, new policies adopted, and a programme of action designed for the next five-year period.

By October 2005, we had completed the preparatory work in the wards and districts. We were now headed for the provinces, an area which Ncube and his group deemed important for their party takeover project. After the split, the districts continued with the provincial congresses. The only area where we had some difficulties was in rural Matabeleland, where the structures had aligned themselves to Ncube and his group. Bulawayo rejected Ncube and Sibanda. Our provincial congress there was largely successful, thanks to the efforts of executive members Gertrude Mtombeni and Thokozani Khupe. These two leaders, who later took each other on for the post of vice-president at the March 2006 congress, flatly refused to follow Ncube's tribal agenda.

I was keen to see the MDC's national congress succeed. Ncube and his group seemed unsure about how they would come out of that process and they appeared reluctant to subject themselves once more to the people for a fresh mandate. I tried on several occasions to strike a deal to reunite the leadership, saying to Sibanda: 'Please let us deal with this problem for the sake of our country.'

We asked Professor Brian Raftopoulos, previously of the University of Zimbabwe and now heavily involved with the work of civil society and the MDC, to mediate. He tried and tried, but failed to make headway.

Ncube and his group kept shifting the goalposts. At one time, they demanded that their political posts should not be contested at the pending party congress. They stated that they did not want their positions challenged and wanted me to endorse that position, a promise impossible to keep in a democratic party the size of the MDC.

There were various instances of both direct and indirect contact between Sibanda and me, facilitated by businessman Jameson Timba and my family lawyer Innocent Chagonda. Sibanda's relatives often called me, saying that Gibson was wrong. They pleaded with me to accept him back. I told them that I was open to suggestions and discussion. It was all rather embarrassing – we had worked closely together for more than 20 years and were close friends rather than just colleagues. Unfortunately, it would appear that the death of his wife Zodwa caused a lot of problems for Sibanda. Zodwa had a strong personality and was very focused in her political views. General opinion was that Zodwa's death could be responsible for Sibanda's total loss of political direction.

When I persisted in my efforts to find common ground, proposing that pro-Senate candidates withdraw and that public recriminations stop, Sibanda went public and complained that I was trying to woo him back to the party, which was unacceptable. At that point, I decided to let sleeping dogs lie.

Both the party and I were under siege. I could hardly imagine having to fight on two fronts: my former colleagues as well as Mugabe. The credibility of the MDC itself was seriously affected and many of the MDC's wealthy supporters ceased to help us financially. People started to ask me: 'So, what now?' We had let them down; they had sacrificed their lives for the MDC, and their hopes were suddenly dashed. The party was now without a sound technical administrative unit.

Zanu PF took this opportunity to deploy the entire state machinery against us and many of my former colleagues became a ready source of leakages. They still had close connections in the party who divulged strategic information on our plans and programmes. These were quickly conveyed to Mugabe, who descended on us, directing poisoned arrows at the heart of the party. My relevance and legitimacy as a potential president of Zimbabwe was severely put to the test as people wondered whether I still possessed the stamina and political gravitas to pursue the call and to step up to the podium for another shot.

The solution, as I saw it, rested with the people. If they wanted me out, it was their right to say so. Because of lack of resources it became impossible for us to have the MDC congress in December 2005 as we had originally planned. We postponed it to March 2006 while we embarked on a fund-raising campaign.

I went on a countrywide tour, thanks to the invaluable support I received from business people Makone, Murisi Zwizwai, Jameson Timba and others, to address public meetings and rallies and to assure the people that all was not lost. At my first rally in Bulawayo I was deeply moved by the public response, as the dominant feeling was for unity and transformation. I was humbled by the fact that the MDC's supporters still considered us to be committed to the ideals we had originally set ourselves. Now, with Isaac Matongo, Lucia Matibenga and Nelson Chamisa, I articulated my vision and began to see a recovery of hope.

While I was at the lowest point in my political career, abandoned by top lieutenants and betrayed by people I considered to be friends, Amai Edwin provided a pivotal anchor in my life.

I cannot imagine how I survived the pressure, the talk, the accusations and counter-accusations, the allegations of tribalism and of political ineptitude, and the blame for splitting the MDC. I could easily have buckled under the pressure if Amai Edwin had doubted me or withdrawn her warm encouragement. Where else would I have gone for comfort? I felt isolated and deserted. Even my children could not understand what had hit me. Amai Ed thus became the only trustworthy and honest person I could rely on.

She and I had started off as a simple family. Through our involvement with the people and the sincerity with which we expressed our thoughts, we found ourselves as leaders – symbols of an extremely difficult struggle. We never hid our mistakes or failures from the public, nor did we seek to distort or cover up our shortcomings. Neither of us had a university degree and our academic backgrounds were far from impressive. Yet we were never ashamed of or embarrassed about who we were.

We believed in the people; we knew that in a struggle there is a fine line between staff, activists and politicians. My staff – Mudzingwa, Bango, Makore, Murira, Professor Mukonoweshuro, Makone, Edith Munyaka and even the office orderlies – faced the same challenges as the rest of the country. Together with the politicians, they were in the trenches. Their observations, advice and assistance were fundamental to our cause. For that very reason I had refused to let Ncube fire my personal bodyguards, Nhamo Musekiwa and Washington Gaga. They played a vital role in ensuring the success of the overall party programmes through the support they extended to my work – in most cases without a regular source of income.

We made it through those ugly days. Over the years, I had learnt to swim through vicious currents; to survive the most chaotic of climates. After weathering the storm, in early December 2005 I issued a statement in which I said if Mugabe thought he would get an early Christmas gift out of a dead MDC, all he had received was a rude wake-up call.

Mugabe had attempted a brutal cleansing of MDC supporters in the cities and had engineered internal plots against us. Now the MDC had managed to cleanse itself; we were steadfastly on the road again.

ENDNOTES

1   'Mugabe spies have a secret', *LA Times*, 20 November 2008 http://articles. latimes.com/2008/nov/20/world/fg-cio20
2   Solidarity Peace Trust (27 June 2005). 'Interim report on the Zimbabwean government's "urban cleansing" and forced eviction campaign, May/June 2005.' http://www.solidaritypeacetrust.org/download/report-files/discarding_the_filth.pdf
3   'Report of the Fact-Finding Mission to Zimbabwe to assess the Scope and Impact of Operation Murambatsvina, by the UN Special Envoy on Human Settlements Issues in Zimbabwe, Mrs Anna Kajumulo Tibaijuka.' 18 July 2005 http://ww2.unhabitat.org/documents/ZimbabweReport.pdf UN report on Zim.government
4   The full results were widely published. See, among others, www.eisa.org.za/ PDF/zim05ser.pdf for a complete list of returns

CHAPTER TWENTY-THREE
TORTURE'S REWARD

We should no longer have been surprised by the monstrous brutality of the Mugabe regime. Yet we were in for a shock that even we – an opposition leadership hardened to the mindless state-sponsored thuggery – would find hard to credit. One day in March 2007, men clad in police uniforms hauled me out of my car and hit me with an iron bar, fracturing my skull. I lost so much blood lying on the hot tarmac near Harare Central Police Station that I lost consciousness and could have died there.

My status as effective leader of the opposition gained me no quarter. Meanwhile, fellow leaders and activists were also picked up and beaten mercilessly with iron bars and wooden planks, and were insulted, whipped and kicked, leaving them with broken limbs and serious internal injuries. Also caught in the dragnet were photo-journalist Tsvangirai Mukwazhi and two other journalists reporting for the foreign media. Chairperson of the NCA Glen View constituency, Gift Tandare, was shot and killed in Highfield that same day. We would later declare him our national hero.

It took an emergency application in court – attended by foreign diplomats – to get us released from the clutches of our captors in order to receive medical treatment. Pictures were splashed over world newspapers and widely broadcast showing me with a swollen face and bandaged head, surrounded by colleagues with a range of equally painful injuries. World reaction was one of abhorrence. Now African leaders could no longer continue to watch in silence. In his response, Mugabe looked utterly stupid trying to defend the actions of a police force that was now clearly the criminal arm of a repressive state.

The MDC's internal difficulties paled into insignificance beside this vicious physical onslaught. Obviously the resilience of the MDC in bouncing back from a party breakaway had stretched Mugabe's patience. It had provoked the ruling party to resort to outright bodily assaults on those who dared to question the right of Zanu PF to govern as it pleased – murder and mayhem included. If the razing of urban homes in Operation Murambatsvina had been an act of madness, this latest episode indicated the sheer barbarity of the hoodlums Mugabe now depended on to keep himself in power.

Yet all it did for him was whip up further international condemnation and finally, at long last, spur African leaders to a concerted effort to find a solution.

It had taken almost two years from the 2005 elections to bring us to the point where we were so brutally attacked. In that period, new faces showed themselves in the MDC's leadership and new challenges presented themselves.

After the official split with the Ncube group, new opportunities availed themselves to other politicians inside the MDC for senior party positions. The party started the search for fresh blood. By the end of December 2005, we were almost through with our provincial congresses and there were radical changes to the party leadership countrywide.

Only Morgan Femai, the original Harare provincial chief, retained his position. Other provinces came up with a fresh set of leaders, all drawn from the districts. By then Roy Bennett was out of jail and he never considered joining the Ncube group. In fact, Bennett worked hard to convince Manicaland province to stay with us when it seemed unsure about which way to turn.

Not to be outdone, in February 2006 Ncube and his group organised their own separate congress. Ncube was looking for a party leader. Various names were thrown around, but none from amongst the rebels. I wondered why. If they chose to leave the MDC because of my poor leadership qualities, why were they now desperate for a leader? Why were Sibanda or Ncube himself scared to take over? After all, they had declared that I was a dictator and put themselves forward as leaders in their own right. I failed to understand their motivation – to seek to oust your leader and then struggle to find a replacement.

They knew they were on shaky ground. To worsen their position, while campaigning for the Senate in Binga in October 2005, Sibanda was quoted as advocating a separate state for Matabeleland. He was said to have compared the province's position to that of Lesotho, arguing that if the tiny mountain kingdom could survive as a sovereign state while completely surrounded by South Africa, Matabeleland could easily do the same. The statement was, to say the least, unfortunate for the rebel cause, if not completely self-indulgent for those ethnically inclined to regard the region as special and separate. Secession has never been part of a Matabeleland agenda.

Regarding leadership of the rebels, Chimanikire thought he had it made. In fact, he was talking as if he was already their chief spokesman and obvious leader – denigrating me and explaining his own political vision, with strong support from state media. For the first time, he was a darling of the ZBC and *The Herald* commanding a lot of media space simply because of his incessant attacks on me. Then suddenly the world collapsed around him.

Ncube and his group had shifted their focus to former student leader Arthur Mutambara. How he was selected remains a mystery. Mutambara had led anti-government protests at the University of Zimbabwe in the late 1980s which resulted in his arrest and imprisonment. A student of robotics, he held an Oxford doctorate and was running a technology company in Johannesburg when the Ncube group approached him to offer him the position of president of the breakaway group.

It was an extraordinary gamble. With Mutambara now a clear favourite to lead the group, all hell broke loose. Chimanikire directed his acerbic tongue at Mutambara, accusing him of opportunism and of reaping fruits that he had never planted or nursed. A fight erupted between Ncube and Chimanikire, leaving both stony-faced and embarrassed before a restless public. In the process, hundreds of their supporters started to come back home, to the mainstream MDC.

By bringing in Mutambara, Ncube and his advisers sought to paint a picture of a national movement with a leader who had credible academic and business credentials. The decision was clearly opportunistic and outrightly dishonest: they wanted to hoodwink the majority Shona voters into believing that Mutambara, a Shona, was a perfect replacement for Tsvangirai. However, the stigma of being a mere ethnic splinter group brought their party considerable shame and lack of direction.

The mere idea of 'renting' a leader – a highly inexperienced one at that – was unheard of in the history of political parties and voluntary organisations in Zimbabwe. Indeed, Mutambara's entry into politics was one of the most opportunistic moves I have ever witnessed anywhere. The act contributed significantly to the splinter group's undoing – but by then they had already lost the plot.

Given that the group's core accusation against me was that I had flouted the MDC constitution, the entire proceedings at their so-called congress was simply a farce. Mutambara was imposed on the ashen-faced gang; he made a highly contradictory and confused statement saying he was against the Senate election and yet was now leading a pro-Senate ethnic group. That issue was now in the past, he added. 'Tsvangirai is my hero,' he bellowed to a bemused group baying for my blood.

When I read his speech, I simply shrugged my shoulders in resignation and amazement and told Amai Edwin: 'The more the merrier!'

I had lost touch with Mutambara long before we formed the

MDC. I last met him in 1989 when he was arrested during the student demonstrations against legislative changes that students believed attacked academic freedom. I saw him again after the formation of the MDC when Nelson Chamisa brought him to me for a meeting at which he demanded a position in the party. I told him that I had no power to impose him on the membership. What he had to do was work his way up the party structures.

After perusing a copy of his inaugural speech I realised that one could easily pass through law school, a university or any structured technical training course and still come out totally unfinished as a human being. The speech exposed him as a politically illiterate newcomer, a lay intellectual, requiring time and space to grow up. The narrow technical traits our universities prize as higher learning can easily block our access to wisdom, deform our morals and deplete our intuitive gifts to a point where common sense ceases to be common.

Mutambara's opportunism and public demeanour inspired no confidence that he could confront a dictator in a post-colonial African setting. How would he fight black-on-black oppression in a geographical neighbourhood awash with nostalgic memories of historical victories in liberation wars, deep emotions about race and, above all, with a record of turning a blind eye to the excesses of its erstwhile national comrades-in-arms? Mobilising the poor against a despot is more dangerous and far tougher than pursuing a degree in the comfort of a cosy university, especially one in an advanced and consolidated democracy like Britain or the US.

Mugabe's cabinet had, at various times, included no fewer than ten ministers with earned doctorates from reputable Western universities. They openly boasted to the world about their nationalistic and academic leadership qualities. But with their impressive academic qualifications and understanding of economics as a science, it surprised me that they printed money as a solution, just like semi-literate Idi Amin of Uganda in the 1970s.

Lawyers Lovemore Madhuku, Innocent Chagonda and Selby Hwacha – then Mutambara's close friends – were said to have briefed him at length about Zimbabwe and warned him against taking up the post. Mutambara had been out of Zimbabwe for a long time in cushy circumstances, mainly in the United States and South Africa. He knew little about our struggle, let alone the local price of a loaf of bread – then running into trillions of Zimbabwe dollars whenever it was available on the informal market. But, as a privileged geek, he allowed ambition to kill any doubts.

People expected instant delivery of relief, not Mutambara's inaugural forecast that Zimbabwe might have to wait for up to 30 years to realise a national vision and total freedom. Twenty to 30 more years of suffering? Why?

Mutambara's statements were mixed with doses of nationalist references to the war. He praised Zimbabwean nationalist liberation heroes and offered disjointed phrases about national branding, economics and development. Each time he spoke at a public meeting, more Zimbabweans looked to me, in the mainstream MDC, for sense and national direction. Those who followed him, initially out of respect for his impressive academic qualifications, became even more confused and sceptical about his belief systems.

In March 2006, we convened a proper MDC congress – proper, in terms of the dictates of our founding constitution. The meeting, attended by delegates from all over the country and purely on a voluntary basis, became a major political statement in Zimbabwe's struggle against Mugabe's dictatorship. The commitment exhibited by our party members was phenomenal. Sibanda and the splinter group seemed unclear what their next move should be.

When an interim disciplinary committee, headed by Dr Tichaona Mudzingwa, summoned them for a hearing on the eve of our congress, they indicated a willingness to present their case. Through a lawyer, they asked for more details and later confirmed that they would attend the congress, only to back out at the last moment. They were then officially suspended from the party, pending a determination at congress.

We expected about 5 000 delegates, drawn from our structures, to attend the congress. But we ended up with 18 000. We didn't pay for them to come. They sold their goats, their poultry and other assets just to be at that historic meeting – to revive and to renew the movement. This testimony of a people's dedication to the democratic struggle was incredibly encouraging.

After three days of intense debate, we mapped out the future for Zimbabwe. We charted a course to legitimacy, putting together several signposts to guide our political programme. We identified the need for additional pressure on Mugabe in order to lead the way to a negotiated settlement with a transitional government. A new constitution would have to be drawn up, followed by free and fair elections.

Thokozani Khupe was elected my new deputy, ahead of Gertrude Mtombeni. Khupe, a veteran activist, former railway unionist and secretary of the ZCTU Women's Advisory Council, was a founder member of the MDC. In 2000 she was elected MP for Makokoba in Bulawayo and she retained the seat in 2005. It was a pleasure to have her on board – especially as she would prove her worth in the 2008 election when she would beat Welshman Ncube for the same seat.

Isaac Matongo and Lucia Matibenga retained their posts as national chairman and the leader of the women's assembly respectively. Lovemore Moyo, the new Matabeleland South provincial chairman, took over as Matongo's deputy. Tendai Biti became the new secretary general, after a tight contest with Tapiwa Mashakada, Elton Mangoma and Ian Makone. Mashakada stood again for the deputy secretary general's post and won. I appointed Ian Makone as secretary for elections in the national executive, a decision that irked some in the leadership as Makone and his wife Theresa are close family friends.

Roy Bennett was unchallenged for the post of treasurer. Then, suddenly, Bennett had to flee Zimbabwe after Mugabe tagged him for arrest, forcing us to create a post of deputy treasurer. The state wanted to charge Bennett with treason, saying he had acquired guns and ammunition intended for a bid to assassinate Mugabe. Bennett went into exile in South Africa where he remained until February 2009. The national council later chose Elton Mangoma as Bennett's deputy.

Elias Mudzuri, the former mayor of Harare, flew in from Cambridge,

Massachusetts, where he was studying public administration at Harvard University and was elected organising secretary. Morgan Komichi, the Matabeleland North provincial chairman, was elected his deputy. I had to intervene to secure Komichi's election. Young Dennis Murira, a member of my staff, was challenging him for the post but I felt I needed Komichi's maturity and experience as a former provincial leader.

Mudzuri left for Harvard immediately after his election to complete his studies. When he returned home, there were petty differences between him, his deputy and some senior officials in the national executive committee. In the strained atmosphere after the 2005 elections, fractiousness was common. Another row erupted between Matongo and Matibenga. I think the friction emanated from differences between Evelyn Masaiti, the secretary in the Women's Assembly and Matongo's wife. Masaiti did not see eye to eye with Matibenga. I intervened and resolved the differences, but not in the Women's Assembly. It appeared Matibenga was having trouble keeping the unit together. The women ganged up on her, dominating debate for much of the year.

The stand-off threatened the party once more. Matibenga, a senior politician with a strong trade union background, fought a spirited battle for survival. She is a very effective public speaker but the revolt in the assembly weakened her significantly. I intervened again and tried to make the women see the danger their disagreements posed for the MDC. But I failed to reconcile their differences.

Matibenga then took the fight to the rest of the party when the women decided to have a vote of no confidence in her leadership. Again, I felt I had a personal responsibility to resolve the conflict. The issue became messy and so acrimonious that it was highly divisive. Theresa Makone, supported by Masaiti and Matongo, was behind the challenge on Matibenga's leadership. The CIO took full advantage by actively nursing the conflict. In the end, after the national council intervened, an interim leadership led by Makone – a highly assertive business person – took over.

I could understand the women's concerns about Matibenga's leadership style. I knew that she had many other commitments and was stretching herself too far. She was still heavily involved in the ZCTU, in SATUCC and in other regional bodies. On the other hand, Matibenga was a hard worker and a committed trade unionist and politician. The Matibenga/ Makone fracas dominated debate in the party for much of 2006 and together with other spats it fell to me to spend a large part of the second quarter of 2006 trying to build a cohesive team. The new leaders were so different and fights could erupt so easily within their ranks, with a potential to cascade downwards and contaminate other party structures.

However, the MDC's internal difficulties and personal rifts had no major effect on our alliances with our civil society partners. Working with the Christian Alliance – an assembly of progressive church leaders – we organised a national day of prayer for Zimbabwe on 11 March 2007. All looked set for a successful gathering. It was time to relax.

A day before the event, Amai Edwin arranged a party to celebrate my fifty-fifth birthday. I knew nothing about the party when I returned from Johannesburg where, the night before, I had addressed the annual foreign correspondents dinner. With a few senior party leaders, friends and family, we ate and danced the Saturday night away. A fantastic, home-made cake was sliced up and consumed in the midst of fine speeches while the wine flowed freely. Many showed off their dancing skills, with complex footwork and wriggling behinds – Zimbabwean style – in an electric, but mature and relaxed atmosphere. Such moments of levity were a most necessary antidote to the crushing burden of politics – tinged by fear – that never left us. And well we might have felt that.

On the morning of Sunday, 11 March 2007, we were all set to congregate at Zimbabwe Grounds in Highfield where the prayer meeting was to be held. Then, to my consternation, I received reports that Zanu PF militias, the police and paramilitary forces had sealed off the area. This was just a moment of supplication to the Almighty, after all – why should it bring the police out in force?

Earlier, police cordoned off the offices of the Crisis Coalition of Zimbabwe and those of the Christian Alliance in central Harare. The state suspended normal activity in Highfield, banning church services and other Sunday business. Nevertheless, with clear consciences, we set out on the journey to the stadium. Along the way we thought it wise to stop at the Young Women's Christian Association (YWCA) centre in the adjacent suburb of Kambuzuma to receive reports from our advance teams. When we arrived at the centre, I could see dozens of state agents hanging about. Something was up.

So I decided to leave my own car and to travel into Highfield with Mudzuri in his car. All roads were closed. Police prevented any traffic from entering the suburb. We found an opening in a small side road, shielded by maize fields and tall grass, and drove around the township in order to make a personal assessment of the situation.

There was nobody in sight, other than hundreds of police officers wearing Israeli-made riot control gear with water tank cannons and tear-smoke canisters. What was going on? Had Mugabe decided on a final crackdown? An earlier meeting, scheduled for 18 February, had been thwarted in a similar manner, despite a court order barring the police from interference. After visiting the prayer venue and finding it totally deserted, we drove out and Mudzuri dropped me off at home.

Meanwhile Tendai Biti, the secretary general, and 30 other senior officials and activists were intercepted and taken to Machipisa police station in Highfield. Mutambara and his officials were also picked up but they were quickly taken out of the area. As I sat at home waiting for the rest of the leadership to return for a meeting, I received a call from Machipisa informing me that my officials had been arrested. I waited for additional information but there was an ominous silence – no more telephone calls – and when I tried to reach my people there was no reply.

Concerned, I drove to Machipisa police station. On arrival, I was pulled out of my car with my driver and aides and thrown into a fenced courtyard between the main charge office and the police cells. I saw to my horror that my colleagues were being beaten to a pulp. There was agonised screaming as men and women in police uniforms attacked the hapless MDC leaders and activists with iron bars, whips, booted feet and wooden planks.

I had gone to the police station to try to find out what was happening, never suspecting that I was falling into a trap. Suddenly I was struck on the head, close to the right eye, with an iron bar. I was roughly pushed to the ground, as were my assistants, Nhamo Musekiwa and Carter Mudzingwa, and driver Simba Mujeye.

We were mercilessly beaten amid a stream of verbal abuse. The attack on me lasted for about 20 minutes but my colleagues endured the brutality for much longer. I was worried by the amount of blood I was losing and feared that that was it; that this would be the end of me.

Groggy as we were, we were ordered to move to a waiting drop-side, open truck, told to lie down and driven to Harare Central Police Station. Sekai Holland, Grace Kwinjeh, a one-legged activist whose name I never got to know, Madhuku, Biti, Mangoma, Bango, Chamisa, Mudzingwa and several activists from the MDC and the NCA could hardly walk.

After alighting on the hot tarmac near Harare Central, we were ordered to lie face-down, before being shepherded inside the station's parched grass grounds. There we were advised to 'rest' for a while. There was blood everywhere. I finally passed out, oblivious to my surroundings for an indefinite period. Madhuku suddenly sprang up and started to remonstrate with a senior police officer: 'How can you treat a national political leader like this?' he demanded, referring to me. 'What kind of society is this …?' Officers dashed towards Madhuku, ordering him to shut up and remain flat on the ground.

I feared the worst for all of us and dreaded a repeat of the beatings. Later in the day, we were back on the hot truck – to be dropped off at various police stations. I was taken to Harare's Borrowdale police station. This continued until early evening as my colleagues were being separated and shunted off to various centres. What was our crime?

For two days, injured and uncared-for, we shared cells with common criminals, unsure of our fate. I was lucky in that a sympathetic police officer from Borrowdale police station secretly called Amai Edwin and advised her of my whereabouts.

She promptly brought food and water. My other colleagues spent two days without anyone knowing their whereabouts or their fate. The situation was far worse for Grace Kwinjeh, who was followed by military intelligence operatives at Braeside police station and singled out for a further beating, despite her already broken bones, causing her serious internal injuries and a ruptured eardrum.

The attacks paralysed the MDC For 48 hours. Once again, my staff – Professor Mukonoweshuro, Makone, Mudzingwa and Murira – mounted an aggressive international campaign, alerting most diplomatic missions to our plight. Vice-president Thokozani Khupe other senior party officials played a key role in directing and coordinating the effort. For two days, the MDC's lawyers struggled to locate the entire group. Two High Court orders were secured, ordering the police to say where we were and to release us. As usual, Mugabe ignored the court orders.

On Tuesday morning we were taken back to Harare Central. I saw that Mutambara and his group were already there. I did not know that they had been arrested as well, but they were not assaulted. After the police recorded statements, we were taken to the magistrate's court. The place resembled a military camp; heavily armed police were both in and outside the courts – something to which our lawyers, led by Advocate Eric Matinenga, vehemently objected. Our lawyers further argued that before any formal charges were made, we needed medical attention.

Eventually, the magistrate ordered that I be allowed to see a doctor. I refused, insisting that we had all suffered the same fate and had to be treated in the same way. My injuries were far less serious than those of Holland and Kwinjeh, who could hardly remain upright during the short proceedings. Finally, the state gave in and ambulances were brought to ferry the group to a private clinic. Under police guard, many were detained for treatment and surgery.

So severe were the injuries to Holland and Kwinjeh that doctors recommended that they be flown to South Africa for specialist attention. Mugabe callously refused to allow this, forcing the MDC to resort to the courts again for relief. The whole story was now in the open. Almost all Western diplomats accredited to Harare were at the courts to get a glimpse of limping, badly bruised MDC activists. African diplomats tend to shy away from such matters, perhaps for fear of being accused of interfering in the internal affairs of sovereign states – the traditional guiding philosophy of the African Union!

Publicity had its outcome. The torture brought its rewards. For the first time, SADC convened an extraordinary meeting in Tanzania. A few days later, SADC forced Mugabe to talk to us – and that was when the negotiations began, with a limited degree of seriousness. Mugabe thought he could still wriggle out of any responsibility. The talks dragged on for the next 18 months without much progress.

Then, quite capriciously, Mugabe unilaterally decreed an election date for 29 March 2008, leaving us with little time to prepare. Equally surprisingly, Mutambara and the MDC splinter group approached me with a proposal for unity. Sincerely believing that this could finally put an end to our differences, I welcomed the move and put together a negotiating team. But after long hours of debate and discussion, we failed to agree on a common position. The more I thought about it, the less I trusted the motives behind their sudden change in attitude.

To Mutambara and Ncube, I was suddenly the founding president of the MDC, worthy of respect. I found this behaviour disingenuous: only a year before they had told the world that I was a dictator, worse than Mugabe. The plan was for the united MDC to back my candidature but with far-reaching trade-offs – all designed to benefit their beleaguered camp.

One point of contention was a demand that we share the parliamentary and local government seats equally. Mutambara had already identified a safe seat in Harare's northern suburbs. Except for the Bulawayo-based politicians, others in the group were also beginning to carve out areas of influence, even though they knew that alone or with Mutambara as their leader they stood no chance.

On their own, they wouldn't be able to exert any influence: they were much too small, totally unable to field a sufficient number of candidates countrywide. The main fear in the MDC, however, was that absorbing them back into our team, as passengers, as it were, was likely to dishearten our supporters. Such a scenario would have guaranteed Zanu PF a clear victory.

I was fairly flexible, guided by the long view and seriously believing in unity. The rest of the party refused to accede to Mutambara's demands. The

MDC resolved to go into the election alone despite my spirited appeals and arguments for unity of purpose. When a negative national council decision was communicated to Mutambara, he went ballistic, calling me an 'intellectual midget' who was unable to dictate orders to my party, a weak and indecisive leader, and a man completely lacking in what he called political gravitas.

From a barrage of public statements denigrating my person it was clear that Mutambara was a very disappointed man. He had hoped to ride on Tsvangirai's back to secure unearned power while his colleagues saw the opportunity as a sanitised way of returning to the party. Once again, the Ncube group was desperate for a leader. Mutambara was a lightweight without a political brand and unsuitable as a presidential candidate.

CHAPTER TWENTY-FOUR

VICTORY AND FLIGHT

If a week is a long time in politics, a year is an absolute eternity. The year 2008 dawned with high hopes for the success of the MDC in elections, with the possibility that I myself might take the presidency. Yet it was in this year, after winning the elections, that I found myself on the run from a vengeful ruling clique that refused to give up power. Having lost to the MDC, military elements in Zanu PF carried out what can only be described as a quiet coup – keeping Robert Mugabe as president but in effect taking control behind the scenes. Our spirits soared with victory and then plunged as the year dragged us through the depths of despair.

Things began hopefully. In January 2008, in a meeting with Mugabe, Simba Makoni assured the old man that news stories in the privately owned media indicating a potential split in Zanu PF were baseless and that he was still a loyal member of the party. This was despite the fact that he had contested a Zanu PF primary election for a parliamentary seat in Manicaland and lost. But the day after Mugabe announced 7 February as the date for the nomination of candidates for the 2008 election, Makoni made a surprise about turn, offering himself to the nation as an independent presidential candidate. He claimed to have a large following within Zanu PF, ready to defect and to support his bid. There was turmoil in Mugabe's camp. In general, the disorder caused by Makoni's arrival on the scene was both a curse and a blessing: it rekindled the people's interest in politics. There was a sudden upsurge in the registration of new voters, mainly among young people.

To Arthur Mutambara, Makoni came as an unexpected gift. He knew Makoni wanted a back-up team. He seized the opportunity and offered him support. Sensing danger, and to contain the emerging threat from within Zanu PF, Mugabe postponed the dates for the nominating process to find time to whip his fracturing party back into line. To amplify the confusion, Dumiso Dabengwa, a former ZAPU intelligence supremo, and Thenjiwe Lesabe – both of them fellow Zanu PF Kremlin-style politburo members – deserted Mugabe and sided with Makoni. There were whispers of more earth-shaking defections from Zanu PF.

Makoni's sudden presence as a player caused havoc within the MDC's middle-class and business support base. Many saw Makoni as a great candidate, a fighter from within Mugabe's inner circle, and a politician assumed to have the backing of the Solomon Mujuru faction of Zanu PF. The importance of the Mujuru faction, in the eyes of the propertied class, rested on a distorted view that, as a retired army general, Mujuru controlled the military and the security establishment – then seen as a significant factor in a stable power transfer in the event of a collapse of Mugabe's rule.

Unfortunately for him, Makoni's new party, Mavambo/Kusile/Dawn (MKD) was so loose that its threat to my candidature was minimal. I knew that Makoni would cream off some of my supporters and fence-sitters. But his main catchment area by far appeared to be his former home ground, Zanu PF. For a while, I was a bit unsettled by suggestions that I should work with Makoni. There was a lot of pressure, especially from some sections of the business and diplomatic communities for me to allow Makoni to be the lead candidate.

After listening to his public statements, it dawned on me that Makoni's views were essentially in line with Zanu PF values; his political philosophy was essentially in accordance with Zanu PF's policies. Such an ideological position was at variance with the founding values of the MDC. I tried to argue that I already had a team while Makoni was still searching for one, but some of my supporters refused to hear me out.

I told them that taking Makoni on board would cause dissension within our ranks. I believe I was proved right in the end. Working with Makoni under such unclear circumstances would have been political suicide. The sparkle went out of his temporary glitter after his assumed handler, General Mujuru, publicly disowned him. Mujuru's rejection was a big blow to Makoni's claims that he had dozens of sleeping Zanu PF giants ready to cross the floor from Zanu PF to his one-man organisation.

Meanwhile our national council shored up our campaign by announcing that it was fully ready to take on Mugabe, Makoni and any other aspirants in the presidential race. The council was raring to go. Earlier, we had rejected Mutambara's attempt to talk us into an elite pact. Although the MDC had expressed discontent with the gerrymandering of constituencies, a biased demarcation of electoral boundaries and the attendant confusion that followed the process, we had nevertheless readied ourselves for a tough contest.

We managed to field candidates in 209 parliamentary constituencies; all but a few hundred seats in some 1 958 local councils; and 59 of the 60 Senate seats on offer.

I accepted a request from our party leaders in western Zimbabwe to let Jonathan Moyo take the Tsholotsho parliamentary constituency on the understanding that by so doing, we would avoid splitting the vote in favour of Zanu PF. With hindsight, this was a serious mistake and we gained nothing from it.

Other than that, by and large, I fielded what I considered to be a strong national team despite some setbacks. Problems arose especially in the Midlands, where, due to unending political turf squabbles, some areas fielded two candidates from the MDC. Despite our protests to the ZEC for their disqualification, these constituencies went into an election with two individuals registered as MDC candidates. This confused the voters and split the vote. Zimbabwe uses the 'first past the post' electoral system. If a party fails to whip its candidates into line and two officials from the same organisation lodge their papers using the same party name and symbols, these candidates split the party's votes among themselves. What this means is that a minority party candidate can slightly edge the two out. I did my best to persuade the feuding candidates to give each other a chance for the sake of the party. I failed. And of course it was against the rules, but the Zanu PF-aligned nomination courts accepted their nomination papers in order to split the MDC vote.

As I campaigned I could feel that I had the upper hand. My main problem was money. Makoni, as a new and exciting kid on the block, was an instant attraction within big business, the diplomatic community and in certain circles of wealthy financiers. They all rushed to him.

With his photogenic, wrinkle-free face and lanky, agile frame, Makoni temporarily stole the limelight as the political Casanova of the time. His courage was buoyed by public street shows, which attracted easily persuaded urban onlookers. Zimbabweans waylaid Makoni's entourage in dilapidated shopping malls and dusty streets as he embarked on his walkabout-style campaign. Little did Makoni and his team know that the curious bystanders cheering them on were merely interested in MKD's handouts – in the form of cash, gifts, food and trinkets which they lavishly distributed among the people.

We went into the election on a shoestring budget. Much of our support came by way of small donations from supporters and friends, and through fuel coupons from our external branches, many of which adopted a number of constituencies. Unlike previous elections, the campaign period was relatively free of direct violence. Restrictions on public meetings were relaxed and the MDC worked around the clock, sending out our message deep into the countryside. We even made tremendous inroads in rural Mashonaland thanks to limited violence. For the first time, we were able to penetrate that Zanu PF heartland.

Our message made a lot of sense. The entire country was like a place coming out of a war, with no functioning schools, hospitals or other public amenities. There was a cry for rehabilitation, for recovery and for reconstruction. Hunger and famine were everywhere, roads were impassable and the people were racked by poverty and years of state-sponsored violence. We spoke of the need for a fresh start; Zimbabwe was at the end of its tether and badly in need of radical change.

For two months, we stirred up the entire country with a cacophony of MDC voices clamouring for change. While on the campaign trail, I noticed that Zanu PF was extremely weak on the ground. Zanu PF candidates were struggling to make sense of their party's message of one hundred per cent black empowerment, given the sorry state of our rural areas. Zanu PF could no longer talk of land reform. Poverty and extreme food shortages had turned the so-called new farmers into hunter-gatherers. Poaching had replaced agriculture in the invaded commercial farms. People ate what they gathered, literally on a day to day basis.

On the morning of Saturday, 29 March 2008, Amai Ed and I received numerous calls from all over Zimbabwe. There was much excitement and a phenomenal turnout. People began to queue at polling stations from as early as dawn, especially in the rural areas. Their interest in this race meant a lot to me. Mugabe and Zanu PF thrived on apathy; a huge turnout always favoured the MDC.

At about 10 o'clock in the morning, we left for Avondale Primary School near our Harare home to cast our ballots. There was a winding queue of excited voters. After a brief chat with a few along the way, we went into the station. My aides asked the presiding officer if we could be allowed to jump the queue, which was duly agreed to.

I could feel my heart lift as I completed the ballots and placed them in the four respective ballot boxes: for the local ward councillor, the MP, the senator and the president.

After dropping Amai Ed at home, I went around Harare visiting various polling stations. I returned home later that afternoon to prepare myself for a long night of reports and accounts from my staff, my party agents, candidates and senior officials all over Zimbabwe.

At around midnight, news of results began to filter in. All indications were that we had done extremely well everywhere, even in areas where we lost. We were awake the entire night, sifting through the news from all over the country. At dawn on Sunday, I began to receive the real results from most of our candidates – both winners and losers. By the end of the day, I knew I had won the election. The bulk of figures reflected a definite victory in parliament. At the time, we estimated that we had about 120 parliamentary seats.

There was a slight delay in the collation of presidential figures, but I was positive that if I had won control of the legislature, there was no way I could have lost the presidency. The results began to trickle in on Monday morning – and they showed an even more positive trend. There were many areas where I was ahead of Mugabe, other presidential hopefuls and even my own MPs and senators.

Mugabe had failed to realise that as a person he was a separate election issue. Many in his party felt comfortable to retain their Zanu PF legislators, especially outside his Mashonaland West base, but no longer saw Mugabe as fit for the presidency.

There were several separate campaigns within the main Zanu PF campaign. I know of many Zanu PF candidates who openly pleaded with their supporters to feel free in their choice for a president. Some argued that they now wanted Makoni to take over Zanu PF from Mugabe. There was a deep division in Zanu PF between these two campaigns – one for the local representative and the other for a president.

We created our own national centre to receive and collate the results. Looking back, I now realise that this was a mistake, that we failed to handle this aspect properly. We should have insisted that as a country we needed a single centre, open to the media, to handle all the results and to publish and broadcast them whenever they became available. Initially we did propose the setting up of such a facility, but Zanu PF argued that it would render useless the role of the Electoral Commission. I am sure this refusal was grounded in Zanu PF's fear that the nation would tend to see our figures as more credible than those from the ZEC.

We experienced serious communication difficulties. The police distorted the figures as many senior officers were keen to see Zanu PF remain in power. We did not have an immediate and effective alternative set of statistics. This was unfortunate – a potential source of national instability. Our limitations and communication failures affected the collation of figures and results and distorted the outcome in a fundamental way. I know that, in hindsight, it is always easy to blame poor planning and ineptitude, but resources equal results. Without money, the MDC did the best it could under the circumstances.

To add to the confusion, the Zimbabwe Electoral Support Network (ZESN) – a civil society umbrella body – analysed a sample from the stations they surveyed and came up with an estimated result which showed that although I had won the presidential election, my victory was insufficient for me to assume power. This estimate denied me an outright majority, giving Mugabe and Zanu PF a momentary whiff of comfort.

But I was convinced that I had won the election. I saw the behaviour of the official electoral commission as a way to lull Zanu PF supporters into believing that all was well on Mugabe's part. For instance, the ZEC would announce results from Chiredzi South, 500 kilometres south of Harare where Zanu PF would have won, ahead of the tally in central Harare, in favour of the MDC. In their broadcasts, the electoral commission, still headed by Chiweshe, made sure that whenever our legislator was the victor, the next winner or two would have to come from Zanu PF – as a way of managing Zanu PF's emotions. For close to 72 hours Zimbabwe was on a knife-edge, completely unaware of what the final official result was.

In the end, Chiweshe told us that we had won 99 seats, Zanu PF, 97 seats, and Mutambara, 10. Jonathan Moyo, an independent, also made it to parliament. We now controlled the legislature. Then everything suddenly turned sour. After completing the announcement of the parliamentary returns in which Zanu PF was a clear loser, the ZEC imposed a blackout on the presidential outcome. I protested, but to no avail. In exasperation we agreed to go public with our figures. Biti announced my victory over Mugabe to the world, suggesting a clear lead that did not even require a run-off election. Biti's figures were based on the returns the MDC compiled from each polling station.

Chiweshe and his team dug in, claiming that they were still working out the figures – a process that went on for five solid weeks. In the meantime, Biti was in trouble. The police were after him with threats of all sorts of charges. It was clear that Mugabe was very disappointed. He was under the impression that everything was under control. When the election results became public, his advisers had to find a way of retaining power by refusing to accept the reality.

That was the cause of the delay in the official announcement of both the parliamentary and presidential results; the manipulation behind the scenes; the power struggles in Zanu PF; as well as the vexed question of how to give up power – or at least to save the party and its leader from humiliation. I saw that the hardliners were not ready to give up power, a position later confirmed by Mugabe. Mugabe did not know or understand what had hit him. I heard later that he had to be persuaded to put on a brave face, to concede that he had lost – but not sufficiently to give up power.

In the interim, I started to prepare an alternative administration. I had a transitional team devising a transitional mechanism and suggesting various departments and ministries.

All that was left were firm appointments and taking over the government. In the midst of all this, I received a telephone call from Elton Mangoma saying that Zanu PF politburo member Nicholas Goche had been in touch, indicating that he needed to talk to the MDC on the transitional mechanisms now that we had won the elections. According to Goche, Mugabe had agreed to step down and to ensure a smooth power transfer there was a need for us to take some of their senior Zanu PF winners into a coalition administration.

Previous elections in 2000, 2002 and 2005 were confused fights. In 2008, Mugabe and Zanu PF had no choice other than to accept that they had lost. No matter how hard they tried to adjust the figures or delay the announcement, the evidence was too overwhelming. It was an outright win – and Goche's mission confirmed this development. Goche did not speak of a run-off. He was pleading for Zanu PF's accommodation in our government, an MDC government. Before the military generals stepped in, Goche suggested that we take five of their senior officials into our new administration. I was relieved to hear about Goche's move. He told us that by Sunday, 30 March 2008, Mugabe already had the full results. Here was a trusted negotiator appointed by Mugabe coming to reason with us. I never thought he could be on a fishing expedition.

I was surprised, therefore, to hear Thabo Mbeki tell a press conference that there was going to be a run-off in the presidential election long before the results were announced. There were other comments here and there, even in SADC, to the effect that there would never be an outright winner. I wondered where their information was coming from. Mugabe soon joined the run-off chorus. How did he know, when ZEC was still holding on to the official results? How did Mbeki know? What was this run-off business all about? I was unaware that the law had been changed to deny a winner without 50 per cent plus one vote to take over government. It must have slipped my mind at the time when it went through parliament. I did not know that in such an event, a run-off would be needed between the two leading candidates.

The military, Mugabe and Mbeki started to make a case for a run-off. They knew that such a contest would be held in a climate of intense intimidation and violence. Some of the responses to my victory from SADC were so mealy-mouthed that I felt completely isolated. It was a terrible mistake for some respectable African leaders to endorse Mugabe's open fraud.

I felt demoralised and helpless by the turn of events. I had won two elections in a row but still failed to execute the people's mandate. For a moment I did not know what to do. I had no arms of war. I lacked the necessary wherewithal to force myself into power to fulfil the people's wish.

I had believed that Goche had Mugabe's mandate. If he was fishing, then he had made a very adventurous move. Our talks with him continued throughout Tuesday, 1 April. But when an uncompromising Zanu PF clique met Mugabe the following day, things changed even more dramatically. Military and security chiefs and some senior Zanu PF hardliners refused to give in.

A civil-military junta took over and refused to hand over power to the MDC. The hardliners were mere followers; the real political managers, as in 2000 and 2002, were from the military. It was an armed takeover of government. They refused to budge, denouncing the election results and whipping Mugabe into line through a soft coup d'état.

Goche suddenly disappeared from the scene; all communication channels were cut off; he even ignored Mangoma's telephone calls. Under pressure from his security chiefs, Mugabe turned on Goche and obviously succeeded in terrifying and gagging him. In subsequent public statements, Mugabe publicly confirmed that he had been approached by war veterans and received the order. He said he no choice but to comply. I understood later that the JOC had intervened, ordering Mugabe and Zanu PF to stay in office. This body coordinated the police, military and intelligence services, and had gained sway over all national affairs, including the economy.

Mugabe threw a tantrum, spluttering unconnected emotions: liberation war credentials; the uselessness of the ballot in a nation's sovereignty; guns to protect the nation against imperialists and their puppets – Mugabe's usual sobs. As a hostage with a temporary lease on life, he became totally pigheaded and off-topic and he condemned the elections, claiming the ballot was rigged in my favour. It all amounted to a lot of incomprehensible whimpering. Naturally, he accused whites and the West of attempting to bring about regime change by covert and overt means: secretly stage-managing the opposition in Zimbabwe while imposing economic sanctions on the country.

On the instructions of the JOC, in April 2008 the police raided the MDC headquarters, Harvest House, and the offices of the ZESN in Harare and arrested 215 'activists'. These included women and children who were not activists but refugees displaced by the post-election violence in rural Mashonaland. The raid involved about 500 police officers and Zanu PF youth militias in military uniform. Most of those picked up were nursing serious injuries from the violence. The police seized computers, office files and party records. They said they were looking for evidence that the organisation had been infiltrated by the MDC to manipulate the results and what they described as 'subversive material likely to be used to overthrow a constitutionally elected government'. We challenged the raid in court and won. The High Court ordered that those arrested be released, but the police refused to do so immediately.

The US government strongly criticised Mugabe for failing Zimbabwe, remarks which seemed to anger Harare even further. Soon afterwards, the UN Security Council convened a special session on Zimbabwe with the view of dispatching a special envoy to Harare. But Mbeki blocked the move, thus giving Mugabe an opportunity to denounce the UN as harbouring a 'sinister, racist and colonial' attitude.

We tried without success to communicate with some top officials in the military. Military generals were part of the Zanu PF structures and decision-making machinery. By refusing to go, Mugabe was now the de facto leader of a military junta, not a legitimate government. As a loser but with the backing of the military, Mugabe foisted himself upon the nation.

By delaying the announcement of the final score, Chiweshe was manipulating the vote to create grounds for a run-off. Under a run-off election, conducted by the military, Mugabe expected to force a win in order to claim some form of legitimacy.

I don't know whether or not Mugabe informed Mbeki about his predicament but, surprisingly, Mbeki quickly threw himself into the ring, saying the result was inconclusive. Mugabe then ordered Chiweshe to come up with an inconclusive result. Chiweshe had a hard time manipulating a result which everyone already knew about – hence the unreasonable delay of five weeks.

While the nation waited uneasily, Dr Tichaona Mudzingwa, our party portfolio secretary for defence, a senior war veteran and a retired colonel, revived his contacts to ascertain the mood of the military. At no point did he seek to incite his former comrades to rebel; he merely wanted to evaluate the mood. This was important. As the party that had won the election, there was no way we could ignore the feelings of the military. We had to open up our lines of communication. Up to this point, we had never had any live communication channels with the military – and this was our first attempt at getting there.

After extensive checks, Dr Mudzingwa reported that he found a positive attitude towards Mugabe's loss within the security forces. I never assigned him to this specific mission; it was his own initiative. However, he did encounter some pockets of resistance to change, especially at the top. In his view, the problem lay with a few commanders. But generally, Dr Mudzingwa told me, he was assured of cooperation during the transition and a smooth power transfer, should Mugabe openly accept the people's verdict. As far as the security forces were concerned, they were professionals keen to support the government of the day and to respect the wish of the people.

Intense anxiety built up locally and abroad over the delays in the announcement of the presidential election results. I constantly voiced my frustration in my regular briefs to the diplomatic community.

I thought Africa could seize on the moment and confront Mugabe. Maybe it did behind the scenes – but I doubt it. Africa, as my home, is my natural source of comfort. But Africa and its attitude towards change can spawn major disappointment at the same time. Africa always deceives itself into believing that all is well, when everybody – friend and foe alike – can see through such an open lie. We rush to cry 'victim' when many of our woes are self-inflicted. Africans are notorious for self-delusion and denial; we work so hard to please, to be polite, even when it is totally unnecessary and dangerous.

There was no harm to Africa if it rose and told Mugabe off as a way of expressing solidarity with the people of Zimbabwe. The so-called principle of non-interference in the sovereign affairs of our neighbours is a cover for political corruption, indecision and a desire to deny the evidence of malpractices and unprofessional conduct.

In Harare, the civil-military junta could read the people's mood: the people felt betrayed by the so-called democratic system. Although they appeared calm, deep in their hearts they were rebellious and frustrated – impossible to govern. So the junta turned its attention to me. It began to mount pressure against me, whispering threats and planning to take me out. I really feared for my life. The merchants of violence and proponents of a failed state were out to liquidate me, while Africa watched from a safe distance and remained mum.

While I was chairing a meeting of our national executive at Harvest House, news began to pour in of nationwide violence against my supporters, my agents and our miserable workers and peasants. Mugabe and the military had once again launched a blitz on the nation in an onslaught Mugabe code-named *Operation Mavhotera Papi*. Loosely translated, it means 'Operation how did you vote?'

Thousands were displaced and began to trek to our offices in Harare for refuge, often covering long distances on foot. Senior military officials had taken charge of various provinces, coordinating a campaign of reprisals and retribution against a defenceless population.

The ballot papers were moved to a secret location without consultation and my election agents Chris Mbanga and Morgan Komichi were told bluntly by Chiweshe: 'Here is the result. Take it or leave it.' The ZEC knew that the figures would not add up – and their fiddling became so obvious that the announced result was a sick joke. They took some of the ballots in my favour and donated them to both Makoni and Mugabe.

The ZEC told the nation, five weeks after the election, that Mugabe had secured 1,079,730 votes – or 43.2 per cent – against my 1,195,562 which they said translated to 47.9 per cent. The remainder was shared between Makoni and an unknown candidate identified as Langton Towungana.

As Harare is the window to the world because of the large numbers of foreign aid workers and diplomats, I was informed that part of the plan involved getting straight at my person as quickly as possible in order to minimise Mugabe's embarrassment. This time Mugabe was determined to strike at what he called the 'head of the MDC snake', Morgan Tsvangirai.

Things had taken a turn for the worse, much worse. Given the numerous reports of plots against my life, I decided to take action. I left the national executive meeting in session, politely proffering a lame excuse to wash my hands. In my mind, Mugabe's behaviour was a cause for serious concern. I drove straight home, deep in thought. Where is SADC? Where is Africa?

Why can't they respect the voice of Zimbabwe?

I couldn't go to South Africa. I feared Mbeki's personal hostility towards me. I couldn't go to Mozambique; I had doubts about my security there too. Malawi was out; Bingu wa Mutharika was Mugabe's bosom buddy. His close relations worked as Mugabe's security advisers in the secret service. He owned a commercial farm in Kadoma, 140 kilometres west of Harare. The Malawi leader was facing a revolt from his party and parliament. As president, he was in a most precarious position, considered illegitimate by his own people. Zambia was tricky, unpredictable, weak and non-committal. With slight intimidation from Mugabe, Lusaka could change its face so easily.

So, I opted for Botswana. President Ian Khama was a sympathetic ally: he had come out very strongly against what was happening in Harare. He strongly condemned Mugabe and the deteriorating situation and flatly refused to be cajoled into submission; nor did he buy into the outdated Zanu PF anti-West nationalistic mantra. I did not know Khama personally, but because of his passion for stability in Zimbabwe, he had advised me through an emissary that I should feel free to come to Botswana whenever I felt threatened. It was only natural that a friendship should develop between us, even though circumstances had pushed us towards each other.

Yes, Khama had a military background, but we shared the same values on democracy. He is a young leader, a product of my generation; he has different views from those of older African nationalists. We share a similar vision for the region, for SADC and for Africa. As I prepared for a desperate journey out of my motherland, I saw through the weaknesses of the much-quoted African template of solutions to Africa's problems. There are always serious divisions and conflicting visions, never unanimity. In Zimbabwe's case, for instance, the continent knew Mugabe had lost an election for the second time in a row but still failed to reach a common position with his opposition. Senior Nigerian politicians later told me that while they accepted that elections can be rigged, when that happens, no responsible leader should be allowed to unleash a national army on to unarmed civilians simply to claim victory. That was a fundamental point.

In our case, it was obvious that Mugabe lost the election but was refusing to give up power; yet there remained a general acceptance that Mugabe should stay in office. In 2002, there were doubts about me as an individual and as a politician; there were questions over the size of my muscle to take over the state. Questions were often raised as to whether my leadership could lead to sustainable peace and security in Zimbabwe.

It was clear in 2008 that Africa still clung to that same viewpoint. Many African leaders felt that an MDC administration could prove a recipe for general destabilisation of our society. There was opposition in the military and within the partisan security sector; and there was a general solidarity with Mugabe because of his liberation record.

But I think, over time, through our diplomatic forays in Africa, a fresh perspective began to emerge. A new generation of leaders was in power. These included Jakaya Kikwete of Tanzania, Levy Mwanawasa of Zambia, Raila Odinga of Kenya and Ian Khama in Botswana. Even South Africa was not unanimous in its position: there were divisions in the ANC and within its alliance partners. Progressively, many started to search for alternatives to the Zimbabwean crisis and to grant us an audience.

In Mozambique, there was a change of attitude as well after Joaquim Chissano retired. President Armando Guebuza appeared more cautious and measured. This was good news to us because historically Mozambique tended to be sympathetic to Mugabe. Another surprise to me was the changed thinking of a veteran and stubborn African fighter, President José Eduardo dos Santos of Angola. Initially he had supported Mugabe, but later felt his actions were unjustified. This only reinforced my belief in the power and influence of peer pressure. It works, and I think it worked on Mugabe in the end.

As I sat in my study considering a variety of options and thinking about the security threat against my person, I figured out a plan to work hard on Africa. I needed to raise the budding momentum for democracy.

Soon after dusk, I sneaked out of Harare in the company of family friend Pearson Mungofa, the MP for Highfield, and Dr Mudzingwa, our security chief, and headed for Bulawayo with the intention of getting into Botswana under the cover of darkness. Ian Makone had made all the arrangements with Khama's office.

Between Bulawayo and the Plumtree border post, Mungofa and Dr Mudzingwa, who were in the lead vehicle, suddenly rammed into a broken-down bus that was obstructing the poorly lit road. The collision was so serious that the two were only saved by the vehicle's airbags. My car almost crashed into them from behind, but my alert driver, Simba Mujeye, quickly swerved off the road and we avoided harm. Mungofa's latest family acquisition, a new, all-terrain car was completely destroyed. I stopped a few metres away to check. When I realised that none of us were injured, I resumed my journey with Mujeye and a single aide. We arrived at the border post, cleared ourselves and made it safely into Botswana.

I was immediately accorded high-level state protection and we set off for Gaborone. I was accommodated in a state house where I was free to stay for as long as I wished, according to Khama, who kept me up to date on Zimbabwean CIO spy missions sent to check on my activities.

Zanu PF's immediate response was to mount a negative propaganda campaign against me while intensifying its brutality against the people at home. I received a continuous stream of news of thousands of internal refugees and displaced persons now camping at our party headquarters in Harare. Food was short and many needed medical care. The whole of the countryside was unsafe. Zanu PF had deployed the military in full force, targeting our election agents and civil servants, especially teachers, for unrestrained punishment.

I knew time was not on my side, so I took the opportunity to visit our neighbours on a diplomatic initiative: Tanzania, Zambia, Angola, South Africa and Mozambique. The only country I did not visit was Malawi, but my main intention was to impart the message to all 14 SADC countries that a common understanding must be reached.

While I was away, there was mounting turmoil in the MDC. A leadership crisis was emerging and they needed assurance from me about what I was doing. For its part, Zanu PF was adding fuel to a roaring blaze. Mugabe thought an opportunity remained for him to mount an effective assault against the MDC and me. No one in the MDC leadership possessed the necessary pulling power, in my absence, to keep the party together. We had won an election, that was true. But we lost political power to a civil-military junta.

The country was in a serious crisis. Mugabe and the junta could not even appoint a substantive cabinet.

With its leader away from home, the MDC was beginning to feel the strain. The party was saddled with hundreds of internal refugees at its Harare office. I felt that I had to return to Zimbabwe to stabilise the party and to face the consequences. I decided to leave Botswana via South Africa, where I prepared for my return. I called the MDC leadership – the standing committee – to Johannesburg for a situation analysis and review. We then started to work on my return.

But I had made some inroads through my diplomatic offensive while in Gaborone. The whole world now condemned what was happening in Zimbabwe. Large parts of Africa and beyond were now on my side – and therefore I knew that Mugabe would not dare touch me.

Over the years, I have learnt that Mugabe is a pathological coward, a man who easily gets angry if he feels he can bully another while using his peers as guards. If you stand up to him, he quickly claims a victim image – distorting Zimbabwe's colonial history and blaming the country's sensitive past for his own mistakes.

From Harare airport, I drove straight to the Avenues Clinic to visit survivors of Zanu PF's spree of violence, most of them from Mashonaland provinces. The hospital was full of seriously injured people with broken limbs, perforated buttocks and the marks of barbed wire whips all over their bodies. It was a sorry sight. When I walked in, they lifted their mangled bodies, smiled and urged me to soldier on. 'Together to the end, Mr President,' one young man shouted, comforted by my unexpected visit.

I then had a press conference at the Meikles Hotel, visited the refugees at Harvest House, and convened an executive council meeting before going home.

Despite the traumatic scenes in the hospital and at Harvest House, the executive decided to go into the run-off election. If no one – especially in Africa – could see for themselves and accept that we had won this election, then our choices were severely limited. We had to take part in the run-off.

Earlier, SADC as a bloc insisted that all contestants must certify the election result as correct for Zimbabwe to have a legitimate administration. Mugabe persisted in disputing my victory, together with his service chiefs and Mbeki. I didn't see any reason in arguing and told them that if the circumstances required a run-off poll, we should proceed with it for the sake of a smooth transition. I had no problems with that. I knew I was going to win again.

I didn't mind having to go through the process again, even though I knew that my victory in the 29 March 2008 election had been stolen from me. My only worry was the impact of the involvement of the military on an already bullied civilian population in the supposedly democratic process.

Once more I energised the campaign teams. I was ready to finish Mugabe off, but the ground we were to traverse was now very bumpy indeed. I spent ten days in Matabeleland, only to realise that the whole state machinery had been mobilised into action against the people. Police and soldiers stopped my campaign motorcade at every imaginable place, banning my meetings, harassing MDC supporters and blocking me from entering certain areas.

Any discerning Zimbabwean could see that Mugabe and Zanu PF were spoiling for a fight, a war. They had put the nation under siege and were constantly looking for avenues to ignite conflict. For the first ten days after my return, I attempted to go out to the rural areas. In Matabeleland, at every station, my convoy was stopped and searched while my officials were arrested and only released at night. This was obviously a strategy to prevent me from going anywhere.

When I went to Lupane in Matabeleland North, my car was impounded, leaving me stranded. In Kwekwe in central Zimbabwe, my convoy was stopped for the whole day, only to be allowed to proceed to a meeting venue in the evening. On my way to nearby Gweru, I was intercepted, searched and delayed. The same thing happened in Shurugwi. I was told that the police were acting on orders from above – an indirect reference to police commissioner Augustine Chihuri and Mugabe. No one in the lower ranks of the police force would authorise any of my meetings.

If this was an attempt to stop my campaign for a run-off poll it was succeeding. I was forced to ask myself what the point of campaigning was. My supporters were being killed and displaced from their homes and businesses. It was not possible to work under such horrendous conditions.

The north and north-eastern part of Zimbabwe, the Mashonaland provinces, were literally turned into no-go areas. Those who came to my meetings were followed at night and attacked. Internally displaced people were coming to Harvest House in their thousands. On two occasions, Mugabe rounded them up for further beatings before they were detained and ordered to leave Harare. I could see no reason for remaining in such a flawed race. To achieve what?

The situation was so bad that there was no way I was going to compete with Mugabe and the military: they had informed all civil servants that they were going to vote under instructions. The junta ordered our supporters to feign illiteracy, even school headmasters, so that they could be assisted in casting their ballots.

Every area had a military and Zanu PF militia base: there were operational zones all over the country and travel restrictions were imposed on everybody. An informal curfew was imposed and travellers from towns and cities were barred from entering the communal areas. They were told to keep Tsvangirai's 'political virus' out of the countryside.

As Election Day approached I convened a national executive committee meeting to review the situation. I informed my colleagues that I felt I was literally under house arrest. Hardly could I leave home without being subjected to visible enemy surveillance – four to six unmarked cars with strangers in thuggish balaclavas and dark glasses followed me everywhere. The situation was becoming desperate. The numbers of refugees at Harvest House kept rising. Despite being routinely rounded up, detained and 'deported' to their rural homes, new arrivals continued to stream in – mostly the badly injured, the maimed, and the totally confused and mentally traumatised.

The executive committee recommended that our national council – our supreme policy review organ in between congresses – call off my participation in the run-off. It was clearly going to be a futile exercise. If Mugabe wanted a war I was not going to be part of it; if Mugabe wanted an election, then it was important that it be under fair conditions. The decision that I should withdraw was unanimous, but we decided not to announce it immediately. We delayed it right up to a week before the scheduled sham election.

The decision did not go down well with Mugabe and Zanu PF. Instead of celebrating an assured victory, they intensified the pressure on the MDC and on me personally. Abductions and torture were scaled up. There was additional chaos in the rural areas, with militants insisting that every person must come out and vote in the one-candidate contest.

Churches and other religious services were interrupted and religious parishes came under heavy political strain. Many, especially in the rural areas, closed their doors completely. Their lay preachers were accused of praying for 'Mugabe's death'. Sunday services were replaced with Zanu PF brainwashing meetings, at which the sole item on the agenda was to denounce Tsvangirai and the MDC. The entire country became a lawless jungle – a failed state.

Even Somalia, without a functional government since the departure of dictator Siad Barre, could hardly be compared with Zimbabwe in June 2008. Mugabe was totally out of his wits, ready to burn down the whole house while searching for a rat in a food cupboard (as Zimbabweans metaphorically refer to the frantic actions of a madman).

Zimbabwe was completely on its knees. Apart from vast tracts of desolate land now littered with pole-and-mud shacks occupied by hungry and open-mouthed refugee/settlers, nothing was breathing. Like all counterfeit leaders, Mugabe turned on me as his scapegoat. It was a pitiful experience; emotions were running high and the whole national burden, once again, landed on my shoulders with the weight of a ton of bricks. I needed fresh air.

My passport had run out of blank pages so I could not even leave the country. I needed space. I was in danger, but I hung on to my spirit. I moved my family to South Africa and tried to stay put at home in Harare but the political heat was unbearable. Real danger lurked on the horizon. By then, about 200 of my agents had been abducted and murdered. Scores of other cases, especially in remote areas, went unreported.

The military, the secret service and Zanu PF militias, loaded with printed cash from the Reserve Bank of Zimbabwe and using unmarked vehicles, ran the show. To this day, the fate of dozens of activists is unknown. Neither the party nor their families know what happened to them. They simply vanished after being abducted in broad daylight by Mugabe's men and women. And he continued to exert undue pressure on me.

In the light of this, I was advised to seek sanctuary in an embassy for my personal security. I decided to avoid the embassies of leading Western nations: I needed to get into a chancery of a small country, generally considered to be neutral and less sensational. I also knew that if I went into an African embassy, Mugabe's agents would simply walk in and pluck me out. Mugabe would apply pressure and blackmail to have me handed over to his agents. I desperately needed a secure place and decided to approach the Dutch embassy in Harare – where I was willingly accepted. After a about week I went back home.

MDC negotiators informed me that Mugabe's emissaries were totally inflexible; Zanu PF gave its negotiators a highly restrictive mandate. This was unconstructive and though the negotiations went on for a long time they were totally unproductive. There was virtually no movement.

It was an exasperating and harrowing time. Our nation was at a standstill. Food and medicines were critically short. Nobody wanted to do business with Zimbabwe and people could hardly afford to buy anything anyway as inflation was ratcheting up on an hourly basis. The prices of basic commodities, now only available on the informal market, were changing four or five times a day.

The banks were short of bearer cheque notes, then used as money. Queues of extremely poor millionaires, billionaires, trillionaires, quadrillionaires and sextillionaires – some with even more worthless bank notes – formed everywhere in Zimbabwe because hyper-inflation eroded the value of the bearer-cheques every hour. Schools and hospitals remained shut.

I contacted Mbeki and warned him that our talks were getting nowhere. As long as the main players, the party leaders, remained removed from direct action to thrash out the pertinent details, the situation was definitely not going to change. I persuaded Mbeki to see the need for some degree of collaboration – for a relationship, no matter how loose, between Mugabe and me. I was convinced that despite Mugabe's unacceptable behaviour, there had to be a common position that could be used to guide our negotiators.

Mbeki understood my point. And one day, in the form of a completely unexpected phone call, Mugabe sent me a message, indicating that he was ready to have a face-to-face meeting.

CHAPTER TWENTY-FIVE
REGIME CHANGE

I never tried to find out how Mbeki persuaded Mugabe to agree to meet me. Given Mugabe's fiery rhetoric and his deep, personal hatred for Morgan Tsvangirai, I was extremely surprised by the invitation. My mind raced back to our MDC congress resolution of March 2006 where we decided to drag Mugabe, in shame, to the negotiating table. The man was a national disgrace and had better own up to it. Our intention was to force him to recognise the superior political insights of ordinary Zimbabweans.

I took a leisurely walk in my garden, repeatedly saying to myself: the mountain has finally accepted that it needs to have a bath in a tiny pond down the river. Finally I had dismantled the monolith to its last pebble.

Details of the meeting arrived. A dinner was arranged for us at the former Sheraton Hotel, now named Rainbow Towers. At the agreed time, wearing a grey business suit and striped necktie, I went into one of private function rooms at the hotel, ready for what would probably be my longest dinner in 58 years.

My last meeting with Mugabe had ended in acrimony a decade before when I was the secretary general of the ZCTU. That time he had treated my colleagues and me as pieces of dirt and openly challenged us to get out and form our own political party. We had least expected that kind of behaviour when what we intended was to inform him that the workers were suffering. Among the issues we had hoped to address were rising corruption and lack of good governance. As head of state and government, it was important that he listened to our pleas for help. Instead, Mugabe had accused us of hiding behind the trade union movement. With the gusto and arrogance of a confident heavy-weight boxing champion he challenged us to enter Zimbabwe's political ring. His remarks left us baffled, angry and determined to respond. He had demonstrated clearly that he was not prepared to listen to what he called a bunch of political upstarts.

As I entered the Rainbow Towers meeting room, I was shocked to see a frail senior citizen huddled on a chair at a corner table. I had not seen Mugabe at close range for more than ten years. He certainly looked much older than I expected. He stared at me with an ashen face, looking deeply troubled. He reminded me of my late father, Dzingirai-Chibwe. In fact, Mugabe was older than my father had been when he died. I wondered why Mugabe's close friends and relatives didn't insist on his retirement. Surely a person of his age should be allowed to rest?

As he struggled to rise to greet me, I quickly moved closer to spare him the trouble, echoing his clan totem, Zimbabwean style. 'Gushungo?' I said. The term 'Gushungo' identified Mugabe by his lineage and was a mark of respect. I smiled and stretched out my hand. 'My pleasure to meet you. How is your family? And you?'

'Mr Tsvangirai?' was all he could say, with a firm handshake. The politeness was warm and engaging; not even the slightest hint of acrimony could be detected.

After the pleasantries, I quickly proceeded to the main subject of our meeting. But Mugabe interjected, pointing to bowls of food – an inviting array of dishes neatly arranged on the other side of the table.

I had not noticed the sumptuous dishes when I entered the room. My eyes were focused on Mugabe. My mind was on the business of the day and my concern was the fate of the Zimbabwean people. Two days before, I had attended the funeral of a close relative and two family friends who died in a cholera epidemic, now still in its initial stages, in Harare's Budiriro suburb. I knew that I should not allow myself to be distracted from the true reason for our meeting and that now was the moment for me to begin talking. I politely declined his invitation to eat.

His face lit up for a moment, but he quickly composed himself. Resorting to an old Zimbabwean tactic of changing the topic, Mugabe looked at me thoughtfully and said: 'You know, Morgan, many Zimbabweans perceive me as a murderer. They say Mugabe kills people. This is far from the truth!'

I burst out laughing – that usual, natural and unpolished laugh Zimbabweans are familiar with. I was disarmed. I stood up, picked up a plate and a fork and took a small helping of a succulent vegetable salad. As I picked out the carefully sliced tomato and lettuce, I remembered a story told about Mugabe and his perceived desire to murder opponents.

When the late Enos Chikowore, then a senior Zanu PF member, was admitted to a hospital in Kadoma a few years earlier, Mugabe felt compelled to pay him a visit to check on his condition. At the expected time of the visit Chikowore sneaked out of the hospital ward and Mugabe arrived to find him gone. A search was conducted but the patient was nowhere to be found. After Mugabe left, Chikowore came out of a closet and told friends and relatives that anyone Mugabe sees in hospital seldom survives. '*Ane ruvhuno*,' Chikowore reportedly said. This meant that Mugabe's juju breaks people's spines. Chikowore survived his illness.

After Mugabe's light reference to his perceived murderous traits, I felt that it would be unfair for me to reinforce that perception. I felt persuaded to have dinner with him. Then I returned to the reason for our meeting, breaking the ice with a hard point in our political dispute.

'*Gushungo*, our nation is crying out for peace. Why are our people dying? They say you have unleashed violence on the entire nation.'

'No, no, no. Tsvangirai, I am not a violent person,' he retorted. 'What do you mean? I have never killed a human being,' he continued in protest.

'But *Gushungo*, I have the evidence,' I said.

He mumbled something I failed to catch, but quickly came back. 'Fine, if you have the evidence, that is good. Maybe at our next meeting you should bring along the facts.'

I agreed.

'You must realise that I defeated you in the election,' he said, seemingly ignoring the subject of violence which I was keen to pursue.

'Which one, *Gushungo*? 29 March 2008?' I asked calmly.

'No, no, no. You probably won that by a tiny margin, but ...'

'Mr President,' I chipped in seeing that we were getting nowhere. 'We must help our negotiators today. There has been no progress since they began the interparty dialogue.' I threw the conversation back to our real agenda. 'With all due respect, I came here on the understanding that we could identify the areas where we are in agreement and to clear any sticking points.'

Again, Mugabe veered off course launching into his trademark tirade against the whites, colonialism, the British, land and sanctions. I listened to the all too familiar Mugabe diatribe, giving him a chance to cool down. As he spoke, I could see deep anti-white passion in his eyes and the intensity of his emotion. The veins around his ageing neck jutted out, full of rage and fury. I expected this from a man who had lost power, fame and national respect. It was a sad spectacle. I have never seen a man at such a debased level trying to cover up his humiliation through an emotional outburst. Here was an ashamed, elderly Zimbabwean, desperate to be heard by a person young enough to be his child.

Eventually, I told him that our political stalemate had arisen out of the recently disputed elections. I assured him that he had nothing to fear as he had a clear legacy of leading the liberation struggle, which he was now putting at risk. It was my assessment that we had to find a solution, otherwise our country would stay mired in a crisis with the potential for open conflict.

Mugabe leaned forward, demonstrating an intense interest to listen. He nodded three or four times as I explained myself and I felt heartened that I had scored my first victory as a political negotiator with a difficult opponent. True, every conflict has its own peculiar roots and an assortment of dimensions to deal with, so I summoned what I thought were my mental strengths to keep the discussion flowing and to seize his interest in my views and vision. At that point he realised that he had to act responsibly and in a civil manner. For my part, I did everything possible in terms of our African culture to show respect, even listening patiently when he veered off into irrelevance. All in all, he showed some restraint and a degree of underlying respect for me.

Mugabe searched for, and rearranged, his thoughts. His body language and line of questioning told me that he was trying hard to assess my character. He began to listen to me as I went through the pertinent issues confronting the nation. I was impressed. He was a good listener.

We talked for one and half hours – as I had expected, it was the longest dinner in my life. This was surprising – but what astounded me more was that, by the end of our meeting, Mugabe seemed to have changed his attitude towards me. The desire to vilify and humiliate me seemed to have dissipated, at least temporarily.

As a parting shot, I took up the question of violence again. He assured me that he would welcome the evidence and suggested that we meet again the following Thursday. When I left the room to return to my Harare home, Mugabe looked a bit confused, possibly about his reading of my character and my vision for Zimbabwe. I think he realised that he had become a willing victim of his own propaganda.

I gather that after the meeting Mugabe initially felt some mistrust towards me, although at the time neither his body language nor his words betrayed any sense of this. We were talking to each other, not talking past each other. He seemed nervous about doing business with me and looked puzzled about what kind of person I was. I was later to learn that he confided in a close family friend that he now had a totally different impression of me. This was a happy sign that we had finally made some progress.

But when I followed up on his proposed meeting for the following Thursday, I was told that there was no other meeting set down for Mugabe and me. I think he was advised against getting the evidence of killings as he would not know what to do with it. So he avoided the meeting altogether and it would only be much later, at the actual negotiating table, that the next cycle of meetings would be on the cards.

I could see that circumstances were pushing Mugabe to talk to us although he remained full of defiance. At some point he would have no option but to reach a compromise. That was what kept me in the room. Mugabe considered himself to be a generous giver of power which he could none the less withdraw at will. As he put it, he was under no obligation 'to receive strangers' into his government. From the MDC's side, I explained that we remained steadfast in our demand for responsibility *with* meaningful authority.

The parliamentary elections had taken place in March 2008; it was only in February 2009 that we formed a coalition government with Mugabe as president and me as prime minister.

The protracted negotiations were orchestrated by President Thabo Mbeki of South Africa in his role as the mediator appointed by SADC. Mbeki himself would be ousted from power in September 2008, forced by the ANC to resign after he had lost the party leadership to Jacob Zuma, but SADC kept Mbeki on in the facilitating role in Zimbabwe for the time being.

As the process moved forward it was apparent that Mugabe was refusing to honour his part of the deal. With hindsight, I can understand that. He was about to lose a lot of executive power and faced an uncertain future. In frustration and without an escape route, he resorted in the end to shouting, 'I am giving you power!' To which I coolly retorted, 'You are not *giving* us anything; we won the mandate of the people.'

Each time I reminded him of his election loss, his pain was obvious. With furrowed forehead, he would blurt out angrily: 'You will soon be in cabinet, you have to learn! You have to know how government works. Why do you want everything now?'

Mugabe evidently hoped for an arrangement similar to the Zanu PF/ PF-Zapu solution, the so-called Unity Accord of 1987, in which Zanu

PF co-opted its junior partner to administration without changing tack. Such a deal, an elite pact, could destroy the MDC and I refused to agree to it. We were coming in as equal partners: sharing responsibilities in a coalition. That required changing the whole political matrix.

One could see that Mugabe was still in a state of denial. The election result was obviously a big blow to him and he kept insisting that he had won it. There were numerous moments when the talks turned confrontational.

Mutambara, seeing a chance to take a stealthy lick at power opportunistically and from the periphery, kept urging us to consider Zimbabwe's national interest, as if his whole motivation as a spoiler was in the national interest.

I must say, though, that the process of dialogue was an interesting experience as we watched Zanu PF being forced into making numerous compromises. To behold Mugabe moving from a position of total denial to grudging acceptance of an agreement was our biggest victory. I was determined to force him to stretch his skin to breaking point which, given his attitude towards the MDC and me personally, he finally had to do because I had narrowed his options substantially. The whole course of discussions exposed him in a terrible way. If he had worked with us ten years before, he could have had a profoundly better political career with the admiration of his people and the world to carry him into retirement. Now, here he was, making a fool of his impressive achievements as an intellectual, liberation icon and politician.

The first face-to-face with Mugabe had taken place in July 2008 and this was followed by negotiations between our parties in Pretoria.

The drawing up of the Memorandum of Understanding (MoU) at the end of July 2008 signalled that we were making some progress towards a full agreement. I could see that Mbeki was keen to get the Zimbabwe story behind him as quickly as possible, even to the extent of papering over some clear cracks and contentious issues.

The period between the signing of the agreement and my swearing-in as prime minister in February 2009 was a kind of interregnum during which all the signs pointed to a cynical abrogation of the agreement by the ruling junta. But we were committed, and went into government.

I kept a keen eye on Mugabe's behaviour throughout the talks. I felt sorry for him. Despite his advanced age, he was prepared to work late, sometimes spending an entire night in the negotiations. I was actually surprised. He stuck to his position, with eyes wide open and a clear mind, keeping track of every point in the discussion. Finally, what we got was far from being totally unreasonable, although it is one thing to sign an agreement and another to get it implemented fully; to commit each other to the letter and spirit of the pact.

Mbeki kept pressing Mugabe, nudging him to concede defeat although he was carefully biased towards Zanu PF and the old man. Mbeki's relationship with Mugabe, though not uncomplicated, provided protection for Mugabe in international forums including the African Union.[1] I understood Mbeki's liberation war background and his inherent respect for 'Uncle Bob', as he constantly referred to him.

My own assessment was that Mugabe ran out of alternatives. He was forced to deal with me, while Mbeki was exerting his pressure so that he could scoop a trophy and salvage the little that was left of his tattered legacy. Mbeki appeared to push hard to get me any position in government, thinking that was enough to satisfy me. I argued that it was not about a position for me personally in government; it was about a genuine need for a division of labour and an equitable distribution of power. We were not going into this agreement to be a junior partner in government, to get responsibility without authority.

We wanted to be satisfied about roles: if I was going to be prime minister, what did that mean? I kept the question on the table. Neither Mugabe nor Mbeki could respond in a satisfactory manner. Mbeki had seriously underrated me and his approach was obviously slanted by his admiration for Mugabe. But he also knew that unless he succeeded in helping us find a solution that satisfied both parties, he would have nothing to show for his intervention. He must have calculated that he had to push Mugabe to the point of no return.

During the discussion around the composition of the transitional government, I recall Mugabe persistently stressing that he had never known of a head of state who was not head of government – even though this is a common international practice; he was desperately trying to cling to power at all costs. We therefore had to create the office of the council of ministers with a prime minister tasked to monitor government business. He finally accepted that position.

By 15 September 2008, when the leaders of SADC witnessed the signing of the power-sharing document, I could see that we had worn Mugabe down significantly. Officially called an Interparty Political Agreement the document came to be known as the Global Political Agreement (GPA). Mugabe's real dilemma now was how to sell the idea to the military junta and to his hardliners. It was a tough call. Mugabe had been forced into a major climb-down from 29 years of unchallenged rule in which he always had the last word. Now this despot was to be a mere partner of Morgan Tsvangirai, a man he loathed, along with an erstwhile student activist and academic, Arthur Mutambara.

He may have been consoled by the fact that the political agreement we finally reached was vague. In June, Mbeki had proposed that Mugabe take up a position as titular president with executive powers transferred to me as prime minister. Ncube and Mutambara would have none of this. Whatever their motivation, I wondered why they would want Mugabe at the helm and delay transition even further. I found their behaviour strange, and not in the national interest.

The final agreement, however, provided for Mugabe to remain as executive president at the head of a large cabinet evenly divided between the two major parties with me as prime minister. A few posts were allocated to Mutambara who would become one of two deputy prime ministers (the other to be from my MDC party).

There was both joy and scepticism at the announcement of the agreement. While international observers and many in Zimbabwe hailed the newfound spirit of cooperation leading to shared power, it was evident that the transitional government was bound to face serious problems.

Mugabe would enjoy some form of flexibility as we tried to implement the pact. For his part, Mbeki was impatient and happy to shake the dust of Zimbabwe off his shoes after imposing a patched-up agreement with many holes. Vague as it was, the agreement still did not satisfy Mugabe and he launched an apparent strategy to force the MDC and me out of the transition. We refused to give in to his puerile tactics.

In October 2008, Mbeki needed Mugabe, Mutambara and me to attend a SADC summit in Swaziland. My passport had run out of pages. I needed a new one. Mugabe refused to allow this. His government officials gave me a temporary travel document, arguing that the state had run out of paper. I ignored that meeting and left for Johannesburg, feeling that Mugabe's behaviour was completely ridiculous. To a great extent, it only exposed his insincerity. I decided to put my foot down and declared that I was not returning to Zimbabwe until I received a new passport. I went to Botswana. Mugabe wanted to keep me caged in Zimbabwe, using a mere passport as a negotiation lever. I realised, however, that if I did not maintain an international profile, nothing was going to move. I stayed in Africa, travelling around the continent.

Despite Mugabe's wanting the world to believe that I was travelling without documents, my passport was still valid – it had only run out of blank pages. I therefore made arrangements with various governments and was granted entry without any problems. In Europe, the French, who had invited me to speak at a development conference in Strasbourg in November 2008, facilitated my travel. After visiting France, I also spent some time in Germany.

After months of haggling over the passport issue, the document was finally delivered to me at State House in Gaborone on Christmas Day 2008. By then the pressure on the MDC to join the government, both at home and in SADC, was intense.

Cholera was ravaging our nation; the state was struggling to pay civil servants; food was critically short; and national anxieties and fears were high. A spirit of uncertainty hovered over the entire nation. Few Zimbabweans will ever forget what we went through as 2008 drew to a close.

Mugabe was desperate for a safety valve. All his efforts to safeguard his position – propaganda, violence, intolerance, murder and dictatorship – had failed. He pulled out his last trick aimed at the African continent, accusing Botswana of training Zimbabwean rebels and dissidents on my behalf. He further accused Botswana of beaming hostile propaganda messages into Zimbabwe. He tried hard to undermine Khama and to denigrate Botswana for taking a stand against his regime. Chinamasa took the matter to SADC, forcing the group to investigate. As expected, SADC found nothing to validate Mugabe's claims.

Mugabe's supporters in the military and security sectors had never concealed their unhappiness with the interparty agreement and sought to frustrate it at every turn. The military abducted and tortured 38 MDC supporters, including top MDC officials Gandi Mudzingwa and Kisimusi Dhlamini, and pro-democracy activist, Jestina Mukoko. Unbelievably, a two-year-old toddler, Nigel Mutemagau, was caught up in the swoop and spent several months in unlawful detention with his activist parents, Violet Mupfuranhehwe and Collen Mutemagau. They were accused of recruiting Zimbabweans for military training in Botswana.

The worsening political situation, despite the interparty political agreement, forced South Africa and SADC to intervene again. At a SADC meeting in Pretoria in January 2009, it became clear that if we failed to implement the arrangement, no matter how imperfect it was, the consequences would be dire. According to the new thinking within the South African government, as long Morgan Tsvangirai and the MDC were not part of the new regime, there was no solution to the crisis.

During the interregnum, Mbeki left office and was no longer a player in the Zimbabwe crisis. South Africa's interim president, Kgalema Petrus Motlanthe, who chaired the meeting, advised SADC leaders to find a solution, no matter how defective it might be at the beginning.

I must commend Motlanthe for his political maturity, flexibility and the firm stance he took. Because of his past as a trade unionist, I think he understood my background. Unlike Mbeki, Motlanthe was honest and forthright. He showed an interest in building trust, while emphasising the need for fairness. He acknowledged that Mugabe had a stake in Zimbabwe and implored me to coexist with him as a fellow citizen and compatriot. Privately, he advised me that the best shot, in terms of influence, was for me to get into the new government, citing his own experiences in South Africa where, during the talks that culminated in an all-race election in 1994, extremists sympathetic to the previous government killed senior ANC leader Chris Hani in an attempt to scuttle the dialogue. He said if the ANC had remained out of the negotiating process, there was no way the violence in South Africa could have been stopped. The same was possible for Zimbabwe.

Motlanthe was equally forceful or persuasive with Mugabe. We spent the whole night in the meeting in Pretoria trying to find the best way to implement the power-sharing deal. Even before that meeting, however, there had been progress. We had decided to share power practically by allocating state departments and ministries to the different parties to the agreement and ensuring that there be fairness in the process.

The allocation of cabinet posts became a thorny issue. Zanu PF wanted the MDC to head economic and social ministries while they retained control of the security and production sector. That became a sticking point. We wanted at least ten ministries, including those related to the security sector, to be shared equally. We then agreed that if Zanu PF took the defence and intelligence portfolios, we should have those responsible for home affairs and finance. But Zanu remained adamant that they control the ministry of home affairs. We finally secured finance, but not the other. We then appealed to SADC, as underwriters to the agreement, to step in.

Our impression of which ministries carried the most weight was, at that time, well off the mark, as we have now found out while in government. The individual performance, influence and alliances of a minister can have a huge effect on the outcomes. A minister responsible for water and sanitation can have as much impact on the general population as his or her counterpart responsible for security.

What Zanu PF failed to understand was that the social ministries actually dealt with our lives. To them, power is translated in terms of security; but security without sound national economic performance means nothing. Although I know that national security is important, in terms of political advantage it comes out second on the list of measurable outcomes.

At last, we agreed that the ministry of home affairs be shared by ministers from both the MDC and Zanu PF. We did our best to maintain the view that if we were unable to influence change, there was no need for us to be in government. If we were unable to introduce fundamental reforms necessary for transformation, there was no point in our being part of the administration.

The duties, responsibilities and powers of the president and the prime minister were unclear at the start and remain so even today. The difference between the roles of cabinet (chaired by Mugabe) and that of the council of ministers (which I chaired) was also vague. Worse still, the position of the two vice-presidents (both from Zanu PF) – was another source of confusion, another expensive layer of political dust in this transition.

Mbeki was right in his initial June 2008 proposal that Mugabe be stripped of his executive powers and become a ceremonial president. But the hawks in Mugabe's military junta would have none of it. Our case was also complicated by the refusal of Ncube and Mutambara to allow our party to play a leading role in Zimbabwean affairs, despite our victory in the March 2008 election. Ncube often tended to side with Zanu PF simply to place limits on the executive authority the MDC and I could assume in the transition. I never figured out what he thought Mutambara and their group could gain from this – other than to delay Zimbabwe's transformation into a full democracy.

The other weakness of our compromise pertains to that section of the agreement which dealt with our appalling national circumstances. Zimbabwe had become one of the poorest countries on earth, totally dependent on the donor community for basic essentials. To shore up his own support, and contrary to our advice, Mugabe appointed an inflated cabinet and made numerous other government postings. Establishing a large bureaucracy through an expensive and unsustainable administration simply to accommodate cronies is an unnecessary and indeed crippling expense.

We also failed to discuss the role of women in the transition. Women, who constitute the majority of our people and have arguably had the hardest time of all, needed recognition and representation. Their NGOs and local associations had been extremely vocal since the foundation of several women's organisations in the 1980s, demanding alternatives to the patriarchal Zimbabwe society. Institutionalised male dominance has kept the state and status of women marginal but they have not been passive victims,[2] and constitutional reforms must recognise them as full citizens.

Despite these obvious flaws in the agreement, Mugabe and Zanu PF had no desire to continue negotiating for mutually acceptable solutions. In fact, they tried to alter the entire agreement in their favour, without consultation and in fundamental ways. After we signed the original document on 11 September 2009, Mugabe – through Chinamasa – changed a key part by deceptively sneaking in an amended document for public signature four days later, witnessed by foreign heads of state and government. I was extremely disappointed by Zanu PF's dishonesty.

Chinamasa unilaterally deleted an important clause which required deputy presidents and deputy prime ministers to lose their voting rights in parliament. If they were already legislators, they would be replaced by appointed non-constituency MPs from their own political parties. He also took out another clause which mandated the president and the prime minister to make senior government appointments. This paved the way for Gideon Gono and Johannes Tomana, who were subsequently employed as central bank governor and attorney general respectively. Chinamasa's deception allowed Mugabe to appoint provincial governors without the consultation that was supposed to be the norm.

The Gono and Tomana issue derailed progress and strained relations in the inclusive government in a significant way. Although it has sucked in SADC, it remains unresolved. The unilateral allotment of posts of provincial governors to Mugabe's associates remains a contentious point but he is adamant that they stay in office, unconstitutionally.

Chinamasa made sure that the section of the agreement, which deals with external interference in our internal affairs, omitted a pertinent UN principle tasking the international community to protect the innocent, wherever they are in the world, in cases of callous political exposure to danger and in times of humanitarian emergencies. Our president and his party were in no way willing to accede to outside intervention to prevent the kind of brutalities we had seen over so many years, such as the mass killings in Matabeleland, unwarranted attacks on women, the demolition of shanty town homes in Harare, and the victimisation of impoverished rural dwellers if they dared to vote for the MDC.

Mugabe and Zanu PF knew that we would see through all of this but their intention was to wear us down through endless bickering and the erosion of our political brand. They hoped the nation would get tired of waiting for real transformation and become demoralised, retreating into apathy. The long-term aim, of course, was to undermine support for the MDC by creating the impression that we were wasting our time and theirs.

Mugabe and the junta, again using Chinamasa, unilaterally altered a draft bill on the setting up of a National Security Council, which was passed by parliament in February 2009, clearly disfiguring the agreed legal content. What Mugabe failed to achieve through furtive editing, he compensated for by ensuring remnants of his civil-military junta sabotage the letter and spirit of the accord. We were not treated as partners but as the enemy. Zanu PF could not grasp the simple fact that there had been a regime change in Harare. It was crazy for anyone to think that there had been a shift of power in Zimbabwe.

For example, the periodic review mechanism was stalled for unexplained reasons. Economic recovery remained constrained by lawlessness, especially fresh farm invasions. Zimbabwe remains fragile because conditions for democracy are frustrated at every turn. The healing process is gasping for life as Zanu PF violence is still endemic in the rural areas. Intolerance is rampant and displaced persons seeking merely to survive are harassed and chased away by rogue elements from the military and the Zanu PF militia. Some 2 442 cases of human rights abuses were recorded in the 30 days after we signed the agreement, and they continue.

In spite of what Mugabe committed himself to, he allowed the civil-military junta to set up a parallel administration that reported directly to him. For them, nothing had changed. Out of nostalgia, they were Mugabe's devotees who reflected his desires and parroted his private thoughts and opinions. These clones are everywhere in key government positions and Mugabe loves them – for their lack of mental and moral independence.

The real crux of power was the military-security establishment. The parallel administration controlled the criminal justice system through Chinamasa and Tomana along with the secret service and elements in military intelligence.

The Public Service Commission, through its chairman Mariyawanda Nzuwa, continued to approve the employment of partisan Zanu PF militias in the civil service. The deployment of party hacks in the rural areas meant that villagers would continue to be harassed and intimidated. Discrimination against the MDC intensified. Chinamasa himself never forgave us for Zanu PF's total loss in his rural Manicaland province.

Mugabe did not spare the trade unions either. In fact, he still loathed the labour movement for spearheading the formation of the MDC. In a short period after the agreement, the ZCTU recorded 2 300 cases of violation of workers' rights at the hands of state security agents through assaults and torture. I grew up with many of these unionists. They shaped my mind, and my destiny. By persecuting them, Mugabe sought to get directly at my soul and to punish my allies. I was embarrassed and placed in an invidious position by the actions of a government I was supposed to be leading as prime minister. I apologised to the workers but could do little to contain the rogue elements.

The police continued to defy court orders with impunity. They arrested 78 workers for trade union work, assaulted 2 306, tortured four – including ZCTU president Lovemore Matombo – and shot three in Zvishavane for demanding their wages at a mine.

None of the barefaced dirty tricks and tactics of the president and Zanu PF were new. They stretched back to those early days when I, among others, had begun to wonder about Mugabe's true credentials as a champion of freedom. After independence he had enacted numerous amendments to the Lancaster House Constitution that gave him sweeping powers. The arsenal of party domination and deceit was familiar to all who had suffered maltreatment. It included electoral irregularities, the perversion of the police and justice system, repressive laws and propaganda and, above all, widespread violence designed to quell dissent and maintain the appearance of popular support.

Yet there were grounds to accept and implement the agreement. We had signed it, we were committed to national reconstruction, and we wanted to make it work. After the SADC meeting in Pretoria in January 2009 urging us to participate or be sidelined, I had returned home, put the matter to the MDC's national council and we had decided to enter into government. To back out would be conceding defeat. Parliament adopted Constitutional Amendment No. 19, introducing the changes necessary to give effect to the Global Political Agreement of September 2008. The interregnum was over. An apparently inclusive government called the Government of National Unity (GNU) came into being. Time was to prove it a government of disunity.

ENDNOTES

1   'Love in a Time of Cholera: Thabo Mbeki's Relationship with Robert Mugabe, 2000-2008'. In: Matyszak, Derek (2010) 'Law, Politics and Zimbabwe's "Unity" Government'. Konrad Adenauer Stiftung, in association with the Research and Advocacy Unit, Harare

2   Ncube, Janah (undated, c 2002). 'The Women's Movement in the Zimbabwe Constitutional Debate: the continuous journey to a gender fair Constitution'

CHAPTER TWENTY-SIX

LIFE AND DEATH

As a cool breeze swept through our leafy garden, I pressed Amai Edwin and the children to get ready for our journey back to our home village of Buhera. We were planning to stay the night in the village before attending a meeting at the Murambinda Business Centre the next day. It was 6 March 2009, and it would be the first time I had been back home as the Prime Minister of the Republic of Zimbabwe. The community was anxiously awaiting us.

My elevation to the premiership was a victory for the people of Buhera, much as it was for the people of Zimbabwe. Those in Buhera had every reason to feel proud to have one of their own in a top national public office, considering how communities throughout the country toiled and suffered with little recognition. Numerous phone calls informed me that thousands of people had walked and gathered overnight to be present at my first rural meeting and to see our family in its new role. Amai Edwin took her time making sure there was sufficient food and drink for those she would later entertain in her thatched kitchen at home in Buhera.

My officials were running around refuelling the cars and doing the last-minute checks on windscreen wipers, tail lights, batteries – anything associated with getting ready for a three-hour drive to a rural area. When all was done, I got into the car next to Amai Ed and off we went, heading south.

I relaxed on the vast back seat, took an occasional nap and cleared my thoughts for my address to the people. Amai Ed occasionally interrupted me with casual chatter as we cruised along the highway.

Then out of nowhere I heard a loud bang. The impact registered before my eyes as a flash and was so strong that it instantly disorientated me. Our heads banged together violently as the car rolled several times and finally landed on its roof. We were thrown out of the vehicle. I quickly got up off the ground, dazed and in shock.

Onlookers from surrounding farms, drawn by the disturbance, assembled at the scene. I looked around the car for Amai Edwin, and caught sight of her raising an open palm: our party symbol and a Zimbabwean greeting sign. As I staggered towards her I saw that she was struggling to breathe. Then, silence. Total silence.

Amai Edwin, at the prime age of 50, my confidante and adviser – almost a mentor – a mother and grandmother, a champion of the struggle for change and democracy in Zimbabwe, could neither open her eyes nor talk to me. Could this be the end, at the 80 kilometre post along the bumpy and narrow Harare-Beitbridge road? No, she is all right, I thought. But I had never felt so powerless. Blood dripped from my face; I was very weak. I sat down in a reflex movement, trying to compose myself.

I heard desperate murmurs from a young man pleading for forgiveness. I later learnt that the lamentation was coming from one Chinoona Mwanda, the driver whose truck had veered on to our side of the road – and killed Amai Edwin.

My wife of many years was no more my living companion in my hour of greatest need.

Mwanda's oncoming single-cab lorry, belonging to the John Snow International medical charity, had swerved into our lane to avoid an unusually large pothole and collided with my Land Cruiser, forcing us off the tarmac and into a deadly spin. Only Amai Edwin was fatally injured. I had head and neck bruising while my aide Benson 'Okolo' Muchinouta and our driver Simba Mujeye sustained only minor injuries.

Too stunned to react coherently, I was taken away from the scene. Our lead security vehicle ferried us to nearby Beatrice Hospital. But given the state of decay in our health delivery system, no meaningful help could be secured there, so we proceeded to the Avenues Clinic in Harare. By then, Amai Edwin could not be helped. Mugabe and his wife Grace came to see me in hospital and to offer their sympathy.

At that moment I did not know how to react. Was this a genuine accident? Was Mugabe involved? Was there anyone trying to take us out? On reflection, I settled for a normal road accident. Others were not so sure. Suspicions of foul play welled up around this terrible event, pointing to Mugabe as the assassin. The perception was fuelled by the behaviour of the police and the security establishment.

Deon Theron, a farmer in the area, rushed to the scene and began to photograph the wreckage. Police arrested him, an act which fed the rumour mill. Theron was in fact the vice-president of Zimbabwe's Commercial Farmers' Union. He was charged with obstructing the police in the course of their duties and his camera was confiscated. According to press reports, Theron said he had asked the police if he could take pictures and was given the go-ahead.

To quell suspicions, I announced that the collision had been an accident. Mistrust of the ruling party and its security forces ran so deep that many in the MDC were not disposed to believe this. To further complicate matters, none of the other Zanu PF senior officials, ministers and members of the military junta dared come near me to offer their condolences or simply express human sympathy.

I understood and accepted the depth of emotion on both sides. Amai Edwin had built a formidable reputation as a pillar of the struggle for a new kind of revolution in Zimbabwe. She did everything possible to work for all Zimbabweans. On the ground her role was far more visible than mine, behind the scenes, inside the party and in contacts with wives and mothers like herself. She had never sought the public spotlight and was content to be seen playing a symbolic role but I knew just how much she had contributed in word and deed.

Three weeks before Amai Edwin's death I had sat at breakfast listening to her as she reminded me of the heavy national burden I was about shoulder. From her words, I knew I was up for a solemn and complicated contract with the people. In terms of the agreement to form a government of national unity, I was officially to assume my duties as prime minister on 11 February 2009.

As my car pulled up outside State House, there was flurry of activity. Officials who for years had been schooled and brainwashed to hate Morgan Tsvangirai and the MDC, now looked eager to receive me and relieved that the nation had a new addition to Zimbabwe's leadership. We found Mugabe waiting for us. He greeted Amai Edwin and me warmly.

As I took the oath of office, I once again quietly recalled my journey from a dusty village in Buhera North to high school in Masvingo, to a weaver's factory in Mutare, to a nickel mine in Bindura, and to a national position as labour organiser in Harare. I had met tens of thousands of people along the way and was conscious that theirs were the concerns of millions. Entering into government was an irreversible process, a measurable outcome of the people's democratic project, and a response to a national need. And, looking back, it struck me that I made far fewer enemies than admirers. While I had experienced a rough fight with Mugabe and could well have been killed by the thugs who beat me up in prison, when he honoured the wishes of the people of Zimbabwe that morning by conferring the position of prime minister on me I was gratified – not just for myself but, in a strange way, for him too. By admitting me and the MDC to government he opened himself to opportunities that might help him salvage a tattered human rights record and reclaim his long-lost image.

Despite all that I had been through during Mugabe's regime, I bore no grudges, nor did I wish to let the past preoccupy me while I performed my official duties. I raised my hand to recite the oath and swore inwardly to honesty and hard work, vowing to forgive my past tormentors as I was now a national leader.

I had never gone out of my way to become a leader. Amongst my colleagues I had merely expressed myself fully and sincerely in a way that articulated their own hopes and grievances, and it was this that had propelled me to the national stage. All that I had wanted was to help my desperate siblings, to get married and raise a normal family in a society that would grant us the space to be ourselves.

Now I was in a position of great authority and had to respond to the demands of an entire nation. I reasoned that I had to ensure that the necessary reforms to facilitate the development of true democracy must be put in place. The road would be bumpy and dangerous, I knew, and I would have to keep both my enemies and my supporters close. My compatriots – the men and women of Zimbabwe who looked to me for leadership – would be my teachers. If some spat in my face and cursed me, as was the everyday behaviour of unrepentant Zanu PF rogues, they would have to be ignored. My pledge was to maintain my composure, decency and dedication to curing the nation's pain, even if this meant taking personal and political risks. I would strive to honour my promise to the people – even in the toughest of circumstances.

The advice I had given to Sessel Zvidzai, soon after his election as executive mayor of Gweru, was to take it easy and to keep an open heart. This was advice I was duty bound to apply to myself. In difficult transitions, genuine results always come late. Transformation is an agonisingly slow process. Change becomes inclusive and meaningful when people see and feel it, but in the interim what is important is to show constant concern for public service and the delivery of visible and measurable outcomes. I have an image of change in my mind: real change and transformation, change for the better, carries tiny gold coins. It takes time and effort to pick them up. At the same time, change sits on a precipice from which it can easily be dislodged.

When the founders of modern-day America laid a solid foundation for inclusion, diehard slave owners and racists may never have dreamt of the possibility of a black man, Barack Obama, being sworn in to lead the United States. When the founders of Mauritius ensured that the vast sugar plantations on the island would form the basis of a first-class economy, hardly did they envisage that Paul Berenger, the socialist-leaning son of a French immigrant, would one day take over as prime minister. When Mahatma Gandhi trekked all the way to the sea to make salt in the traditional way as a protest against the tax on salt, while defiantly preaching non-violence, none of his detractors could fathom that the nation of India would become the world's largest democracy and an impressive economic giant just a few decades later.

When South Africa's white nationalists jailed Nelson Mandela for nearly three decades, little did they foresee that he would he would be freed to save the country from a racial war and, in a tough negotiated transition, ensure the country adopted a non-racial, democratic constitution. Who knows, maybe a descendant of a Malay slave, or that of a Somali refugee, or a San housemaid – all South Africans today – shall one day preside over Pretoria's political life. Similarly, who knows what will happen to a descendant of a former farm worker whose parents were brutalised during the uncertain period of Zanu PF farm seizures, in a future democratic Zimbabwe?

Unbridled hatred, lawlessness and violence are the enemies of progress and justice. A distorted view of what is good and patriotic often leads Africa into wastefulness and unnecessary errors. In our case, we must chide ourselves for taking so long to stand up to Mugabe's dictatorship until at last the situation had deteriorated to the point of utter despair. Mugabe and others had played their part in the liberation war but were well on the way to destroying the country we had won together. They must realise that their time has come and gone – and that they should allow a new leadership, a new generation, to hold the reins while they rest in the shade.

I mused over these issues and many others affecting our place in the world and the future of humankind as we drove home after I had taken my oath of office at State House. I was deep in thought; engrossed in what an outsider might regard as wild reflections, but which expressed my excitement, imaginings and qualms. I only realised we were back home when Amai Edwin tapped me on the knee. As I walked into the house, I resisted a strong urge to apologise to Amai Edwin and to all my children and my grandchildren, Gamuchirai and Anesu, for being an absentee parent for ten years.

Anesu greeted me with his usual, tight little smile and a snort. And when I sat down he quickly jumped on to my lap. I embraced his bouncy frame, lifted him up and took a lazy walk around the garden, mumbling things to him; in fact, mumbling nothing, just enjoying his infant giggles. It was as if he perfectly understood the unusual journey I had travelled over 57 years to that infinitesimal moment. I then sat down to a cup of tea and a crisp, home-made biscuit Anesu's granny, Amai Edwin, had baked the night before.

The business of government absorbed me totally during those first few weeks of the unity arrangement. Immediately after my appointment as prime minister I set out to select the MDC's nominees for the new cabinet, identifying various officials for different ministerial posts. I had never worked in government before, never mind in a shared, coalition government, and therefore knew that it would take a fair amount of adjustment to fully assert myself in my new position.

I picked my cabinet team on the basis of seniority in the party, competence, gender, capacity and loyalty to the MDC. I had worked with a number of the officials for a long time and I knew them well, but the posts were limited so the selection process was naturally difficult. Inclusiveness was the watchword. As a national leader, I felt obliged to recognise and respect all Zimbabweans, especially during this transitional period. People needed to see and experience change and they wanted an inclusive government.

One could probably argue that this was all done for political expediency or convenience, but I deliberately decided to spread power away from the urban areas and dominant ethnic groups. Those who had been generally overlooked for appointments in government must be integrated into the structures: women, the disabled, workers and peasants. We had to respect cultural and other differences and persevere with national integration: tolerance would teach us how to handle various class, ethnic and regional aspirations. I pledged to honour my word and couldn't ignore such fundamental issues after three decades of Zanu PF exclusion.

Roy Bennett, who had been forced into exile after his release from Mutoko Prison in 2006, was back in Harare after Mugabe assured the MDC of his safety. I proposed Bennett's candidature for the cabinet on merit and out of my desire to embrace Zimbabwe's diversity. Bennett, a hard worker, successful businessman and commercial farmer was the most suitable candidate to help the new government revive agriculture, our economic mainstay. With Bennett at the agriculture ministry, I was confident that Zimbabwe would, within a few seasons, reclaim its position as a net food exporter.

Back in July, I had persuaded lawyer and prominent businessman Muchadeyi Masunda, a member of Simba Makoni's party, to take over Harare as mayor. Masunda was to take the city back to its former self and guide the young and inexperienced MDC councillors in their civic duties. I felt my decision was in the best interests of the city's recovery effort.

In my line-up for cabinet, I picked Abednico Bhebe from the Mutambara/Ncube group, suggesting that he take charge of the Water Affairs portfolio. As for the remainder, they all came from within the MDC top ranks, but were carefully selected to reflect the national character of the party. I made sure every region was adequately represented.

But Mutambara thought that by offering Bhebe a government post I was interfering in his party's affairs; he felt slighted and thought I wanted to divide his supporters. My plan was to strengthen the overall position of the pro-democracy movement by nominating individuals I thought were best for a variety of positions. While Mutambara and his top leadership were more sympathetic to Zanu PF, their MPs had a lot in common with us.

After Mutambara's protest, I dropped Bhebe from my shortlist. I picked Eddie Cross MP for a ministerial post with responsibility for public enterprises. But then he had to give way to Gabuza Joel Gabbuza, a member of the tiny, historically marginalised Tonga ethnic group from the Zambezi Basin in the far north-west of Zimbabwe. I made the same consideration in respect of Murisi Zwizwai, a Shangani – another minority clan from the south-east. Also in my line-up was Gorden Moyo, a civil society activist from Bulawayo.

There were sad moments when a few MDC top officials, men and women, literally drove under the cover of darkness to my home, without warning or appointment, to plead for cabinet posts. I refused to enter into such deals. In some cases, organised delegations from Matabeleland North, Harare, Masvingo and other areas knocked at my door to apply pressure for their preferred candidates. Suddenly, there appeared to be a resurgence of ethnic alliances inside the party. I felt very uncomfortable with this behaviour but I stood my ground.

The cabinet appointments process was stressful but I sought opportunities to relax with family and friends. Sometimes I was able to break away from the pressures of office but more often than not I was brought up sharply by some new, untoward development.

One day I learnt that Mugabe was at it again. The police were looking for Roy Bennett, to be charged for attempting to assassinate Mugabe in 2006. When Bennett visited me at home and explained his predicament, I assured him that I would continue to fight for his rights and liberty.

When I submitted the names of our ministers to the new government, Mugabe and Zanu PF were incensed by the appointment of Bennett to both the Senate and as the deputy minister of agriculture designate. As a white Zimbabwean whose farms Mugabe seized during the chaotic land reform programme, Zanu PF saw my appointment of Bennett as an insult. On the day he was supposed to be sworn in as a deputy minister, police arrested him as he was boarding a private aircraft at a small airport near Harare. They took him to Mutare and locked him up.

Meanwhile there was chaos at State House, where Mugabe almost lost control. Every senior Zanu PF official wanted to be a cabinet minister and many were turned away at the main gate. Others pulled rank and forced themselves into the grounds, trying their luck. Time was up; Mugabe had left them out in the cold.

We had to restart the negotiation process, as Mugabe appeared unable to deal with the potentially explosive situation. There was resistance everywhere, mainly from the perennial beneficiaries of the system of patronage. They were not ready to quit and go away. In the end, Mugabe succumbed to pressure and made last-minute changes to his line-up. Later, I discussed these events with him and he conceded that elements in Zanu PF still thought they wielded untrammelled power. But really, what power? I asked. Mugabe simply shrugged his shoulders and remained silent, displaying a troubled mind.

He was caught between the deep blue sea of political change and a vicious internal alliance of devils within Zanu PF. His attempts to navigate through the chaos led to his being accused of selling out and giving in to the MDC's demands.

One thing was clear to me, however. Much as the hardliners may have tried to overturn his directives, Mugabe remained the only Zanu PF politician capable of holding the party together. By talking to us and reaching an agreement, he simultaneously saved these residual elements of chaos from doom and oblivion. This group sometimes acted in an irrational manner, but that was not enough to keep a nation from creeping out of an abyss.

I was allocated an office in the same Munhumutapa Building that houses the offices of the president and cabinet, as well as the Ministry of Foreign Affairs. On Monday, 16 February, I was in office and started to induct all the ministers into their new jobs. I could see most of those from Zanu PF felt a deep sense of gratitude and relief that the MDC was now in government. They had tried, for 29 years, to run a government in a failing state without success. I could feel their respect for my office and me, after decades of vilifying my person at public meetings and in their own circles.

There seemed to be confusion among the general staff, especially the low-level security personnel, many of whom could not grasp what was happening around them. I didn't pay much attention to it, but many looked bewildered and acted awkwardly when dealing with personnel from the MDC. There was confusion too in the state bureaucracy. Some departmental chiefs had been made to feel they were just as powerful as cabinet ministers; conversely, there were ministers who wished to work as the executive heads of departments.

The respect the ministers accorded me seemed to have irked Mugabe, who promptly directed them to report either to his deputies or his office directly. He even tried to force MDC ministers to behave in the same manner. I knew this would eventually lead to conflict, so I organised a retreat and get-together for all ministers and officials at a venue outside Harare.

There were serious capacity deficiencies right across the board. I found myself surrounded by lots of well-read and knowledgeable officials but many lacked the requisite wisdom to handle changing circumstances. I realised then that nearly 30 years of one-party rule had caused a kind of administrative brain damage and stunted the growth of initiative.

It was becoming increasingly clear that had the transitional government failed to take off, Mugabe would have not have sustained his dictatorship beyond February 2009. Uniformed soldiers had already taken to the streets twice, looting shops and randomly beating up ordinary people.

As prime minister I was entitled to an official residence. At first, I was reluctant to move out of my Strathaven home in Harare but I soon realised that official residences are important national symbols. Mugabe told me that Zimbabwe House, opposite State House, where he lived as prime minister in the 1980s, was run down and required extensive renovation. It was dilapidated and uninhabitable. He offered to build a new place for me. I refused. I told him that I could easily find a new official residence, which I did – a place symbolic enough for a prime minister's official residence.

Meanwhile our new ministers and officials from outside Harare were still struggling to find suitable accommodation although the state had plenty of houses currently occupied by undeserving Zanu PF cronies – and, in some cases, the concubines of senior politicians.

With the MDC in government, Zimbabwe came back to life again. We reopened schools immediately; the cholera pandemic was contained; food was back on shop shelves and on family tables; and commerce and industry started to recover their productivity. School children pulled out their uniforms, washed them and, for the first time in nearly two years, sauntered into their classrooms looking neat and eager. Nurses, in their white uniforms, could be seen at bus stops, ready to do what they know best. No one wanted to slide back to the past.

I believe we could have done more in a short space of time if Mugabe and Zanu PF had stopped throwing spanners in the works through a renewed wave of farm invasions, general lawlessness and continued looting of state resources.

We abandoned the local bearer-cheques Mugabe used as the official currency, the Zimbabwe dollar; eliminated the informal market for foreign currency and fuel and introduced a multi-currency system in which Zimbabweans can now use the world's major currencies for business purposes.

For the record, I feel it is important for me to state briefly what I found in Mugabe's empty pantry, the country he boastfully called 'my Zimbabwe'. I seriously underestimated the extent of the damage until I walked into that government office with paint flaking off the walls and broken windows and loose floor tiles.

I shall confine myself to Harare, the capital city and our window to the world, for a sneak preview of what the whole nation looked like. The city could only supply 500 megalitres of water, half of which was lost to leakages because of ageing pipes. Demand was five times that quantity, so large parts of the city went without a drop of water for months, if not years.

A third of the sewerage pipes were blocked and raw matter constantly flowed into people's homes, into water courses and on to the streets. That polluted our main supply dams, leading to a cholera pandemic. Harare urgently needed US$150 million to improve its water supply and sanitation.

Out of 70 refuse and solid waste collection vehicles, only six jalopies were still on the road. Garbage was everywhere. Another US$20 million was required. Half our road and public lights worked, in a city of about three million people; roads were in a deplorable state, having been ignored for ten years – US$40 million was needed.

Despite the eviction of more than two million people under Operation

Murambatsvina in 2005, Harare still faced a staggering housing backlog, conservatively put at one million. Parks, cemeteries, halls and workers' houses were in a state of disrepair. The city had suspended all community services. Public safety was at risk. Only one ambulance was on the road, out of a fleet of 25 in 1999. The remaining three fire tenders, out of an original 16, could not be used on buildings a mere nine floors high.

An estimated US$200 million was necessary to bring basic public services back to the barest acceptable minimum. Hospitals and clinics were either without drugs or had been abandoned. Operating theatres at the referral centres had been shut down ten years ago. Many were vandalised and in a state of disrepair. At least US$100 million was needed to attract staff back and to repair basic infrastructure.

In total, Harare was short of $500 million for a facelift. Other towns and cities had virtually collapsed because of a weak revenue base and lack of economic activity. Close to 90 per cent of the population was now in the informal sector. All our mining and farming centres resembled ghost towns. The state could no longer afford to pay staff. Our tax base had all but collapsed.

The entire nation depended on a trickle of remittances from Zimbabweans in the diaspora and from money laundering. Almost everyone – including nuns and priests, sheiks and imams, faith healers and fortune tellers – was pushed into crime, surviving on the sale of trinkets, smuggled goods and fuel in the informal sector. Literally every Zimbabwean was trying hard to circumvent unjust official controls.

When our finance minister Tendai Biti assumed office, he immediately dumped Chinamasa's poorly devised budget, hurriedly rolled out in January 2009 to pre-empt our entry into the transitional government. Biti crafted a short-term economic recovery plan whose signposts for success depended on a return to the rule of law, peace and stability and a revival of domestic investment. We are still engaged in a running battle with Mugabe and his military chiefs and hardliners to see the plan through. Corruption remains endemic. I suspect our skirmishes with a well-organised and destructive force are likely to take us right into the next general election. Our fight over the control of a precious resource, diamonds, has yet to reach a climax.

Our institutions remain loosely rooted, partisan and weak. To be honest, many look totally irrelevant in a democracy. Our failure to implement the agreement speedily stemmed from an absence of political will and the lack of essential institutions to enforce that will.

Institutions hardly function without the blessing of a culture supported by a committed leadership, a leadership with a shared national vision. For institutions to make a difference, leaders must get out of their shells and be true to what their nation stands for. In Zimbabwe's case, that seems to be a grey area.

One of the main impediments to our work as a coalition is the absence of message discipline. I told Mugabe that if this government has to communicate a single message to the public, if we are going to have a single transitional leadership with a clear reporting structure, with one message aimed at building confidence among Zimbabweans, then the confusion he was fanning through the state media and the bureaucracy was unhelpful. When he refused to heed my message, I launched a newsletter to explain myself to Zimbabwe.

I could not even staff my office adequately. There were numerous blocks along the way. Mugabe wanted to impose his staff on me. I refused. Everything Zanu PF tried to do was meant to stop me from completing my arduous journey to a real prime minister's office.

I am still on the road. I have turned the corner from a narrow footpath into a much wider highway, an arena for official state actors. But I remain the same person, always without a magic wand. I know that with the support of Zimbabwe, together we can perform better. I hold no crystal ball – only an olive branch.

With my solemn vow to serve the people and the encouragement of my wife and colleagues, I was set on a course that seemed if not routine – for nothing is really routine in politics – then at least preordained as a set of necessary moves to secure working relationships and start the process of transformation. On the morning of the car accident, I was to be forcibly reminded that it is not by our own designs that we live or die. Whatever power I enjoyed as prime minister would not shield me from the fierce anguish and family confusion induced by personal loss.

After Amai Edwin's death I spent a night in hospital. Although cleared to return home from the Avenues Clinic the next day, I was anxious about my health. Arrangements were made for me to undergo further checks in Gaborone. In our culture, a spouse is hardly expected to leave home immediately after a partner dies. Mourners come to console a surviving spouse and the children, so one must be at home at all times. I could not fail to be aware of this but as a descendant of a chief and a national leader, I also knew that leaders shaped a nation's culture and could not focus solely on personal matters. I could not risk further complications in our politics merely in order to fulfil a traditional custom. My responsibilities demanded that I break with tradition by taking a step beyond the pressures of the bereavement, not only for the sake of the people but also to look after Amai Edwin's own dream and legacy. For me to continue to raise the children and take on my national role were two sides of the same coin. It was a difficult situation but a decision had to be made and I made it.

I left for Gaborone and went through the hospital rites by undergoing a thorough medical check-up, rested for a day, and then flew back to handle the heartbreak in our family after the loss of our wife and mother. My children were utterly devastated. Edwin, Gari, Vimbai and Rumbi were out of Zimbabwe, with only the twins Vincent and Millicent at home, so everything had to wait until the others returned. I could not imagine what the twins, aged 13, were going through in the familiar setting of our home with the absent presence of Amai Edwin everywhere. I had grown up with both my parents ever present in my life until I started working and finally went into politics, and knew nothing personally about how it feels to be an orphan, especially at such a young age.

And the grandchildren, Gamuchirai and Anesu? I lack the capacity to even think of it. Anesu, Gari's son, was the little darling in the house, our blossoming flower. Gamuchirai, Edwin's daughter, was away with her mother in South Africa. She may have heard little about the family tragedy, or been unable to make any sense of it. But as she reads this work, I am sure she will be able to feel the lightning shock that shot up our spines at the time.

We buried Amai Ed at our family gravesite in Buhera North.

Zimbabweans from all walks of life gave her a resounding send-off. It was a highly emotional moment. May her soul rest in peace.

A commemorative gathering was held at the Glamis Stadium in Harare attended by about 30 000 people who came to pay their respects. Giving the keynote address, MDC secretary general and finance minister Tendai Biti referred to my wife by her known name, Susan, and said she had been an activist and revolutionary in her own right. She believed in the same values as her husband in wishing to bring about democratic change in Zimbabwe through a new, people-driven constitution. Although I have attended hundreds of public gatherings in my time, on this occasion I felt withdrawn into a deep part of myself and was unashamedly in tears. There was a moving personal moment when our eldest son Edwin told the gathering that the Tsvangirai family would not withdraw from the struggle for democracy.

Neither the family nor the party could have coped without the multitudes who spent days trying to console us in our debilitating loss. I have never seen such a large number of Zimbabweans together for a single purpose. I can only thank my fellow citizens for their compassion and sympathy. To us in the Tsvangirai family, the response to Amai Edwin's death showed that she was a true national hero. Her death had shaken Zimbabwe but the response of the people made me feel deeply indebted to the nation. As a family we had become a kind of warehouse of the nation's woes and multiple yearnings. Everything we had all gone through was somehow stored up in our hearts and minds although we were really a simple couple without pretensions. We came from a simple background and we hearkened back to our roots for strength and the renewal of our spirits. I suppose this is why people looked to us for hope and inspiration.

When I first met Amai Edwin in 1976 in Bindura, it never dawned on me that we would part in that unfortunate way – barely three weeks after I had assumed national office. I must acknowledge the generosity of President Jacob Zuma of South Africa in allowing us, as a family now minus Amai Ed, to go through a short 'bereavement rest' in that country. It dawned on me then that I was now like a naked man.

To lose someone you have lived with for 31 years is never easy, especially when you are caught in complex political dynamics that demand shrewd judgement and subtle but decisive moves. I missed Amai Edwin's counsel as the intransigent and highly destructive remnants of the Mugabe clique swirled around our national space.

I was now a single parent, totally unable to wash and iron my undergarments or pack my own clothes for a journey. I could not locate the toothpaste in the bathroom cupboard or even clean my shavers. I had not been shopping for years; I did not know the price of salt or milk or toilet cleaner. These were silly small things but they reinforced my sense of nakedness, being suddenly faced with the complete absence of polished advice, support and guidance. The loss I felt was intense.

For the first time I took a look at the vast size of our bed and our entire bedroom. I began to value and appreciate the intangible power of pillow-talk, or what the American scholar Warren Bennis refers to as 'reflective backtalk'. In every marriage these soft, slow and sobering bedside conversations keep a check on reality. Even when the going gets tough and there are arguments, a couple's life challenges may spread inside the whole house but remain tightly hidden under the roof. Before Amai Edwin's untimely departure I took pillow-talk for granted, but now there was silence.

Whenever I had found myself at an all-time low, utterly humiliated by a leadership squabble and stressed out by the vicissitudes of our democratic struggle, Amai Ed had listened to me, ploughing through my emotions and carefully interrogating my thoughts. In the end, this counselling created options, choices and opportunities.

Vimbai temporarily left a cushy job in Australia to help me with the conversion to single parenthood and the role of a widower with a family to take care of. Each time I fill in immigration forms at airports or similar government documents, I am reminded of that personal status. Sometimes I leave the column blank. When a cheeky officer, a stickler for detail, picks it up, I pretend to have missed the item and dutifully fill it in.

Our eldest son Edwin returned home from South Africa, also to help; and my wife's two sisters played the role of governess and family caretakers. That was a great consolation; but I always felt the absence of my pillar and holistic stabiliser – Amai Ed.

A spouse knows a partner better than anybody else. Our parents only see us as we grow up from childhood through youth to adulthood – and sometimes they do not know the whole of what goes on. The moment one leaves home for high school, the world takes charge. A wife, on the other hand, sees or senses it all. Amai Edwin gave me a chance to realise my full potential as a human being. She was a consummate listener, posing fearless and honest challenges, and we had blossomed together into mature, communicative adults over a period of three decades. We experienced everything together. I missed the comfort, the fun, chiding, laughter and the togetherness of our marriage.

Dark anxieties hovered over me. I was afraid of turning into a rotting cabbage with nothing fresh or spontaneous in my reactions, but I did my best to keep my emotions under careful guard and not disclose too much of what I was feeling. To manage the loss, I constantly questioned my feelings and checked my physical condition for any worrying signs. But I survived those dark days. Through prayer, games of golf, idle chat with friends, and solitary reflection, I slowly regained my private soul and personal stability. Amai Edwin's capacity to pull me out of despair and a sense of rejection in times of hardship became more pronounced in the first few weeks after her untimely departure. She had made me see the immense, soothing power of prayer.

As for my official duties, I took a very short rest and was soon back at work, compelling myself and others to stay focused on the MDC's goals. I was afraid of the worst, worrying about the dangers of personal withdrawal and political paralysis in the midst of the strife and disenchantment that surrounded our nascent national transition.

When I made my maiden speech to parliament as the newly installed prime minister, I spelt out my vision for the transition and announced that I needed to develop a 100-day emergency recovery plan. With this in mind, a cabinet retreat was arranged at Victoria Falls, far from the proverbial madding crowds of Harare. Apart from focusing on hard business, the forum was designed to develop rapport among my mixed cabinet colleagues. I knew my MDC team's weaknesses, and mine too;

we were all fresh from the opposition, an area far easier than being in government. We needed to understand the entire apparatus of the state and to be clear on all vital cogs of policy advocacy, priorities, policy making, and implementation dynamics inside the huge bureaucratic configuration of a dictatorship in a hard transition to a democracy.

When I arrived at Victoria Falls amidst a jovial and highly optimistic cross-party mix of politicians, I heaved a huge sigh of relief. At last we were firmly on the path towards unity of purpose. We were on the road to serve our people and to save Zimbabwe from a further plunge into an even deeper crisis. Barely a few hours into our cordial discussions, I was interrupted from the chair and informed of an urgent telephone call.

The news was devastating: Anesu had followed his granny, Amai Edwin. That morning the toddler sneaked out of the house, perhaps looking for his grandmother. Playing around the swimming pool area, he fell into the deep blue water and drowned. I simply did not know how to deal with this. I remained outside the conference room for a while, staring into an empty sky.

'My Lord and Amai Ed, kindly save us from further harm ...' I whispered to myself. 'Amai Ed, your family needs you badly. God, please guide us ...'

One or two tears quickly dried as they dripped down my cheeks. What a desolate moment! I steeled myself and flew back to Harare. The family was in mourning again – after barely three weeks the agony was renewed. I have never been through such an agonising time.

The loss of Amai Edwin and our subsequent family tragedy raised a lot of compassion for me across the ranks of government. There was newfound respect across the political divide. All ministers, at least on the surface, including those in Zanu PF who seemed in the past to have hardened their hearts as sworn enemies, now appeared to respond to me as a real person with a living soul and human feelings. This spirit contributed in some way to the softening of hostility. After years of incessant brainwashing, Zanu PF ministers and government officials soon came to embrace the new political dispensation, accepting that my role could not be wished away. But the ball was still in the air, especially for residual hard-line elements.

Despite the loss of Amai Edwin and Anesu's fatal mishap, I thought I had managed to break through the initial resistance amongst opponents in the transitional government. It was possible to build footbridges across our historical divisions and differences.

I was dead wrong.

CHAPTER TWENTY-SEVEN

TOGETHER TO THE END!

I signed the Global Political Agreement because my belief in Zimbabwe and its peoples ran deeper than the scars I bore from my ten-year struggle against Mugabe's dictatorship. I went into an openly loveless marriage out of my hope for the future. That hope was, and still is, far stronger than the grief I felt for the needless suffering in my personal past.

For more than two years I worked hard to make the loveless marriage with Mugabe work. Serious problems threatened our strange union but I remained pragmatic and positive. Mugabe was unsure whether he needed the MDC, despite his advanced age and desperation to clear his soiled record. In one of our routine Monday meetings, he confided that the hawks in Zanu PF were piling pressure on him for conceding to the demands of the interparty agreement that had led to the current coalition.

The situation was equally difficult for me; similar accusations were being made against me – not from the same sources, though. The people were getting impatient with the slow pace of change, with Zanu PF's reluctance to honour what it committed itself to, with delays in a full return to peace and security.

My experiences spurred me to dig deeper into the African political psyche and to sharpen my vision as an African, born in a colonial setting and matured under a post-colonial tyranny. For the transition to survive, I had to be cautious. Publicly, I went out of my way to assure the nation that all was well. I forfeited my militancy and never sought to humiliate Mugabe as an opponent. I could see the dangers of taking off my boxing gloves and engaging in yet another political fracas with Mugabe and Zanu PF. Had I done otherwise the transitional government would have collapsed within weeks of its formation.

The private sector, civil society, villagers and peasants, the MDC and the international community were anxious about the pace of change. I found myself deep in a steamy melting pot. Only hope kept me going in the face of extreme provocation and unfulfilled Zanu PF pledges. My biggest headache stemmed from a reluctance to embrace change from the security sector – a fundamental requirement for stability and national renewal. The security establishment has a decisive and compelling influence on whatever the transitional government might seek to do.

While Zimbabwe bore the classic hallmarks of a post-war conflict, the 15 September 2008 peace deal was a purely political agreement. It left the status of a highly politicised security sector intact. That was a mistake. By the time I raised the subject for national consideration, Mugabe and Zanu PF had become terrified and withdrew to their traditional comfort zone – the military – for safety.

I realise now that any talk of 'security sector reform' must refer to a long-term programme, perhaps over the next generation. To shift the outlook and behaviour of the security establishment from what it has become – an enforcer of the nationalist mantra of the Mugabe regime – to what it needs to be – the underwriter of a true democratic dispensation – is going to be a monumental and time-consuming task. Habits die hard. The dogs of war, once they have their teeth into victims, cannot easily be wrestled from their grip and retrained as watchdogs for peace and non-partisan national, humane and human security. What we needed in the transitional period was alignment of the security sector to the goals of the Global Agreement. That this alignment did not occur was an indictment of Mugabe's own breach of faith: he had signed but he did not carry out the spirit of the agreement by calling his security forces to order. The security forces should be enablers, not spoilers, of change.

One of the weaknesses of the negotiating process leading to the agreement was that the parties met on unequal terms. Ours was not a traditional ceasefire agreement as had happened when the forces of Ian Smith agreed to lay down arms if those of Joshua Nkomo and Robert Mugabe did the same. Or, again, our negotiations did not resemble the settlement reached between Nkomo and Mugabe when Zipra and Zanla ended their quarrel. The MDC did not come to the table backed by an armed force seeking an end to civil war, but as a political party and opposition grouping seeking true democracy. We did not have a standing army to be integrated into the national army. Indeed, we had eschewed civil war as a matter of principle and we aimed for change through electoral processes under the proper rule of law. There should have been detailed discussion of how the security elements currently answering to Zanu PF would align themselves with the spirit of the transition.

The omission was a serious one. We were left with a situation where security chiefs and their underlings remained loyal to Mugabe and could carry on bullying and brutalising the people in order to maintain Zanu PF supremacy. That put the nation's renaissance in danger. The agreed plan for justice, national healing and reconciliation was interpreted as a matter of life and death, especially by the architects of the instability and the chaos we had seen in the past. We knew that heads of military, police and intelligence services were frightened of being sacked and having their perks taken away. An investigation into dirty land deals and corruption involving security personnel was certain to turn up incontrovertible evidence of widespread misuse of powers. With so much to hide, the establishment closed ranks against us and continued its rampage of terror.

The whole aspect of what I call 'human security' rather than regime security and protection needs to be addressed from several angles once we are through the transition period. Apart from non-partisanship in the security forces themselves, a number of key considerations must be addressed. These would include what to do about the flood of returning Zimbabwean refugees who are likely to come home once there is a prospect of real change for the better. Also on the agenda would be the role of peacekeepers in communities; genuine policing and national defence by the army and air force; how to handle street crime; and upholding the rule of law in order to achieve national freedom – the very thing that we had expected liberation parties to bring us at independence but which they had failed to deliver. None of this could be achieved during a transitional period of a mere two years as originally stipulated in the agreement.

In March 2009, parliament passed a law that established the National Security Council (NSC) to oversee the work of the military. It took me another four months to meet with the service chiefs. Expectedly, the meeting exposed high mistrust among our security elites regarding the changed political circumstances. They have dominated civilian life for the past three decades and see themselves as the real political managers of Zimbabwe. Many are so embedded in Zanu PF that they loathe any attempt at reform, leaving the transition in limbo. The result, inevitably, has been a disjointed national reform programme, much policy confusion and distortion of the national vision of change. The efficacy of the political, economic and social agenda is in question.

At independence in 1980, the integration of the three separate armies – the Rhodesian forces, Zanla and Zipra – opened the way for national stability, economic recovery and post-war reconstruction. It gave the people confidence to start picking up the pieces and rebuilding their lives. While the situation today is vastly different from what it was at that time, we needed to adopt a similar position to assure the nation of peace. The people wanted to see how the security sector could be placed within the civilian order, with effective oversight, after 30 years of abuse.

Although we have an economic statement to guide our recovery plan, there remain serious differences over fundamentals like the constitution-making process, the need for a shared political culture, a shared vision, transitional and economic justice and the fate of the security forces.

Our differences in the new government surfaced early when Defence Minister Emmerson Mnangagwa declared that the defence forces, as a matter of priority, would ensure that the land reform programme was never reversed. It was a source of pride, he indicated. Where in the world has a nation's land policy been determined by soldiers, except under a military government?

The deep involvement of the military in civilian life has proved a major setback to Zimbabwe's plan to crawl back on to the rails. Any civilian advancement project that I attempted to put in place was seen as an act that strengthened the MDC. It attracted the attention of the security establishment and was sabotaged, often before it even took off, with the connivance of Mugabe and Zanu PF.

I fully understand the historical background of Zimbabwe's security forces: Zanla was a liberation army with its own political ideology, outlook and loyalties. That I can't take away from them. As we move towards a phase of full democracy, these institutions must be depoliticised and professionalised. They must behave and be seen as national, non-partisan entities and not as extensions of an interest group, Zanu PF.

I believe that in any transition, pockets of resistance will always remain. When one of the signatories of a political agreement engages in unlawful means to realise personal political goals, the nation is short-changed. From the day I took my oath of office, rifts have emerged because of the behaviour of perpetually nostalgic, confused elements fighting against holistic transformation and change. It appears Mugabe does not know how to handle them.

After the February 2000 referendum the security sector became heavily involved in the campaign to liquidate the MDC. They assisted in the wholesale destruction of commercial agriculture. And earlier, during the disturbances in Matabeleland, the security forces played a leading role in suppression. All of this has placed Mugabe and Zanu PF in a kind of permanent revolution frame of mind, imposing a virtual state of emergency on society.

A war psychosis, a quasi state of emergency, such as that which has prevailed in Zimbabwe during the past 30 years, can only survive in a climate of lawlessness. It distorts the definition of national interest and replaces public concerns with personal interests. It leads to polarisation as it sees any form of civil dissent and civic organisation as a threat. Coexistence becomes impossible unless this psychosis is wiped out.

I wish to acknowledge the lack of space in this memoir for me to go into detail about my new experience in the changed political arena. The MDC's struggle took on a different complexion now that I was in government. I shall, however, attempt to present a summary of the issues, the frustrations and the barriers along the way which impacted negatively on the nation's search for a lasting solution to the political impasse.

First, I think it is important to state my personal credo: why I am in politics, how I see my role, what motivates me to keep going despite torture and double-dealing by the regime, and how – despite my sceptical view of some of our neighbouring African leaders – I embrace the African approach to conciliation and nation-building through mutual understanding based on our human commonality. I know that I have been perceived as a rough-and-ready politician rather than a statesman, someone who sprang from the ranks of trade unionists and lacks the polish to symbolise the aspirations of a new Zimbabwe. I have to smile at the memory of my early experiences in statecraft when – lacking a steady income as the leader of a new party, and without even a business suit to my name – I wore my boots and leather jacket to meetings with diplomats, business people and other political agenda-setters. No wonder they had trouble sizing me up and drew the conclusion that I was a flaming radical!

Both Amai Edwin and I needed a finishing school – but we learnt on the job. She found out it was not etiquette to serve wine in an enamel mug, or to lay a table for a dinner function without a tablecloth. My wonderful wife had supported us in the hardest of times by being a simple housewife, a mother and personal, family mentor, trading jerseys over the border in South Africa. She had no pretensions. She worked with people, not over them. For my part, trade union work had taught me to be a listener, content to sit in meetings trying to sense the mood before pronouncing what seemed to be the consensus. This is the African way and perhaps my origins in a chiefly line gave me the self-possession to wait and watch, picking up signals that could finally be expressed as a group decision.

I see my role as that of a transitional leader with the goal of putting in place the institutions of democracy that will protect Zimbabwe from dictatorship now and in the future. Once that job is done, and by then it is my sincere hope that Zimbabweans will have clear leadership succession mechanisms, I could happily make way for successors. Lack of constitutional checks and balances was a major drawback of the Lancaster House Agreement and is the main reason why Zimbabwe's political structures have remained so fragile after more than three decades of independence. Although I have my reservations about South Africa as the dominant commercial presence in our region, I can only admire the constitution that was drawn up in negotiations between all players at the end of apartheid. There are checks and balances in South Africa. The judiciary has affirmed its independence by sending laws back to parliament for review. Certain state institutions were created to strengthen South Africa's democracy by standing outside of the executive, legislature and judiciary: the Public Protector, the Human Rights Commission, the Commission on Gender Equality, the Commission to promote cultures, religious and language communities, the Electoral Commission and the Auditor General. And, of course, rights to freedom of expression which also guarantee media freedom are essential to allow open debate and expose corruption and abuse of power.

Without such independent arbiters with real powers, a country with a dominant party like Zanu PF can quickly sink into the mire of self-serving legalism that has characterised Zimbabwe. Political appointees have warped our weak institutions to the point where the whims of one man become law, whether constitutional or not. In March 2007 our party leadership was detained and beaten by security forces. I suffered a fractured skull, while several senior officials suffered serious internal injuries and needed emergency operations in South Africa. Mugabe refused to let them fly out of the country. We got a court injunction to overrule the travel ban – so at least in that instance a limit was put on arbitrary executive authority

– but it is hard to forgive or forget the sheer inhumanity of it all. While I lay in intensive care in a Harare hospital, Mugabe told western countries which criticised his government to 'go and hang'.[1] Meanwhile, Edward Chikomba, the part-time television photographer who took photos of our group after we emerged from torture and smuggled the images out of the country, was abducted from his home and his murdered body discovered some days later in a distant village.[2] No one has ever been brought to book for these crimes.

I went into politics not as a career choice but in response to a burning desire for change from a nation already in a crisis of governance, and as a patriotic necessity. Such are the horrors that have been visited upon us as a people that one simply has to stand up for what is right. I have confronted Mugabe many times over the well-documented violence perpetrated by the security forces. His answer has been to deny complicity and say that violence is endemic in African society and is basically a fact of life that we should learn to live with. This is utterly unacceptable. Even if violence were endemic, it should be treated as a kind of 'public health problem' to be dealt with at the level of communities where education, stakeholder involvement, policing, and respect for others must replace brute force and criminality. But in Zimbabwe's case we are facing state-sponsored violence. This does not arise at ground level but is ordered from the top. It is not a public health problem but a regime public policy problem. It must be stopped by political means.

That, then, is what I stand for – normal human decency and a return to the principles of an African culture that avows the value of community life and personal freedom. Politics in a democratic society is about deliberating on what matters most, hearing oppositional views, and acting with sufficient consensus to carry decisions through. We will not have a democracy in Zimbabwe until the nationalists who seized control of the state cease to regard themselves as the sole champions of liberation and, by extension, the ultimate underwriters of the people's freedom. Their victory against colonialism has, in reality, meant a new form of oppression to us as a nation. We need a restatement of the nature of citizenship, to be inclusive of all, participatory, humane and respectful of dissent.

Mugabe and Zanu PF exploited the inherent weaknesses in the 2008 Global Agreement to frustrate holistic institutional reforms. They maintained the pressure on civil society and the MDC, sponsoring lawlessness especially among poor peasants in the rural areas and workers on commercial farms, refusing to honour their part of the deal – all for partisan political ends.

My analysis of Mugabe's behaviour is that he saw us as a temporary lifeline to enable him to rise from an abyss. This was despite my numerous assurances, sincerely expressed, that we are serious about a long-term role in government and aim to bring about transformation in the wider society. The MDC's involvement was seen as a quick fix. Mugabe's attitude was a selfish and opportunistic way of handling a crisis as deep as that of Zimbabwe.

A visitor to Zimbabwe in the past two and half years could be excused for assuming that there were two governments running the country. In spite of what Mugabe committed himself to, it remained Zanu PF's policy to undermine my executive authority at every turn. To most of Zanu PF's senior officials, nothing had changed. And, as with all dictatorships, Mugabe appears to be loyal to his hardliners, and not the other way round. At almost all my Monday meetings with Mugabe, I found myself raising one issue after the other. Sometimes the old man did not even know what was happening in his own party, in particular he did not know about blockages to progress. Each time I confronted him about the negative behaviour of some of his officials, he expressed shock and surprise.

For example, while the agreement required parliament to set up a committee to work on a new constitution within two months of the new government coming into office, Zanu PF hardliners were uncomfortable with the plan which led to constant political bickering and public disturbances in July 2009. The mayhem stopped immediately after Mugabe publicly called his supporters to order.

Fresh conflicts almost derailed the process before it even began. Mugabe declared his intention, early on, to impose his own views on the new constitution. Zanu PF militants disrupted consultative meetings, leading to outbursts of violence. These events discouraged civil society from participating fully in the process.

In the meantime, I desperately tried to avoid a constitutional crisis by working tirelessly to make the transitional arrangement work, despite Mugabe's clear breaches of the agreement. I thought that was the right thing to do. Mugabe, as a human being like all of us, is subject to certain idiosyncrasies and natural frailties; he needed a chance to prove himself and to show remorse. But when the pattern continued into October 2009, I could no longer keep quiet. The whole thing was fast turning into a complete farce. I pulled out.

SADC woke up to the reality that all was not well and convened an emergency summit of its subcommittee on defence and security in Maputo. At that meeting, I realised that Mutambara was no longer interested in the struggle for democracy. Ultimately his boss, Welshman Ncube – clearly embarrassed by his antics and puerile political behaviour – booted him out of the splinter group in January 2011, leaving him with egg on his face. Today his political career is in tatters, with Mugabe as his only supporter. Previously, I had thought he had a superb chance of moving up the ladder if only he would exercise some self-restraint and patience. Each time he opened his mouth, I felt isolated because he was so far off the mark. He showered praise on Mugabe for what he described as his fantastic work for Zimbabwe, saying, much to my amusement, that Mugabe's record was a perfect generational legacy worth emulating. It meant that I was a lone voice in the call for order.

I was happy when SADC understood my concerns and tried hard to nudge Mugabe to see reason. Knowing the weaknesses of SADC, Mugabe left Maputo unchanged. He knew that the regional body could do nothing to force him to comply with the terms of the power-sharing agreement.

Although I reported to my state office soon after the Maputo meeting, I was worried about the setbacks. They eroded investor confidence, pulverised public morale and polarised Zimbabwe even further.

Back in Harare, Mugabe was at it again, saying his party would no longer listen to any person or organisation other than its politburo – which he chairs. Mugabe heightened political tensions, making public utterances that were highly divisive and promoted hate speech. This was at a time when close to two million people still required food aid, mostly sourced from foreign donors.

The constitution-making process, an indispensable requirement for political and economic reform, was hopelessly delayed by the interference of Zanu PF and the military, which disrupted public hearings.

The level of participation in almost all areas failed to meet public expectations. Women and youths felt intimidated by the tense atmosphere and a genuine fear of reprisals from Zanu PF. The public's fears were amplified by the inflammatory reports from a partisan public media, which severely undermined any view that differed from that of Zanu PF.

As the prime minister, I could not guarantee the nation peace and security as long as Mugabe and Zanu PF intensified their assault, in connivance with a biased police force and criminal justice system. Despite the assurances I received from both South Africa and Zanu PF, Bennett was back in prison, having to endure a long trial on a trumped-up charge of treason. The prosecution in this case was unusually led by none other than Johannes Tomana, the attorney general who made no secret of his allegiance to Zanu PF.

When it became clear that the case was going nowhere, Bennett was slapped with another charge, that of hoarding maize at his farm in 2001. It was now 2010 – a classic case of justice delayed! This was ridiculous and totally against the letter and spirit of the interparty agreement. For the record, the agreement committed each one of us 'to act in a manner that demonstrates respect for the democratic values of justice, fairness, openness, tolerance, equality, respect of all persons and human rights'.

It was clear that Bennett, as a Zimbabwean, was being persecuted for being white, for his senior position as the treasurer of the MDC, and for his background as a commercial farmer who lost all his possessions and lifetime savings to state-sponsored, marauding gangs. Again, this was out of line with what Mugabe had committed himself to. Our agreement required us to accept and acknowledge tolerance, the rule of law, non-racialism and common citizenship as the bedrock of democracy.

Through the interparty agreement, I thought we had taken an initial step to craft a value system guided by universal principles of the rule of law. I was mistaken. Mugabe and Zanu PF always behaved according to partisan and selfish norms.

I thought our prosecution policy was to be guided by our new environment. Once again, I was wrong. Mugabe and Zanu PF continued with a persecution strategy designed to draw the nation back to the dark days of policy flip-flops, political corruption, intemperance and hate. I am in favour of a separate and independent prosecuting authority, devoid of any political contamination. Such an office should then ensure that everybody, from peasant to president, is equal before the law.

Traditional leaders, an essential part of our largely rural society, remained under Mugabe's direction. This made the process of national healing, as part of my reform agenda, impossible. Ultimately, the MDC noted that the people had had enough of Zanu PF's abuses. They took a stand and urged Mugabe to return Zimbabwe to order. But through rank madness, he turned a blind eye to our pleas.

I stopped shielding Mugabe from the ire of the people, regretting my earlier position – that of temporarily covering up Zanu PF's acts of sabotage of the transitional arrangement. Mugabe's failure to make significant moves left me sorely disappointed. He had betrayed the trust that I had personally invested in him, purely out of an open heart and sympathy for his very advanced age. He even failed, dismally, to respect Zimbabweans.

At its August 2010 annual summit in Windhoek, SADC showed signs of exasperation with Mugabe. It gave Zimbabwe a 30-day ultimatum to sort itself out. Based on the fact that SADC has no plan to enforce political resolutions, Mugabe simply looked away. I started to hear influential SADC leaders, including Jacob Zuma of South Africa, suggesting that a lasting solution lay in another general election – but one based on a strict observance of the requirements of the agreement. In Zimbabwe, given my personal experiences, an election has never proved to be a panacea for our deeply entrenched weaknesses and shortfalls in governance. An election for the sake of an election can be a traumatic experience. Without sufficient safeguards and guarantees for a free and fair electoral process, conducted in line with universal norms and standards, such a poll is a waste of time and a source of political instability. To pass a legitimacy test, any future election designed to restore a normal society in Zimbabwe must be open to international observation and monitoring – before, during and after the event. An election must unite the people.

If SADC fails to rein in Mugabe to respect the transitional arrangement that the regional grouping itself swore to oversee, the least it can do is ensure that Harare conducts a legitimate election to break the impasse and resolve the national crisis.

As 2010 drew to a close, Mugabe and Zanu PF were already in an election mood, campaigning and trying to cover the ground they lost in 2008. In the middle of all this, I was concerned about the lack of action and enthusiasm from SADC. A lot of work needed to be done during the transition to prepare for the elections, if Zimbabwe was to avoid falling back into the past. Countless Zimbabweans have taken risks to get the country to where it is now; some even gave their lives for change.

I am determined to consult the majority for a collective, national guide about the future. In today's changing world, the power of democracy and the irresistible force of popular will shall always prevail. Gone are the days of command, control and closure of space for a people determined to free themselves. Gone are the days when strength was measured through military might, force, armour, violence and an ability to intimidate the people. Zimbabweans proved that fallacy wrong in 2008. They will speak out again. The people understand Mugabe's predilection for dominance and control, and have long moved ahead of him.

Unfortunately, experience is never transferable. Experience is a generational lesson. Every nation must learn things for itself. What is fundamental is that experience is never taught. As Africans we hardly learnt anything from the experiences of others. We had to go through our own experience, despite the fact that we had a large pool of fairly well-educated and trained manpower and a vibrant economic infrastructure in 1980.

Try to tell an adolescent about life's dangers. In most cases, it doesn't follow that he or she will respond in a reasoned, positive manner. It is very difficult to advise a teenager about the vagaries and temptations of life, let alone the efficacy of human experience.

I have learnt over the years that people have to go through their own set of experiences in order to rebuild their lives from their own history, from their past, and from their own legacy. Much of the pain and uncertainty can be avoided if, as leaders, we help to set up open societies.

I always searched for an out-and-out, authentic tipping point as a signpost for progress. I urged the MDC to celebrate these small victories and acknowledge them as significant movements towards our broader national goal. I used these benchmarks to comfort myself in the belief that we were still moving, though at a frustratingly slow pace. In politics, one must constantly be on the lookout for what may, on the surface, appear as insignificant changes. The cumulative impact of small victories can easily overwhelm an opponent.

Small victories may help convert potential landmines into definite gold mines. One's opponent normally dismisses them out of a human weakness to protect and defend a bigger share of the bread loaf. By the time the crust crumbles, there will be nothing inside. An ant, given its size, may seem insignificant, but over time ants can cause a once strong roof to cave in very suddenly.

When a leader loses a normal habit of listening to the people – and in 30 years of public service I have seen enough to know that Mugabe and Zanu PF are afraid of the people – then that person's political future is doomed.

In my regular meetings with Mugabe, I often reminded him of the dangers of underrating the collective intelligence and wisdom of a nation. I told him that my involvement in the coalition government was a stabilising force and that he risked losing my presence at his own peril in the sunset stage of his life. The restoration of Zimbabwe's legitimacy was of paramount importance, I said, and as the two principal leaders it remained our key responsibility.

After one such discussion in January 2010, Mugabe unilaterally changed ministerial mandates, stripping away the powers of most of our MDC ministers and handing them over to his Zanu PF colleagues. So ridiculous were the changes that Chinamasa was assigned to administer 94 Acts of Parliament while some of our ministers from the MDC were reduced to spectators without any responsibility for policy formulation and implementation. The idea was to get us to restart the negotiation process midway through the agreement.

Peace and national security must reflect the changed expectations of all citizens, national institutions and state organs in a plural political system. Mugabe nodded in agreement when I said this; but continued to act in a manner that ran contrary and that was difficult to understand.

As Zimbabweans toiled with the heavy baggage of their past up a rocky and steep mountain slope, I was happy to note that they remained focused on their dream of arriving at a rich, secure and lush valley on the other side. Now that together we are on the last long haul, we still need to maintain our vigilance. A political transition, as an interval between chaos and order, is generally a period of uncertainty; it offers saboteurs an opportunity to try out all forms of tricks to maintain the turmoil.

When power is shared between a winner and two losers, those without the people's mandate are always guided by self-interest and tend to gang up against the winner. Losers want more time for rebranding, and can be very dangerous.

I took over a state that was completely broke. I managed to stabilise the situation, allow for aid inflows, deal with a massive humanitarian emergency and contain a runaway cholera epidemic. As I look back today, I think that as Africans we must constantly talk to ourselves and search for a sustainable way to deal with the political culture inside the continent. We must always opt for what is best for our people. We must never stop laughing at ourselves. The traditional political technique, strengthened by Mugabe and Zanu PF, has always been for public officials and their supporters to please their leaders. Today there is no excuse for craven subordination to authority figures. With its abundance of talent, Africa, and Zimbabwe in particular, should not be crying out for authentic and responsive leadership.

We must move with the times; attend to changing public demands and contexts; recognise our failures; and always pair fast-evolving societal moments with our own inborn and acquired habits for relevance.

Post-colonial Africa lags behind in leadership monitoring and evaluation, with dire consequences for the people. At the end of the Cold War, many an African leader had to be pushed out of office after clinging to the one-party state philosophy for decades.

To Zimbabwe, a tenuous transition like the one we are experiencing radiates fluidity; a clouded outlook; real danger but also real possibilities. A post-conflict transition must be experienced only once in a person's political lifetime. Power-sharing agreements hardly resolve conflicts in a holistic way because of unending suspicions and inherent hatred between former competitors.

Reform will bring losses to tradition and patriarchy; losses to perceptions of political royalty; losses from our inheritance; fears of the unknown; fears of change; and losses from patronage and advantage. We must manage the losses, save our institutional memory and history, and preserve our core values and those cultural aspects which define us. Our leaders, at all levels, must carry the torch and the symbols of our national desires and ideals. Central to our work must be the national question, inclusion and the extension of freedom.

The ideals of inclusion and freedom are nothing new. We fought against colonialism together in our quest for the extension of our basic liberties. Freedom is the least expensive commodity, requiring merely a will and effective public participation.

Politics, from our sad experience, matters. With inclusion, freedom and a stream of reality checks, our dreams can be realised. We can arrive at our goals with our ideals intact and alive. Meaningful results rarely arrive early, but significant shifts can still be felt. They are seen. They are visible. Economic contagions, social effects and political epidemics move faster than political processes which are always subject to negotiation and compromises.

With another nail-biting election in the air, my message remains that tomorrow will be better. Let us stick together, right to the end.

ENDNOTES

1   'Mugabe tells critics to "go and hang"'. *Financial Times*, 14 March 2007
    http://www.ft.com/cms/s/0/078c36a0-d1d2-11db-b921-000b5df10621.
    html#ixzz1PESDFr7c

2   Zimbabwe journalist murdered 'over leaked Tsvangirai pictures'. *The
    Independent*, London, 4 April 2007 http://www.independent.co.uk/news/
    world/africa/zimbabwe-journalist-murdered-over-leaked-tsvangirai-
    pictures-443267.html

WORKS CONSULTED

Allport, R. 'Operation Quartz – Rhodesia 1980'. http://www.rhodesia.nl/quartz. htm

Barclay, Philip (2011). *Zimbabwe: Years of Hope and Despair*. London: Bloomsbury

Bates, Robert H (2008). *When Things Fell Apart: State Failure in Late-century Africa*. Cambridge University Press

Bay, Edna G & Donham, Donald Lewis (eds) (2006). *States of Violence: Politics, Youth, and Memory in Contemporary Africa*. Charlottesville: University of Virginia Press

Campbell, Horace (2003). *Reclaiming Zimbabwe: The Exhaustion of the Patriarchal Model of Liberation*. Cape Town: David Philip Publishers

Catholic Commission for Justice and Peace/Legal Resources Foundation (2008). *Gukurahundi in Zimbabwe: A Report on the Disturbances in Matabeleland and the Midlands, 1980-1988*. Columbia University Press

Chikuhwa, Jacob W (2004). *A Crisis of Governance: Zimbabwe*. New York: Algora Publishing

Chung, Fay & Kaarsholm, Preben (2006). *Re-living the Second Chimurenga: memories from the liberation*. Sterling, Va: Stylus Publishing

Columbia Encyclopedia (2008). 6th Edition http://www.encyclopedia.com/ doc/1E1-RhodNyas.html

Compagnon, Daniel (2010). *A Predictable Tragedy: Robert Mugabe and the Collapse of Zimbabwe*. Philadelphia: University of Pennsylvania Press

Creighton, Thomas Richmond Mandell (1997). *Southern Rhodesia and the Central African Federation: The Anatomy of Partnership*. Westport, Connecticut: Greenwood Press

Flower, Ken (1987). *Serving Secretly: An Intelligence Chief on Record: Rhodesia into Zimbabwe, 1964-81*. London: John Murray Publishers

Garfield Todd, Judith (2007). *Through the darkness: a life in Zimbabwe.* Johannesburg: Zebra

Government of Zimbabwe. *Zimbabwe Government of National Unity of 2009, House of Assembly of Zimbabwe, Zimbabwe Temporary Cabinet of 2009.* Books LLC.

Hudleston, Sarah (2008). *Face of Courage: A Biography of Morgan Tsvangirai.* Cape Town: Double Storey

Hughes, Matthew (2003). 'Fighting for White Rule in Africa: the Central African Federation, Katanga and the Congo Crisis, 1958-65'. *International History Review,* 15(3): 592-613

Human Rights Watch (undated). *Sleight of Hand: Repression of the Media and the Illusion of Reform in Zimbabwe.* Kindle Edition, Amazon Digital Services

Kriger, Norma J (2003). *Guerrilla veterans in post-war Zimbabwe: symbolic and violent politics, 1980-1987.* Cambridge University Press

Kriger, Norma J (1992). *Zimbabwe's guerrilla war: peasant voices.* Volume 70 of African Studies Series. Cambridge University Press

MacQuarrie-Collins, J C (2001). *History of Zimbabwe: Black Kings, White Overlords.* The Pentland Press

Masaka, Dennis (2010). *Zimbabwe's Government of National Unity (GNU): A Panacea to an Economy in a State of Crisis?* LAP LAMBERT Academic Publishing

Matyszak, Derek (2010). *'Law, Politics and Zimbabwe's "Unity" Government'.* Konrad Adenauer Stiftung, in association with the Research and Advocacy Unit, Harare

Nkomo, Joshua (2001). *The Story of My Life.* Harare: Sapes Books

Nkomo, Joshua (1984). *The Story of My Life.* London: Methuen

Pongweni, Alec J C (1983). *Songs that Won the Liberation War.* Harare: College Press

Raftopoulos, Brian & Mlambo, Alois (eds) (2009). *Becoming Zimbabwe: A History from the Pre-colonial Period to 2008.* Harare: Weaver Press

Ranger, T O (author) & Bhebe, Ngwabi (editor) (1996). *Society in Zimbabwe's Liberation War (Social History of Africa).* Oxford: James Currey, 2nd revised edition

Rubert, C & Rasmussen, Kent R (2001). *Historical Dictionary of Zimbabwe.* Lanham, MD: The Scarecrow Press, 3rd edition

Smith, Ian (1997). *The Great Betrayal: The Memoirs of Ian Douglas Smith.* Brisbane: Blake Publishing

Williams, Gwyneth & Hackland, Brian (1998). *The dictionary of contemporary politics of southern Africa.* London: Taylor & Francis

Zvobgo, C J M (2009). *A History of Zimbabwe, 1890-2000 and Postscript, Zimbabwe, 2001-2008.* Cambridge Scholars Publishing

SELECTED INDEX

Joint Operations Command (JOC) 309,310
Jongwe, Learnmore 258,297,389,391,428

Kabila, Laurent 182,186-7,275
Kadenge, Phineas 226
Kagurabadza, Misheck 397
Kahiya, Vincent 367
Kanengoni, Elias 135,136
Kangai, Kumbirai 68,79,80,82,83,191
Kanyenze, Godfrey 146,155,208,226
Karakadzai, Mike 189,311
Kasukuwere, Saviour 311,410
Kaunda, Kenneth 44,46,134,143,165,166, 167,168-70
Khama, Ian 490,491
Khumalo, Raphael 367
Khupe, Thokozani 201,203,240,258,458, 469,474
Kikwete, Jakaya 491
Kissinger, Henry 53,54
Kombayi, Patrick 136,158,219,241-2,281
Komichi, Morgan 489
Kondo, Timothy 196-7,201-3,206
Kwaramba, Rudo 226
Kwinjeh, Grace 187,240,258,449,473,474

Laing, Richard 59,71
Lancaster House Agreement 59,62,64,67, 116,117
Legault, Alexandre 359,360,364
Lesabe, Thenjiwe 478
Liberation War (Second Chimurenga) 32-3,50-1,54,56,62,64-5,66
Loewenson, Rene 233

Mabhena, Welshman 202
Mabika, Talent 299-300,343
Machiridza, Tonderayi 392
Made, Joseph 311,313,325
Madhuku, Lovemore 257,417,467,473
Madiro, Mike 430
Mafudze, Hilda 437
Magaya, Taurai 391
Magoche, Emmanuel 136
Mahlunge, Yvonne 240,258,449

Makarau, Rita 345,346
Makone, Ian 388,450,454,459,460,469, 474,491
Makone, Theresa 469,470
Makoni, Simba 311-12,431,477-9,480,482
Makore, James 315,403,404,406,460
Makore, Kumbirai 201,203,240
Makova, Claudius 332,335
Makuwaza, Remus 230,238,240,258,294
Makuwe, Bernard 301
Makwarimba, Alfred 109
Makwavarara, Sekesayi 397
Malunga, Sidney 158,216
Mandaza, Ibbo 187,234,235
Mandela, Nelson 134,175,275
Mangadze, Levi 46,55
Mangoma, Elton 469,473,484
Manhanga, Trevor 395
Manyika, Elliot 404
Manyonda, Kenneth 291,300,301,343-4
Mapaura, Joel 344
Marchi, Itai 412
Martins, Jose 227
Marumahoko, Reuben 345
Masaiti, Evelyn 470
Masawi, Ephraim 410
Maseko, Jevan 311
Masepe, Alois 136
Mashakada, Tapiwa 348,398,469
Masuku, Lookout 94,95,96
Masuku, Nhlanhla 410
Masunda, Muchadeyi 524
Mataure, Mike 158,202
Matchaba-Hove, Reginald 230
Matekenya, Richard 44,45
Matibenga, Lucia 258,294,394,437,449, 460,469,470-1
Matimba, Brighton 451
Matinenga, Eric 362,474
Matiza, J B 311
Matombo, Lovemore 109,514
Matongo, Isaac 227,230,238,240,257,315, 348,394,403,448,454,456,460,469,470
Matsanga, David Nyekorach 413
Mavhangira, Susan 394
Mawema, Michael 5
Mawere, Mutumwa 412
Maya, Shakespeare 384
Mbalekwa, Pearson 447

Young, Andrew 57

Zembe, Wurayayi 136
Zhou, Happius 400
Zimbabwe Congress of Trade Unions
(ZCTU) 81,82-3,123-5,141-
2,144,145,161-2,181,206,211-
12,215,225,228-229,236-41,440
Zimbabwe National War Veterans
Association 133. *See also* War veterans

Zimondi, Paradzai 310
Zimunya, Tom 301
Zindoga, Isidore Manhando 214
Ziswa, Valentine 258
Ziyambi, Vernanda 345
Zulu, Nomalanga 202
Zuma, Jacob 532,548
Zvinavashe, Vitalis 188,310,373-4,390,418
Zvobgo, Eddison 107,186,234,367
Zwizwai, Murisi 459,525